Art for Yale

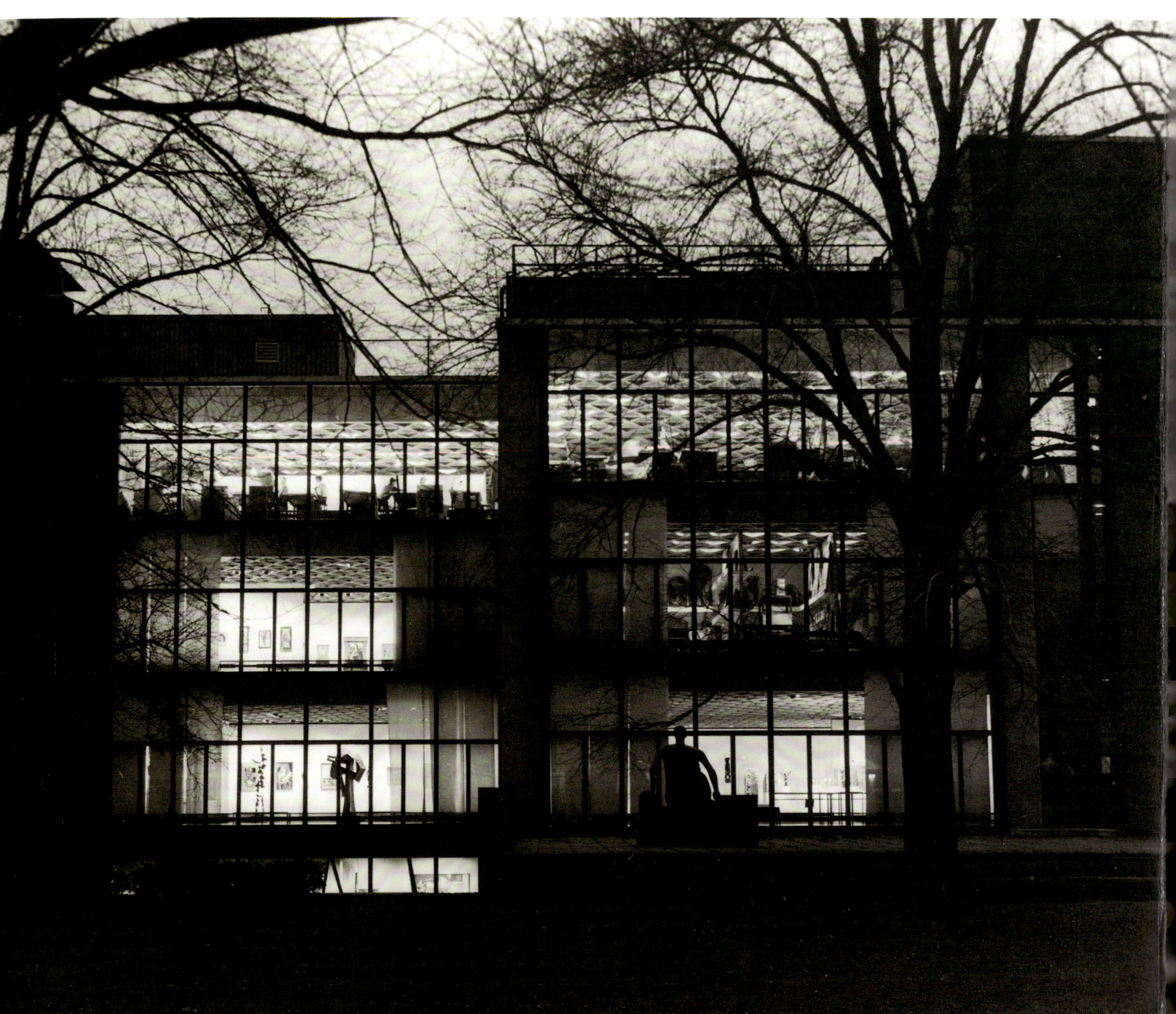

SUSAN B. MATHESON

Art for Yale

A History of the Yale University Art Gallery

YALE UNIVERSITY ART GALLERY

Published in conjunction with *Art for Yale: Defining Moments*, an exhibition organized at the Yale University Art Gallery in celebration of the Tercentennial of Yale University and shown at the Yale University Art Gallery, New Haven, Connecticut, April 19 – August 19, 2001

Funded by a grant from the Robert Lehman Foundation, Inc.

Cover: John Trumbull, *The Declaration of Independence, July 4, 1776* (detail), Trumbull Collection, Yale University Art Gallery

Frontispiece: Louis I. Kahn, *Yale University Art Gallery and Design Center*, 1953. Photograph ca. 1959, courtesy Yale University Art Gallery Archives

P. O. Box 208271, New Haven, Connecticut 06520-8271

ISBN numbers: cloth 0-89467-953-8; paperback 0-89467-955-4

Library of Congress Control Number: 2001098322

Edited by Joyce Ippolito
Designed by Katy Homans with production by Nerissa Vales
Printed by Meridian Printing, East Greenwich, Rhode Island, under the supervision of Daniel Frank

Contents

Director's Foreword VI

Acknowledgements IX

CHAPTER 1 Introduction: The Collegiate Collections 3

CHAPTER 2 Colonel Trumbull and his Collection 11

CHAPTER 3 The Missionary, the *Wolf*, and the 1858 Exhibition 23

CHAPTER 4 The Yale School of the Fine Arts 37

CHAPTER 5 The James Jackson Jarves Collection 45

CHAPTER 6 New Teachers, Old Pots, and Old Masters 55

CHAPTER 7 The Gallery of Fine Arts 69

CHAPTER 8 Francis P. Garvan and the Mabel Brady Garvan Collection of American Art 89

CHAPTER 9 Digging and Teaching 111

CHAPTER 10 Katherine Dreier and the Société Anonyme 121

CHAPTER 11 "A New Building for the Arts at Yale" 145

CHAPTER 12 A Magnet for Visitors and Art 171

CHAPTER 13 Modern and Contemporary 201

CHAPTER 14 "Towards Independence" 227

CHAPTER 15 "Art For Yale: Defining Moments" 247

Endnotes 260

Selected Bibliography 267

Exhibitions 1858–2001 271
Elise K. Kenney

Index 295

Foreword

On the occasion of Yale's Tercentennial, President Richard Levin asked that each school and museum at the University recognize this notable occasion by calling special attention to the role that human imagination and creativity have played in the learning life of the institution. The exhibition *Art for Yale: Defining Moments* and the accompanying book *Art for Yale: A History of the Yale University Art Gallery* celebrate this momentous anniversary with two major presentations of the history of the Yale University Art Gallery. Both tell the story of an extraordinary institution as seen through the growth of its permanent collections from the time of its founding in 1832 with John Trumbull's gift of his history paintings to the beginning of the twenty-first century.

Yale has long enjoyed the distinction not only of recognizing the importance of exposing students to original works of art during the progress of an academic education but of being the first college in the United States to build a museum specifically for its art collection. From the small neoclassical Trumbull Gallery on the old campus, to Street Hall in 1866, to the Swartwout building in 1928, to Louis Kahn's magnificent art gallery of 1953, the Yale Art Gallery's history is an inspiring story of generation after generation of alumni and teachers, curators and collectors, who believed in the emotional and intellectual power of original works of art. They shared the belief that great works of cultural, historic, or aesthetic value should be an integral part of every Yale student's education. Today we are the beneficiaries of their commitment to this vision of a university art gallery, to the unique role of a "teaching" museum. Everything we do in the Art Gallery has the ultimate purpose of helping people to see. Each distinguished object that enters the collection helps us do our job better.

The permanent collection is the core of a museum's identity. It is what gives the museum its character, and forms the foundation for its activities—education, research, conservation and preservation, exhibitions and publications. Long before there was a Yale Art Gallery, art came to Yale, beginning in 1718 with Elihu Yale's gift of Sir Godfrey Kneller's *Portrait of George I* to the then Collegiate School. Since then the collections have grown through hundreds of gifts and bequests to more than 85,000 objects, given with myriad intentions, and reflecting the full range of artistic expression from virtually every culture from ancient times to the present. Supported with endowments for student internships, research, conservation, and publications, these far-sighted and generous donations from alumni/ae and friends continue to leave a mark on generations of young people. By their example, these donors have set the standard for our acquisitions and programs in this new century.

Structured around the defining moments of the Art Gallery's history, the exhibition, which was conceived and organized by Helen A. Cooper, the Holcombe T. Green Curator of American Paintings and Sculpture, and this book, written by Susan B. Matheson, the Molly and Walter Bareiss Curator of Ancient Art, tell a many-layered story, of collections and donors, curators, directors, and faculty, of the growth of the museum as seen through its architecture, of the role of the Art Gallery in the teaching and making of art and art history at Yale, and the interaction of the Gallery with New Haven and the art world at large.

Art for Yale: Defining Moments and *Art for Yale: A History of the Yale University Art Gallery* are made possible by the Robert Lehman Foundation, named for Mr. Lehman, B.A. 1913, an extraordinary collector and benefactor of the Yale University Art Gallery. We are most grateful to the Foundation and to its President, Philip H. Isles, and its Board of Directors.

Today, as in the past, the Art Gallery is continuously being transformed by those who walk through its doors, who by their presence and benefactions give meaning to the art within its walls. We are proud to be a part of this distinguished history as we continue to build its future.

Jock Reynolds
Henry J. Heinz II Director

CONTRIBUTORS TO RESEARCH

Patricia E. Kane, Curator of American Decorative Arts

David L. Barquist, Associate Curator of American Decorative Arts

Helen A. Cooper, Holcombe T. Green Curator of American Painting and Sculpture

Robin Jaffee Frank, Associate Curator of American Painting and Sculpture

Megan Doyon, Museum Assistant, Ancient Art

David Ake Sensabaugh, Curator of Asian Art

Sadako Ohki, Assistant Curator of Asian Art

Mary L. Kordak, Jan and Frederick Mayer Curator of Education

Ellen Alvord, Assistant Curator of Education

Jennifer Gross, Seymour H. Knox, Jr., Curator of European and Contemporary Art

Joanna Weber, Assistant Curator of European and Contemporary Art

Suzanne Boorsch, Curator of Prints, Drawings, and Photographs

Elisabeth Hodermarksy, Assistant Curator of Prints, Drawings, and Photographs

Mark Aronson, Chief Conservator

Patricia Sherwin Garland, Senior Conservator of Paintings

Elise K. Kenney, Archivist

Louisa Cunningham, Deputy Director, Finance and Administration

Jock Reynolds, Henry J. Heinz II Director

Acknowledgements

This book complements the exhibition *Art for Yale: Defining Moments*, which was shown at the Yale Art Gallery from April 19 to August 19, 2001, in celebration of the Tercentennial of Yale University. Organized by Helen A. Cooper, the Holcombe T. Green Curator of American Paintings and Sculpture, *Defining Moments* traced the history of the Yale University Art Gallery by displaying the highlights of its collection in sequence with a narrative timeline of the significant events in the life of the Gallery, the University, and the museum world. Since most of the works in the exhibition are well published, the decision was made to produce this history rather than a traditional exhibition catalogue with extensive entries on each object. I am grateful to our director, Jock Reynolds, for inviting me to undertake the book, thereby providing me with the chance to fulfill a dream that many of us have had for the Gallery for years, and to Helen Cooper, for endorsing the idea of a narrative history as the complement to her exhibition and offering her support and wise advice throughout.

Because this book is the only published record of *Defining Moments*, the vast majority of the works included in the exhibition are included here as well. Like the exhibition, this book is thus based on the collaborative effort of my curatorial colleagues at the Gallery, who recommended to Helen Cooper the works from which she chose to represent their respective parts of the collection. It is a pleasure to thank these colleagues here, not only for their initial wisdom and creativity in choosing the best and most captivating objects, but also for their unfailing generosity in sharing their knowledge of their collections, reviewing text, and answering the myriad questions of an author outside their fields who must constantly have seemed to be in over her head. Their names are listed as contributors on page viii. I am also grateful to my colleagues Mark Aronson and Patricia Garland for helpful information on conservation issues and to Mary Kordak and Ellen Alvord for information and suggestions about our education department and programming.

Primary sources are fundamental to any institutional history, and the fun of a project like this is in the discovery of letters, notes, and other documents that reveal new details about the people and events that are woven into the narrative. The Gallery's archives would not have existed as a resource for either the exhibition or this book without the dedicated efforts over more than a decade of our indefatigable archivist, Elise K. Kenney, who has single-handedly created a working archive out of the Gallery's disparate historical files. Her invaluable work compiling a list of the Gallery's exhibitions appears as an appendix in this volume. Her comprehensive knowledge of the Gallery's history, framed in the context of the broader knowledge of the University that she has gleaned from the Yale University archives, guided this project throughout, as she checked my facts and served as my historical conscience. If my emphasis is in some cases not what hers would have been, the sin of omission is mine. I thank her profoundly, as we all do, for her dedication to the Gallery, and on a personal level for her patience, good humor, and unbelievably hard work. Judith A. Schiff, Chief Research Archivist, and William R. Massa, Jr., Public Services Archivist, Manuscripts and Archives Collection, Sterling Memorial Library, and their colleagues in the Yale collection were unfailingly generous to both Elise Kenney and me in their assistance with the archives of Yale's presidents, treasurers, and other officers, councils, and committees, and with many of the archival photographs that add flavor to this volume.

A book of this nature depends on the work of others, both past and present. Museum staff, faculty, students, donors, and outside scholars who have contributed to our knowledge about the Yale collections have provided the facts and interpretations of individual works of art discussed in these pages. Many of these individuals remain anonymous, their work recorded in the museum's permanent files. While it is thus impossible to recognize each contribution to the collective record of the collection, it is imperative that I acknowledge my heavy reliance on the research contained in the permanent files and my debt to those who created them. I have also relied heavily on the published catalogues, books, and articles touching on the collection, but rather than weigh the text of this book down with meticulous documentation, I have chosen to list in the Selected Bibliography (pp. 267–270) the books and catalogues to which I have referred. The reader should consult these catalogues for further information on individual works of art and their makers. The *Yale University Art Gallery Bulletin*, published since 1926, has been an invaluable resource for information about donors, exhibitions, and programs, as well as on objects, collections, and museum staff.

I offer very special thanks to Professor Jules D. Prown, who generously read the entire manuscript and wisely and gently did much to improve it. He has been deeply involved in the Gallery for decades, and his unique perspective of having been curator and interim director of the Gallery, an intensive user of the collections in his teaching, and director of the Yale Center for British Art made him the ideal critic.

I am also grateful to Professor Robert L. Herbert, who kindly brought his extraordinary expertise on the Société Anonyme to bear on my chapter on Katherine Dreier. Professor Vincent Scully suggested including the exhibition *Ars in Urbe* and generously shared his views on its significance. Professor William H. Pierson, Jr., related stories of life in the School of the Fine Arts when he was a student in painting here in the 1930s. Professor Charles H. Sawyer graciously responded to questions about various issues related to his tenure as Director of the Division of the Arts. Professor Alexander Purves has been a constant source of insight into the Kahn building, and John Cohen shared many personal anecdotes about Kahn's teaching and design of the Gallery. Professor George Heard Hamilton was very helpful with questions relating to modern art at the Gallery, and I am grateful to him and to his son, Richard Heard Hamilton, for permission to reproduce the *Linear Construction* by Naum Gabo in chapter 11. Caroline Rollins has always been a fountain of information on Gallery life, and her written summary of the Gallery's history is something I have consulted with appreciation. Victoria J. Solan, Shelley Hagen, and Baird Jarmon, graduate students in the History of Art department, provided helpful research on a variety of topics. Barbara L. Narendra, the Archivist at the Peabody Museum of Natural History at Yale, was exceptionally helpful in tracking down facts from the Peabody Museum's early history that related to that of the Gallery. Marie N. Weltzien, Director of Public Information at the Gallery, helped enormously in locating publicity and illustrations for the Gallery's past exhibitions and programs.

My warmest thanks go to Megan Doyon, the unfailingly professional and able Museum Assistant in my department, who willingly and with good spirit sacrificed her expected work on the ancient collections to support this project in innumerable ways. I am grateful for her patience and energy and for making us all laugh at the right time, and hope that what she has learned about the Gallery through this undertaking will compensate for the deferral of her work on ancient art.

The heart of a book about an art museum must surely be the images of the works of art in its collection, and here, as with the collection records, this book owes its existence to Gallery colleagues past and present. Not all their names are known, and I have not been able to attribute every image to a specific photographer, but I cannot fail to thank our photographers Emiddio de Cusati, Joseph Szaszfai, Regina Montfort, Michael Agee, Carl Kaufmann, and now Alex Contreras and Susan Cole for the extraordinary visual record that, beginning in 1936, they, in sequence, have created. In addition, it is a pleasure to thank Janet Zullo, Digital Imaging Assistant Project Manager, for her excellent printing; John ffrench, Digital Imaging Project Manager, for lending his department to the project and for his commitment to the highest standards; and Suzanne Warner, Service Representative, Rights and Reproductions Department, for her constant assistance with existing images. Special thanks are offered to the administrative assistants in the curatorial departments, all of whom responded willingly to innumerable requests for images and information: Nancy Yates, Joanne Thompson, American Decorative Arts; Janet Miller, American Painting and Sculpture; Ami Potter, Asian Art; Yvonne Morant, European and Contemporary Art; and Russell Lord, Prints, Drawings, and Photographs.

Louisa Cunningham, Deputy Director for Finance and Administration, and her department, notably Charlene Senical, Assistant Business Manager, Noreen Mattei, Financial Assistant, and Maria D'Urso, Financial Coordinator, helped enormously with information about donors and funds supporting the collections and programs, as well as with managing the many financial details associated with the project.

The manuscript was edited by Joyce Ippolito, to whom I am especially grateful for her meticulous work and for her patience with an irregular schedule and short deadlines. Her precision and care were exemplary, while her sensitivity to the material supported the atmosphere that I was trying to create. I am fortunate to have had Elise K. Kenney, who, in addition to being the Gallery's archivist, is an experienced editor, as a second reader of the manuscript, and I benefited greatly from her editorial help.

The raw material of text and images has been transformed into a crisp and elegant book by Katy Homans, whose design achieves perfectly a balance between the traditional and the modern that in its own way evokes the Yale Art Gallery. Her response to the material was flawless, and the final result surpasses even my ambitious vision. My very special thanks go to Katy and to her able assistant Nerissa Vales. Equally, my sincere thanks go to Daniel Frank of Meridian Printing, who oversaw the publication of the book with thorough dedication and an unsurpassed standard of quality. He truly deserves his reputation as the best.

Both the exhibition *Art for Yale: Defining Moments* and this book have been funded by the extraordinary generosity of the Robert Lehman Foundation, Inc. As a history of the Yale University Art Gallery, this book is but a beginning. There will no doubt be others in the future, as the Gallery grows and continues to flourish and as it expands its vital teaching mission at Yale and in the community. I hope that this volume, like the *Defining Moments* exhibition, provides an approachable introduction to the museum, its collections, and the people who brought them together, and will serve as a record of a key part of this distinguished University in its tercentennial year. Like the exhibition, it is offered warmly as a token of thanks to the generous donors who have made the Yale University Art Gallery possible.

Susan B. Matheson
The Molly and Walter Bareiss Curator of Ancient Art
Chief Curator

Art for Yale

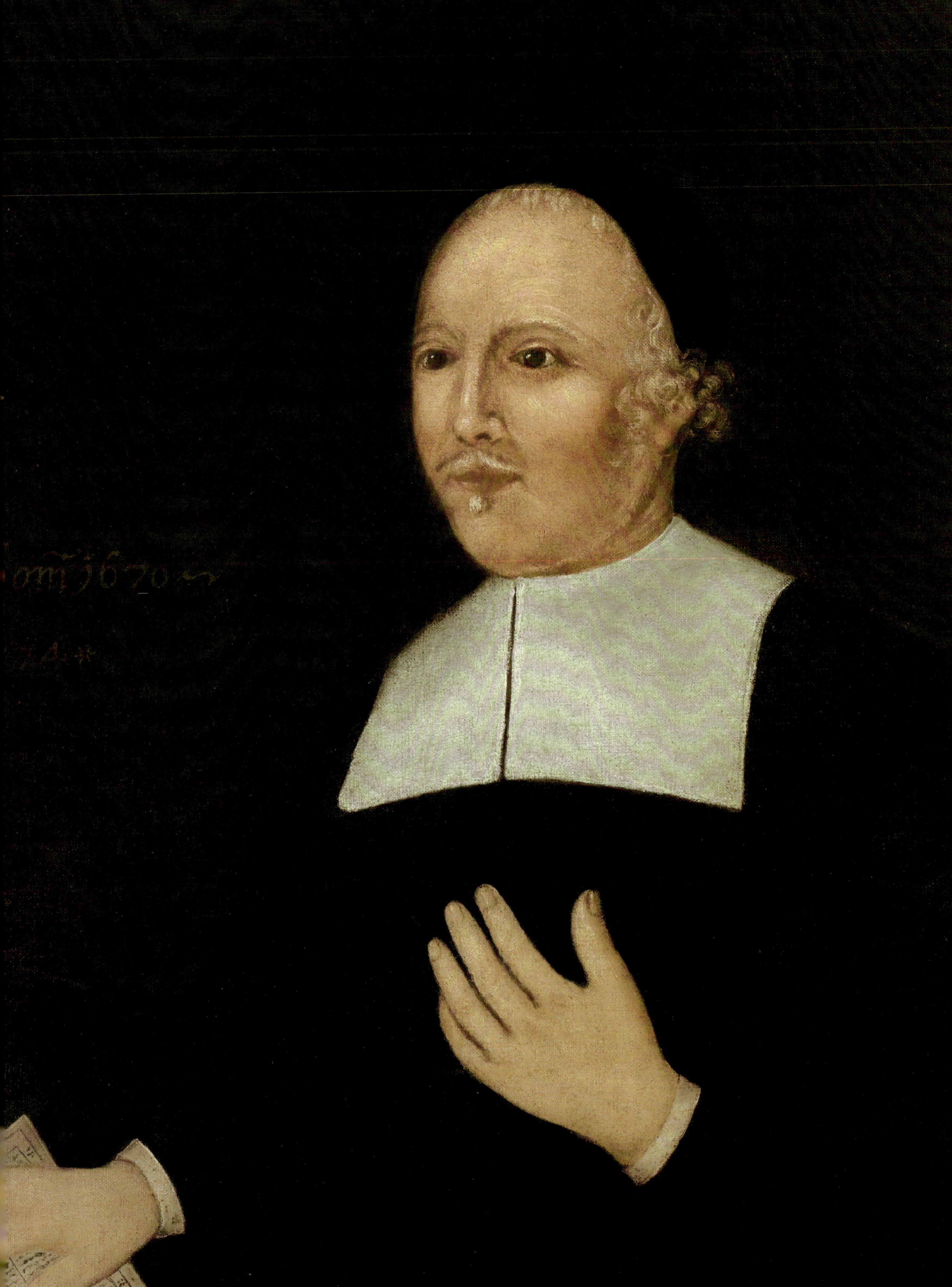
1670

CHAPTER I

Introduction: The Collegiate Collection

Yale University began collecting art well before the United States of America was an independent nation. As is being celebrated in this tercentennial year, Yale University marks its founding in 1701, with the start of the Collegiate School in Saybrook, Connecticut. Its history as Yale College and as a collector of art began shortly thereafter, in 1718. It was in that year, two years after the Collegiate School had moved to New Haven (1716), that Governor Elihu Yale gave it £650 and several boxes of books. In return for his generosity, the school was named "Yale College." Accompanying the donation of funds and books, the cornerstones of any college, was Governor Yale's third gift, a *Portrait of King George I* by the British artist Sir Godfrey Kneller (fig. 1). Yale College's first acquisition of a work of art is thus rooted in its earliest history.

The Kneller portrait was the foundation of a collection that has grown to more than eighty-five thousand works of art in fields ranging from American and British through Asian, European, African, Precolumbian, and ancient Mediterranean art. Among them are some of the best of their kind in the world. During the first phase of its growth, this was simply the collegiate collection. Not until 1832, with the acquisition of paintings by Colonel John Trumbull and the erection of the Trumbull Gallery to house them, can one speak of the existence of a college art museum at Yale, or for that matter anywhere in the United States. The Yale University Art Gallery is the oldest university art museum in America.[1] This book traces the history of the museum, its collections, and the people whose generosity and wisdom have endowed them.

THE COLLEGIATE COLLECTION

The collection grew slowly at first: prior to 1832, fewer than thirty-five acquisitions are recorded. Almost all of them are American portraits. Many had ties to the history of Yale, often given by students in honor of their professors, while others portrayed important public figures of the day. All would have been considered images of noble souls who would have been worthy role models for aspiring students. In acquiring portraits with these ideals in mind, Yale was acting in a manner consistent with other New England colleges. Dartmouth and Bowdoin Colleges both had significant portrait

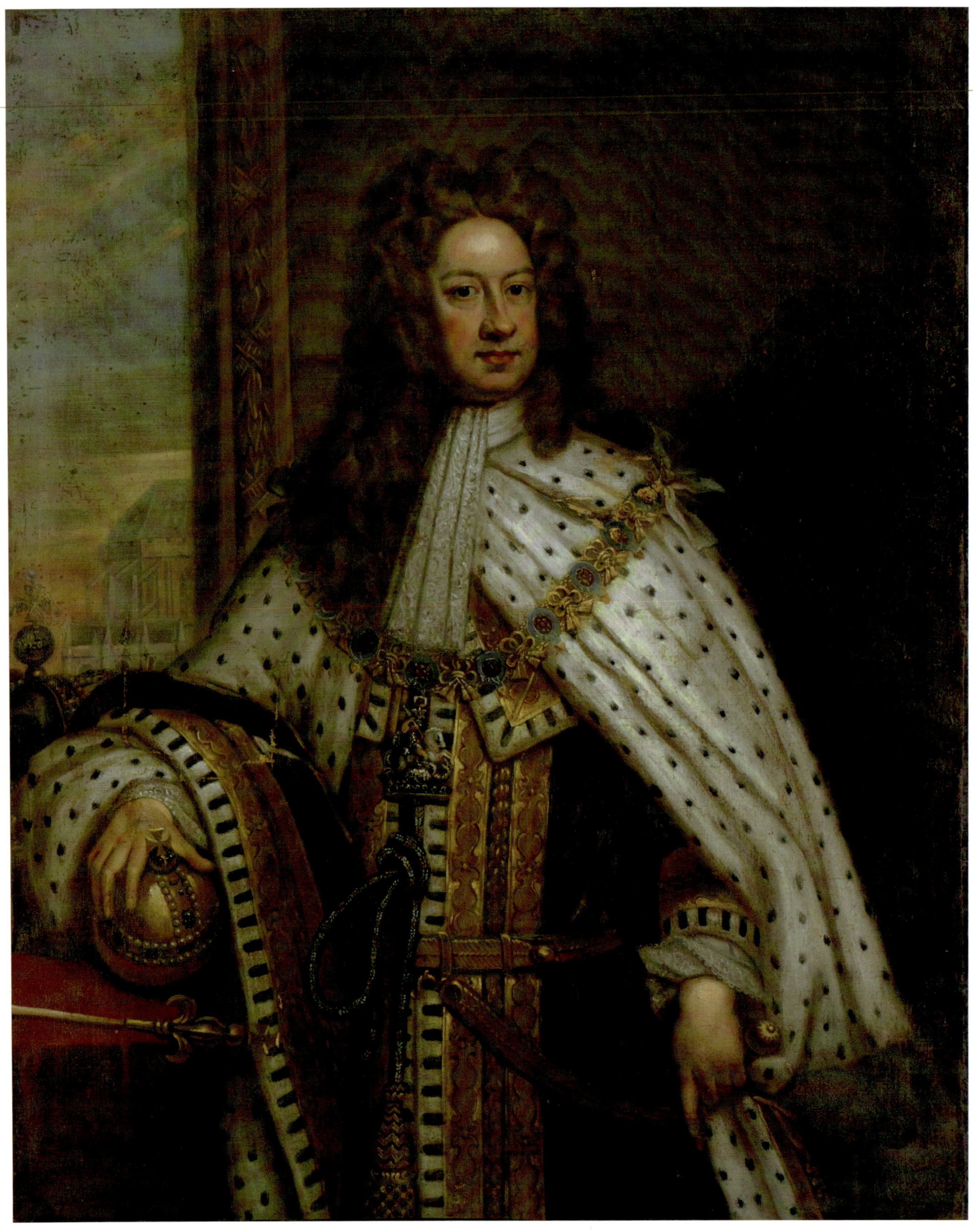

FIG. 1
Sir Godfrey Kneller
King George I, early 18th century
Oil on canvas, 127.3 x 103.5 cm
Gift of Governor Elihu Yale
1718.1

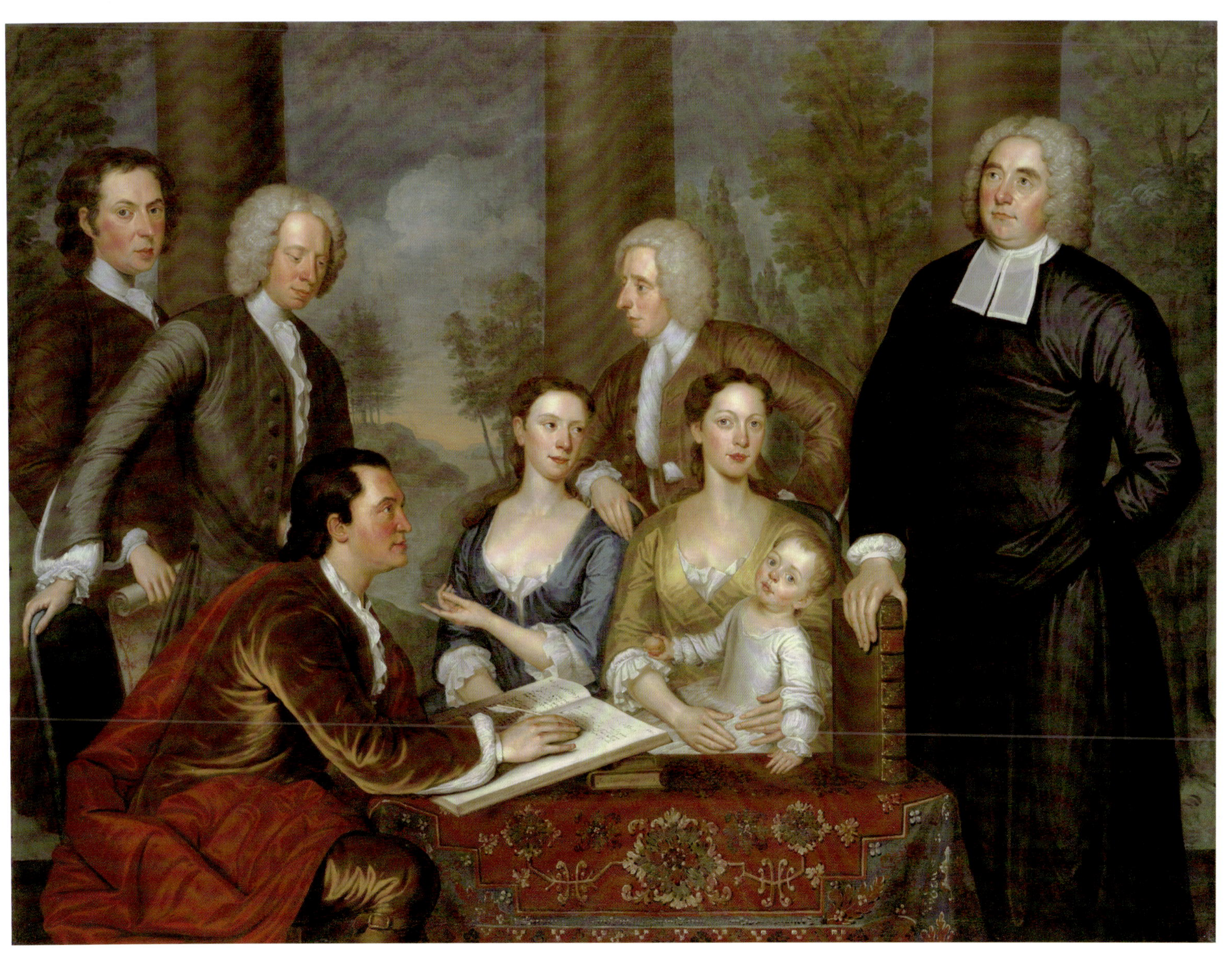

FIG. 2
John Smibert
Dean Berkeley and His Entourage (The Bermuda Group), 1729–31
Oil on canvas, 176.5 x 236.2 cm
Gift of Isaac Lothrop
1808.1

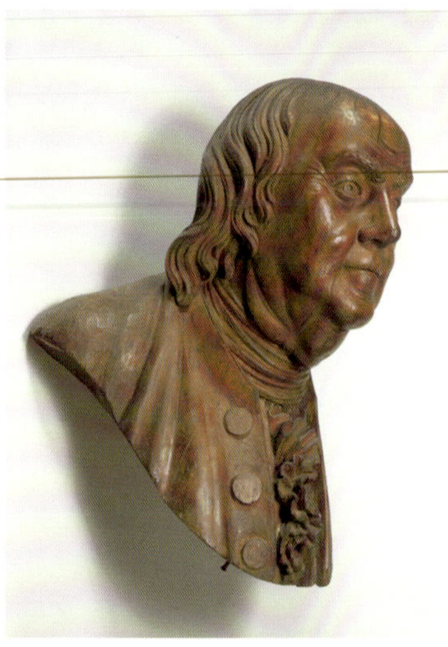

FIG. 3
William Rush
Benjamin Franklin, 1787
North American white pine, 54.6 x 40.0 x 38.1 cm
Yale University Art Gallery
1804.4

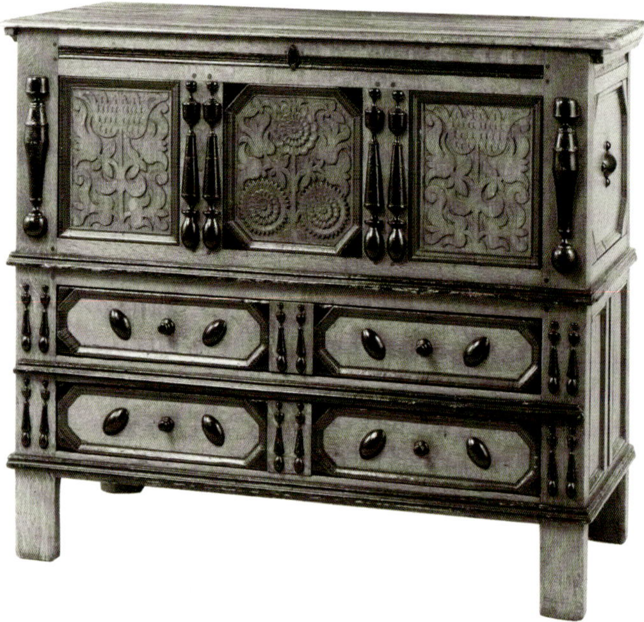

FIG. 4
Possibly by Peter Blin
Chest with Drawers, 1670–1710
Perhaps cedar, 101.6 x 121.0 x 54.3 cm
Donor unknown
1800.4

FIG. 5
The Davenport Limner
John Davenport, 1670
Oil on canvas, 69.2 x 58.4 cm
Yale University Art Gallery
1750.1

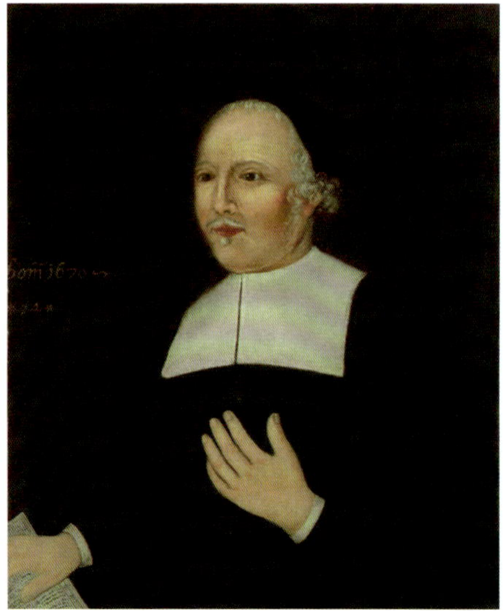

collections before 1832.[2] In concentrating on portraits, Yale was also reflecting general attitudes toward collecting and commissioning art in the early years of the American Republic. Most loyal Yankees looked on collecting Old Masters as a hobby of the wealthy European aristocracy that was decadent, self-indulgent, and wasteful of the resources and attention that should be devoted to the development of the new nation.[3] For both the aspiring artist and the institutional collector, portraiture was the only acceptable art form. There were exceptions, of course, and the attitude changed by the middle of the nineteenth century, but for a New England college founded and run by Congregational ministers the dominant attitude was bound to prevail.[4] Although the idea of acquiring works of art as moralizing reminders of great figures of the past diminished over the years and finally disappeared by the late nineteenth century, the acquisition and commissioning of portraits of "Yale Worthies" as commemoratives continue to the present day.

Several aspects of the early history of the collection are particularly important. First, there is the prominence of American art, which arguably remains the star of the Yale Art Gallery's collections. Yale began acquiring what are now recognized as world-class collections of American paintings, sculpture, and decorative arts well before 1832. The first works of American painting came into the collection in 1720, a pair of portraits of *Anne, Queen of England* (1665–1714) and her consort *George, Prince of Denmark* (1653–1708) by J. Cooper, a little-known artist apparently trained as a carriage painter who copied these portraits from engravings.[5] Another important early acquisition is John Smibert's *Dean Berkeley and His Entourage (The Bermuda Group)*, the gift of Isaac Lothrop in 1808 (fig. 2). The first acquisition of American sculpture was the portrait of Benjamin Franklin by William Rush, acquired in 1804 (fig. 3). More than fifty years earlier (1753), Franklin had been awarded an honorary M.A. degree by Yale. The first American decorative arts acquisitions, a chest of drawers possibly by Peter Blin (fig. 4) and an eighteenth-century desk with later bookcases, came in 1800.

Second, already cited, is the importance of portraiture and the link to the history both of Yale and of the times. Such acquisitions intertwine the themes of history, early Yale, alumni donors, and living artists. The acquisition in 1750 of the portrait of *John Davenport* by the painter known as the Davenport Limner after this painting (fig. 5), for example, reflects Yale's early history. John Davenport (1597–1669/70) was the founder and first minister of the New Haven Colony. An eloquent preacher, he served as pastor of First Church (Congregational) for thirty years. The acquisition of his portrait embodies the fundamental link between Yale College and the Congregational Church that stretched from the school's founding well into the nineteenth century. The first Yale purchase of a work of art was also a portrait tied to Yale's history, a likeness of a professor, Reverend Elisha Williams, painted by Reuben Moulthrop in 1795.

A portrait given in 1790 of the Reverend Nehemiah Strong (1728/29–1807), Professor of Mathematics and Natural Philosophy, by Ralph Earl (fig. 6), underscores the church–college link. Born in Northampton, Massachusetts, in 1728/29, Strong was ordained a minister in Simsbury, Connecticut, in 1761. He was Yale's first Professor of Mathematics and Natural Philosophy, a post created in 1770, and remained on the faculty until 1781. He also practiced law, tutored in private schools, and published a series of almanacs and a book on astronomy.[6] Because Strong was a Yale graduate (B.A. 1755, M.A. 1758), this acquisition also signaled the importance of Yale alumni in the growth of the College's art collections. Equally significant is the fact that Earl's portrait of Nehemiah Strong was the gift of the artist, establishing as early as 1790 the key role of living artists in the history of Yale's collections and museum.[7]

Other early acquisitions included portraits by two prominent painters of the time, Gilbert Stuart and Samuel F. B. Morse (B.A. 1810, M.A. 1816, LL.D. 1846). Three portraits by Stuart entered the College's collection in 1830, two years after the artist's death, and five portraits by Morse were given to Yale before 1830. One of these, the portrait of Eli Whitney (1822), was the gift in 1827 of George Hoadley (B.A. 1801). It was the first work of art to be given by an individual Yale alumnus, establishing, along with early donations by colleagues and classmates of Yale graduates, the tradition of alumni giving that dominates the Gallery's subsequent history. Morse's portrait of *Alexander Metcalf Fisher*

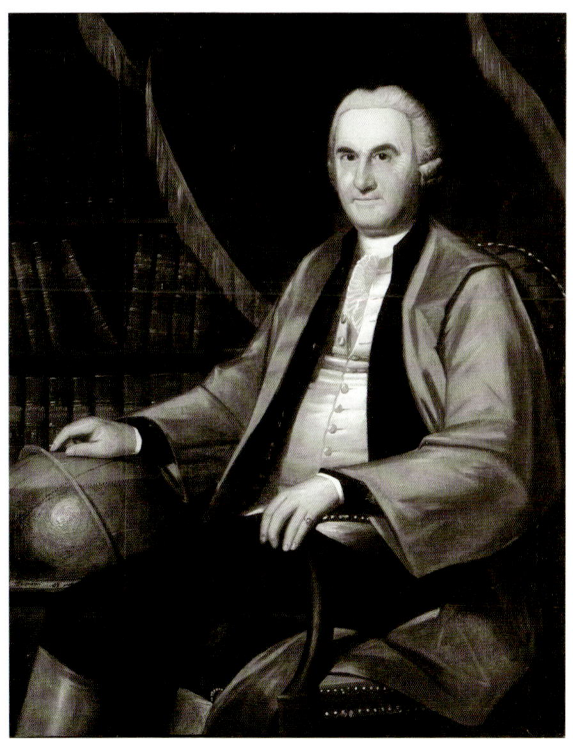

FIG. 6
Ralph Earl
Reverend Nehemiah Strong, 1790
Oil on canvas, 172.1 x 96.5 cm
Gift of Ralph Earl
1790.1

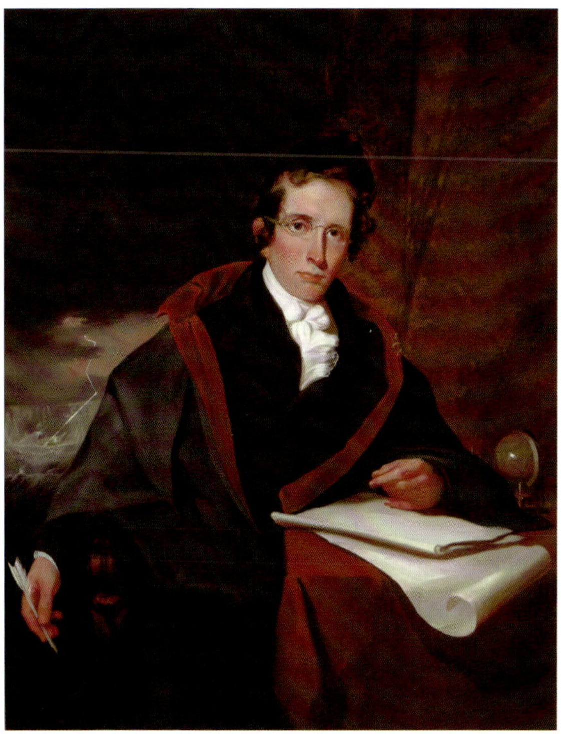

FIG. 7
Samuel F. B. Morse
Alexander Metcalf Fisher, 1822
Oil on canvas, 112.7 x 58.9 cm
Gift of Colleagues of the Sitter
1822.1

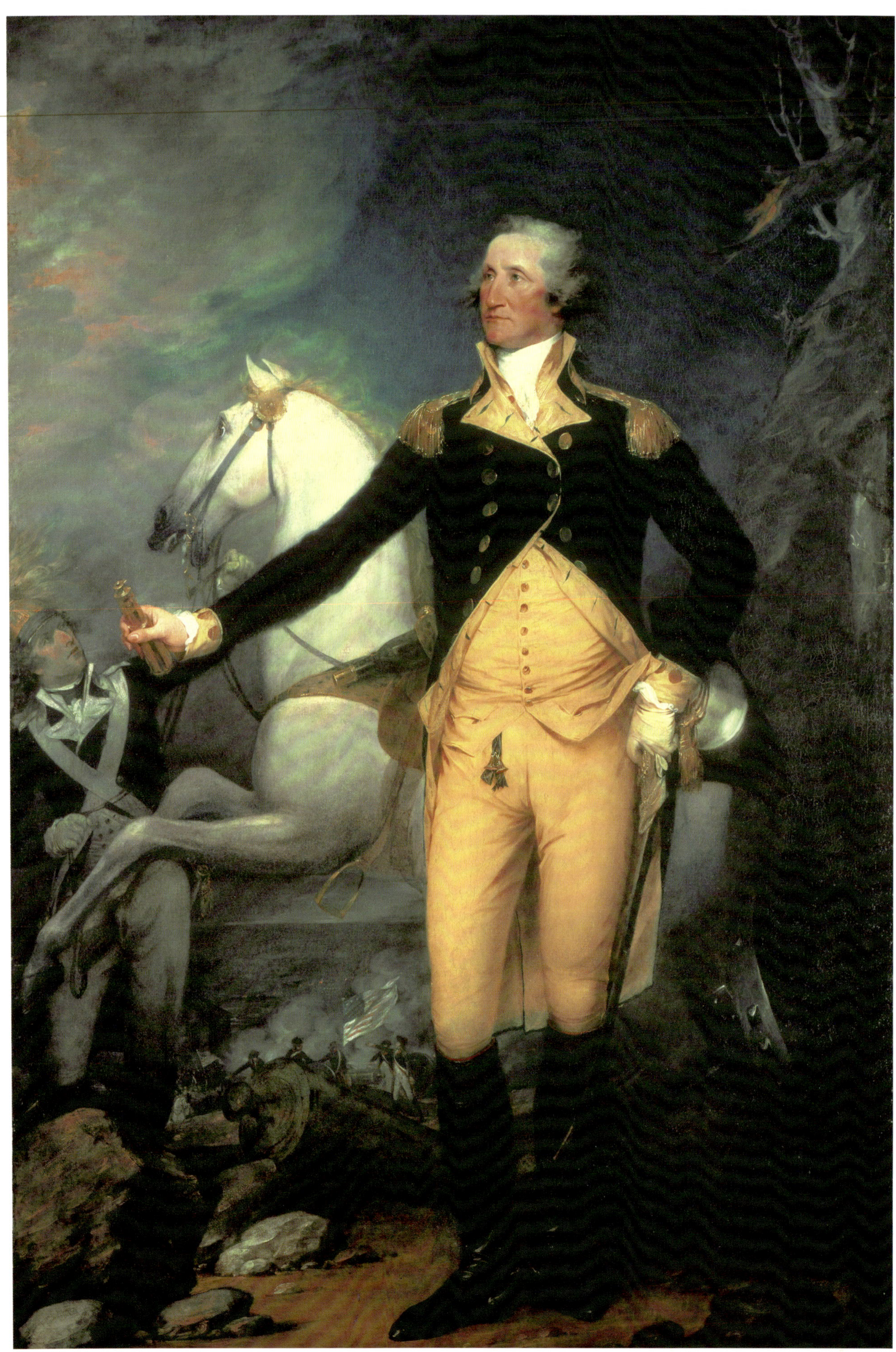

(fig. 7), painted in 1822, was a gift to the College by the sitter's colleagues the same year. The portrait commemorates Fisher, a Yale graduate (B.A. 1813, M.A. 1816) who as a youthful professor of mathematics perished in the sinking of the *Albion* on a transatlantic crossing in 1822. A second portrait of Fisher, a marble bust by the sculptor Hezekiah Augur, a prominent New Haven artist, was donated by the sitter's Yale classmates in 1827.

Equally prominent at the time was Nathaniel Jocelyn, a number of whose portraits of Hillhouses, Woolseys, Streets, and other distinguished members of the Yale and New Haven communities came into the Yale collection in the 1820s and '30s. Jocelyn's portraits had been exhibited at the National Academy in New York, but unlike most artists associated with the Academy, who had studios in New York, he maintained his studio in New Haven, painting portraits to supply frequent demand while also serving as head of the art department of the American Bank Note Company.[8] Jocelyn's best-known work is his portrait of Cinqué, the leader of the Amistad slaves, now in the collection of the New Haven Colony Historical Society.

The most significant encounter between Yale and a living artist was that with John Trumbull. This relationship began as early as 1792 with Trumbull's submission of a design for the Yale campus.[9] Ultimately, with the acquisition of Trumbull's Revolutionary War paintings and the opening of the Trumbull Gallery in 1832, it led to the transition from a collegiate collection to an art museum.

Three portraits by John Trumbull entered the Yale collection before 1832. The first painting was his portrait of his father, Governor Jonathan Trumbull (LL.D. 1779), given to Yale by the artist's brother, Lt. Governor Jonathan Trumbull (LL.D. 1797), in 1797.[10] Also acquired was a portrait of Timothy Dwight (B.A. 1769, president of Yale 1795–1817), given by the Class of 1817 in the year of the president's death. The most important was his portrait of *General George Washington at the Battle of Trenton* (1792; fig. 8). Acquired in 1806 as a gift of the Society of the Cincinnati in Connecticut, Trumbull's portrait was viewed by General Lafayette when he visited the College in 1824.[11] The portrait of Washington was a major commission at the time, and it is now recognized as one of Trumbull's finest portraits. Trumbull considered his service as Washington's aide-de-camp to be one of the key moments in his life. Truly a defining moment for the artist, it set the stage for the Revolutionary War pictures that would make his career and become the cornerstone of the Trumbull Gallery and Yale's American paintings collection.

FIG. 8
John Trumbull
General Washington at the Battle of Trenton, 1792
Oil on canvas, 235.0 x 160.0 cm
Gift of the Society of the Cincinnati in Connecticut
1806.1

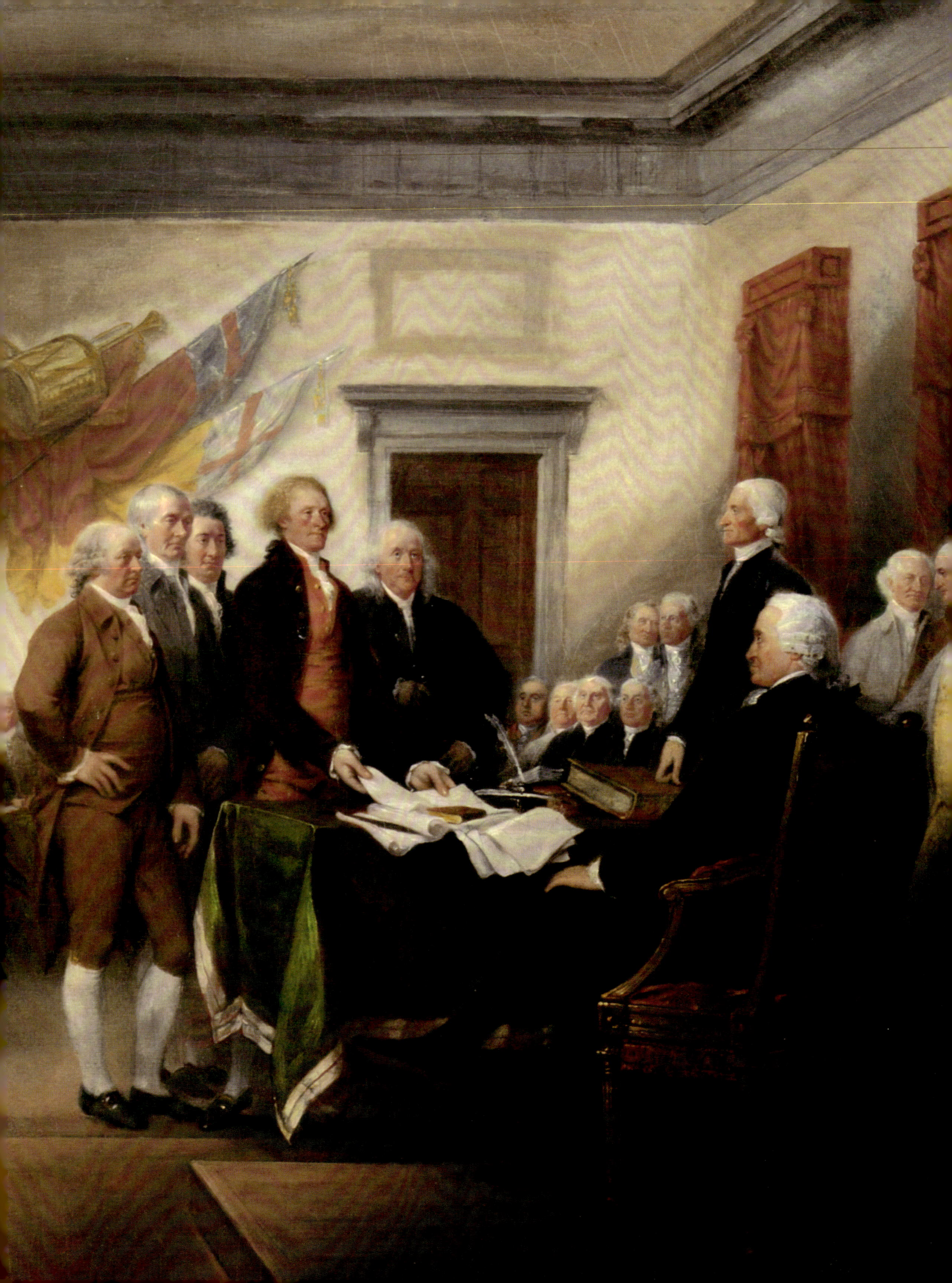

CHAPTER 2

Colonel Trumbull and His Collection

The Yale Art Gallery's mission to collect, preserve, and exhibit original works of art, including works of living artists, and to teach art and the history of art from these originals is grounded in the acquisition of the Trumbull Collection and the building of the Gallery to house it. These two events marked the founding of the Yale University Art Gallery in 1832.

John Trumbull (fig. 9) was born in Lebanon, Connecticut, in 1756.[1] He was the son of Jonathan Trumbull, then a representative to the Connecticut General Assembly and later the governor of Connecticut, and his wife, Faith, who was descended from John Robinson, the Pilgrim leader who came on the Mayflower. Sent to Harvard to study law instead of to the celebrated colonial portraitist John Singleton Copley to study painting, as he had wished, Trumbull nevertheless visited Copley in Cambridge and taught himself painting by copying works from books and from the portraits that hung on the walls of the college. He graduated in 1773 (the youngest man in his class) and returned to Lebanon. Trumbull entered the war for independence in 1775 as an adjutant of the First Regiment of Connecticut, but General Washington soon appointed him as an aide-de-camp. By the next year he was a deputy adjutant general, with the rank of colonel. He was sent to Fort Ticonderoga, where he made a major contribution to the war effort in the form of a plan for strengthening and defending the fort. After the British retreated from Ticonderoga, Trumbull rejoined Washington at Trenton. His war experience and his contact with Washington and other key figures later provided the subjects of his most celebrated paintings.

Trumbull resigned his commission in 1777 and, after several failed business attempts, resumed painting. Determined to pursue his art studies abroad, in 1780 he went to London to study with Benjamin West. Gilbert Stuart was a fellow student and became Trumbull's close friend, a relationship that ultimately yielded a portrait of Trumbull by Stuart. Refusing to keep his anti-British sentiments quiet, and perhaps as a reprisal for the hanging of Major André, Trumbull was arrested for treason and spent almost eight months in a British prison, where he occupied himself by painting and drawing. Returning to Connecticut, Trumbull struggled to

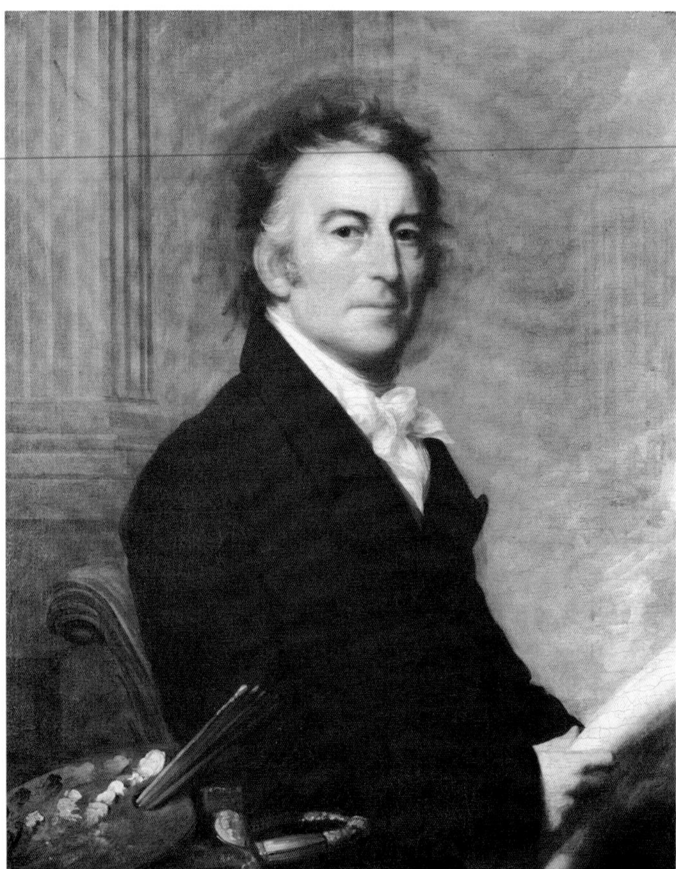

FIG. 9
Samuel Lovett Waldo and William Jewett
Colonel John Trumbull, ca. 1821
Oil on canvas, 83.8 x 66.0 cm
Gift of Alfred Wild Silliman and Benjamin Silliman IV, B.A. 1870, M.A. 1873
1920.23

convince his father that he should pursue painting as a career, and the governor at last relented.

In 1784 Trumbull returned to London, to West's studio. Here he began his Revolutionary War pictures, completing *The Death of General Warren at the Battle of Bunker's Hill* and *The Death of General Montgomery in the Attack on Quebec,* both now at Yale. Trumbull visited Paris in 1786, where he was the guest of Thomas Jefferson and became acquainted with the preeminent artists and intellectuals of the day. Trumbull began *The Declaration of Independence* (fig. 10) in Paris, basing his painting on the description of the event and the plan of the room that Jefferson provided (fig. 11) and adjusting it after discussions with Jefferson and John Adams.[2] Each figure in the painting required an individual likeness, which resulted in an American odyssey for Trumbull as he sought each signer/member of the Continental Congress for a portrait. After his return to America from London in 1789, Trumbull spent the next five years painting miniature portraits of the celebrated individuals who had witnessed the great events of the Revolutionary War. These miniature portraits, many of which came to Yale with the Trumbull Collection, served as the basis for Trumbull's large-scale portraits and the likenesses of these individuals in historical paintings such as the *Declaration of Independence.*

The *Declaration* was finally completed in 1817. It was exhibited in the young nation's House of Representatives, and it inspired Congress to commission the artist to create four large paintings of Revolutionary War subjects, including the *Declaration of Independence,* to decorate the Capitol Rotunda. Trumbull copied the *Declaration* now at Yale, but before installing the new large version in Washington, he toured it to New York, Boston, Baltimore, and Philadelphia, where it was exhibited in Independence Hall. Thousands of visitors paid to see it. Trumbull's painting had become an American icon. The fame of the *Declaration* and its companion Revolutionary War paintings was a significant factor in Yale's decision to acquire the paintings in 1832.

Trumbull was thus well established as the nation's premier American history painter by the time Yale acquired his Revolutionary War series in 1832. Prior to this, however, he had made a career as a well-known

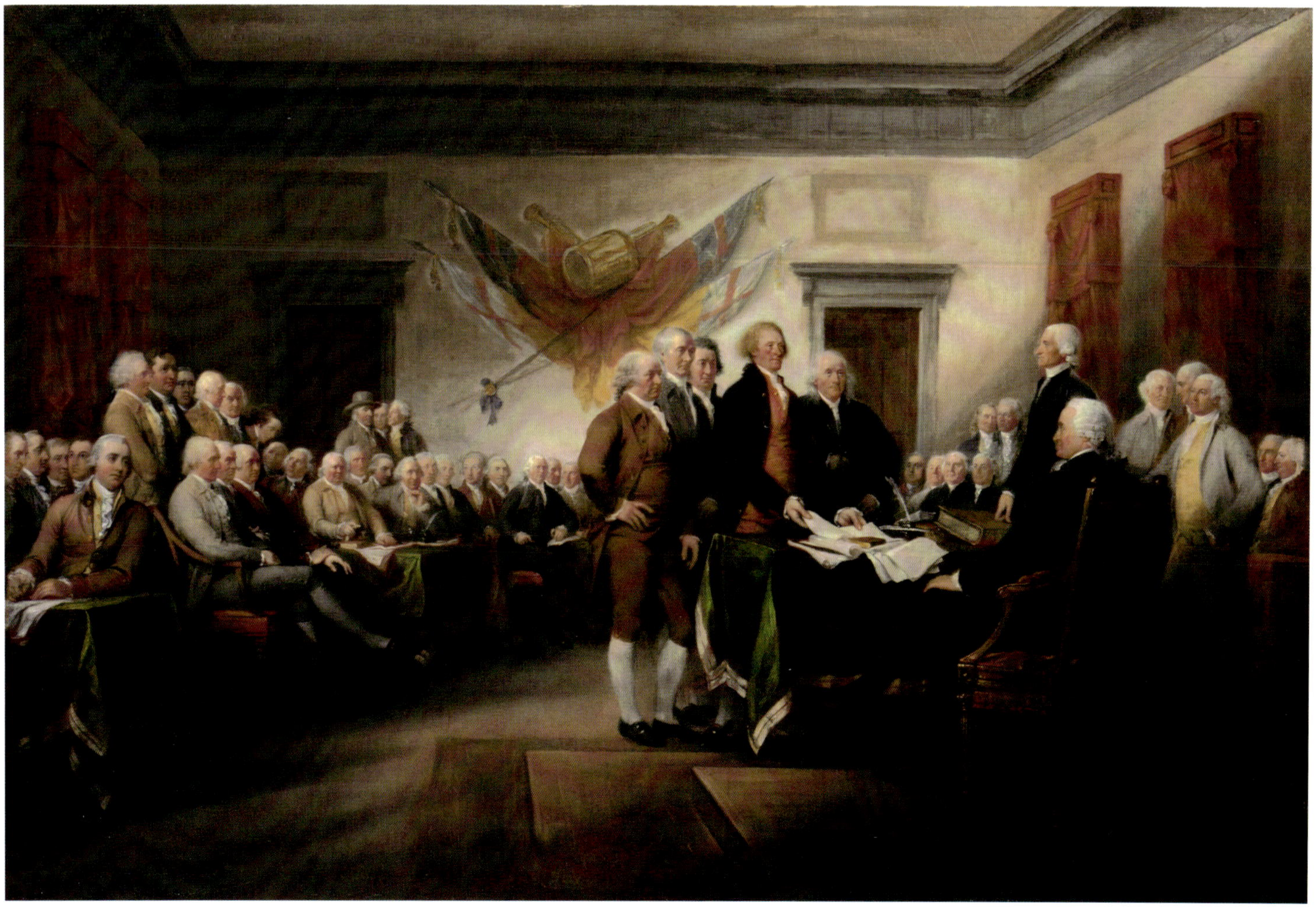

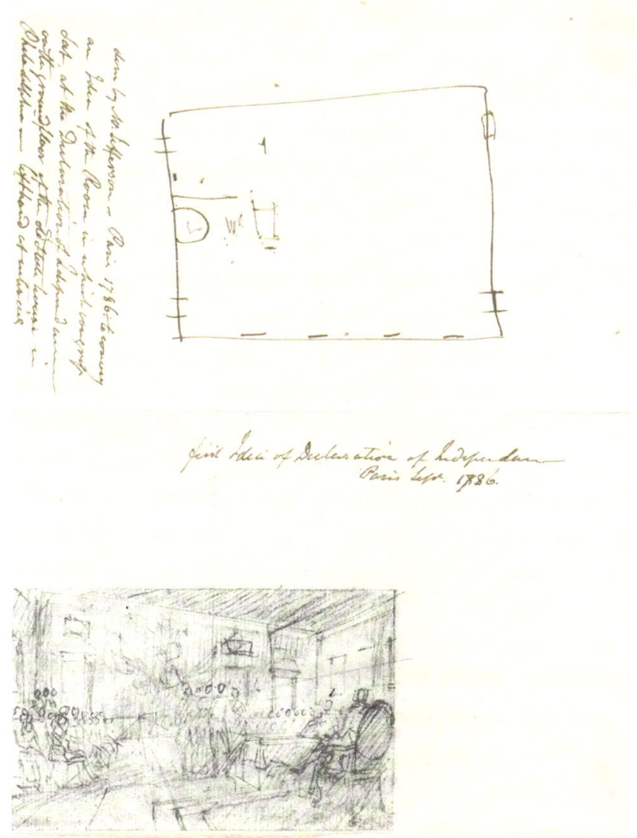

FIG. 10
John Trumbull
The Declaration of Independence, July 4, 1776, 1786–1820
Oil on canvas, 53.0 x 78.7 cm
Trumbull Collection
1832.3

FIG. 11
John Trumbull and
Thomas Jefferson
First Idea for the Declaration of Independence, Paris, September 1786, 1786
Graphite and brown ink, 23.0 x 17.6 cm
Gift of Mr. Ernest A. Bigelow
1926.8.2

portrait painter, sharing the spotlight with Gilbert Stuart and Charles Willson Peale. Beginning with portraits of family members, by 1790 and 1791 he was receiving commissions for portraits of George Washington and Governor George Clinton for City Hall in New York.[3] Between 1805 and 1808 he painted national figures like Alexander Hamilton and distinguished New Yorkers like DeWitt Clinton and Edward Livingston, also for City Hall.

These powerful contacts resulted in Trumbull's being elected vice president of the American Academy of Arts in 1805, which was founded by Edward Livingston's brother Robert and run by a board of New York's most prominent business and professional men.[4] Beginning in 1817 Trumbull served as the Academy's president for nineteen years. For nearly half of his tenure, the Academy was the only institution in New York devoted to the arts. Trumbull worked to promote the Academy and artists, and under him the Academy's exhibitions flourished and its collections grew. His efforts accomplished much toward his goals of increased audience and patronage for the arts. He designed and oversaw the erection of a new building for the Academy in 1831, a timely manifestation of the architectural talents that he would bring to bear in the design of the Trumbull Gallery at Yale.

Trumbull's involvement in the American Academy and his championship through it of contemporary artists and the study of art are important for his activities at Yale. Art academies were growing in popularity, largely based on the success of European art academies. Samuel F. B. Morse had already attempted to found an art academy in New Haven in 1821, based on London's Royal Academy.[5] Although that attempt failed, Morse, who had advocated the idea of governance by artists at the new National Academy, remained interested in bringing an art school/academy to Yale. The major art academies in America had collections, largely of plaster casts and copies in oil of famous European masterpieces, which were used to teach art students to draw, model, and paint. Any art academy in New Haven or at Yale would have to have a collection as well, and a building in which students could learn from these collections. Although nothing in the surviving documentation of the arrangements between Yale and Trumbull specifically states this, it is not unlikely that the idea of an academy was part of Trumbull's thinking when he agreed to establish a gallery of art at Yale. The strongest documentary evidence is the provision in the agreement that a portion of the proceeds from admission fees to the Trumbull Gallery was to go to the support of indigent students. In any case, it is hardly insignificant that the founder of the gallery was an artist and academy president, and that his founding gift was a collection of paintings, the foundation of the sort of collection he had helped to build for the Academy in New York.

The acquisition of the Trumbull Collection by Yale was arranged in 1831, when Colonel Trumbull was seventy-five years old. Living in New York, a widower, financially distressed, and without a means of livelihood beyond the basic subsistence he could earn from a few portrait commissions, Trumbull had only one asset that could conceivably be converted into an income—his paintings. He still owned the small American history series, including the *Declaration of Independence*, that was the basis of the Capitol Rotunda paintings, as well as his portrait miniatures of so many of the key figures in the Revolutionary War and the early years of the American Republic, most of whom were now dead. In ceding these paintings to Yale for an annuity of $1,000 a year, Trumbull not only ensured a lifetime income for himself but also guaranteed that his paintings would stay together and be seen, adding to his fame.

Trumbull made his proposal through Benjamin Silliman (fig. 12), who described the scene in his "Reminiscences," which are preserved in the archives at Yale.[6] Silliman, professor of chemistry at Yale and the husband of Trumbull's niece, Harriet, paid a visit to his uncle-in-law in New York in July 1830. The deeply distressed Trumbull spoke from his heart about his anguish at the thought that his paintings, his visual record of the birth of the nation, might be neglected or destroyed after his death, his legacy to his country lost forever. Silliman asked the artist, "And what, Sir, do you intend to do with them?" Trumbull replied, "I will give them to Yale College to be exhibited forever for the benefit of poor students provided the College will pay me a competent annuity for the remainder of my life." "Are you in earnest, Sir?" asked Silliman. "Certainly I am," replied the artist. "Am I then at liberty to go home and act upon this suggestion?" "You are at liberty and I authorize you to say so from me." "The proposition, Sir, is as grateful to me as it is surprising. I will return then, Sir, forthwith to New Haven," finished Silliman.

It was an extraordinary offer and one that met with an enthusiastic response among Silliman's colleagues at Yale, but it came at a particularly difficult time in the financial life of the College. In 1825, Yale had suffered a tremendous loss as a result of the failure of the Eagle Bank of New Haven, in which it had invested heavily.[7] The loss of $21,000 represented more than two-thirds of the College's annual income for that year, and it left the school with an annual fund of only $1,800, exclusive of library funds. Debts stood at $19,000, including $10,000 owed on the purchase, negotiated by Silliman, of the Gibbs Collection of minerals, which had been exhibited as a loan in Connecticut Hall since 1812. A fundraising campaign had been undertaken to pay for the Gibbs Collection, raising $10,000 but making it difficult to return so soon to the same sources for additional money. An approach to the State Legislature, which had given financial support to the College in the past, yielded no help this time. Little progress toward recovery had been achieved by the time Trumbull made his offer in 1831.

In spite of this dire situation, President Jeremiah Day (Yale B.A. 1795, M.A. 1798, president 1817–46) and his colleagues decided to proceed. A proposal came from Daniel Wadsworth of Hartford, who was, like Silliman, related to Trumbull by marriage, that the paintings should be divided between Hartford and New Haven, or travel back and forth between the two cities twice a year. Both proposals were initially endorsed but ultimately rejected by Trumbull, and a permanent home in New Haven was fixed. The annuity of $1,000 was agreed upon, and it was funded personally by Silliman, Wadsworth, President Day, Stephen Twining, and Professor Chauncey A. Goodrich. Yale also agreed to erect a building to house the paintings on the campus. This picture gallery was to be fireproof, and it was to be completed and open by the first of October, 1832. Admission was to be charged to see the paintings and the proceeds used to pay the annuity, if necessary, or, if not, to "be perpetually appropriated towards defraying the expense of educating poor scholars in Yale

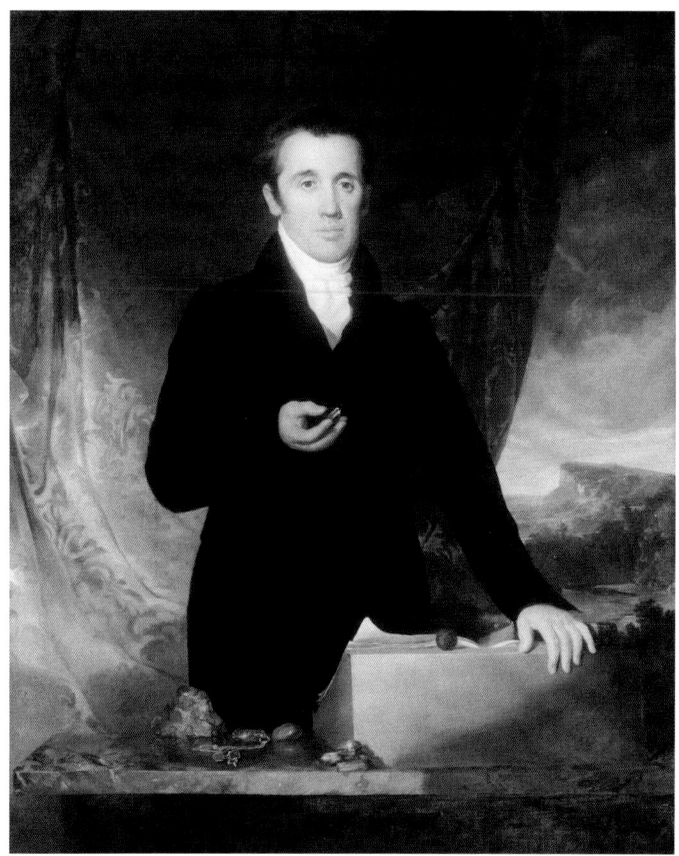

FIG. 12
Samuel F. B. Morse
Benjamin Silliman, 1825
Oil on canvas, 140.3 x 112.4 cm
Gift of Bartlett Arkell, B.A. 1886, M.A. 1898
1940.117

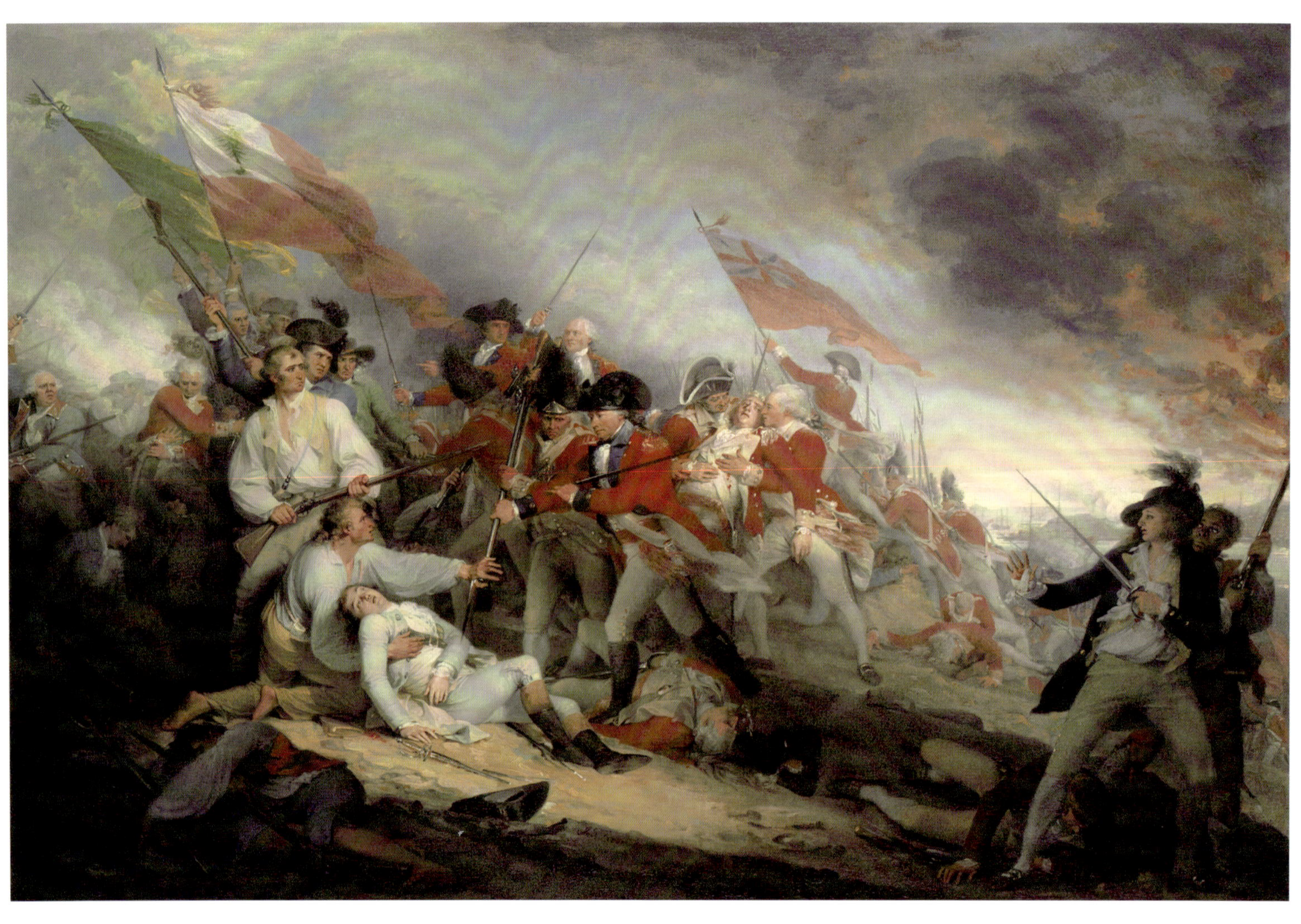

FIG. 13
John Trumbull
Death of General Warren at the Battle of Bunker's Hill, 17 June 1775, 1786
Oil on canvas, 65.1 x 95.6 cm
Trumbull Collection
1832.1

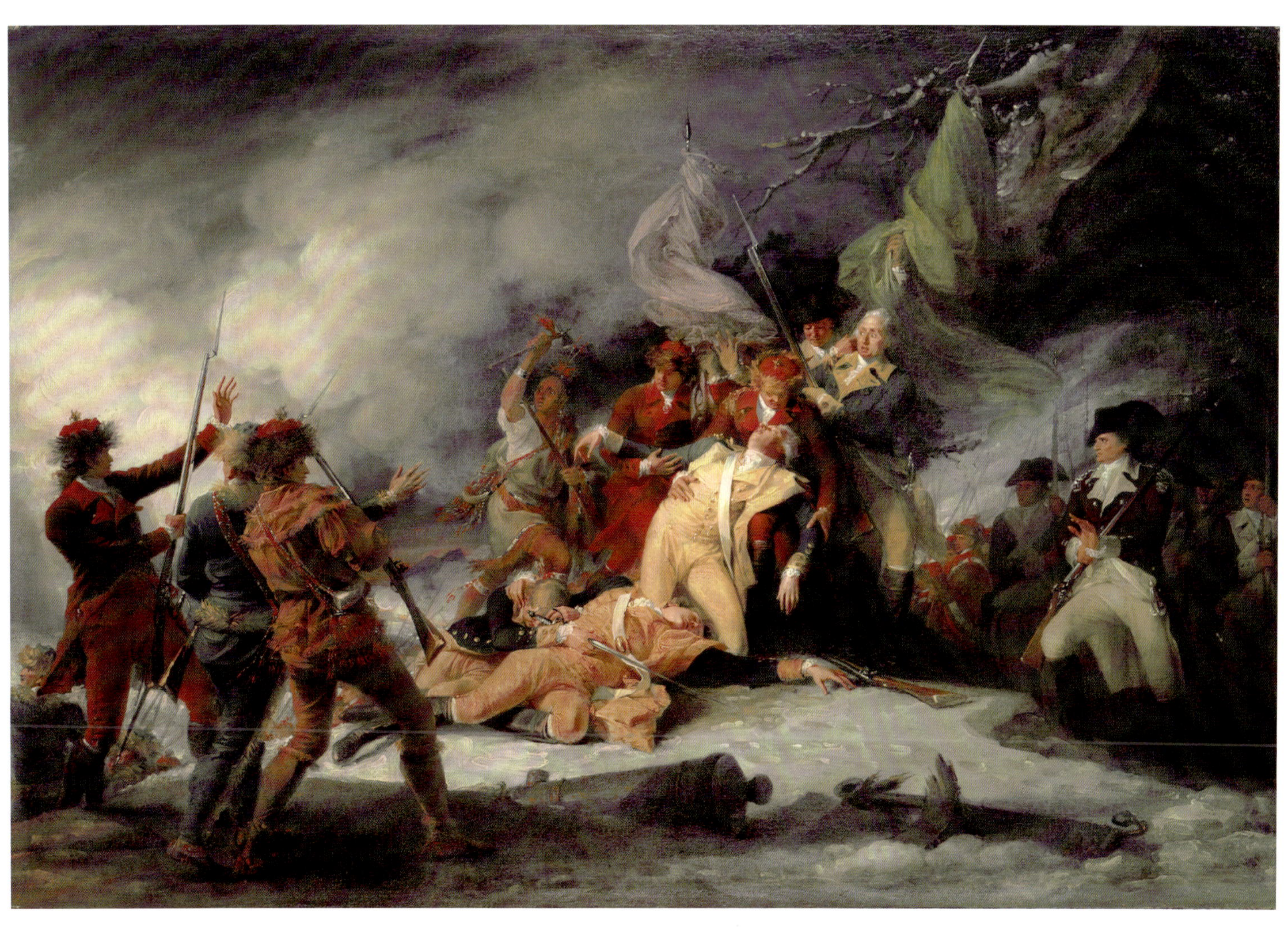

FIG. 14
John Trumbull
Death of General Montgomery in the Attack on Quebec, 31 December 1775, 1786
Oil on canvas, 62.5 x 94.0 cm
Trumbull Collection
1832.2

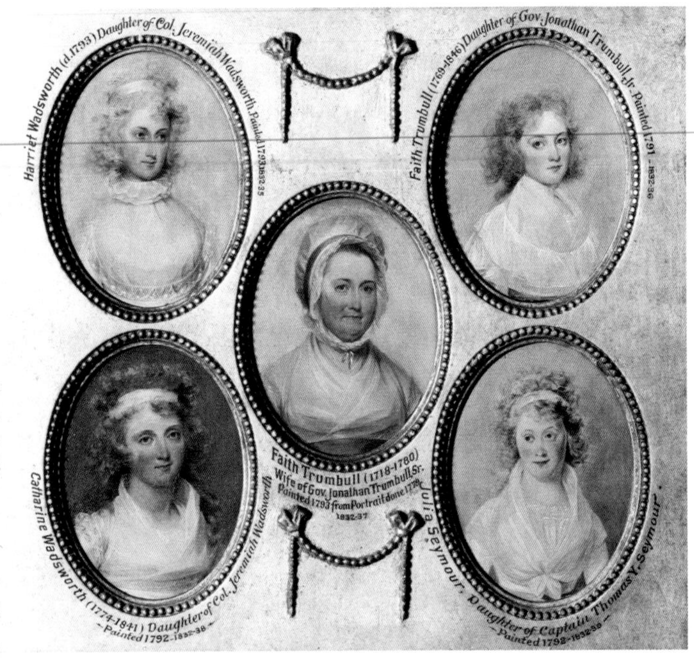

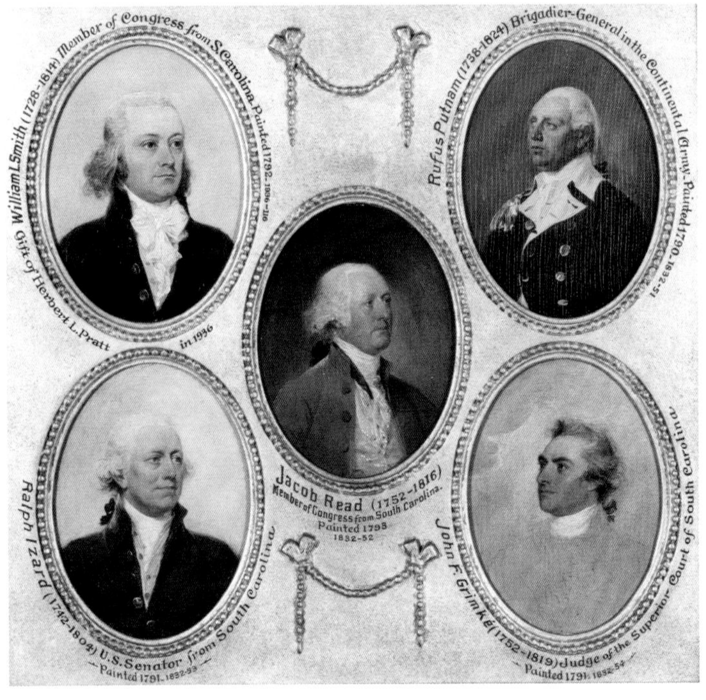

FIG. 15
John Trumbull
Miniature Portraits, ca. 1793
Oil on wood, each approximately 9.8 x 7.3 cm
Trumbull Collection
1832.50–54, 1832.35–39

College."[8] A similar arrangement to support poor students was to continue after Trumbull's death. Silliman went back to the State Legislature seeking funds for the building, and this time met with success: a grant of $7,000 was given for the purpose. The proposals for the collection and gallery were accepted by the Yale Corporation in September 1831, and the indenture between Trumbull and the University was executed on December 19, 1831.[9]

The paintings that came to Yale are listed as part of the indenture agreement. They include the eight original paintings of subjects from the Revolutionary War (figs. 13–14),[10] eight religious paintings,[11] four portraits, and six frames, each holding five miniature portraits (fig. 15) representing individuals who played important roles in the Revolution, painted from life as described above. For both Trumbull and Yale, the religious pictures offered educational value equal to that of the Revolutionary War pictures, the former to foster pious sentiments as the latter inspired patriotism.

The Picture Gallery at Yale, to be built behind the Old Brick Row, was designed by Trumbull himself (fig. 16). According to Silliman, Trumbull had learned architecture while a prisoner in London.[12] He was a close friend of the prominent architect Ithiel Town of New Haven (fig. 17), and likely influenced by Town's preferences in his choice of Greek Revival as the style of the building. A drawing by Town and his junior partner Alexander Jackson Davis of a "Pinacotheca for Colonel Trumbull" survives (1831; fig. 18).[13] It shows a building with a Doric-columned porch at one end, much closer to a traditional Greek temple than was the gallery as ultimately built (fig. 19). In Trumbull's design, the Doric porch was replaced by a modest central entrance, flanked by Doric columns, piercing the lower story of the long side of the building. Doric pilasters adorn the exterior walls and mark the building's corners. Above the door in silver letters was the inscription TRUMBULL GALLERY.

Inside, there were two large rooms for paintings on the upper floor. Silliman describes them in some detail, and quotes Trumbull as saying that he consulted Town on their proportions.[14] Each room was slightly over thirty feet square (30'3"), with a fifteen-foot ceiling. The galleries were lit by skylights. The walls were covered

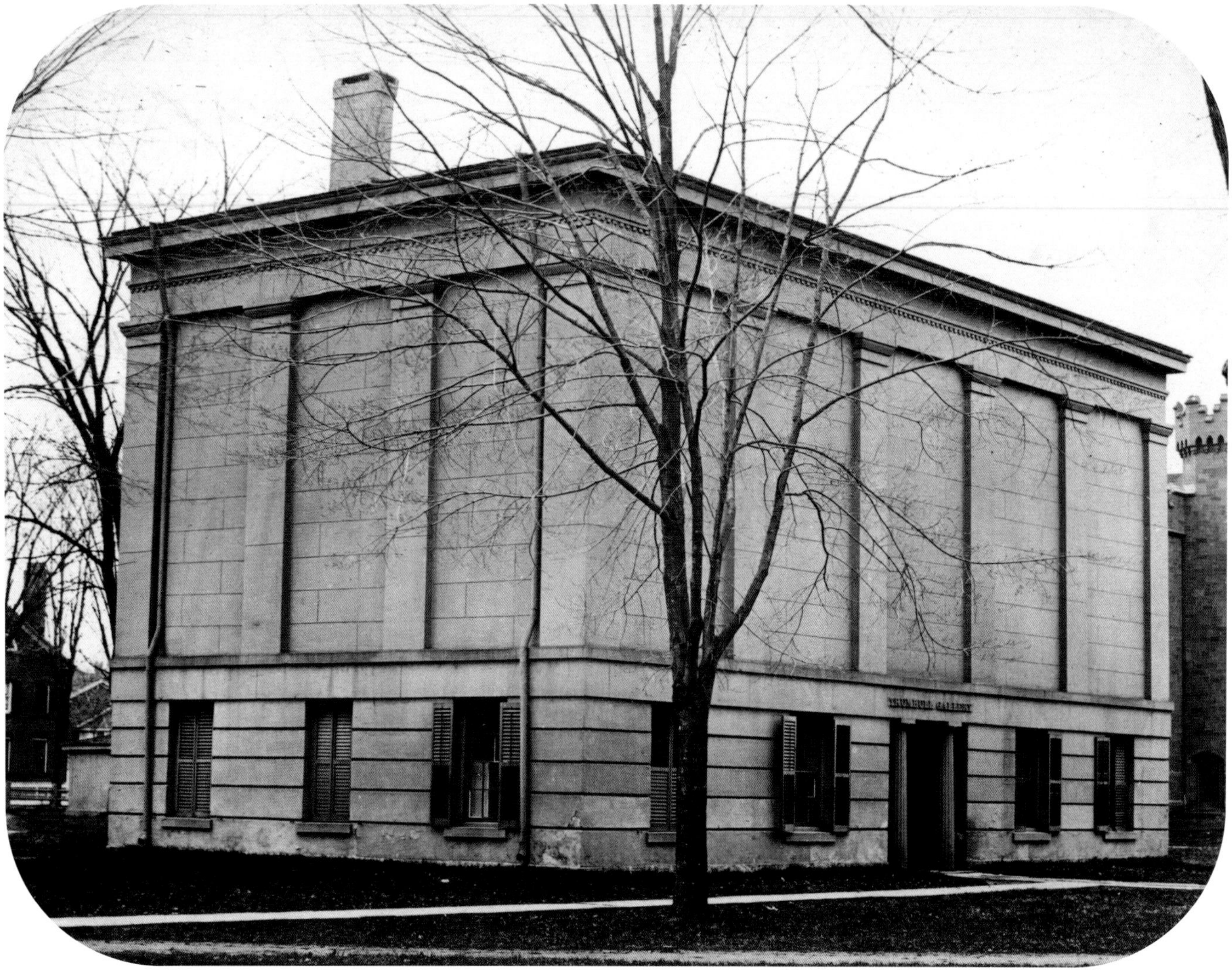

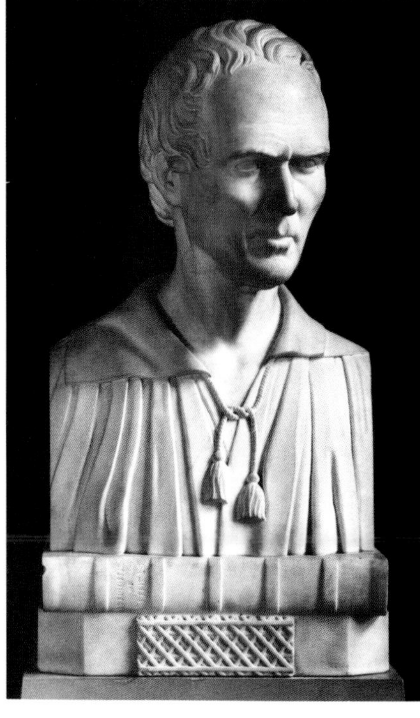

FIG. 16
John Trumbull
The Trumbull Gallery, 1831
Photograph, 1865, courtesy
Manuscripts and Archives, Sterling
Memorial Library, Yale University

FIG. 17
Chauncey Bradley Ives
Ithiel Town, 1842
Marble, 66.0 x 36.8 x 28.6 cm
Gift of Dr. William Thompson Peters,
B.A. 1825, M.D. 1830
1844.3

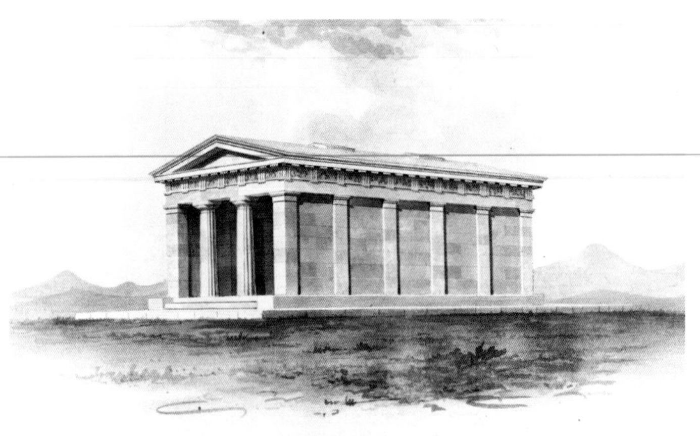

FIG. 18
Ithiel Town and A. J. Davis
Pinacotheca for Colonel Trumbull, 1831
Watercolor
Beinecke Rare Book and Manuscript Library, Yale University

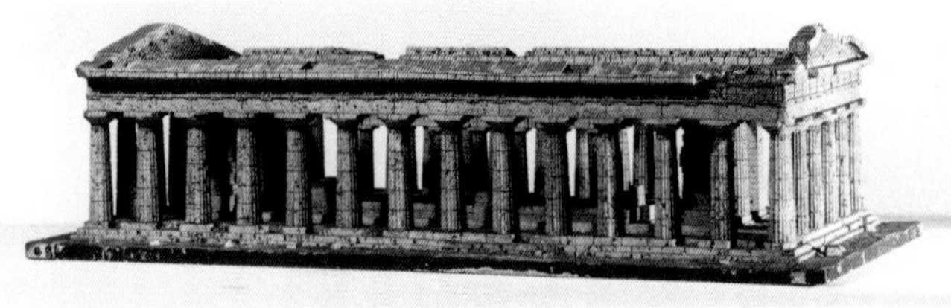

FIG. 19
John McAdam
Temple at Paestum, before 1835
Cork and wood, 23.0 x 83.0 cm with base
Gift of John McAdam of Scotland through William McCracken
1835.10

with red moreen, the carpets were green, and the room was furnished with stools, settees, and chairs of curly maple with cane seats.

Colonel Trumbull, who had personally escorted his paintings from New York on the steamship, also personally oversaw their installation in the new Gallery. It opened on October 25, 1832. Two catalogues of the paintings on view, published in 1835, appear to record the original hanging. One of the two galleries, the north one, was devoted to Trumbull's paintings. These included the Revolutionary War series and the portrait miniatures related to them, as well as the religious pictures and other portraits listed in the indenture. Included as well were other paintings by Trumbull not covered by the indenture but now at Yale, notably the *Death of Paulus Emilius at the Battle of Cannae*, painted when the artist was eighteen, and several portraits of members of Trumbull's family. Also displayed was the full-length portrait of *General Washington at the Battle of Trenton* (1792), which had been acquired by Yale in 1806, as noted above.

The south gallery was largely devoted to portraits by artists other than Trumbull. These included the early acquisitions noted above, among them the Kneller *George I* and the Smibert *Bishop Berkeley and His Entourage (The Bermuda Group)*. Prominent in this gallery were portraits of distinguished Yale and New Haven citizens, including *President Jeremiah Day*, by Samuel F. B. Morse; *Professor Nehemiah Strong*, by Ralph Earl (described above); *Professor Silliman*, by Morse; *Eli Whitney*, again by Morse; *Roger Sherman*, after a portrait by Earl; and *James Hillhouse*, copied from John Vanderlyn by Nathaniel Jocelyn. Also displayed here were several naval battle scenes from the War of 1812, a self-portrait of Major John André drawn the morning before his execution, maps of Virginia and South Carolina, a view of Rome, and two cork models of Greek temples at Paestum, in southern Italy (fig. 19). As years went by, other portraits, including marbles, were added to the south gallery; these are listed in a revised catalogue dated 1852.

The *Connecticut Journal* announced on October 30 that "Colonel Trumbull's paintings . . . are now ready for exhibition."[15] Among those who came to see them were students and New Haven citizens. Tourists arrived by steamship from New York and Philadelphia. Some came from the South, as New Haven was now a popular summer spot for Southern families.[16] Distinguished visitors to New Haven generally included Yale College in their itinerary, along with Ithiel Town's Greek Revival State House on the Green and the city's churches and factories. Charles Dickens, visiting New Haven in 1842, wrote of Yale College, "The effect is very like that of an old cathedral yard in England, . . . seeming to bring about a compromise between town and country."[17] Daniel Webster, Presidents Andrew Jackson and James Polk, Senator Sam Houston of Texas, Frederick Douglas, and President Lincoln all visited New Haven prior to the Civil War, and no doubt saw something of Yale. It is likely that a Yale visit would have included the Trumbull Gallery and its famous Revolutionary War paintings; it was certainly so for Jackson.[18]

Trumbull moved from New York City to New Haven to live with the Sillimans in 1837. Here he could keep track of the care of his paintings, and be in touch with students. "Uncle is quite busy with committees from college requesting him to address them on the subject of the pictures. He meets the Senior Class on Saturday, the Sophomores on Wednesday next. He laughs a good deal at his having taken up the trade," Henrietta Silliman wrote to her sister, Maria, in October 1839.[19] These were surely the earliest art history lectures given at Yale, and they inaugurated a tradition of teaching from original works of art that remains the heart of the Yale Art Gallery's mission.

Trumbull died on November 10, 1843, at the age of eighty-seven. Silliman, in his "Reminiscences," recorded the patriot-artist's thoughts about his final resting place:

> Soon after the arrangement of his pictures was completed in 1832, he said to me one day when we were in the Gallery, "It is my wish to be interred beneath this Gallery." Looking around on the pictures he added with emotion, "These are my children. Those whom they represent have all gone before me. Let me be buried with my family—I have long lived among the dead."[20]

He was buried, according to his wishes, beneath the Trumbull Gallery in a stone tomb below his paintings and next to his wife.

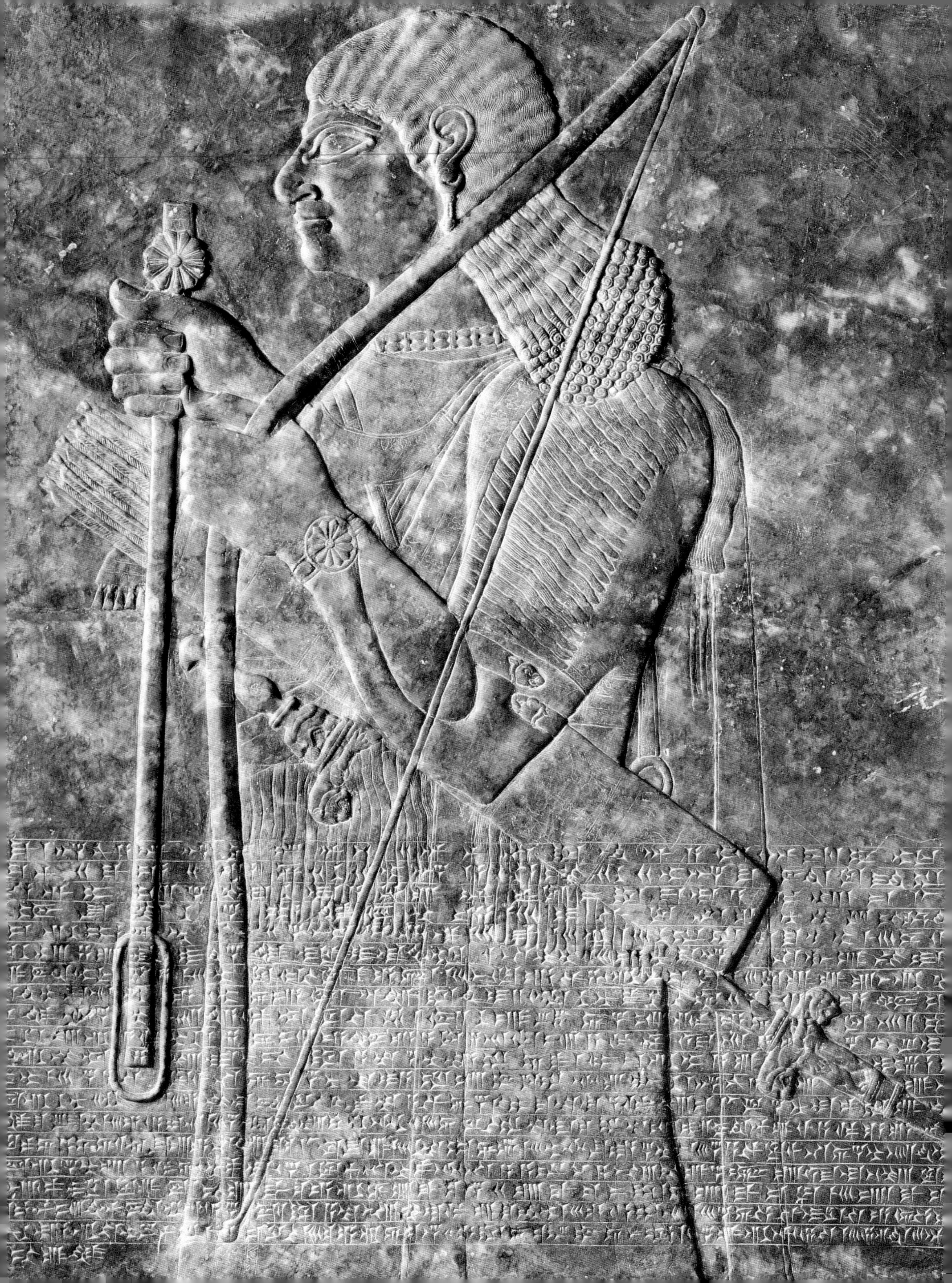

CHAPTER 3

The Missionary, the *Wolf*, and the 1858 Exhibition

The Trumbull Gallery remained Yale's art museum for more than thirty years. During that time the collections continued to grow, and new additions were installed in the south gallery. A revised catalogue of the south gallery's contents, published in 1852, indicates that portraits were still the most frequent new acquisitions.[1] A number of Trumbull's paintings that had been exhibited in the north gallery as loans but were not included in the indenture officially became part of the collection in 1840. The biggest change was the introduction of sculpture. All of it was American, by contemporary artists. Three were copies of famous portraits of celebrated figures from ancient Greece and Rome (*Homer*, *Demosthenes* [fig. 20], and *Cicero*) by Thomas Crawford, one of America's premier neoclassical sculptors and an artist at the height of his popularity. Lent to Yale shortly after their creation in 1837 by Professor Edward E. Salisbury (B.A. 1832), these portraits became part of the permanent collection by gift in 1900.

A portrait bust of *Ithiel Town* (1842; fig. 17) by Chauncey B. Ives was donated to Yale by W. T. Peters (B.A. 1825, M.D. 1830), in 1844—the thirtieth anniversary of the first medical degree awarded by Yale. Ithiel Town was a prominent and wealthy New Haven resident, not associated with Yale. An important architect of the neoclassical style and a pioneer of the Gothic Revival in America, Town was the designer of the Gothic Trinity Church on the Green (1813–14) and the Greek Revival State House (1824). He was a partner with Alexander Jackson Davis, and a friend of Trumbull, whose architectural drawings were probably influenced by Town's style. The acquisition of this portrait indicates a recognition of the importance of architecture as a discipline, later to be seen in the founding of a program, a department, and ultimately a school of architecture.

A major work by the sculptor Hezekiah Augur, *Jephthah and His Daughter* (fig. 21), was presented to Yale by "The Citizens of New Haven and the Officers of Yale College" in 1835.[2] Augur, a New Haven resident, received an honorary degree from Yale in 1833. That same year, he joined other New Haven citizens and Yale faculty in founding the Society for Architectural and Rural Improvement in an effort to improve the appearance of the city. Augur's best-known work and said to be the first ideal multiple-figure statue group by an

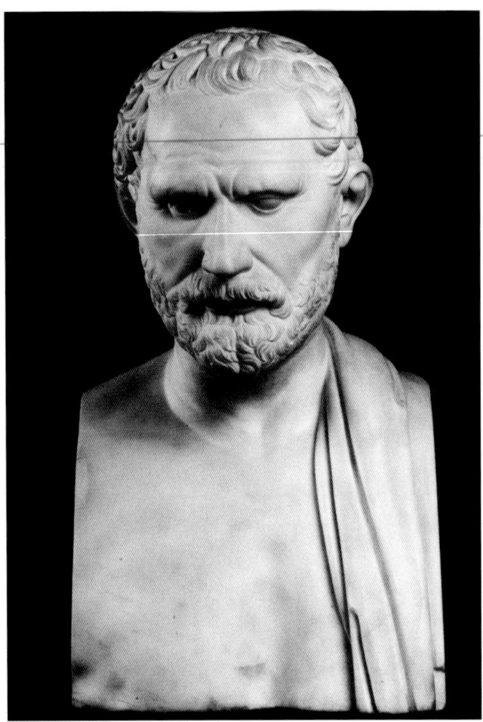

FIG. 20
Thomas Crawford
Demosthenes, 1837
Marble, 54.6 x 30.5 x 28.6 cm
Presented to Yale College by Professor Edward E. Salisbury, B.A. 1832, M.A. 1835, LL.D. 1869
1900.57

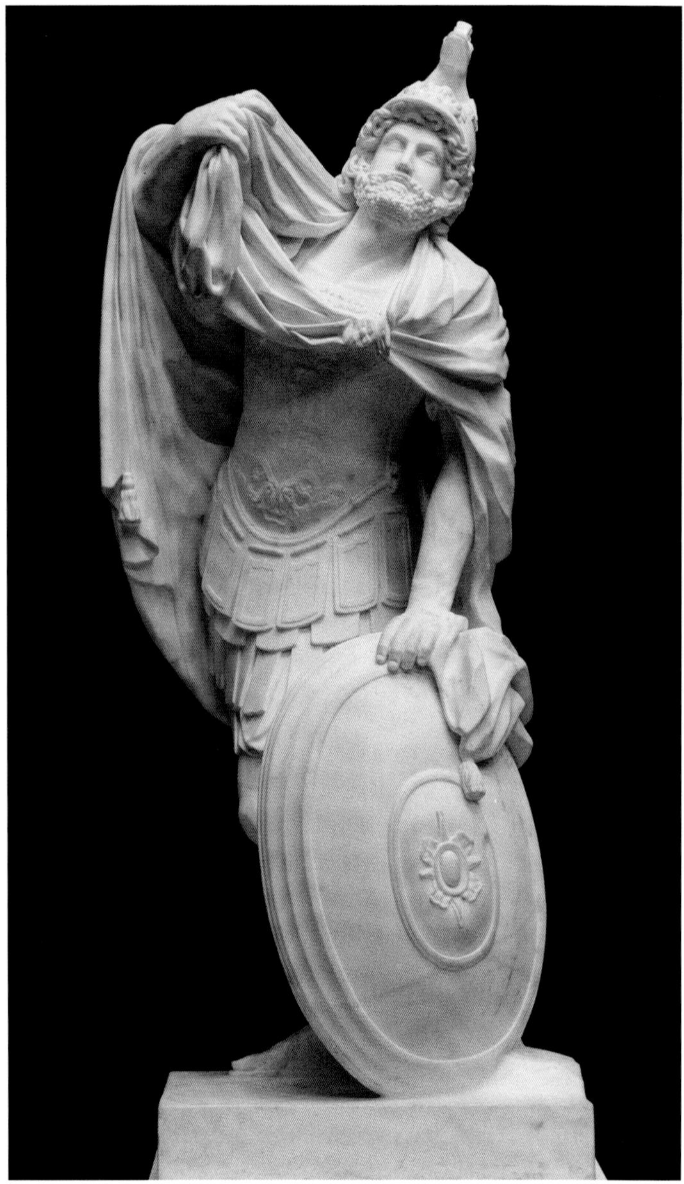

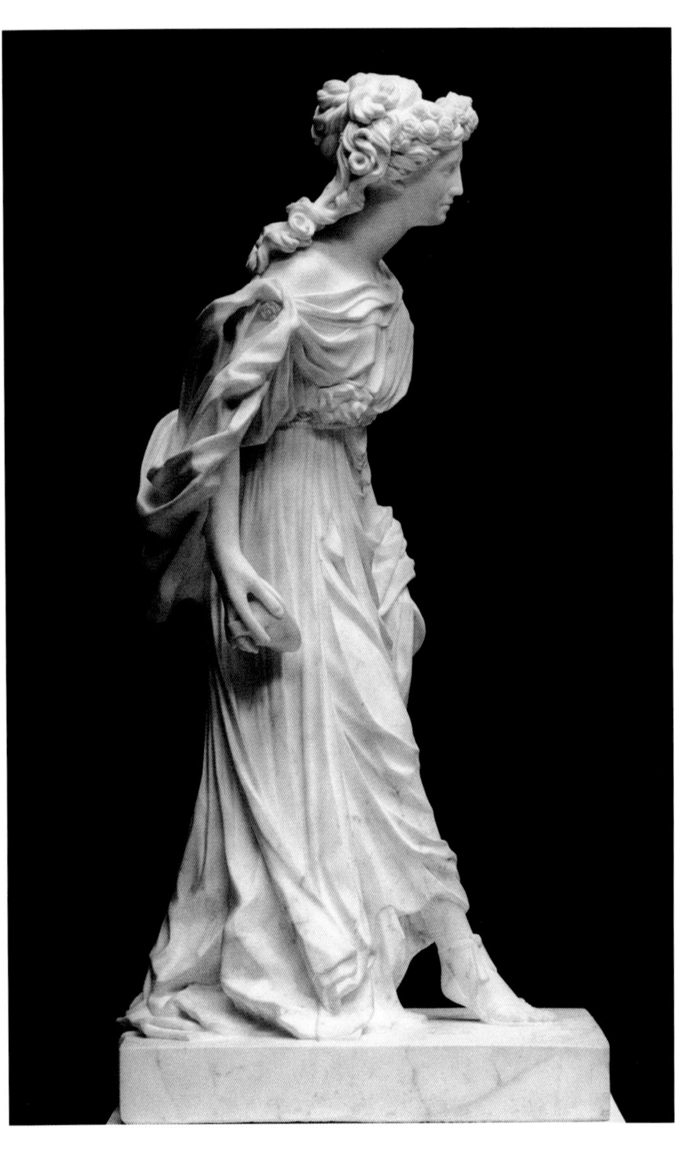

FIG. 21
Hezekiah Augur
Jephthah and His Daughter, 1828–32
Marble, Jephthah: 111.8 x 47.0 x 39.4 cm; Daughter: 91.4 x 44.5 x 34.3 cm
Gift of the Citizens of New Haven
1835.11a,b

American sculptor, *Jephthah and His Daughter* represents a biblical subject drawn from the *Book of Judges*, 11.30–39. The story of Jephthah tells of a Hebrew military leader who must sacrifice his daughter in exchange for victory as a result of a vow he made to God to offer up the first person who greeted him when he returned home. Old Testament subjects were popular among neoclassical sculptors both for their moral content and for their similarity to stories from classical antiquity. Augur, known for his neoclassical work, has shown the figures in Roman dress.

Paintings by Nathaniel Jocelyn, another New Haven artist whose portraits had been part of the Yale collection since the 1820s, continued to be given to the College. Jocelyn's portrait of Benjamin Silliman, who played such a key role in the acquisition of the Trumbull paintings and the founding of the Gallery, became part of the collection in 1850, the gift of John Berwick Legare, Esquire, B.A. 1815, of Charleston, South Carolina. Jocelyn's painting joined the portrait of Silliman by Gilbert Stuart already at Yale. Robert Ball Hughes's marble portrait of John Trumbull (fig. 22) also entered the collection at this time, purchased by the College on July 29, 1851, for display in the Trumbull Gallery.

Two key acquisitions in the field of American decorative arts in this period were closely tied to Yale's history. The first is a silver and tortoiseshell snuff box made by John Obrisset for Elihu Yale, probably in London between 1710 and 1720. The box bears a portrait of Yale and his family crest and coat of arms. Ezra Stiles (B.A. 1746), president of Yale between 1778 and 1795, acquired this box in 1788, and until recently it was believed that he donated it to Yale College at that time. Research has shown, however, that it was subsequently owned by Stiles's son-in-law and given to Yale in 1832. The second is the so-called President's Chair, a wainscot chair by an unknown Connecticut maker dating to 1640–60 (fig. 23). Said to have been purchased in 1672 by the Reverend Abraham Pierson, who in 1701 became Rector of the Collegiate School that became Yale College, the chair was given to Yale in 1841 by the Reverend John E. Bray. Since that time it has served as the inaugural chair of the president of Yale.

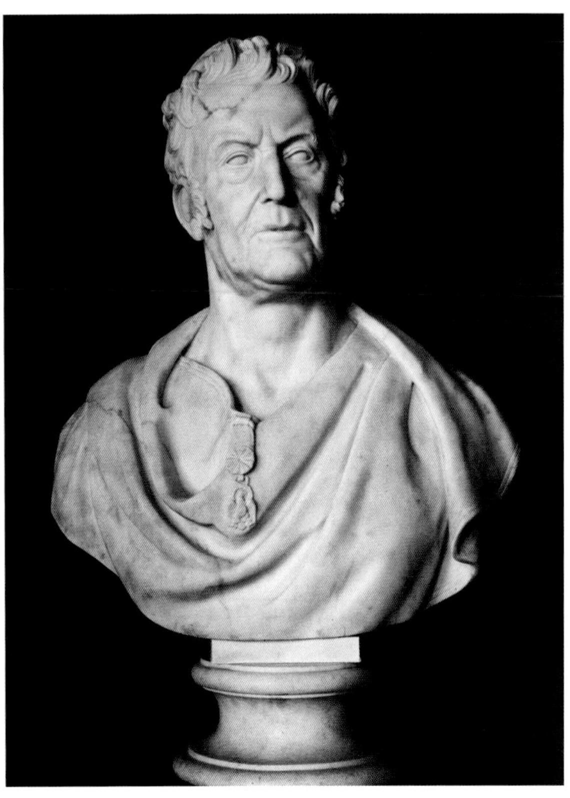

FIG. 22
Robert Ball Hughes
John Trumbull, ca. 1834
Marble, 61 x 51.4 x 23.5 cm
University Purchase
1851.2

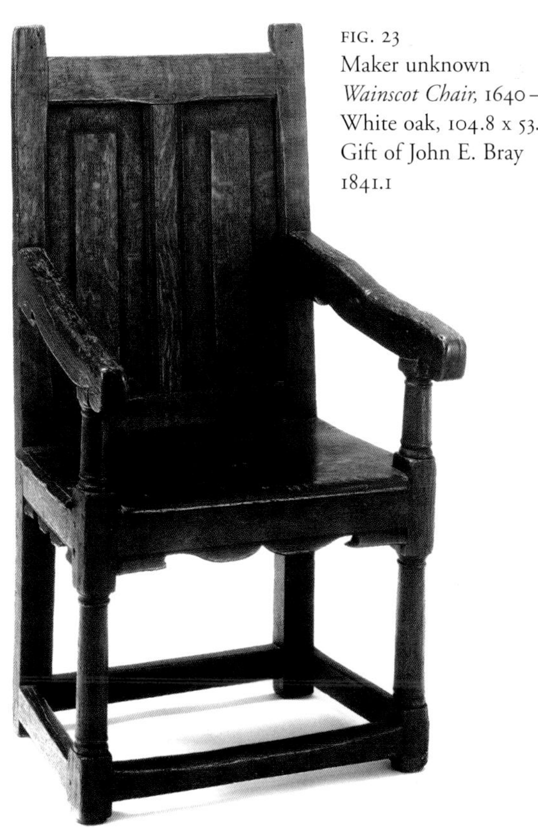

FIG. 23
Maker unknown
Wainscot Chair, 1640–60
White oak, 104.8 x 53.2 x 35.2 cm
Gift of John E. Bray
1841.1

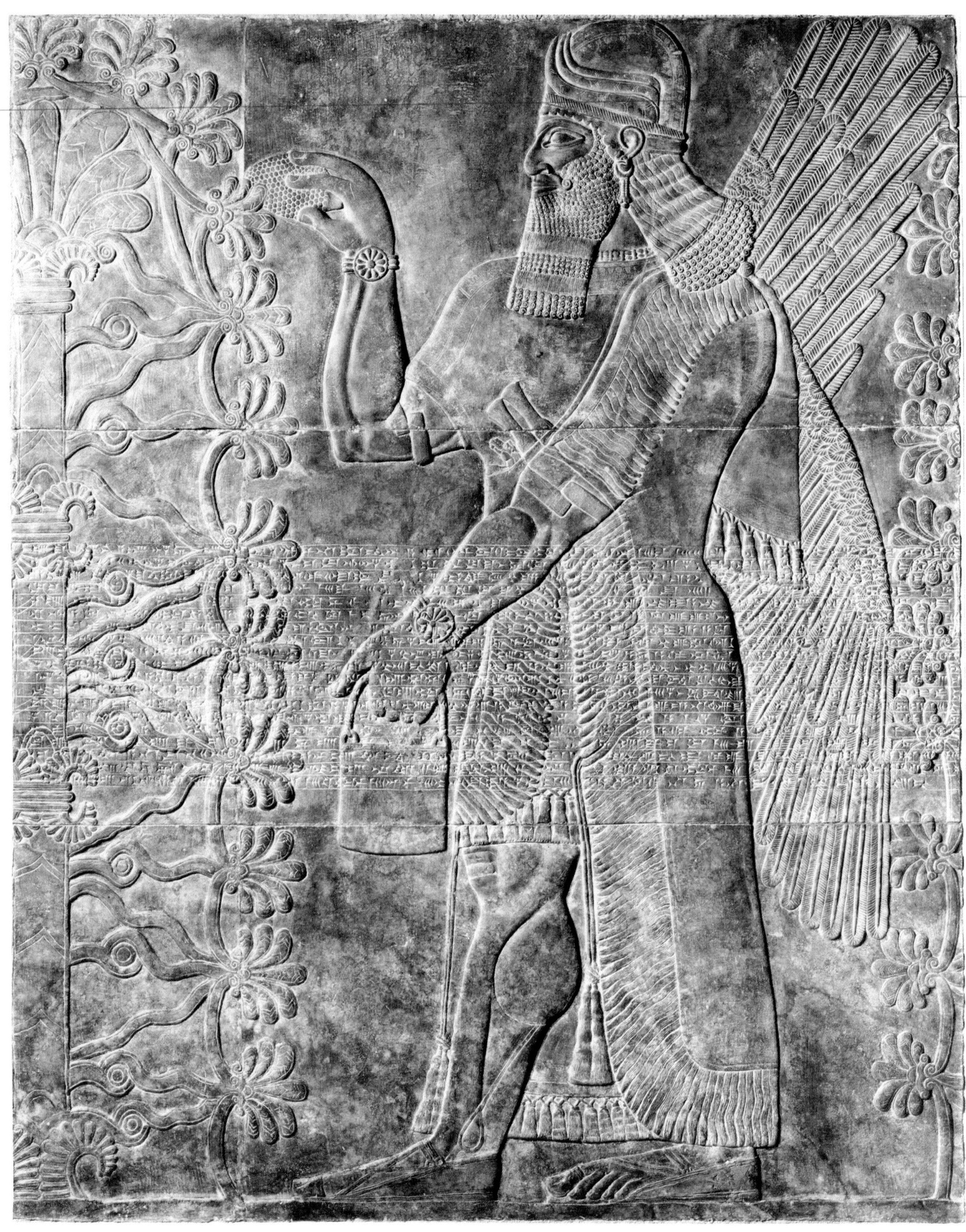

FIG. 24
Maker unknown
Relief of Human-Headed Genie Watering Sacred Tree, 883–859 B.C.
Gypseous alabaster, 224.8 x 184.8 cm
Yale University Purchase
1854.1

The first major departure from the pattern of collecting American art and copies of European Old Masters came in 1854 with the purchase of four monumental stone reliefs from the ancient palace of the Assyrian king Assurnasirpal II at Nimrud (in modern Iraq; figs. 24 and 25). The reliefs came from the celebrated excavations of the Assyrian royal palace by the British archaeologist Austen Henry Layard. Dating from the ninth century B.C., the palace was discovered by Layard in 1850. The majority of the palace's sculpture, consisting of massive stone figures of semi-divine beings in hybrid human/animal form and row upon row of relief sculpture showing royal lion hunts and processions honoring the king, was bought by the British Museum. Their arrival at the museum was a front-page story in the *Illustrated London News.* During the course of the excavations, some of the sculpture from the palace became available through Layard's agents to private buyers. Among these prospective buyers was a group of American colleges and theological seminaries led by Yale.[3]

Several American institutions were interested in buying one or more of the reliefs. Bowdoin, Amherst, and Williams Colleges, and the Episcopal Theological Seminary in Alexandria, Virginia, all sent their own representatives to Iraq to negotiate the purchases. Reverend William Frederic Williams (fig. 26) was empowered to negotiate on behalf of Yale, as well as for Dartmouth and the Union Theological Seminary in Utica, New York, his hometown. Williams, known as Fred, attended Yale briefly in 1838 before leaving to study at Auburn Theological Seminary.[4] After graduation, he served as a Christian missionary in Turkey before being sent to Mosul, near the site of the Assyrian palace excavations. His brother, Samuel Wells Williams (Hon. M.A. 1877), and his nephew, Frederick Wells Williams (B.A. 1879), both served on the Yale faculty, and they were the first major donors of Chinese art to Yale.[5]

Correspondence in 1852–54 between "Assyrian" Williams and his sponsors in New Haven is preserved in the Art Gallery's archives. It provides a vivid picture of the course of the negotiations and the difficulties, including 105°F heat, that Williams endured in completing the deal and arranging for transport. This acquisition was the direct result of the continued influence of the Congregational Church on Yale.

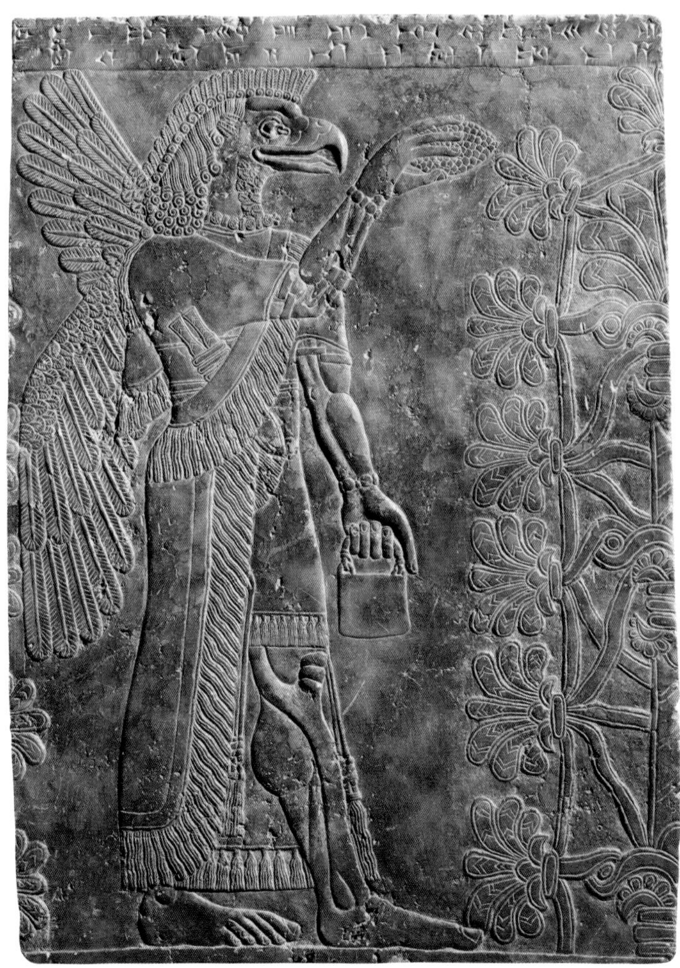

FIG. 25
Maker unknown
Relief of Eagle-Headed Genie Watering Sacred Tree, 883–859 B.C.
Gypseous alabaster, 109.0 x 77.0 cm
Yale University Purchase
1854.3

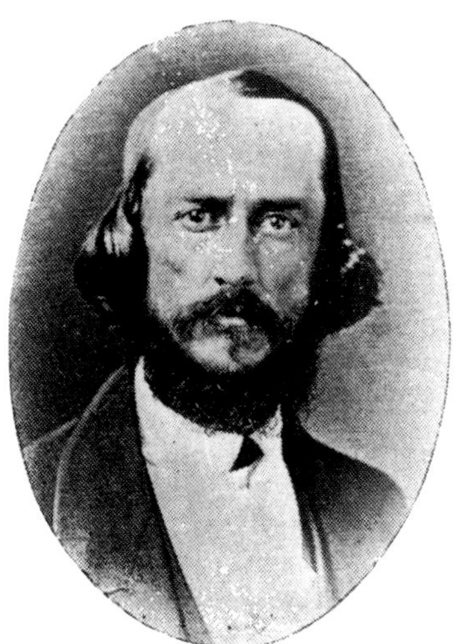

FIG. 26
William Frederic Williams
Photograph, from E. Dunbar, *Talcott Williams: Gentleman of the Fourth Estate* (Brooklyn, 1936)

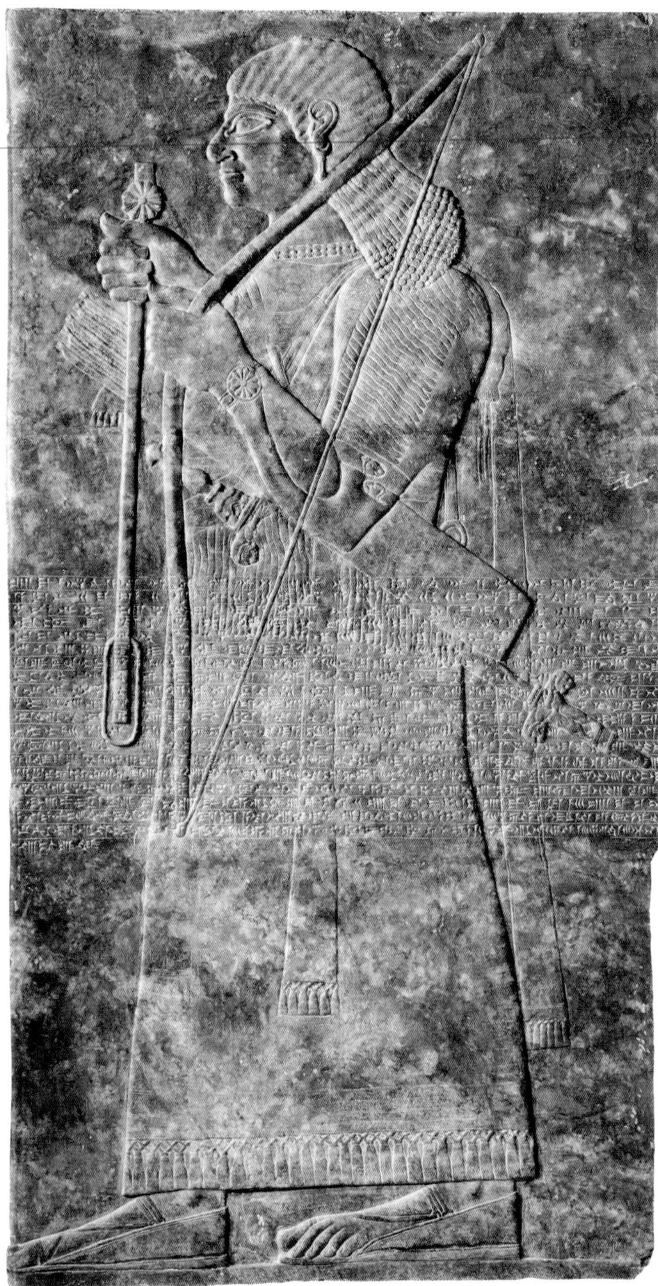

FIG. 27
Maker unknown
Assyrian Relief of an Arms Bearer,
883–859 B.C.
Gypseous alabaster, 225.0 x 110.0 cm
Yale University Purchase
1854.2.1

Williams's letters are written to the Reverend Leonard Bacon (B.A. 1820), pastor of the First Church (Congregational) in New Haven, who had helped raise the money for the purchase. Reverend Bacon sent $250 to Williams in Mosul, with instructions to use it for purchase and shipping. Missionaries from other institutions were buying as well. Williams College was represented by Dwight W. Marsh, while Bowdoin commissioned Dr. Henri Byron Haskell (B.A., Bowdoin College, 1855) to acquire whatever he could for his alma mater. Amherst College sent a representative and Yale's Williams was also commissioned to purchase reliefs for the Union Theological Seminary in Utica, New York. Williams described his efforts:

> Dr. Lobdell on behalf of Amherst insisted on having equal chance with Yale and Union. We of course could not go to the mound as rival claimants and so as one party we brought away six slabs and divided them into three lots as evenly as we could and then I chose first for Yale, second for Union and the third went to Amherst. . . . Yale gets a Eunuch [fig. 27] in perfect order and with one half of the sacred tree which belongs behind the figure. This is the only unwinged figure that goes to the U.S. and on that account, though it is some smaller I prized it higher than the others; and a horned headed divinity with a cone and half a tree *before* it to which it is offering the cone [fig. 24]. This also is perfect. . . . I send also to Yale a small Nisroch [a semi-divine figure; fig. 25], and a small kneeling figure. . . . You see therefore I send you the best lot.[6]

Shipping the reliefs to New York in 1853 was no small challenge. The choice of shipping by water down the Tigris River meant sending them by ship around Cape Horn, while sending them overland meant two months by camel caravan. The land route was considered safer, and was what Williams chose, but stone slabs ten feet high and a foot thick could not be borne intact by any beast of burden. Williams, and others who chose the same route, were forced to cut the slabs down for shipment, cutting them into smaller pieces and reducing their thickness by nearly 75 percent.

> Ours will be packed this week and the caravan expects to leave in a fortnight. I have taken the utmost possible pains in packing that they may reach you as good as they now are. The wool in which they are packed cost here 3¢ a pound. I guess it will sell for that in Connecticut. . . . I want Yale to know that their indebtedness is to Dr. Bacon only for the opportunity of getting [the] slabs to New Haven. If only I were able, it would give me more pleasure than you can guess if I could make a buchsheesh of the whole expense, but it is only the rich who are privileged with such luxuries.[7]

Once the reliefs reached the Mediterranean, they were shipped on board the *Wolf* to New York, and thence by steamer to New Haven. The total cost for the purchase, bribes, and shipping to New York came to $212, well below the $250 sum sent by Reverend Bacon.[8] The fact that Williams could not afford to make a present of the $212 cost attests to the austerity of life for Christian missionaries in the mid-nineteenth-century Middle East. Williams gave tirelessly of his time and effort, however, and he was deeply concerned that the reliefs reach Yale safely and be properly cared for once they arrived. "Don't let those who wash, in their zeal, wash off the black paint of hair or beard nor the black and red of the shoes, as that is as old as Sardanapalus."[9] The paint on the shoes, at least, survives today.

While we now value these reliefs as major works of art (in 1994 a fragmentary figure from one such relief was sold at auction in London for $12 million to the Shumei family for their new museum in Kyoto, Japan), in the mid-nineteenth century their primary role in the American mind was as tangible proof of the literal truth of the Bible.[10] In the *Book of Isaiah*, the prophet speaks twice of the fate of the Assyrians at God's hands:

> The Assyrians will be terror-stricken at the voice of the Lord, when he smites with his rod. And every stroke of the staff of punishment which the Lord lays upon them will be to the sound of timbrels and lyres; battling with brandished arm he will fight with them. For a burning place has long been prepared, yea, for the king it is made ready, its pyre made deep and wide, with fire and wood in abundance; the breath of the Lord, like a stream of brimstone, kindles it. (*Isaiah* 30.31–33)
>
> "And the Assyrian shall fall by a sword, not of man; and a sword, not of man shall devour him; and he shall flee from the sword, and his young men shall be put to forced labor. His rock shall pass away in terror, and his officers desert the standard in panic," says the Lord. . . . For the palace will be forsaken, the populous city deserted; the hill and the watch-tower will become dens forever, a joy of wild asses, a pasture of flocks. (*Isaiah* 31.8–9; 32.14)

What better proof of the truth of this prophecy than the discovery of the ruined palace of the great Assyrian king? What better incentive to young people to go forth and preach the word of God than this new and tangible proof that the words of the Bible are true? What better recruiting poster for the Divinity School at Yale and its fellow theological institutions than one (or better more) of these evangelically charged reliefs?

Reverend Bacon and Yale were of like mind as to the importance of this acquisition, and Reverend Williams succeeded admirably in the charge they had given him. In the end, the reliefs arrived safely in New Haven. Now valued as monuments of one of the greatest of the ancient Near Eastern civilizations, Yale's Assyrian reliefs anchor the Gallery's ancient art collection.

THE YALE CAMPUS AT MID-CENTURY

New Yale buildings joined the Trumbull Gallery behind the Old Brick Row that faced the New Haven Green (fig. 28). The campus was still confined to the block now known as the Old Campus, bounded by College, Chapel, High, and Elm Streets. Connecticut Hall, which still stands, was part of the Old Brick Row, together with the North and South Colleges, the Atheneum, the Lyceum, Berkeley Hall, the Chapel, and the Divinity College. In front of them stood the Yale Fence, extending the length of the College, Chapel, and Elm Street sides of the campus. The Trumbull Gallery stood behind the Chapel, facing the Green. Approximately in line with it were the Old Laboratory, site of Professor Silliman's scientific experiments from 1820 on, and The Cabinet, into which the mineral collections

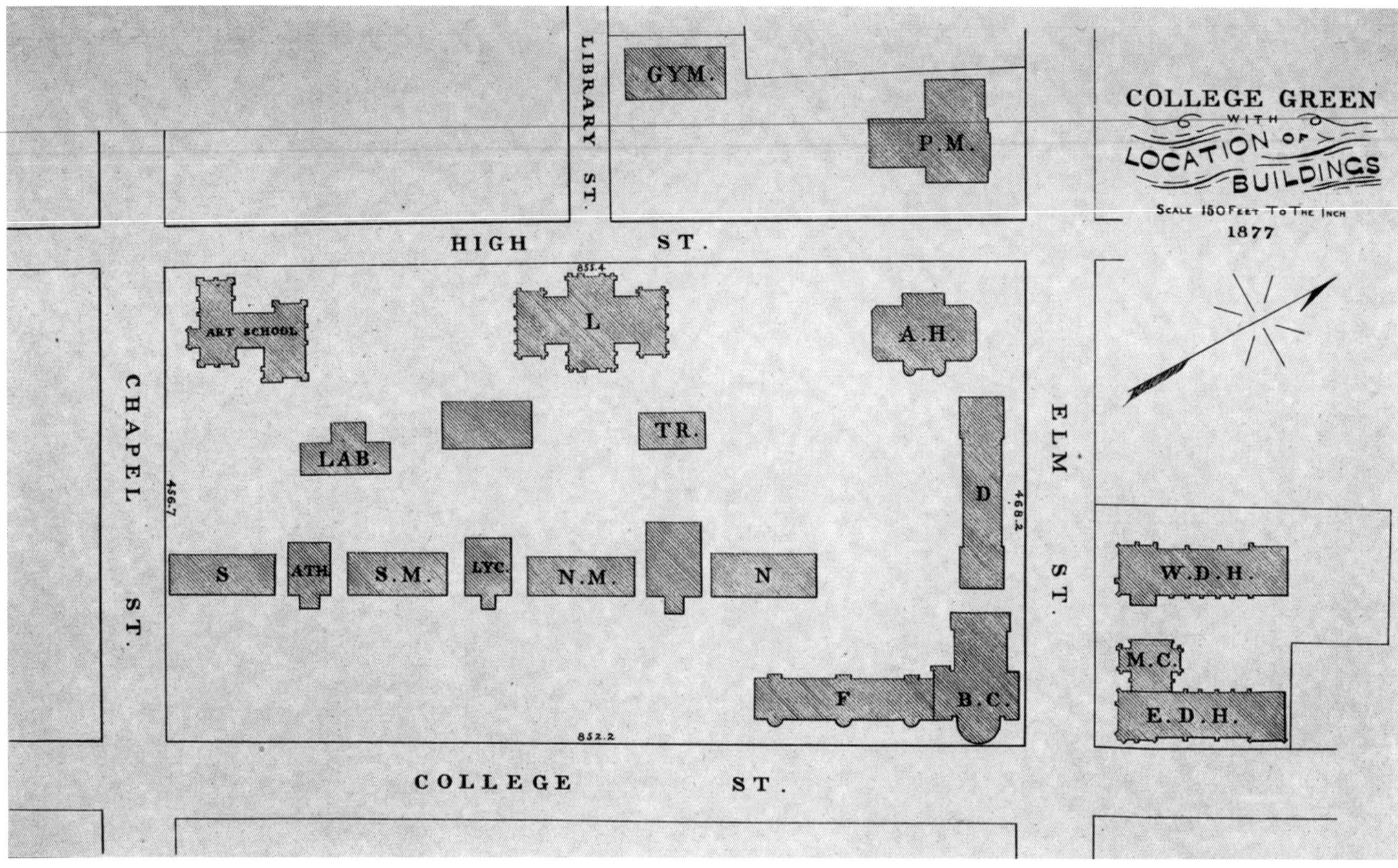

FIG.28
William L. Kingsley
College Green with Location of Buildings, 1877
From William L. Kingsley, *Yale College: A Sketch of Its History* (New York, 1879)

Key to buildings:
TR: Trumbull Gallery
AH: Alumni Hall
LAB: Old Laboratory
L: Library
Art School: Street Hall
S–N: Old Brick Row
D: Durfee
B.C.: Battell Chapel
F: Farnam

moved in 1819, followed in subsequent years by several academic departments and a newspaper reading room.

A new library opened in 1842, almost directly behind the Trumbull Gallery. Designed by Henry Austin and based on Kings College Chapel in Cambridge, it was the first Gothic Revival–style building at Yale. The library housed not only the College's books but also the extensive collections of the literary and religious societies known as the Linonian Society and the Brothers in Unity. These societies also owned works of art, especially portraits and sculpture based on the antique. Other works of art belonging to the College and now a part of the Yale Art Gallery's collection were also exhibited in the library. Records indicate that the Chauncey B. Ives marble portrait of President Jeremiah Day as well as drawings by D. W. Coit were displayed there in 1858.[11] The Austin building, with the later additions of Chittenden and Linsly Halls, served as the College's library until 1931, when the books were transferred to the new Sterling Memorial Library. The "Old Library" now serves Yale as Dwight Memorial Chapel and Dwight Hall.

Between 1851 and 1853, a second Gothic Revival

building rose to the north of Austin's library, standing on the corner of High and Elm Streets. This building, known as the Alumni Building or Alumni Hall (fig. 29), was designed by Alexander Jackson Davis, the partner of Ithiel Town and apparent pioneer of the term "Collegiate Gothic." Funds were raised from students, faculty, and alumni, including Augustus Russell Street (B.A. 1812), Professor Edward Elbridge Salisbury, and Benjamin Silliman, Jr. (B.A. 1837), son of the famous scientist, professor of chemistry, and nephew-in-law of John Trumbull.[12] Serving primarily as the site for the admission tests and the semiannual examinations required of all Yale students, the building's large examination rooms had walls that were used for displaying works of art. Judging from old photographs, these were mainly portraits. At one point in its history, however, Alumni Hall provided the stage for a key event in the history of the Yale Art Gallery, namely the first temporary loan exhibition ever mounted at Yale.

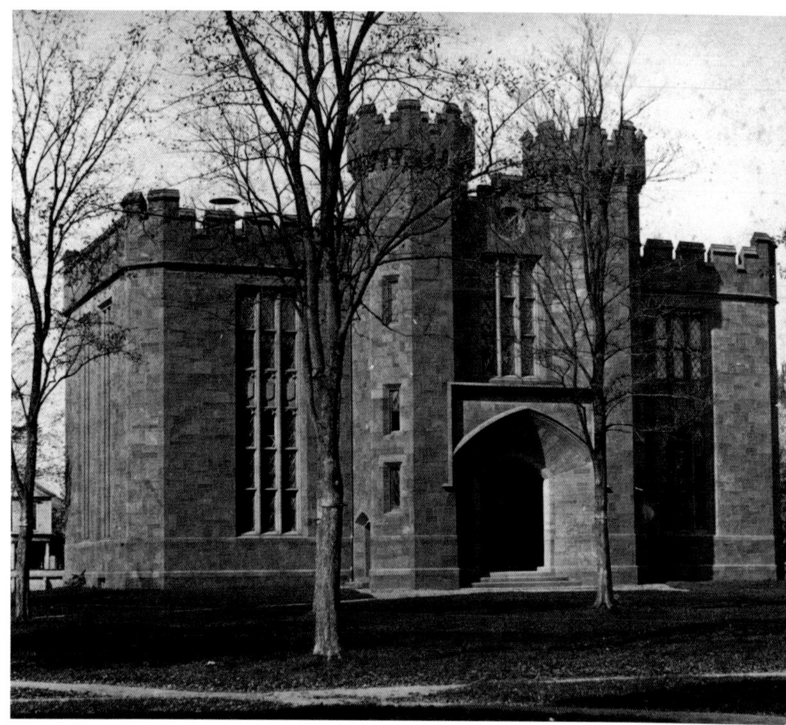

FIG. 29
A. J. Davis, *Alumni Hall* (1851–53)
Photograph, 1860s, courtesy Manuscripts and Archives, Sterling Memorial Library, Yale University

THE 1858 EXHIBITION

The Alumni Hall loan exhibition of 1858 was organized by Yale faculty, students, and alumni, headed by Professor Edward E. Salisbury. The exhibition committee included Aaron Nicholas Skinner (B.A. 1823 and former mayor of New Haven), John Addison Porter (B.A. 1842 and professor of chemistry), W. L. Kingsley (B.A. 1843), editor of the prominent periodical *The New Englander and Yale Review*, who later wrote valuable histories of Yale, F. J. Betts (B.A. 1864), Benjamin Silliman, Jr., and Daniel Coit Gilman (B.A. 1852, M.A., LL.D. 1889). The stated aim of the exhibition was "to awaken and gratify a love of the Fine Arts among the citizens of New Haven and the students of Yale College."[13] More than 250 works of art are listed in the exhibition catalogue. Most are paintings, ranging (if the attributions can be believed) from originals by European artists including Poussin, Paulus Bril, and David Teniers, to copies after European masters such as Raphael, Domenichino, and Claude Lorrain, as well as American portraits, history, genre, and landscape paintings by a wide range of both well-known and now-forgotten artists. Portraits by Van Dyck and Benjamin West were included. One of the Teniers paintings represented the same subject, *Jephthah*

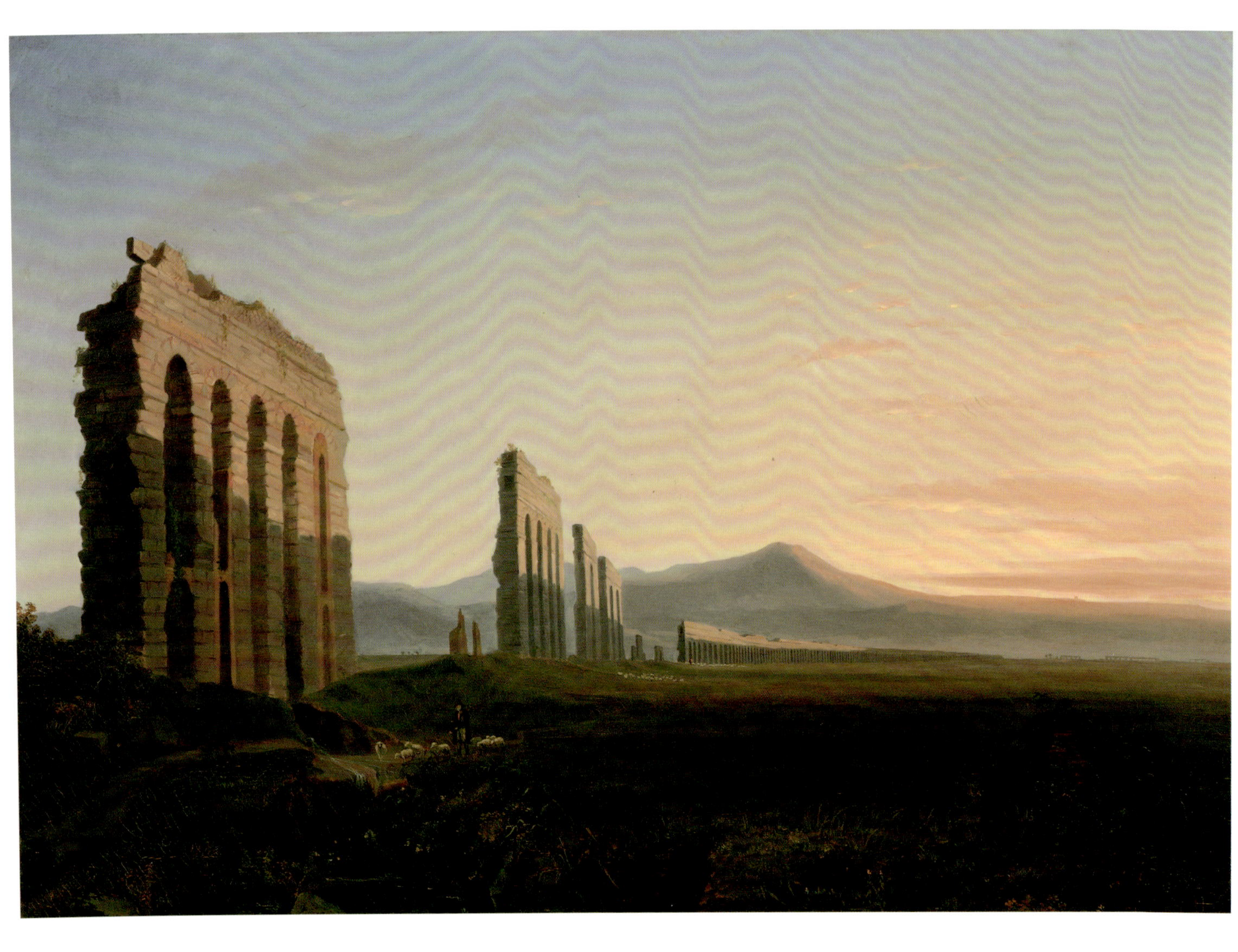

FIG. 30
Benjamin Champney
View of the Roman Campagna, 1846
Oil on canvas, 78.7 x 109.9 cm
Yale University Art Gallery
1900.15

and His Daughter, that Hezekiah Augur had produced in marble for Yale.

Most of the American paintings were contemporary art at the time, although the artists (e.g., Inness, Durand, Cropsey, Kensett, Cole, and Church) are now considered American "Old Masters"; some of these paintings were lent by the artists; some were for sale. Loans came from Yale faculty (e.g., Professor Salisbury), alumni (e.g., C. L. Elliott, B.A. 1857), and New Haven residents, as well as from collectors elsewhere in Connecticut (particularly Hartford, Lyme, and Norwich) and New York City. Only a few ended up in the Yale collection. A notable acquisition was the Benjamin Champney painting of the Claudian aqueduct outside of Rome (fig. 30), a favorite subject of American painters in Italy. It was lent to the 1858 exhibition by A. R. Street, a Yale graduate and wealthy, well-traveled New Haven citizen who would play a critical role in the Yale Art Gallery's history. There was one loan from another museum, a portrait of Isaac of York by Washington Allston lent by the Boston Athenaeum.

Around fifty "Engravings, Sketches, and Miniatures" were shown in a separate room. These included sketches of landscapes in Europe and America and copies after European Old Masters on paper and in miniature on porcelain and ivory. Fifteen sculptures were displayed. The subjects represented by this group attest to the continuing popularity of the neoclassical style. Casts of portraits of Cicero (borrowed from the College Library) and Augustus stood with Crawford's *Homer, Cicero,* and *Demosthenes* (fig. 20). Also shown was Horatio Greenough's *Aristides* (now known to be a copy of the portrait of *Aeschines* from the Villa of the Papyri at Herculaneum, now in the National Archaeological Museum in Naples), lent by Professor Salisbury and ultimately bequeathed by him to Yale in 1919. Another major work by Greenough, *The Angel Abdiel* (fig. 31), was shown, again lent by Professor Salisbury and bequeathed at his death. Two works by Hezekiah Augur, a head of Apollo and an image of *Resignation,* were lent by James Augur, the brother of the artist.[14] The few nonclassical works were portraits (Napoleon) or personifications (a classical concept) like Augur's *Resignation.*

The 1858 exhibition was also the occasion of one

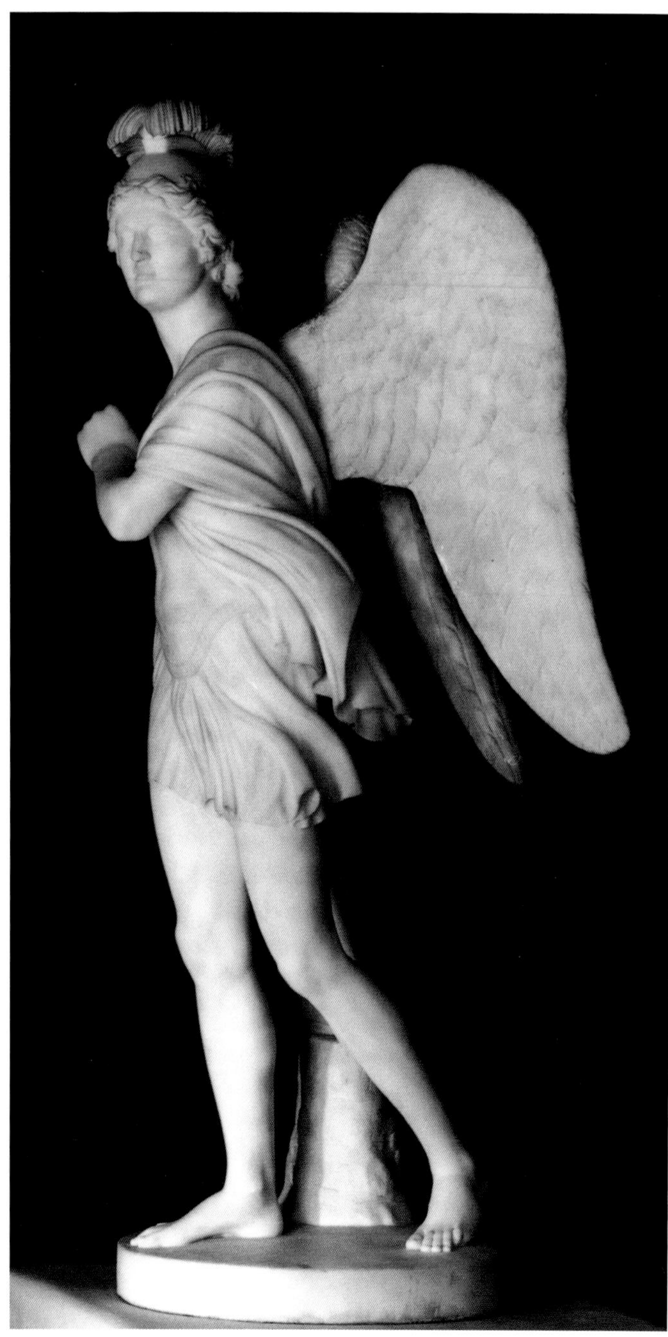

FIG. 31
Horatio Greenough
The Angel Abdiel, 1839
Marble, 104.1 x 42.5 x 36.8 cm
Bequest of Professor Edward E. Salisbury, B.A. 1832, M.A. 1835, LL.D. 1869
1919.13

of the first commissions of a work of art by Yale. The Linonian Society, whose books and art works were kept in the Austin library, was preparing, in 1857, to share a debating room in the new Alumni Building with the Brothers in Unity. Seeking to furnish the chamber with appropriate works of art and finding that a copy of Raphael's *School of Athens* was beyond their budget, the Linonians commissioned instead marble copies of ancient Greek statues of Demosthenes and Sophocles from a Connecticut sculptor, Edward Sheffield Bartholomew.[15] Both ancient statues were in Rome, where Bartholomew was in residence. Both were well known to students of ancient art, and the choice was endorsed by the society's advisers at Yale as "admirable illustrations of ancient skill." Moreover, the men represented were "appropriately remembered in a society avowedly devoted to eloquence and literature." The value of portraits of role models seen in Yale's earliest acquisitions was still evident. Bartholomew's untimely death in May of 1858 at the age of thirty-six meant that these statues were his last works, and that they were delayed in arriving in New Haven. They did not arrive in time to be part of the exhibition, but they were hailed when they finally did come in late summer. Their present location is unknown.

Daniel Coit Gilman published an extensive article on the exhibition and its catalogue in the widely read *New Englander and Yale Review* shortly after the exhibition closed. A member of the exhibition planning committee, Gilman was College Librarian in 1858 and later professor of physical and political geography (1863–72). He was thus in a good position to explicate the goals of the exhibition and the educational purpose it served in the eyes of the College, as well as describe it in detail. Gilman reports that the exhibition, which was on view from June to August, was visited by six or seven thousand persons. It was also a financial success. Admission of 25 cents for a single visit was charged, and the catalogue cost an additional 10 cents. Total expenses were $2,074.07, while total receipts were $2,200.10. Gilman attributes the success to the quality of the works of art: "Many competent judges declared that so large a variety of meritorious works of Art had very seldom been collected in America." Although a few copies of European Old Masters were admitted because, as Gilman says, "one of the chief designs of the exhibition was the instruction of students," Gilman concludes that "the chief value of the collection consisted in the large number of original works by early and modern masters, which were thus temporarily brought together."

The stated goal of the exhibition, to awaken a love of the fine arts, was advanced through a series of lectures offered during its run. Gilman describes their purpose: "To instruct the college students and others who might listen, by informing them somewhat of the history of the fine arts, and by directing their attention to the principles of taste, a course of lectures was given by various gentlemen, during several successive weeks."[16] Five formal lectures were given. Professor Salisbury spoke on Michelangelo; Mr. Deming of Hartford spoke on the late Edward Sheffield Bartholomew, whose statues of Demosthenes and Sophocles were still awaited; Professor George W. Greene of New York spoke on Thomas Cole; Professor Andrew Dickson White, then of Michigan, later on the faculty at Yale, and ultimately president of Cornell, spoke on medieval cathedrals and sculptors; and Donald Grant Mitchell, a popular New Haven author (writing under the name of I. K. Marvell), spoke on the principles that should guide students in a talk entitled "How to Look at Paintings." In addition to these lectures, less formal lectures were given in the gallery with the original works of art, much as Trumbull had done in 1839. The pattern of teaching art history from original works of art that survives today at Yale had begun.

The legacy of the 1858 exhibition was profound, both for New Haven and for Yale. Suddenly, there was a reason for the culturally astute to visit New Haven. The exhibition was reviewed in journals and newspapers from Boston (the *Boston Transcript* and the *Boston Journal*) to New York (the *New York Times* and the *New York Tribune*). The *New York Tribune* reviewer stated that, in his opinion, the show was "one of the finest collections of paintings and other works of art ever formed in this country." Connecticut reviewers beyond New Haven (the *New Haven Courier*) included the *Hartford Times* and the *Waterbury American*.[17] There is no question, on the basis of attendance alone, that the exhibition reawakened interest in the fine arts in New Haven and at Yale, which had become somewhat dormant after the initial years of the Trumbull Gallery. This re-engagement with art had been one of the organizers' goals. The sight of so many fine works of art in private hands encouraged the growth of local private collecting, both of Old Masters and contemporary art. In the following years, the show inspired numerous exhibitions organized by Yale, the New Haven Sketch Club, and a commercial New Haven gallery known as Cutler's Art Shop, extending beyond the end of the nineteenth century.

The exhibition raised serious issues about the study of art, and the fact that it was mounted and shown at a college provoked a dialogue in the press about artistic training in American higher education. The influential journal *The Congregationalist* praised the exhibition for providing the opportunity to study original art, noting that while many acknowledged the value of studying art history, few American universities had made any provision for doing so. Yale had made a better effort than many, but the exhibition provided even its host institution with an important opportunity for its students beyond that offered by the Trumbull Gallery and its collections. The emphasis in this dialogue was primarily on art history. Practical education in art was not yet recognized as part of a traditional university curriculum, with drawing being taught only as part of training for medical, engineering, and military careers. Although one of the reviewers, Louis Bail, a local New Haven artist and art teacher, praised the show for giving him the opportunity to learn from original works of art and went on to say that he hoped to establish public education in the arts, it was some time before this took place.[18] When it did start at the university level, it was at Yale, where Bail was Instructor in Drawing from 1865–73.

Gilman, in his review of the 1858 exhibition and catalogue, described the event as a major forward step by Yale College toward the goal of ensuring that the "educated young men yearly leaving our colleges in companies of thousands are well instructed in the principles of artistic as well as literary taste."[19] Gilman had a vision for the future: "It is greatly hoped that among the friends of the college some one interested in the Fine Arts will be encouraged to provide the means for the purchase of particular works or for the annual delivery of a course of lectures. But our desires do not rest here. We should rejoice to see in all our colleges successful efforts to secure the recognition of the Fine Arts as an important branch of academic discipline."[20] Several specific proposals followed, among them the establishment of a fund whose annual income could be used to buy engravings after famous paintings and copies of ancient statues, originals of both being too expensive. Such a fund was long in coming, but the acquisition of the copies, especially plaster casts of ancient Greek and Roman statues, began immediately and was an important part of the growth of the teaching collection during the second half of the nineteenth century.

Apart from these acquisitions, the established pattern of acquiring primarily portraits continued until after the Civil War, when the landmark Jarves Collection of early Italian paintings was purchased (see chapter 5). Among the portraits acquired after 1858 was the first photograph to enter the permanent collection, a portrait of Mrs. Hepsa Ely Silliman, aged eighty-three, the sister-in-law of Benjamin Silliman, Sr., as the gift of her children.

Daniel Coit Gilman was something of a visionary when it came to the future of art museums, especially at universities:

> We sincerely hope that the day is not too distant when the increasing wealth of our country, the rapidly spreading acquaintance with the galleries of Europe, and the increasing cultivation of society, will be manifested in permanent Art collections, in frequent occasional exhibitions, and in courses of lectures appropriate to both; and particularly that the students in our colleges and universities may have their attention directed to such principles of taste, and to such examples of the beautiful, as will fit them in after life to be in this respect, as in others, the enlighteners of public opinion and the guides of public outlay.[21]

The Civil War delayed the realization of this dream, but by 1864 a generous donor, inspired by his involvement in the 1858 exhibition and his experiences in Europe, came forward to provide a building that would embody this vision and more.

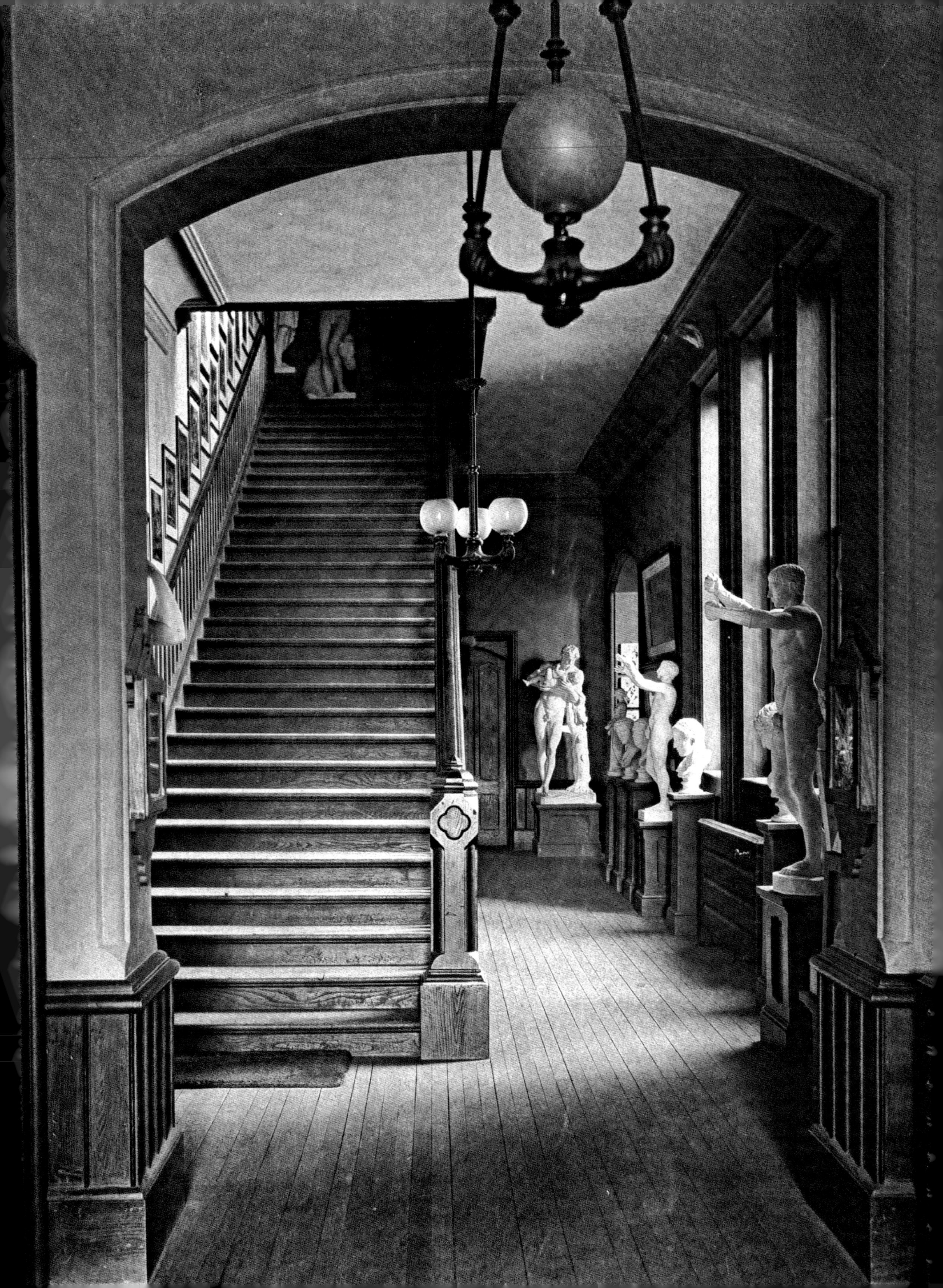

CHAPTER 4

The Yale School of the Fine Arts

In 1864, Augustus Russell Street offered to build a School of Art for Yale. "To the President and Fellows of Yale College," he wrote, "Gentlemen: I hereby propose to cause the erection, at my sole expense, of a building on the College grounds, to be used for a School of the fine arts."[1] With the acceptance of Street's offer, the College undertook to create the first school of art on an American college campus and to build, as part of this school, new galleries for exhibiting works of art.

Augustus Russell Street (1791–1866) was a native of New Haven and a graduate of Yale College (B.A. 1812; fig. 32). He was a "wealthy and public-spirited citizen," in the words of John Ferguson Weir, the first professor of painting and design and director of the School of the Fine Arts.[2] Street was a generous benefactor to Yale, endowing a professorship in ecclesiastical history and another in modern languages before beginning his plans for the School of Art. Married to Caroline Mary Leffingwell, daughter of a prominent New Haven family, Street and his wife had lived for many years in Europe, where they became devoted to art. Street collected art—he was one of the lenders to the 1858 exhibition—and he was particularly interested in the training of artists. The École des Beaux-Arts in Paris seems to have inspired his vision for an art school at Yale. The 1858 exhibition and the discussion about art education that it generated appear to have been the catalyst for Street's proposal, and the success of the exhibition and associated lectures prepared the ground for the College's acceptance of the offer.[3] As Professor Weir wrote, the lectures inspired a renewed interest in art and resulted in "a decided recognition, on the part of the friends and officers of Yale, of the important influence which art culture might exert on college students, and the desirableness of careful attention to it during an academic course."[4]

Street's vision and the specifics of his proposal embodied his dual allegiance to his alma mater and his city: "The building [is] to be located on the corner of Chapel and High Streets, . . . to have one front with entrance on Chapel Street, and another entrance on the College grounds."[5] Instruction was to be offered to both students from New Haven and local towns and students from Yale College. The role of the School was to train students of both sexes who desired to pursue

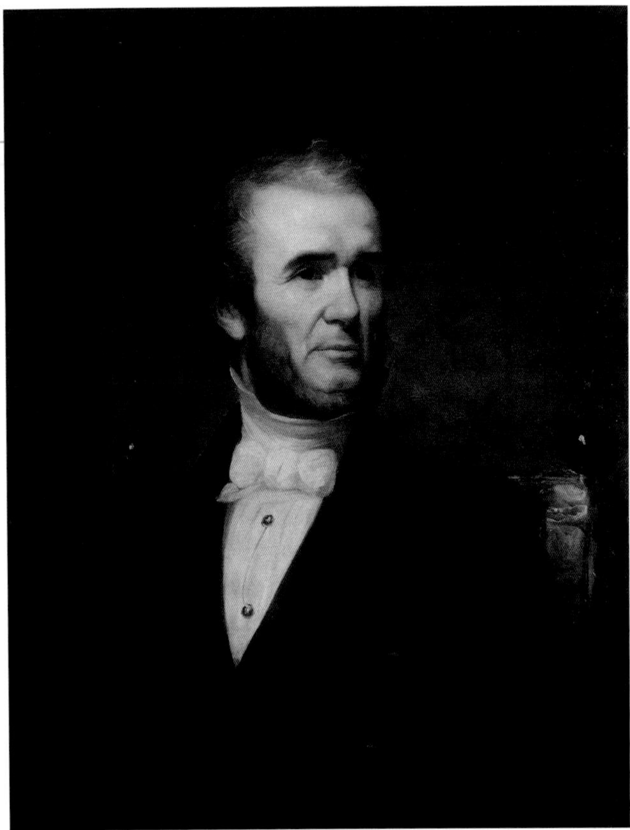

FIG. 32
Nathaniel Jocelyn
Augustus Russell Street, ca. 1840–50
Oil on canvas, 76.8 x 64.1 cm
Gift of Mrs. Augustus Russell Street Foote
1918.1

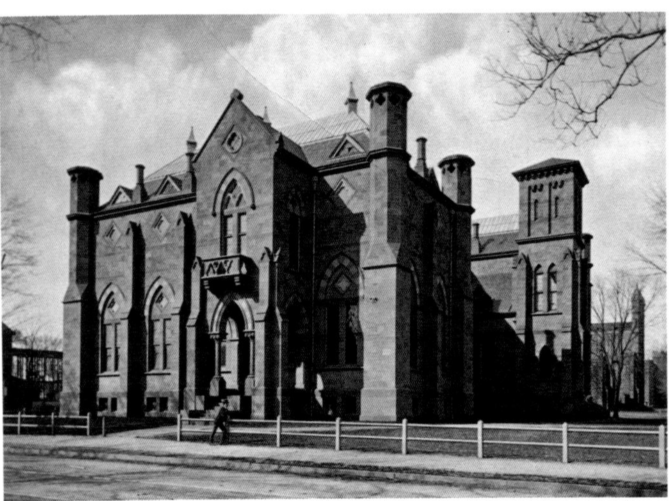

FIG. 33
P. B. Wight
The Yale School of the Fine Arts, 1864
View of the southeast corner from Chapel Street
Photograph courtesy Manuscripts and Archives, Sterling Memorial Library, Yale University

art as a profession, as well as to educate those who wished to learn about and appreciate art. Street's own words reflect the goals stated for the 1858 exhibition and very nearly echo D. C. Gilman's words:

> . . . a School of Art in Yale College, for the purpose of providing instruction in, and diffusing a knowledge of, the arts of drawing, designing, painting, sculpture, and other of the fine arts, under such regulations for the admission of pupils of both sexes, and for the method and course of instruction, as said [Yale] Corporation, from time to time, shall prescribe, it being among the objects of this gift to provide, for those desiring to pursue either of the fine arts as a profession, the means of instruction and improvement, and to awaken a taste for, and appreciation of, the fine arts, among the undergraduates of the college, and others.[6]

The 1858 exhibition had also clearly revealed the value of expanded exhibition space beyond that offered by the now crowded Trumbull Gallery. Street's proposal addressed this need by giving equal attention to exhibition and teaching space in the new building, which was "to be constructed and arranged in such a way as to be convenient for collections in the Fine Arts, as also for the uses of a school of instruction in the same."[7]

The College engaged Peter Bonnett Wight as architect for the new building. Wight was relatively unknown at the time, but he had recently won the competition for the new National Academy of Design in New York (1861, building completed in 1865), and the Ruskinian Gothic style that he used for the Academy appears to have influenced the Yale committee's choice in his favor. Ground was broken on August 13, 1864, by former Yale President Jeremiah Day and John Foote, Street's grandson. The cornerstone was laid on November 16, 1864, by Yale President Theodore Woolsey, while Professor Edward Elbridge Salisbury gave the address. Wight's design was true to its Ruskinian sources on the outside (fig. 33), with towers and turrets, arched windows, and multicolored stone for chromatic effect. As Street had specified, the building had an entrance on Chapel Street and another on the campus. The basic plan was that of an irregular letter "H," its irregularity another homage to Gothic style.

The interior was divided into three floors. The first floor and basement were studios and classrooms, and the second floor was given over to exhibition galleries. The upper floor and its galleries were reached by a broad staircase that led up from the Chapel Street entrance (fig. 34). There were two main picture galleries, both placed on an east-west axis, one extending along the Chapel Street side, the other on the campus side. Both were lit by skylights and had ceilings over thirty feet high. The gallery on the north side featured an oriel window with a view of the campus, while the south gallery overlooked Chapel Street from a small room over the entrance. The building was complete enough to be opened in 1866, and in July of that year the Yale Corporation voted to transfer the paintings and other works of art that had been displayed in the Trumbull Gallery to the galleries in the new School of the Fine Arts. In January 1867, art books were transferred from the main (Austin) library to the new art library in the School. The bodies of Colonel and Mrs. Trumbull were transferred into a specially built vault in the new building, in accordance with the artist's wishes to be buried beneath his portrait of George Washington.

The south (Chapel Street) gallery was designated for the Trumbull Collection, while the north (campus) gallery was to be used for European and other American paintings and marble copies after ancient Greek and Roman statues, along the lines of what was shown in the 1858 exhibition. These two large galleries were joined by a smaller one, lit by windows, designed for the display of engravings, photographs, and casts. The hallway adjacent to the staircase on all floors could also be (and was) used as a gallery, again combining works on paper with casts.

These two smaller galleries were particularly didactic in focus. Copying masterworks of the past, whether paintings or sculpture, was a standard method of learning for art students in the later nineteenth century. While European students could copy originals in the museums of Paris or Rome, American students needed access to some intermediate form of reproduction. As Gilman and others had stated, black-and-white engravings and photographs were the most desirable reproductions of famous paintings, and plaster casts were of equal value to marble copies of ancient statues for

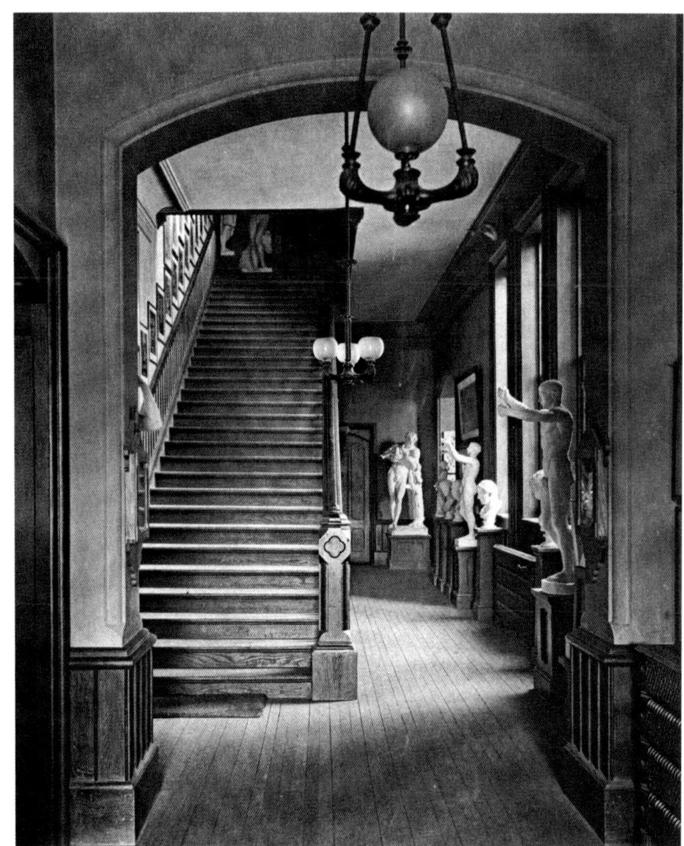

FIG. 34
P. B. Wight
The Yale School of the Fine Arts
Main staircase, 1864, with plaster casts in the hallway
Photograph, before 1878, courtesy Manuscripts and Archives, Sterling Memorial Library, Yale University

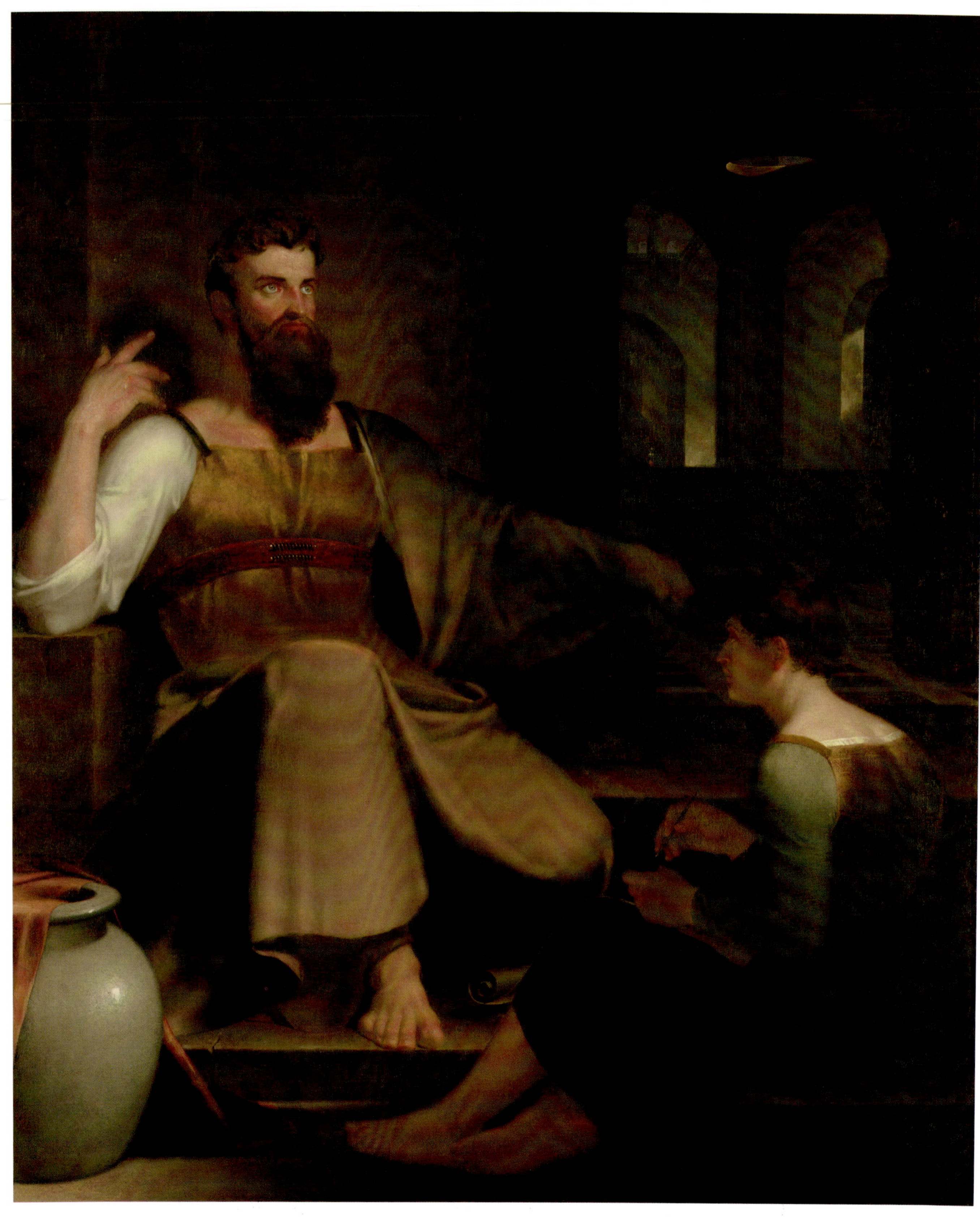

FIG. 35
Washington Allston
Jeremiah Dictating His Prophecy of the Destruction of Jerusalem to Baruch the Scribe, 1820
Oil on canvas, 227.0 x 189.9 cm
Gift of Samuel F. B. Morse, B.A. 1810
1866.1

teaching purposes, and far less expensive. Continuous effort and funding were devoted to increasing Yale's cast collection, and it rapidly claimed display space outside the classroom. Casts lined the hallways (fig. 34), the *Laocoön* was squeezed under the stairs, and casts of the Parthenon frieze and pediments rapidly filled the small galleries. Other casts were integrated into the main picture galleries. A cast of Ghiberti's bronze doors in Florence, purchased by J. F. Weir in 1873 for $1,049.60, stood at one end of the north gallery. Acquisition of additional plaster casts was funded by the proceeds from admission charged to exhibitions of contemporary American art.

Several important additions to the collections were made around the time the new School of the Fine Arts building opened, inspired by the new exhibition space that it featured. According to Gilman,[8] Samuel F. B. Morse made the first donation to the new galleries, by purchasing for Yale the monumental oil painting by Washington Allston of *Jeremiah Dictating His Prophecy of the Destruction of Jerusalem to Baruch the Scribe* (1820; fig. 35). Morse gave two of his own works the same year, the large oil painting of the *Dying Hercules* (1812; fig. 36) and a plaster model of the Hercules figure for the painting. The first piece of American silver to enter the collection was also acquired in 1866, an eighteenth-century tankard by Elias Pelletreau (ca. 1760–75; fig. 37) that had once belonged to Naphtali Daggett, the sixth president of Yale.

Loans were also displayed in the galleries, and in 1867 the first of the major summer loan exhibitions to be mounted periodically between 1867 and 1890 was installed. There were also more or less annual winter exhibitions of student work.

By an agreement reached in July 1865 between President Theodore Dwight Woolsey (B.A. 1820) and A. R. Street, the School was to be governed by a five-person Art Council, although approval of the Yale Corporation was needed to spend the School's funds. Initially, the council consisted of President Woolsey, ex officio, Professors Noah Porter (B.A. 1831), Edward Elbridge Salisbury, Donald G. Mitchell (B.A. 1841), all of New Haven, and Daniel Huntington of New York, the president of the National Academy of Design. The council began meeting in January of 1866, and the

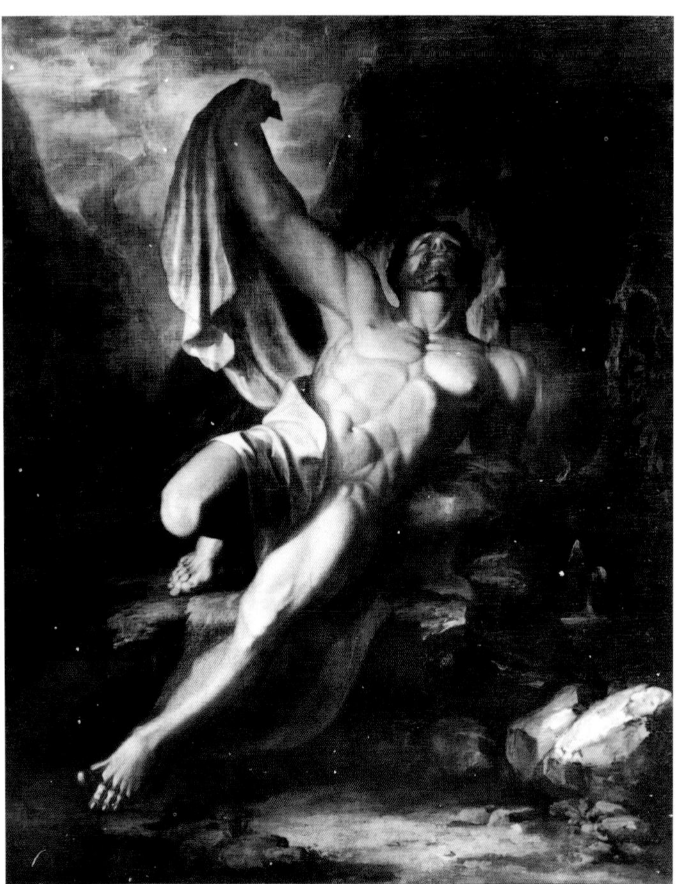

FIG. 36
Samuel F. B. Morse
Dying Hercules, 1812
Oil on canvas, 244.5 x 198.4 cm
Gift of the Artist
1866.3

FIG. 37
Elias Pelletreau
Tankard, ca. 1760–75
Silver, 21.3 cm
Yale University Art Gallery
1866.5

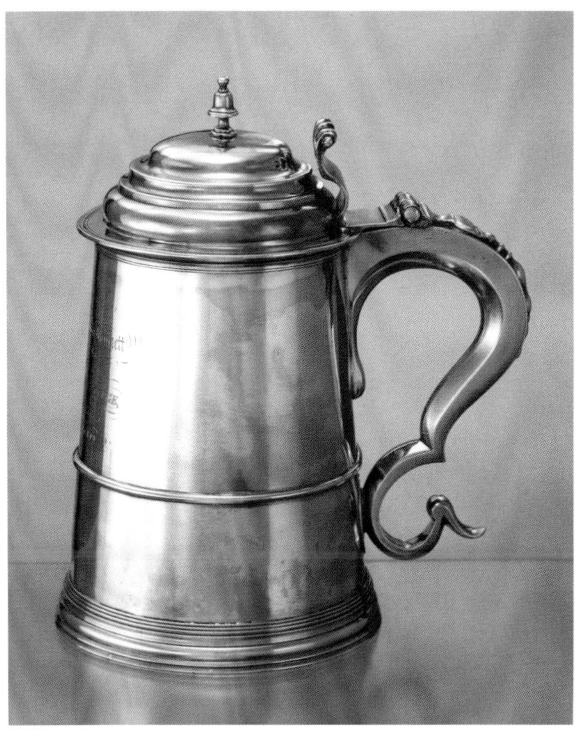

minutes of its meetings through May 1887 are preserved. These minutes confirm the idea that the initial impulse for an art school at Yale should be attributed to the 1858 exhibition, and propose that the new School might be inaugurated with a similar show. This was, in fact, done. The minutes also reveal that the council envisioned a school that was a national center for eminent artists, including painters, sculptors, and architects, and that they wanted to bring artists "of decided genius" to teach. Artists who did come would be given free studio space, although no salary. An artist, again unsalaried, would be sought to direct the School, and in the interim an unpaid "lover of art" would be appointed "Curator of the School."

The Art Council was also considering strategies for increasing the collections. They hoped that interest generated by exhibitions and lectures

> might be expected to lead to a gradual accumulation of works of art in the School — paintings, marbles, casts, models, engravings, and the like — some left on permanent deposit by the exhibitors; some sent home by graduates of the University on their foreign travels, inspired by what they had seen and, while pursuing their education in favor of the fine arts, or in the way of special intimation of what would be desirable for the art collections to be gathered in the School; some contributed by American artists resident abroad; and some bequeathed by persons desirous of thus expressing their interest in the establishment. The accumulation would, indeed, be somewhat miscellaneous; but a wise control on the part of those in charge under the College Corporation would bring it into order, and form a unity at once honorable and effective for the School. These permanent collections should be open to view without any fee for admission.[9]

The College was not providing much financial support for the School — the School counted on "an empty treasury"[10] — and the Council agreed immediately on the need for an endowment. In the meanwhile, Gilman, F. J. Betts, R. S. Fellowes, and others were charged with raising funds for equipment from contributions from the citizens of New Haven. Given the fact that the College did not encourage its students to take courses at the School (and indeed did not give students credit for such courses toward a Yale College degree until 1891), while Yale studio space and classes were available to local residents, it was not an inappropriate suggestion.

The building was sufficiently complete to be opened at Commencement in June 1866, although when Augustus Russell Street died in mid-June, the building he had donated was in fact still unfinished, unfurnished, and largely unstaffed. His widow, Caroline Leffingwell Street, began overseeing the funding that her husband had provided for the School, retaining control of it until her death, when it became an endowment. Relations between Mrs. Street and the Art Council were not smooth, although it is not clear at whose door the blame for this situation lay. In December Mrs. Street wrote to President Woolsey, stating her concern that the building was underused, insufficiently appreciated, and likely to be vandalized. She urged the immediate transfer of the works of art from the Trumbull Gallery, which had already been approved by the Corporation. This was done in January 1867. Whatever the difficulties, however, Mrs. Street never relinquished her interest in the School, and ultimately, by bequest, she endowed the first professorship of painting and design. John Ferguson Weir was the first Leffingwell Professor, a title he held, along with that of director of the School of the Fine Arts, from 1878 until 1913.

In early 1867, the painter Nathaniel Jocelyn moved into a studio in the School and began offering classes. He also arranged for students to rent studio space in the School. In January, Jocelyn was charged with taking care of "the art building and its contents,"[11] apparently making him the interim curator called for by the Art Council. He was in any case responsible for arranging the Trumbull paintings when they were brought to the School from the Trumbull Gallery.

THE 1867 EXHIBITION

The Art Council's proposal for an inaugural loan exhibition resulted in the *First Annual Exhibition of the Yale School of the Fine Arts, Founded as a Department of Yale College, by the Late Augustus Russell Street of New*

Haven, Conn. in the summer of 1867. Since the goal of the exhibition was to raise money, opening hours were long: daily from 9:00 a.m.–7:00 p.m. and Wednesday evenings until 11:00. Free admission was suspended during the exhibition; an individual ticket cost 25 cents, a season ticket $1.00. A catalogue was published.

The exhibition was installed in the two large paintings galleries and the corridor gallery on the second floor of the new School of the Fine Arts. The content and format were modeled on the 1858 Alumni Hall exhibition, but this one included fewer European Old Masters and was heavily weighted toward contemporary American art. Some of the work was for sale. Yale's own paintings were featured again. The Trumbull paintings took a wall of the south gallery, and the newly acquired Allston and Morse paintings were shown as well. Included in this exhibition, not counting the Trumbulls, were 206 oil paintings; 81 watercolors and drawings, displayed in the corridor gallery; a pair of Wedgwood tiles with scenes from the life of Achilles, likely from a larger cycle; and 10 sculptures. Among the statuary were Yale's three familiar Crawfords and the Augur *Jephthah and His Daughter* as well as the Robert Ball Hughes portrait of Trumbull; new were three of the popular John Rogers groups, *Uncle Ned's School*, *Taking the Oath*, and the *Charity Patient*.

Many of the artists exhibiting were members of the National Academy. Among them were some now famous names: A. Bierstadt, J. F. Cropsey, Sanford R. Gifford, William Troost Richards, and J. F. Kensett, as well as painters who may be less well known today but were appreciated and collected at the time, notably Daniel Huntington, William Hart, J. B. Flagg, and Louis Lang. Painters with current or future Yale and New Haven connections included Nathaniel Jocelyn and John Ferguson Weir. The majority of the paintings were landscapes and genre subjects, but there were also portraits, mostly of Yale and New Haven figures like Benjamin Silliman, the Reverend Leonard Bacon, Samuel F. B. Morse, and Augustus Russell Street himself. Among the works on paper were several designs and drawings by Richard Morris Hunt of gates in Central Park and another Hunt drawing of a monument in Trinity Church (presumably Richard Upjohn's important Gothic Revival Trinity Church in New York).

Proceeds from the exhibition ($4,270.80) were used to pay expenses, and after those were covered, $700 was devoted to buying plaster casts, largely of the Parthenon sculptures. Purchases were overseen by Professor Salisbury and Charles C. Perkins of Boston, a dealer and conservator who was known as an expert in Italian sculpture.[12] Additional casts were added in early 1868, purchased from London, Paris, and Berlin. These cast acquisitions were well within the parameters of a standard teaching collection for an art school. The next major collection to come to Yale was not.

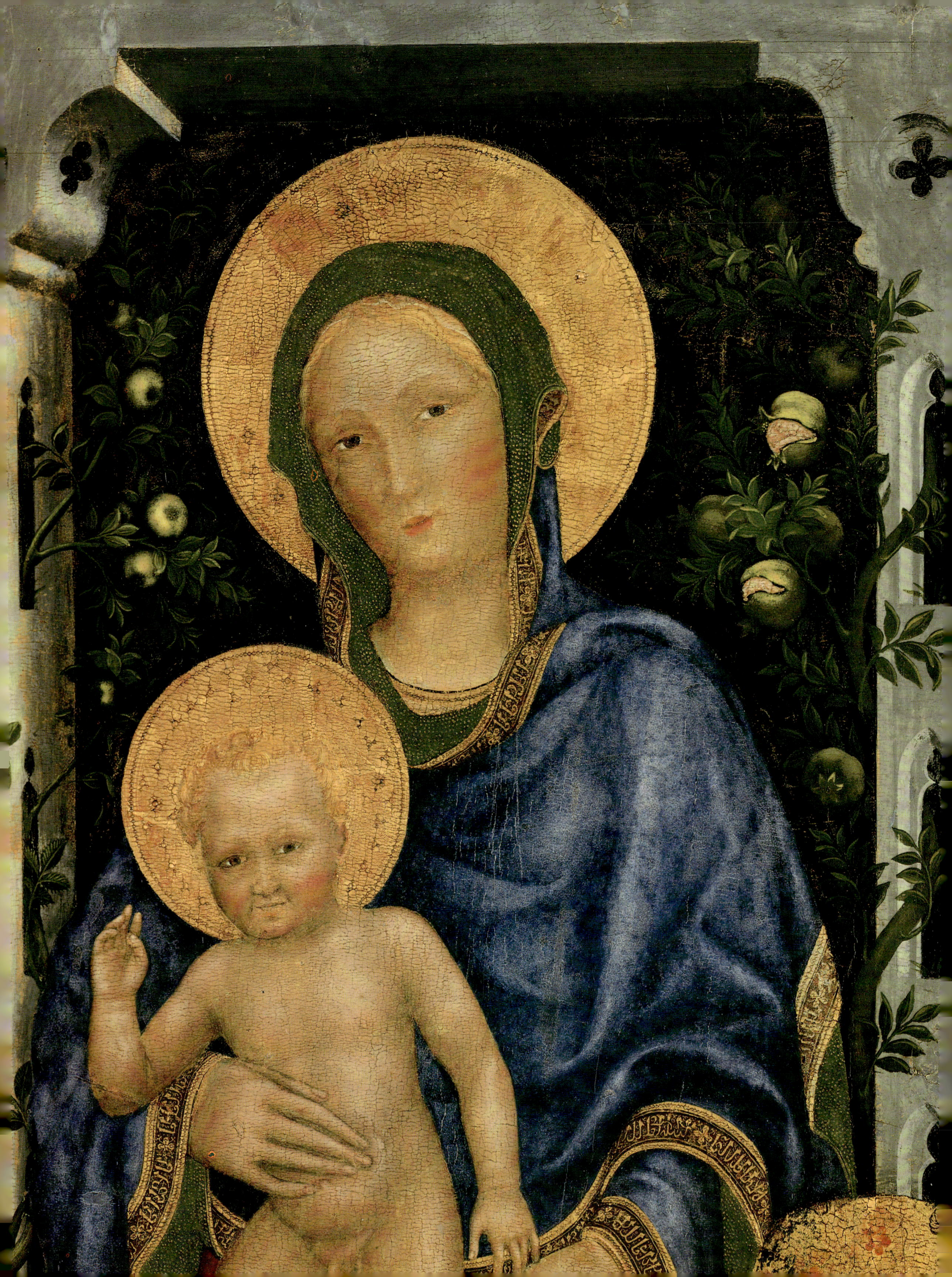

CHAPTER 5

The James Jackson Jarves Collection

On December 4, 1867, the Prudential Committee of the Yale Corporation voted to authorize a loan of $20,000 to James Jackson Jarves "on the deposit of his collection of paintings."[1] The collection consisted of 119 Italian Old Master paintings, ranging from ca. A.D. 1200 to the "best periods of Italian art" (fig. 38). With Jarves's attributions, the paintings bore names like Giotto, Cimabue, Duccio, Massaccio, Fra Angelico, Raphael, and Ghirlandaio. The term of the loan was for three years, and the pictures were to be installed in the galleries in the School of the Fine Arts. Nowhere else in America could such a collection be seen.

James Jackson Jarves was a native of Boston who began his search for fortune as a publisher and entrepreneur in Hawaii. Failing completely after eleven years of struggle, he moved to Europe. In Paris and Florence he discovered art, and he became an avid collector of Old Master paintings. He specialized in early Italian paintings long before they were fashionable or even respected. Frequently the artists whose works Jarves bought were called "Primitives." Nevertheless, he amassed what remains today, in spite of changing attributions, one of the most significant collections of early Italian painting outside Europe.

The decision by Yale to exhibit these paintings was not an obvious one. It came about because of the perception and intrepidity of a few key Yale faculty members. The first was Lewis R. Packard (B.A. 1856), who, just appointed as Hillhouse Professor of Greek, met Jarves on a transatlantic crossing in June 1867. Jarves told Packard of his pictures and of his unfulfilled desire that they should reside in a museum in Boston or New York, and offered to sell them to Yale for $40,000, allegedly a fraction of their cost. Packard communicated the offer to a friend at Yale, the librarian Addison Van Name (B.A. 1858), with the request that Van Name put the question to Professor Edward Salisbury. Salisbury was receptive, and further information about the collection was sent to him.

The Jarves Collection was already well known. It had been exhibited at the New York Institute of Fine Arts in 1860 and at the New-York Historical Society in 1863. Leonard W. Jerome (Winston Churchill's maternal grandfather) had attempted to buy the Jarves pictures in 1859 with a plan of endowing a gallery for them in

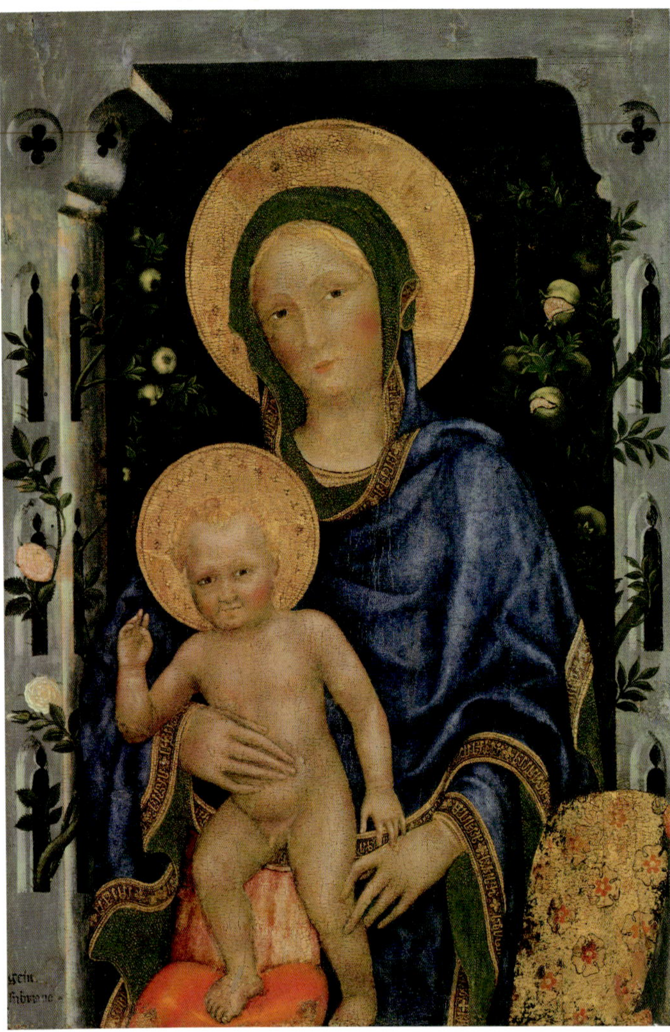

FIG. 38
Gentile da Fabriano
Madonna and Child, ca. 1424–25
Tempera on panel, 91.4 x 62.9 cm
University Purchase from James Jackson Jarves
1871.66

New York, and Jarves claimed that Mr. Corcoran wished to acquire them for the gallery he was building in Washington. Clarence Cook, the art critic for the *New York Daily Tribune*, had published a notice in the August 1867 issue of the *Galaxy*, a New York monthly, that the collection was for sale, along with a plea that some wealthy New Yorker buy it for the city as the basis for a metropolitan picture gallery.[2] This appeal failed, but the idea of a gallery took hold: in 1870 the Metropolitan Museum of Art was founded. Only later did the Metropolitan acquire its early Italian paintings.[3]

Charles Eliot Norton, one of the cultural leaders of Boston and a trustee of the Boston Athenaeum, had worked continuously to have the Jarves pictures acquired by the Athenaeum, although without success, from 1859 until they were deposited at Yale. Norton had also first met Jarves on a transatlantic crossing, in this case in 1855, and he had visited Jarves and his pictures in Florence in 1857. As part of his campaign, Norton collected testimonials from all over the world from supporters as diverse as Harriet Beecher Stowe, Sir Charles Eastlake, T. A. Trollope, and Signore Bucci, the director of the Uffizi Gallery in Florence, but it was not enough. The Athenaeum had never shown pictures like Jarves's Italian paintings, having focused instead on contemporary American and British artists, and its patrons were not interested in contributing to the purchase.[4] Norton was a graceful loser, and he was confident in his assurances that the collection would bring distinction to Yale and New Haven when he wrote to Jarves on December 8, 1867:

> I was truly glad to learn . . . that the arrangement had been completed by which your collection was secured for New Haven. I, indeed, regret & shall not cease to regret, that your generous intent in regard to Boston was not responded to in a more generous spirit, and that we have consequently lost this precious gallery from our immediate neighborhood. But as we could not keep it here, I am glad it is so near us, & gone to a place where it finds at once a building admirably fitted for its safekeeping & display. The acquisition of the collection by the College at New Haven will have a great effect on the future development of the college, & on the culture of New England generally.[5]

Elsewhere Norton wrote:

> It is several years since I saw the collection, and I have no doubt that its value and importance have been much increased by the additions which Mr. Jarves has made to it; but even as I knew it, it was a collection of the highest value in this country, as illustrating by well chosen examples the historic development and progress of Italian art. There are few collections in Europe, if we exclude the galleries in the great capitals, which surpass it in this important respect, and very few in which the proportion of valuable and interesting pictures is so great as compared with the whole number. Such a collection would make a truly magnificent foundation for a gallery, and the institution which should acquire it, would have an easy prëeminence over all other schools of art in America.[6]

Congratulatory articles about the loan appeared in the *New York Daily Tribune*, *The New Englander and Yale Review*, and *The Nation*, but there remained some concern over the possible reception of the pictures by the public. Gilman, writing in *The New Englander and Yale Review*, warned that:

> Such pictures must not be looked at with the same eye for entertainment and amusement, with which people are accustomed to run through the annual exhibitions of modern pictures. There is need of the same appreciative inquiry and study which is needed for the works of Dante or Homer. The aims of the painters, their beliefs, their surroundings, their aspirations, must be borne in mind, or the visitor will turn away unrewarded by the sight.[7]

Russell Sturgis, Jr., a New York architect and a Ruskinian like his friend and fellow architect P. B. Wight, was asked to prepare a catalogue of the paintings.[8] Sturgis was a member of the committee charged by the Art Council with arranging for the reception and display of the pictures. Other members were Professor Salisbury, who paid for the catalogue, Professor Gilman, who wrote about the collection for *The New Englander and Yale Review*, and Luther Maynard Jones (B.A. 1860), a New York attorney who was, along with Sturgis, Jarves's official representative in the negotiations with Yale. Sturgis attempted to address the possible public concern and misunderstanding of the pictures in his introduction to the catalogue. He discussed authenticity and the notion of "Primitives," offered explanatory and historical notes on each picture, and provided a historical table of the general sweep of Italian art. Going far beyond the simple lists of works that made up the catalogues of the 1858 and 1867 loan exhibitions at Yale, Sturgis's catalogue of the Jarves pictures is the first at Yale, and apparently in any American museum, to approach a modern scholarly exhibition catalogue. Also included as further encouragement for the viewer were some of the testimonial letters from the earlier catalogue of the collection from its showing in New York in 1860, which described the pictures as the "Unique Jarves Collection of Old Masters."[9]

The Jarves pictures were hung in the north gallery of the School of the Fine Arts building (fig. 39), whose Ruskinian Gothic architecture, based by the architect's own admission on Italian sources, was especially suitable for them. Jarves supervised the hanging personally. The gallery did not open at once, however. Concerns about the public reaction caused College officials to delay the opening until Sturgis's catalogue was ready, and when the gallery did open to the public in May 1868, it was opened without a formal ceremony or reception.

The undergraduate student newspaper, the *College Courant*, ancestor of the *Yale Daily News*, reacted at first with conservative disdain (city residents frequently complained that the college students were too conservative). In a piece written by a student who had gained unauthorized entry before the gallery was open, the writer says that "one hour's study of Bierstadt's 'Yosemite Valley' would, for me, be worth more than all of this collection."[10] The same writer appears to have been granted an official viewing a year later, and he reports on this visit in a more positive vein in the *Courant* of March 6, 1869.[11] The difference seems to have been Sturgis's catalogue, which the student actually read.

The installation that Jarves arranged remained in place until 1892, when, following conservation, the pictures were rehung with new labels. The original hanging was chronological. Like many nineteenth-century displays, the pictures were densely hung, often one above

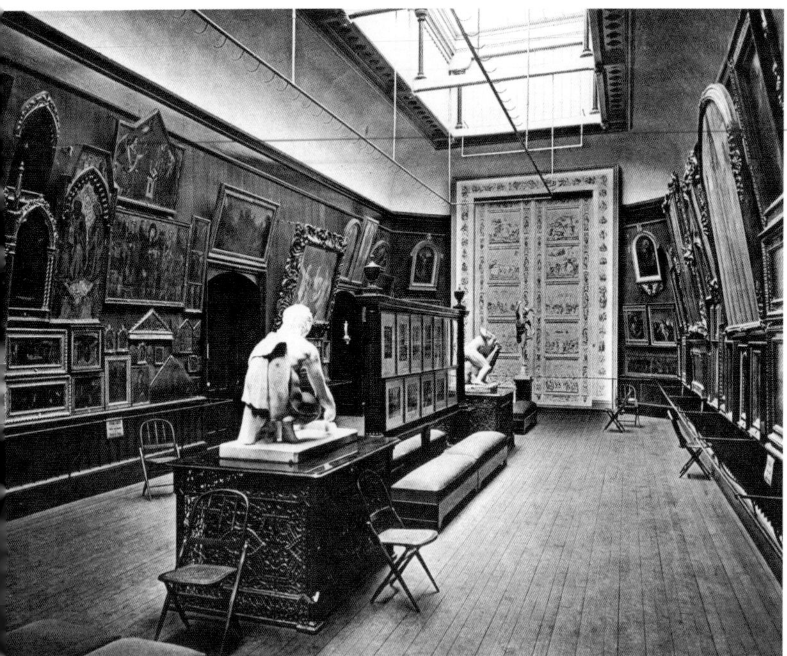

FIG. 39
P. B. Wight
The Yale School of the Fine Arts
Paintings Gallery, with Jarves pictures, casts, and works on paper, 1868–78
Photograph, before 1878, courtesy Manuscripts and Archives, Sterling Memorial Library, Yale University

another, sometimes as many as five deep. Their ornate Gothic-style gold frames and their rich jewel-like colors were cause for much comment. Several *cassoni* were part of the collection and included in the display, and the Jarves material was complemented by the copies and casts from the antique and the cast of Ghiberti's bronze doors.

Among the pictures are some extremely important works, even with today's less ambitious attributions, including the *Virgin and Child Enthroned with Saints Leonard and Peter* by the Master of the Magdalen, the *Hercules and Deianira* by Antonio del Pollaiuolo (fig. 40), two fragments from a Temptation of Saint Anthony cycle on an altarpiece by the Master of the Osservanza Triptych (figs. 41a and b), a *Portrait of a Lady with a Rabbit* by Ridolfo Ghirlandaio (fig. 42), and an *Annunciation* by Neroccio de' Landi (fig. 43).

The terms of the agreement of 1867 stipulated that Jarves was to repay the loan in three years, or forfeit the pictures that had been deposited as collateral. The pictures being his only significant asset, Jarves was obliged to put them up for sale to raise the $20,000 he owed. An auction was arranged for November 9, 1871, to be held in the gallery where the pictures hung at Yale. The sale was advertised in the New York and Boston press, a catalogue was prepared, and an auctioneer was brought in from Boston.[12] Jarves had expected to sell the pictures individually in order to raise the necessary funds, but the day before the auction he learned that the College would only permit the sale of the collection en bloc. Jarves was devastated—he had been well aware, based on past experience, that there was no individual nor any institution in either Boston or New York who could or would bid on the whole collection.

The auctioneer began the sale shortly before noon with a statement that had he known of the College's lien on the pictures the sale would never have been advertised as it was. To say that the pictures could be sold individually only on the condition that the total price realized by the whole collection would exceed $20,000 was unrealistic, "a farce," at best, and the only solution was therefore to sell the collection as a whole to a single bidder. The College bid $22,000, and no further bids being offered, the collection was sold to Yale.

There appear to have been several reasons why no

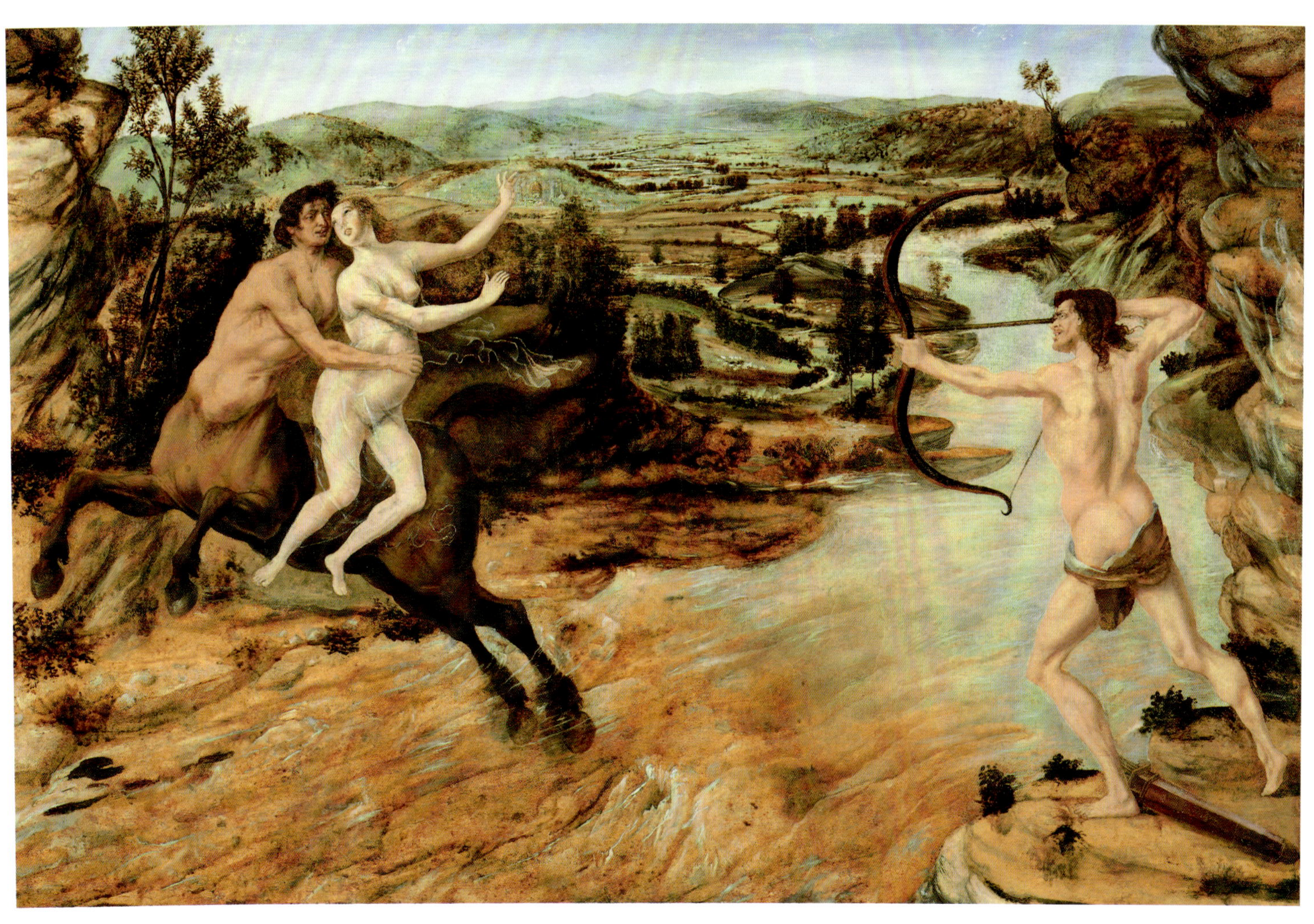

FIG. 40
Antonio del Pollaiuolo
Hercules and Deianira, ca. 1470
Oil on canvas, transferred from panel,
52.6 x 79.7 cm
University Purchase from James
Jackson Jarves
1871.42

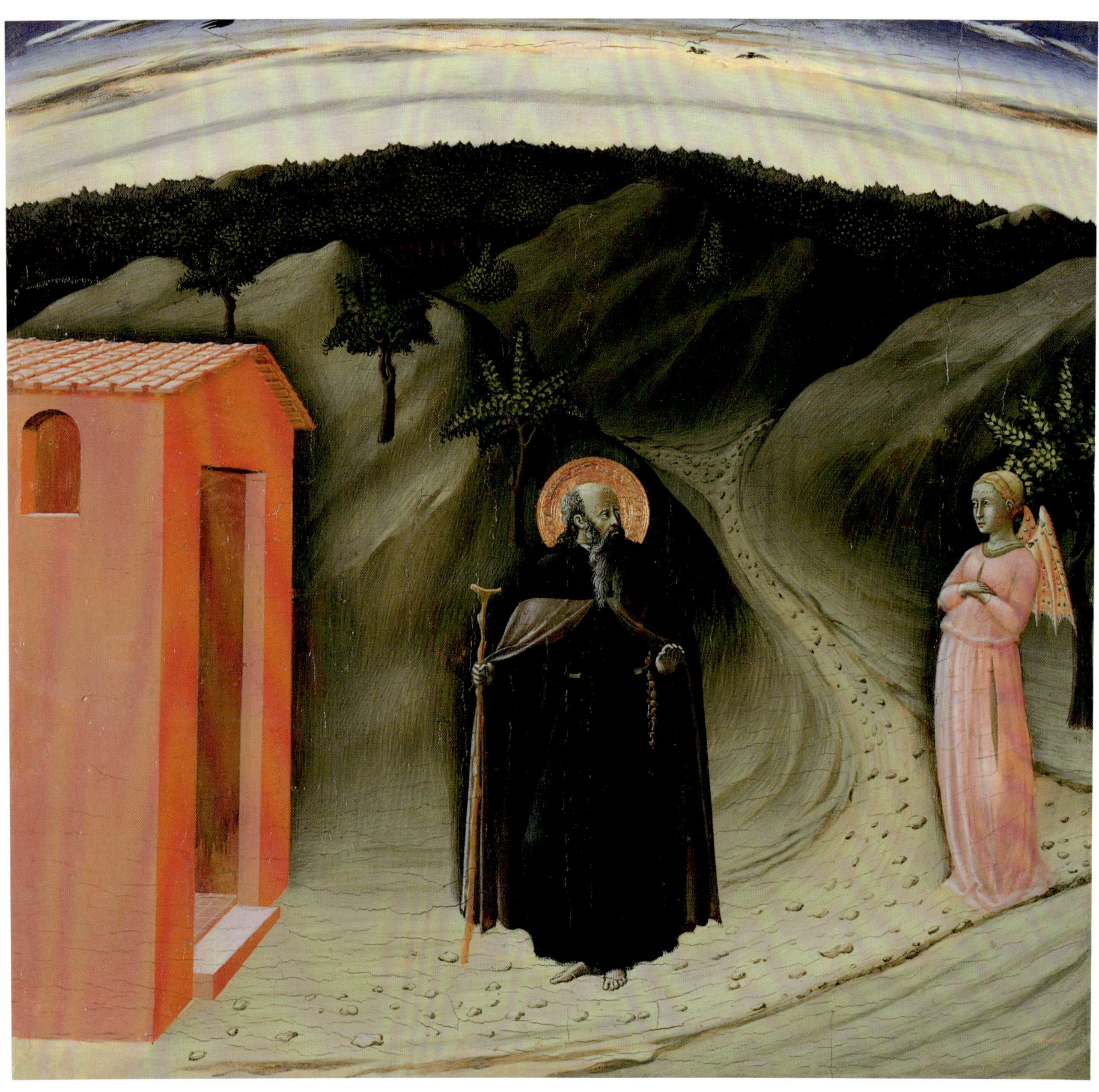

FIG. 41a
Master of the Osservanza Triptych
Temptation of Saint Anthony Abbot, ca. 1430
Tempera and gold on panel, 37.8 x 40.2 cm
University Purchase from James Jackson Jarves
1871.57

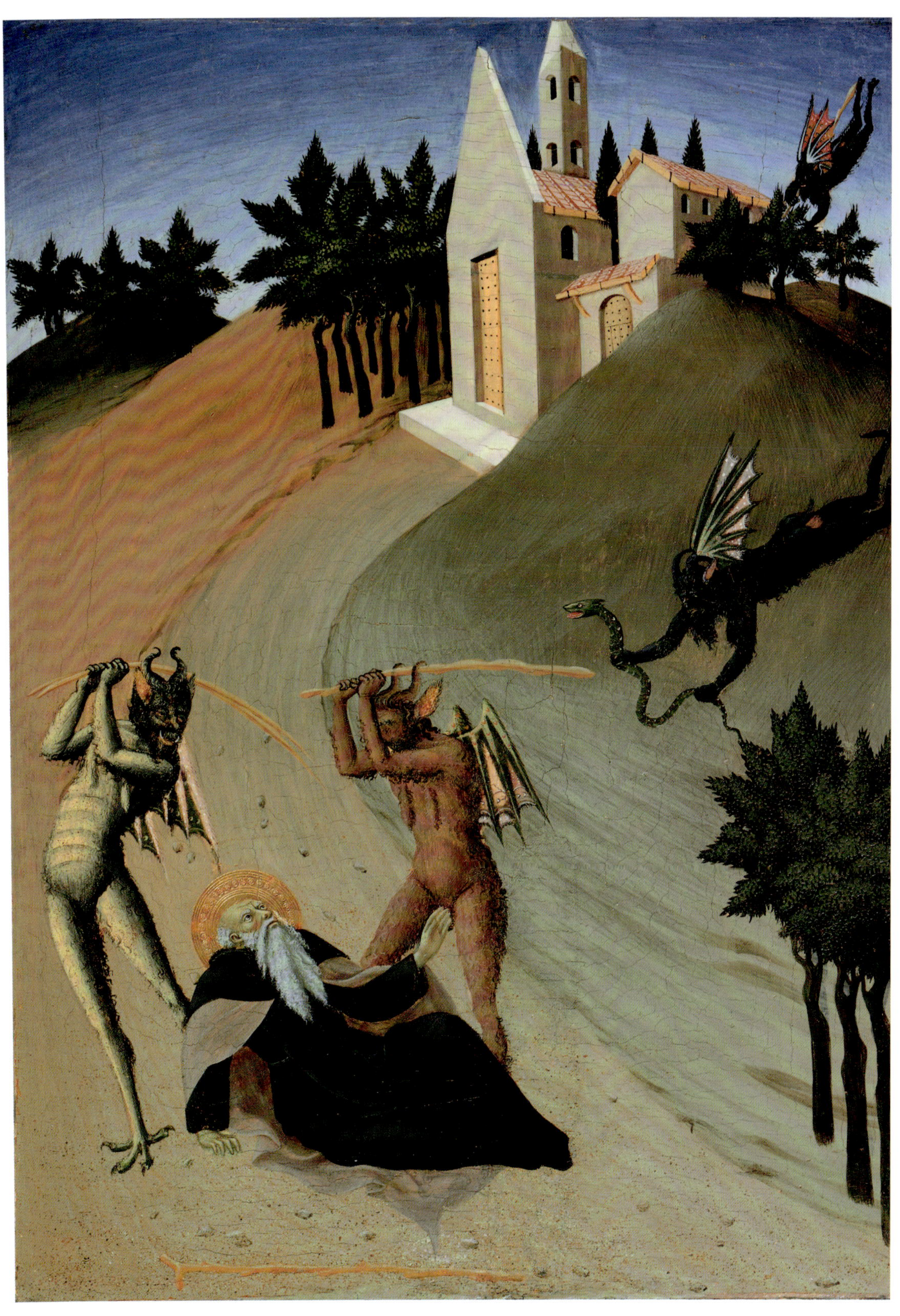

FIG. 41b
Master of the Osservanza Triptych
Saint Anthony Abbot Tormented by Demons,
ca. 1430
Tempera and gold on panel, 47.5 x 34.3 cm
University Purchase from James Jackson Jarves
1871.58

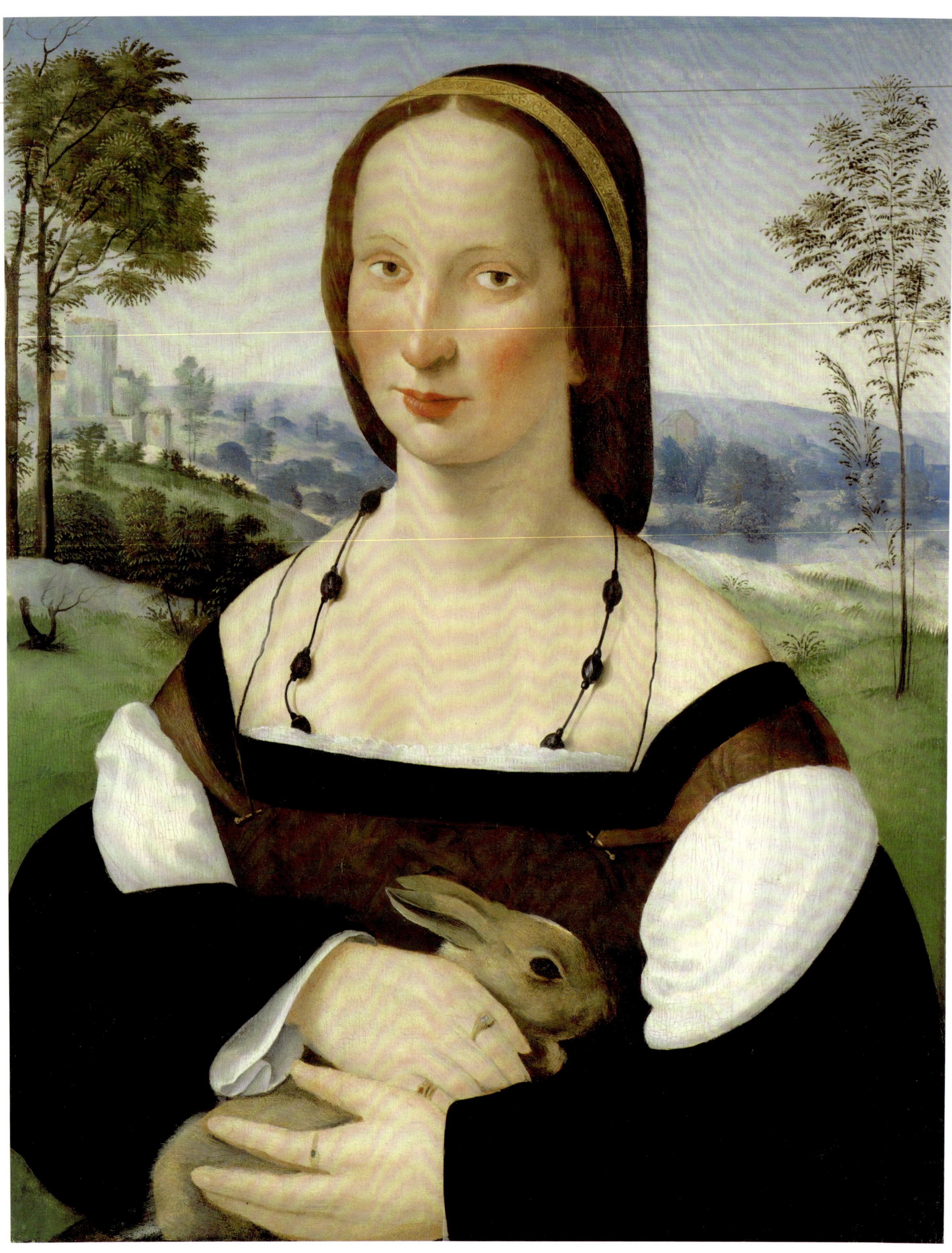

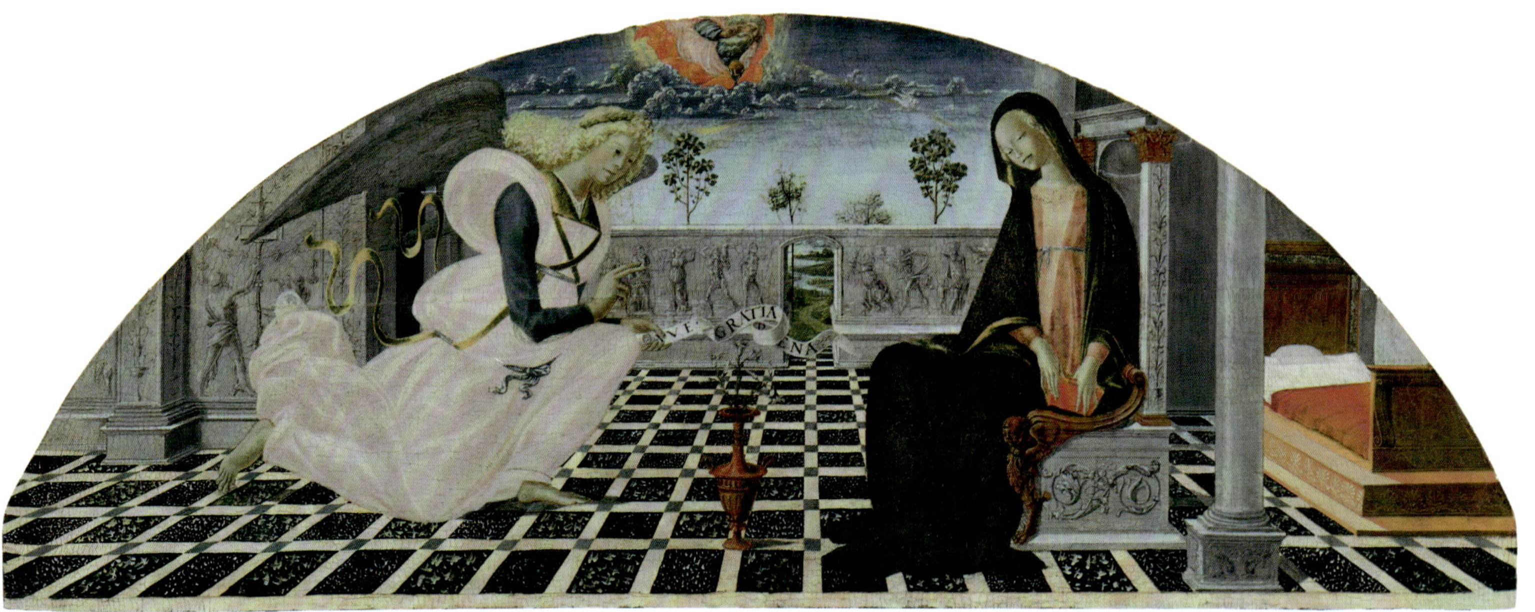

one bid against Yale for the collection. Most obvious was the requirement to buy the whole collection and the general perception that it would sell for between $60,000 and $75,000. There was also the perception that with the College's lien on the pictures it would be impossible to obtain clear title to them, either singly or as a group. In addition, many individuals and institutions were still recovering financially from the Civil War, which put such a major investment beyond their reach. Finally, there was simply not yet enough interest in early Italian art in America to generate a real market. The Jarves Collection was a pioneering effort in this field, complete and well known at a time when both the Boston Museum of Fine Arts and the Metropolitan Museum were only beginning their collections.

Yale's purchase was something of a risk, and it was apparently not universally endorsed at the College. Even Daniel Cady Eaton (B.A. 1857), the newly arrived Professor of History of the Criticism of Art, did not support the purchase, which must have given President Noah Porter pause. Porter, Kingsley, John Ferguson Weir, and many others at Yale were behind it, however, and it therefore went forward. Once the purchase was complete, most in the press and at other universities agreed that the collection brought distinction to Yale.

For Jarves, the resolution was not happy, and he complained about it publicly in the press and in letters to President Porter and others at Yale. He suffered further from personal attacks in the press, and he believed that his integrity had been questioned in the transaction. He felt he had been abandoned by his friend and official representative in the negotiations with Yale, Russell Sturgis, who was supposed to get him $60,000 for the pictures. Jarves's response to these attacks was to accuse Yale of less than honorable dealings. Although some details of the events leading up to the sale remain unexplained, there is no evidence (nor did anyone other than Jarves seriously believe) that Yale acted improperly. And no one would now argue that the president and faculty showed anything less than prescience and courage in acquiring this magnificent collection.

FIG. 42
Ridolfo Ghirlandaio
Portrait of a Lady with a Rabbit, ca. 1530
Oil on panel, 58.4 x 45.1 cm
University Purchase from James Jackson Jarves
1871.72

FIG. 43
Neroccio di Bartolommeo de' Landi
Annunciation
Tempera on panel, 48.3 x 128.6 cm
University Purchase from James Jackson Jarves
1871.63

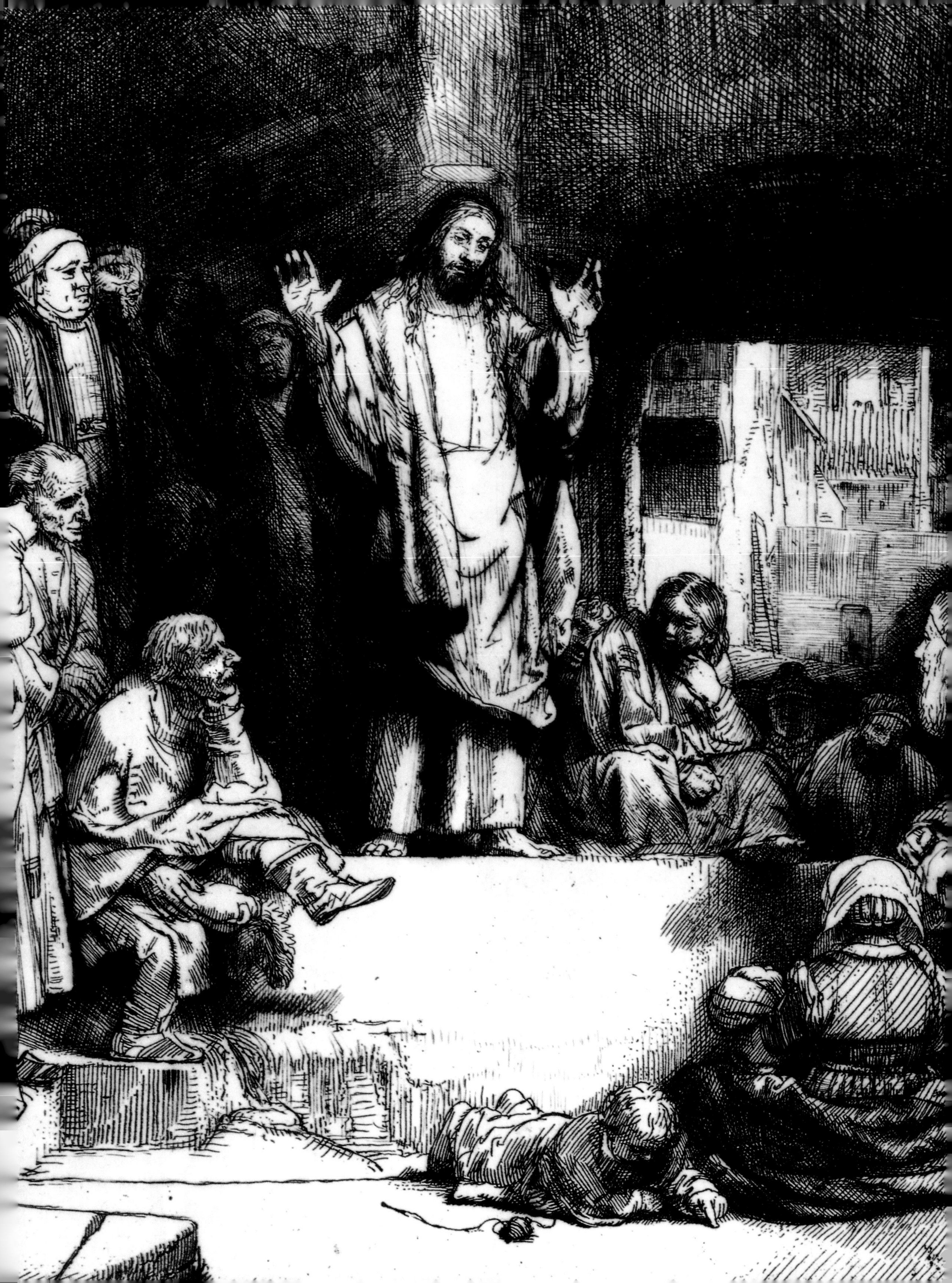

CHAPTER 6

New Teachers, Old Masters, and Old Pots

Other significant events during these post–Civil War years advanced the School of the Fine Arts along the lines envisioned by A. R. Street. In 1869, Mrs. Caroline Street, the founder's widow, provided an anonymous endowment for a professor of painting and design, who would also serve as the dean or director of the School—only after her death in August 1877 did this become the Leffingwell Professorship of Painting and Design. John Ferguson Weir, a well-known painter, was named to the dual post in 1869 (fig. 44). Son of the painter Robert Walter Weir and, along with his half-brother Julian Alden Weir, a student of their father, J. F. Weir was born and educated at West Point. After service in the Civil War, he took up his painting career in New York, at the famous Tenth Street Studio. He remained in New York through much of the 1860s. Weir was elected to the National Academy, celebrated for his painting *The Gun Foundry*, and made a member of the Century Club.

Weir, who was a key voice in favor of purchasing the Jarves Collection, as has been noted, was the guiding force behind the School until his retirement in June 1913. Once he undertook his duties, he essentially replaced the Art Council in the day-to-day decisions about program, acquisitions, and exhibitions, although the Art Council retained the responsibility for appointing the faculty. His was the vision that guided the program.

A professor of drawing was added in 1871, with funding again provided anonymously by Mrs. Street. John H. Niemeyer (Hon. M.A. 1874) was appointed and served in the position until 1908. A professor of perspective was endowed the same year by Henry Young of New York. The Art Council recommended its own termination as well as that of the position of director of the School as soon as the professorships of architecture and sculpture should be filled. President Noah Porter, who had succeeded President Woolsey in October 1871 following the latter's retirement in June, also succeeded him on the Council, filling the president's spot. Not unexpectedly, Professor Edward E. Salisbury was elected to another Council term.

The Second Loan Exhibition was held in 1870, the next in the series of summer exhibitions that had begun in 1867 and that, in Weir's words, "attracted attention

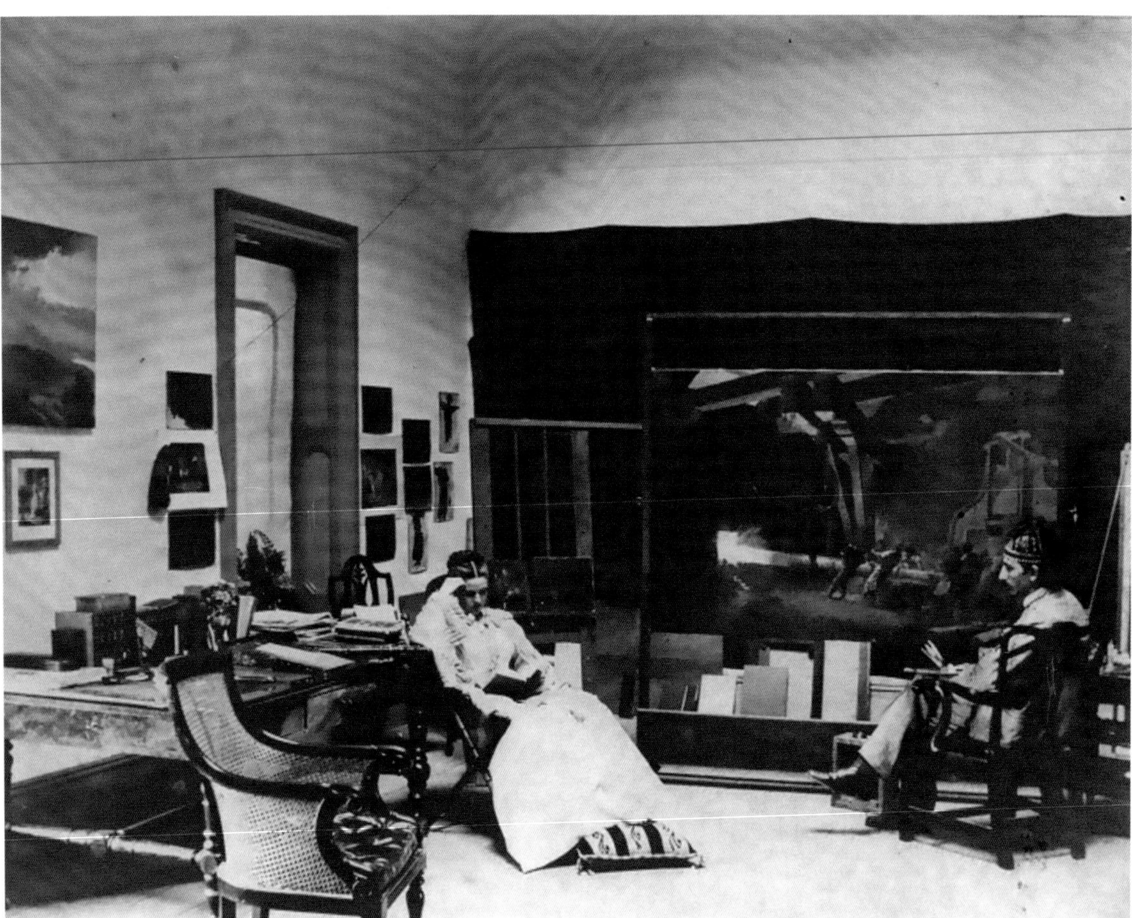

FIG. 44
John Ferguson Weir and His Wife in His Studio
Photograph, ca. 1865
courtesy Manuscripts and Archives, Sterling Memorial Library, Yale University

to the school through their marked excellence, serving the purpose not only of elevating and directing the taste for art, and awakening a general interest in the institution, but yielding funds by which the collection of casts has been largely increased."[1] The shows consisted of works selected by Weir from "private galleries in New York City and elsewhere," and "prominent masterpieces . . . from . . . private collections."[2] The exhibition of 1870, designed to show "the character and progress of American art,"[3] drew 12,000 visitors. It netted $1,296.04, which once again went to buy plaster casts for the teaching collection.

Another of Weir's many responsibilities was the care of the collections. Having observed that direct sunlight from the skylights was damaging the paintings in the galleries, in 1874 he had the skylights "of both galleries painted with zinc white and turpentine with just sufficient oil to hold the color."[4] He also urged the conversion from coal to steam heat because the coal was causing dirt problems. Mrs. Street donated the money for the conversion. Later, in 1886, Weir arranged for protective glass to be placed over some of the Jarves paintings to shield them from temperature change, a project that continued periodically at least until 1901. He also arranged for a ground glass ceiling to be installed in the Jarves gallery to improve the light. Around 1890, a two-year project to restore the Jarves pictures was begun.[5] Restoration of some of the Trumbull portraits was undertaken in 1893–94.

Caroline Street died on August 24, 1877. In her will, she left an endowment of $75,000, primarily for faculty salaries, and several works of art to the School of the Fine Arts. In spite of a strained relationship with some at Yale and especially with the School's architect, P. B. Wight, she had continued to support the School in the spirit of her husband's vision and deserves a respected place in the list of Yale's generous donors.

Even with Mrs. Street's bequest, by 1878 the School was $15,000 in debt to the College, and the Art Council proposed that the College should begin to pay part of the School's expenses, especially for the upkeep of the collections.[6] The College contributed $1,000 per year to the School between 1881 and 1884, but significant financial support was not forthcoming until 1891.

Student enrollment at the School increased throughout the 1870s. There were twenty-six students in 1876, for example, most of whom were enrolled in the three-year course. In addition, some seventy-one students from the Sheffield Scientific School took courses in drawing. The links between the School of the Fine Arts and its fellow professional schools were stronger than were those between the Art School and Yale College. The professional schools as a group (including Medicine, Divinity, and Law) were quite separate from the College at this time, both financially and programmatically. The majority of the students at the School of the Fine Arts in these years were women, which further distanced the School from the male undergraduate College. Most of the art students were from New Haven and local communities, fulfilling Street's vision of a professional training school. Some Yale College students stayed on after earning their B.A. to take the three-year art course, but the primary contribution the School of the Fine Arts made to Yale College life was through its lectures, collections, and exhibitions.

A new professor of history of art, James Mason Hoppin, was appointed, without salary, in 1879. Hoppin (1820–1906) was a Yale graduate (B.A. 1840), a theologian, and professor of divinity at Yale for nineteen years before being named to the post in history of art. He was not a trained art historian, but his connections with Yale's art collections went back many years; as a child he had heard Trumbull lecture in front of his pictures in the Trumbull Gallery. Hoppin had family connections to the Streets: his brother married Augustus Russell Street's sister. Hoppin held his professorship from 1879–99. January 1879 also marked the beginning of instruction in architecture, with Harrison Wheeler Lindsley, PH.B. 1872, and a student at the École des Beaux-Arts, as the instructor for its two students. Lindsley held the architecture post from 1879–87, and returned to teach perspective in 1892 and 1893.

The first exhibition dedicated to the collection of a Yale alumnus took place in 1882, when the collection of American marine and landscape paintings belonging to Robbins Battell (B.A. 1839, M.A. 1842) was put on display. Many of the paintings in the exhibition remained in the family until the death of Robbins Battell's daughter Ellen. They were bequeathed to the College along with a trust to maintain them, the house in Norfolk, Connecticut, in which they were displayed, and the music program that Ellen and her husband Carl Stoeckel established, for which the Battell Stoeckel Estate is known today. Among the paintings in the Ellen Battell Stoeckel Trust are *Ruins at Baalbek*, by Frederic Edwin Church (1889; fig. 45), the *View of the White Mountains, New Hampshire* by Thomas Cole (ca. 1827), *On the Winooski River*, by Sanford R. Gifford (ca. 1855–65), and a number of paintings by George Inness.

The first display of Chinese art at Yale, a collection of "Chinese Curios and Porcelains," was installed in cases in the paintings galleries in June 1885. Gathered by Samuel Wells Williams, eminent Chinese historian and professor at Yale, the collection was placed on loan to the School in 1884 after his death by his son, Frederick Wells Williams (B.A. 1879). These objects were later installed as a separate collection and ultimately given to Yale, as described more fully below.

John Ferguson Weir was the first to articulate a vision for a separate art museum at Yale. According to the minutes of the Faculty of the School of the Fine Arts meeting of March 26, 1891, "By this arrangement [a separate art museum] it was hoped that the collections now in the Art building would be cared for by the Corporation as all other collections of the University had been for a long time. Such an arrangement would release the Art Faculty from considerable expense, and would throw the collection open to the whole University."[7] Weir further requested "that for the purpose of providing for an Art Museum, a suitable building should be erected in close proximity to and in connection with the Art School, and the expense of a Curator and necessary outlay for repairs and additions, etc. be regarded in future as properly falling under the charge of the University Fund."[8] By May of that year, the Corporation had accepted responsibility for the expenses of maintaining a museum, but a new building was yet to come.[9]

The financial commitment by the Corporation was linked to increased interest on the part of the College in the art history courses offered by the School of the Fine Arts. Beginning in this same year, 1891, the School's lecture courses were available to Yale undergraduates for credit on a regular basis. Course offerings

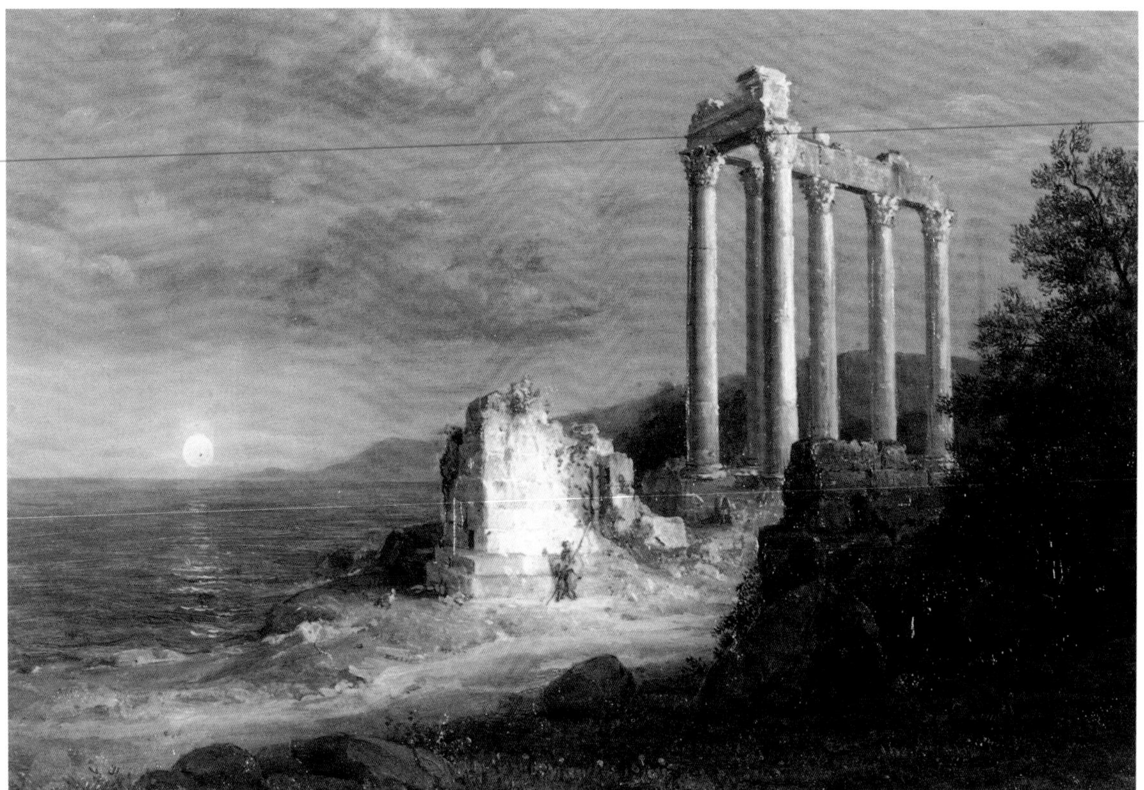

FIG. 45
Frederic Edwin Church
Ruins at Baalbek, ca. 1870–1880, 1889
Oil on canvas, 22.9 x 30.5 cm
Ellen Battell Stoeckel Trust

included European, Asian, and ancient art. Also in 1891, the Corporation granted permission to the School to award Bachelor of Fine Arts (B.F.A.) degrees. The first B.F.A. was given to Josephine Miles Lewis. Shortly thereafter, in 1900, the requirements for the B.F.A. brought a creative response from one of the many Yale School of Art students who went on to achieve success and fame, when Frederic Remington donated his recent painting *The Scream of the Shrapnel at San Juan Hill* (1898; fig. 46), and a drawing, *Spurring His Horse in Pursuit* (1878), in lieu of submitting a thesis. Irene Weir, John Ferguson Weir's niece earned a B.F.A. in 1906.

In 1890, a collection of drawings and European paintings was acquired by purchase from the estate of Robert W. Weir, father of John Ferguson Weir. In 1897, two full-sized seventeenth-century carved wood confessionals, bought in 1855 by Colonel Bradford Alden from a suppressed convent in Ghent, were purchased from the Alden estate. Exhibited in several places within the School of the Fine Arts, the Alden confessionals appear in many of the early photographs of the classrooms and studios.

Yale's bicentennial in 1901 was marked by two exhibitions organized by Professor Weir. One was a historical exhibition of American art, in which the works of Trumbull and Samuel F. B. Morse were prominent. The other comprised 192 works by former students and present faculty of the School. In the same year, on a sadder note, the Trumbull Gallery, which had been converted in 1867 into the treasurer's office and altered architecturally to accommodate this function, was demolished.

The early twentieth century brought the deaths of two important figures in the School's early history, Professors Edward Elbridge Salisbury, B.A. 1832, M.A. 1835, LL.D. 1869 (d. 1901), and James Mason Hoppin, B.A. 1840 (d. 1906). Both left substantial bequests to the School. Salisbury's included three sculptures by Horatio Greenough (*Aeschines, Abdiel, The Angel Warning St. John*), all of which had been on loan and two of which had been included in the 1858 exhibition. Hoppin left $60,000 toward the endowment of a professorship in architecture—the beginning of the Department of Architecture at Yale.

Weir's vision of a separate building for the museum would not be realized for many years, but in 1907 plans were made for an addition to the School of the Fine Arts building that would provide significantly more gallery space. The goal was to consolidate all of the collections on one floor, while providing additional classroom and studio space at the same time. Weir apparently

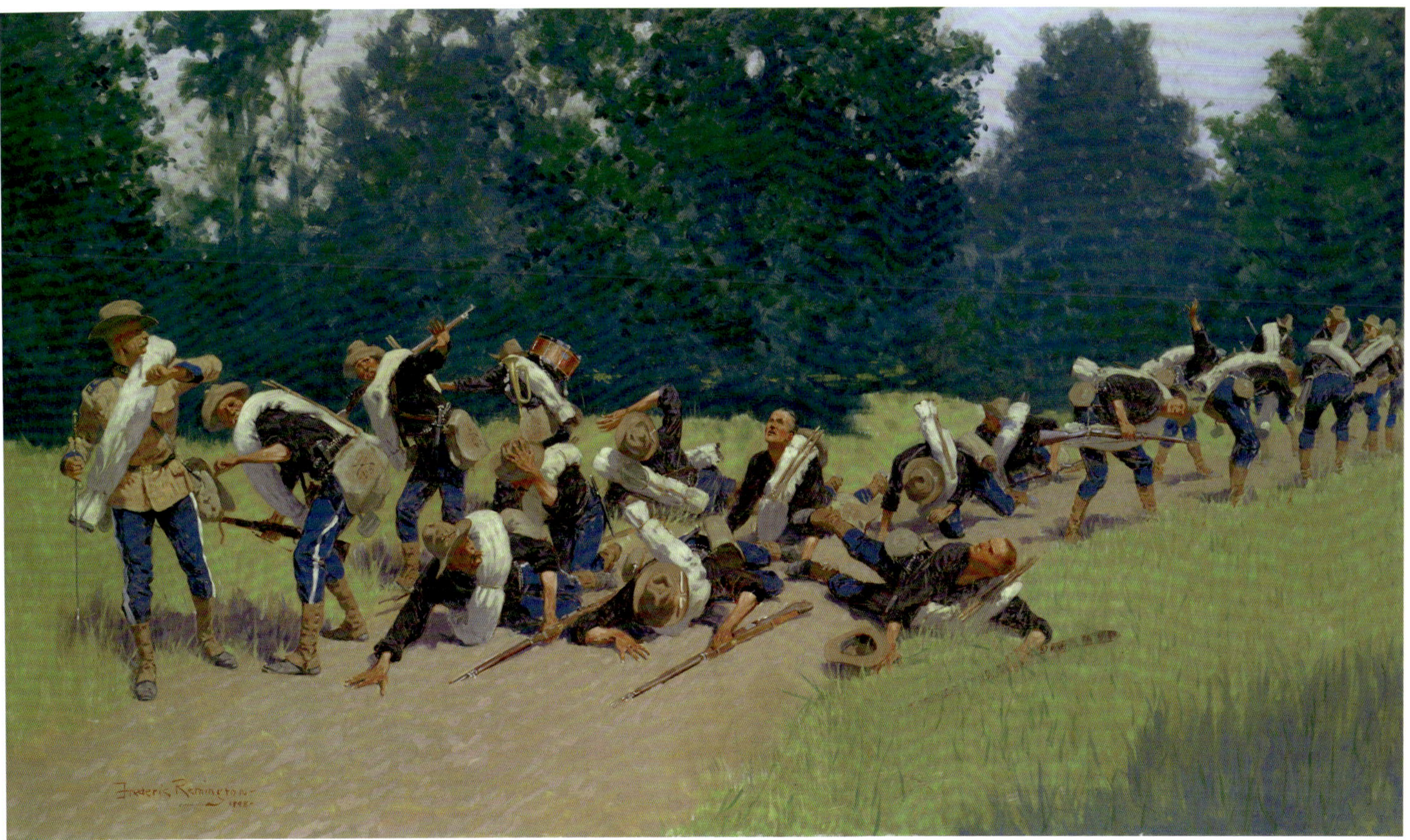

designed the addition himself. The classrooms were available for use in the fall of 1910. The opening of the new galleries on February 17, 1911, was reported in the *New Haven Register*, which described in detail how the collections were installed.[10] The expansion was funded by J. Davenport Wheeler (PH.B. 1858), who at the same time (1909) donated $15,000 anonymously toward the endowment of the architecture program that had been begun by Professor Hoppin's bequest. Richard Henry Dana had joined the faculty the previous year as Instructor in Architecture, and there was increasing interest in expanding this program. A further gift of $60,000 for the program was given anonymously in 1911, in memory of Richard S. Fellowes, a graduate of the Yale Class of 1832. The son-in-law of Fellowes, J. Davenport Wheeler had been active in his own right in the fund-raising effort to equip the School of the Fine Arts.

The addition to the building extended it on all three floors at the northwest corner on the High Street side. The extension provided three new exhibition galleries and six new classrooms, totaling 6,204 square feet of space. A new large gallery (68 x 30') divided into three sections provided a new home for the Jarves

FIG. 46
Frederic Remington
The Scream of the Shrapnel at San Juan Hill, 1898
Oil on canvas, 89.5 x 154.0 cm
Gift of the artist
1900.2

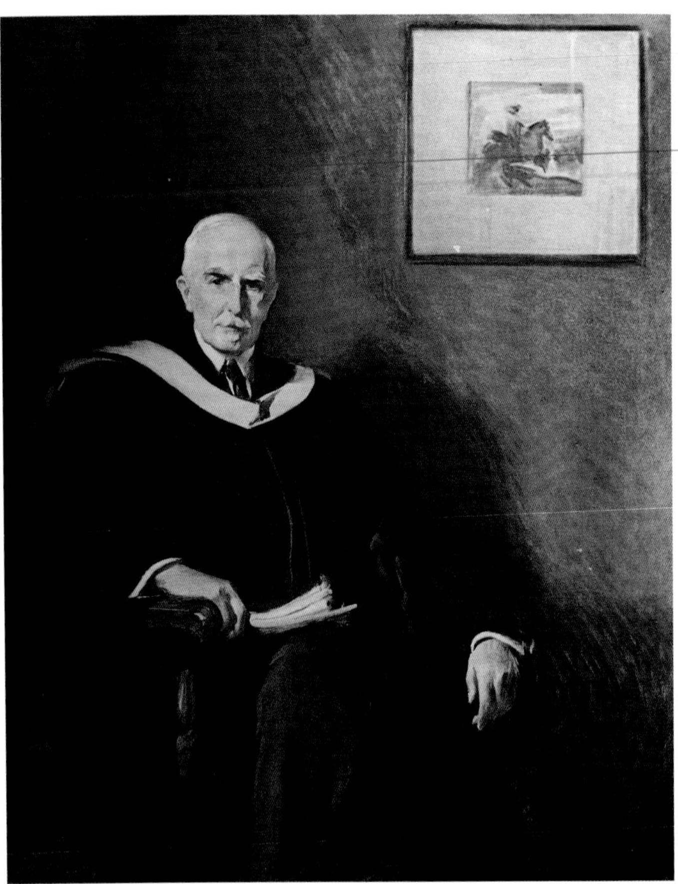

FIG. 47
John White Alexander
John Ferguson Weir, 1913
Oil on canvas, 163.8 x 137.2 cm
Gift of Colleagues, Friends, and Students of the Sitter
1913.681

Collection, as well as for a new installation of Asian art. The S. Wells Williams Collection of Chinese porcelain was displayed in this new gallery. According to the *Register* report, this collection had not been exhibited before, but it had been on loan since 1885 and at least part of it had been shown in display cases in the paintings galleries—the *Register* may have meant "exhibited separately." Moving the Jarves pictures to the new galleries permitted the consolidation of all of the plaster casts in the north gallery where the Jarves Collection had previously been displayed, making the collection much more useful for art students to draw from and for students of classical art, as the *Register* reporter noted.

Still thinking of expansion, Weir envisioned in 1910 an extension of the building across High Street, linked by a bridge. This idea would take form in 1928 with the construction of the Egerton Swartwout building. Weir retired in 1913, having overseen the School and the collections for nearly half a century. His dedication to art, artists, and teaching, and the energy and commitment with which he implemented his vision for the School and a teaching museum, shaped both as we know them today. On the occasion of his retirement, his students, colleagues, and friends commissioned a portrait of him (fig. 47), as was traditional. Weir himself donated works of art, mostly French prints, to Yale.

Throughout this period the collections continued to grow. The Davenport Wheeler Collection of Furniture and Tapestries was given to Yale in 1910, by the same donor who had funded the expansion of the School. J. Davenport Wheeler's gifts of European drawings in 1911 and 1913 were among the earliest acquisitions in this field,[11] supplementing the European drawings purchased from the estate of Robert W. Weir in 1890. As a graduate of the class of 1858, Wheeler may well have seen the Alumni Hall exhibition during that summer and been inspired to give his collection to his alma mater as a result.

Two major collections of antiquities from the ancient Mediterranean world came to Yale in 1912 and 1913, adding more than two thousand objects to the College's holdings. Both collections were purchased, and their acquisition reflected a continued commitment to the study of classical civilization and biblical history at Yale. Classics had been a fundamental part of the Yale

College curriculum since the school's founding, and its central role had been reaffirmed in a report to the president in 1828.[12] Greek and Latin were still part of the core courses required of undergraduates under the curriculum reform of 1911, although by 1917 only one or the other was required. The continuing importance of the Divinity School ensured the need for courses in ancient languages and anything else related to the early history of Christianity. Thus the acquisition goals for the art museum were designed to reach a broad range of Yale students beyond those already interested in art.

The College was also actively acquiring Egyptian antiquities at this time, both through gifts and through sponsorship of excavations in Egypt, which yielded antiquities for the sponsoring institutions' collections. Most of this material, however, went to the Peabody Museum of Natural History, founded in 1873; the Gallery did not begin acquiring significant Egyptian art until the 1920s. The College Library was beginning its collection of Babylonian objects, especially written documents in the form of tablets and seals that are now the core of Yale's internationally renowned Babylonian Collection. In the early twentieth century, both of these collections were displayed in Osborn Hall.

The first of the Gallery's Mediterranean collections was the Whiting Palestinian Collection (1912; fig. 48), formed in Jerusalem by John David Whiting in 1910–11. Designed as an encyclopedic survey of the pottery and other antiquities of biblical lands, the collection ranged from the Chalcolithic period to the fall of the Roman Empire. Originally housed and displayed at the Divinity School and catalogued in 1962 by a divinity student as his PH.D. thesis, it is now displayed at the Divinity School, the Art Gallery, and several theological schools outside of Yale.

Greek vases are at the heart of the second of the two collections, the Rebecca Darlington Stoddard Collection of Greek and Italian Pottery. Two important Athenian panathenaic prize amphorae by the Kleophrades Painter (ca. 480 B.C.) had come to Yale in 1909, the gift of Frederic W. Stephens, B.A. 1858, but the Stoddard Collection brought with a single purchase a comprehensive collection of more than nine hundred vases from Greece and Italy dating from the Bronze Age through the Roman period. The collection was

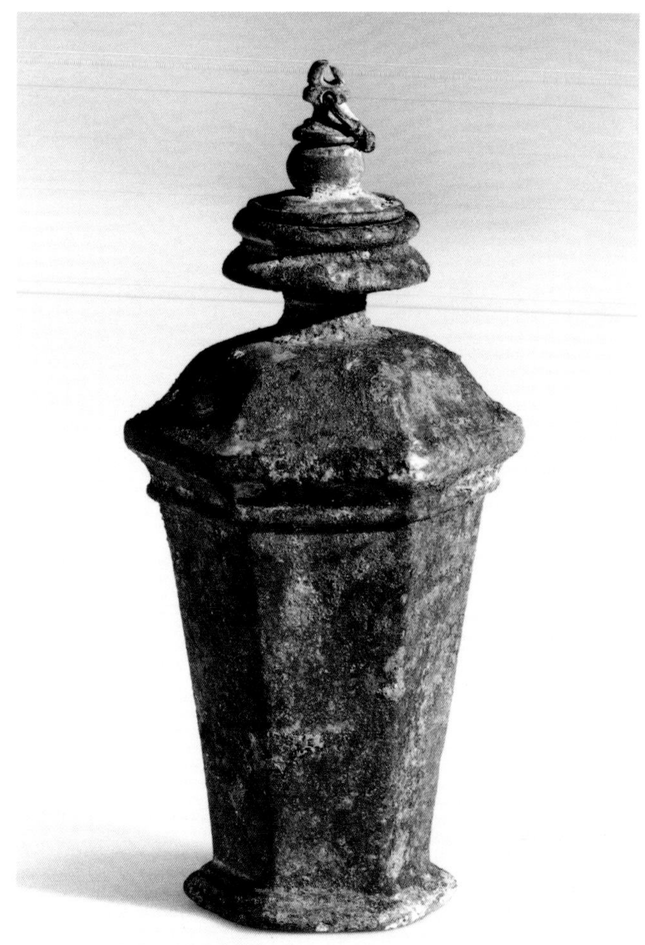

FIG. 48
Maker unknown
Amphoriskos, 1st century A.D.
Bronze, 13.3 x 6.8 x 6.8 cm
Whiting Palestinian Collection
1912.1013

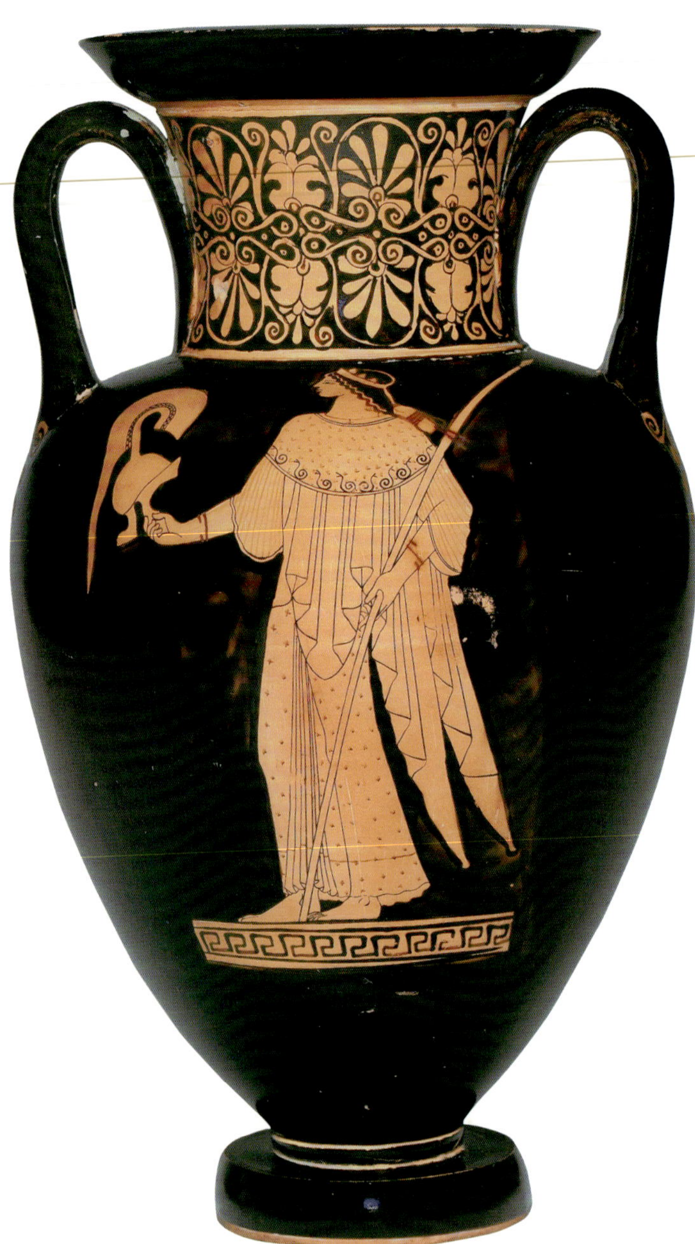

FIG. 49
Berlin Painter
Red-Figure Nolan Amphora showing Athena, ca. 480 B.C.
Terracotta, 32.7 x 20 cm
Gift of Rebecca Darlington Stoddard
1913.133

FIG. 50
Painter of the Yale Oinochoe
Red-Figure Oinochoe showing Poseidon and Theseus, ca. 470–460 B.C.
Terracotta, 40.3 x 26.1 cm
Gift of Rebecca Darlington Stoddard
1913.143

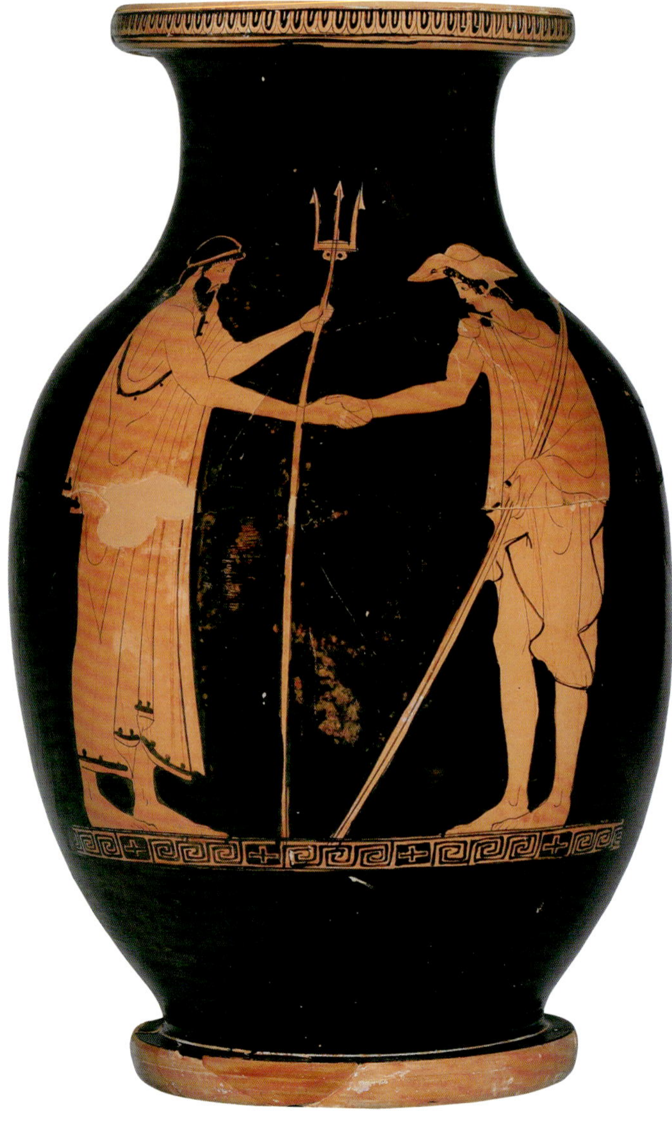

assembled by a distinguished German scholar, Dr. Paul Arndt, and it was particularly designed as a survey collection for a teaching museum. It was one of several such collections that he created for university museums in Europe. When this collection came on the market in Paris, Professor Paul V. C. Baur of Yale's Classics Department urged that it be acquired. Shortly before this, Rebecca Darlington Stoddard had offered to do something for Yale, her husband's alma mater, and when asked, she agreed to have her gift used for this collection. Mr. and Mrs. Stoddard (Louis E. Stoddard, B.A. 1899) lived in New Haven, in a Palladian-style house on Prospect Street that they commissioned in 1905 from Peabody and Stearns of Boston.[13] Mrs. Stoddard was pleased that the vases would be made available to local residents as well as to Yale. The collection was bought at auction in Paris in late 1912, but sadly, Mrs. Stoddard died in childbirth before it could reach New Haven and never saw it. The collection was opened to the public in January 1914, displayed in the President's Reception Room in Memorial (now Woolsey) Hall.

Today the Stoddard Collection is the core of the Gallery's holdings of Greek art. Its stars are an amphora by the Berlin Painter (fig. 49) and two vases whose painters are named for their vases at Yale, the Yale Oinochoe (fig. 50) and the Yale Lekythos. The collection has been supplemented by gift and purchase, including a black-figure amphora by Group E (fig. 51), a red-figure krater by the Aegisthus Painter, and a white ground lekythos by the Painter of Munich 2335, and it continues to grow, always in the spirit of the teaching collection named for Mrs. Stoddard.

The fiftieth anniversary of the founding of the School of the Fine Arts was celebrated in 1916. The anniversary was marked by an address by Professor and Director Emeritus John Ferguson Weir. In his speech, Weir spoke of "what may now properly be termed the Yale Art Museum."[14] He emphasized the significance of the major collections now owned by the museum having been acquired by purchase rather than gift, which made possible a coherent plan of development for the collections that made them more valuable for teaching purposes than collections of "personal gifts capriciously brought together"[15] could have been, and he praised the

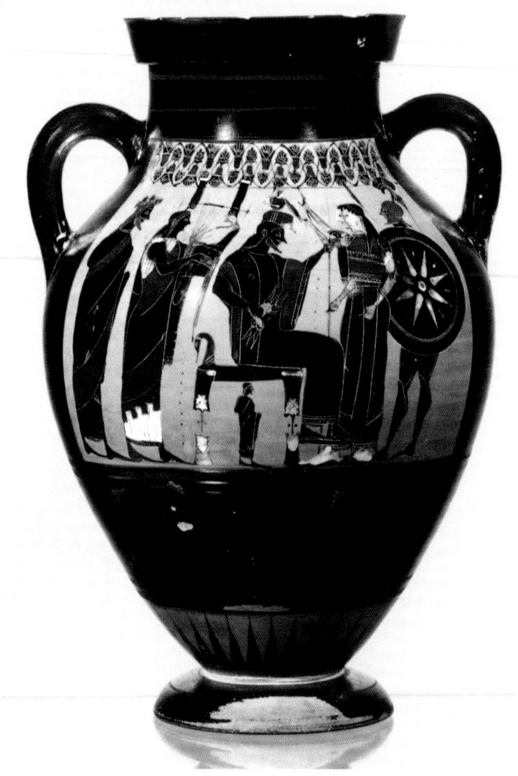

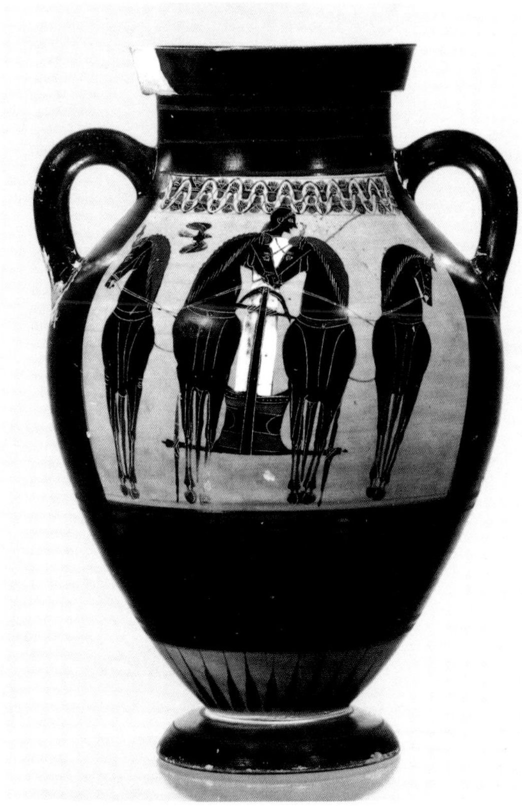

FIG. 51
Attributed to a Painter in Group E
Black-Figure Amphora, SIDE A: *Birth of Athena*; SIDE B: *Four Horse Chariot*, ca. 540 B.C.
Terracotta, 40.9 x 29 cm
Leonard C. Hanna, Jr., B.A. 1913, Fund
1983.22

wisdom of the University authorities and their readiness to act when such opportunities arose.

Weir was succeeded as director in fall 1913 by William Sergeant Kendall, who served as Leffingwell Professor from 1913 to 1922. Like Weir, Kendall was an artist, and a member of the National Academy. An exhibition of the new director's paintings, drawings, and sculpture, accompanied by a small display of works by other faculty members, was shown in the south gallery to mark the start of his tenure, and he was awarded an honorary M.A. Several of Kendall's paintings are part of the Gallery's collection, among them portraits of President William Howard Taft (B.A. 1878) and Yale President Arthur Twining Hadley (B.A. 1876, LL.D. 1899).

Beginning to plan for the future, in 1916 the Faculty officially discussed plans for a department of the history of art for the first time. "The desirability of a serious course in the history of Renaissance painting"[16] was voiced as well, by Arthur Kingsley Porter (B.A. 1904, B.F.A. 1917), who was lecturer in the history of architecture from 1915–17. Porter believed strongly that art history should be integrated into programs for training artists such as that at Yale, and be made available to all undergraduates. So committed was he to this idea that in 1916 he offered Yale a bequest of half a million dollars for the establishment of a "Faculty of the History of Art in the College." It did not matter to Porter whether the department became part of the College or of the Art School, so long as its courses were open to academic students and counted toward the B.A. degree. Writing to Yale's President Arthur Twining Hadley, Porter argued, "It is because I am certain that the adequate study of the history of art would tend to raise, rather than lower, the present loose standard of scholarship, that I am so anxious to see it added to the curriculum."[17] The economic realities of World War I intervened, however, and prevented Yale from establishing any new departments; after the war Porter went to Harvard, and the idea of a history of art department at Yale was shelved.

The years during World War I and through 1920 were quiet for the School of Art and its museum, with no major loan exhibitions and few key acquisitions for the collection. Special exhibitions consisted primarily of the annual exhibitions of the New Haven Paint and Clay Club, a local organization founded in 1900 that included both artists and collectors, continuing the long-standing link between the School and the city. Although the Club's annual exhibitions were dominated by the work of its members, well-known painters were also invited to participate. As a result, Yale students and New Haven residents had the opportunity to see works by Childe Hassam, Edward Steichen, Julian Alden Weir, and others, as well as additional works lent by local collectors.[18] Yale continued to host these annual exhibitions through 1926. Notable among the acquisitions of this decade were the portrait by John Trumbull of *Dr. Lemuel Hopkins* (1793; fig. 52) and the Salisbury bequest, mentioned above.

The Fritz Achelis Memorial Collection of Old Master Prints was given in 1925, establishing the Print Department, the first phase of what is now the Gallery's largest collection, namely prints, drawings, and photographs. A lifelong resident of New York, where he was a successful industrialist and a generous patron of music and art, Frederick (Fritz) Achelis was known as an enthusiastic and discerning collector of prints. Shortly after he died in 1924, his son, Frederick George Achelis, B.A. 1907, donated his father's collection of Dürer and Rembrandt prints to Yale as a memorial to his interest in art. There had been gifts of prints and drawings before, as noted above, but the quality and quantity of the Achelis Collection elevated Yale's holding of works of art on paper to a level commensurate with established print rooms in other museums. Included in this major collection of around 125 prints were some of the most important works by Rembrandt and Dürer. Among them were Rembrandt's etchings *Christ Preaching (La Petite Tombe)* (fig. 53), *Christ with the Sick around Him Receiving Little Children ("The Hundred Guilder Print")*, and *The Windmill*, and Dürer's engraving *Adam and Eve* (fig. 54). The arrival of this collection triggered the creation of a print room in the School of Fine Arts building (possibly in the northwest corner of the 1911 addition), the appointment of the first curator of prints, Carl A. Lohmann, in 1926, and a course in prints, apparently the first at Yale, taught by Theodore Sizer from 1929 until the early 1950s.

Carl Lohmann, the new curator, was a Yale graduate (B.A. 1910), but he did not have a background in art.

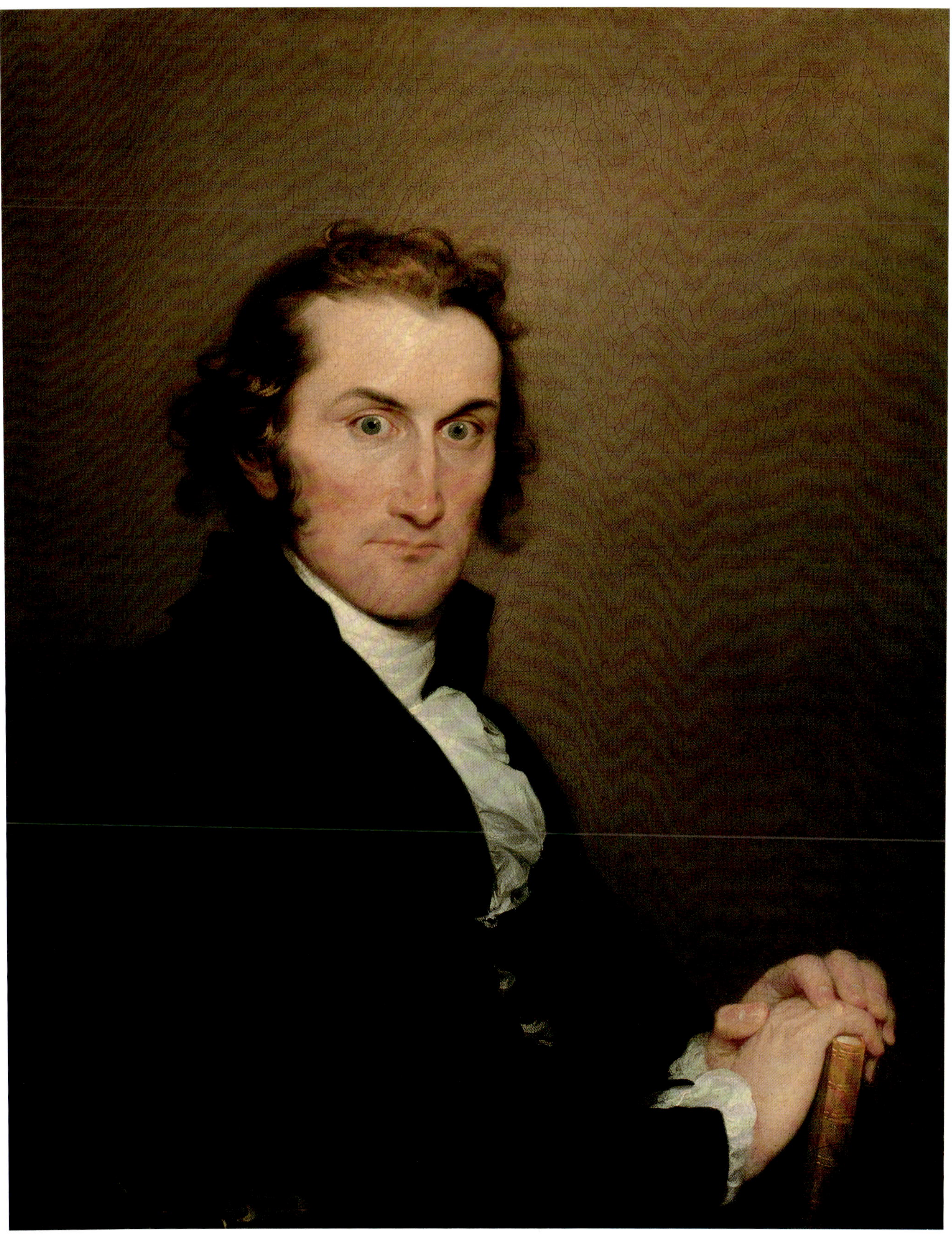

FIG. 52
John Trumbull
Dr. Lemuel Hopkins, 1793
Oil on canvas, 76.8 x 61.6 cm
Gift of Miss Elizabeth Sill
1914.1

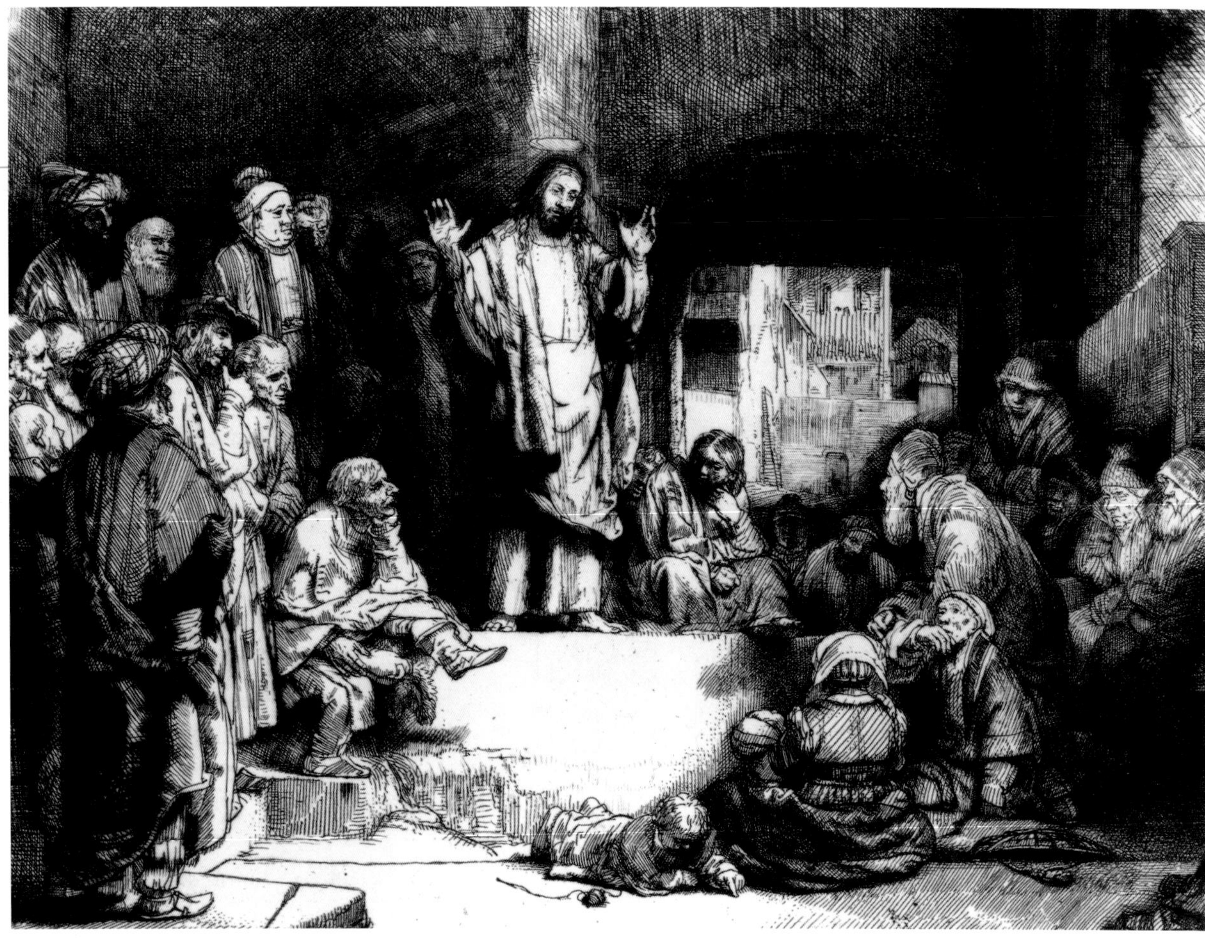

After leaving Yale, where he was one of the founders of the Whiffenpoofs, he studied music in Germany for a year. After time in business and in the service during World War I, he returned to Yale in 1925 as secretary to the Alumni Advisory Board. Two years later he was appointed secretary of the University, a post he held until his retirement in 1953. He is credited with founding the print collection at Yale, and he served as its curator from 1926 to 1930 and again from 1946 until 1957. He was a member of the Governing Board of the Art Gallery from 1940 to 1957. He was an expert on the history of Yale, and the University awarded him two honorary degrees when he retired.

Three English Chinoiserie tapestries that had belonged to Elihu Yale were given to the Gallery in 1927 by Edward Harkness (B.A. 1897). Apparently in less than perfect condition when they arrived, the tapestries were not exhibited until 1949, after their conservation was complete. This first showing was doubly celebratory, because 1949 marked the tercentennial of the birth of Elihu Yale, and the tapestries were displayed as part of the Gallery's exhibition *Elihu Yale and the Collegiate School.*

But the major thrust of the prosperous and optimistic 1920s was the campaign for a new building for the art collections. The chronic need for additional space for exhibiting and storing the collections had not been fully met by the addition to the School of Fine Arts building in 1911, and it rapidly became critical. The galleries were too small to house the growing permanent collection—the Stoddard Collection of Greek vases, for example, was still exhibited in Memorial Hall—and the permanent collection had to be either removed or covered with temporary screens when a special exhibition was installed. Reports to the College in 1921 and 1922 outlined the needs, and with funding donated by Edward Harkness, planning for a new building was begun.

FIG. 53
Rembrandt Harmensz van Rijn
Christ Preaching (La Petite Tombe), ca. 1652
Etching, 15.6 x 20.9 cm
Fritz Achelis Memorial Collection, Gift of Frederick George Achelis, B.A. 1907
1925.134

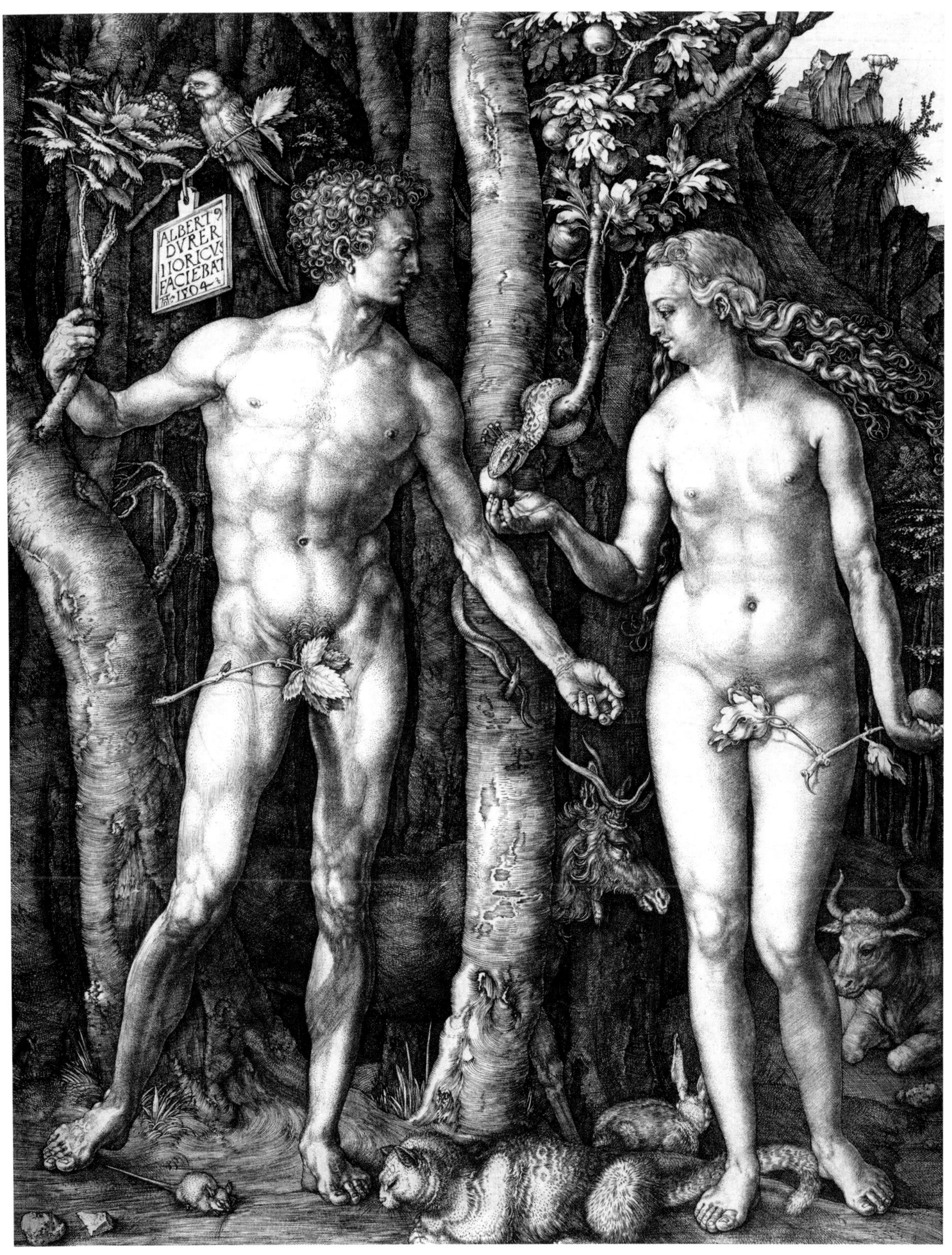

FIG. 54
Albrecht Dürer
Adam and Eve, 1504
Engraving on laid paper, 24.4 x 19.3 cm
Fritz Achelis Memorial Collection, Gift of
Frederick George Achelis, B.A. 1907
Reacquired 1972 with Henry J. Heinz II
B.A. 1931, Everett V. Meeks, B.A. 1901, and
Stephen Carlton Clark, B.A. 1903, Funds
1925.29

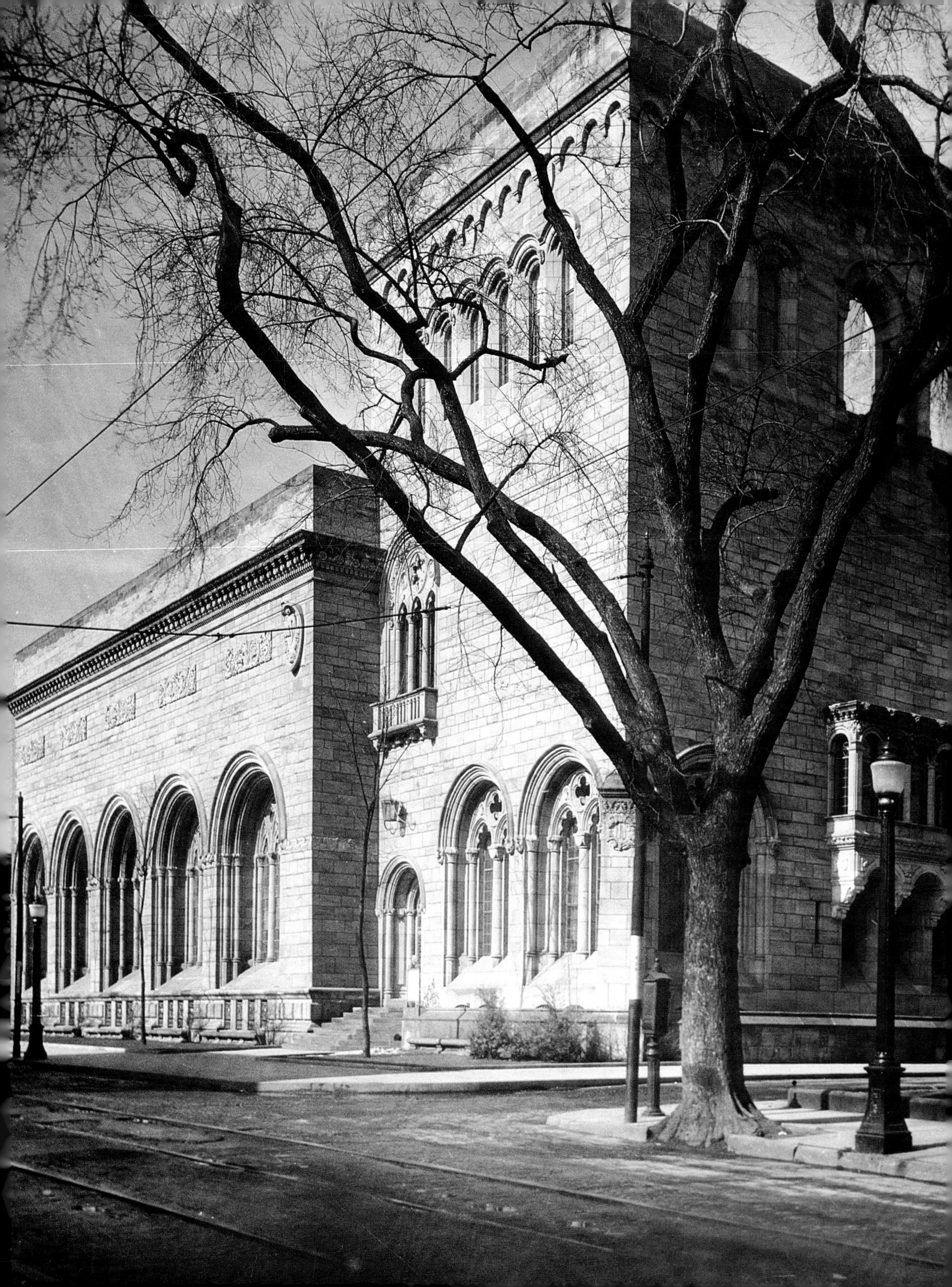

CHAPTER 7

The Gallery of Fine Arts

In 1921, William Sergeant Kendall, who had succeeded John Ferguson Weir as director of the School of the Fine Arts in 1913, submitted expansion plans for the School and its galleries to the Committee for Architectural Plan.[1] These plans, which included a bridge over High Street, were developed by Hyman I. Feldman, B.F.A. 1920, based on his proposal for his B.F.A. thesis—a vivid example of student involvement in the important activities of the School and art museum at Yale. Little progress on the plans had been made when Kendall left in 1922 and was succeeded by Everett V. Meeks.

Everett Victor Meeks (fig. 55) served as dean of the School of the Fine Arts from 1922 to 1947.[2] An architect rather than a painter, educated in Paris in the Beaux-Arts tradition, as at home with Greek temples as with the American landscape, Meeks brought a different perspective to the School than that of his predecessors. As a practicing architect with the distinguished New York Beaux-Arts firm of Carrère and Hastings, Meeks had the practical background on which the School was based, but he combined it with an upbringing and lifestyle of cultured privilege quite antithetical to Yale's Congregational past. Notwithstanding his renowned devotion to the finer creature comforts, Dean Meeks was energetic, hardworking, and committed to the growth of the School, particularly the Department of Architecture. He expanded course offerings, integrated the study of architecture with that of painting and sculpture, increased enrollment, and engineered the move of the architecture department into Weir Hall. Most critical for our story, it was Meeks who created the new Gallery of Fine Arts that John Ferguson Weir had envisioned on the other side of High Street.

Upon taking office, Meeks immediately reiterated to President James Roland Angell that the need for expansion was critical. Galleries were being used as classrooms, limiting access to the collections and forcing some of them into storage, and the existing building was not fireproof, thus putting the collections at risk. The president agreed that expansion was needed, and a variety of proposals were considered. Among them was a new building on Pierson-Sage Square (at the corner of Sachem Street on the parcel bordered by Edwards Street, Prospect Street, and Whitney Avenue),

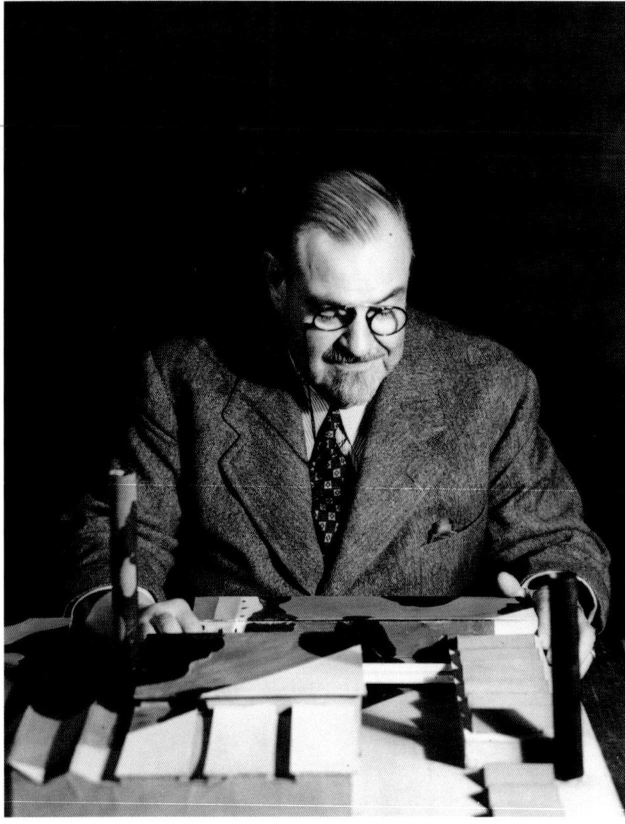

FIG. 55
Everett V. Meeks examining Philip Goodwin's model for the expansion of the Gallery of Fine Arts, ca. 1941
Photograph courtesy Yale University Art Gallery Archives

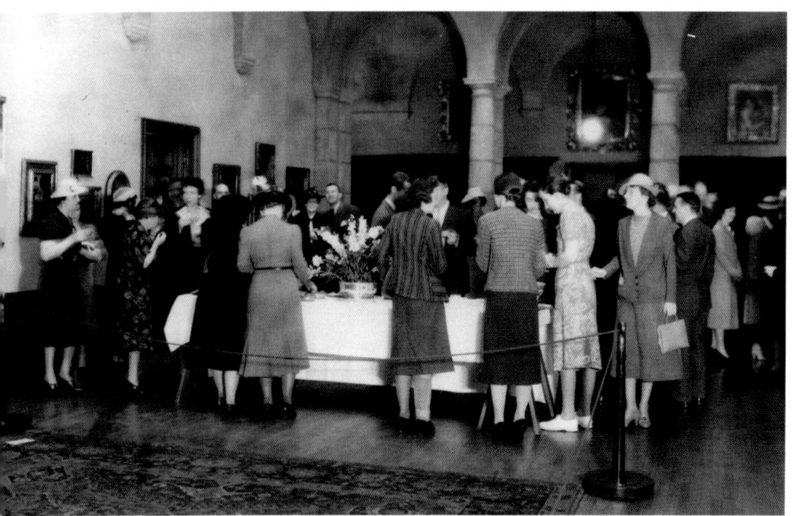

FIG. 56
Associates Event, ca. 1935–40
Photograph courtesy Yale University Art Gallery Archives

near the new Peabody Museum of Natural History building. Although the idea of siting the new museums together was appealing, this proposal was rejected because the terms of Augustus Street's gift required that the School of Art building and galleries be located on Chapel and High Streets. Another proposal recommended renovating the buildings on the "Miller Property" (now Weir Hall) for classrooms and studios, thereby returning the gallery spaces to their original function. This idea was folded into subsequent plans. In 1924, using funds donated by Edward S. Harkness, the University purchased the land along Chapel Street between High and York Streets and set it aside for the School of Art's expansion. In June of that same year the University's Committee on Architectural Plan recommended to the Corporation that a plan be drawn up for a fireproof building for the collections on the Chapel Street site. This emphasis on collections, as opposed to classrooms and studio space, was key to the ultimate disposition of the spaces, consolidating display spaces in the new building, with fireproofing and climate control, and concentrating (with a few exceptions) the classroom and studio spaces in the old building.

The first choice for architect for the new building was James Gamble Rogers (B.A. 1889, Hon. M.A. 1921), consulting architect to the University and subsequently the designer of the residential colleges. Declining the offer, Rogers recommended Egerton Swartwout, B.A. 1891, a well-known New York architect who was noted for his buildings in the Beaux-Arts style and thus a good match for Everett Meeks with his similar grounding in Beaux-Arts architecture. It was understood from the start that, because of funding limitations, the project would be completed in phases, but given its complexity, it was deemed advisable to design the entire building at once. Working with Meeks and taking into account the requests of the faculty, Swartwout presented a draft plan that included galleries along Chapel Street, a library, and offices. The latter were to be in two wings that were perpendicular to the Chapel Street facade and connected the new galleries with Weir Hall.

Dean Meeks embarked on a campaign to raise money for the building and acquire art for the collections. To assist him, Meeks formed a committee of twenty men led by Maitland Griggs (B.A. 1896) in 1925, naming them the Associates in Fine Arts at Yale (fig. 56). This organization, which has evolved over the past seventy-five years into the Members of the Yale Art Museums, has played a key role in the collaboration between the museum and New Haven in advancing the museum's educational programs in the community. One of the committee's first endeavors was to begin publication of the *Bulletin of the Associates in Fine Arts at Yale University*, a periodical designed both to inform readers about the activities of the museum and to make them aware of the museum's financial and collection needs in the hope that readers might respond with donations of money and art. The second issue of the *Bulletin* (June 1926) contained the article and plans for the new museum, and the announcement of a $1 million gift from Edward S. Harkness toward the building. Subsequent issues chronicled the work on the building and described additions to the collection. The December 1928 issue announced the opening of the building, and in describing the contents of the galleries it made specific pleas for donations of works of art to fill gaps in the collections, notably in the areas of Japanese color woodblock prints, Persian and Indian miniatures, Chinese sculpture and bronzes, Near Eastern brocades and velvets, and ancient Roman art. During the 1930s, '40s, and '50s, the Associates in Fine Arts provided funds of their own as a group to purchase works of art, adding important Chinese and Persian sculptures (fig. 57), paintings, and American decorative arts to the collection.

The final plan by Swartwout was presented to the Committee on Architectural Plan on March 13, 1925, and approved by the Corporation in June. This design included the bridge over High Street, which was to contain two small classrooms and a picture gallery (fig. 58). The permission of the New Haven Board of Aldermen was needed in order to bridge a city street, but it was granted and the plan went forward. A massive three-story tower anchored the High Street end of the building, designed to accommodate offices for the dean and secretary of the School of Fine Arts and the curator of the Museum, two classrooms, five studios for faculty and advanced students, and a gallery large enough to display the collections. The main facade stretched from the tower, which was slightly recessed, to York Street.

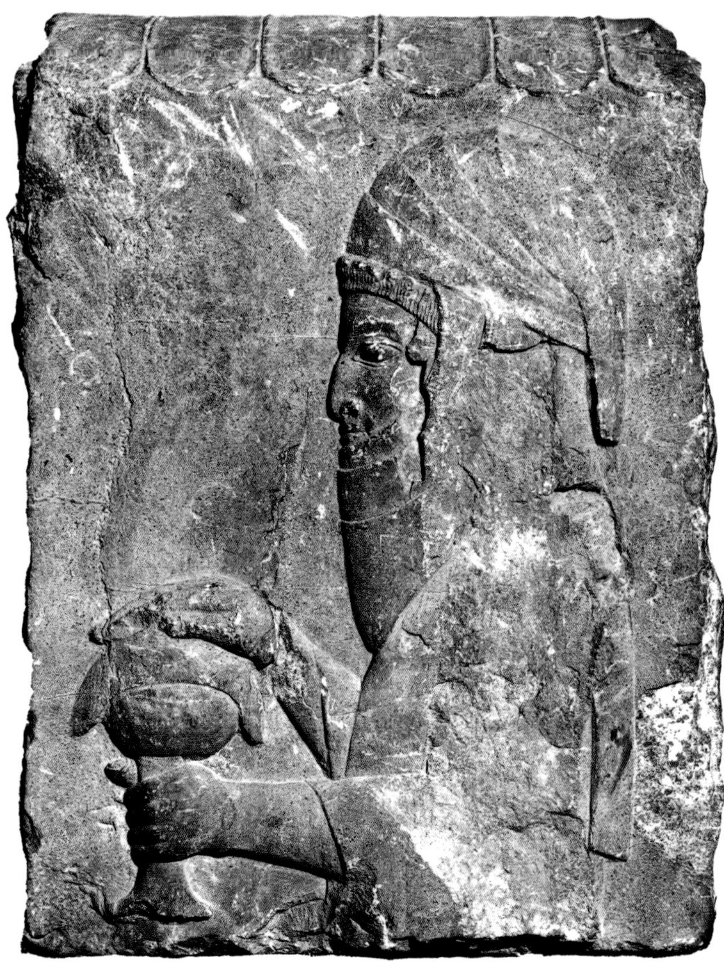

FIG. 57
Maker unknown
Persepolis Relief, 6th century B.C.
Limestone, 33.0 x 24.1x 9.1 cm
Gift of the Associates in Fine Arts
1933.10

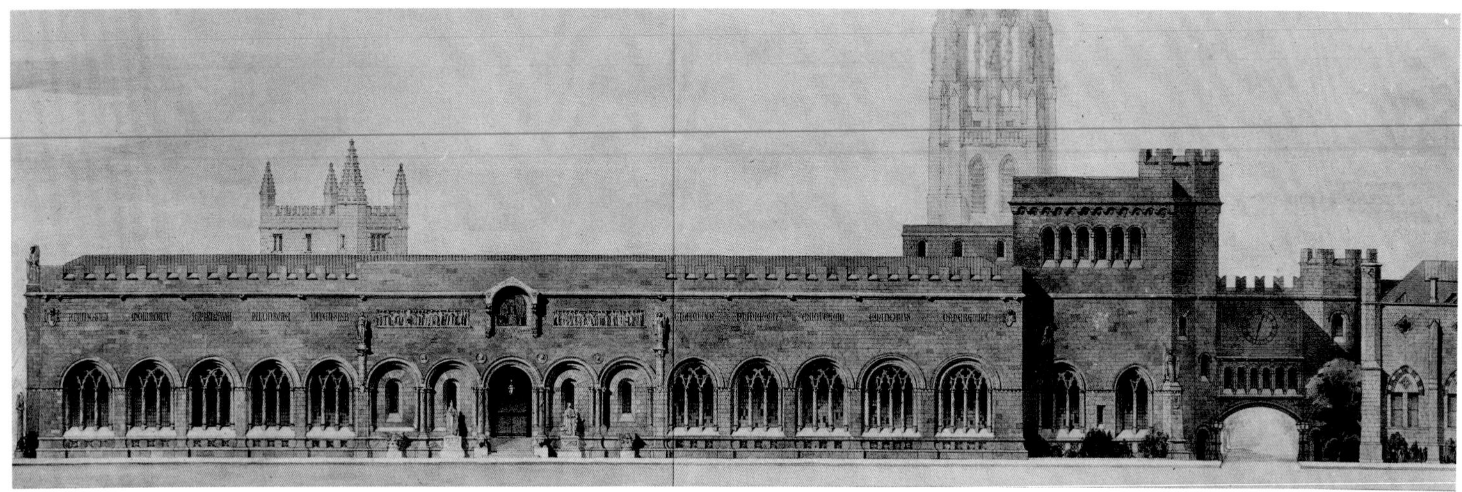

FIG. 58
Egerton Swartwout
Proposed New Building for the Gallery of Fine Arts, Yale University, 1926
Pen and ink and watercolor
Photograph courtesy Manuscripts and Archives, Sterling Memorial Library, Yale University

It featured a monumental central entrance set into a row of arched windows. The entrance comprised an arched doorway flanked on each side by two arched and traceried windows, the whole set off by engaged columns that rose nearly to the roof line. Carved in stone over the entrance was the name of the new building: GALLERY OF FINE ARTS.

It was agreed from the start that the new building had to be in the Gothic style, in order to conform to the style favored throughout the University. Although Swartwout was accustomed to working in neoclassical style, he accepted the challenge and became immersed in the study of variants on the Gothic in a search for the most appropriate setting for the Yale collections. The prominence of the Jarves Collection was the strongest force at work on his decision, and it led him to work in a modified Italian Gothic style. Scholars have identified elements of several Florentine Gothic buildings in Swartwout's design, notably the Palace of the Bargello and the Davanzati Palace, as well as echoes of towers of the Tuscan hill town of San Gimignano.[3] Swartwout was careful to use traditional methods of construction like true stone vaults wherever possible, "so that students may not be inclined to feel that it is mere archaeological exercise of a passé subject to study true vaults, walls, arches, and the 'bones' of the antecedents of the modern buildings."[4] This was not the Ruskinian truth to medieval techniques that drove Peter Bonnett Wight in his design for the School of the Fine Arts, but rather an effort to make the very building in which the students worked a case study and an inspiration.

The portion of the building that was to be built in the first phase comprised the bridge, the tower, and the main gallery building up to the start of the central entrance (fig. 58). The library wing and other parts of the building linking it to Weir Hall were not included. The decision to build only phase one necessitated some revisions in the plan to accommodate the most basic functions of the program, and the windows on the first floor of the tower were reduced in order to create space for a main entrance.

The program specified the locations of collections in the new building. The Jarves Collection, recognized as one of the most important collections of Italian paintings in America or abroad, should be "placed in the most important position on the main gallery floor."[5] The Trumbull Revolutionary War paintings were to be displayed as a group with the miniatures, with the larger Trumbull paintings hung together as a second group. Also to be shown in the new galleries were the S. Wells Williams Collection of Chinese porcelains, on loan since 1885 and displayed in one of the 1911 galleries in the School of the Fine Arts; plaster casts, with a separate gallery designated for the Parthenon casts; the Alden wood carvings; and modern art, which was envisioned as a growing collection.

Equally important and particularly ambitious was the plan to unite the University's art collections, then dispersed in several locations on campus, in the Gallery of Fine Arts. These diaspora collections included the Stoddard Collection of Greek and Italian Vases (shown in Memorial, now Woolsey, Hall), the Whiting Palestinian Collection (stored in the Day Mission Library), Egyptian, Classical, and Near Eastern antiquities (housed in the Osborn Botanical Laboratory, the Classics Department in Phelps Hall, and the Osborn Zoological Laboratory, respectively), and ancient coins (kept in the University library). The Alden wood carvings, which had been shown in one of the classrooms in the School of the Fine Arts building, had since been moved partly to Woolsey Hall and partly to storage.

A gallery for contemporary exhibitions was included in the plan, as were several modest galleries for prints and other small works of art. The contemporary gallery, which was to be just inside the main entrance, could be used either for loan shows or for exhibitions of student work. The plan also called for a lecture room that would seat four hundred, a smaller one for one hundred and fifty, and two classrooms for sixty students each. Space for student assistants to work with the museum staff was included, making this the first plan to recognize a practice that remains fundamental to the functioning of the museum today.

This design evolved further, however, and plans published in the June 1926 issue of the *Bulletin of the Associates in Fine Arts* represent some changes from the plan that the Corporation approved. In the 1926 plan, the first floor gallery, which opened off the entrance, was to house sculpture and plaster casts. The main galleries were on the second floor: later Italian art in the High Street bridge gallery, the Jarves Collection in the tower gallery, the Trumbull and early American paintings in the long central gallery of the main building, flanked on the north and south sides by small galleries for other permanent collections and loans. A separate room was devoted to the Trumbull miniatures, another to the Alden wood carvings. A special gallery was designed for prints, inspired by the recent acquisition of the Achelis Collection of Old Master prints, anchored by Dürers and Rembrandts.

Construction began in the fall of 1926. In February 1927, Theodore Sizer (fig. 59) was appointed curator of Painting and Sculpture and associate professor of the History of Art, to start officially in September. Prior to coming to Yale, Sizer had been curator of Prints and Oriental Art at the Cleveland Museum of Art and a visiting fellow in a number of European print rooms. According to the President's Report for 1926–27, "he comes to us in the fall with a wide knowledge of museum work at the time we are planning to move into our new building," a move that Sizer was hired to supervise.[6] Sizer made several changes to the interior gallery spaces in order, in his view, to make them better for hanging pictures. In the case of the gallery designed for the Trumbull paintings, he asked that Swartwout's Italian Gothic cornice be replaced with one that Trumbull had designed for the Congregational Church in Lebanon, Connecticut, which Sizer had obtained from the church.

These changes were minor, however, and they had little effect on the overall Italian Gothic appearance of

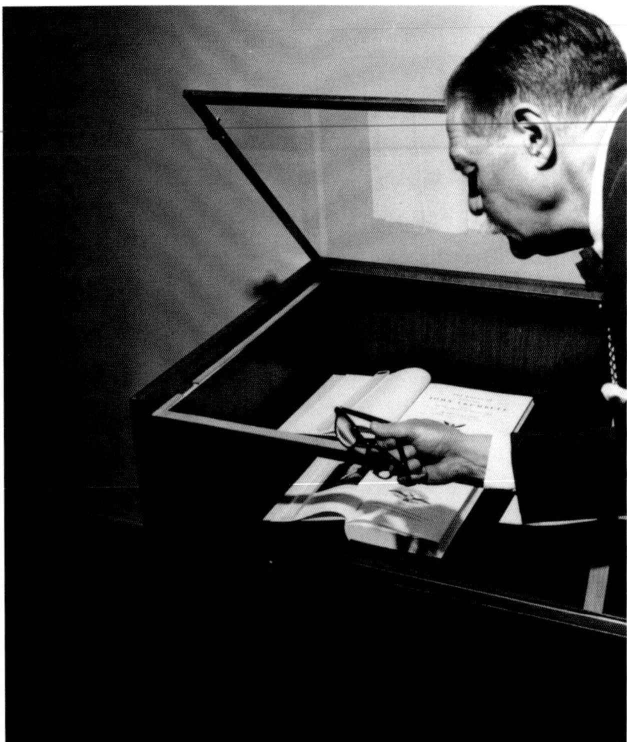

FIG. 59
Theodore Sizer, ca. 1960
Photograph courtesy Yale University Art Gallery Archives

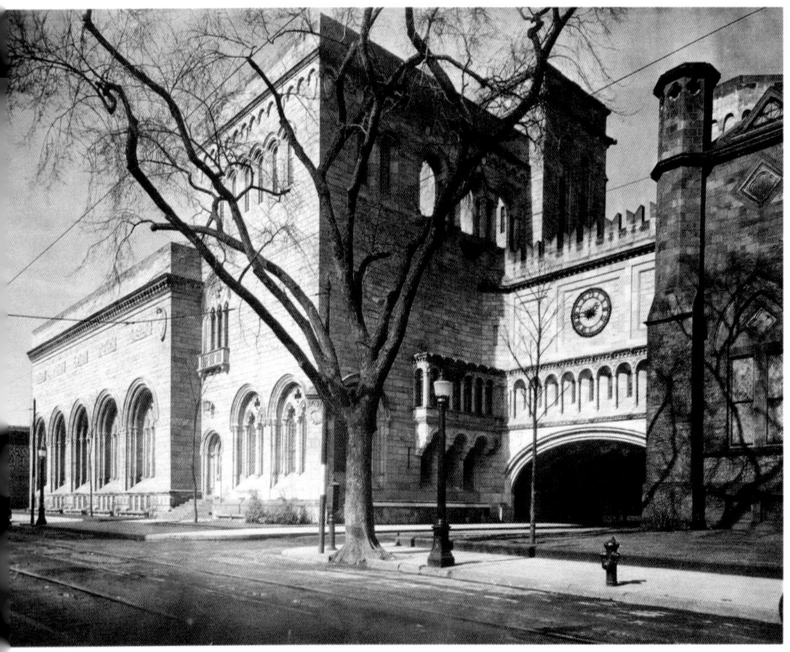

FIG. 60
Egerton Swartwout
Gallery of Fine Arts, 1928
Photograph courtesy Yale University Art Gallery Archives

Swartwout's design. The architect, no doubt encouraged by Meeks and actually assisted by Sizer, went to great lengths to provide detailing of the highest quality, by, for instance, commissioning Samuel Yellin of Philadelphia, a master metalworker, to create the clock faces and the magnificent iron gates that graced the interior. In many cases the architectural detail was as laden with symbolic meaning as that of any true Gothic building. The relief sculptures on the High Street bridge, for example, carved by George Hubert from models prepared by Henry Hering, represented winged undraped female figures symbolizing Architecture, Sculpture, Painting, and Drama. The shields in the sculpture hall, researched and drawn by Theodore Sizer, bore the coats of arms of great patrons of art—among them the Medici, the Gonzagas, Francis I, Louis XIV, Philip II of Spain, Charles I of England, and Horace Walpole.

The Gallery of Fine Arts (fig. 60) opened on September 27, 1928, with an opening celebration on Alumni Day, February 29, 1929. The primary change in the distribution of the collections between the final plans and the actual display was that the Italian and American galleries were switched. The Italian pictures occupied the large east-west gallery with its pendentives, while the American paintings were displayed in the gallery on the bridge for which Sizer had obtained the Trumbull cornice from the Lebanon church.

Parts of the building remained unfinished when the building opened, as described in the December 1928 *Bulletin.* Still in process was the Trumbull room, designed for the artist's Revolutionary War pictures and miniatures and planned to include loans of furniture from Francis P. and Mabel Brady Garvan, the first pieces of American furniture from this extraordinary collection, soon to come to Yale, to be exhibited at the Gallery. Also incomplete were three small galleries on the south side of the second floor, to be devoted to Egyptian, Assyrian and Babylonian, Greek and Roman, early Christian, and Near and Far Eastern art. Featured in the early Christian gallery were to be mosaics and other antiquities from the excavations Yale was currently undertaking at the city of Gerasa in Jordan, if the necessary money could be raised to ship the mosaics to New Haven. The S. Wells Williams Collection of

Chinese porcelain, still on loan, was to be the focus of the Asian gallery. The completion of these galleries was expected by midwinter 1929.

With the opening of the Gallery of Fine Arts in 1928, the museum entered a new phase in which it was to a much greater extent a separate conceptual and physical entity from the School of Art. This is not to say that they were separately governed, or that the Gallery was any less involved in the teaching mission of the University. Edward V. Meeks held the dual title dean of the School of Art and director of the Gallery of Fine Arts. Theodore Sizer was the first to hold the title of director of the Gallery on its own, beginning in February 1940. The Gallery continued to mount exhibitions and make acquisitions that were related to courses taught. Until 1963, when the Schools of Art and Architecture moved into the Paul Rudolph building, and classroom and studio space, the art library, and the slide and photograph collection used for teaching were periodically located under the Gallery's roof. A two-story lecture hall in what is now two floors of exhibition galleries functioned, like the present McNeil Auditorium, as a shared classroom and public event space. What differed was that most of the spaces in the new building were devoted to galleries or to offices and workspaces associated with the care and study of the collections. The new entrance brought visitors directly into the Gallery of Fine Arts and deposited them into galleries filled with art. Such an entrance immediately signaled that one was in a museum, in contrast to the previous need to mount the stairs to reach galleries that must have seemed like an adjunct to the School of Art, as indeed they were.

The new building proved to be a magnet for art. The years of planning and construction and the subsequent plans for expansion during the decade between 1928 and 1938 brought gifts and other acquisitions in every major field that transformed collections and displays and in some cases inaugurated whole curatorial departments.

ASIAN ART

Asian art is a case in point. In spite of the passionate interest for Asian, particularly Japanese, art among European artists and composers of the late nineteenth and early twentieth centuries, and despite the installation of several loans and loan exhibitions of Japanese and Chinese art in the School of Fine Arts, no Asian art had entered the permanent collection at Yale prior to 1928.

Nineteen twenty-eight and twenty-nine, however, brought the gift of a substantial portion of the Williams family collection of Chinese art. This was the first of two collections of Chinese art donated to the Gallery by this family. The first is the S. Wells Williams Collection, bequeathed in 1928 by Frederick Wells Williams, B.A. 1879, Hon. M.A. 1924, in memory of his father, Samuel Wells Williams (1812–1884; Hon. M.A. 1877). The second came to Yale in 1949, as gifts from Frederick's widow, Frances Wayland Williams.

Included in the 1928 bequest was a portrait (fig. 61) by John Ferguson Weir of the father, Samuel Wells Williams, known as Wells, a prominent Sinologist and Yale professor. The 1928 issue of the *Bulletin of the Associates in Fine Arts* describes him as a philologist, a historian, a diplomatist, and a teacher. A Utica, New York, native, he went to China as a missionary printer in 1833, learned Chinese, and published the first Chinese-English dictionary as well as his book *The Middle Kingdom* (1847), a history of China that remained the standard in English for half a century. Also in 1847, he married Sarah Walworth, and the following year the couple returned to China. Wells next learned Japanese, and because of his knowledge of these two languages he was appointed by the U.S. government to be the interpreter on Admiral Perry's expedition to Japan (1854). In 1855 he was appointed Secretary and Interpreter to the U.S. Legation and established his residence in Peking. It was between this date and their permanent return to the United States in 1877 that Mr. and Mrs. Williams formed their collection of Chinese art. Upon their return from China, Mr. Williams became Professor of Chinese Language and Civilization at Yale, a post he held until his death in 1884.

At his death, his son, Frederick, arranged with his friend Professor and Director John Ferguson Weir that

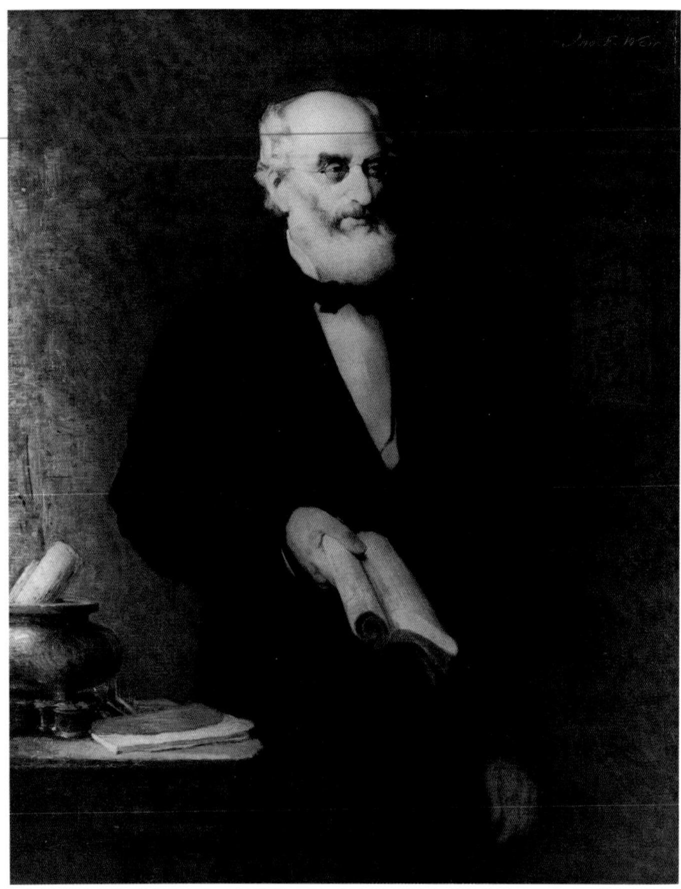

FIG. 61
John Ferguson Weir
Samuel Wells Williams, ca. 1880
Oil on canvas, 86.4 x 68.6 cm
Gift of Mrs. Dalton V. Garstin
1949.50

the Wells Williams Collection would be lent to the School of the Fine Arts. Placed on exhibition in cases in the center of the paintings galleries until a special gallery for Asian art was created in the 1911 renovation of the School, the collection remained on loan until Frederick's bequest of it to Yale in 1928.

Frederick, born in 1856, was the fifth son of S. Wells Williams, and he succeeded his father as Professor of Chinese Language and Civilization at Yale. Although Frederick appears to have been the first in the Williams family to graduate from Yale College, the family had a previous connection to the University collections. S. Wells Williams was the brother of William Frederic Williams, the missionary who acquired the Assyrian reliefs for Yale in 1854. Frederick was thus William Frederic's nephew, and he may have been encouraged by his uncle to attend Yale.

This founding collection of Asian art included rich holdings in Chinese porcelain (fig. 62), and in 1929, an important Buddhist votive stele from the Northern Qi Dynasty (550–577 C.E.; fig. 63) was added to the bequest. The second collection of Chinese art associated with the Williams family is the Wayland Wells Williams Collection, given by Frederick's widow, Mrs. Frederick Wells Williams (née Frances Wayland) in 1947, '48, and '49, in honor of their son, Wayland Wells Williams, Yale Class of 1910. Included in this collection are several fine Ming Dynasty vessels, including the first example of blue-and-white porcelain to come to Yale (fig. 64). These gifts approximately doubled Yale's holdings of Chinese porcelain, and they extended the involvement of the Williams family with the Yale collections into the third generation.

Also in 1928, Maitland F. Griggs, B.A. 1896, donated an earthenware figure of a court attendant from the Northern Wei Dynasty (fig. 65), dating, like the Buddhist votive stele, to the sixth century C.E. This figure was the first of the Griggs family's gifts in Asian art. Also aiding the formative stages of the Asian collection, in 1930 the Associates in Fine Arts donated an image of Guanyin, the bodhisattva of compassion, sculpted of limestone in the eleventh or twelfth century C.E. (Liao or Jin Dynasty; fig. 66). This sculpture was among the first Associates' gifts of works of art to the Gallery.

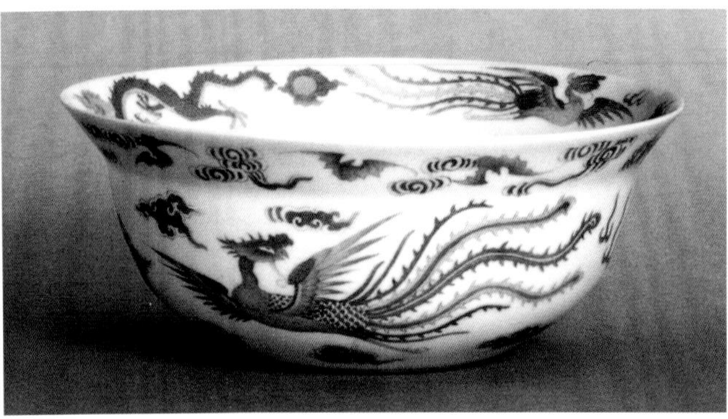

FIG. 62
Maker unknown
Bowl, 1798
Porcelain, 4.4 x 4.3 cm
S. Wells Williams Collection; bequest of F. Wells Williams
1928.201

FIG. 64
Maker unknown
Ming Dynasty Pilgrim Bottle
Porcelain, blue glaze, 25.4 x 19.1 cm
Collection of Wayland Wells Williams, B.A. 1910; gift of Mrs. Frances Wayland Williams
1949.289

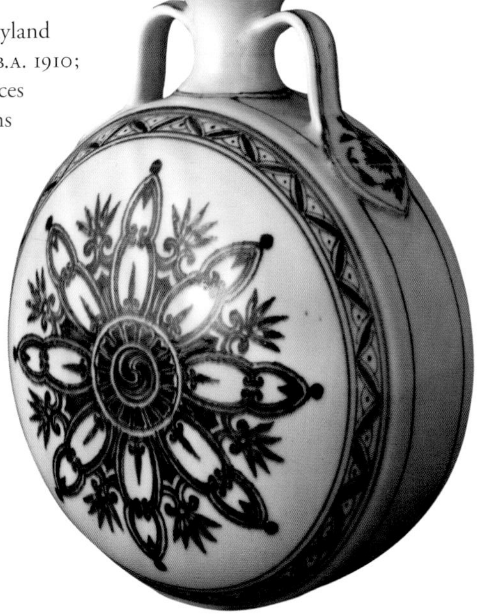

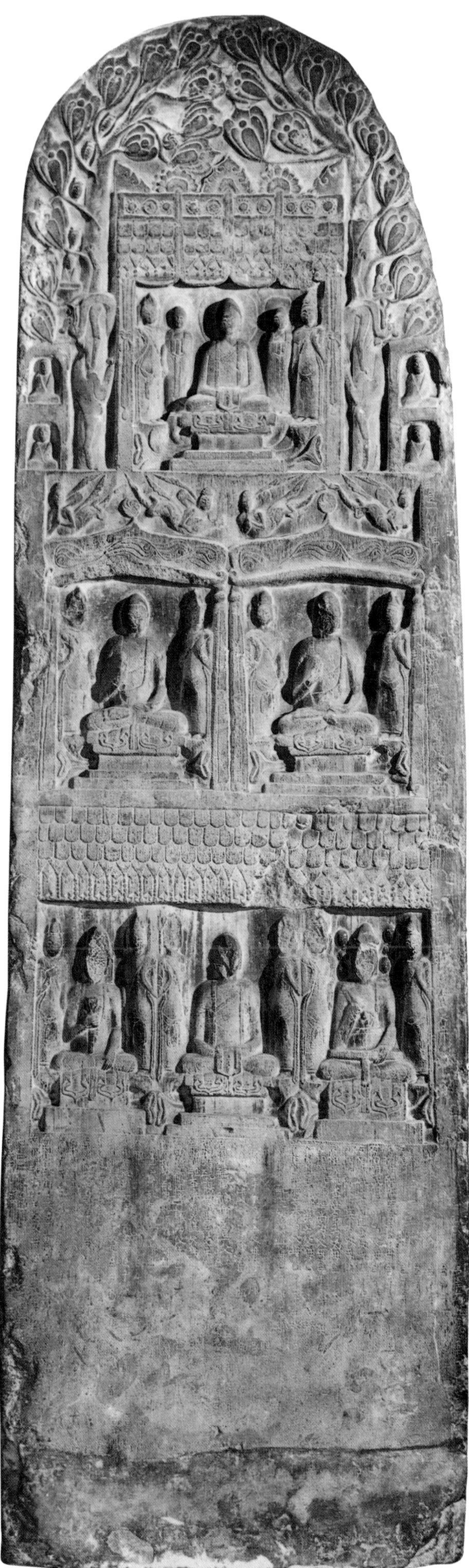

FIG. 63
Maker unknown
Buddhist Votive Stele, 6th century C.E.
Gray limestone, 208.3 x 66.0 x 20.3 cm
F. Wells Williams, B.A. 1879, Collection
1929.45

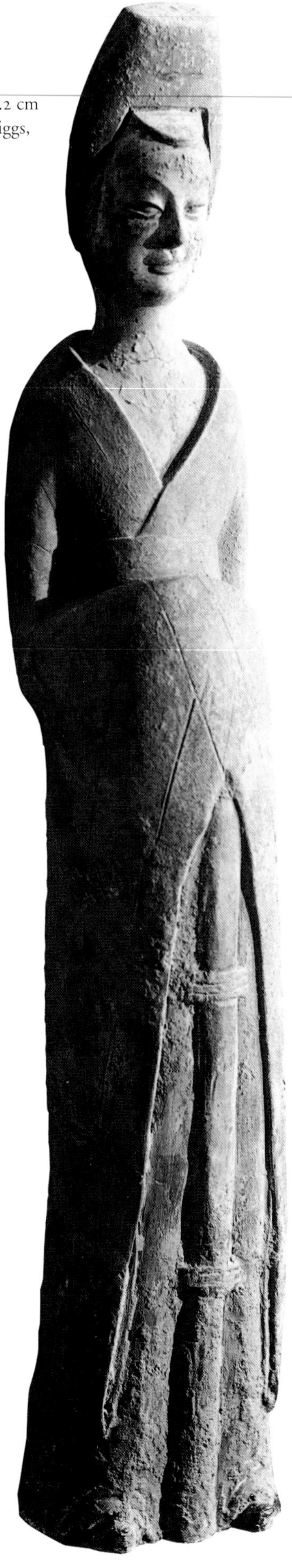

FIG. 65
Maker unknown
Standing Attendant,
6th century C.E.
Earthenware, 59.7 x 10.2 cm
Gift of Maitland F. Griggs, B.A. 1896
1928.382

The first Chinese painting to enter the collection was a Qing Dynasty landscape painting given in 1930 by T. Lawrason Riggs (B.A. 1910; fig. 67), followed shortly thereafter by the important fragment of a painted banner showing Sri Maha-Devi from the Tang Dynasty (9th century; fig. 68). The gift of Ada Small (Mrs. William H.) Moore in 1937, the Tang Dynasty painting marks the beginning of a pivotal donor relationship for the Asian department that lasted until Mrs. Moore's death in 1955, at the age of ninety-six. Mrs. Moore's gifts to the Asian department included Chinese paintings, porcelains, and bronzes, Japanese prints, Persian pottery, rugs, and tapestries, Luristan bronzes, and her important collection of Near and Far Eastern textiles. A passionate collector, widowed early, and an intrepid traveler, she journeyed widely in China, Japan, India, the Near East, and Greece. She sailed the Nile and the Yangtze. She met Mahatma Gandhi when she was in India, and stayed with maharajahs there. Her grandson, Bishop Paul Moore, Jr., Yale B.A. 1941, Hon. M.A. 1965, and a former member of the Yale Corporation, recalls stories of these travels, some drawn from the round-the-world trip on a sailing yacht that she took in 1922. He particularly remembers the trip to the Middle East that she took in the early 1930s, during which she began to collect ancient cylinder seals, a new field that became an enduring focus. Told by her travel agent that the trip was too dangerous for an elderly lady (she was then in her seventies) unless she went by plane, she promptly chartered three planes for herself, her traveling companions, and their baggage, and took off.

Throughout her travels, she acquired not only objects but a lifelong interest in scholarly research, archaeological excavations, and the preservation of cultural property. She was a major supporter of the work of the Byzantine Institute in the uncovering of the mosaics at Hagia Sophia in Istanbul and paid for repairs at the Golden Temple at Amritsar in India. She built a museum for the Corinth excavations run by the American School of Classical Studies at Athens, donated generously to the Oriental Institute of Chicago's excavations in Persepolis, and built a scientific library for the American College in Teheran.

Mrs. Moore filled her New York townhouse with the objects she collected, and added to her holdings

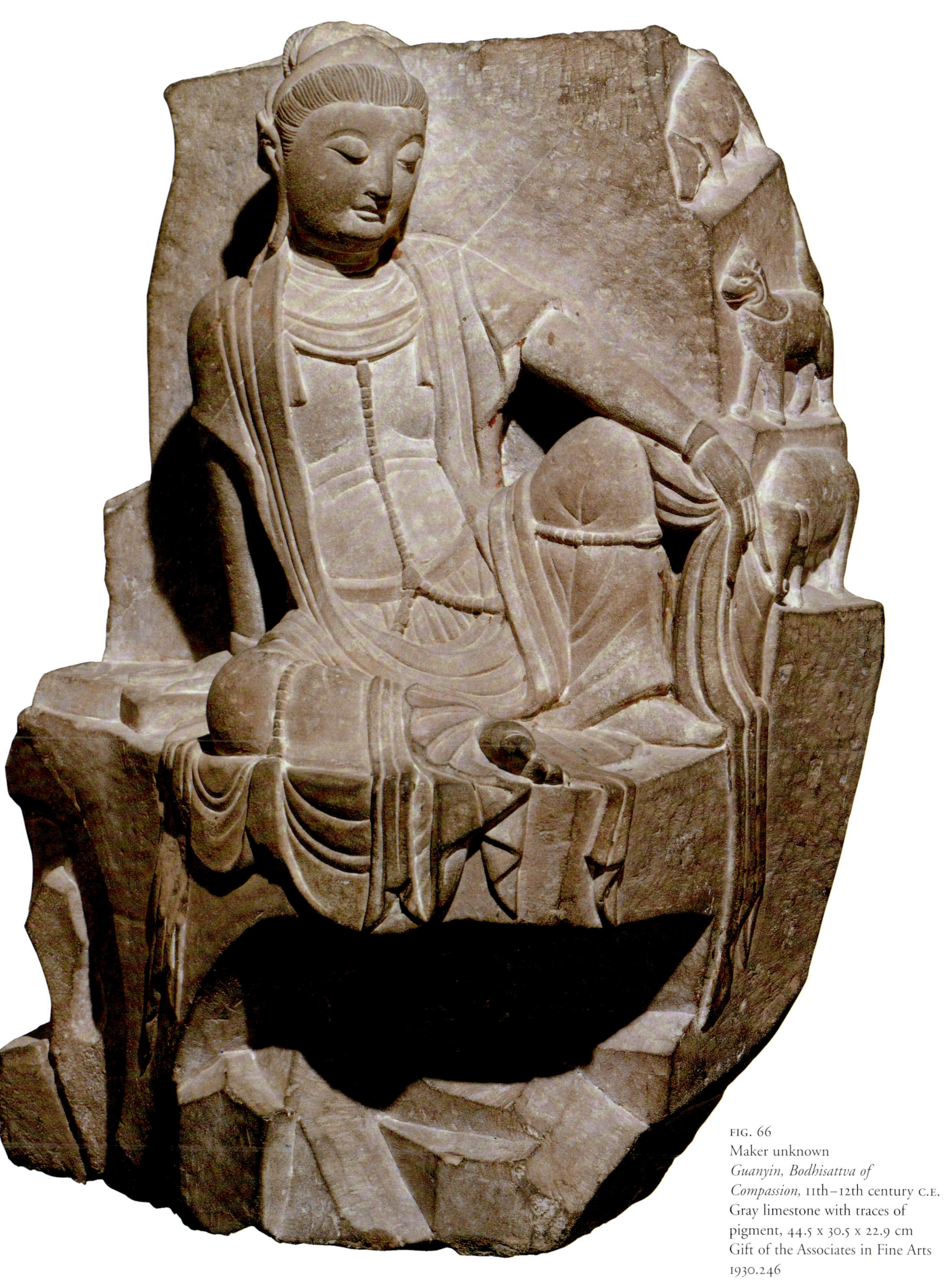

FIG. 66
Maker unknown
Guanyin, Bodhisattva of Compassion, 11th–12th century C.E.
Gray limestone with traces of pigment, 44.5 x 30.5 x 22.9 cm
Gift of the Associates in Fine Arts
1930.246

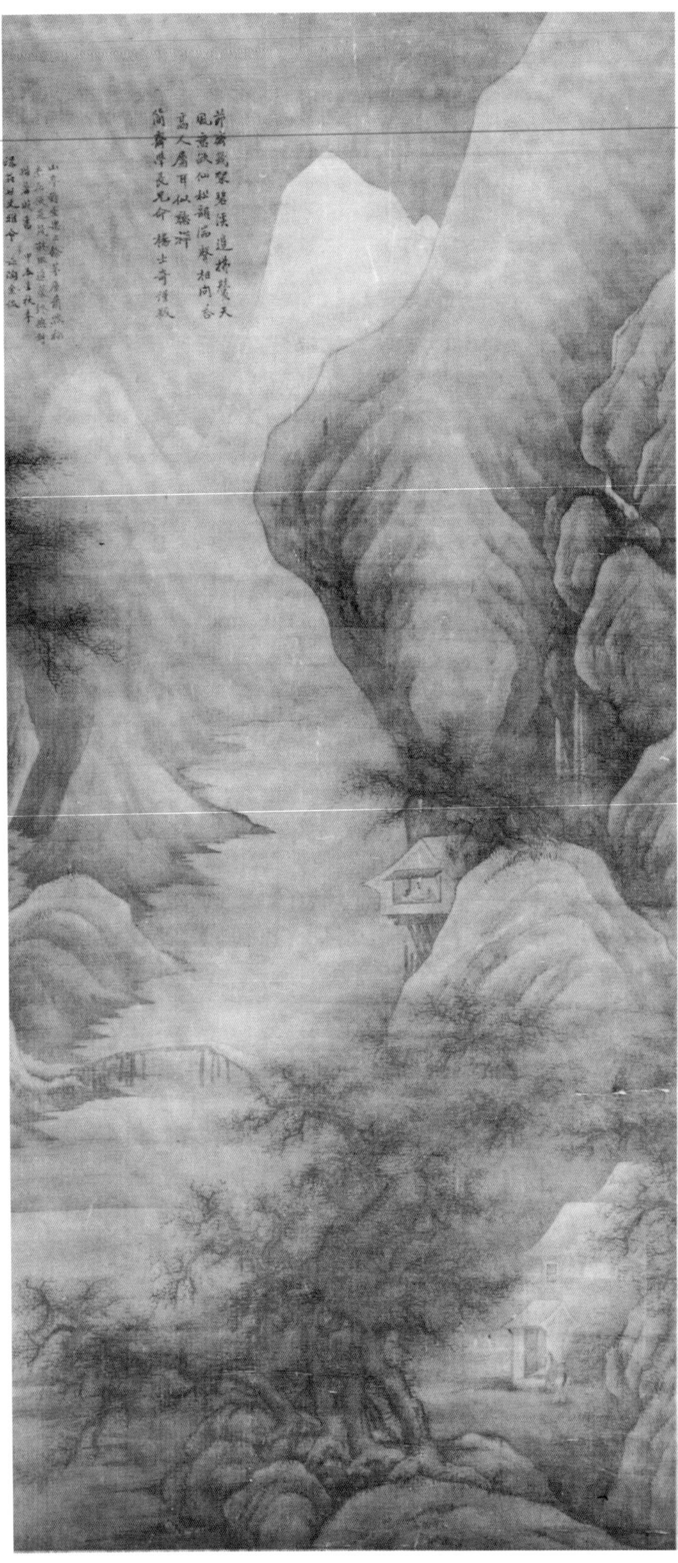

FIG. 67
Jin Kan
Landscape, late Ming, early Qing Dynasty
Ink and color on silk, 254.0 x 101.9 x 85.7 cm
Gift of T. Lawrason Riggs, B.A. 1910
1930.30

with purchases from prominent dealers. Photographs of her in her library (fig. 69), where much of her collection was displayed and enjoyed, show her surrounded by Chinese porcelains and ancient Roman glass, another major collecting interest that resulted in an important collection for Yale. The original gift of textiles in 1937 comprised 869 pieces, and additions were made to the collections almost yearly. The strength of the collection is in the Iranian material, notably a rare Sassanian tapestry fragment (6th–8th century C.E.; fig. 70), Seljuk period textiles, and later pieces spanning the sixteenth to nineteenth centuries. Other parts of the collection include Japanese, Coptic, North African, Greek Island, Turkish, Indian, South Asian, Chinese, and even Peruvian textiles. Additional Iranian material, notably Luristan bronzes, early pots from Tepe Sialk, and a fine collection of Persian glazed pottery, complements the Iranian textiles.

Well over two hundred Japanese prints were given by Mrs. Moore, including several early prints as well as works by some of the famous eighteenth- and nineteenth-century artists. The extensive Chinese porcelain collection included many examples of celadon, blue-and-white (fig. 71), and later types such as peach bloom. Especially important were some of the Chinese bronzes in the Moore Collection, such as the late Shang Dynasty owl-shaped *Zun* (fig. 72), *Fang yi*, and *Jue* (fig. 73). Subsequent to 1937, Mrs. Moore's gifts of Chinese paintings were concentrated in 1952–54. Among them were other early works, such as a *Tantric Buddhist Charm* from the late Tang Dynasty, two album-leaf portraits, *Zhu Guan* and *Du Yan*, from "The Five Old Men of Suiyang" dating to the eleventh century, and a rare *Winter Landscape* attributed to Li Shan (active ca. 1150–1201). Later paintings include the fourteenth-century hanging scroll *Ink Plum* by Wang Mian (fig. 74).

Mrs. Moore's gifts honored the memories of two of her sons, Hobart Moore, who graduated from Yale in 1900 but died of consumption at the age of twenty-five, and Edward Small Moore, who died in 1948, having also attended Yale, as had her third son, Paul Moore (B.A. 1903). It was because of her sons' Yale connection that Mrs. Moore chose Yale for her collections. Her contributions to the Gallery extended beyond her collections: she served as a member of the

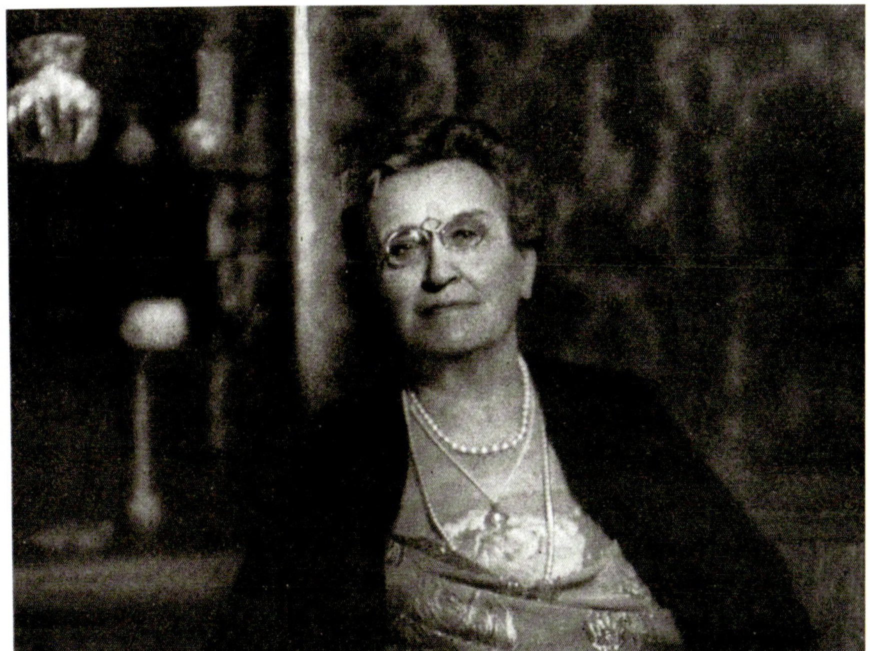

FIG. 69
Mrs. Moore in her Library,
date unknown
Photograph courtesy
Yale University Art Gallery
Archives

FIG. 68
Artist unknown
Sri Maha-Devi, 9th century C.E.
Woven textile with plaster and
painted in ink and color,
24.3 x 20.6 cm
The Hobart and Edward Small
Moore Memorial Collection, gift of
Mrs. William H. Moore
1937.5576

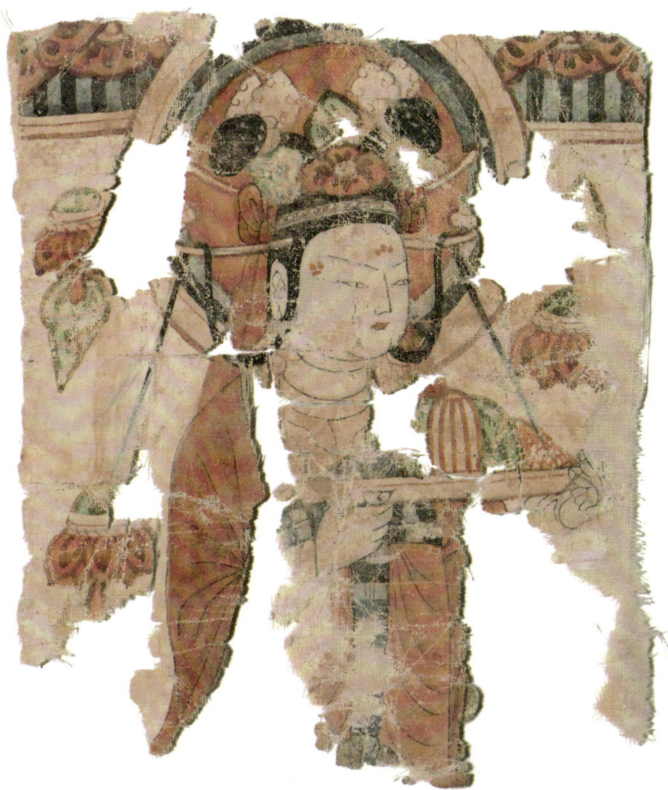

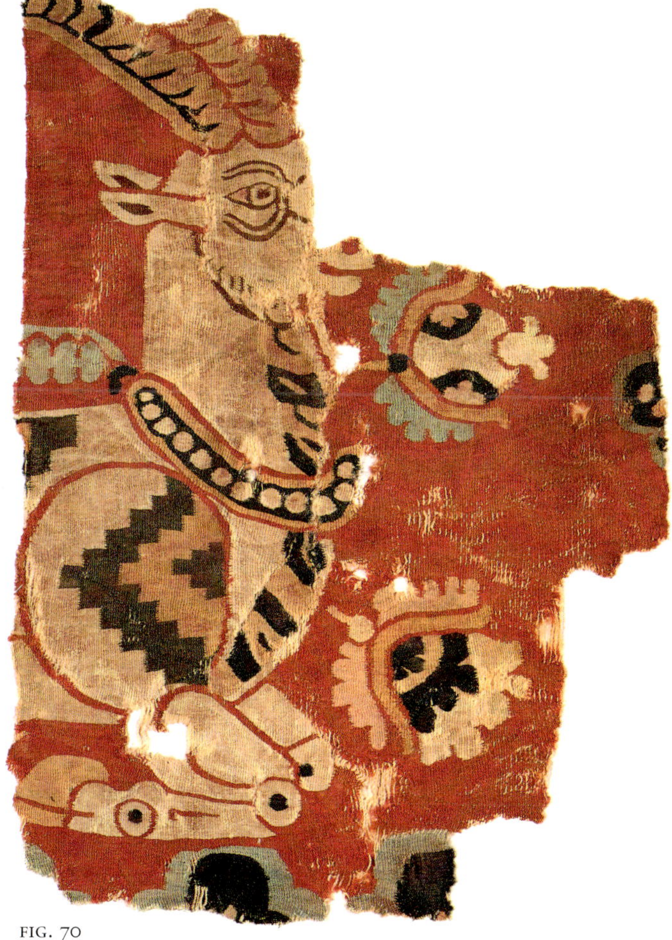

FIG. 70
Maker unknown
Tapestry Fragment, probably 6th–8th
century C.E.
Wool tapestry weave, 38.0 x 27.5 cm
The Hobart and Edward Small Moore
Memorial Collection, gift of Mrs.
William H. Moore
1937.4604

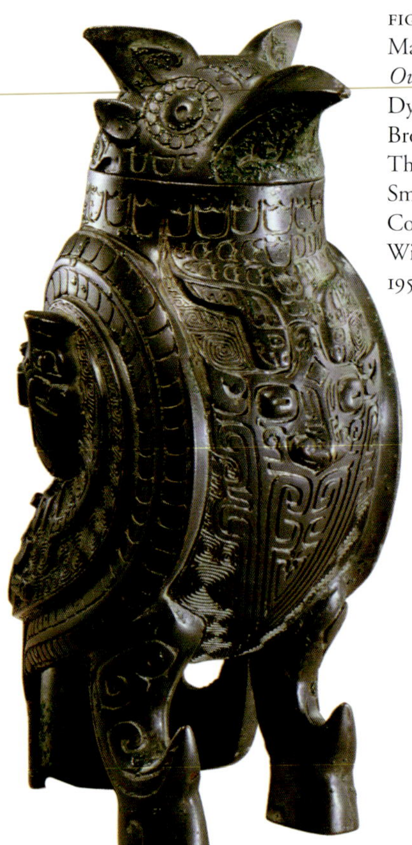

FIG. 72
Maker unknown
Owl-shaped Zun, late Shang Dynasty
Bronze, 20.7 x 9.8 cm
The Hobart and Edward Small Moore Memorial Collection, gift of Mrs. William H. Moore
1954.48.7

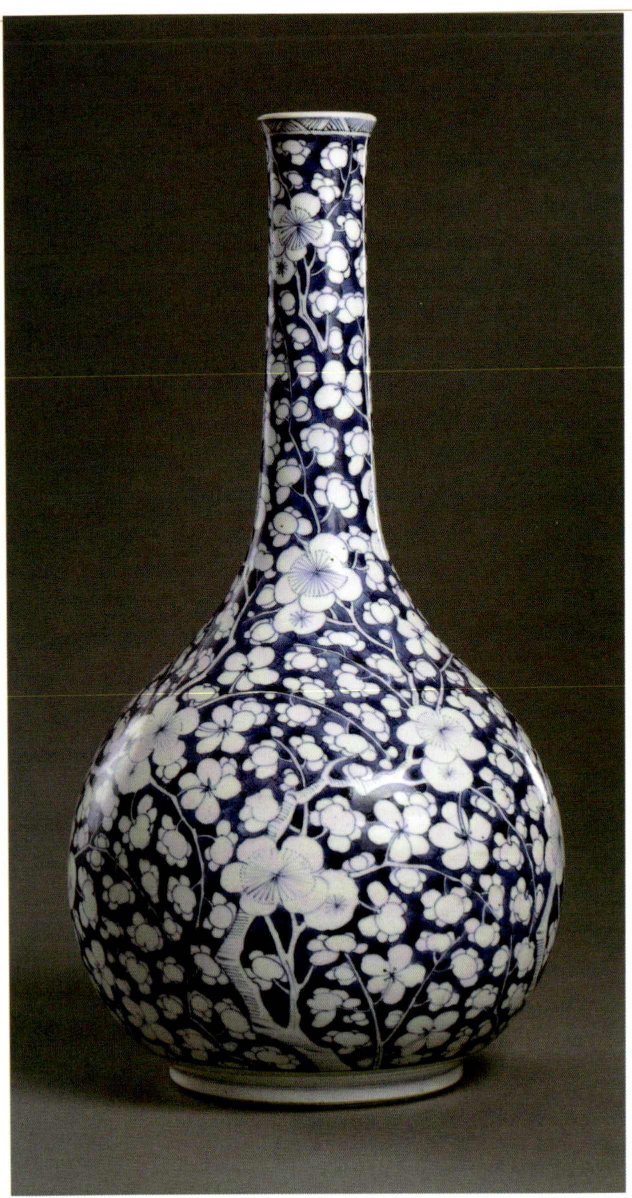

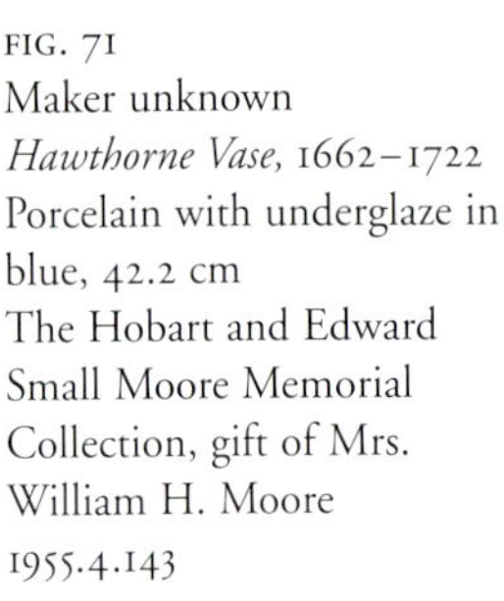

FIG. 71
Maker unknown
Hawthorne Vase, 1662–1722
Porcelain with underglaze in blue, 42.2 cm
The Hobart and Edward Small Moore Memorial Collection, gift of Mrs. William H. Moore
1955.4.143

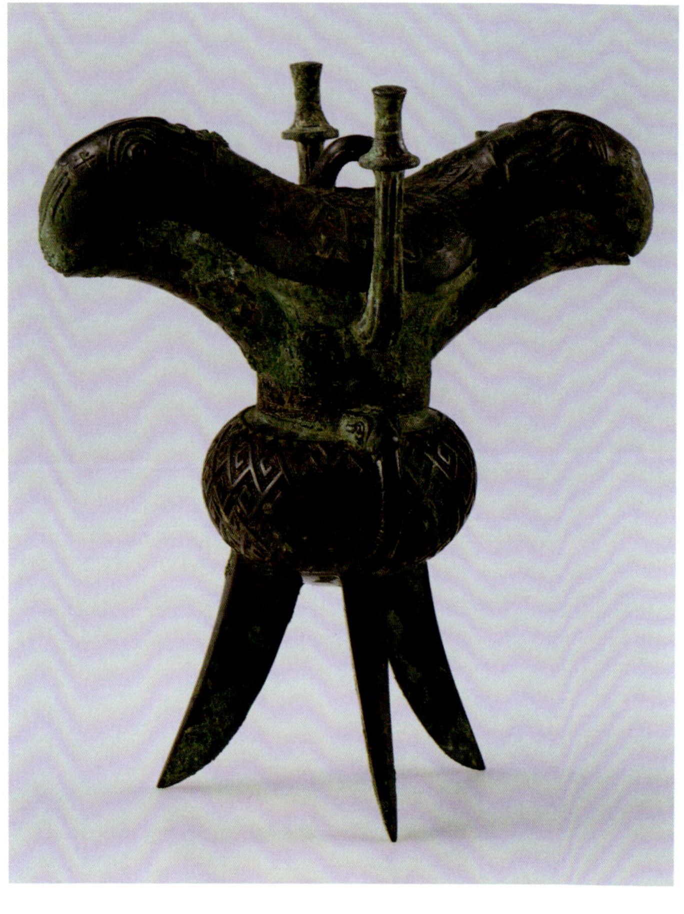

FIG. 73
Maker unknown
Jue, 13th–10th centuries B.C.E.
Bronze, 24.5 x 19.7 cm
The Hobart and Edward Small Moore Memorial Collection, gift of Mrs. William H. Moore
1954.48.11

OPPOSITE: FIG. 74
Wang Mian, d. 1359
Ink Plum, ca. 1355
Hanging scroll, ink on paper, 114.8 x 26.0 cm
The Hobart and Edward Small Moore Memorial Collection, gift of Mrs. William H. Moore
1954.40.3

Governing Board and was a generous donor to the construction costs of the Kahn building. In her will, Mrs. Moore left an endowment for the Asian department. The family connection with the Gallery continued with the generous support of her surviving son, Paul, and his wife, Fanny Hanna Moore, who was a member of the Governing Board of the Gallery and the first woman to receive the Yale medal for her service to the University.

The culmination of this first stage of the Asian collections took place shortly after the end of the 1928–38 decade, when an important group of ceramics from the Changsha region, at the time one of the most extensive collections of its kind outside East Asia, was exhibited at the Gallery in 1939. Given in 1940 by John Hadley Cox, B.A. 1935, it is now the core of Yale's early Chinese ceramic collection.

The John Hadley Cox Collection of Changsha ceramics represented a significant new initiative in Asian art. Previous acquisitions of ceramics, the gifts of the Williams family in 1928 and 1949 (figs. 62 and 64), had been porcelain and stoneware from the fourteenth century to the Republic. The Cox material was earlier, some of it much earlier, and it was specifically given as the basis for a study collection designed to represent the potter's art from the third century B.C.E. to the fourteenth century C.E.

John Hadley Cox spent the two years following his graduation from Yale as a teacher in China, as part of the Yale-in-China program. He was stationed in Changsha, the capital of the Hunan province in south central China. While he was there, excavations for a municipal building project uncovered a large number of tombs and artifacts, mostly of the state of Chu dating to the last Eastern Zhou period, ca. fifth–third centuries B.C.E. Cox became interested in the finds and in early Chinese history, and he assembled an extensive collection of early Chinese ceramics. In 1937, he offered to give forty ceramic objects, primarily from the Changsha area, to Yale. Ceramics from the Changsha region are particularly important in the history of high-fired green glazes in China and in the Tang Dynasty development of painting under the glaze. Enthusiasm greeted the offer, and the Cox proposal proved to be the foundation of a collection of ceramics from the

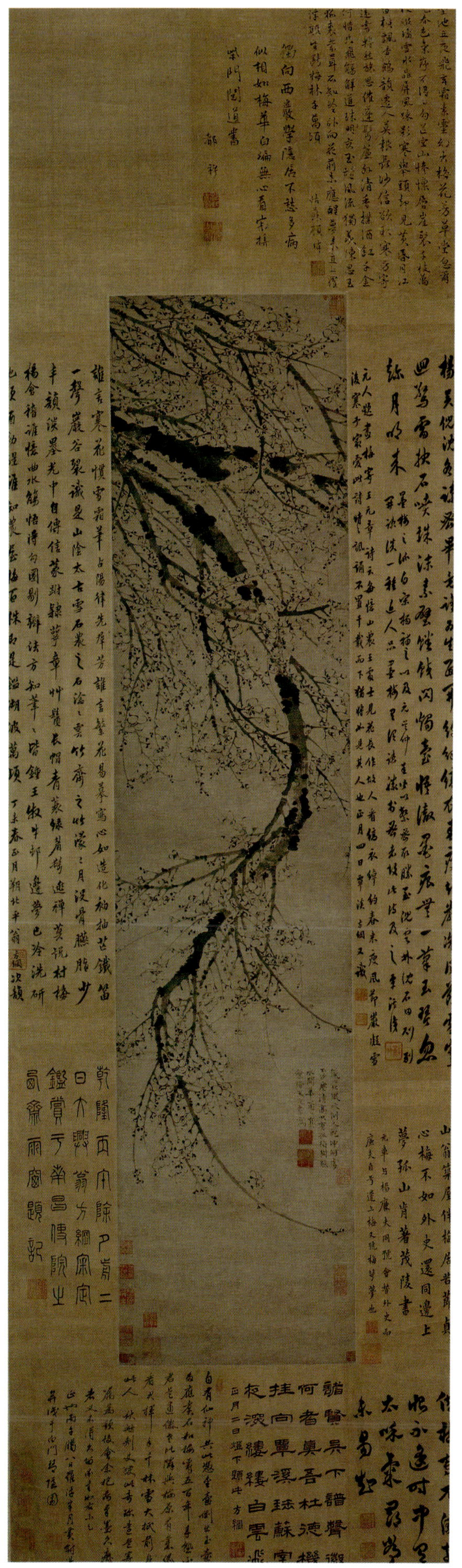

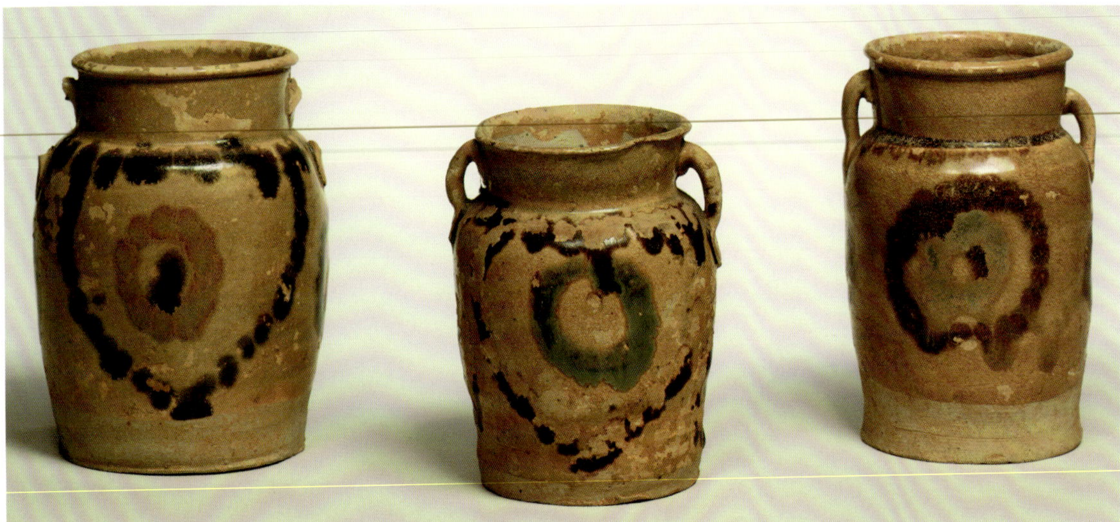

FIG. 75
Maker unknown
Changsha Ceramics,
Tang Dynasty, 8th–9th centuries C.E.
Stoneware, yellow-green glaze, brown and blue underglaze painting, 7.3–8.6 cm
Gift of John Hadley Cox, B.A. 1935
1940.383, 1940.384, 1940.830A

Changsha region of Hunan that grew to some two hundred pieces with his extensive gift in 1940 of ceramics spanning over a thousand years of ceramic history in the Changsha area (fig. 75). This gift, plus the gifts and financial support of the Gallery's other great patron of Asian art, Ada Small Moore, including her gift of a Han Dynasty *Covered Bowl (Gui)* acquired by Cox in Changsha, allowed the collection to become the most representative of its kind outside of China. Subsequently, key gifts of Chinese art, especially ceramics, have come from Dr. Yale Kneeland, Jr. (B.A. 1922), George Hopper Fitch (B.A. 1932) and Mrs. Fitch, and Molly and Walter Bareiss (B.S. 1940S). Recent purchases in Chinese art have concentrated on painting, early ceramics, and earthenware sculpture.

Japanese art has been a more recent interest for the collection, building on what had been a collection limited largely to Japanese prints. A pair of six-fold screens by Yamamoto Soken showing *Birds and Flowers of the Twelve Months* was purchased in 1986. A special focus on contemporary Japanese ceramics, thanks to generous gifts from Molly and Walter Bareiss such as the porcelain sculpture with celadon glaze by Fukami Sueharu, *View of Distant Sea II*, is complemented by an interest in historical Japanese vessels such as the fifteenth-century Shigaraki jar purchased with a gift from the Bareisses. But we are ahead of our story.

Other important gifts and loans of collections and individual works of art that came to Yale around 1928 were installed in the new galleries and noted in the *Bulletin*. Prominent among these was the group of five late Romanesque stone sculptures from the Church of Saint Martin at Angers (1185–95), representing the Virgin and Child, Saint Andrew, the Apostle John, and two bishops (fig. 76), given in 1926 by Maitland F. Griggs (B.A. 1896). In 1929, Mr. Griggs established the first endowed fund for acquisitions with a gift of $100,000, "the income from which shall be used solely in acquiring works of art for exhibition and study in the Gallery of Arts."[7] Purchases were to be made "upon the recommendation of the Committee on Accessions," which had been established two years earlier by the Yale Corporation. At Griggs's request, purchases were credited as gifts of the Associates in Fine Arts at Yale during his lifetime, and the name of the fund was changed to honor its donor after his death in 1943. Since this generous gift, the Griggs Fund has supported the purchase of a broad range of works of art including Roman portraits, European paintings and drawings, Asian art, and American art, notably the pair of portraits of Mr. and Mrs. Isaac Smith by John Singleton Copley (figs. 77a and 77b). The Griggs family has donated works of art in other fields, notably early Italian paintings in 1943, a field in which their support continues today.

The Angers sculptures were installed in the Gallery of Fine Arts in the Sculpture Hall on the first floor. Shown with them were two of the Assyrian reliefs from the palace of Assurnasirpal II, purchased in 1854, Greek, Roman, and Renaissance casts, and a collection of Near Eastern carpets on loan from George Hewitt Myers (B.A. 1898, M.F.A. 1902), founder of the Textile Museum in Washington, D.C.

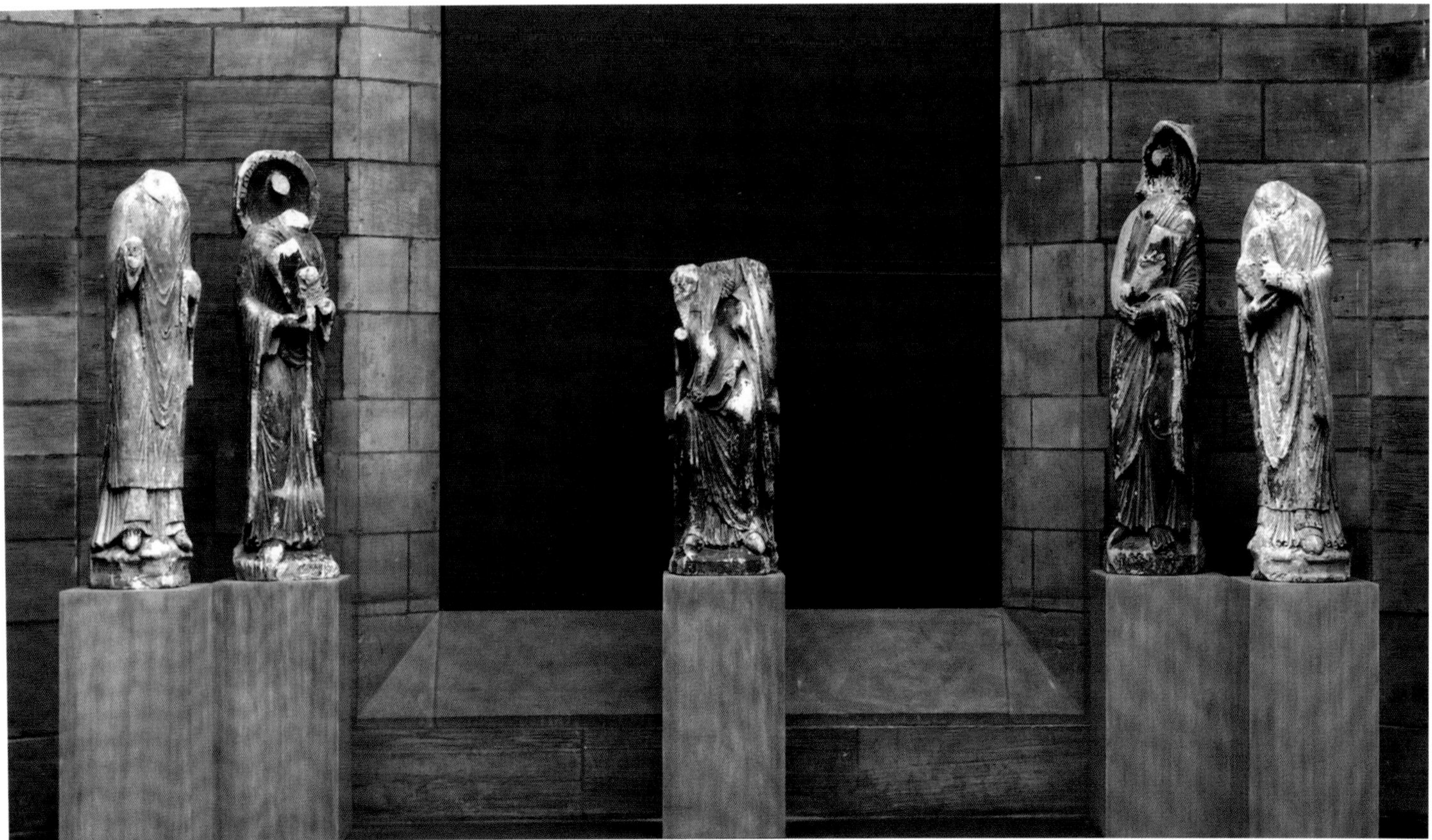

A key acquisition was also made for the American decorative arts collection while Swartwout's building was under way, requiring a major change in building plans to accommodate it. In 1926, at the suggestion of George Dudley Seymour (Hon. M.A. 1913), the University purchased the Curtis-Rose House, built in North Branford, Connecticut, in 1710, as it was about to be demolished to make way for the New Haven Water Company's new reservoir. The two principal rooms from this house were installed in the new Gallery of Fine Arts, which was modified so that the four windows and staircase could be installed in their proper relative positions. The restoration of the rooms, which included the removal of layers of wallpaper and paint to recover the original surfaces, was overseen by J. Frederick Kelly, B.A. 1915, already recognized as an authority in early colonial architecture. The rooms were furnished with period furniture exclusively from Connecticut, lent by Francis P. and Mabel Brady Garvan, apparently their first loans to Yale. Also displayed in one of the rooms were some of Yale's earliest acquisitions, including the portraits of Queen Anne of Denmark and her Consort, George, and the portrait of John Davenport by the Davenport Limner (fig. 5).

Additional portraits from the University's early collections were shown in the gallery spaces devoted to American and English eighteenth- and early nineteenth-century art. Included here were Sir Godfrey Kneller's portrait of George I, presented by Elihu Yale in 1718; a portrait of Elihu Yale by an English artist, Enoch Zeeman; three portraits by Ralph Earl, including that of Roger Sherman; and John Smibert's *Dean Berkeley and His Entourage (The Bermuda Group)*. Portraits by John Singleton Copley, Samuel F. B. Morse, John Wesley Jarvis, and Gilbert Stuart were also shown in this gallery.

FIG. 76
Artist unknown, French
Five figures from the Church of St. Martin of Angers, 1185–1195
Polychromed limestone
max. dimensions: 195.6 x 45.7 x 43.8 cm
Gift of Maitland F. Griggs, B.A. 1896
1926.15-.19

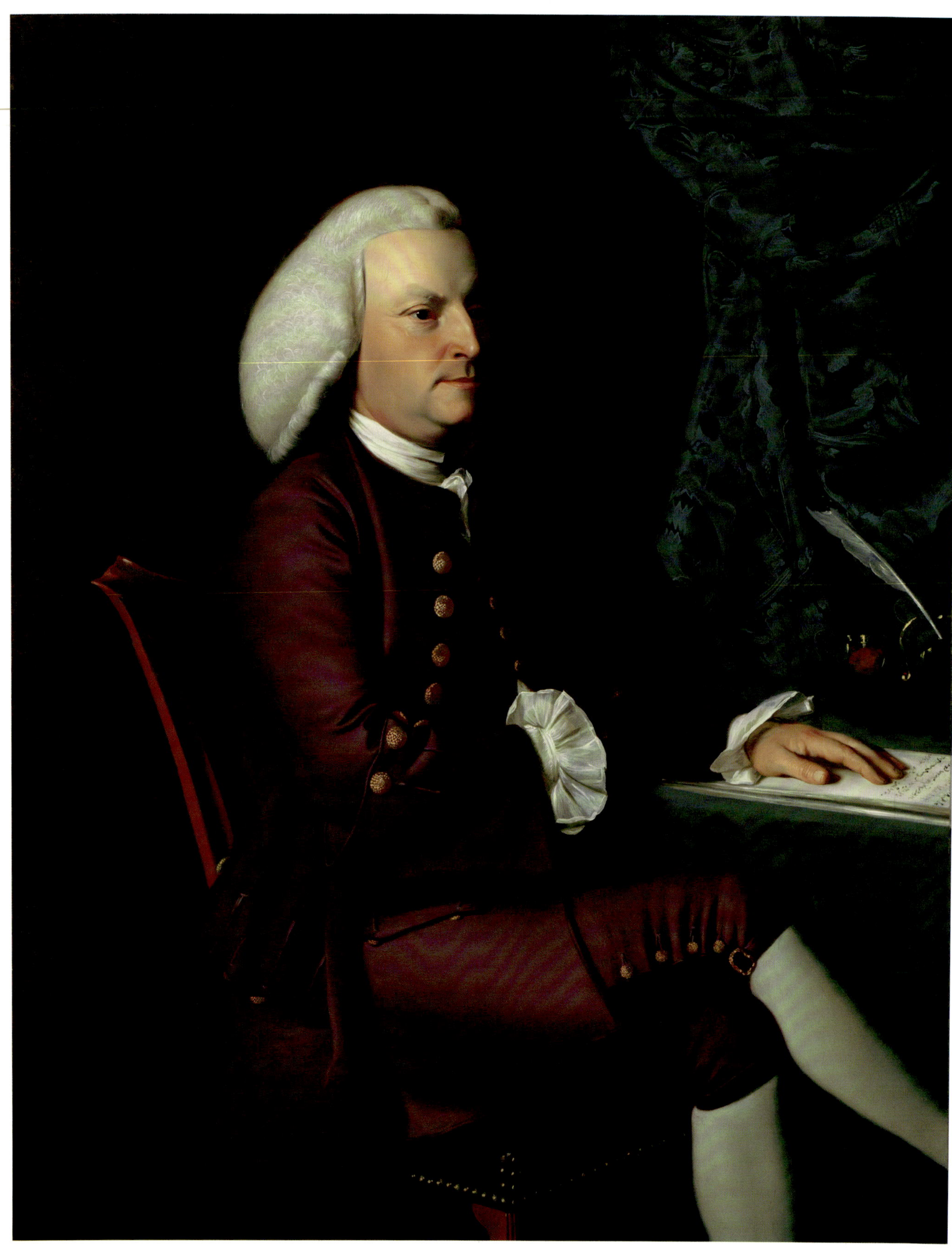

FIG.77a
John Singleton Copley
Isaac Smith, 1769
Oil on canvas, 127.3 x 101.9 cm
The Maitland F. Griggs, B.A. 1896, Fund
1941.73

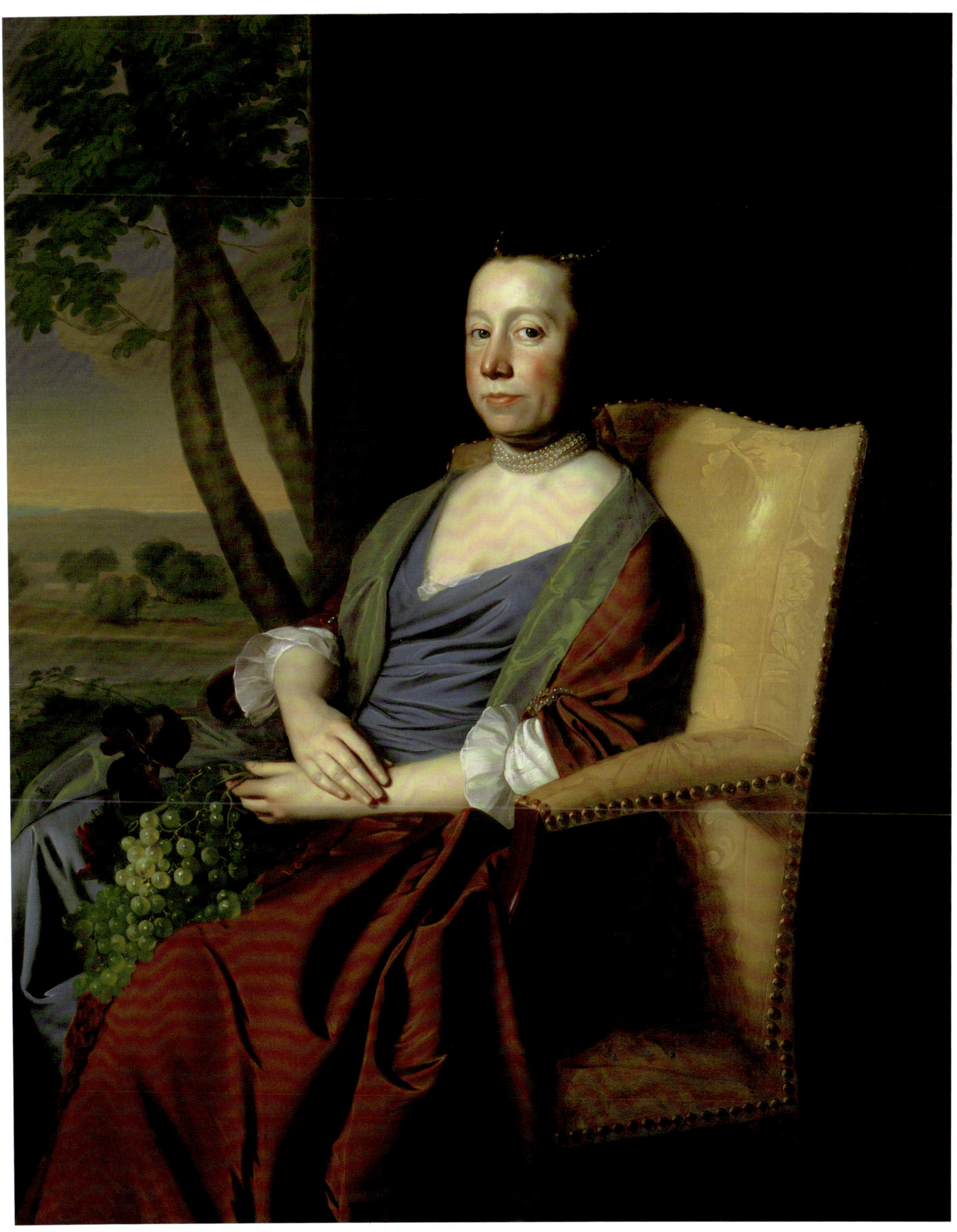

FIG. 77b
John Singleton Copley
Mrs. Isaac Smith (Elizabeth Storer), 1769
Oil on canvas, 127.3 x 101.9 cm
The Maitland F. Griggs, B.A. 1896, Fund
1941.74

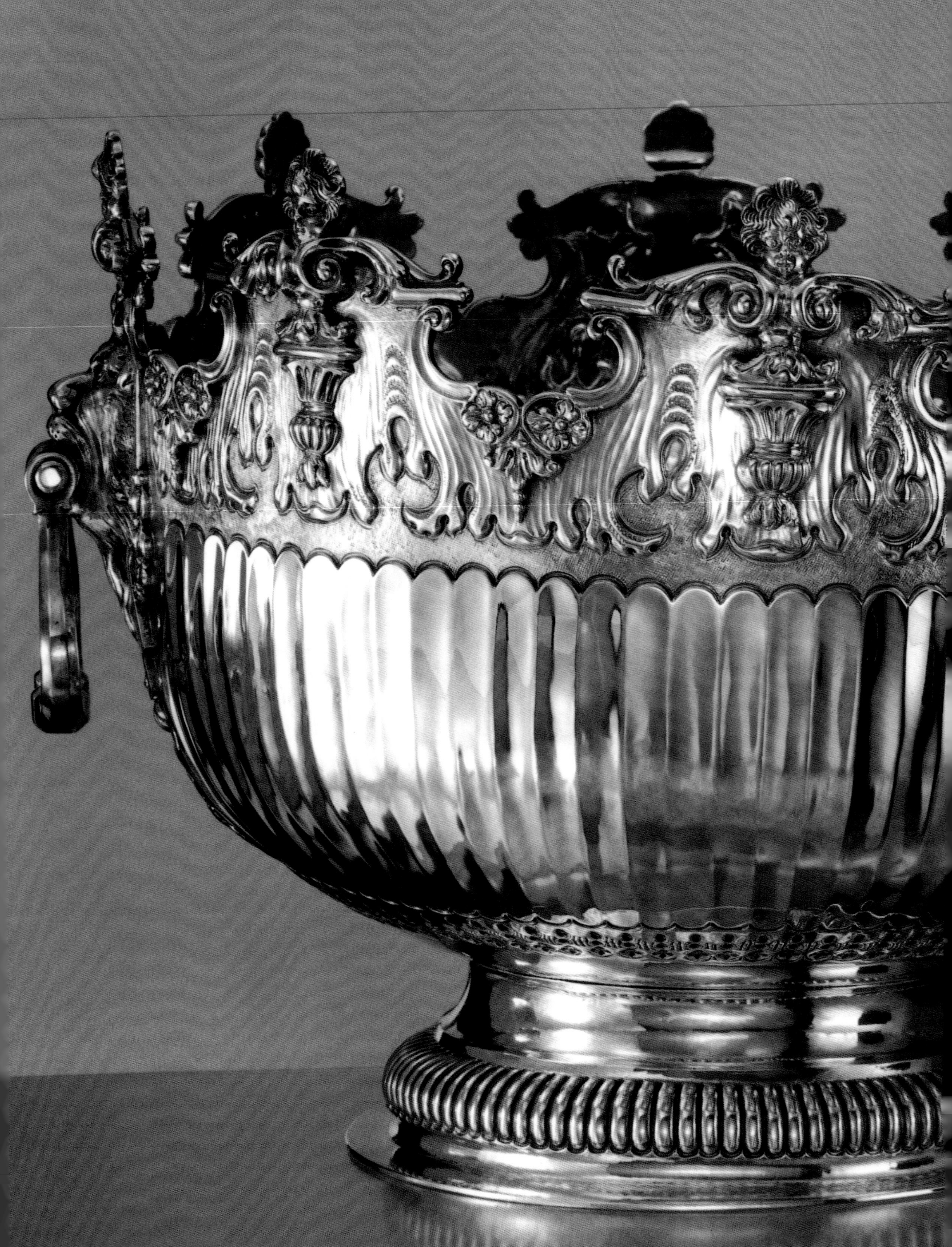

CHAPTER 8

Francis P. Garvan and the Mabel Brady Garvan Collections of American Art

The loans of American furniture to the new Gallery of Fine Arts by Francis P. Garvan and his wife, Mabel Brady Garvan, initiated a relationship that would make the Yale Art Gallery preeminent among university museums and one of the best among all museums that collect American art. Mr. Garvan's gift to the Gallery in 1930 of some five thousand works of American decorative arts inaugurated the Mabel Brady Garvan Collection, which would grow in time to more than ten thousand objects, many the most important and beautiful of their kind. In accepting the collection in 1930, Dean Everett V. Meeks said, as reported in the *New York Times*, "the quality and wealth of material placed here by Mr. and Mrs. Garvan are making our Gallery a place of pilgrimage."[1]

Francis P. Garvan (fig. 78) was born in East Hartford, Connecticut, in 1875.[2] After graduating from Yale (B.A. 1897), where he was a member of the track team, he earned his law degree from New York Law School in 1899. Following World War I, President Woodrow Wilson named him to direct the Chemical Foundation, Inc., an organization formed to develop a chemical industry in America. Garvan was viewed as the first American to recognize the importance of chemical research and manufacturing for a secure and prosperous nation, and he devoted himself to advancing this cause through the Foundation for the rest of his life. The esteem in which the industry held him is reflected in the publication of a "Francis P. Garvan Memorial Issue" by the *Made in America Monthly*, which included tributes characterizing him as a trail-blazer, a patriotic American, and a man who lived for others.[3]

Garvan began collecting American art in the mid-1910s, a few years after marrying Mabel Brady of Albany, New York. "I asked Mr. Garvan how he began collecting," wrote Charles Messer Stowe in an article published at the time of the Garvan gift to Yale, "and what motive he had in getting together the remarkable examples of past craftsmanship which he owned. Both of them [he and Mrs. Garvan] thought that better craftsmanship and more beauty were to be obtained in the furniture of former years than in that of the then present. So in buying for their home they bought antiques, at first English furniture. It was on their

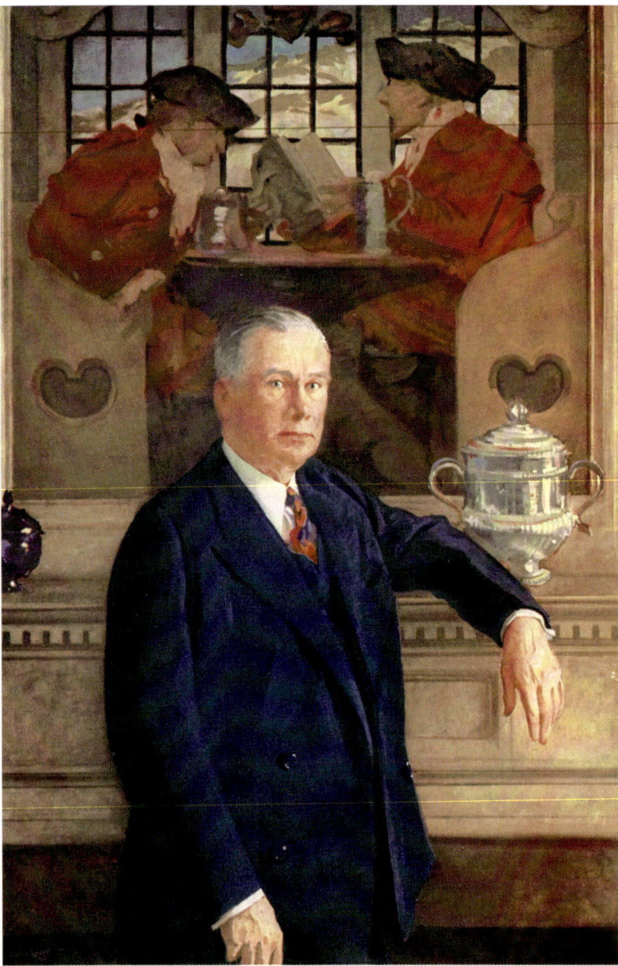

FIG. 78
Augustus Vincent Tack
Portrait of Francis P. Garvan, ca. 1930
Oil on canvas, 151 x 99.7 cm
Bequest of Mabel Brady Garvan
1980.18.1

wedding trip that they bought their first piece, and soon their small apartment was full.

"Then Mr. Garvan found that he had been bilked in some of the pieces he had bought, that some of the English antiques were fakes, so he and his wife decided to buy only American things and they dumped about $40,000 worth of articles they had acquired, mostly English, and started in to replace them with those of American manufacture. They took the wise step of getting competent advice on their purchases after that, a policy which has been adhered to ever since. The result is that there are no doubtful pieces in the thousands that make up the Garvan collections, and by the same token these are so much the more valuable for study and for comparison."[4] Garvan described his personal approach to avoiding fakes: "I had eight years experience in the District Attorney's office here in New York, and I try every piece as I would a murderer. It must be proven innocent of every charge that can be brought against it before I accept it."[5]

At first, collecting was simply a pleasure. "The collector is well repaid for any efforts he puts forth," Garvan stated. "There is a joy that cannot be compared with anything else in acquiring a genuine article to add to one's collection. It takes constant study, constant watchfulness and long training of eye and fingers. During the war [World War I] I was working on an average about eighteen hours a day. The last half hour before I went to sleep I gave to antiques, reading auction catalogues, books, magazines, studying my own catalogue, looking at the photographs of what we had assembled. That half hour rested me as nothing else could."[6] His reputation grew with his collection, as Messer relates: "But as he got on in the world and outgrew the small apartment in which he first set up housekeeping, Mr. Garvan continued to buy beyond the needs of his house and presently became known as a collector."[7]

In assembling his collections, Garvan strove to obtain the best as well as the most representative objects of their kind: "He sought the rare, early, and 'finest' objects."[8] Objects in poor condition were rejected. Histories of ownership that could be traced were important, partly to guard against forgeries, partly for the added historical dimension that they provided.

FIG. 82
Maker unknown, Newport, Rhode Island
Desk and Bookcase, 1765–90
Mahogany, chestnut, white pine, American black cherry, 272.4 x 113.5 x 64.0 cm
Mabel Brady Garvan Collection
1940.320

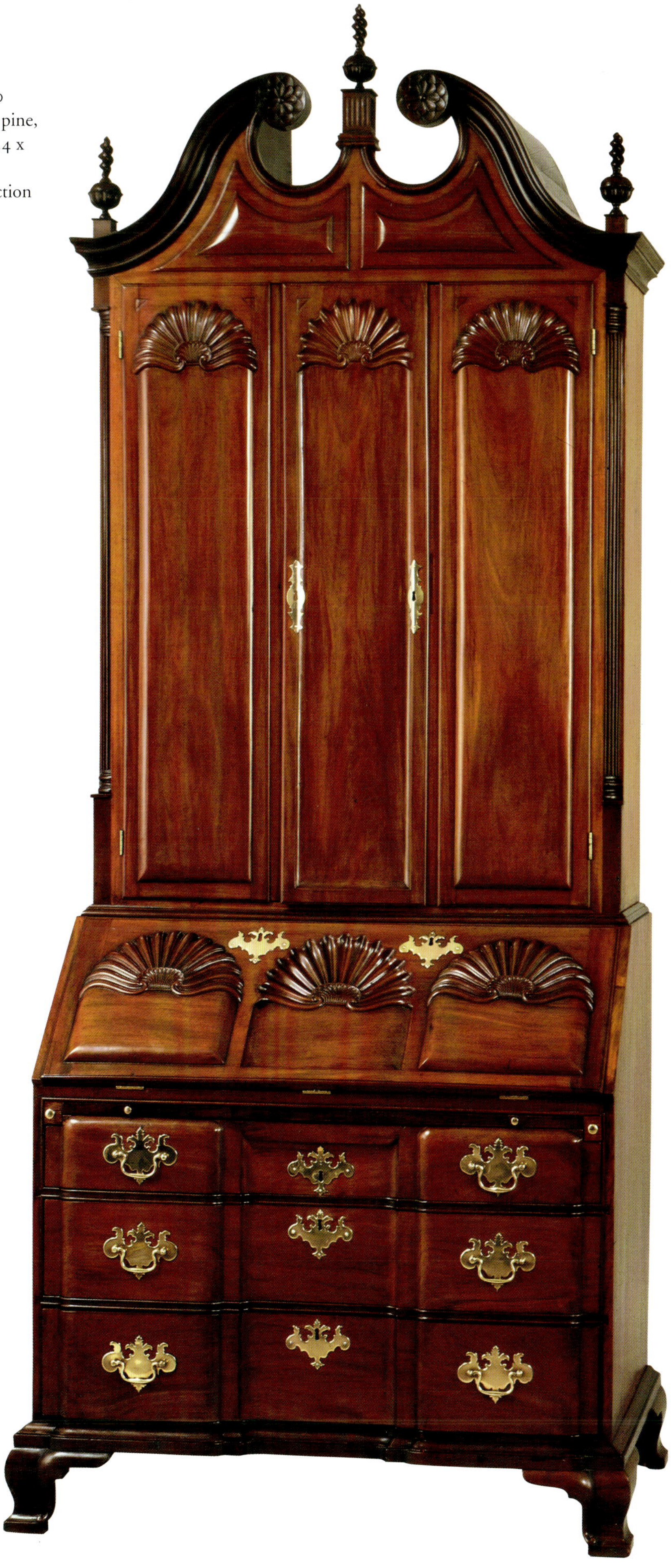

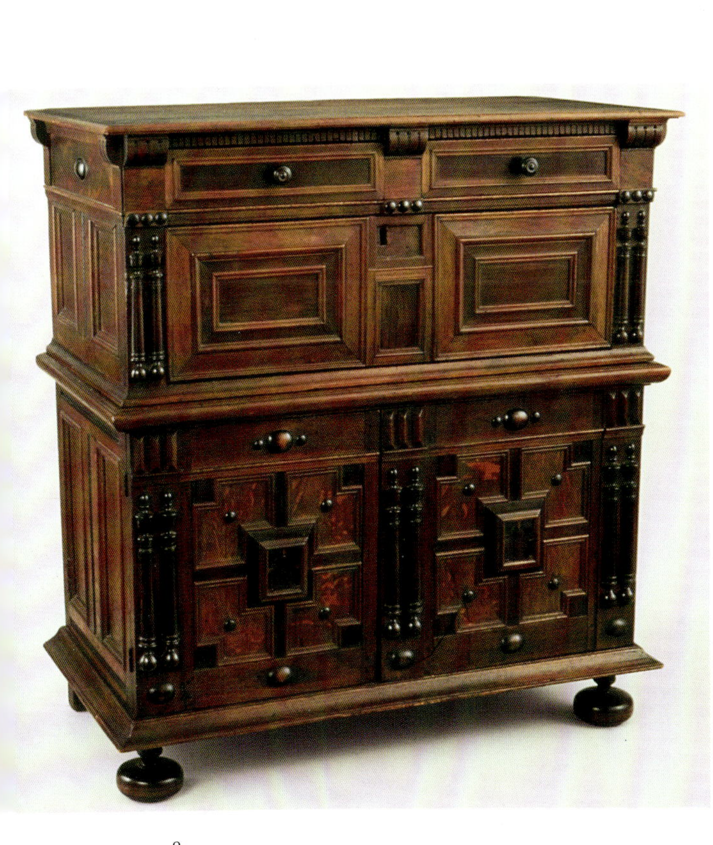

FIG. 81
Maker unknown, Boston
Chest of Drawers with Doors, ca. 1650–75
White oak, red oak, and other woods, 124.1 x 115.3 x 60 cm
Mabel Brady Garvan Collection
1930.2109

FIG. 83
Maker unknown
Lancaster, Pennsylvania
High Chest of Drawers,
ca. 1760–80
American black cherry and other woods, 240.1 x 111.8 x 58.5 cm
Mabel Brady Garvan Collection
1930.2632

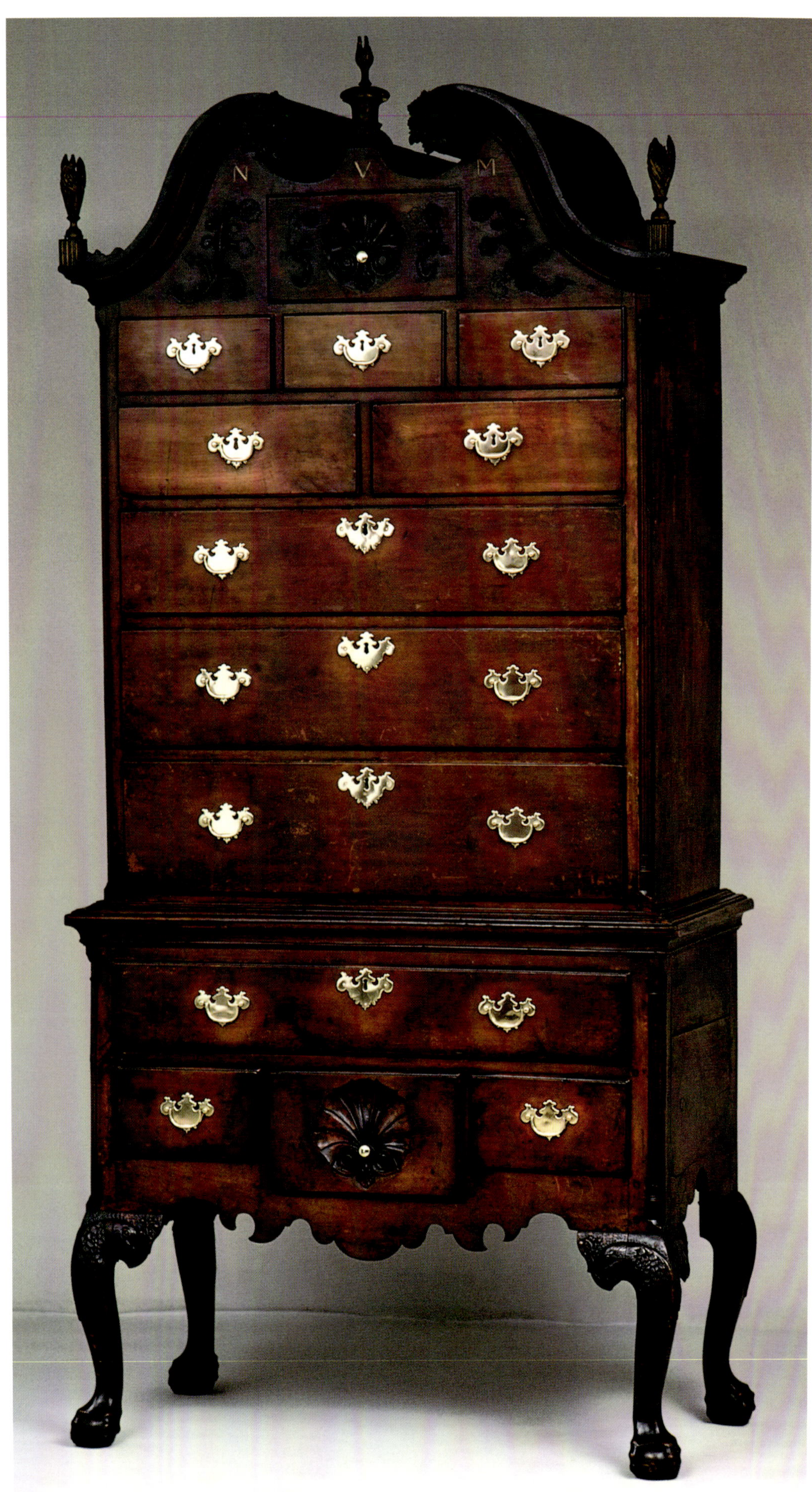

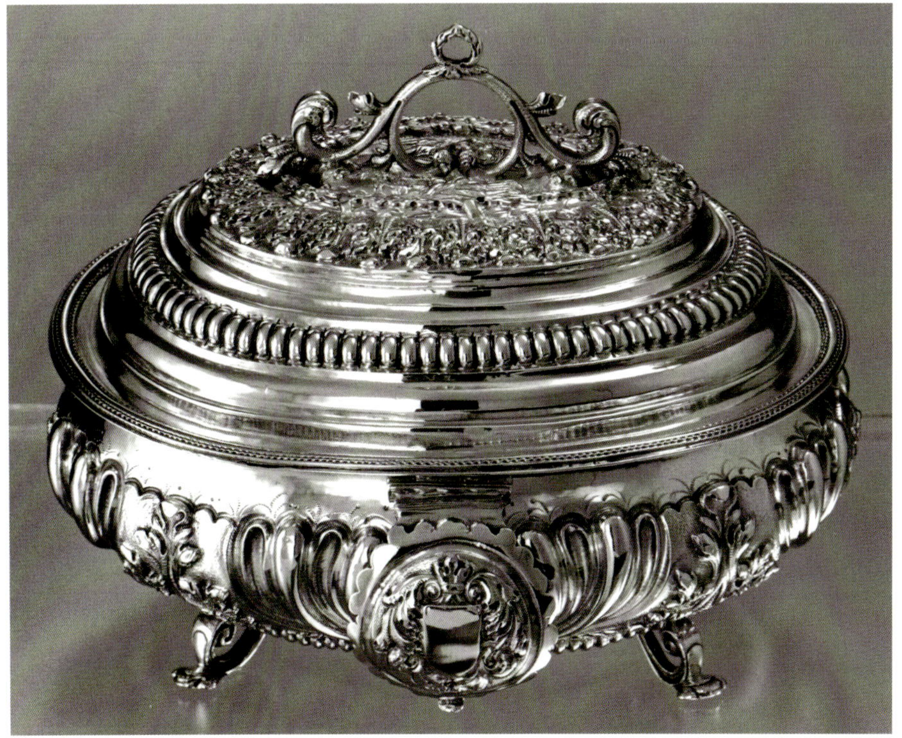

FIG. 84
Edward Winslow
Sugar Box, ca. 1700–1710
Silver, 13.7 x 16.8 x 19.8 cm
Mabel Brady Garvan Collection
1935.152

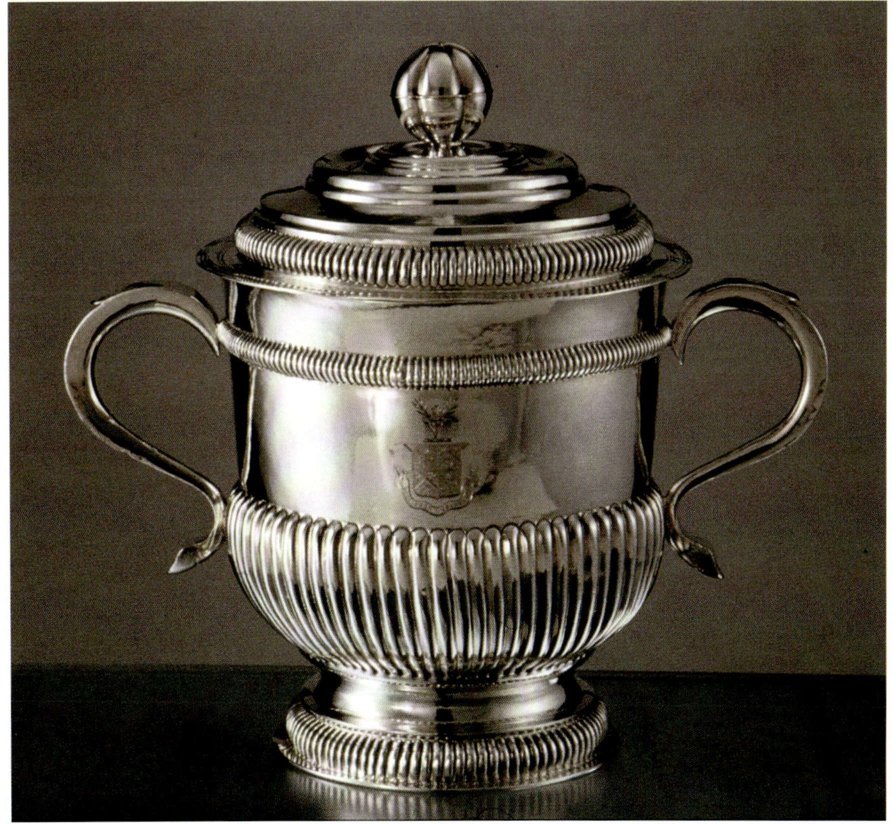

FIG. 85
Edward Winslow
Two-handled Covered Cup, ca. 1710–15
Silver, 27.6 x 30 cm
Mabel Brady Garvan Collection
1932.47

Cup of ca. 1710–15 (fig. 85). The *Cup* is the prized piece shown in the portrait of Garvan reproduced here (fig. 78).

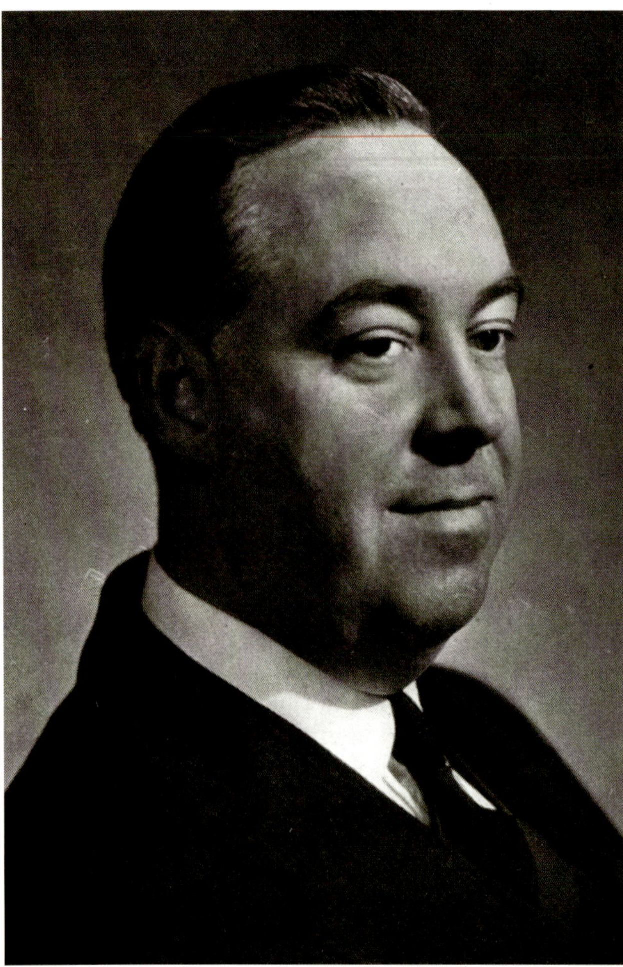

FIG. 86
John Marshall Phillips, ca. 1948
Photograph courtesy Yale University Art Gallery Archives

The importance of the acquisition of the *Sugar Box* was emphasized by John Marshall Phillips (fig. 86), curator of American silver, who organized a champagne party to celebrate its arrival. Phillips joined the Art Gallery staff in 1930. His letter of application for the post was addressed to Garvan, rather than to anyone at Yale, and Theodore Sizer, director at the time, later described his surprise when Phillips presented himself in the director's office to begin work.[15] Although only a few years out of college and holding degrees in English and law rather than art, Phillips was already a skilled connoisseur by the time he arrived at Yale. Having earned money as an undergraduate by buying and selling silver, as he relates in his letter of application, he established his scholarly credentials by publishing a catalogue of the collection of early American silver owned by Maurice Brix of Philadelphia in April 1930.

Once at Yale, Phillips established a laboratory where he systematically examined thousands of pieces of silver from the Garvan Collection for authenticity, and provided a similar service free for the public. He was credited in the press with uncovering legions of forgeries and saving collectors and institutions millions of dollars.[16] Serving in London in the Art Looting Unit of the Office of Strategic Services after the fall of Germany in World War II and assigned to recover Dutch masterpieces stolen by the Nazis, Phillips examined captured documents relating to Dutch art in the collections of, among others, Hermann Goering. Among these documents, he found a letter proving that several paintings said to be by Vermeer were in fact forgeries. Phillips had already suspected them. A seventeenth-century pewter tankard appeared in each of these paintings, but Phillips noticed something about the tankard that had escaped previous experts—namely, that the thumb piece on its lid was a nineteenth-century restoration. Ultimately, as a result of Phillips's discoveries, all of these "Vermeers" were revealed to be the work of the now notorious Johannes van Meegeren.[17]

Phillips was also a member of the faculty from the time he arrived at Yale, and beginning in 1932 he used the Garvan Collection to teach a popular and influential course on early American arts and crafts, soon to be known to all as "Pots and Pans." Frank B. Stone, who in 1933 worked for Phillips in one of the newly created undergraduate "bursary assistant" jobs, took the course, which also included American prints. "A high point," he said, "was an excursion to the Met & Brooklyn collections, followed by a gourmet dinner given us at the Lynx Club by Francis P. Garvan, the patron of the great collection of Americana. . . . My 16-hour a week job as the Bursary Assistant was wide ranging. Routine at first, inventorying, but checking the inventory of the great Whitney print collection displayed in the new Gym. The Currier and Ives were comprehensive, but when I got to the Bellows lithos & a painting on the Boxing Floor, the coach detained me to tell me one of his memories of Dempsey. . . . There was the polishing of the silver and the setting-up of exhibitions, especially the celebration when Johnny Phillips bought the Winslow Box for the collection."[18]

Named curator of the Garvan Collection in 1935, Phillips organized numerous exhibitions, including major shows on early American silver in 1935 and 1939 and, in 1949, the first exhibition since 1730 of the paintings of John Smibert. His book *American Silver* was also published in 1949. Internationally renowned, he was elected a Livery and Freeman of the Worshipful Company of Goldsmiths of the city of London, one of only three Americans to have been so honored. Phillips was named assistant director of the Gallery in 1946, acting director in 1947, and became director, as well as professor of history of art, in 1948; he held these last two posts along with that of curator until his sudden death in 1953, at the age of forty-eight.

Throughout the 1930s the Garvan Collection continued to grow. Faced with diminished resources as the Depression continued, Garvan focused on silver and prints. Families forced by the economic situation to sell extraordinary pieces of silver found a buyer in Garvan. He added several major works to the collection in this way, including the *Two-handled Cup* by Jacob Hurd, known as the "Tyng Cup," having been presented to Commodore Tyng in 1744 by the merchants of Boston in gratitude for his successful routing of French privateers from the Massachusetts coast (fig. 87). Here again, as was typical of Garvan and his wish to be

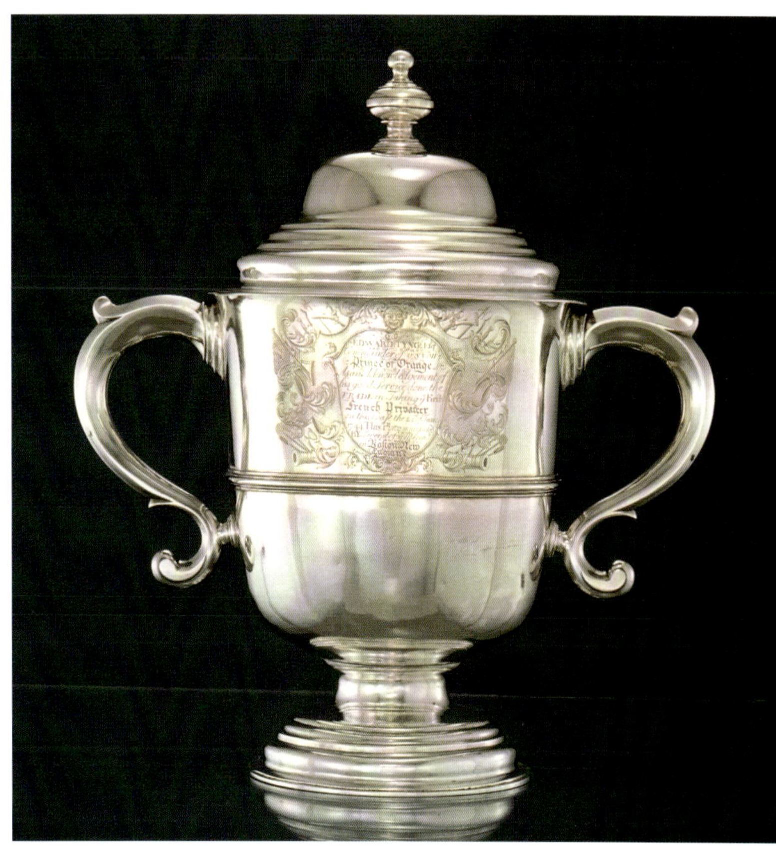

FIG. 87
Jacob Hurd
Two-handled Covered Cup (Tyng Cup), 1744
Silver, 38.4 x 34.9 cm
Mabel Brady Garvan Collection
1932.48

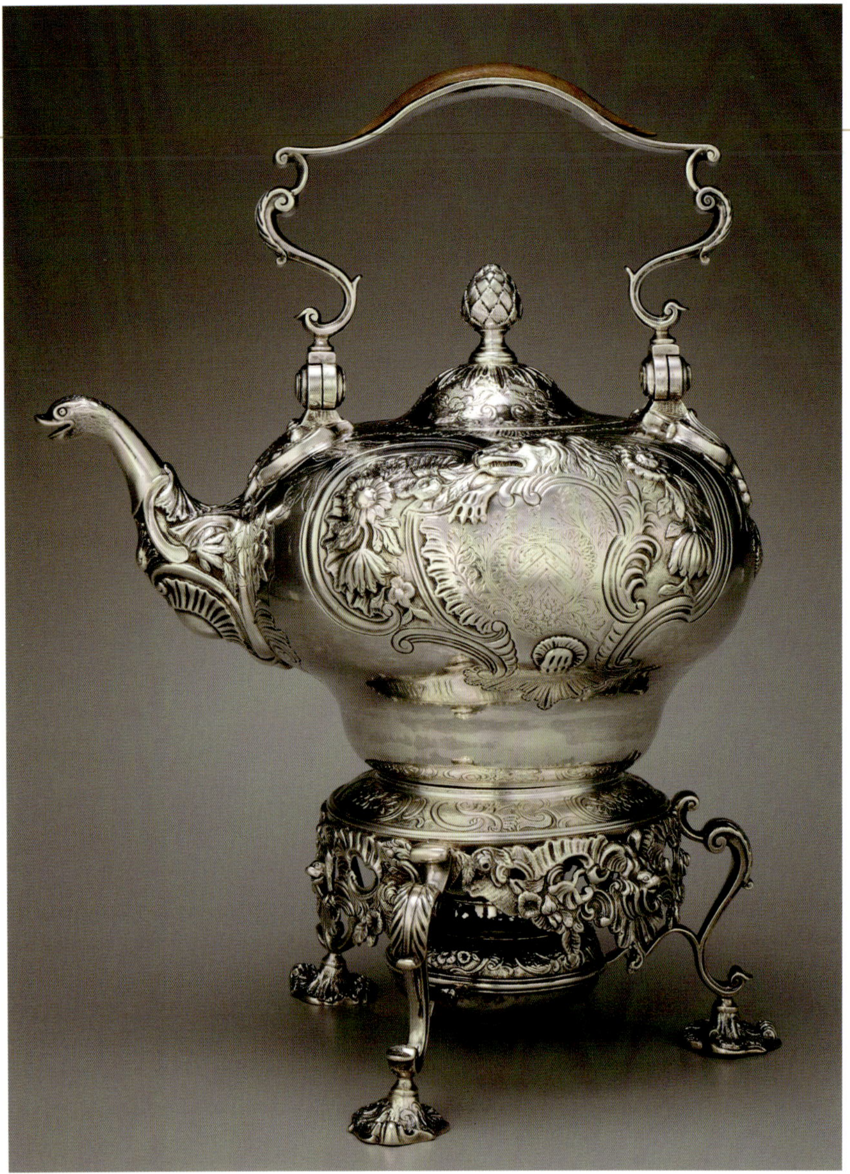

FIG. 88
Joseph Richardson, Sr.
Tea Kettle on Stand,
ca. 1745–55
Silver, 28.1 x 28.3 cm
Mabel Brady Garvan Collection
1932.93

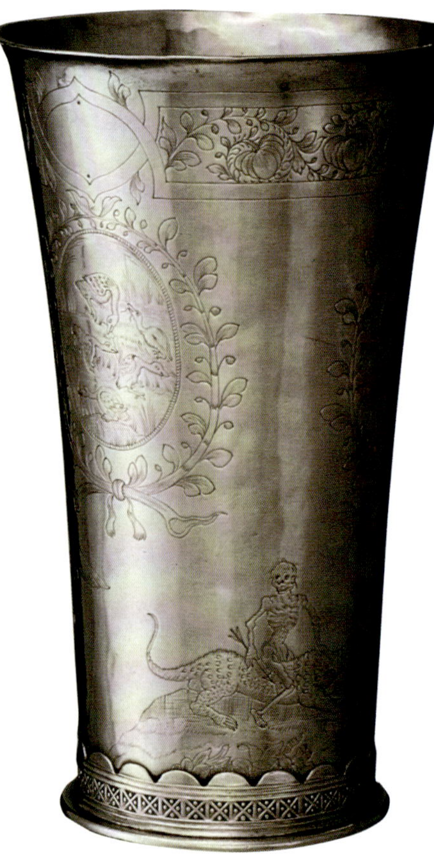

FIG. 89
Cornelius van der Burch
Beaker, 1685
Silver, 20.3 cm
Mabel Brady Garvan Collection
1932.100

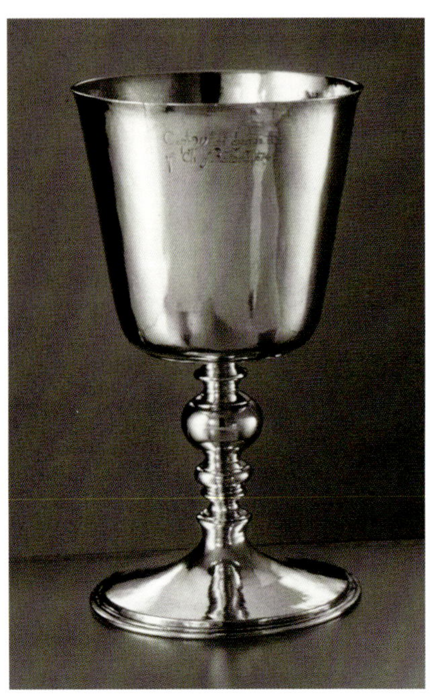

FIG. 90
Robert Sanderson and John Hull
Wine Cup, ca. 1665
Silver, 18.6 cm
Mabel Brady Garvan Collection
1936.137

comprehensive, several works by Hurd, another Boston silversmith, are included in the collection. Joseph Richardson, Sr.'s *Tea Kettle on Stand* of ca. 1745–55, an outstanding example of Philadelphia craftsmanship (fig. 88), and the *Beaker* by Cornelius van der Burch, a New York City silversmith (1685; fig. 89), were also given in 1932. Several pieces by Myer Myers added to the collection in 1936 are rare works by an important Jewish silversmith working in New York City from the mid-eighteenth century, complementing the group of Myer Myers objects given in 1930.[19] The elegant *Wine Cup* by Robert Sanderson and John Hull, created in Boston ca. 1665 (fig. 90), was also acquired in 1936, as part of Garvan's purchase of all of the communion silver from the Rehoboth Church.

Thanks to Garvan, Yale possesses the largest and most important collection of early American gold in any institution. Several particularly significant gold objects were part of the Garvan gift in 1930, including the so-called *Freedom Box* by Samuel Johnson, engraved by Peter Maverick (fig. 91). Made in 1784 in New York City, this box was given to Major General Frederic Wilhelm Augustus, Baron von Steuben, on October 11, 1784. This was the same year in which Baron von Steuben received a gold-hilted sword and an official vote of thanks from the United States Congress for his distinguished service, notably his training of U.S. troops at Valley Forge and elsewhere in a version of Prussian discipline and his universally adopted manual on military regulations and discipline, during the Revolutionary War. The sword, made by the British silversmith John Bennett II, also came to Yale with the Garvan gift in 1930. The *Freedom Box* bears engraving on its cover showing the arms, crest, and motto of the city of New York, and on the sides an inscription stating: "PRESENTED BY THE CORPORATION OF THE CITY OF NEW YORK WITH THE FREEDOM OF THE CITY." Inscriptions on the bottom of the box indicate that it was bequeathed to Baron von Steuben's aide-de-camp, friend, and ultimately his adopted son, William North, who in turn bequeathed it to his own son, William Augustus Stephen North. Baron von Steuben's portrait by Ralph Earl is also in the Yale collection (fig. 92). The circumstances in which this box was made and the role of its owner as a hero of the Revolution were, given

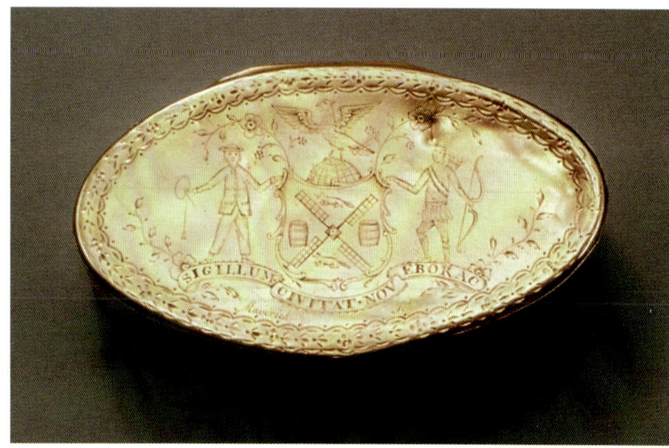

FIG. 91
Samuel Johnson, maker, Peter Maverick, engraver
Freedom Box, 1784
Gold, 18 x 83 x 49 mm
Mabel Brady Garvan Collection
1930.1100

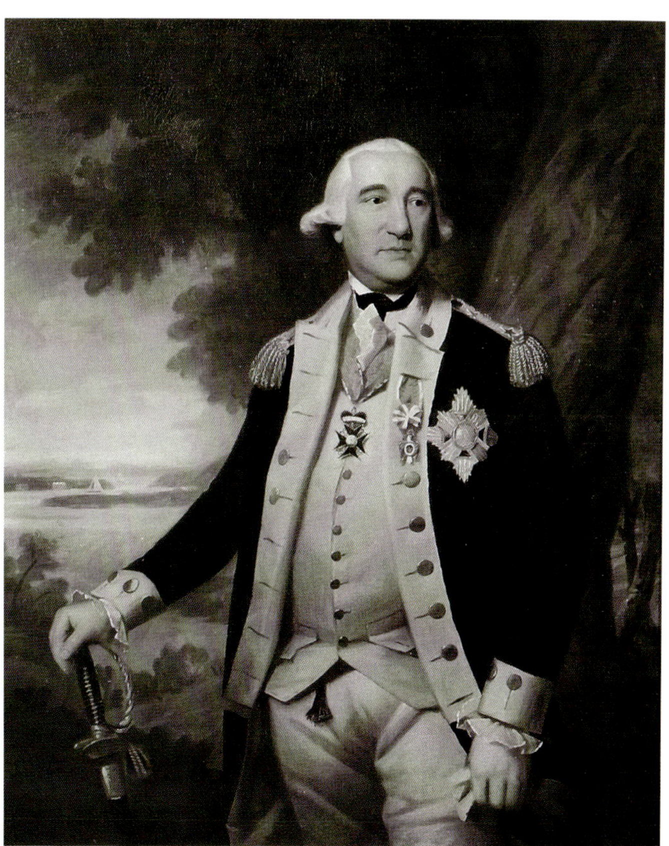

FIG. 92
Ralph Earl
Major General Frederic Wilhelm Augustus, Baron von Steuben, ca. 1786
Oil on canvas, 126.4 x 105.1 cm
Gift of Mrs. Paul Moore in memory of Howard Melville Hanna, Jr., B.A. 1931
1939.14

FIG. 93
Daniel Christian Fueter
Rattle, ca. 1765
Gold and coral, 13.2 cm
Mabel Brady Garvan Collection: Gift of Mrs. Francis P. Garvan, James R. Graham, Walter M. Jeffords, and Mrs. Paul Moore
1942.91

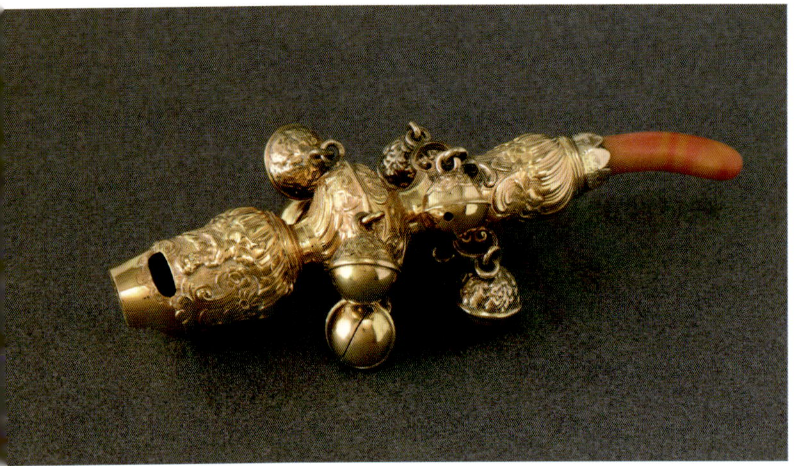

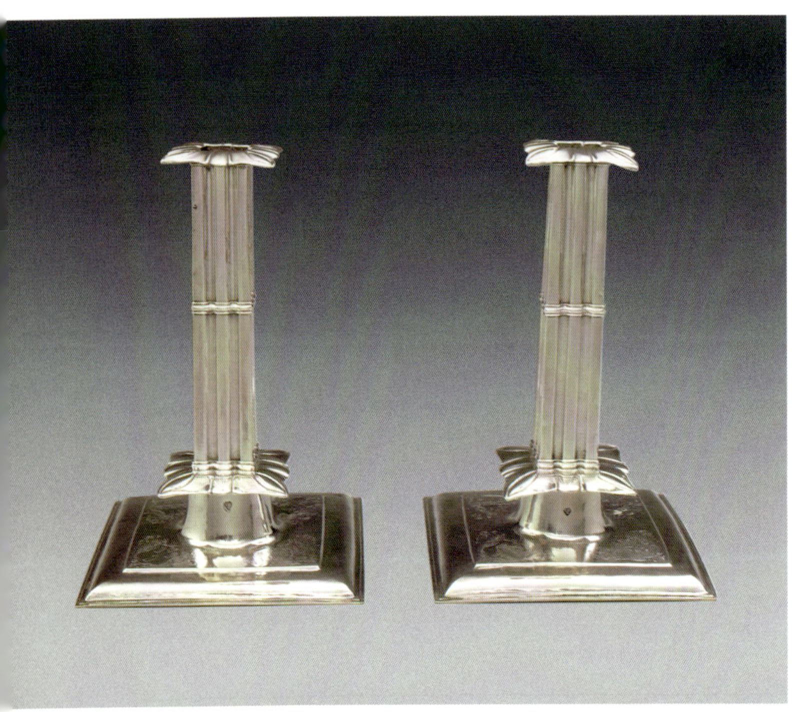

FIG. 94
Jeremiah Dummer
Pair of Candlesticks, ca. 1685
Silver, each 27.5 x 18.9 x 18.9 cm
Mabel Brady Garvan Collection
1935.234 and 1953.22.1

Garvan's interest in American history and the Trumbull paintings at Yale, associations that made a compelling argument for acquiring this work for the collection. The Gallery continued to acquire early American gold after Garvan's death. Among these later acquisitions is the rare gold rattle with gold bells and a smooth coral end for sucking (fig. 93). Made by Daniel Christian Fueter, a Swiss silversmith active in New York, around 1765, it remains one of the most important pieces in the Yale collection.

Acquisitions since Mr. Garvan's death in 1937 have built on the strengths of his collection and also expanded its range into the late nineteenth and twentieth centuries. John Marshall Phillips acquired important works in silver, such as the *Candlestick* (one of a pair) by Jeremiah Dummer of Boston (ca. 1685; fig. 94) that matches the one given by Garvan in 1935. John Coney's *Monteith Bowl* (ca. 1705; fig. 95) broadened the range of works by this Boston craftsman previously given to Yale. Phillips, followed by Meyric R. Rogers and Jules D. Prown, his successors as curators of the Garvan Collection from 1958 to 1968, continued to pursue Garvan's goal of a comprehensive collection of the best examples available, and they did not hesitate to upgrade the collection when the opportunity arose. All continued Garvan's focus on Colonial and Federal period artifacts. Charles F. Montgomery, curator from 1970 to 1978, expanded the range of the collection to include works from the later nineteenth century and the modern era. Patricia E. Kane, curator since 1978, has continued to expand the furniture collection in these areas, including pieces by Gustav Stickley, Henry and Charles Sumner Greene, Donald Deskey, Frank Gehry, and Judy McKie. Late nineteenth-century silver acquired since 1970 includes works by Tiffany and Company and the Gorham Manufacturing Company. Patricia Kane has focused extensively on twentieth-century and contemporary silver, adding important works by Elizabeth Copeland, the Kalo Shops, Ilonka Karasz, Ralph T. Walker for the firm of Graff, Washbourne, and Dunn, Hans Christiansen, and Michael Graves (*Tea and Coffee Service*, for Officina Alessi, 1984–85; fig. 96).

Garvan's strategy for collecting silver and furniture carried over into his collecting in pewter, ceramics, glass, and other materials. As with silver, most of

FIG. 95
John Coney
Montieth Bowl, ca. 1705
Silver, 21.9 cm
Mabel Brady Garvan Collection
1948.148

FIG. 96
Michael Graves
Tea and Coffee Service, 1984–85
Silver, plastic, and blue enamel,
21.0 x 27.0 cm
Funded by Jeanette Cressler, the Mabel Brady Garvan and Leonard C. Hanna, Jr., B.A. 1913, Funds, the Barra Foundation, Mrs. Alfred E. Bissell, the Dobson Foundation, Virginia and Leonard Marx Foundation, Dr. and Mrs. Matthew Newman, and Theodore E. Stebbins, Jr., B.A. 1960, in honor of Mrs. Charles F. Montgomery.
1985.91.1.1–6

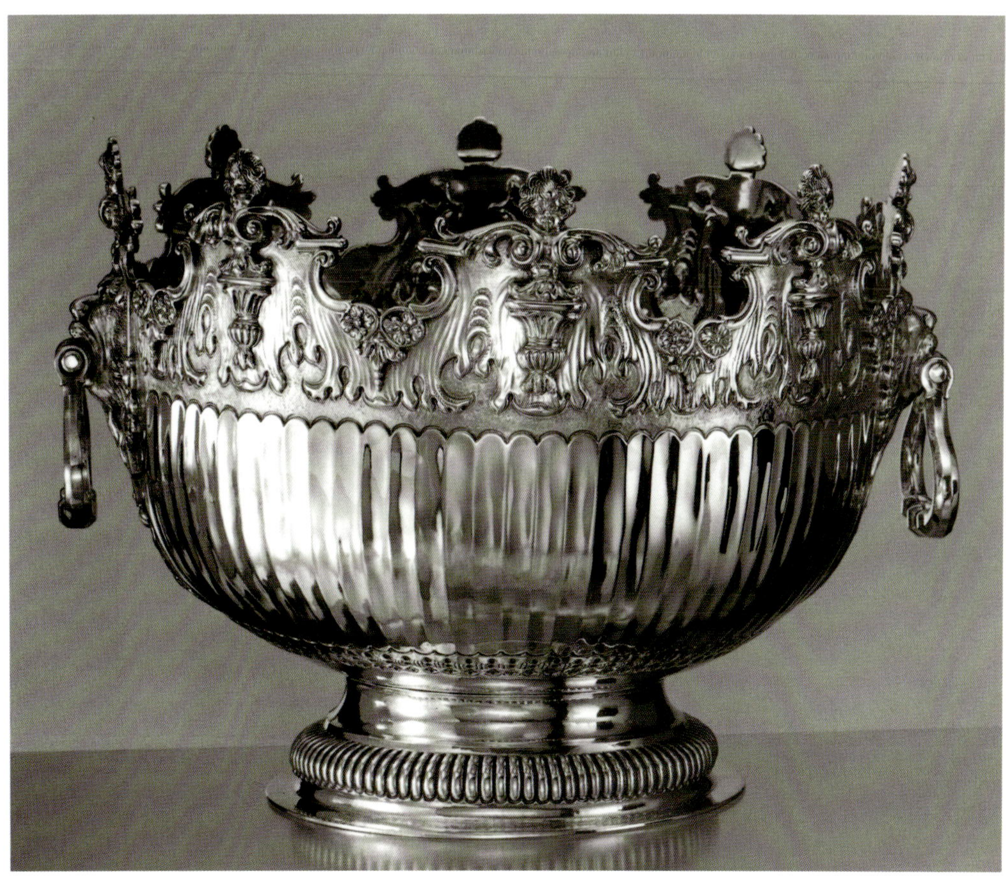

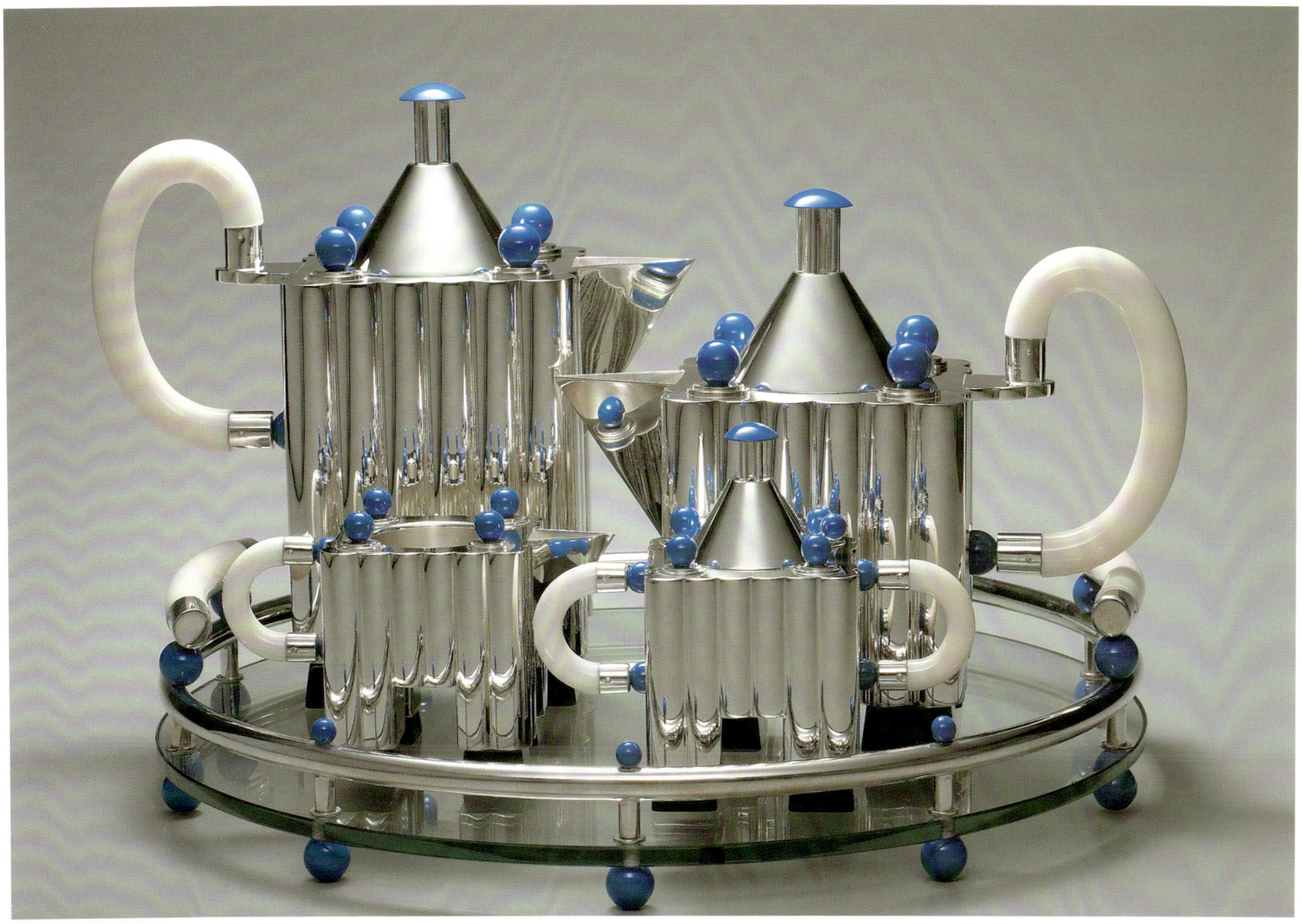

Garvan's purchases in pewter were from the eighteenth and early nineteenth centuries, and he strove to acquire rare and fine examples in this base metal as he had in the more precious mediums. The purchase of Louis Guerineau Myers's collection of some 375 pieces in 1929 provided an unusually strong foundation. Myers was a pioneering scholar of pewter whose books influenced Garvan, and his collection, begun in 1904, contained outstanding pieces by Henry Will and Simon Edgell. Francis Bassett, Johan Christoph Heyne, Boardman and Company, Daniel Curtis, and George Richardson are also represented in the Garvan Collection. Having begun his pewter collection in 1917 and generally having paid no more than $50 for a piece, Garvan was collecting largely for himself at first. By the late 1920s, however, once he had begun to consider giving his holdings to Yale, he began to increase the scope of the pewter collection and to pay top prices to obtain rare or important objects. The collection that Garvan donated to Yale was the first major collection of pewter to enter an American museum.[20]

Garvan also donated an important collection of iron, found with the assistance of Frank McCarthy, who scouted out examples in houses throughout New England. Garvan's glass collecting seems to have aimed at assembling pieces representative of regional workshops and the broad range of glassmaking techniques and vessel shapes. In this endeavor, he was aided by Rhea Mansfield Knittle, a prominent scholar whose *Early American Glass*, published in 1927, was considered the best synthesis of the field. Whatever material he was collecting, Garvan strove to secure the best available advice and when possible purchased from distinguished collections. In ceramics, Garvan bought extensively from the collection of Dr. Edwin Atlee Barber, whose *Marks of American Potters* published in 1904 remained the standard reference work for decades, when the collection was auctioned in Philadelphia in 1917, after Dr. Barber's death. Garvan's purchases in this field encompassed stonewares, earthenwares, and porcelain made throughout the colonies and the United States, as well as English ceramics and Chinese export porcelain, including a plate made for George Washington around 1783. The Garvan Collection also includes several textiles. In each of these media, as in furniture and silver, late nineteenth- and twentieth-century works have been added to the collection in recent years. Other new directions in which the collection is now being expanded include the broadening of Garvan's focus on work of the northeastern United States to encompass decorative arts from other regions of the country.

In addition to his extraordinary collections of American decorative arts, Garvan collected paintings, sculpture, and prints. His particular interest was subject matter, and this is reflected in the Whitney Collections of Sporting Art, his first gift to Yale of works other than decorative arts. Revealing his own personal interest in athletics and his belief in athletics as an important component of education, he stated, "Culture include[s] the cultivation of the body to its highest perfection, . . . sport is more than play, . . . it is a proving ground for the exemplification of the laws of right living and fair play."[21] The collection was given in memory of Garvan's two Yale College friends Harry Payne Whitney (B.A. 1894) and Payne Whitney (B.A. 1898), and meant to hang in the Payne Whitney Gymnasium. Included in it are representations of almost every American sport, another example of Garvan's drive to be comprehensive.

The collection includes forty-nine paintings, twenty sculptures, and nearly nine hundred prints, largely by artists of the second half of the nineteenth century. It was this collection that Frank Stone spent time as a bursary assistant cataloguing in 1933. Among the artists are Thomas Eakins, George Bellows, Frederic Remington, and Currier and Ives. Some of the paintings, notably Eakins's *Taking the Count* (1898; fig. 97) and *John Biglin in a Single Scull* (1874; fig. 98), which now hang in the Art Gallery, were the first works by these artists to enter the Yale collection. Hunting scenes and horse portraits were favored themes, and they are represented by the best American artists working on those subjects, including Arthur F. Tait and Edward Troye. In contrast to the paintings and prints that are primarily from the nineteenth century, the sculpture in the Whitney Collections dates to the first three decades of the twentieth. Paul Manship and Robert Tait McKenzie are among the popular sculptors represented in the collection. Works by both evoke Greek ideal forms, echoing the Olympic feeling of Garvan's statement of the value of athletics.

Although the founding gift for the Mabel Brady

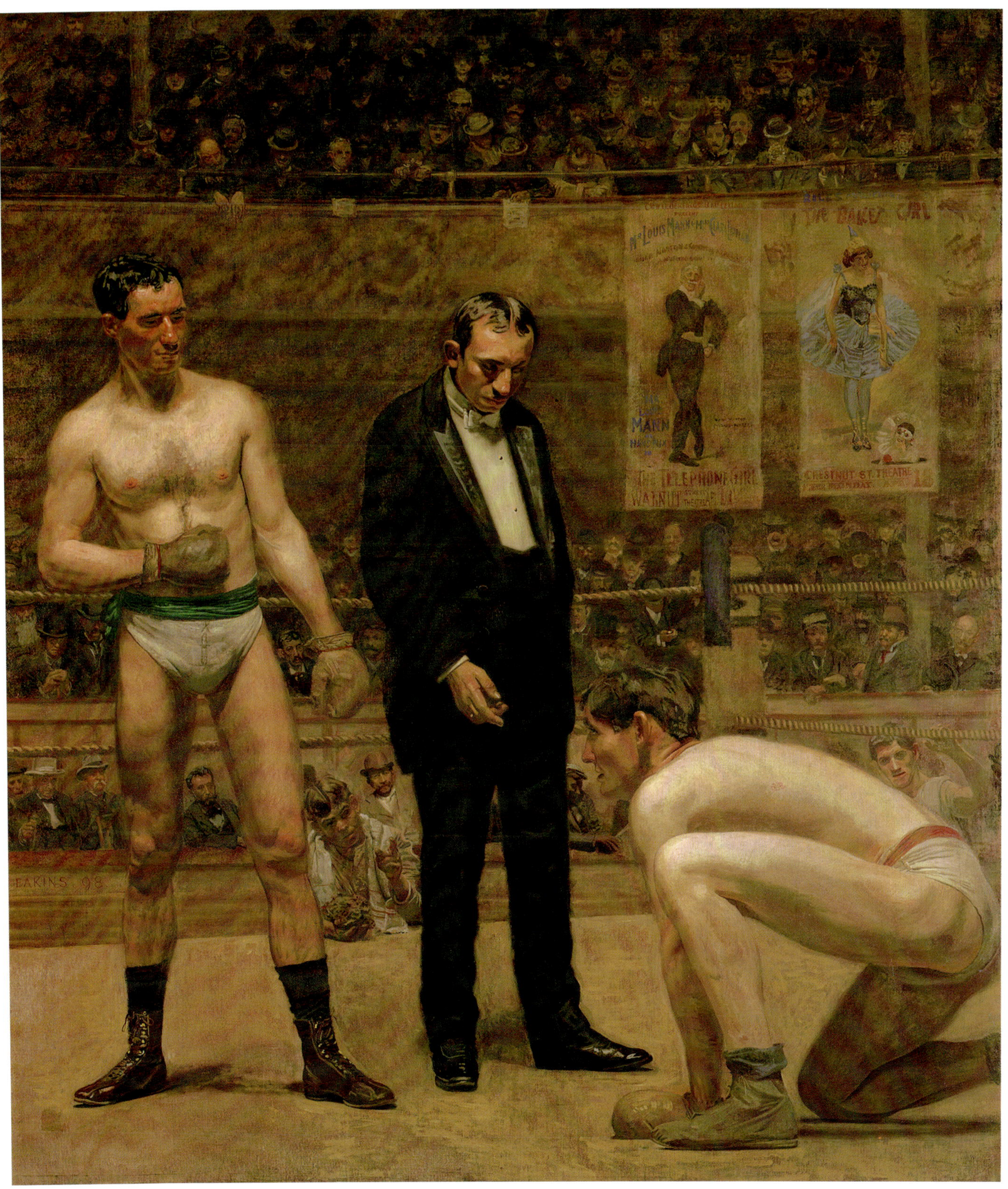

FIG. 97
Thomas Eakins
Taking the Count, 1898
Oil on canvas, 244.5 x 214 cm
Whitney Collections of Sporting Art, given in memory of Harry Payne Whitney, B.A. 1894, and Payne Whitney, B.A. 1898, by Francis P. Garvan, B.A. 1897 (Hon.) M.A. 1922
1932.262

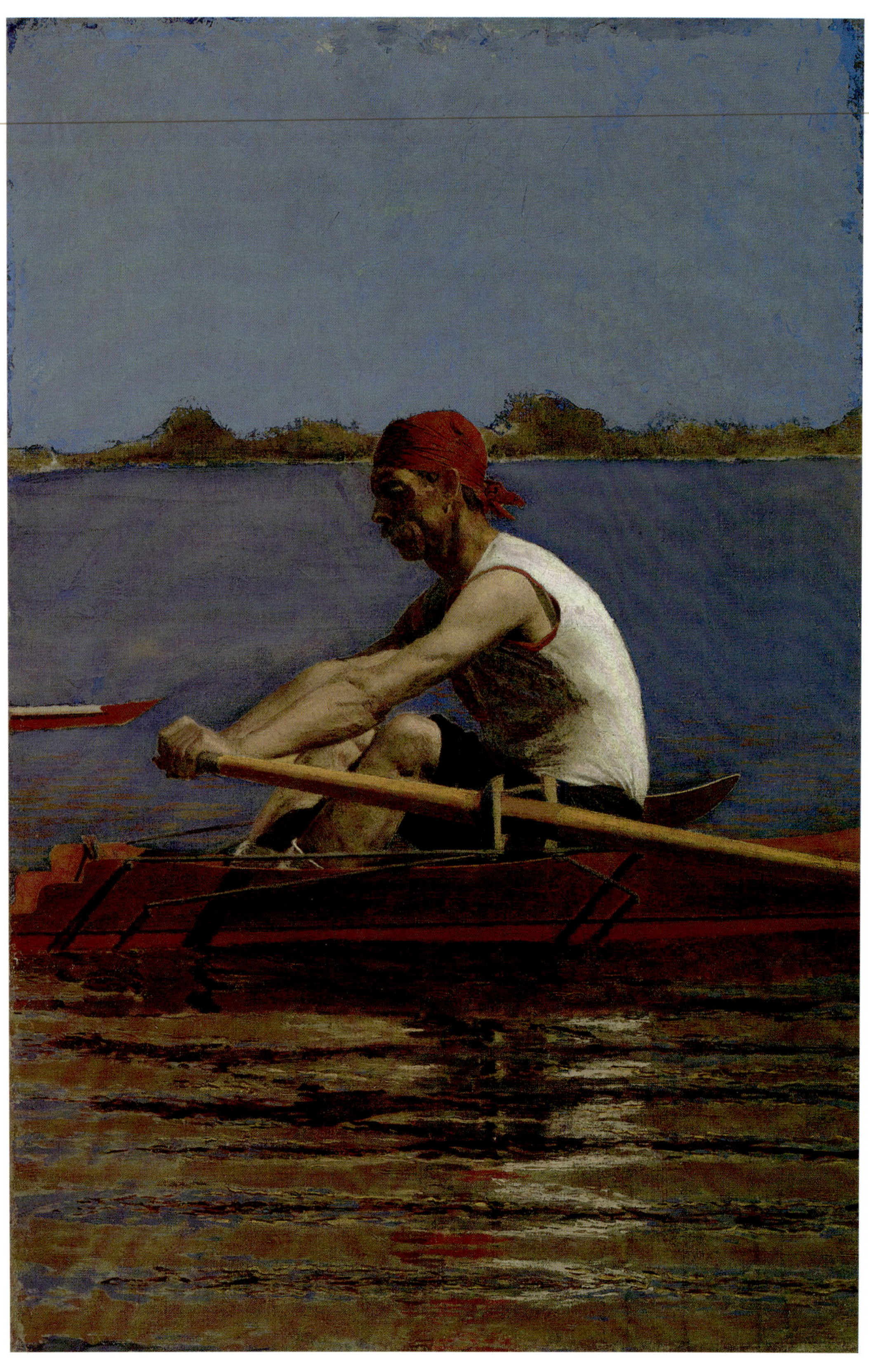

FIG. 98
Thomas Eakins
John Biglin in a Single Scull, 1874
Oil on canvas, 65.4 x 43.8 cm
Whitney Collections of Sporting Art, given in memory of Harry Payne Whitney, B.A. 1894, and Payne Whitney, B.A. 1898, by Francis P. Garvan, B.A. 1897 (Hon.), 1922
1932.263

Garvan Collection in 1930 did not include paintings, sculpture, or prints, works in all these media were subsequently added to the collection. Garvan assembled an extensive collection of paintings in the 1920s and early 1930s, and although many of them were on loan to the Gallery at the time of his death in 1937, after his death many of these loans were dispersed or sold. Nevertheless, seventy American paintings, some of them important, came to the Gallery as part of the Garvan Collection, and fifteen or more have subsequently been added by refining the collection.

The majority of the paintings in the Garvan Collection are portraits. Among them are the portrait of *William Buckland* (1789; fig. 99) and two portrait miniatures by Charles Willson Peale, one of *Mrs. George Washington (Martha Dandridge Custis)*, dated 1772. Two paintings by John Trumbull are part of the Garvan Collection: *Lieutenant Thomas Grosvenor (1744–1825) and His Negro Servant* (ca. 1797), and *Norwich Falls* (or *The Falls of the Yantic at Norwich*) (1806). John Smibert's portrait of *Edward Winslow*, the Boston silversmith whose treasured *Sugar Box* Garvan had earlier given to Yale, was bought and presented because of this connection. Similarly, Garvan bought and presented a portrait of Commodore Tyng, the original recipient of the Tyng cup (formerly attributed to John Smibert; now conceded to be by an unknown artist). A portrait of the commodore's wife by John Smibert was later acquired for the Gallery by the Associates in Fine Arts. Garvan was particularly interested in American subjects, as is revealed by his purchase of paintings such as the three views of Charleston by S. Barnard (1831), a *Moonlit Landscape with Indians* attributed to Ralph Albert Blakelock (1880), the *Capture of the "Serapis" by John Paul Jones* by James Hamilton (1854), *Illustrations for Tom Sawyer* by John George Brown (1899), and John Quidor, *Ichabod Crane Flying from the Headless Horseman* (ca. 1828; fig. 100). Other paintings originally owned by Mr. Garvan were added to the Mabel Brady Garvan Collection after his death, including *Street Scene with Snow (57th Street, NYC)*, by Robert Henri (1902; fig. 101). Henri was a member of the Ashcan School, a group of early twentieth-century realist painters who regularly exhibited in New York. Contemporary critics praised Henri's realism as particularly American, an idea that would have added to his appeal for Garvan.

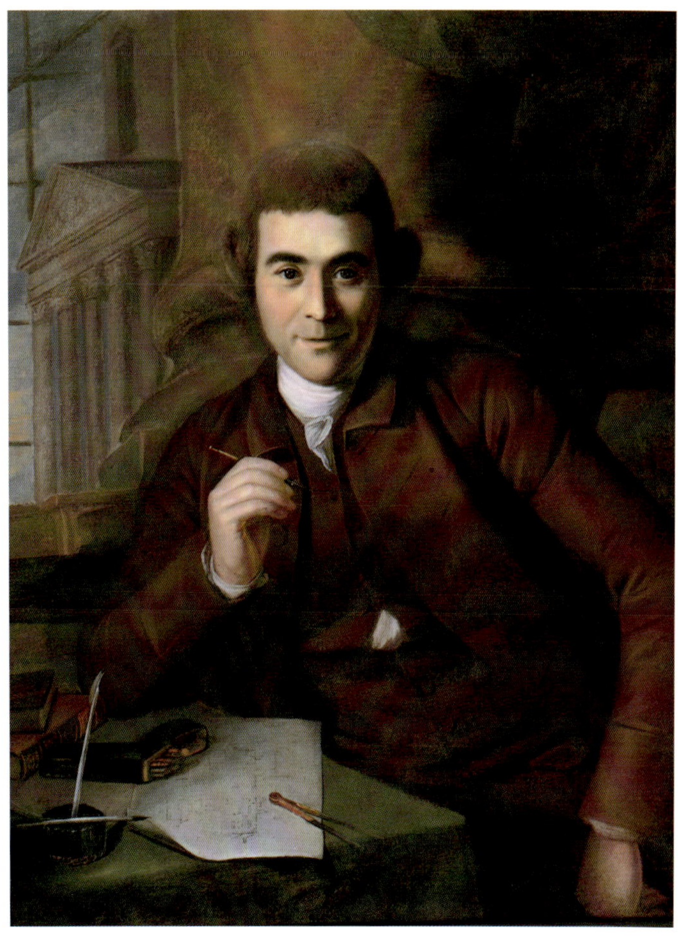

FIG. 99
Charles Willson Peale
William Buckland, 1789
Oil on canvas, 69.9 x 93 cm
Mabel Brady Garvan Collection
1934.303

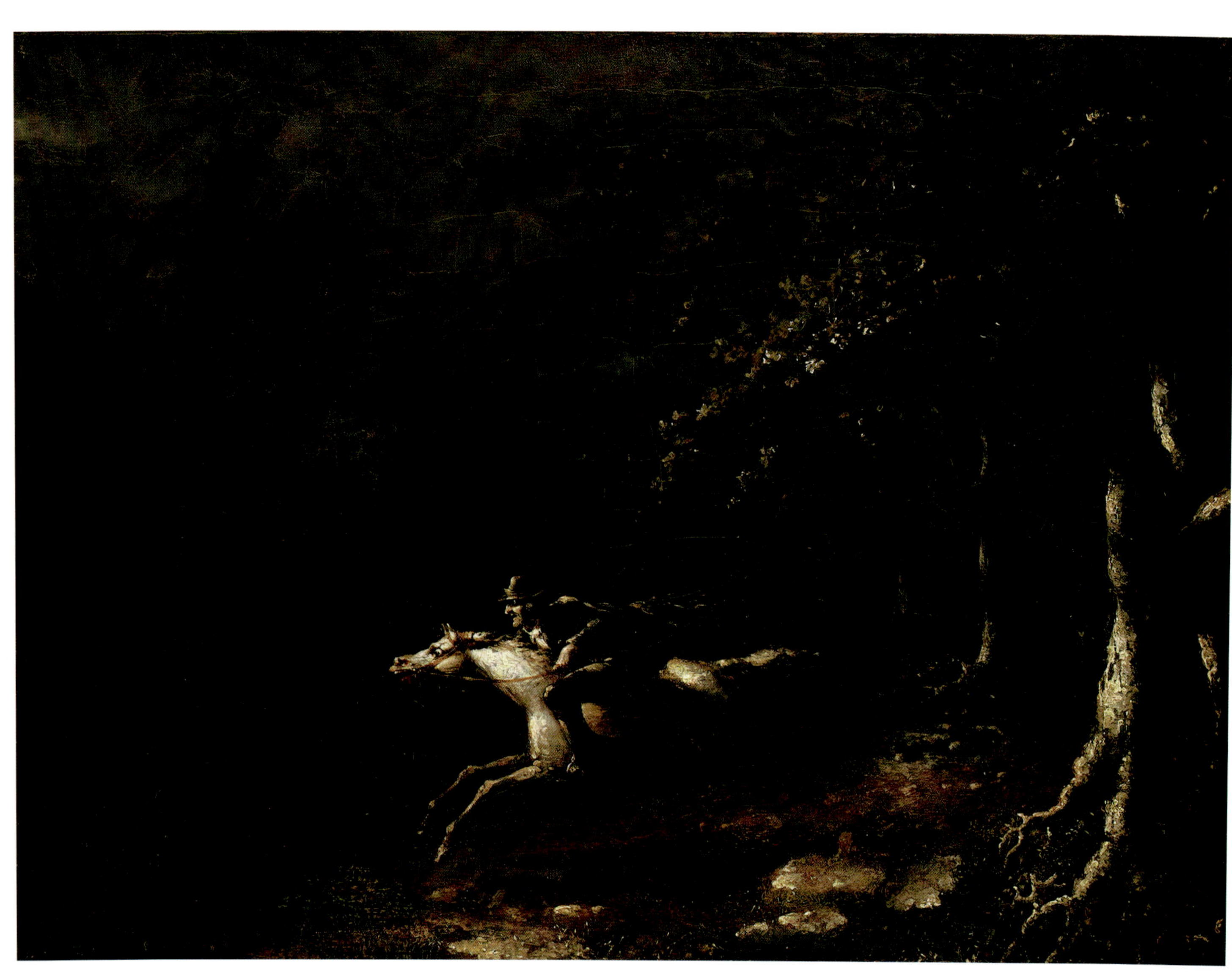

FIG. 100
John Quidor
Ichabod Crane Flying from the Headless Horseman, ca. 1828
Oil on canvas, 57.5 x 76.4 cm
Mabel Brady Garvan Collection
1948.68

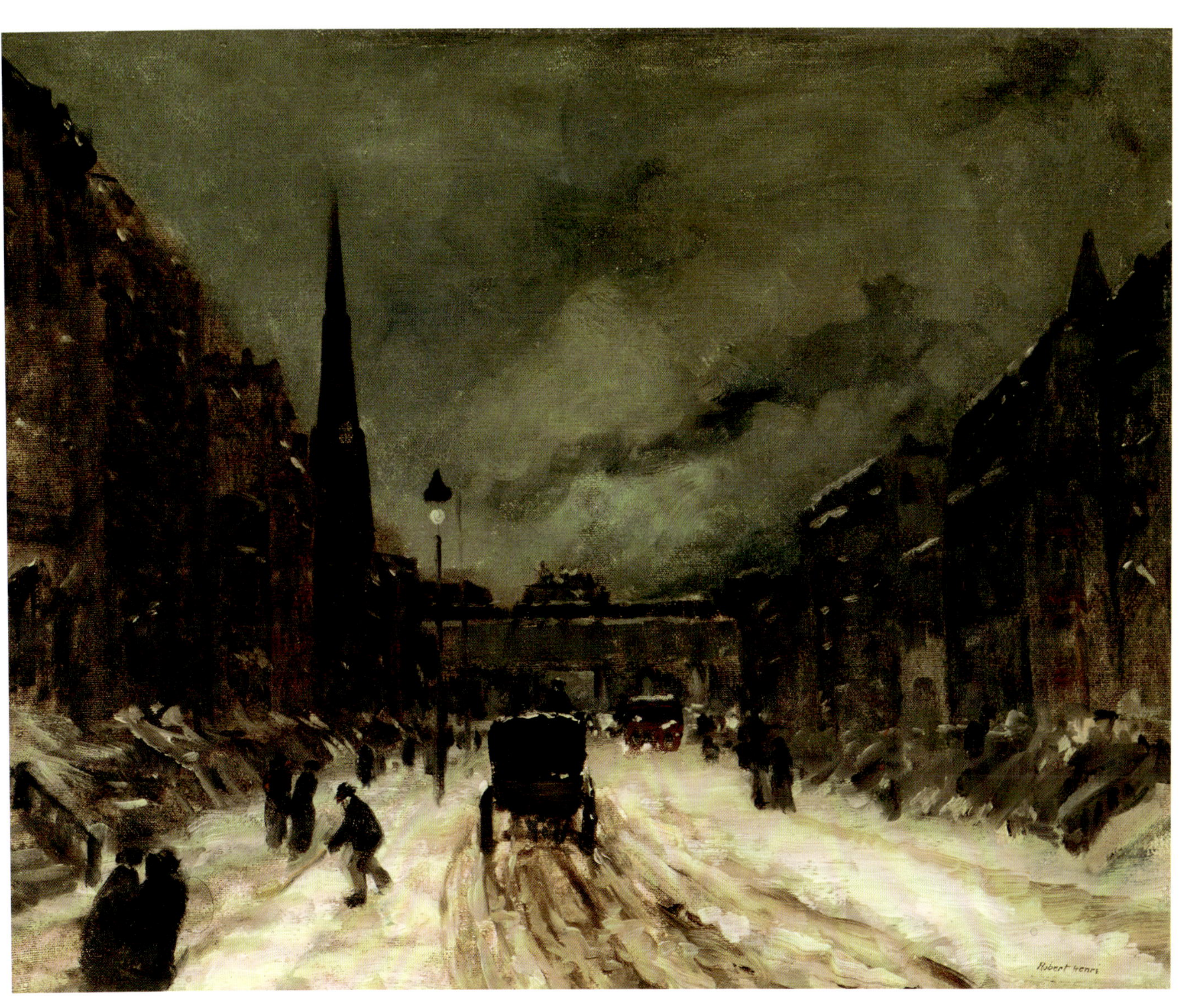

FIG. 101
Robert Henri
Street Scene with Snow (57th Street, NYC), 1902
Oil on canvas, 66 x 81.3 cm
Mabel Brady Garvan Collection
1947.185

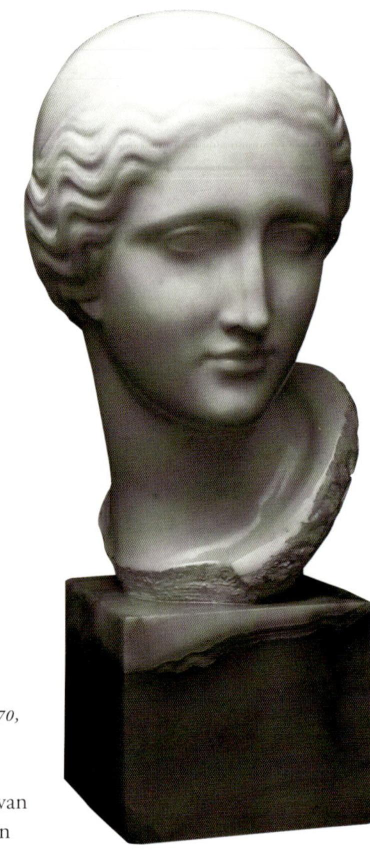

FIG. 102
Elie Nadelman
Classical Head, ca. 1910
Marble, 36.8 x 24.1 x 27.3 cm
Gift of Mrs. Francis P. Garvan
1950.724

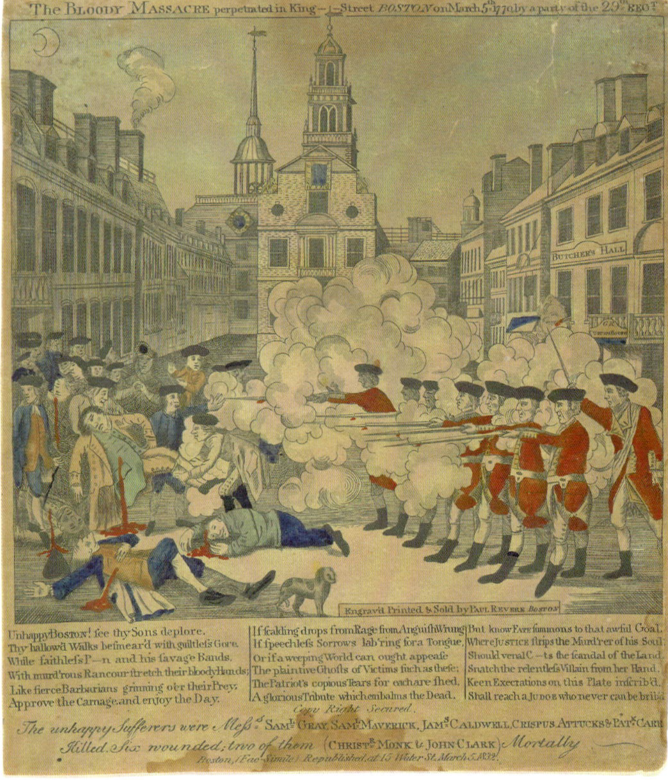

FIG. 103
Paul Revere II
Bloody Massacre, Boston, 1770, ca. 1770 (restrike 1832)
Engraving, 25.4 x 22.9 cm
Gift of Mrs. Francis P. Garvan for the Mabel Brady Garvan Collection
1950.124

The sculpture in the Garvan Collection can likewise be divided into nineteenth-century and contemporary works. The nineteenth century is represented by the popular John Rogers groups, widely owned by the public for their subjects, which were often commemorative or inspirational although generally secular. More than forty of these groups came to the Gallery. Early twentieth-century sculpture in the Garvan Collection features work by the sculptor Elie Nadelman. His *Classical Head* (fig. 102), evoking ancient Greek style, and the portrait of the Garvan's daughter *Patricia Garvan,* who died as a young girl, were gifts to the Gallery from Mabel Brady Garvan.

Mr. and Mrs. Garvan gave five thousand prints to Yale in 1934, comprising a collection heavily weighted toward portraits and historical events in America up to the time of the Civil War. As with his collection of sporting art, the subject was the important feature. The collection was ultimately edited down to two thousand prints, among which are significant groups of military and naval battle scenes from the Revolutionary War, the War of 1812, and the Civil War, and a group associated with the cult of George Washington that gripped the young nation after the death of the Father of the Country. It also now includes famous single images such as the *Bloody Massacre* by Paul Revere II, a political broadside of 1770 that commemorated the firing on colonial civilians in Boston by British troops now commonly known as the Boston Massacre (fig. 103). Among the portraits is a mezzotint of Cotton Mather (1728) by Peter Pelham, the first print in this technique to have been produced in America.

Had Mr. Garvan lived beyond his untimely death in 1937, he would no doubt have continued to add to the collections as well as to develop his idea for disseminating knowledge about them and American art in general to all Americans. His family has continued generously to build on his goals, both for the collection and for the interpretation of it in publication and installation in the galleries of the Mabel Brady Garvan and Related Collections of American Art at Yale. In giving this extraordinary collection and sharing his vision for it, Francis P. Garvan established what remains one of the premier collections of American decorative arts in the world and ensured that the Yale Art Gallery would always be a leader in this field.

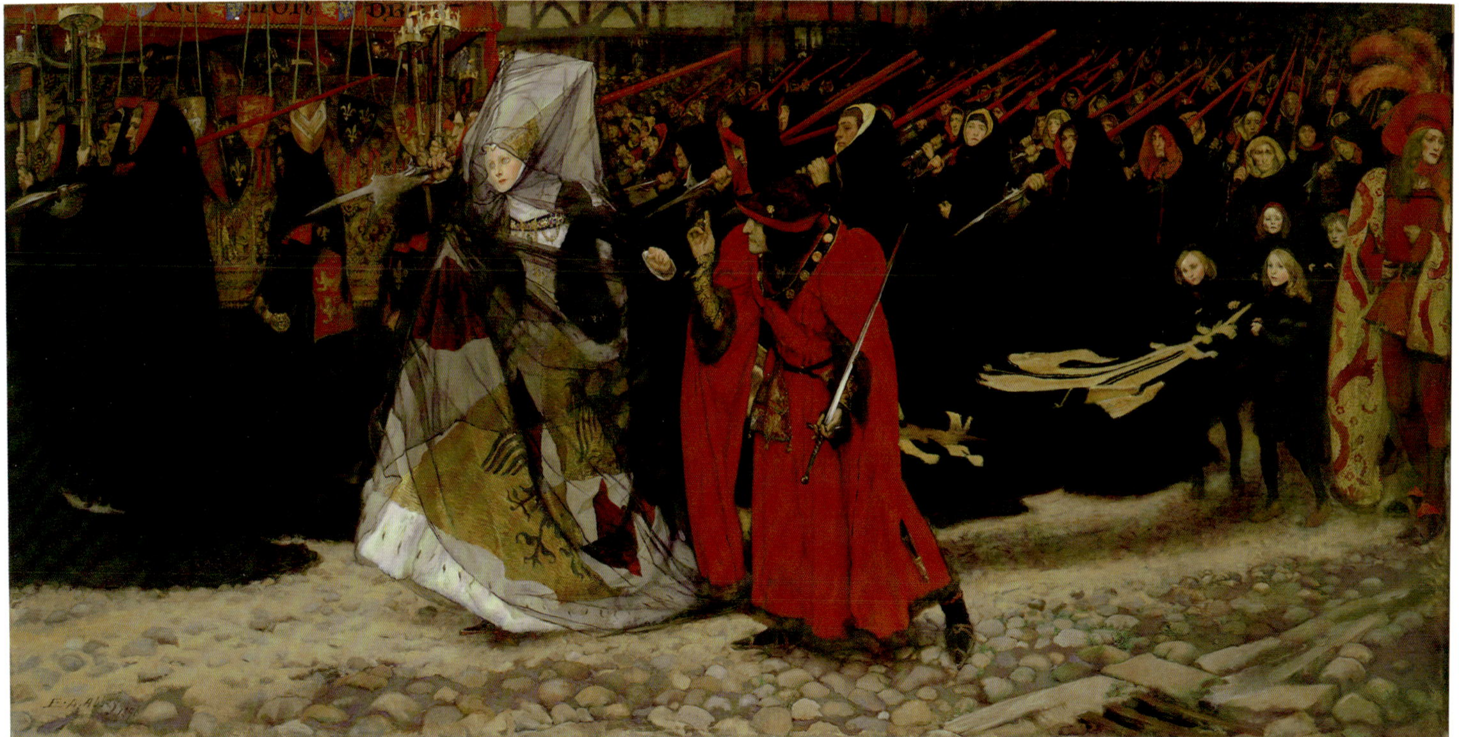

One important collection of American paintings and works on paper that came in during this acquisition-rich decade was not inspired by the Garvan Collection but was rather an homage to the continuing close relationship between the Gallery and the School of Art. The Edwin Austin Abbey Memorial Collection, given in 1937, comprises over three thousand paintings and watercolors, drawings, and prints by Abbey, the vast majority, at least in numbers, of his life's work.[22] Abbey (1852–1911) received an honorary M.A. from Yale in 1897. After his death, his widow spent the remainder of her life reassembling the artist's oeuvre, succeeding in acquiring almost everything apart from the murals in the Boston Public Library and the Pennsylvania State Capitol Building in Harrisburg, the *Coronation of Edward VII*, which hangs in Buckingham Palace, and four large canvases now in other museums.

Abbey, a prolific and popular book illustrator, was known especially for his illustrations of scenes from plays and novels. His most impressive and engaging works are the major Shakespearean paintings, including *Richard, Duke of Gloucester, and the Lady Anne* from *Richard III* (fig. 104), and *The Play Scene in "Hamlet"* (act 3, scene 2). Yale owns studies for four additional major works based on Shakespeare, *King Lear, Henry VIII, Two Gentlemen of Verona*, and *Twelfth Night*, large canvases now in the Metropolitan Museum, the Corcoran Gallery, and the Walker Art Museum in Liverpool, England. Illustrations of dramatic scenes from popular novels, such as the meeting of Rebecca and Rowena from *Ivanhoe* by Sir Walter Scott, are among the Abbey drawings now at Yale. The mural paintings are represented by drawings and oil sketches, including the several studies for the mural still to be seen in the capitol rotunda in Harrisburg, Pennsylvania.

FIG. 104
Edward Austin Abbey
Richard, Duke of Gloucester, and the Lady Anne, 1896
Oil on canvas, 133.7 x 265.1 cm
Edwin Austin Abbey Memorial Collection
1937.2224

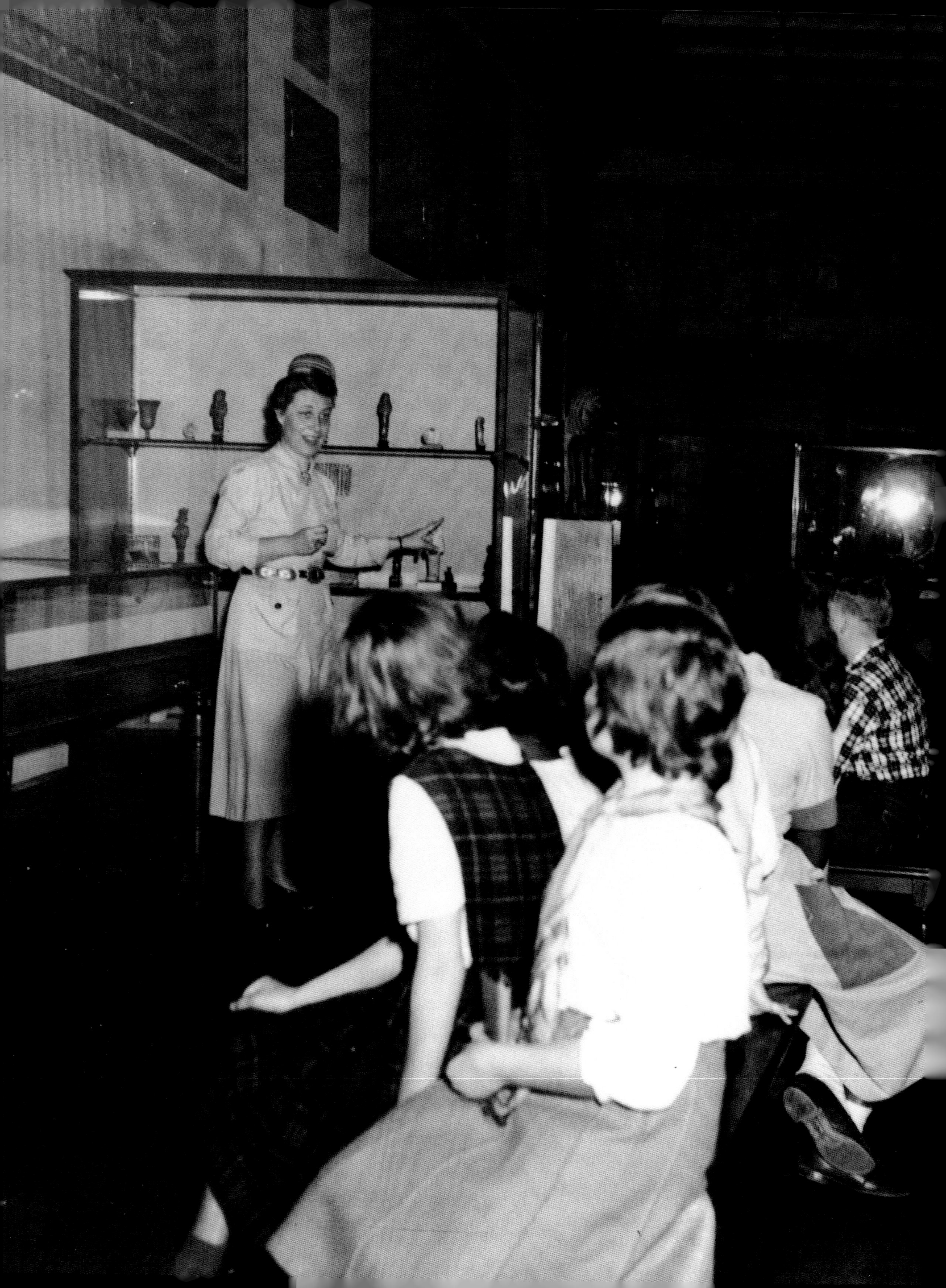

CHAPTER 9

Digging and Teaching

Brief mention has already been made of the early Christian mosaics and other finds from the excavations at Gerasa in Jordan that were installed in the new Gallery of Fine Arts. The Gerasa excavations were undertaken jointly with the British School of Archaeology in Jerusalem from 1928–30 and with the American Schools of Oriental Research from 1930–31 and 1933–34. Yale's participation was funded at first by a $5,000 loan from the Graduate School in 1928 that was repaid with donations from "devoted friends of Yale and of archaeology, in New Haven and its immediate vicinity, [who contributed] small gifts, ranging from $20 to $500."[1] As a result of its participation, Yale received an important sixth-century mosaic with views of the ancient cities of Alexandria and Memphis (fig. 105), as well as several other mosaics from the early Byzantine churches for which the site was renowned. An article in the *Bulletin* on the excavations pleaded for money to cover the cost of shipping these mosaics to New Haven.[2] The same *Bulletin* article also stated the need for an additional $10,000 to cover the costs of a second season; all of these funds were raised.

Excavation was an important method for adding to the Yale collections in ancient Mediterranean art. Early in the twentieth century, the University had been one of the sponsors of the Egypt Exploration Fund, a British organization that assembled funding from educational institutions and museums in support of excavations in Egypt. In return for their funding support, contributing institutions received a portion of the division of finds at the end of the excavation season. This system brought major works of art and archaeological artifacts to numerous American and British institutions like Yale, and it was successful in encouraging support for continuing projects. Yale received some outstanding Egyptian sculpture as part of its share over a decade. This material was directed to the Peabody Museum of Natural History rather than to the Gallery, perhaps reflecting contemporary attitudes about archaeological material but more likely because most of the Egyptian art that Yale already owned was housed at the Peabody. The Barringer Collection of Egyptian art, which includes Yale's finest Egyptian sculptures, came to the Peabody in 1890 as the result of the efforts of Othniel C. Marsh, whose close contact with the Natural History Museum determined

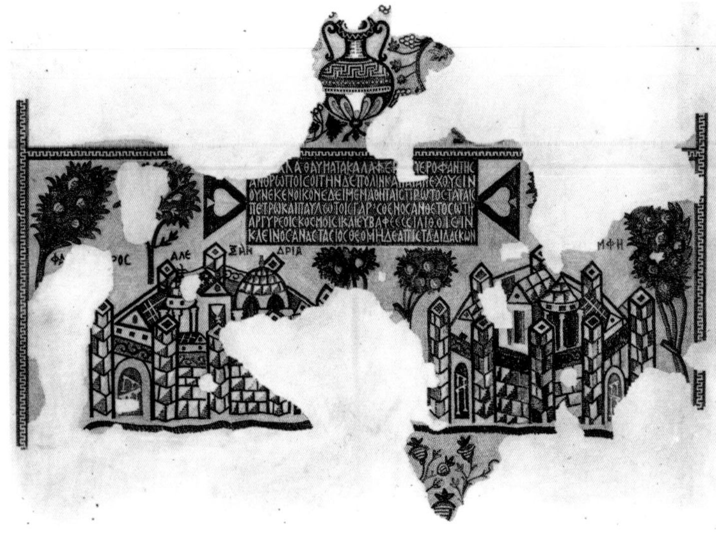

Fig. 105
Maker unknown
Mosaic Floor, depicting the Cities of Alexandria and Memphis,
ca. A.D. 540, from a watercolor drawing
Limestone tesserae,
396.25 x 609.6 cm
Excavated by the Yale-British School Archaeological Expedition, 1928–29
1932.1735

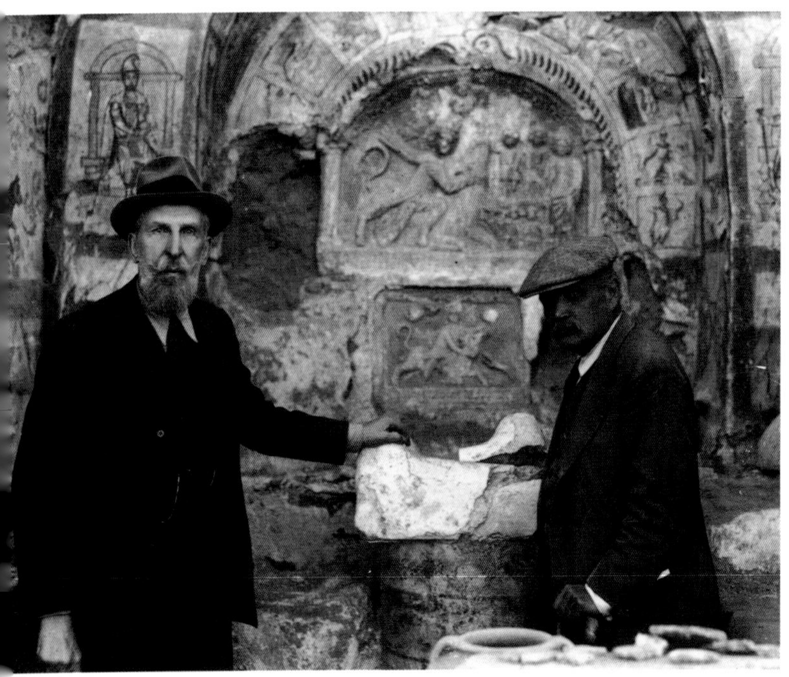

Fig. 109
Photographer unknown
Franz Cumont (left) and Michael I. Rostovtzeff in the Mithraeum at Dura-Europos, 1932
Photograph courtesy of the Dura-Europos Archive, Yale University Art Gallery

the collection's home. Some of the Peabody's finest pieces have frequently been exhibited at the Gallery.[3]

The Gallery did not begin to acquire Egyptian art until 1920, when Ludlow S. Bull (B.A. 1907), then curator of Egyptian art at the Metropolitan Museum of Art in New York, became a consultant curator at the Gallery as well. Bull was an active buyer in Egypt on the Gallery's behalf for the next twenty-seven years, beginning with a fine collection of predynastic pottery in 1920 and acquiring important Middle Kingdom wooden coffins and several stone sculptures (fig. 106). Appointed to the Yale faculty in 1924, Bull was named to a newly created post of curator of Egyptian art at the Gallery in 1930. In 1936, parts of the collection of Garrett Chatfield Pier were purchased at auction for Yale by Bull and some of his classmates, adding some outstanding small objects to the collection. Important donations were made in the 1950s by Fred Olsen (fig. 107), better known for the Precolumbian art he gave to Yale, and in the 1990s by William Kelly Simpson, B.A. 1947, M.A., 1948, PH.D. 1954, professor of Egyptology at Yale and former curator of Egyptian and Near Eastern art at the Museum of Fine Arts, Boston (fig. 108). Professor Simpson's excavations in Egypt, a joint project with the University of Pennsylvania, have added further material to the Peabody Museum's collection.

The Yale-French excavations at Dura-Europos were a far more extensive project and had a much greater impact on the Gallery's ancient art collections.[4] The Dura excavations represented a collaboration between the Gallery and the Department of Classics, led by Professor Michael I. Rostovtzeff (fig. 109). Once the Latin tutor to the czar's children, Rostovtzeff had fled Russia during the Revolution, taking refuge first in Oxford and then in the United States, where he began teaching at the University of Wisconsin. He completed his career as Sterling Professor of Ancient History and Classical Archaeology at Yale, a post he held from 1925–39. The preeminent economic historian of the ancient Greek and Roman world of his day, Rostovtzeff used his stature to secure for Yale a partnership with the French Academy of Inscriptions and Letters on this exciting new excavation. Working with Yale's president, James Roland Angell, he arranged funding from the Rockefeller Foundation for the duration of the project.

Fig. 106
Maker unknown
Pair Statue of Djehuty-em-hab and Iay,
ca. 1200–1085 B.C.
Red sandstone,
48 x 28.5 x 21 cm
Gift of Ludlow S. Bull,
B.A., 1907, and the
Associates in Fine Arts
1947.81

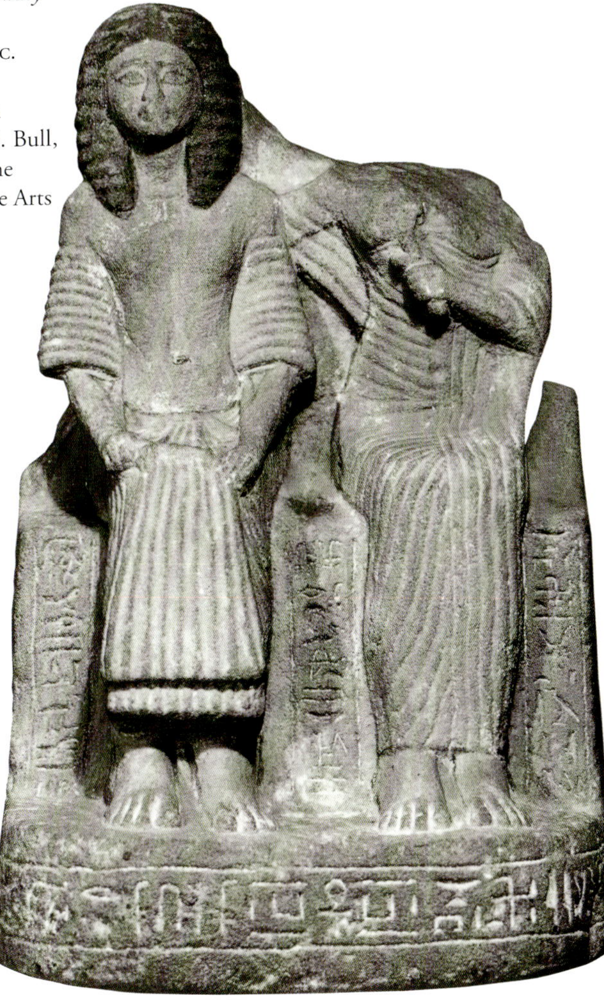

Fig. 107
Maker unknown
Relief Depicting a Sunshade Bearer, ca. 2040 B.C.
Painted limestone, 19.5 x 13 cm
Gift of Mr. and Mrs. Fred Olsen
1956.33.87

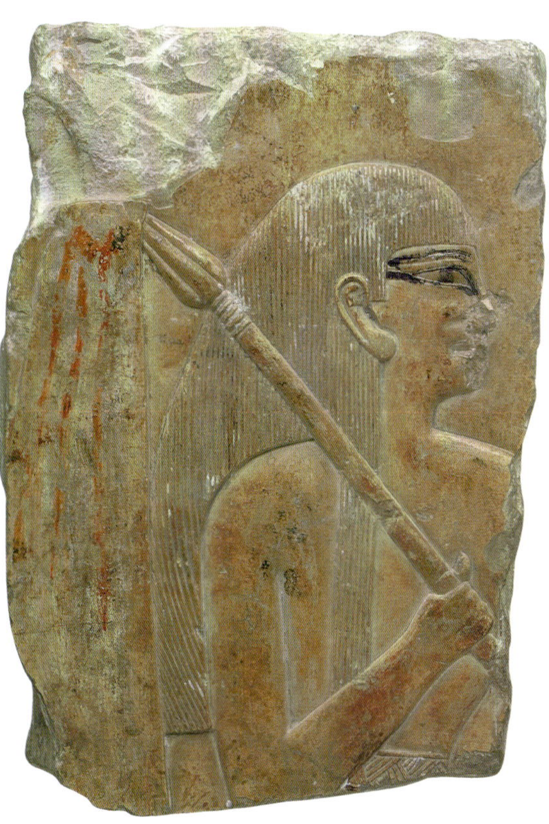

Fig. 108
Maker unknown
Stele of Hetep-neb and His Wife, ca. 2150 B.C.
Painted limestone,
48.5 x 83.5 x .9 cm
Gift of William Kelly
Simpson, B.A. 1947,
M.A. 1948, PH.D. 1954
1992.9.1

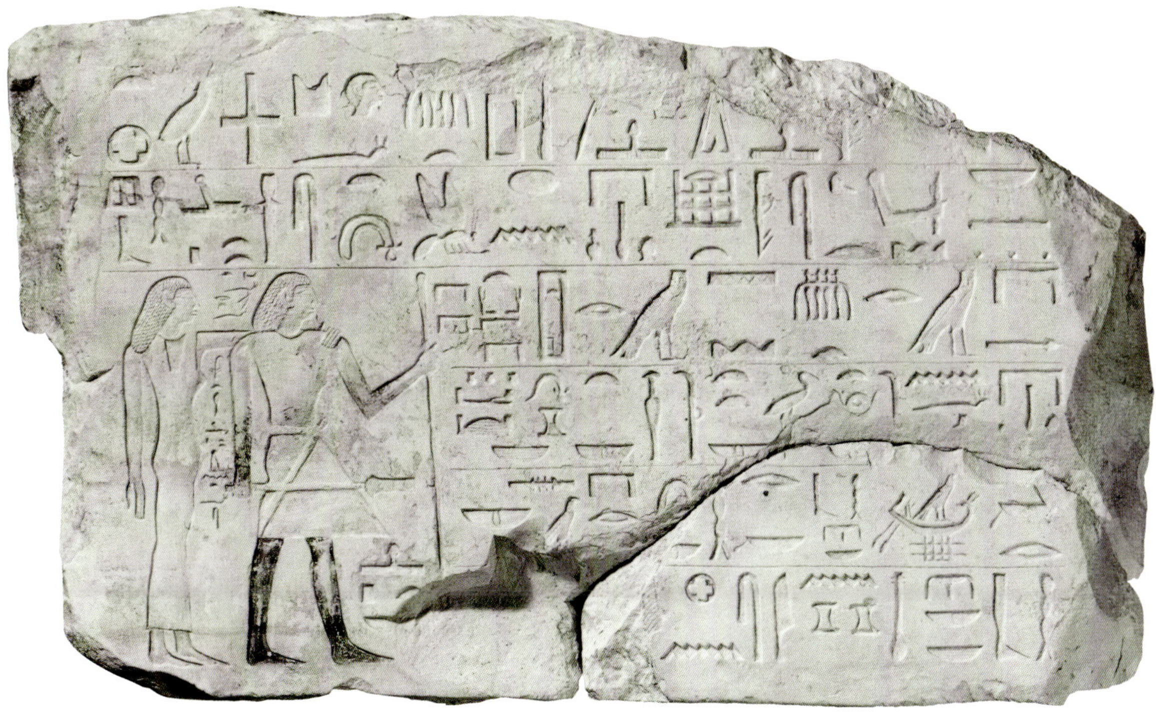

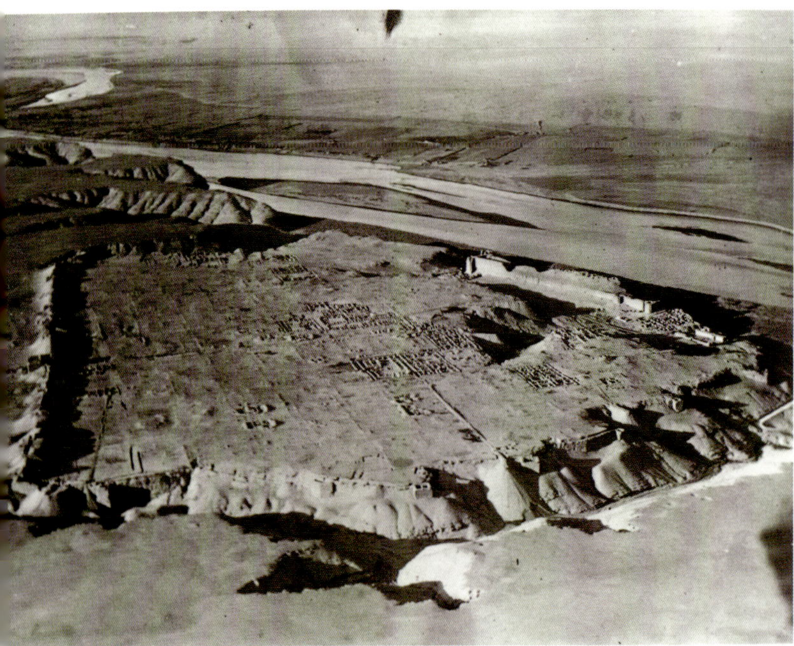

Fig. 110
Photographer unknown
View of Dura-Europos from the air, 1932
Photograph courtesy of the Dura-Europos Archive, Yale University Art Gallery

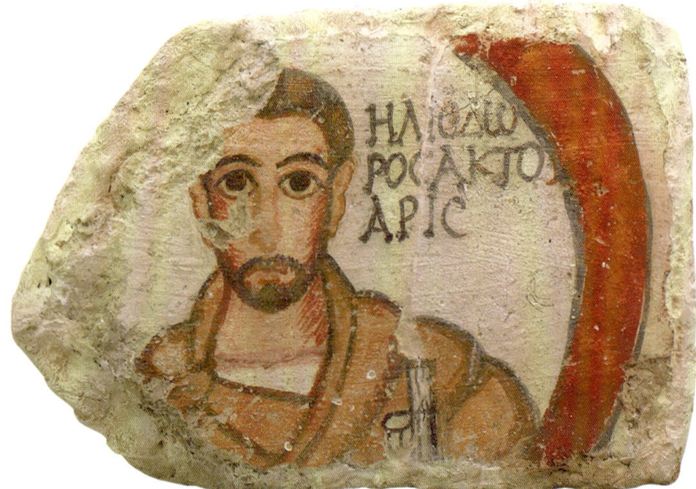

Fig. 111
Maker unknown
Heliodoros, ca. A.D. 200–256
Painted plaster, 30.5 x 44 cm
Yale-French Excavations at Dura-Europos
1933.292

For a decade, Yale faculty and students from several academic departments and the School of Art worked on the site and the annual shipments of excavation finds that came to the Gallery for study, cataloguing, storage, and display. The entire excavation archive, including photographs, diaries, and plans, also came to Yale, where it is now the focus of a computer database project that will ultimately make it accessible worldwide as a research tool.

In the end, over 10,000 objects came to the Gallery between 1929 and 1938, forming a unique record of life in an ancient city situated on the Euphrates River in modern Syria, on the eastern border of the ancient Roman empire (fig. 110). The Gallery's holdings of wall paintings (fig. 111), sculpture, pottery, glass, textiles, and other objects used in the daily lives of the city's residents, complemented by the coins and written documents from the site now housed in Yale's Sterling and Beinecke Libraries, reveal the richly varied culture of a city whose Greek roots from its Hellenistic colonial foundation were transformed under Parthian rule by the prosperous caravan trade into a thriving near-eastern market. The city ended its life as a Roman military outpost, finally succumbing to the Sassanian Persians after more than five centuries of history. The Dura Collection, best known for its Mithraeum, early Christian paintings, and other religious art, along with the synagogue and other finds from the city housed in the Archaeological Museum in Damascus, remains a key to understanding ancient religion and art. Like the Jarves paintings and the Garvan Collections, the Dura-Europos Collection is one of the Gallery's pilgrimage collections.

One other significant part of Yale's ancient art collection, glass, was established during this decade.[5] The ancient glass collection at Yale is one of the best in the country. The Gerasa and especially the Dura excavations brought important holdings of excavated glass, albeit largely fragments, to the collection. Beginning with a handful of pieces in the Whiting Palestinian Collection (1912), the glass collection languished until 1930, when the Anna Rosalie Mansfield Collection was presented as a gift in honor of his wife by Burton Mansfield, graduate of Yale (PH.B. 1875, LL.B. 1878) and a prominent New Haven lawyer, bank president, patron of the arts, and collector of paintings. This gift was followed by the purchase of an exceptional Amarna period piece, an inlay showing a princess from the court of Akhenaten, from the Garrett Chatfield Pier Collection of Egyptian art in 1936. Since the 1930s, the glass collection has evolved through gifts and bequests into precisely the sort of holding appropriate to a teaching museum, one that is representative of nearly the complete range of styles and techniques, and features many pieces of outstanding quality. The growth of the collection culminated in the 1950s with the gift of Robert Lehman, B.A. 1913, in 1953, and the bequest of the Hobart and Edward Small Moore Memorial Collection, by Mrs. William H. Moore in 1955.

The Moore Collection is the heart of Yale's holdings of ancient glass, representing more than half of the glass from sources other than Dura and Gerasa, and including the best pieces in the collection. Mrs. Moore formed her collection over more than thirty years, striving to be comprehensive and seeking the finest examples of each type, as had Francis P. Garvan for American decorative arts. Among her rarest and finest pieces are the signed mold-blown jar by the master glassmaker Ennion (fig. 112), the large beaker with Dionysos and figures of seasons, a particularly fine mosaic glass bowl (fig. 113), two bottles in the shape of the Greek goddess Tyche, and a purple glass drinking vessel decorated with ornament and an inscription incised in gold leaf. One of her mold-blown bottles was made from the same mold as one from which fragments were excavated at Dura-Europos, reuniting at Yale two objects from the same ancient workshop, seemingly against all odds.

The explosive growth of the Gallery's collections in the decade following the opening of the Gallery of Fine Arts in 1928 generated a critical need for curatorial expertise and care. This need was met in 1930 by the establishment of ten curatorships by Dean Everett Meeks, who was director of the Gallery as well as dean of the School of Art. The new curatorships reflected the Gallery's holdings and focused on three broad areas: paintings, sculpture, and works on paper; American decorative arts; and ancient Mediterranean art. Holding the positions in the first group were Theodore Sizer (paintings and sculpture), H. Emerson Tuttle, B.A. 1914 (prints), and James Whitney Barney, B.A. 1900 (drawings). Appointed as curators of decorative arts were

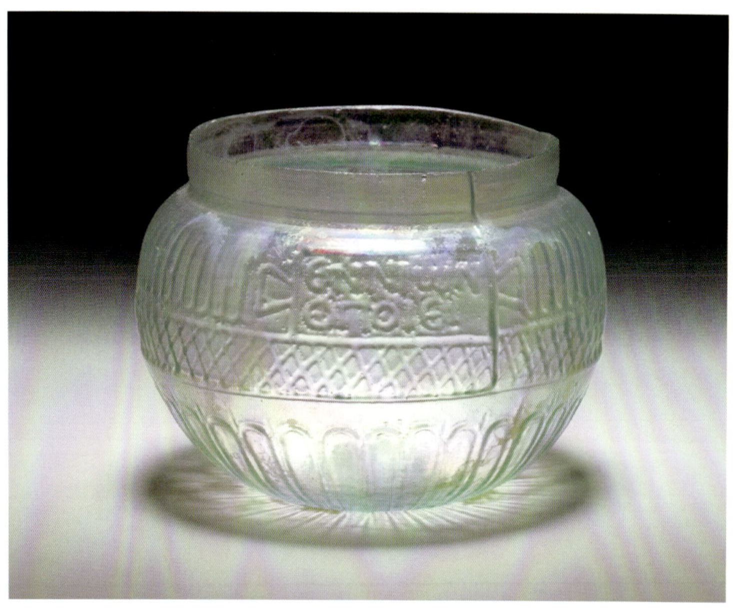

Fig. 112
Ennion
Jar signed ENNIΩN EΠOIEI,
1st century A.D.
Transparent bluish-green glass, 16.5 x 22.4 cm
The Hobart and Edward Small Moore Memorial Collection, gift of Mrs. William H. Moore
1955.6.66

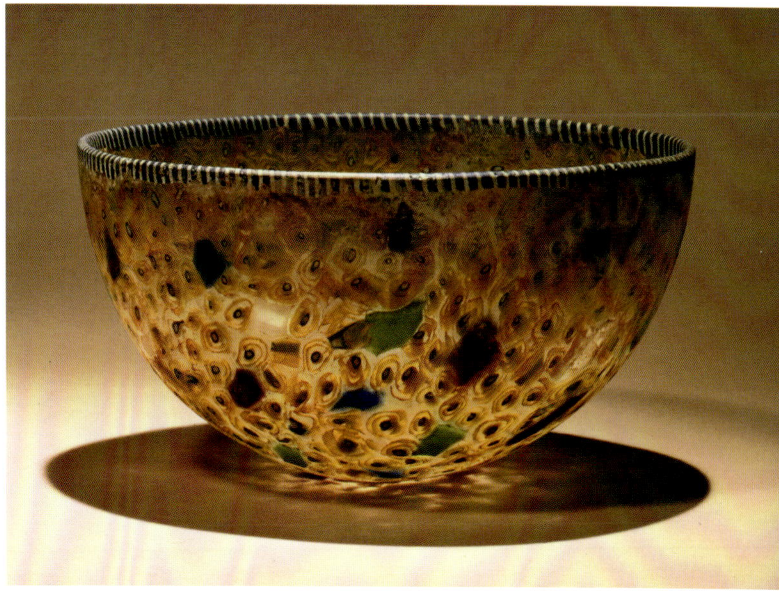

Fig. 113
Maker unknown
Mosaic Glass Bowl,
late 2nd–1st century B.C.
Glass, 7.8 x 14.1 cm
The Hobart and Edward Small Moore Memorial Collection, gift of Mrs. William H. Moore
1955.6.20

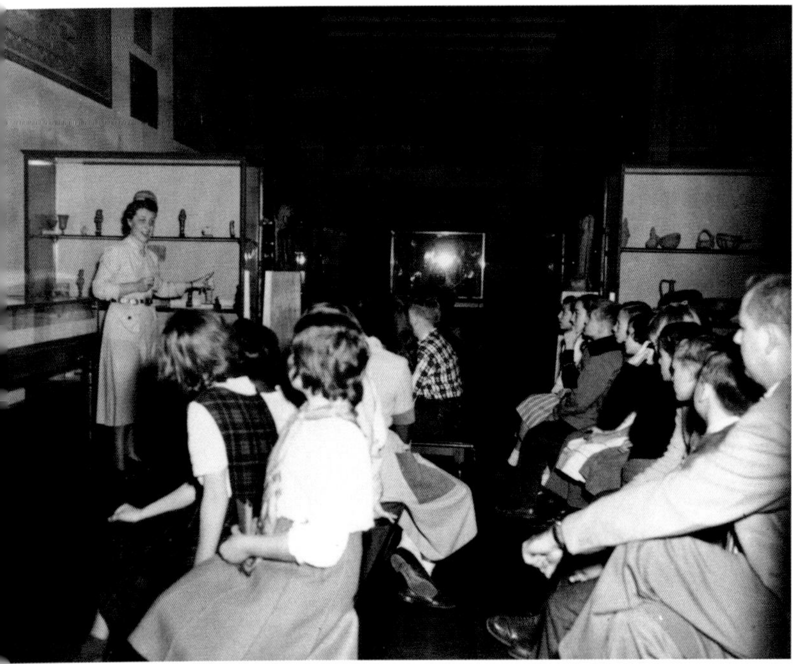

Fig. 114
A. Elizabeth Chase teaching from the Egyptian collection, 1949
Photograph courtesy Yale University Art Gallery Archives

Charles Nagel, B.A. 1923 (decorative arts), E. Alfred Jones (silver, with John Marshall Phillips serving as assistant curator, and succeeding Jones as curator in 1935), and George Hewitt Myers, B.A. 1898 (textiles, later to serve as director of the textile museum in Washington, D.C.). Four curators were given responsibility for ancient Mediterranean art: Ludlow Bull (Egyptian art; he was simultaneously curator of Egyptian art at the Metropolitan Museum of Art); Raymond P. Dougherty (the Babylonian Collection, which was later transferred to the library as a separate collection, where it remains today); Paul V. C. Baur (Classical archaeology, which he also taught as a member of the Classics Department; he had formerly been curator of the Stoddard Collection of Greek Vases); and Clark Hopkins (antiquities from Gerasa and Dura; Hopkins would later serve as field director for the Dura excavations).

An equally critical need was felt for the expansion of the Gallery's public education program. A university museum is by definition a teaching museum, fundamentally committed to education as its mission. When such a museum is located in a city such as New Haven, the museum's educational mission embraces the public as well as the university students. Recognizing this dual mission and building on the existing connection between the Gallery and the city, in 1931 Yale established a public education program at the Gallery of Fine Arts and appointed A. Elizabeth Chase as docent (fig. 114). Miss Chase was not the first docent: Leslie Richardson had been appointed as "Museum Assistant and Docent with the rank of Instructor" in History of Art in 1928.[6] Miss Richardson complemented the faculty's classroom teaching by teaching students in the galleries, preserving the close historic link between the Gallery and the School of the Fine Arts. Miss Chase was appointed to serve another audience, the general public. A pioneering effort in the museum world, the new Yale program was part of the larger drive for public education at the time. The University was concerned about the meager attendance at its public art lectures: in 1930 lecture attendance represented only 3,891 out of a total attendance for the museum of 62,375.[7] Miss Chase was charged with creating a program about art in the Gallery that would engage and educate the public, including both adults and children.

The founding of the museum education program was described in the December 1933 issue of the *Yale Alumni Weekly*:

> In 1931, the University, desiring to extend the educational facilities of the Gallery of Fine Arts to clubs, schools, and the general public, established the position of Docent in the Gallery. During the first year, 120 lectures were given, with a total attendance of over 4,000 people, 1,491 of whom were children. Last year, the work was increased more than thirty per cent. Seventy-five classes from public and private schools, some of them from distant parts of the state, visited the Gallery, with a total attendance of more than 2,000 children. Sixty Gallery Talks were given on week-days, and on Saturday and Sunday afternoons. Organized visits to the Gallery were made by many clubs, and lectures were given outside the Gallery to groups too large, or too distant, to make a visit practicable. In all, 160 free lectures and Gallery Talks were given throughout the year, with a total attendance of 5,488, making a grand total, since the work began in 1931, of 280 lectures, with 9,571 people attending.[8]

The public gallery talks were given by Elizabeth Chase, who gave special attention to exhibitions in the galleries and new acquisitions, while regularly lecturing on the permanent collection. Her first series of lectures in the 1935 season focused on the print collection. In 1935 she gave a series of twelve lectures on European arts and crafts as well as a weekend lecture on religion and art in Ancient Egypt.[9] She gave numerous talks on Italian Renaissance paintings and American art—in other words, on the strengths of the collection. Later in the 1930s, she spoke often on the excavations and finds from Dura-Europos. Throughout the 1930s, the number of her lectures increased and the attendance at them grew.

Miss Chase was well qualified for her post. Born in 1906, she earned a B.A. from Radcliffe College in 1927 and an M.A. from Yale in 1943. Widely traveled, she had examined firsthand the buildings and art she taught in New Haven. She was an assistant professor of the History of Art and the first woman to teach an undergraduate course at Yale. Most active in the 1940s and '50s, she taught a course on the history of modern art in the Department of Education (no longer extant) at Yale, for which credit was given toward the B.A. This course regularly included visits to artists' studios. She also taught a course on early American arts and crafts and taught at the summer school at Yale's Norfolk School of Music. From 1946–47, she was on leave from Yale to serve as curator of education at the Brooklyn Museum. Miss Chase arranged scores of public lectures in all fields of art history that were given at the Gallery of Fine Arts. Yale faculty, visiting scholars from American and European universities, and curators from other museums spoke to large audiences on every imaginable topic, often funded by the Ryerson endowment for public lectures. Throughout her career she spoke to and visited hundreds of school groups in the New Haven area and throughout Connecticut. She retired in 1970.

EXHIBITIONS: BEGINNING THE SECOND CENTURY

The Gallery marked the centennial anniversary of its founding in 1932 with a special exhibition celebrating the Trumbull Collection and other American art, organized by Theodore Sizer. On view in the Trumbull Room and the American eighteenth-century gallery between October 29 and November 17, the *Hundredth Anniversary Exhibition* displayed the identical pictures, drawings, prints, maps, and models that had been exhibited in the original Trumbull Gallery. Miscellaneous objects of "Trumbulliana" that had been acquired recently were added to the display.

Shortly thereafter, in 1935, Connecticut marked its tercentenary with a statewide celebration that ran from June 1 to September 30. The Gallery mounted four loan exhibitions during this period that celebrated the history of the state. One focused on paintings by John Trumbull and a second featured paintings by Samuel F. B. Morse, complemented by furniture of the period from the Garvan Collection. Writing about Trumbull's *Signing of the Declaration of Independence* and the holiday marking the same event, the *New Haven Register* suggested, "New Haveners wishing to celebrate this day in a fitting manner can find no more impressive place to visit than that room in the Yale Gallery of Fine Arts where his pictures, his sketch books, and his tool cabinet are now on exhibition."[10] The third exhibition was a show of Connecticut portraits by another prominent American painter, Ralph Earl. The fourth was an exhibition of silver and prints, curated by Charles Nagel, Jr., which received extensive coverage in the *New York Times.*

In 1938, the city of New Haven celebrated its own tercentenary. The primary offering that the Gallery made to the Elm City was to mount an exhibition of portraits of her famous citizens, *Portraits of Distinguished New Haveners.* Included were New Haven inventors, among them Hezekiah Augur (better known today as an artist), Eli Whitney, Abell Buell, Ithiel Town, Charles Goodyear, and Chauncey Jerome; New Haven and Connecticut artists, including George H. Durrie, Chauncey B. Ives, Ralph Earl, John Trumbull, and Nathaniel Jocelyn; and statesmen who were native sons of New Haven. There were views of Yale, and furniture from the Garvan Collection to accompany the portraits. Loans were obtained from the New Haven Colony Historical Society as well as Sterling Memorial Library at Yale.

Another celebratory exhibition featured photographs and drawings of the work of New Haven architects. A third, entitled *New Haven Progress,* was organized by the Gallery but shown at the Charles E. Coxe Gymnasium (now known as Coxe Cage). This building, designed by Lockwood, Greene & Company as a facility for track and indoor baseball practice, opened in 1927 and still remained one of the largest exhibition spaces available on campus. The exhibition was about the creation of the building, but somehow it became a vehicle for "showing the usefulness of the Gallery of Fine Arts to the city." It featured photographs, models, and lectures, notably gallery talks on New Haven architects by Elizabeth Chase. Lenders to this exhibition included the Addison Gallery of American Art at Andover Academy.

The special exhibition schedule during the 1930s was robust, to say the least. From an average of four to five exhibitions staged annually in the 1920s, in the 1930s the number often tripled and even quadrupled in some years. Exhibitions were often short—two weeks was common—although exceptional occasions such as centennial and tercentennial celebrations engendered runs of one to three months. Themes were varied, and an effort was clearly made to focus in turn on each of the media (painting, sculpture, drawing, and architecture) taught at the School of Art. Thus in any given year there would generally be shows of painting, drawing, watercolor, prints, photography, and architecture. Collaborative exhibitions incorporating all the disciplines taught in the School were instituted in the mid-1930s by Dean Meeks as a way to modernize its teaching methods. The basis for each of these exhibitions was a single topic, to which each discipline was expected to respond.

Loan exhibitions linked to the permanent collections, such as *Twelve Pieces of Silver: Cornelius Kierstede, 1647–1753* in 1932, or *Loan Exhibition of Chinese Paintings* in 1933, or *Federal Art in New England,* a 1937 exhibition of paintings, drawings, and prints, are typical. Large faculty and student shows normally were held once a year, and smaller ones were organized more often for each department in the school. At times Yale was a venue for an exhibition organized by the Metropolitan Museum of Art, the American Federation of the Arts, or other institutions, or a group of objects would be borrowed from the Museum of Modern Art, the Addison Gallery of American Art, or another museum or private collection for a brief exhibition. The Associates in Fine Arts organized loan exhibitions, especially shows designed to bring contemporary art to New Haven.

A fairly typical schedule was that of 1934. The year opened with an exhibition of *Contemporary Silver by Georg Jensen,* followed by *Photographs of Persian Architecture* by Arthur Upham Pope, a famous scholar of Persian Art, lent by the American Institute for Persian Art and Archaeology. Next came a show of paintings by Deane Keller (B.A. 1923, B.F.A. 1925, Hon. M.A. 1948), a member of the Yale faculty who taught drawing beginning in 1925, followed by a loan show of *Early American Historical Prints* from the collection of Francis P. Garvan. March opened with prints by H. Emerson Tuttle, the curator of prints, which coincided with a show on early museum architecture. An exhibition of building designs by graduates of the Yale School of Architecture and a show of paintings, drawings, and watercolors by Mrs. Charles Warren, a Yale Art School student, occupied late March and April, while a loan show of replicas of Egyptian wall paintings of the New Kingdom was on view during most of May.

The year's major offering, on view for a month,

was the *Exhibition in Honor of the Centenary of the Death of Lafayette* (fig. 115), curated by John Marshall Phillips. The exhibition included portraits, personal belongings, and other objects of Lafayette memorabilia illustrating the two periods of his life when he was allied with America, namely 1777, as a liberty fighter, and 1824, as the "Nation's Guest." Featured were thirty prints from Francis P. Garvan's collection of prints portraying Lafayette. There were also some objects related to Washington, who had been honored by the Gallery with his own bicentennial exhibition in 1932. This focus on heroes from American history would surely have pleased Trumbull.

The fall of 1934 brought exhibitions of *Rubbings from Chinese Tombstones*; *Architecture: Photographs of French Cathedrals by Clarence Ward of Oberlin College*; photographs and drawings from the Historic American Buildings Survey of Massachusetts, including buildings from 1674 to the early nineteenth century; *American Cities of the '30s, '40s, '50s, before the Civil War*, an exhibition of architectural photographs by Berenice Abbott; and a loan exhibition of photographs by Ansel Adams.

In December, a show of thirty-three reproductions of arms and armor from the Metropolitan Museum of Art was brought to the Gallery to meet the teaching needs of the Departments of Art and Drama. December also featured a two-week loan exhibition of watercolors of the Connecticut countryside by Wayland Wells Williams, B.A. 1910, the son of Frederick and Frances Wayland Wells Williams, the donors of the Chinese porcelain collections and the Buddhist votive stele mentioned earlier. The year's final exhibition was the second annual Christmas show, *The Christmas Story in Art*, curated by A. Elizabeth Chase.

The last major exhibition of the 1930s was *Masterpieces of New England Silver: 1650–1800*, curated by John Marshall Phillips and on view from June through early October 1939 (fig. 116). Two hundred and fifty pieces of domestic and ecclesiastical silver, "important works of New England silversmiths," along with twenty-six pieces of gold, jewelry, and portraits, lent by museums and private collectors, made up the exhibition.[11] The show was one of a collaborative group of exhibitions held in eight museums that focused on different media in American art of this period.

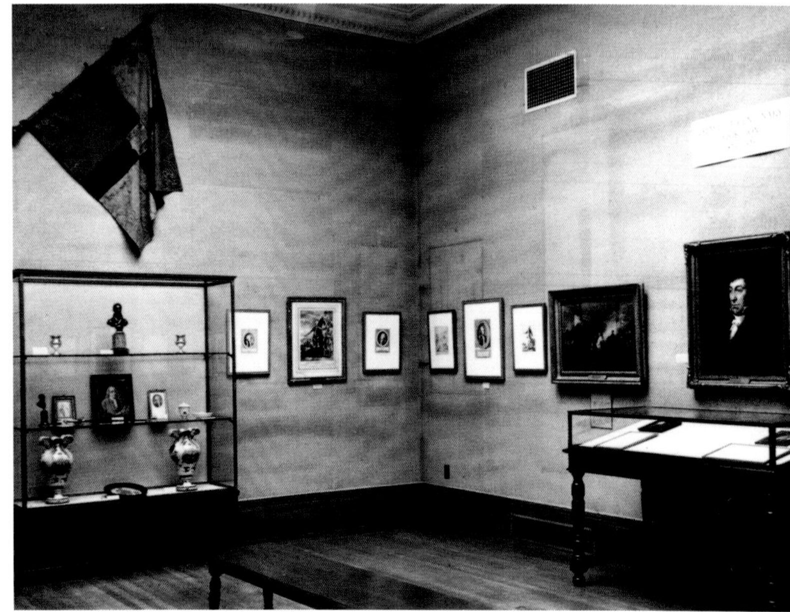

Fig. 115
Exhibition in Honor of the Centenary of the Death of Lafayette, 1934
Photograph courtesy Yale University Art Gallery Archives

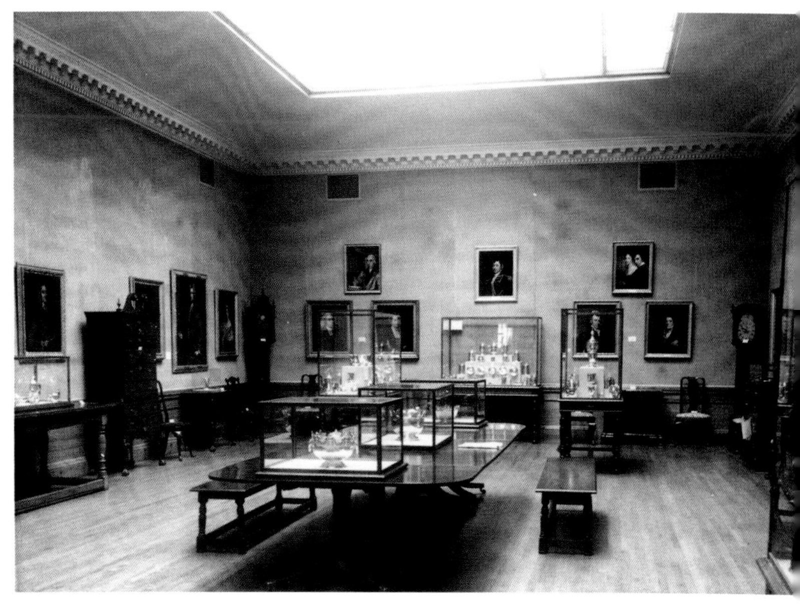

Fig. 116
Masterpieces of New England Silver: 1650–1800, 1939
Photograph courtesy Yale University Art Gallery Archives

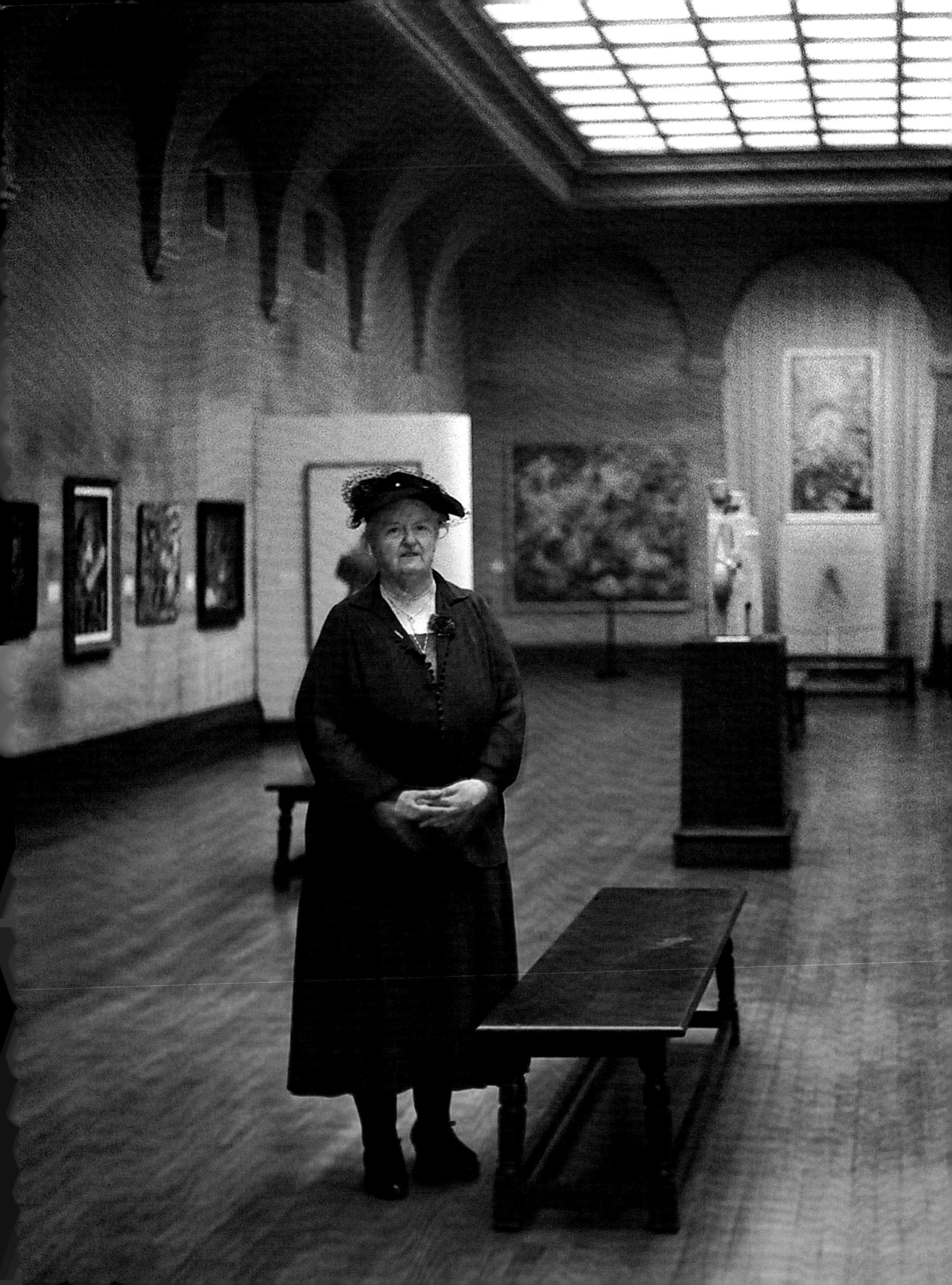

CHAPTER 10

Katherine Dreier and the Société Anonyme

THE DECADE OF THE 1940S: MODERNISM AND WORLD WAR II

Two special exhibitions that took place at the Gallery in 1942 embody the two major forces affecting Yale and its museum during the 1940s, modernism and war. Starting the year, from January 13 through February 22, the first Yale exhibition of the Société Anonyme was held, signaling the arrival of the extraordinary collection of modern art formed by Katherine S. Dreier and Marcel Duchamp. This exhibition, and plans for an extension of the Gallery of Fine Arts that was to be designed in modernist style, marked the transition to modernism as a guiding principle for many of the decisions made by the Gallery and the Art School. Later, from mid-April to mid-June, the Gallery mounted an exhibition called *Our Navy in Action*, an exhibition of paintings reflecting the focus on World War II.

The war effort was observed at the Gallery in two ways. The first concerned the preservation of the collections in case of enemy attack. The immediate solution was to send parts of the collection to caves and museums in Kansas, Ohio, and Missouri. A more longterm solution was to incorporate plans for bombproof storage in the design for the new wing for the Gallery of Fine Arts. The second part of the Gallery's war effort paralleled the explosion of war movies that came out of Hollywood. Exhibitions entitled *National War Poster Exhibition* and *Holland under the Nazis* served, like submarine and air force movies such as *Destination Tokyo* (1943), *Flying Tigers* (1942), and *Bombardier* (1942), to keep the war and the people who fought and suffered in it in the minds of people who saw them. After the war, in June of 1945, an exhibition celebrated the return of the combined Jarves and Griggs Collections of Italian paintings from safekeeping.

The movement toward modernism had a more far-reaching and lasting effect. In architecture at Yale, the transition from Collegiate Gothic and the Beaux-Arts School to modernism is marked by the first modernist design for a Yale building, Philip Goodwin's 1941 plan for a new wing for the Gallery of Fine Arts (fig. 117).[1] Goodwin and Edward Durrell Stone were the architects of the new building erected for the Museum of Modern Art on 11 West 53rd Street in New York, the building that now stands as the core and signature of MoMA's

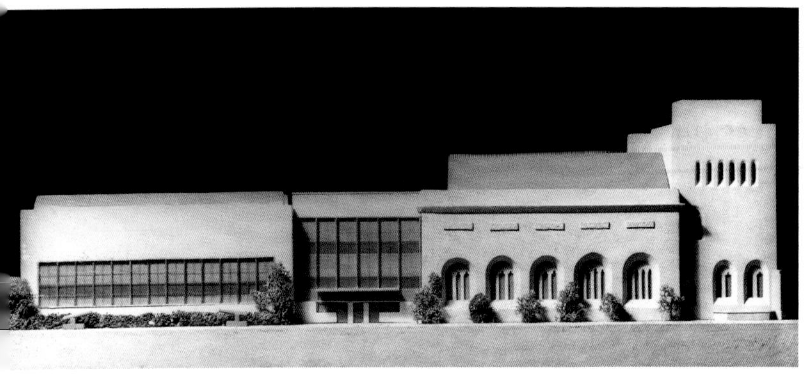

FIG. 117
Philip L. Goodwin
1941 Design Model
Photograph courtesy History of Art Slide and Photograph Collection, Yale University

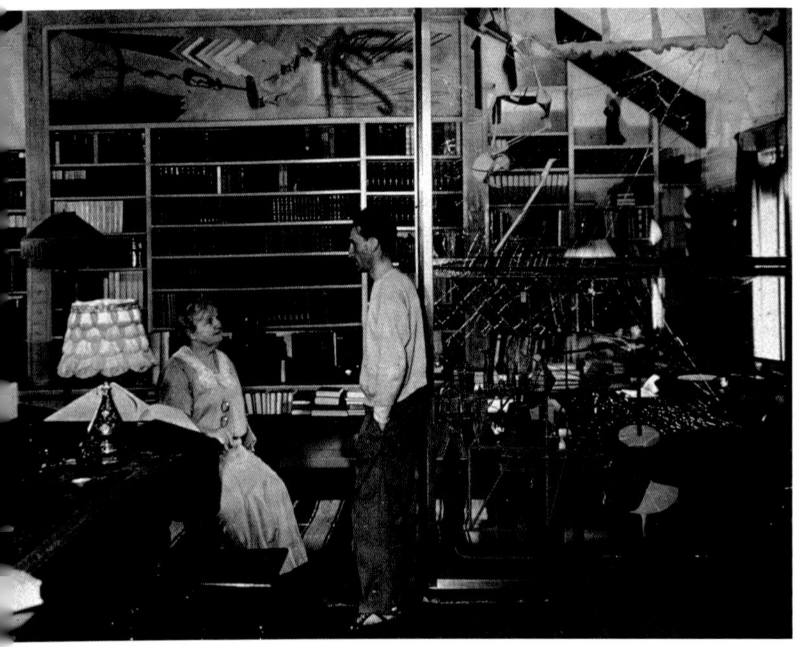

FIG. 118
Katherine Dreier and Marcel Duchamp in Miss Dreier's Library at The Haven, her estate in West Redding, Connecticut, late summer 1936
Photograph courtesy Yale University Art Gallery Archives

complex facade. Goodwin, a graduate of Yale (B.A. 1907), was given the opportunity to design an addition that was to include classrooms, studios, offices, the art library, exhibition galleries, and spaces for many gallery functions such as storage, preparation, and conservation. The design that he proposed in 1941 was closely based on his design for MoMA, both in its modernist facade, stretching around 125 feet from the existing Gallery of Fine Arts building to the corner of York and Chapel Streets, and in its flexible interior, with movable partition walls and abundant natural light. For a variety of reasons, among them financial difficulties and World War II, Goodwin faced delays that lasted a decade and was required to redesign his addition several times. In the end it was never built, but his plans had laid the modernist groundwork for his successor, Louis I. Kahn.

KATHERINE DREIER, MARCEL DUCHAMP, AND THE SOCIÉTÉ ANONYME COLLECTION

The Art Gallery's collections in 1940 were as lacking in examples of modernism as the campus itself. This changed dramatically in 1941, with the transforming gift of the Société Anonyme Collection, followed by additional gifts and the bequest of its principal founder, Katherine S. Dreier.

The Société Anonyme Collection is a remarkable anthology of American and European art from 1920 to 1940.[2] Katherine Dreier (1877–1952; fig. 118), artist, educator, indefatigable lecturer, and collector, founded the Société Anonyme: Museum of Modern Art in New York in 1920 with Marcel Duchamp and Man Ray. The purpose of the Société was to spread the gospel of modern art in America, which Miss Dreier had found to be still mired in the realism of the nineteenth century. The founders' vision was that the chronology of modern art should be developed by artists rather than by critics and art historians, and that contemporary art should be used to educate young Americans.

As the Société's president and funder, Dreier organized traveling exhibitions and lectured tirelessly about modern art throughout the 1920s and '30s. Although not as immediately influential as the Armory Show of 1913, which introduced Duchamp and Cubism to the United States, or Dreier's *International Exhibition of*

Modern Art in Brooklyn in 1926, the Société's exhibitions brought many unfamiliar and often young European artists to the attention of American viewers and collectors. The Société gave some European artists, such as Kandinsky, their first one-artist shows in the United States. Many of these artists came to Dreier's attention during her frequent trips to Europe. Duchamp introduced her to some of them, while she found others herself through her contacts with dealers, especially in Germany, where she often went to visit relatives.

Dreier was a dedicated collector and patron of living artists. Although not wealthy by the standards of the Arensbergs or other major collectors of the day, she had the means to acquire significant works of modern art. As an artist herself, she was often the recipient of gifts of work from fellow artists. She frequently brought works to America for the Société's exhibitions hoping that they would be sold, but when they were not, she typically ended up purchasing them for herself or for the Société. As a result, albeit inadvertently, a permanent collection was gradually formed. Although in the 1920s Dreier's concept of the Société Anonyme: Museum of Modern Art was to be a "museum" of living art without a permanent collection, by the 1930s the collection had accumulated to such an extent that she conceived the idea of the "country museum."

This new venture was presumably envisioned to encompass her own collection and that of the Société. Dreier hoped that the country museum would be housed in her country home in West Redding, Connecticut. She needed funding to convert her rambling country house into a proper museum, and she believed that the endorsement of local schools stating the value of the museum to education would encourage donations. Yale University was identified as a likely supporter of the concept, and in September 1940 Dreier sent her then partner, William Hekking, former director of the Division of Art at the Los Angeles Museum, to meet with Dean Everett Meeks. When this visit produced nothing, Dreier, left on her own after Hekking withdrew from the project, went to call on Yale President Charles Seymour herself. President Seymour sent her to Theodore Sizer, the Gallery's director.

Theodore Sizer was an enthusiastic advocate of modern art and taught courses on it at Yale. He immediately recognized the value of the Société Anonyme Collection to the Art Gallery, whose lack of a collection in this field was of great concern, and to the School of the Fine Arts, where he believed it would be an important resource for art students, the art history program, and the programs in music and drama. Sizer was not interested, however, in Dreier's idea of the country house museum, and after months of negotiation he convinced her of the economic and practical merits of transferring the Société Anonyme Collection to the Art Gallery instead. Not only was the Gallery fireproof, while Dreier's house was not, but by placing the collection at Yale, Dreier would be integrating it into an educational institution that maintained extensive contacts with regional schools through its docent program, thus fulfilling her major educational goal for the "museum." Although Dreier accepted this plan, she continued to encourage Yale to accept her personal collection and her country house.

Finally, in August 1941, at a meeting with Sizer and Wilmarth S. Lewis, the head of the Museums Commission of the Yale Corporation, Dreier agreed to transfer the Société Anonyme Collection without the house and her personal collection. The collection was to be the gift of Katherine S. Dreier and Marcel Duchamp, and it was to be called the Collection Société Anonyme. The terms of the agreement were straightforward and reflected Dreier's and Duchamp's long-standing goals. Additions could be made to the collection, preserving the same requirements as those originally observed. The Société would be dissolved at the death of either Dreier or Duchamp (it was actually dissolved in 1950, prior to either death), and at that point the collection would be closed and no further additions made. While it existed, the Société would arrange exhibitions from time to time, the cost of which would be shared with Yale; Yale would be responsible for traveling these exhibitions. The final agreement, which also clearly stated Yale's obligation to lend works from the collection, was approved by the Yale Corporation in October and signed by Dreier.

Shipment of the collection to Yale began in late October, and by late November 481 objects had been transferred. Dreier, still in charge of the Société although the collection was now owned and managed by Yale,

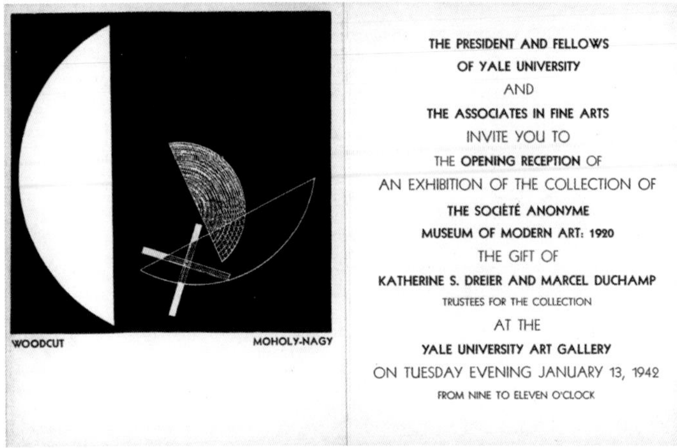
WOODCUT MOHOLY-NAGY

THE PRESIDENT AND FELLOWS
OF YALE UNIVERSITY
AND
THE ASSOCIATES IN FINE ARTS
INVITE YOU TO
THE OPENING RECEPTION OF
AN EXHIBITION OF THE COLLECTION OF
THE SOCIÉTÉ ANONYME
MUSEUM OF MODERN ART: 1920
THE GIFT OF
KATHERINE S. DREIER AND MARCEL DUCHAMP
TRUSTEES FOR THE COLLECTION
AT THE
YALE UNIVERSITY ART GALLERY
ON TUESDAY EVENING JANUARY 13, 1942
FROM NINE TO ELEVEN O'CLOCK

FIG. 119
Invitation to the Société Anonyme Exhibition, 1942
Yale University Art Gallery Archives

launched a fund-raising drive and began pressing the Gallery for an exhibition of the collection. She also paid the Gallery to hire Frederick Hartt, at the beginning of his distinguished career, to catalogue the collection.

To celebrate this extraordinary gift and honor Miss Dreier's wishes, the Gallery staged the major *Exhibition of the Collection of the Société Anonyme Museum of Modern Art: 1920* in 1942, opening on January 13 (fig. 119), a scant five weeks after the United States' entry into World War II. Curated by George Heard Hamilton, instructor in history of art, and shown in the two largest paintings galleries (fig. 120), the exhibition incorporated 127 paintings, sculptures, constructions, and works on paper. It was the first major exhibition of modern art from the permanent collection at Yale. The roster of artists in the exhibition included many of the most important names in early twentieth-century art, notably Léger, Gabo, Kandinsky, Schwitters, Severini, Joseph Stella, Man Ray, Bruce, Moholy-Nagy, Lipschitz, Nolde, and Mondrian, whose two *Fox Trot* paintings (1929 and 1930) were featured prominently. "Those not bound by conventional tastes and prejudices will find in these pictures excitement and stimulation," said one reviewer. Another declared, "With the acquisition of this collection Yale now possesses the largest and most important group of modern art to be owned by any university or college in the country, and can offer unrivaled opportunities for the study and enjoyment of the modern movement."[3]

This inaugural exhibition was followed by frequent displays designed to make the collection available to students. Eighty works were shown at Wesleyan University in March of 1942, a small group was shown at Connecticut College in New London in 1943, another at the Addison Gallery of American Art in 1942, 1947, 1949, and 1952, and there were two exhibitions at Mount Holyoke College in 1945 and 1949. Parts of the collection were constantly on view at the Yale Gallery, and a special display was held at Saybrook College, one of Yale's residential colleges, also in 1943. Loans to other schools further demonstrated the Gallery's commitment to honoring Dreier's, and its own, educational goals.

Duchamp returned to New York from Paris, where he had been living before the war, in 1942. In 1945, the Gallery staged the first American exhibition of the work

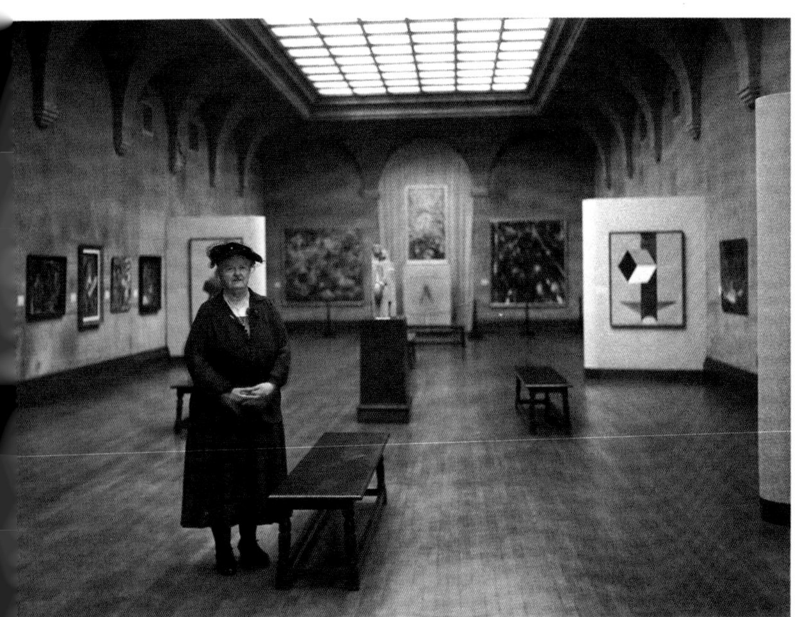

FIG. 120
Katherine Dreier in the Société Anonyme exhibition, 1942
Photograph courtesy Yale University Art Gallery Archives

of the three Duchamp brothers (Duchamp, Raymond Duchamp-Villon, and Jacques Villon), and in 1948 Duchamp was part of the exhibition *Painting and Sculpture by the Directors of the Société Anonyme.* He was represented in the exhibition by his *Rotary Glass Plates,* which were set in motion for the occasion (fig. 121).

Dreier's primary goal at this point was the completion of the catalogue of the Société Anonyme Collection. She and Duchamp collaborated on the research and writing for many of the artists' biographies, and Frederick Hartt's work on the individual objects formed the basis for the entries. George Heard Hamilton, then curator of the Société Anonyme Collection, oversaw the project for the Gallery and contributed enormously to its scholarship and clarity, as well as to keeping Dreier satisfied and the project thus on track. Dreier made numerous additions to the collection while the catalogue was in progress, in an effort to make the collection as representative as possible. Duchamp was consulted on purchases, and both Duchamp and Dreier encouraged artists to donate their own work. Dreier gave works from her own collection to fill gaps. As a result, thirty artists were added to the collection who had not been represented there in 1941. The catalogue, entitled *Collection of the Société Anonyme: Museum of Modern Art 1920,* was published by Yale in 1950. The same year marked the voluntary dissolution of the Société Anonyme by Dreier and Duchamp with a formal declaration on April 30 and a celebratory dinner for President and Mrs. Seymour and other Yale guests hosted by Dreier and Duchamp at the New Haven Lawn Club.

The importance of the collection at the time of its formation was its role in bringing unrecognized and young European and American artists to the fore. Many of these artists are now modern masters, and the collection has grown in importance accordingly. It retains an extra level of value in being a collection representative of its time, both in the artists it includes and in the artists' vision of modern art that it embodies.

Dreier still owned many important works related to the Société Anonyme Collection. They were now housed in the home in Milford, Connecticut, into which she had moved in 1946, having relinquished at last the idea of transforming her West Redding house

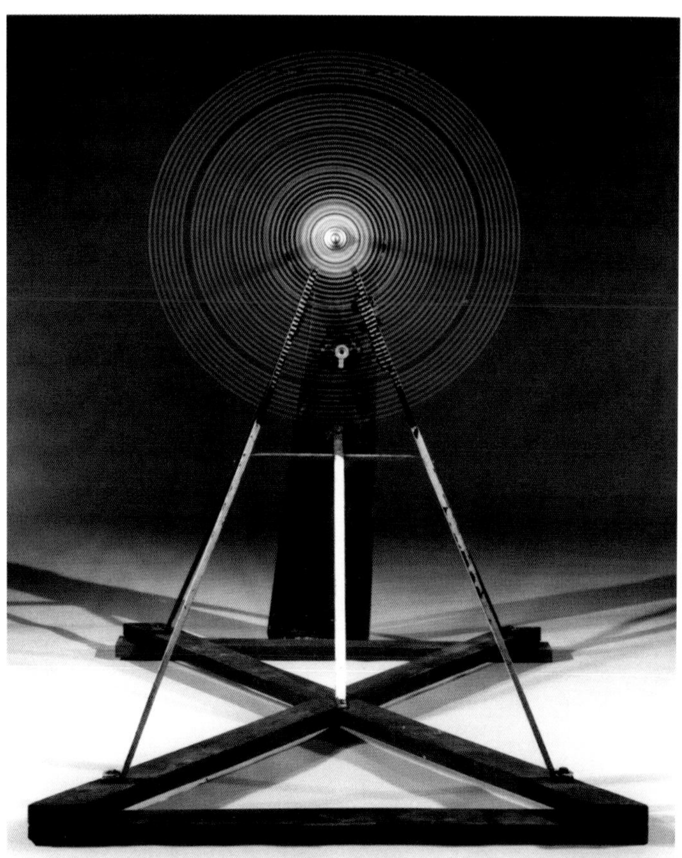

FIG. 121
Marcel Duchamp
Rotary Glass Plates, in motion
Glass, metal, and other media,
166.3 x 98.3 cm
Gift of Collection Société Anonyme
1941.446

into a museum. Dreier's own collection was on a different level than that of the Société. Where the Société's holdings featured works by young artists and "teaching pictures" by established figures, Dreier's personal holdings consisted of major works by major artists. Her collection has been characterized as "outrivalled by no other collections in America except those of the Museum of Modern Art and of Solomon R. Guggenheim."[4]

Although Dreier sold several works between 1941 and 1950, most of the collection was intact when she died in 1952, leaving some works to specific museums, among which seven came to Yale. Included in this group were works by Brancusi (fig. 122), Duchamp-Villon, Ernst, Kakabadzé, Storrs, Villon, and Dreier's own self-portrait. Dreier named Duchamp as the executor charged with distributing the rest of the collection to several institutions that she named in her will. Yale was one of these, receiving by far the largest number. Duchamp included in his selection eleven works that he knew Dreier had particularly prized, including his own *Tu m'* (fig. 123), which Dreier had commissioned in 1918, Man Ray's *Lampshade* (fig. 124), and works by Marc, Halicka, Gabo, Dzubas, Campendonk, Lehmbruck, and Calder. In addition, he selected nearly three hundred other works for Yale, including sculpture, oils, watercolors, gouaches, drawings, collages, prints, and photographs. A few additional works on paper were uncovered among Dreier's papers, which are also at Yale, by the editors of the second major catalogue of the Société Anonyme Collection.[5] Some of the posthumous additions increased the representation of artists already in the collection, such as Lissitzky, Schwitters, Duchamp, and Villon, while in other cases, among them Kirchner, Popova, and Schanker, they were the artist's first works to come to Yale. For some artists, notably Bruce, Covert, Schwitters, Stella, and Villon, Yale has been described as the major American museum for seeing their work.[6]

According to the 1984 catalogue, the combined Société Anonyme and Dreier Collections at Yale total 1,019 works by 180 artists. Although the combined collections unquestionably include major works by artists such as Schwitters, Kandinsky (fig. 125), Klee, Léger (fig. 126), Mondrian (fig. 127), Stella (fig. 128), Man Ray, and others, their unique value for a teaching museum is the comprehensive nature of the holdings, reflecting not only the best, but, as far as could be accomplished by essentially one person, the complete range of the art of two critical decades in the history of modern art. The acquisition of these collections by the Gallery set it on a course of commitment to modern art that ensured its continued partnership with the Yale School of Art. The prominence of modern art in Yale's history of art program completes a productive triad.

Works by artists represented in the combined collections have continued to come to Yale. In 1980, *Mlle. Pogany II* by Brancusi, the bequest of Katharine Ordway, joined the artist's *Yellow Bird* (fig. 122), which was the bequest of Katherine Dreier. In 1969, Jacques Lipchitz's *Guitar Player in Chair* (1922) was acquired with the Director's Purchase Fund. In 1956, H. Wade White, B.A. 1933, donated *Construction in Space with Balance on Two Points* by Naum Gabo (1925). In 1958, relatives of Philip L. Goodwin, B.A. 1907, the architect of the first modernist design for the Art Gallery, donated in Goodwin's memory *The Viaduct* (1925), a painting by Fernand Léger.

The American, Asian, and early European parts of the Gallery's collection also grew in significant ways in 1940 and the years immediately following. American and European gifts built on strengths in the Gallery's collections, while the gifts for the Asian collection represented a new path.

The Yale collection of American paintings was already well known for its important miniatures by John Trumbull and blessed (or saddled) with an extensive collection of other portraits of which many are primarily respected for their subjects. It was on the strength of the best of these portraits, in both large and miniature scale, that John and Lelia Hill Morgan chose to donate their collection of American portraits and miniatures to Yale (1940–45). Morgan knew the Yale collection intimately, having served as curator of American painting from 1931–45.[7] A graduate of Yale (B.A. 1893, LL.B. 1896, Hon. M.A. 1929), Morgan practiced law in New York and was elected to the New York State Legislature, where he served from 1899 to 1903. He was an authority on portraits of George Washington, and a noted collector of American

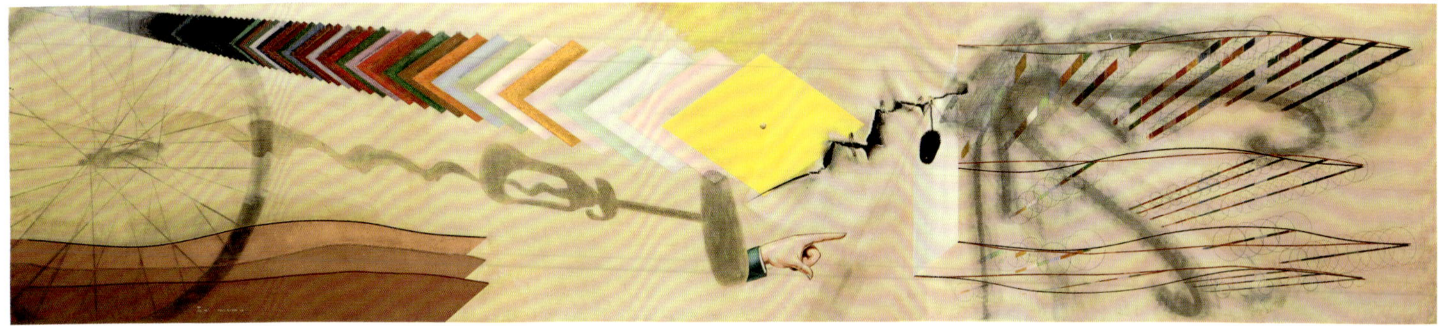

FIG. 123
Marcel Duchamp
Tu m', 1918
Oil on canvas, bottle brush, safety pins, and bolt, 69.8 x 303 cm
Gift from the Estate of Katherine S. Dreier
1953.6.4

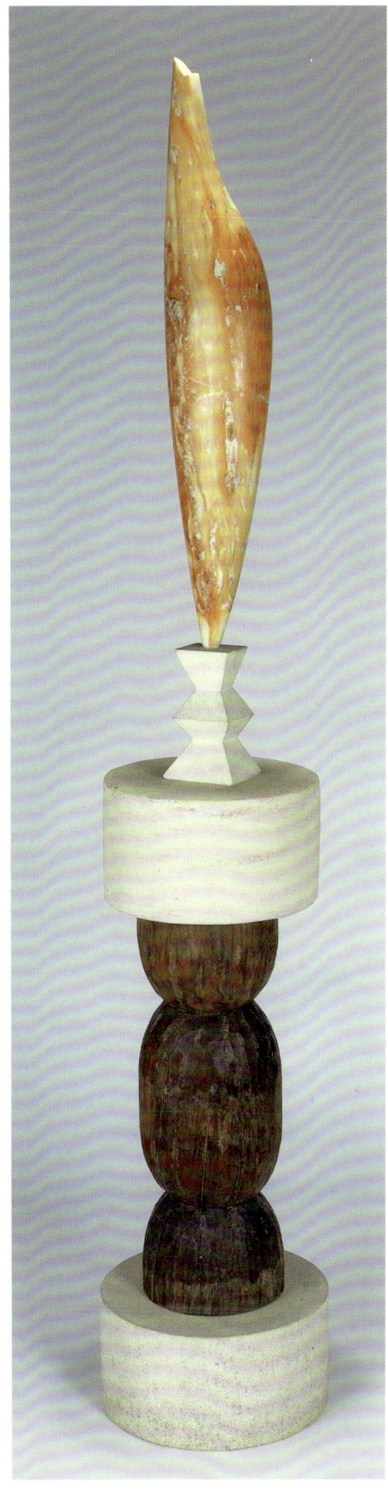

FIG. 122
Constantin Brancusi
Yellow Bird, 1919
Marble, limestone and oak base, 221.6 cm
Bequest of Katherine S. Dreier
1952.30.1

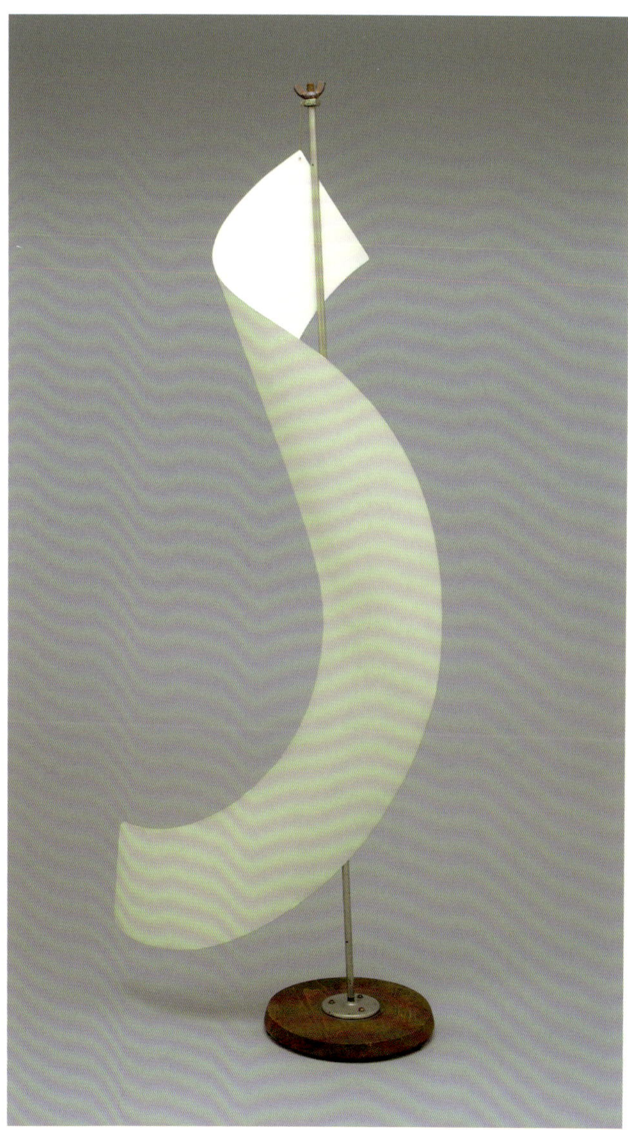

FIG. 124
Man Ray
Lampshade, 1921
Painted tin, metal rod, wing and square bolt, metal flange, round wood base, 115.3 x 7.7 cm
Gift from the estate of Katherine S. Dreier
1953.6.1

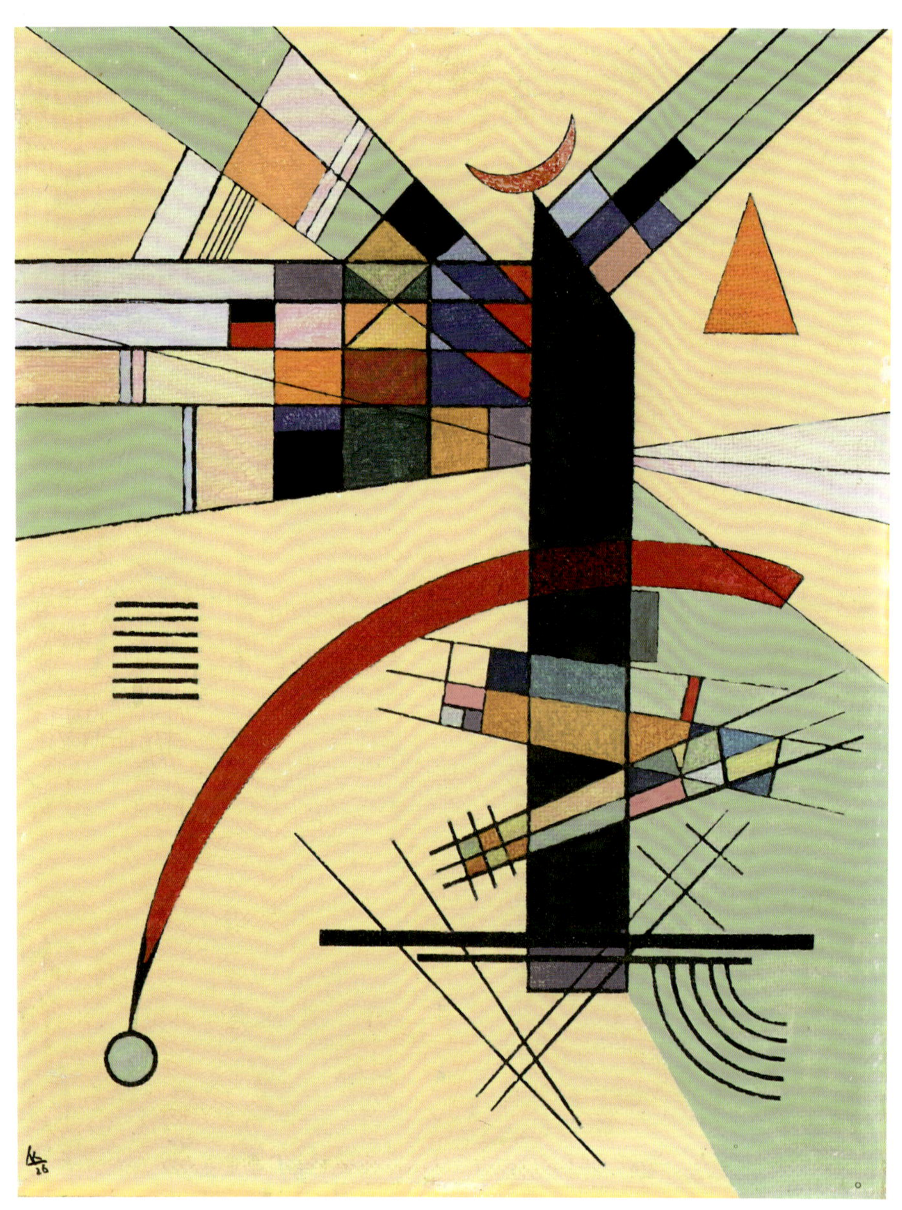

FIG. 125
Wassily Kandinsky
Small Yellow, 1926
Oil on composition board,
41 x 32 cm
Gift of Collection Société
Anonyme
1941.525

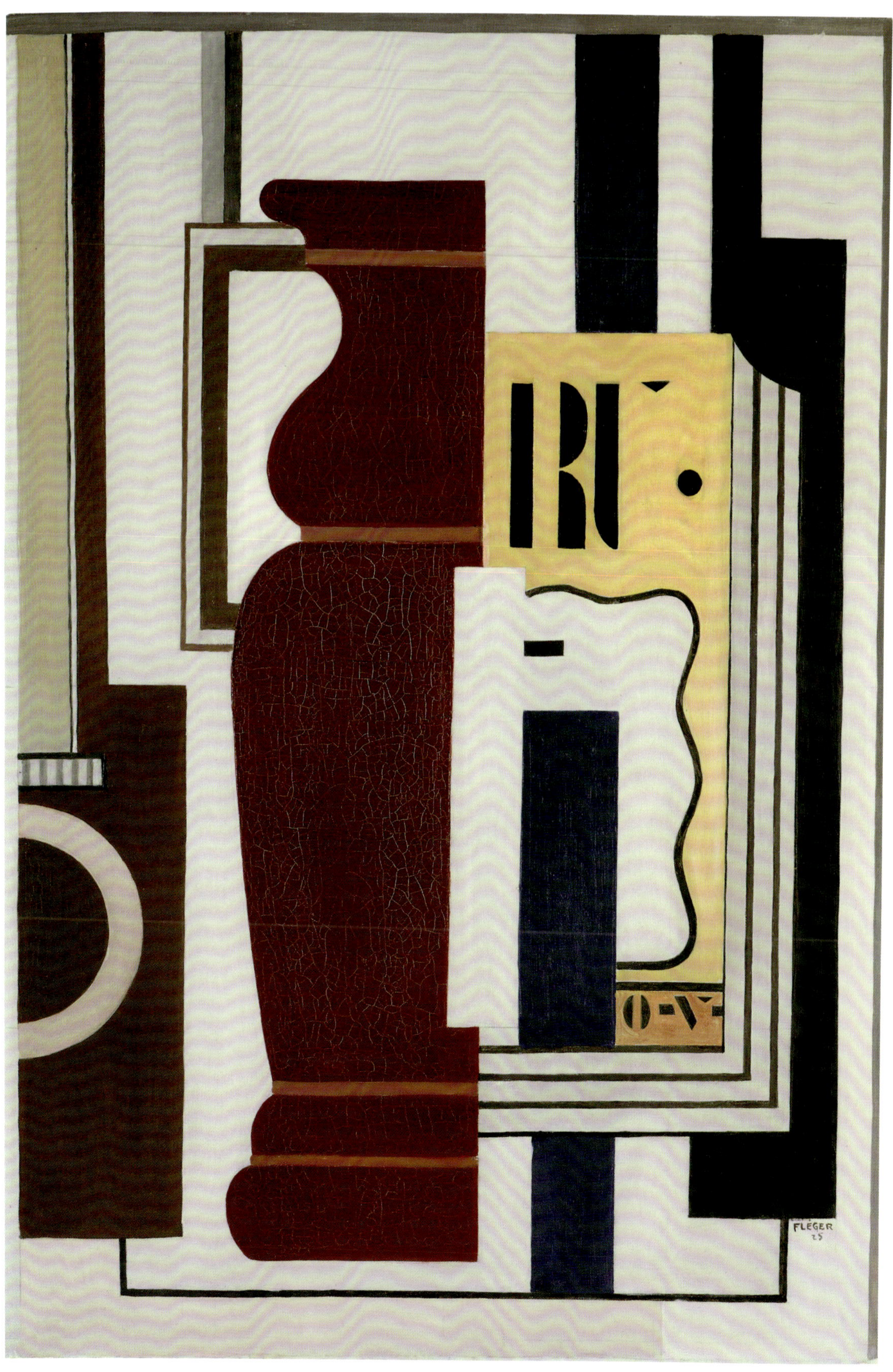

FIG. 126
Fernand Léger
Composition No. VII, 1925
Oil on canvas, mounted on
aluminum, 331.5 x 227.1 cm
Gift of Collection Société Anonyme
1941.542

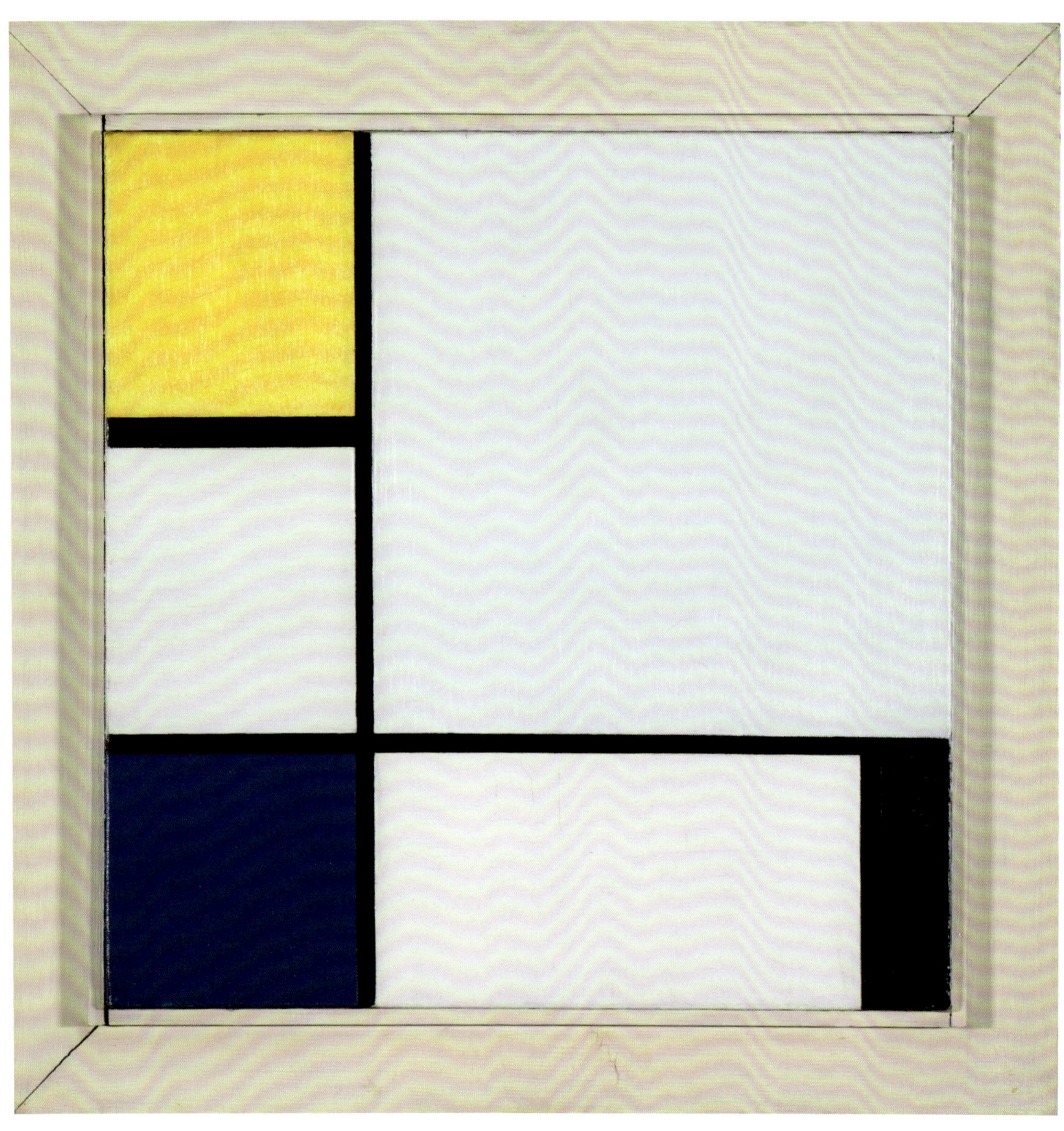

FIG. 127
Piet Mondrian
Composition, 1929
Oil on canvas, 50.6 x 50.3 cm
Gift of Collection Société
Anonyme
1941.603

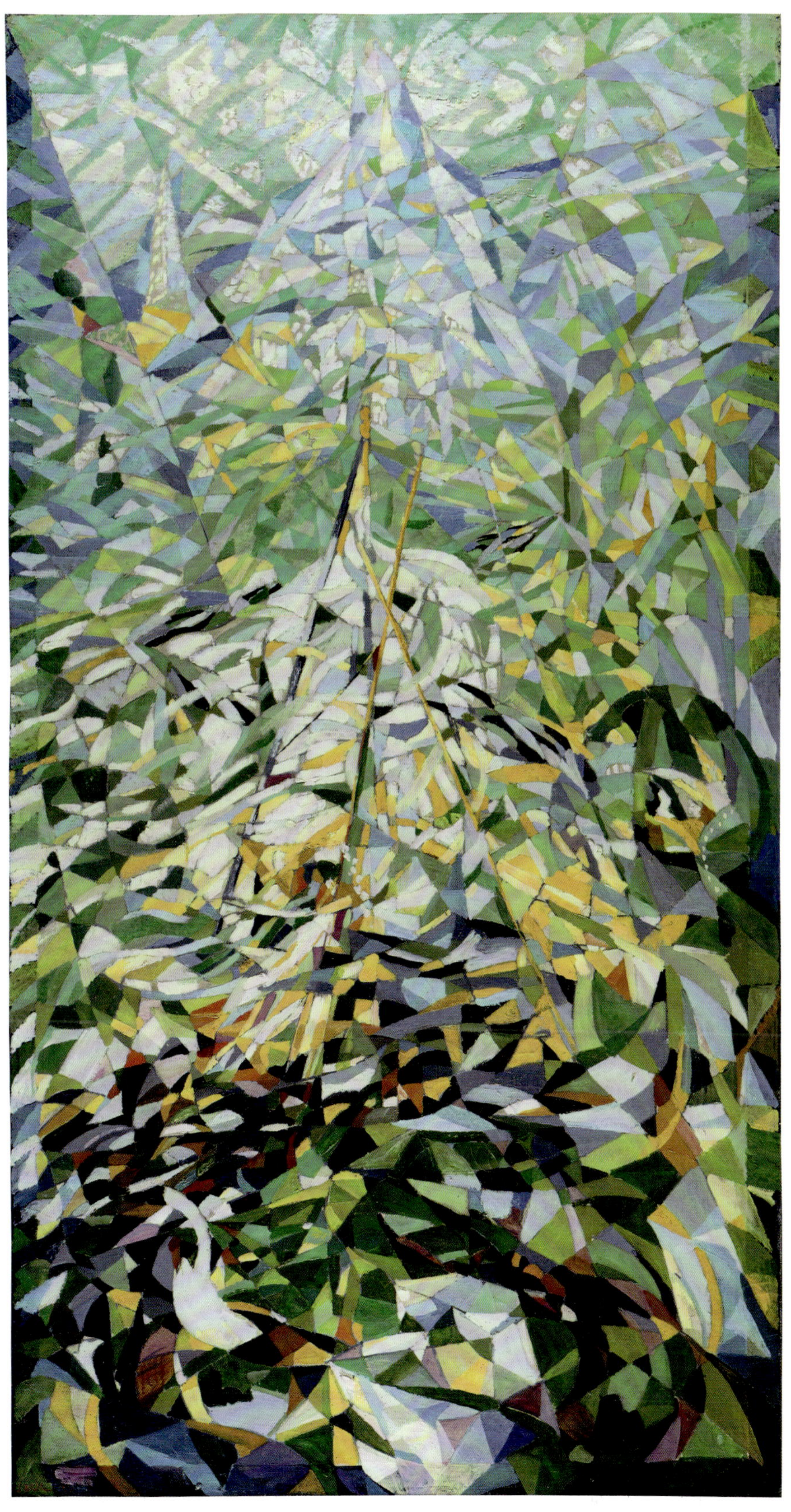

FIG. 128
Joseph Stella
Spring (The Procession),
ca. 1914–16
Oil on canvas, 191.3 x 102.1 cm
Gift of Collection Société
Anonyme
1941.692

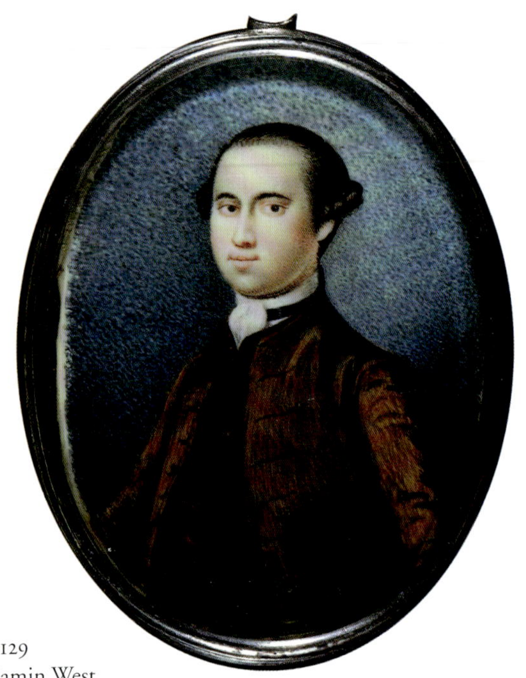

FIG. 129
Benjamin West
Self-Portrait, 1758 or 1759
Watercolor on ivory, 6.4 x 4.6 cm
Lelia A. and John Hill Morgan Collection
1940.529

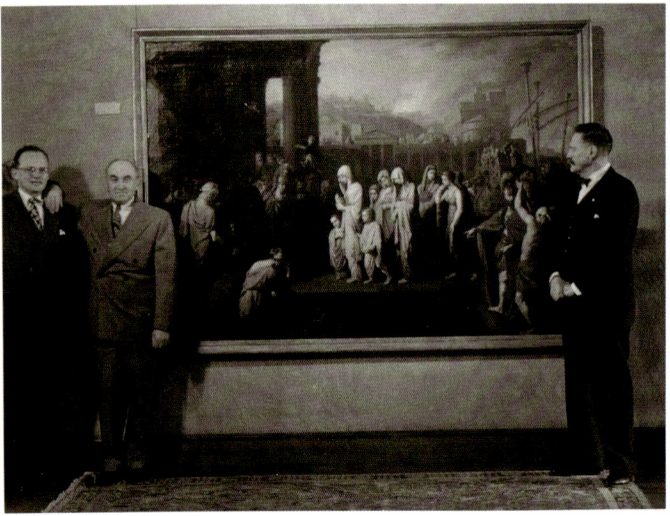

FIG. 130
Louis M. Rabinowitz (center), with George Heard Hamilton (left) and Theodore R. Sizer, 1947
Photograph courtesy Yale University Art Gallery Archives

portraits. His collection had been exhibited at the Metropolitan Museum of Art and the Brooklyn Museum. In 1937, he presented a portrait of John C. Calhoun to Calhoun College at Yale. He had numerous articles on American painting to his credit. The collection given by the Morgans between 1937 and 1951—some of it after his death—is a notable group of American portraits, including a self-portrait miniature by Benjamin West (fig. 129). The Morgans also provided a fund for the purchase of American paintings, which has enabled, among other acquisitions, the purchase of Benjamin West's *Cicero Discovering the Tomb of Archimedes.*

Other important American acquisitions followed. In 1943, the fabulous pair of portraits by John Singleton Copley of Mr. and Mrs. Isaac Smith (1769, the aunt and uncle of Abigail Adams; figs. 77a and 77b), in their original frames, were purchased for the collection with the Maitland Fuller Griggs, B.A. 1896, Fund, with Mr. Griggs's enthusiastic support, as major additions to the already strong American paintings collection. The second major collection of American furniture, following the Garvan Collection, was donated to the Gallery by C. Sanford Bull (B.A. 1893) beginning in 1949. Bull, a Middlebury, Connecticut, collector, focused on New England furniture, and his gift comprised more than thirty pieces from this region. The gift included a chest of drawers from Charleston, South Carolina, as well.

In 1947, Louis M. Rabinowitz gave Benjamin West's monumental neoclassical painting, *Agrippina Landing at Brundisium with the Ashes of Germanicus* (figs. 130 and 131), whose subject, the high moral standards of a distinguished Roman woman, was closely based on the account given by the ancient historian Tacitus. This was the first neoclassical painting by West to enter the collection, followed in 1963 by the purchase of *Cicero Discovering the Tomb of Archimedes,* as mentioned above, and it complemented the self-portrait miniature by West and the unattributed copy of his *Death of General Wolfe at the Heights of Abraham* that Lelia and John Hill Morgan had donated in 1940 and 1943. Given West's role as John Trumbull's teacher, and Trumbull's interest in both historical and neoclassical subject matter, these paintings were important additions to the Yale collection in more ways than one.

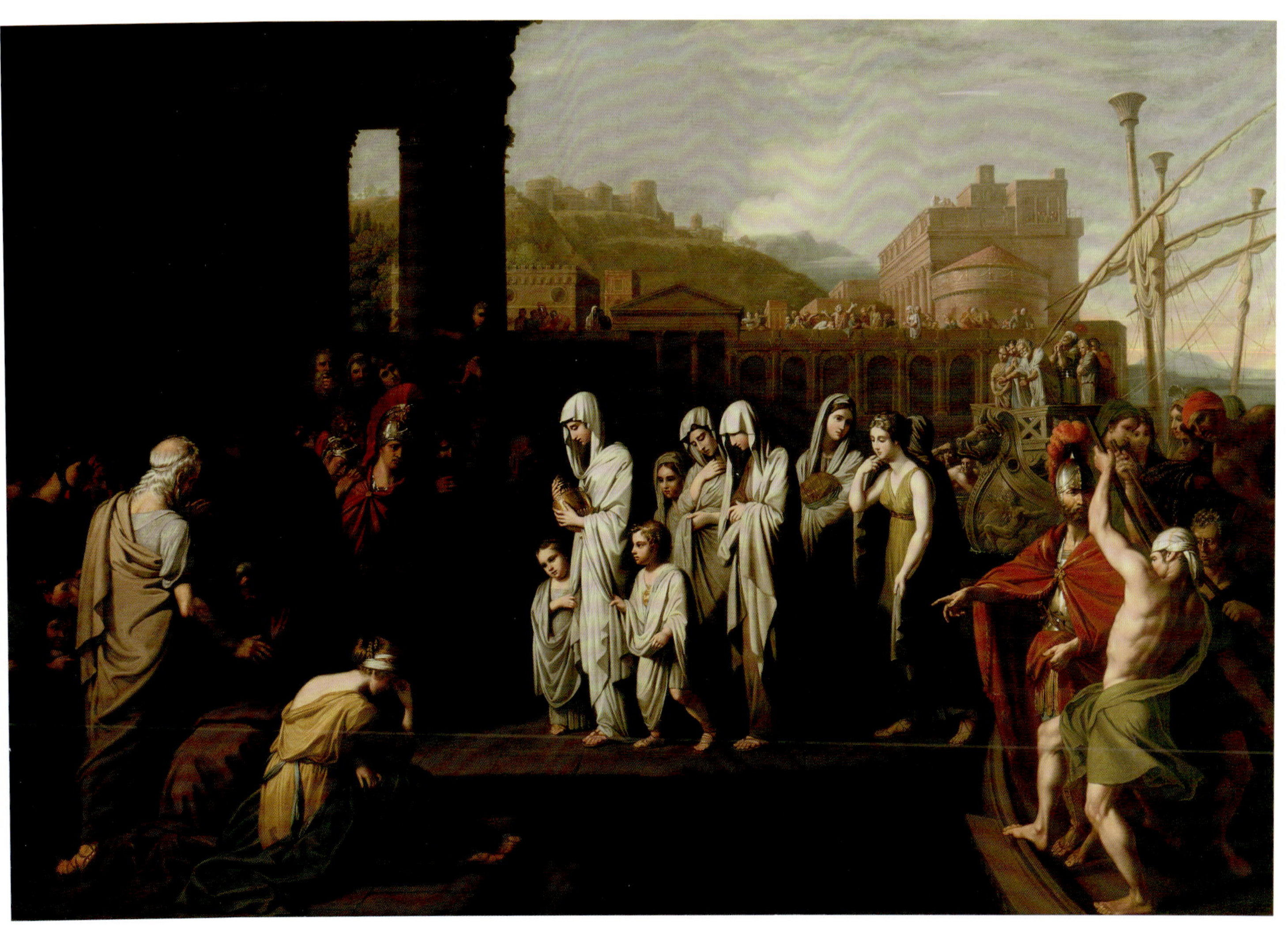

Fig. 131
Benjamin West
Agrippina Landing at Brundisium with the Ashes of Germanicus, 1768
Oil on canvas, 163.8 x 240 cm
Gift of Louis M. Rabinowitz
1947.16

Although he was not a Yale graduate, Louis Rabinowitz had been a generous donor to the academic program, establishing the Rabinowitz Fund for Judaica Research at Yale and funding a chair in Semitic languages and literature. He was an honorary trustee of the Yale Library and served on the Board of Trustees of the Art Gallery Associates during the 1940s and '50s, until his death in 1957. In 1955 he was cited by the University for his services.[8]

West's *Agrippina* was the only American painting that Louis Rabinowitz gave to Yale, but he and his wife were major donors to the European collections. The Rabinowitz gifts of Old Master paintings included Italian, German, and Flemish pictures. During his lifetime, he donated two oil paintings by Giovanni Battista Tiepolo showing *Polymnia, The Muse of Religious Poetry*; and *Thalia and Melpomene, The Muses of Comedy and Tragedy*. After his death, his widow, Hannah D. Rabinowitz, gave major works from their collection, including paintings by Giandomenico Tiepolo, Anthony van Dyck, Lucas Cranach the Elder, Hans Holbein, and Hieronymus Bosch, as well as more than twenty additional Italian paintings from the fourteenth through the sixteenth centuries. The Rabinowitz *Intemperance* by Hieronymous Bosch (fig. 132) is one of the few paintings in America by this extraordinary master of the horrifying and bizarre. The *Crucifixion with the Converted Centurion* is an exemplary work by the sixteenth-century German master Lucas Cranach the Elder (fig. 133). Recently, two fragments from an altarpiece showing the Virgin and the Archangel Gabriel in an Annunciation (fig. 134), believed to be by a follower of Fra Angelico when they were donated as part of the Rabinowitz gift, have been demonstrated to be by Angelico himself. The Rabinowitz gifts both broadened Yale's European holdings and added key works within the framework of the Gallery's existing early Italian collection.

Similarly, the 1943 bequest of early Italian paintings by Maitland Fuller Griggs built on Yale's fundamental European holding, the Jarves Collection. More than fifty Italian Renaissance paintings dating from the fourteenth through the sixteenth centuries, along with European sculpture and textiles, came to the Gallery in the Griggs bequest. Included were important paintings by Giovanni di Paolo, *Madonna and Child with Saints Jerome and Bartholomew*, and Taddeo di Bartolo, *St. Jerome* (fig. 135) and *St. John the Baptist* (fig. 136), among others. No single acquisition since the Jarves Collection has done more than the Griggs bequest to enrich Yale's holdings in early Italian art. In addition, the acquisition fund that Griggs established during his lifetime has continued to fund purchases in early Italian art, as well as in other fields. Such purchases have frequently been chosen to complement existing holdings for use in teaching, as, for example, the rare engraving by Antonio Pollaiuolo *Battle of the Nudes* purchased in 1951 (fig. 137), which provides a wide array of nude male figures for comparison with the nude Hercules in the painting *Hercules and Deianira* by the same artist in the Jarves Collection (fig. 40).

The gifts of Italian and Flemish paintings from Robert Lehman (B.A. 1913) in 1946 further strengthened the late fifteenth- and sixteenth-century parts of the paintings collection, with notable works by Vittore Crivelli (fig. 138), complementing the Carlo Crivelli from the Rabinowitz Collection, and Quentin Massys. Lehman's gifts to the Gallery over the years included not only paintings but also drawings, medals, and pages from illuminated manuscripts. Particularly significant among his gifts are fourteen drawings by Giovanni Battista Tiepolo, among them *Merit and Fame*, a study for a ceiling (fig. 139). In addition to these European works, the Lehman gifts included an important collection of ancient glass.

Important changes in the staff occurred during the 1940s. Theodore Sizer, hired as curator of paintings and sculpture and associate professor of history of art in 1927 and named associate director in 1929 by Everett V. Meeks, served as director from 1940 until his resignation on June 30, 1947 (fig. 140), with a leave of absence for war service from 1942–44. Among the important exhibitions that he brought to Yale was *Art of Australia, 1788–1941*, drawn from Australian collections based on Sizer's selections. Deeply involved as curator in the completion of the Swartwout building, as described earlier, Sizer remained proud of the role he played in this project. Less evident and glamorous, but of fundamental importance to raising the professional standards of the Gallery's management of its collection, was Sizer's

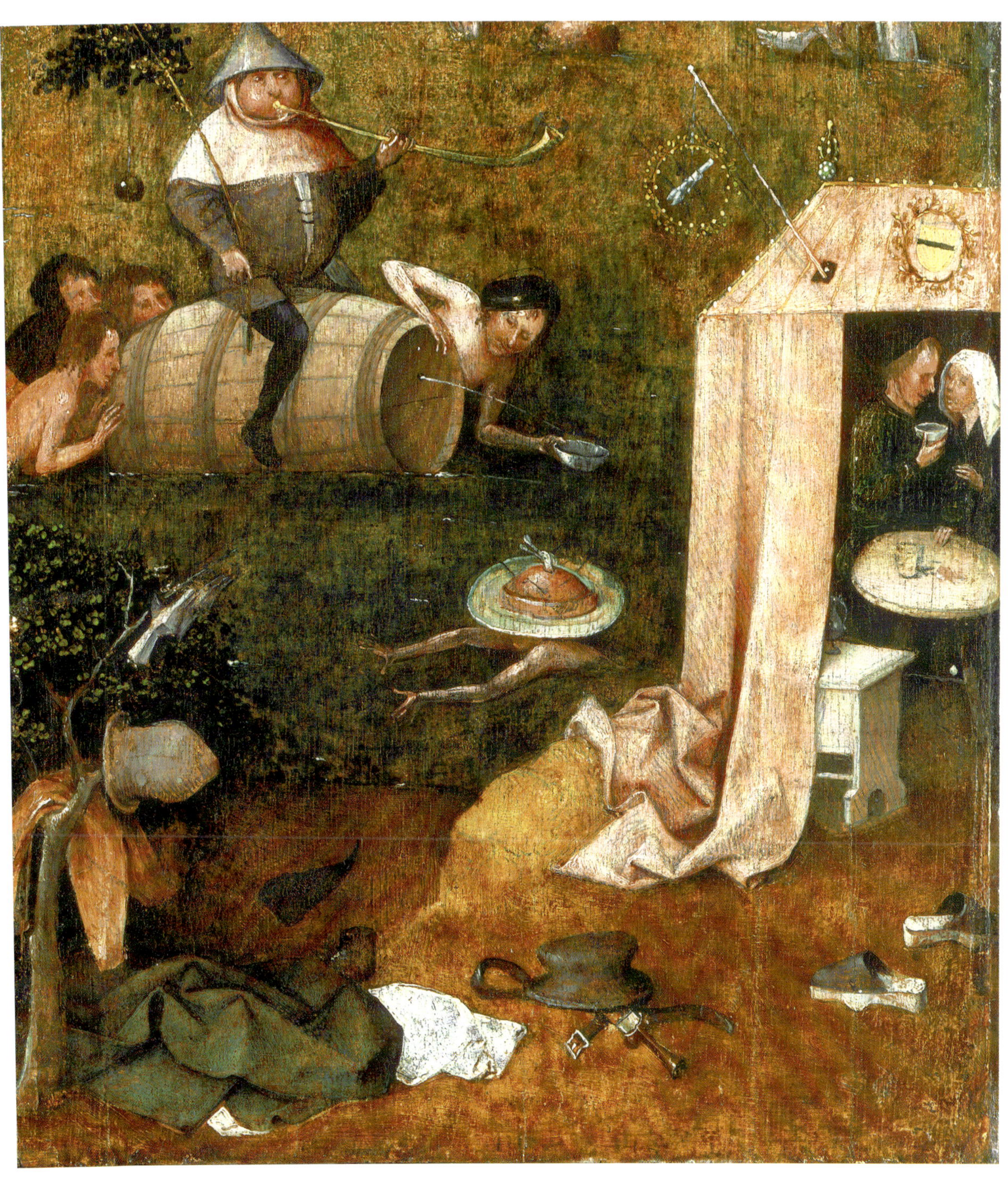

FIG. 132
Hieronymus Bosch
Intemperance, ca. 1500–1515
Oil on panel, 35.9 x 31.4 cm
Gift of Hannah D. and Louis M. Rabinowitz
1959.15.22

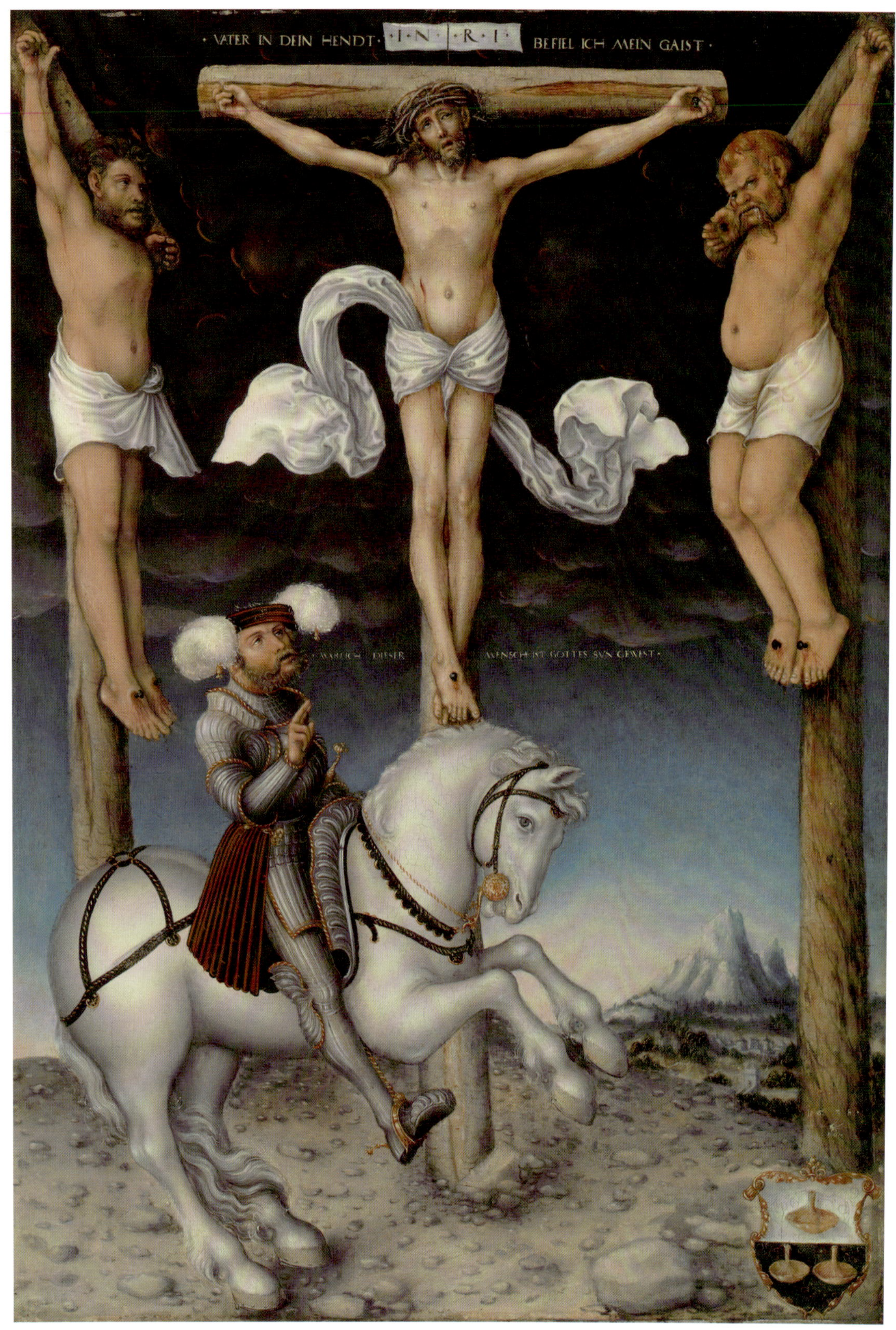

FIG. 133
Lucas Cranach, the Elder
Crucifixion with the Converted Centurion, 1538
Oil on panel, 61.6 x 42.2 x 1.9 cm
Gift of Hannah D. and Louis M. Rabinowitz
1959.15.23

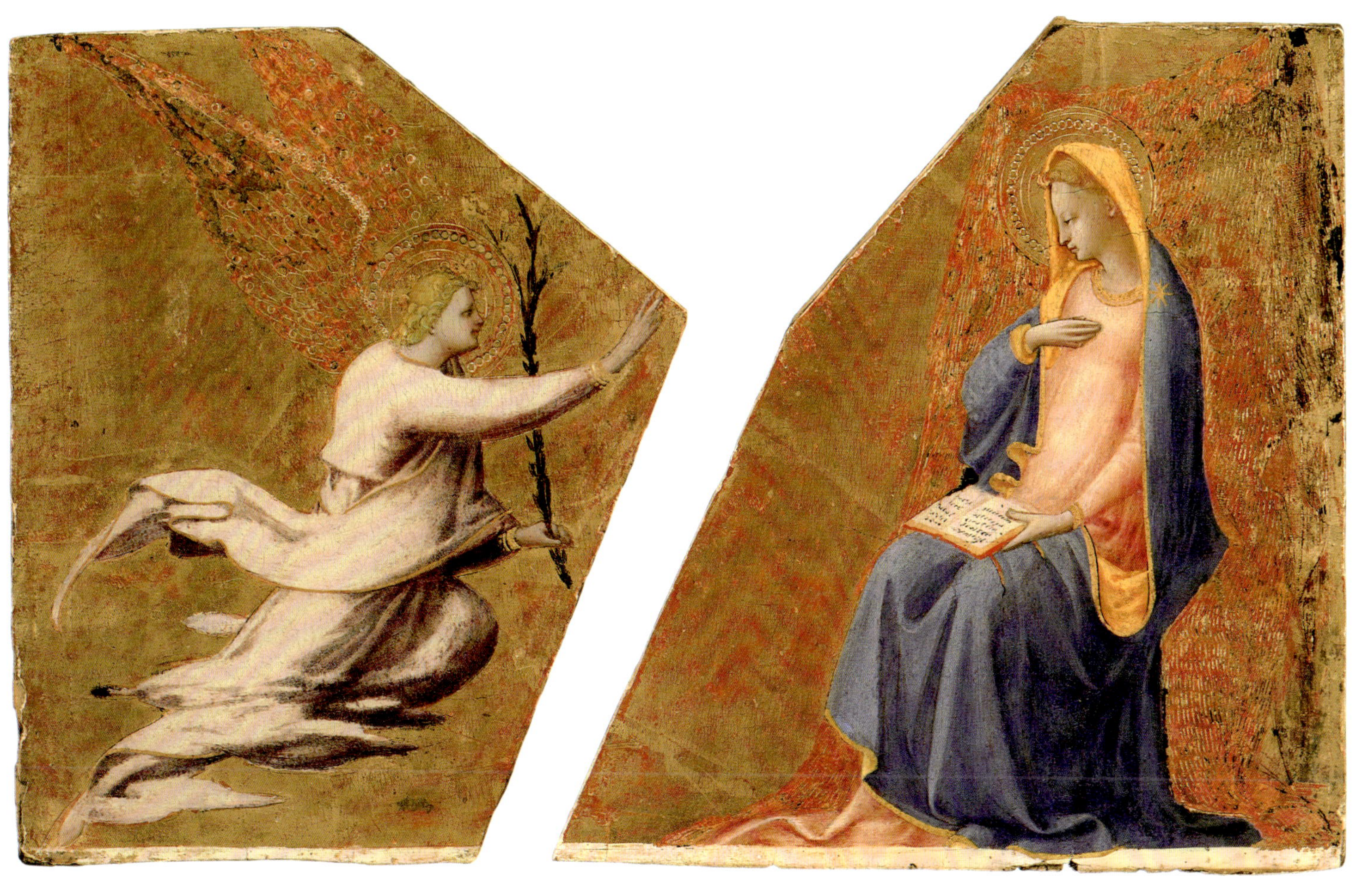

FIG. 134
Fra Angelico
Annunciation, ca. 1440
Tempera on panel, 18.4 x 28.6 cm
Gift of Hannah D. and Louis M.
Rabinowitz
1959.15.6

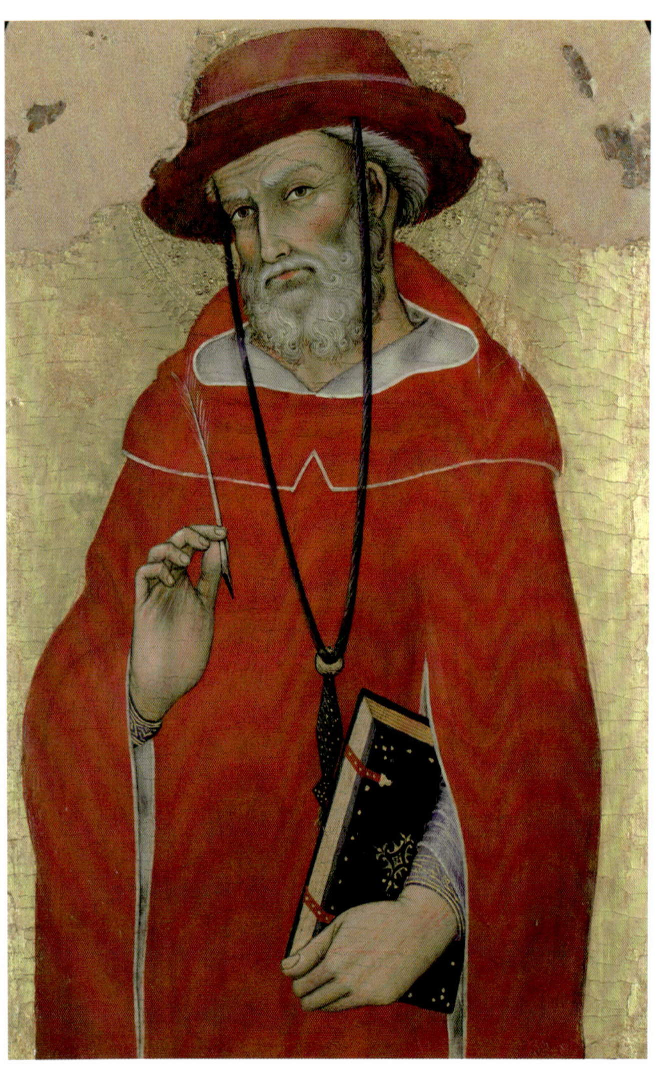

FIG. 135
Taddeo di Bartolo
St. Jerome, ca. 1390
Egg tempera on panel, 50.6 x 36.0 cm
Bequest of Maitland F. Griggs,
B.A. 1896
1943.250

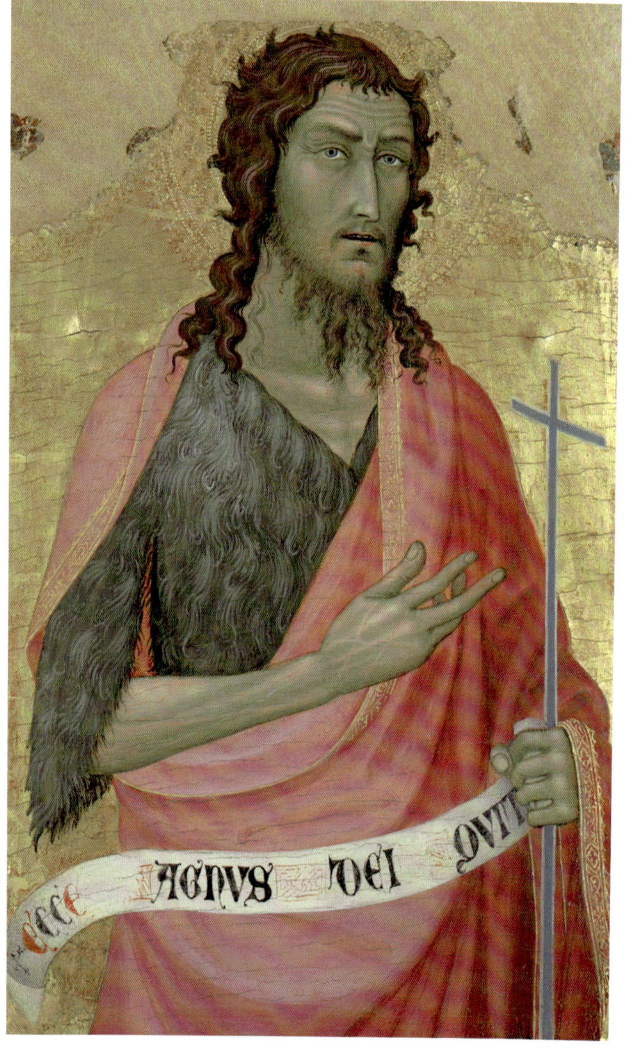

FIG. 136
Taddeo di Bartolo
St. John the Baptist, ca. 1390
Tempera on panel, 50.6 x 36.0 cm
Bequest of Maitland F. Griggs,
B.A. 1896
1943.251

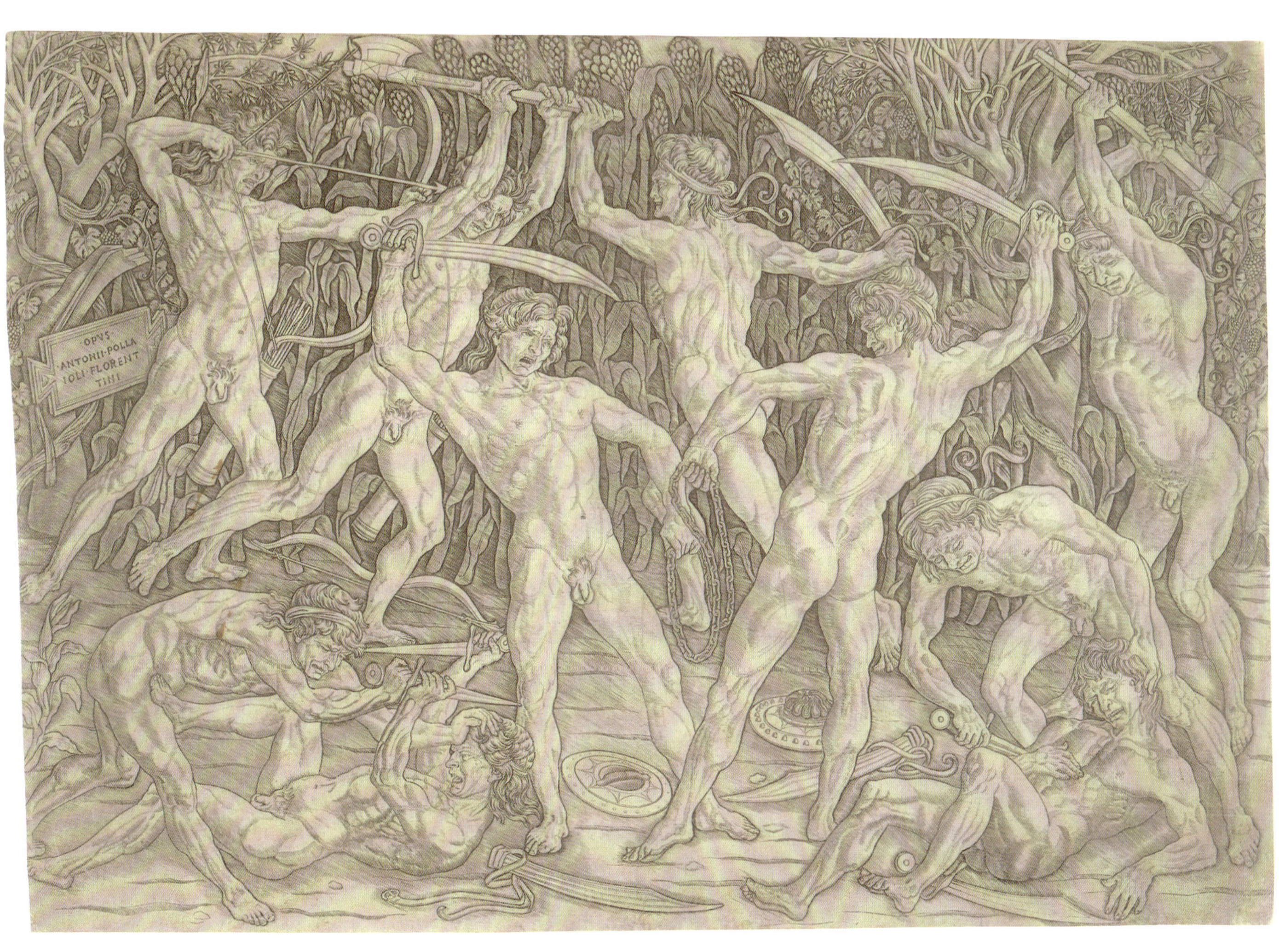

FIG. 137
Antonio del Pollaiuolo
Battle of the Nudes, ca. 1470–75
Engraving, 40 x 58 cm
Maitland F. Griggs, B.A. 1896, Fund
1951.9.18

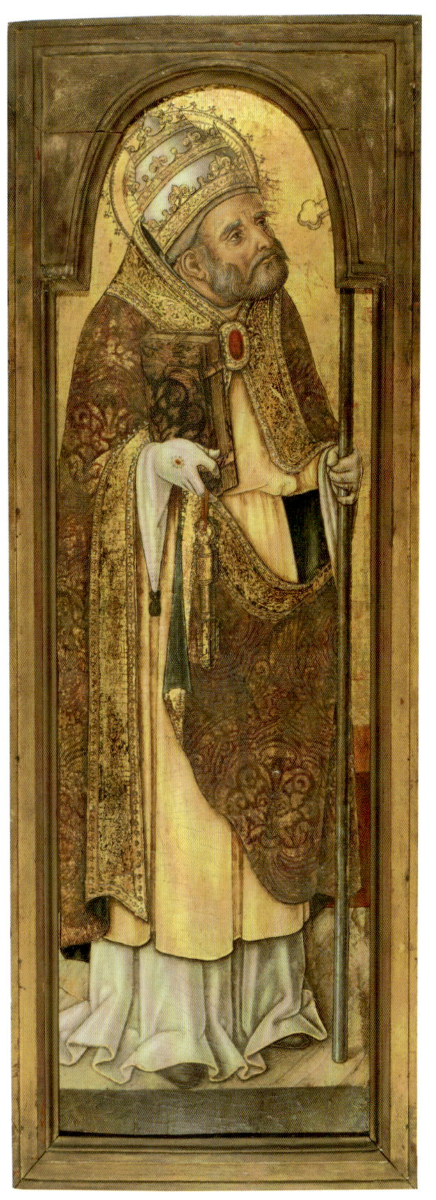

FIG. 138
Vittore Crivelli
St. Peter, ca. 1490–1500
Tempera and gold on panel, 102.2 x 33.5 cm
Gift of Robert Lehman, B.A. 1913
1946.313

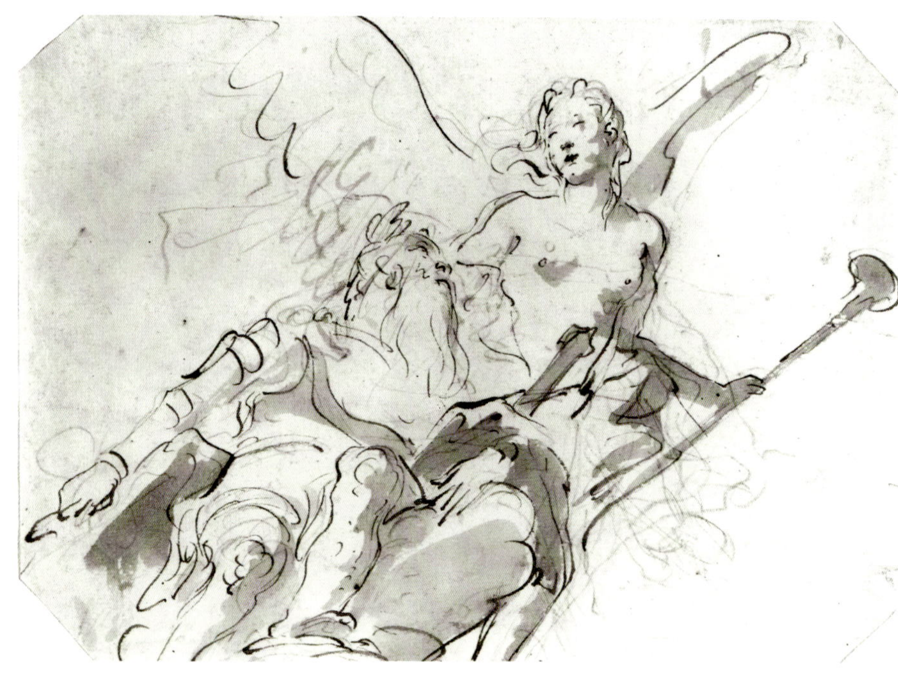

FIG. 139
Giovanni Battista Tiepolo
Merit and Fame, late 1750s
Pen, ink, and wash over sketch in black chalk, 27.9 x 19.6 cm
Gift of Robert Lehman, B.A. 1913
1941.295

massive assault on the Gallery's collection records, the first such comprehensive effort in the Gallery's history. Sizer viewed this as one of his major contributions. In his final report to the Governing Board in 1947, he stated that "he would like to be remembered as one who worked long and hard at the thankless task of getting the scattered records of the objects in the collections—the source, terms of gift or loan and all the rest of the dull but vital data—into some kind of shape, inaugurating the system of cataloguing, curatorial files and records of proceedings. He went through a hundred years of correspondence and extracted notations referring to specific objects. He trusts that no future director will ever have to operate in the dark as he did during his early years at Yale."[9]

Sizer added to the curatorial and education staff and emphasized public education. He taught, as he recorded, 1,406 Yale undergraduate and graduate students, offering courses on prints and museum training. He increased the focus on modern art through acquisitions and exhibitions, especially of the Société Anonyme Collection. In accord with Meeks, Sizer encouraged the shift from the Swartwout plan for expanding the Gallery in the style of the 1928 building to the modernist proposal of Philip Goodwin, which ultimately led to Louis Kahn's landmark design. It was also Sizer who urged the renaming of the Gallery of Fine Arts, Yale University, to the Yale University Art Gallery. A stylish writer, Sizer retired to pursue a life of scholarship, writing, and teaching.

John Marshall Phillips, who had served as curator of American silver beginning in 1932 and curator of the Garvan Collections since 1935, took on the additional duties of assistant director from 1946–47 and acting director in 1947–48. He became director in June 1948, retaining this post and that of curator until his death in 1953.[10] Simultaneously, he held a faculty position in history of art. John Hill Morgan, who had been curator of American painting since 1931, died in office in 1945. After Morgan's death, the position was divided between John Marshall Phillips as curator of the Garvan Collection and George Heard Hamilton as curator of paintings. The titles held by curators changed frequently during the 1930s, '40s, and '50s, at least in part due to the unprecedented growth of the collections. Hamilton,

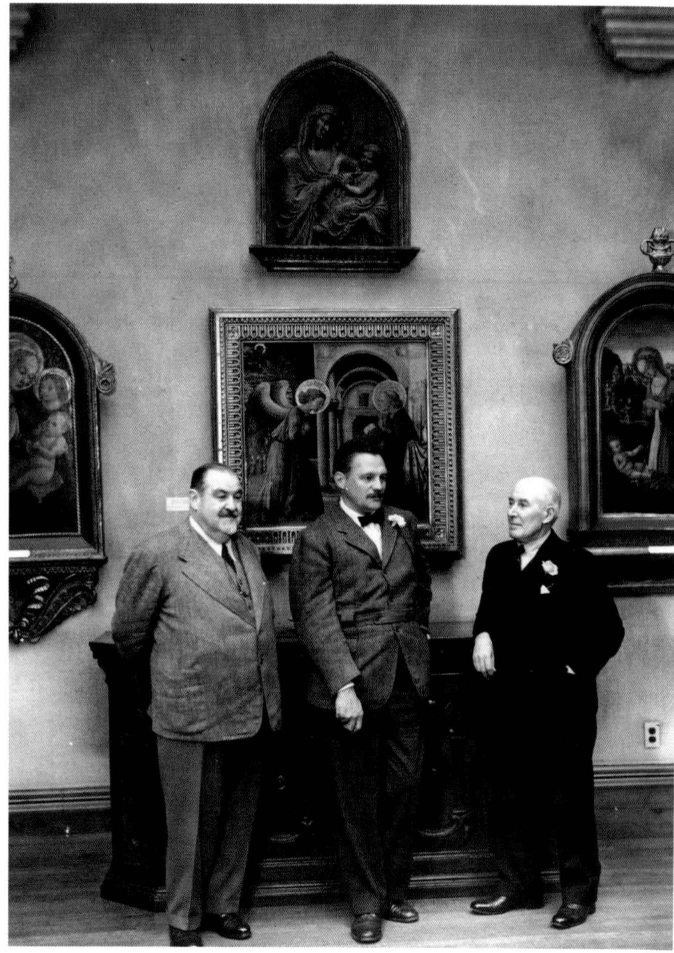

FIG. 140
Theodore Sizer (center), E.V. Meeks (left), and Will Ashton, Director, National Gallery, New South Wales, Sydney, Australia
Photograph courtesy Yale University Art Gallery Archives

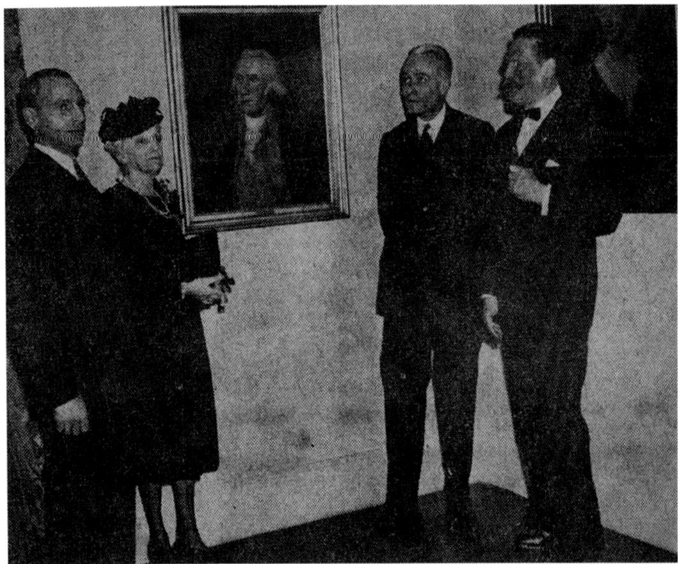

FIG. 141
Lelia Hill Morgan, with William C. Celantano, Mayor of New Haven (left), Wilmarth S. Lewis, and Theodore Sizer (right), at the opening of the exhibition, *New Haven Register*, February 24, 1946

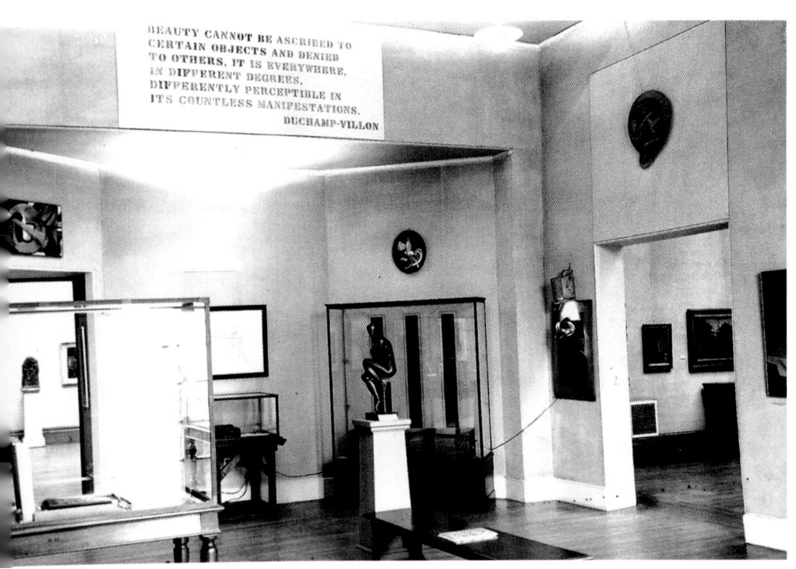

FIG. 142
Duchamp—Duchamp-Villon—Villon, 1945
Photograph courtesy Yale University Art Gallery Archives

for example, was curator of paintings from 1946 to 1949, curator of the Edwin Austin Abbey and Société Anonyme Collections by 1951, and curator of modern art by 1955. In 1949, Charles Seymour became curator of Renaissance art and Sumner McKnight Crosby curator of mediaeval art. Both were primarily faculty members in history of art; faculty members seem often to have been signed on as specialist curators in their fields of expertise, also facilitating their frequent use of the collections in teaching. By 1947, the annual staff list published in the *Bulletin* records positions of docent, assistant docent, restorer, photographer, museum assistant, and secretary to the director in addition to the curatorial and senior administrative staff. By 1948 there was a registrar. Caroline Rollins began her long career at the Gallery in 1949 as membership secretary and editor of the *Bulletin.*

The exhibition schedule continued in the 1940s with the same intensity and commensurate variety of themes that had characterized the previous decade. Shows related to World War II and its aftermath continued into 1947. There were several exhibitions marking the acquisition of new collections, notably the *John Hill Morgan Memorial Exhibition of American Art* (1946; fig. 141). The Société Anonyme Collection inspired numerous exhibitions that drew from Katherine Dreier's collection, the Museum of Modern Art, other private collections, and the holdings of artists. Exhibitions of student and faculty work continued.

The decade's major exhibitions focused on early American painting and twentieth-century art. In 1949, John Marshall Phillips organized *The Smibert Tradition*, an exhibition of paintings by John Smibert, whose pioneering group portrait *Dean Berkeley and His Entourage (The Bermuda Group)* (fig. 2) had come to Yale in 1808. This major show was described in its catalogue as the first exhibition of Smibert's work since 1730, when the first exhibition of his work, and indeed the first art exhibition held in colonial Boston, took place. The Yale exhibition included paintings by Smibert and a few imitators, drawn from the Yale collection, private collections, and the museums in Chicago, Boston, Baltimore, Brooklyn, and New York. As was often the case, the volume of the *Bulletin of the Associates in Fine Arts* that coincided with the exhibition served as its catalogue.

Another first was the Gallery's exhibition of work by Marcel Duchamp and his brothers, Duchamp-Villon and Villon, in 1945 (fig. 142), mentioned earlier. A series of exhibitions in 1945 celebrating the liberation of Italy, France, and Greece from German occupation included an exhibition of French art featuring loans from Walter Bareiss (B.S. 1940s), Stephen Carlton Clark (B.A. 1903), and Edith Wetmore, all subsequently major donors to the Gallery, and George Heard Hamilton (B.A. 1932, PH.D. 1942).

The end of the decade was the occasion of a major loan exhibition of French paintings from alumni collections and friends of Yale that opened at Yale in spring of 1950 and traveled to the National Gallery of Art and the Phillips Collection. The exhibition, which filled all four bays in the Sculpture Hall, was arranged by Charles H. Sawyer, director of the Division of the Arts, John Marshall Phillips, director of the Gallery, and Lamont Moore, the Gallery's associate director. Lenders included Robert Lehman, Paul Mellon (B.A. 1929), the Havemeyers, Edith Wetmore, Stephen Carlton Clark, Mrs. Frank Altschul, and Leonard C. Hanna (B.A. 1913). Attendance was a record-breaking 10,452. Four public lectures were given under the aegis of the Ryerson Fund for Lectures.

During the academic year 1950–51, an "Exhibition of the Week" program was launched. These small, focused exhibitions ranged from a comparison of raised and sunk relief in ancient Egyptian art or the technique of etching as seen in Rembrandt's *The Hundred Guilder Print*, from the Achelis Collection, to a show about fire that featured Currier and Ives prints of fires and the records of the fire company in Bridgeport, borrowed from the Yale library. The term "Yale Worthies," often used for the seemingly innumerable portraits of professors and deans of Yale, was enshrined as the title of an exhibition of such portraits in 1951, staged to celebrate the two hundred and fiftieth anniversary of the University and the publication of the *Yale University Portrait Index*, edited by Josephine Setze.

In 1952, an exhibition presented the recent cleaning of some pictures in the Jarves Collection. *Craftsmanship in American Silver from the Yale Collections* exhibited the work of sixty-four early American silversmiths, revealing the comprehensive range of the Garvan Collection and embodying the scholarly approach to the collection that its curator, John Marshall Phillips, had adopted.

The year 1952 closed with a memorial exhibition to Katherine Dreier, marking the end of a significant relationship in the Gallery's history. The exhibition offered the sole public view of Miss Dreier's personal collection before it was dispersed among several museums according to her will and the efforts of Marcel Duchamp, her executor. Nearly three hundred of these works came to Yale, enriching the Société Anonyme Collection, as described above. Thus ended the Gallery's introduction to modernism.

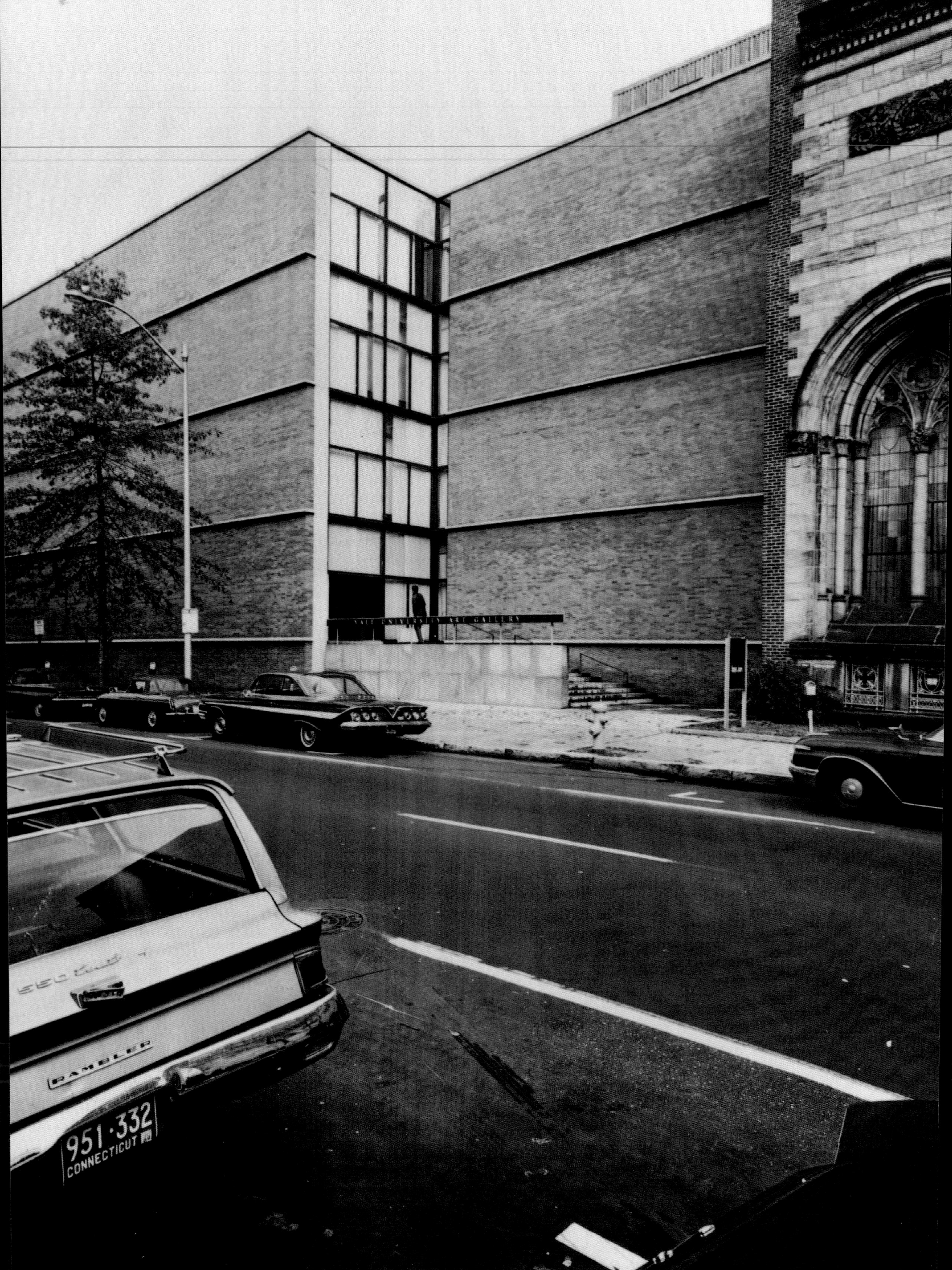
YALE UNIVERSITY ART GALLERY
RAMBLER
951-332
CONNECTICUT

CHAPTER II

"A New Building for the Arts at Yale"

By the end of 1950, the collection included slightly under 50,000 (49,100) objects. Its strengths were essentially as they are now: American art, early Italian art, early twentieth-century art, and ancient art, with growing holdings of prints and drawings, later European art, and Asian art. Two new fields of collecting, African and Precolumbian art, began at Yale in the 1950s. Contemporary art, from both within Yale and without, continued to be a focus for exhibitions, acquisitions, and teaching.

The staff was also growing. John Marshall Phillips was the Gallery's director and Lamont Moore was associate director and administrator. The curatorial staff included a mixture of museum professionals and faculty curators. The *Bulletin* for January 1951 lists curators of the Mabel Brady Garvan Collection (John Marshall Phillips), the Edwin Austin Abbey and Société Anonyme Collections (George Heard Hamilton), the Hobart Moore Memorial Collection of Textiles (Margaret T. J. Rowe), mediaeval art (Sumner McKnight Crosby), Renaissance art (Charles Seymour, Jr.), coins (Alfred R. Bellinger), and sporting art (Robert J. H. Kiphuth). There were honorary curators of Egyptian antiquities (Ludlow Bull), prints (Carl A. Lohmann), textiles (George Hewitt Myers), ancient art (Michael I. Rostovtzeff), and the Babylonian collection (Ferris J. Stephens). A. Elizabeth Chase was the docent, with assistant docent Helen Wade Smith. Mary Mills Hatch was the registrar, a position apparently created in 1948. Andrew Petryn had joined the staff as research assistant in conservation. There was a photographer, a museum assistant, and a secretary to the associate director, who assisted with the daily administration of the museum. In 1951 Caroline Rollins was serving as membership secretary and editor of the *Bulletin*.

Charles H. Sawyer was dean of the School of Fine Arts and director of the Division of Arts, the latter post created in 1947 to oversee the Gallery of Fine Arts and the departments of Painting and Sculpture, Architecture, and Drama. Sawyer's first report to the President, Charles Seymour, reiterated the critical need for the new building for the Gallery. Fund-raising for the building, which was projected to cost $1.5 million, was under way, building on the commitment of $500,000 designated for a new Gallery by the Corporation.

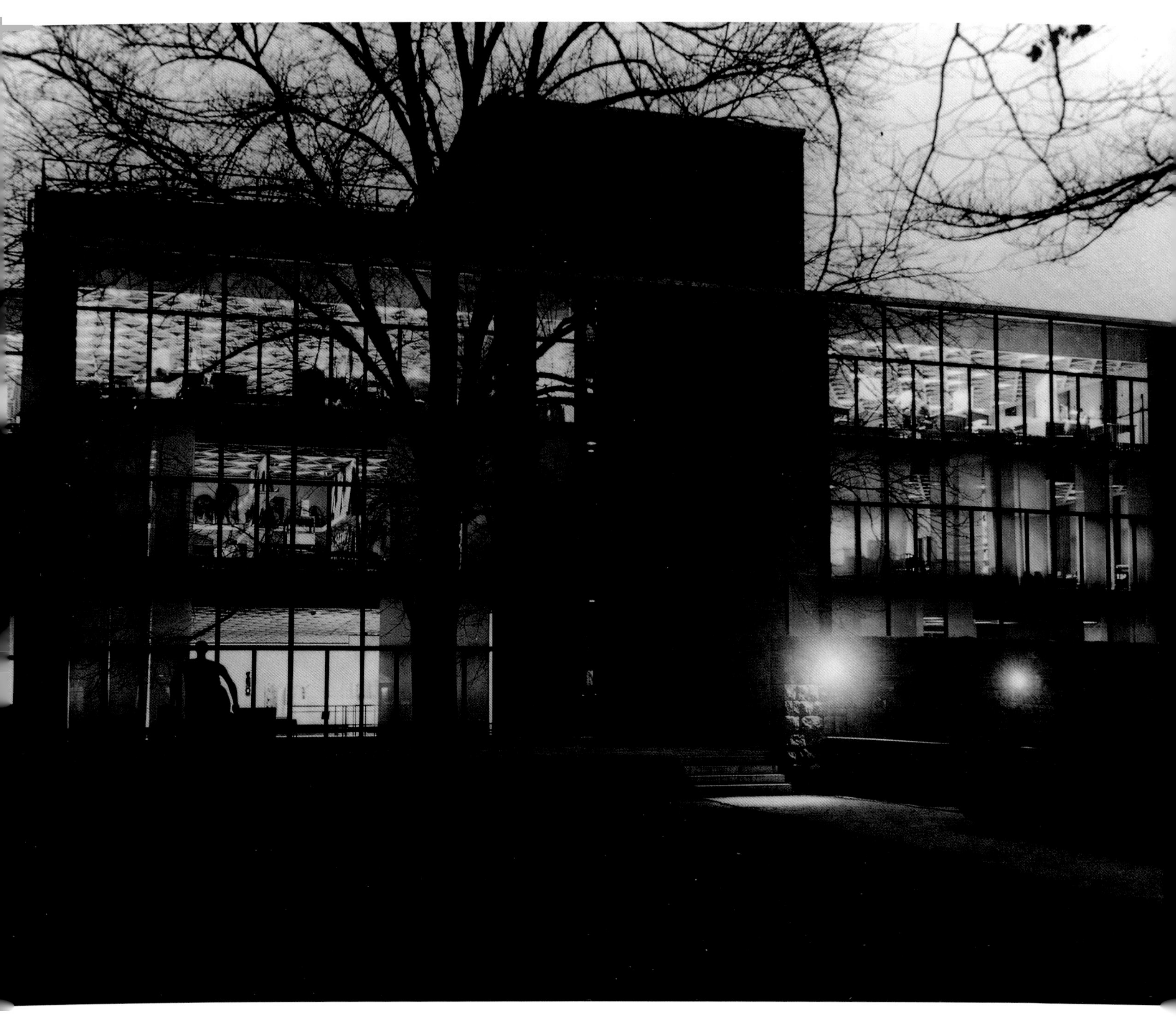

FIG. 143 (front view, p. 144) and
143a (garden view, above)
Louis I. Kahn
Yale University Art Gallery and Design Center, 1953
Photographs, ca. 1959, courtesy Yale University Art Gallery Archives

Numerous trips by Sawyer and John Marshall Phillips yielded $1 million in donations from alumni and friends of the arts at Yale. Phillip Goodwin's design, which had been revised several times since he originally presented it in 1941 (fig. 117), was still the basis for the plans, with construction set to begin in the summer of 1952. In December 1950, however, Goodwin resigned, citing medical reasons. Dean Sawyer and George Howe, professor and chairman of the architecture department, invited Eero Saarinen, chief critic in architecture in the 1940s, to take on the job, but he declined. Saarinen recommended Louis I. Kahn, who had as yet built few public buildings and was not well known, although he had been a visiting critic at Yale since 1947. His modernist style fit the wishes of Dean Sawyer and Professor Howe for the new building. Kahn was in Rome, but he agreed to accept the commission.

The cornerstone ceremonies took place on November 7, 1952, precisely one year before the building was dedicated. Wilmarth S. Lewis (B.A. 1918, Hon. M.A. 1937), scholar, author of *Yale's Collections*, and a member of the Yale Corporation, delivered the address. Mrs. Paul Moore, as vice president of the Trustees of the Associates in Fine Arts at Yale, represented the donors of the building. The Yale Glee Club performed some of the same songs that were sung at the laying of the cornerstone of Street Hall in 1864. Although construction was interrupted by a citywide strike by bricklayers and laborers in May of 1953, the building was sufficiently completed for classes to be held in the fall term, and the dedication took place on schedule on November 6, 1953. Lamont Moore, who had recently been appointed as director to succeed John Marshall Phillips, who had died unexpectedly the previous spring, officially inaugurated the new building.

Kahn's design for the Yale University Art Gallery and Design Center, the first of the triad of museum designs that he created for Yale and the Kimbell Art Museum in Fort Worth, Texas, is rightly considered a landmark in modern architecture (figs. 143 and 143a).[1] Although Goodwin's design and Howe's adaptation of it provided a basis for some of Kahn's thinking, Kahn's final plan goes well beyond the visions of his predecessors. Much has been written about this building and this is not the place to evaluate Kahn's achievement once again, but it is worth noting that much of what is now praised in Kahn's design was already appreciated at the time of the building's dedication. It was both the first modernist building at Yale and a dramatic departure from Yale's earlier museums and American museum architecture as a whole.

The review of the new building in *Perspecta: The Yale Architectural Journal* enumerated Kahn's goals for the building. First, Kahn "set himself the task of creating a space in which the structure and the mechanical equipment—lighting, acoustical and climatic—would all live one life and would become the basic means of artistic expression. Integral unity in form was his first objective."[2] Kahn echoed this thought in a comment made at the opening of the building: "Everything here marches together for the solution."[3] Kahn's second goal, according to *Perspecta*, was permanence. Since future uses of the building could not be anticipated (it was generally understood that there would ultimately be a new art school and that Kahn's building would then become exclusively a museum), it was necessary to create "a universal space, . . . easily adaptable to new patterns of use."[4] Finally, the building should embody Kahn's convictions that "order lies at the root of all architecture," and a "discipline of spirit rather than emotional whims produce[s] works of art."[5]

The primary features of the building that drew the attention of the press and architectural critics in 1953 were its flexibility, the tetrahedral ceiling, and the exposed, unmodified interior surfaces. Flexibility was essential for the varied functions the building was to serve. Until 1963, when the new Art and Architecture building designed by Paul Rudolph opened and the Kahn building became exclusively the Art Gallery, studios and classrooms for painting, sculpture, graphic design, and architecture shared space with offices, classrooms, and exhibition galleries, and the assignment of space to these various functions changed several times. As Vincent Scully, then assistant professor of art and architecture at Yale, described it in the issue of the *Yale Daily News* marking the dedication of the new building,

> The building is conceived as a simple loft space organized around stairway, elevator, and utility centers. In order to provide unimpeded, flexible

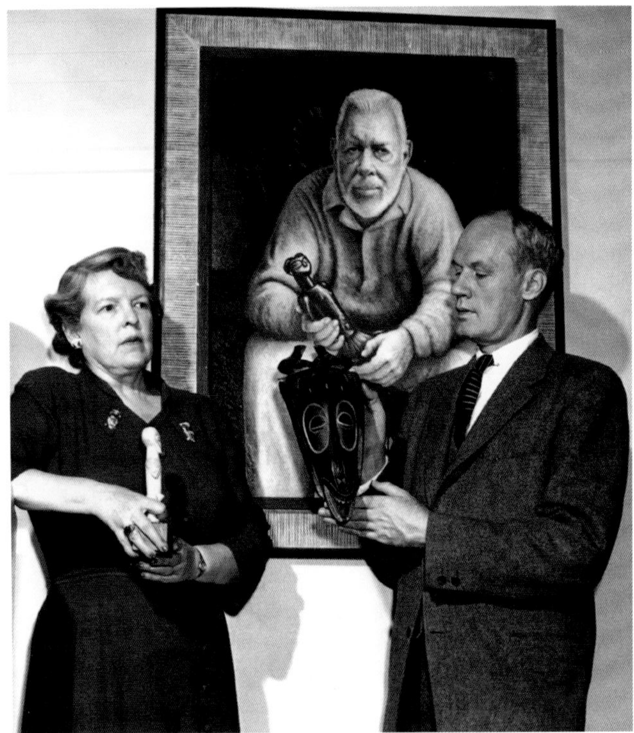

FIG. 144
Lamont Moore and Mrs. Ralph M. Linton, 1954
Photograph courtesy Yale University Art Gallery Archives

FIG. 145
Louis I. Kahn and the tetrahedral ceiling
Photograph courtesy Yale University Art Gallery Archives

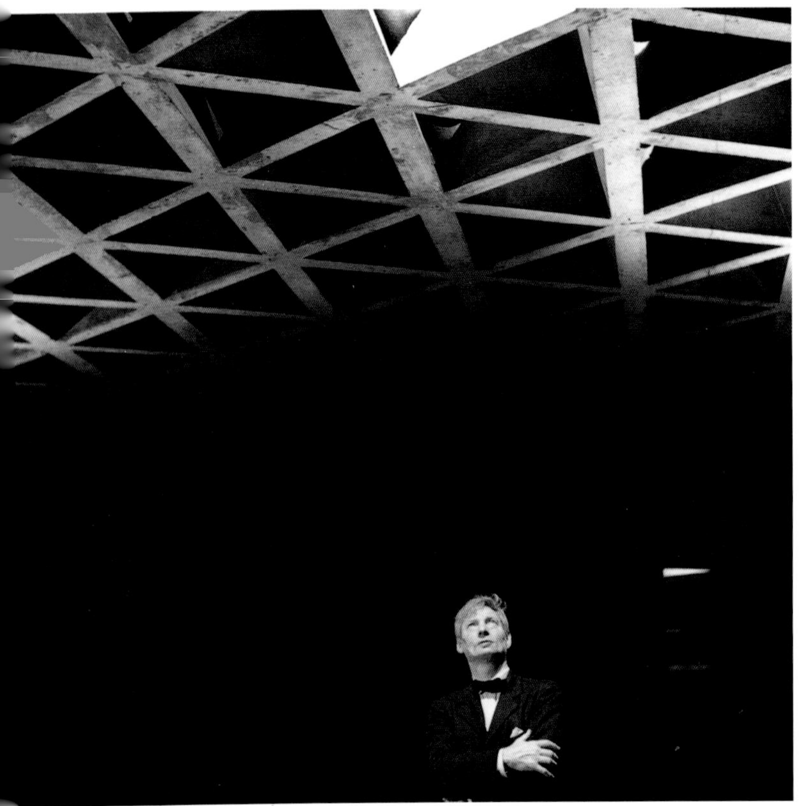

> space about these service cores, Louis I. Kahn has invented a new kind of reinforced concrete slab construction which makes use of a cellular structure of hollow tetrahedrons to form both the ceiling and floor in one homogenous unit. The structural piers of the building are thus meant to support an integrated canopy rather than conventional beams and slabs. With this system, distribution of forces should be almost continuous, and mechanical facilities and lighting devices can be easily installed and concealed. Under the open canopy the spaces of the individual floors assume sweep, power, and dignity.[6]

Flexibility was one of the key charges to the architect. Lamont Moore, the Gallery's new director (fig. 144), said of the building, "It has specifically been designed to be tremendously flexible, as our needs change through the coming years. It is suitable for expanding either gallery or school functions."[7] Kahn himself, in the same dedication issue of the *Yale Daily News* for which Scully wrote, is quoted as saying, "A good building is one which the client cannot destroy by wrong use of space. Almost all the partitions are movable, so whenever space is needed for something else, they can fit the space to suit their need without ruining anything."[8] The movable partitions featured a pogo-stick spring system, created by George Howe, that kept them in position by applying pressure to both floor and ceiling.

The ceiling was designed, in Kahn's words, to "breathe." Air was forced in through each of the triangular ceiling coffers so that there was circulation no matter where the movable walls were placed. The lighting tracks ran along the tops of the tetrahedrons, making the ceiling, as Kahn said, "an electric plug." This ceiling was widely admired. "The chief novelty of the building is its ceiling," wrote Frederick Gutheim in the *New York Herald Tribune* on November 28, 1953.[9] Gutheim noted its important acoustic properties, absorbing sound so that no other acoustic treatment was needed, and praised Kahn's design for using the coffers to screen a functional ceiling, every part of which was available for utilities. The *Tribune* critic went on to say, "The ceiling is thus restored to the room as a controlled element in its design, not abandoned to be cluttered with sprinkler outlets, lighting fixtures, acoustical tile, and heating or air conditioning outlets."

Kahn (fig. 145), in his *Yale Daily News* interview, stated, "I believe in frank architecture." This idea found significant expression in his treatment of the building's interior surfaces. The prominence of the concrete slab ceiling—"Concrete dominates all," wrote Gutheim; "A Tent in Concrete" was the term used by Maude Kemper Riley in *Art Digest* in 1954[10]—was complemented by exposed concrete and gray brick walls. The exposed concrete cylinder encasing the staircase was left in the state from which it emerged from the forms, and other materials—wood, metal, stone—were left unpainted as well. The resulting effect was described by Gutheim as "quiet and modest, composed in a background palette of anonymous materials, relieved by people, lighting, and imaginative architectural detail," and he went on to say that "so perceptively is concrete combined with steel, glass, wood, and other materials, so well is it illuminated, that the effect is as luxurious as travertine."[11]

Two Yale College juniors, T. McCance, Jr., and G. D. Kimball, writing for the special *Yale Daily News* issue, emphasized the way in which the "vast walls of glass take you out into space over the University . . . thus melding with the campus from the inside," and the fact that "the new gallery is set back from the streets to allow room for trees and avoid the crowding effect that many city buildings give their surroundings."[12]

Students in the architecture and design departments who worked in the new building praised it for both design and functionality. In the *Yale Daily News* dedication issue, Avery C. Faulkner, a fourth-year student in the Department of Design in the Architecture School, called the new building "an excellent contemporary environment in which to study contemporary design" having "vastly superior spaces in which to work . . . with lighting, both natural and artificial [that] is rarely equaled in comparable buildings at other universities." It is "an excellent example for the working student. From every important standpoint we are given an opportunity to examine at first hand the results of a practicing architect as he solves one after another of the multitude of problems which confront every designer in the complex, technical age of today. It was particularly beneficial to the student body to have the building a product of its own faculty [Kahn was chief critic in architectural design at Yale] as a graphic representation of theory."[13] Vincent Scully, as quoted by McCance and Kimball in the *Yale Daily News*, echoed the idea that it was appropriate for students to learn modern architecture and design in a contemporary environment, saying that he and his colleagues had chosen a modern style for the building because it was the duty of a college department to experiment in its own field.

Avery Faulkner, the design student just quoted, found the cohabitation of the studios and classrooms with the exhibition spaces and the Gallery's collections beneficial, noting, "We now have the chance to work near the other arts which concern architecture, and to have the products of other students in allied departments available at all times." Maude Kemper Riley also commended this association in the conclusion to her review of the building in *Art Digest*: "It can justly be said that this building represents a new way of thinking and a unique achievement in American university life. . . . Yale's solution may or may not set a pattern for other institutions which also combine departments of fine and applied arts. For Yale, it provides assurance that the old divisions which prevailed between the art object and the creative process are destroyed forever, and that the fine arts will remain as a live, contemporary force in New Haven for generations to come."[14]

The building opened on November 6, 1953, with installations of its permanent collection and *A New Building for the Arts at Yale: Yale University Art Gallery and Design Center*, a special exhibition tracing the history of the Gallery's buildings. Photographs of the interior from the first years show installations of the Jarves Collection, the Angers sculptures, Palmyrene reliefs, and other ancient art, Asian art, and works from the Société Anonyme Collection (fig. 146). Space in the Kahn building was shared between the Gallery, which had the first and third floors and part of the second, and the School of Fine Arts, which had the rest of the second floor and used the basement for graphic design and the fourth floor for architecture. There was also a gallery for works on paper next to the print room, on the second floor, and another for architectural exhibitions. Some gallery space remained in the Swartwout

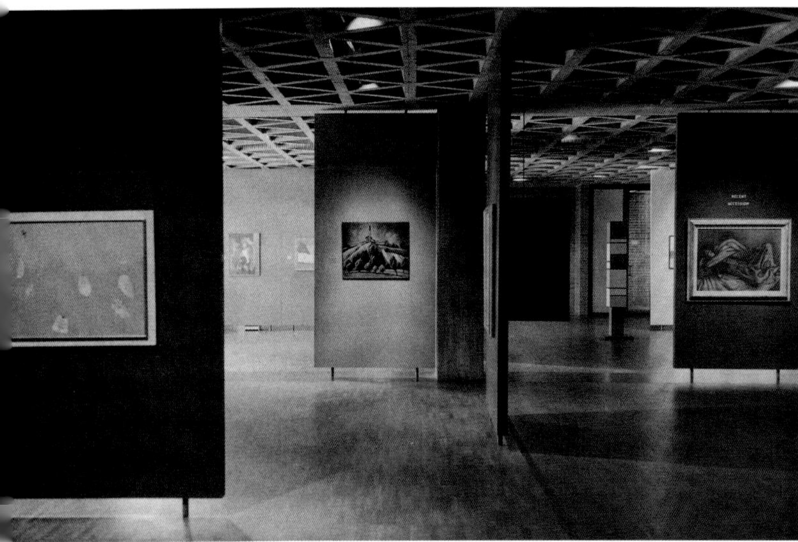

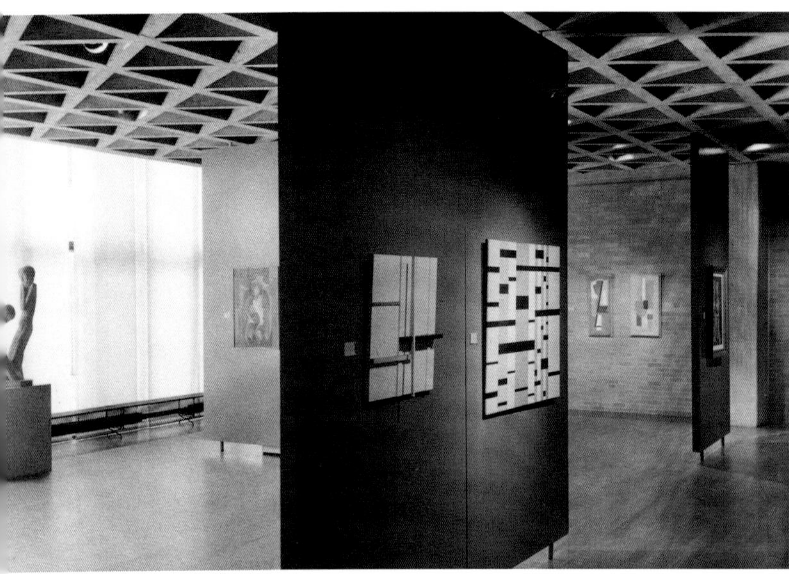

FIG. 146
Permanent collection installations, ca. 1954
Photographs courtesy Yale University Art Gallery Archives

building, notably the Trumbull Gallery and the galleries of American art on the third floor. The remainder of this building was used for the history of art department and library. Studio and classroom space for painting and sculpture remained in Street Hall. Only in 1963, with the completion of the Art and Architecture building, did the original plan to devote the entire Kahn building to Gallery functions take effect.

Overseeing the opening of the Kahn building in November 1953 was one of Lamont Moore's first major official acts as director. Both before this event, as associate director, and after it, as director, Moore was particularly active in the realm of special exhibitions. As is true today, temporary exhibitions were often the primary incentive for visitors, and some of those staged during the 1950s drew record attendance. One such record audience (10,542) viewed a collaborative exhibition by Moore, Charles Sawyer, and John Marshall Phillips of nineteenth-century French paintings borrowed from Yale alumni. French paintings, like American art, have always been popular at Yale. Shown at Yale in May 1950, the exhibition then traveled to the National Gallery of Art. Exhibitions drawn from alumni collections would become increasingly important at time went on. Other well-attended exhibitions during this time included that featuring the Katherine Dreier bequest, described earlier. The new Kahn building also proved to be a magnet for visitors, as the Gallery of Fine Arts had been when it opened in 1928. Attendance increased from 35,000 in 1952 to 87,500 in 1953/54, last matched in the months before the 1929 stock market crash.

"Pictures for a Picture" of Gertrude Stein as a Collector and Writer on Art and Artists (fig. 147), a major exhibition including works by Picasso, Cézanne, Braque, Lipschitz, and others that was shown at Yale and traveled to the Baltimore Museum of Art in the winter/spring of 1951, was also organized by Moore.[15] "*Pictures for a Picture*" marked a shift in emphasis in the exhibition program to modernism, underscoring the close relationship between the Gallery and the School of Art. The exhibition's title is from Miss Stein's *Four in America*, published by Yale University Press in 1947. The thirty-eight paintings, sculptures, and works on paper in the exhibition had mostly been owned by Gertrude Stein, either by herself or jointly with her brother Leo.

Some were borrowed from the Gertrude Stein Collection at Yale,[16] a rich assemblage of manuscripts, letters, photographs, and the works of art remaining from the collection that she gathered and partly sold or gave away during her lifetime. Several of these paintings appear in a photograph from 1910 of Stein's famous studio at 27, rue de Fleurus in Paris, published in the exhibition catalogue. Another part of the exhibition comprised works once owned by two of Stein's distant relatives, the two sisters Miss Etta and Dr. Claribel Cone, who had bequeathed their now famous collection to the Baltimore Museum of Art. Other works formerly owned by Stein were borrowed from additional museums and private collections. Stein's association with Katherine Dreier and her support for the formation of the Société Anonyme Collection is reflected in the inclusion of a Juan Gris painting from the Société Anonyme in the show. Complementing Stein's writings, works by artists about whom she wrote—but by whom no work that she had owned could be secured—were borrowed from other sources. In the catalogue, Moore interweaves his own narrative about Stein's thinking with her writings about art and artists, including this statement on the frequent but unfortunate rejection of contemporary art by the public because they are unwilling to take the trouble to look at it:

> No one is ahead of his time, it is only that the particular variety of creating his time is the one that his contemporaries who also are creating in their own time refuse to accept. . . . For a very long time everybody refuses and then almost without a pause almost everybody accepts. . . . When the acceptance comes, by that acceptance the thing created becomes a classic. . . . And what is the characteristic quality of a classic. The characteristic quality of a classic is that it is beautiful. . . . [T]he trouble is that when [a] first rate work of art . . . becomes a classic because it is accepted the only thing that is important from then on to the majority of the acceptors . . . is that it is so wonderfully beautiful. Of course it is wonderfully beautiful, only when it is still a thing irritating annoying stimulating then all quality of beauty is denied to it. . . . If every one were not so indolent they would realize that beauty

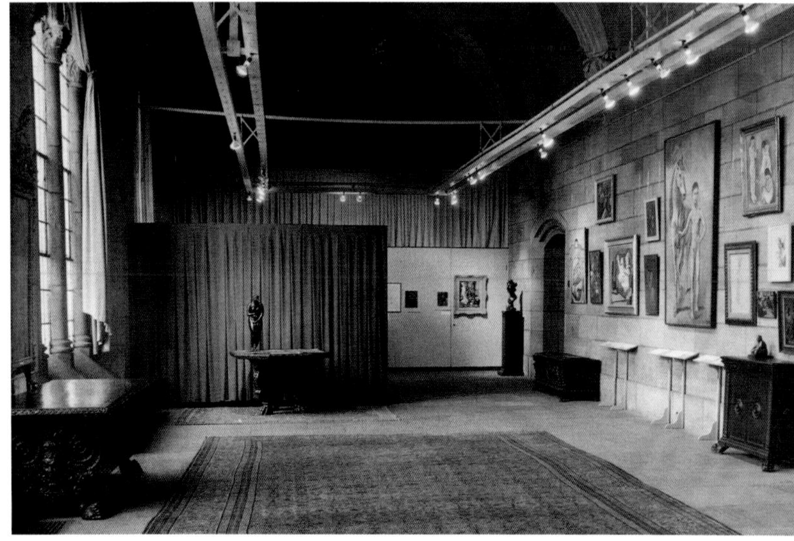

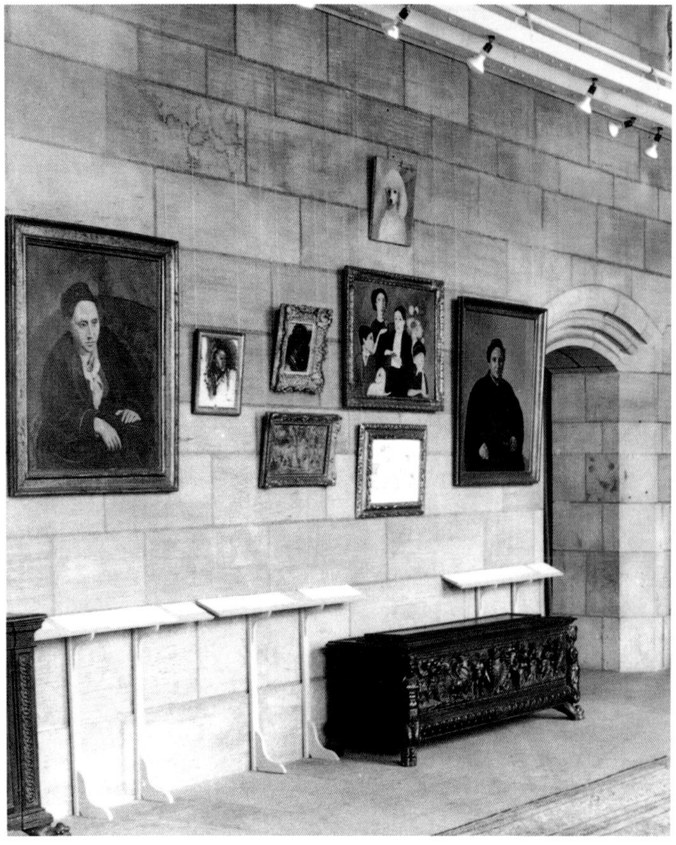

FIG. 147
"Pictures for a Picture" of Gertrude Stein as a Collector and Writer on Art, 1951
Photographs courtesy Yale University Art Gallery Archives

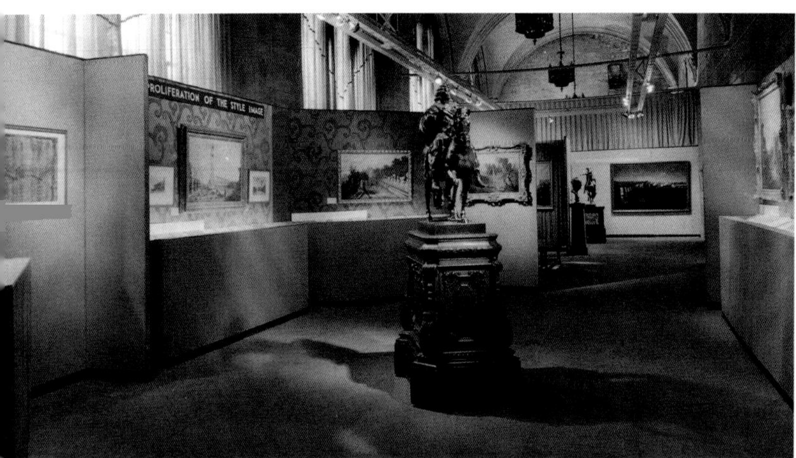

FIG. 148
Ars in Urbe, 1953
Photograph courtesy Yale University Art Gallery Archives

> is beauty even when it is irritating and stimulating not only when it is accepted and classic.[17]

As Moore asks, "What finer plea could one compose for the active participation in a work of art by the beholder than the open-mindedness of looking first instead of rejecting first!"[18] One might add, "What better goal for an exhibition in a teaching museum than to use inspired writing and works of art to encourage people to look?"

Modern architecture was another focus of Moore's at this time—doubtless because beginning in 1949 courses and a degree in city planning were offered at Yale—and in 1950 he brought in the exhibition *Architecture and the City Plan* from the Museum of Modern Art. Moore was the co-curator of *Ars in Urbe* (April–May 1953), a loan exhibition of more than fifty works focusing on civic art and city planning (fig. 148). A collaboration between Moore and Christopher Tunnard, associate professor of city planning and a recent convert to classicism under the inspiration of Gropius, *Ars in Urbe* was described by the curators as "an exhibition of civic art from Renaissance to present times in Europe and the United States as created and revealed by painters, sculptors, architects, scenographers & city planners for kings and emperors, popes and pontiffs, financiers and speculators, and democratic citizens."[19] Vincent Scully describes it as an exhibition about putting the city together and about classical architecture.

Based on the work of a graduate seminar in city planning taught by Tunnard, *Ars in Urbe* explored the influence of ancient Roman monumental architecture and city planning on architectural design from the Renaissance to the modern day, on everything from individual buildings to squares, avenues, bridges, and statues. The exhibition traced the creation, first by painters and sculptors and later by architects, of a style that they believed was the image of ancient Rome. Painters shown used elements of Roman architecture to create visionary cities and imaginary settings for religious and secular subjects, or left contemporary renderings of cities that preserve relatively accurate views of civic environments that have since changed significantly. Sculptors modeled hundreds of equestrian statues after images of Roman emperors (fig. 172). Architects measured ancient Greek and Roman buildings in great detail, using these facts as the basis first for Renaissance buildings, and later for baroque, neoclassical, and even fascist styles in both buildings and city plans, several of which were in the exhibition. The American "classic revival" was shown in Romantic paintings by Thomas Cole and in the designs for the Columbian Exposition of 1893, and its influence on civic plans such as the Mall in Washington, D.C., was explored.

Ars in Urbe was described by one reviewer as "the first show of its type in America."[20] In a review for the *New York Times,* Aline Louchheim (later Saarinen), who was not entirely pleased with the show, commends it for addressing the issue of city planning at a time when the public has lost interest in the subject: "One of the primary excellences . . . of *Ars in Urbe* . . . is that it once again takes city planning down from the specialist's shelf. Without forgetting that city planning is a many-faceted affair or that architecture demands skillful solutions of problems of function and structure, it emphasizes architecture's other requirement—esthetics or delight or beauty or whatever you choose to call the quality which man imposes on materials to create not only a work of art in terms of mass, space, line and coherence but also to shape and express a way of life." [21] The one significant complaint voiced against the exhibition by Louchheim in her *Times* review was what she saw as its implied conclusion that we must return to Roman architecture or Renaissance humanism in order to beautify our cities. Opposing her view to Tunnard, who stated "We at Yale feel that modern artists in the field today are returning to the earlier inspiration for models in contrast to the technological emphasis surrounding us today,"[22] and coincidentally to another reviewer, who said, "Thanks to the painters and engravers whose creative imaginations restored the grandeur of the past and possessed insight into the city spaces of their own times, we can participate vicariously in the humanistic cities, seeking relief from the mechanistic concept of city plans inherited in our own time,"[23] Louchheim was adamant that there were modern examples of city planning that "honor the dignity of man no less than did the Roman or Renaissance architects," and that some of them should have been included. What she saw as a rejection of modern architecture can scarcely have been in the organizers' minds, however. Yale's courses in architecture and city planning, its decade-long negotiation with Philip Goodwin over his modernist designs for an extension to the Swartwout building, and its decision to hire Louis Kahn to undertake the final design for the new Art Gallery clearly contradict such a view. Moore, Tunnard, and Yale itself had made the commitment to modernism, and the subsequent chain of modern buildings by Rudolph, Saarinen, Johnson, and Kahn himself, among others, shows that Yale's commitment would stand. The exhibition opened less than six months before the Kahn art gallery opened, and indeed was shown in the very shadow of the nearly completed modernist building. The purpose of the exhibition was not to deny the value of modern architecture, but to remind the viewers who seemed to value nothing else that there was merit in historical styles as well. In doing so, it encouraged people to look comprehensively at the built environment in which they lived. The value of *Ars in Urbe* was, as Louchheim herself declared, that it reintroduced the idea of civic art to the public mind. According to Vincent Scully, *Ars in Urbe* was a prophetic show of what would happen in the next generation, especially prophetic of the new urbanism at Yale in the 1970s.[24]

The Gallery's interest in contemporary art was embodied in these years in George Heard Hamilton. Hamilton, whose key role in the 1950 catalogue of the Société Anonyme Collection and the memorial exhibition in 1953 commemorating Katherine Dreier's death has already been noted, served the Gallery as curator of painting, of modern art, of the Société Anonyme Collection, and of the Edwin Austin Abbey Collection, as well as editor of the *Bulletin,* at varied times beginning in 1936. Educated at Yale (B.A. 1932, M.A. 1934, PH.D. 1942) and already well established at the Gallery, Hamilton was appointed to the history of art faculty as assistant professor in 1943. He remained on the Gallery staff and on the Yale faculty, becoming full professor in 1956, until he left in 1966 to serve as professor of art at Williams College and director of the Sterling and Francine Clark Art Institute.

As curator and teacher, Hamilton focused primarily on twentieth-century art, and it was thus fitting that he should curate the exhibition *Object and Image in*

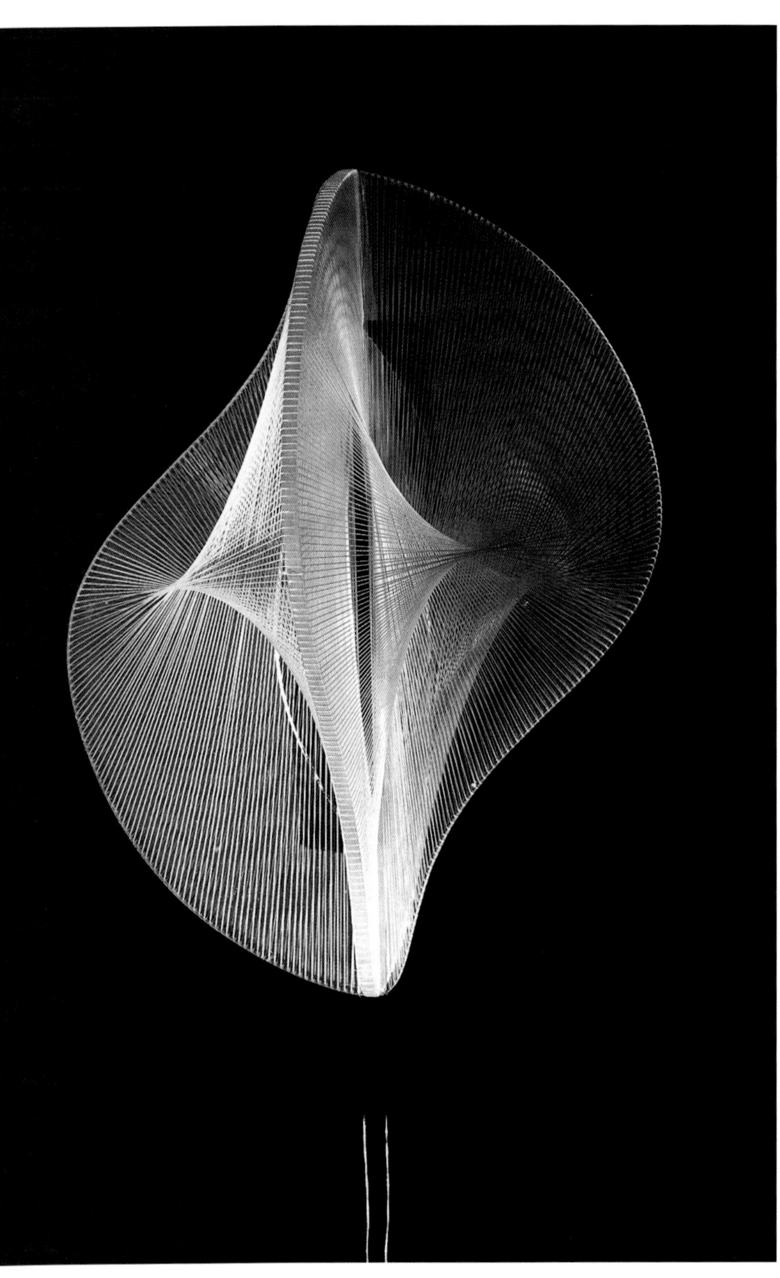

FIG. 149
Naum Gabo
Linear Construction, 1950
Lent by George Heard Hamilton to the exhibition *Object and Image in Modern Art and Poetry*, 1954; collection of Richard Heard Hamilton
Photograph courtesy Yale University Art Gallery Archives

Modern Art and Poetry. This thoughtful and innovative exhibition, on view at the Gallery in the spring of 1954, consisted of thirty-four modern paintings and sculptures assembled from a variety of public and private sources that were arranged in juxtaposition with brief quotations from contemporary poetry. Hamilton took as his inspiration the opening of Jacques Maritain's book *Creative Intuition in Art and Poetry*:

> Art and poetry cannot do without one another. Yet the two words are far from being synonymous. By Art I mean the creative or producing, work-making activity of the human mind. By Poetry I mean, not the particular art which consists in writing verses, but a process both more general and more primary: that intercommunication between the inner being of things and the inner being of the human Self which is a kind of divination. . . . Poetry in this sense, is the secret life of each and all of the arts; another name for what Plato called *mousikè*.[25]

Featured in the exhibition were works from the decade 1943–53, by artists including Naum Gabo (fig. 149), Robert Motherwell, Josef Albers, Mark Rothko, Clyfford Still, and Francis Bacon, and poems by e. e. cummings, W. H. Auden, T. S. Eliot, Wallace Stevens, Dylan Thomas, Robert Penn Warren, Ezra Pound, and William Carlos Williams. In a review for the *New York Herald Tribune*, Emily Genauer described the purpose of the exhibition as follows: "The intent was neither to use the poetry as expository program-notes, so to speak, nor the art to illustrate, in the literal sense, images contained in the lines. It was, rather, to show that artists and poets have a common concern with certain ideas, and to relate parallel (rather than strictly equivalent) expressions dealing with the same basic concepts, insights and symbols."[26] Hamilton explains in the catalogue:

> If at the present time the object is not less important, and the proof is that each of these works when first seen is seen as abstract, each may also be seen in the context of poetic experience, not as translatable into words but as a kind of divination. This is not to say that we can or even should illustrate in the literal sense the work of art with the poem, but rather that the experiences of artist and

poet can be shown to have a common concern with the image alive in the object. Therefore, beside the reproductions of some of these works of art, and elsewhere in these pages, I have placed poetic texts, to suggest other kinds of communication. They have not been selected at random, but neither are they to be taken as strict equivalents. Rather, the variety and the differences, as well as the mysterious correspondences, are to be felt, even when the titles are the same.[27]

Genauer concludes her review with a statement that there is an additional, implicit, value to the exhibition, not stated in its premise—namely, that it "may be considered a powerful and eloquent plea for a return in contemporary art to meaning, to thought, to feeling, to values and to purpose." Hamilton would not have disagreed; in his catalogue essay, he declares, "the work of art, conceived obscurely within the reaches of our imagination and our blood, must have its meanings and reverberations from within and from without our lives. . . . [T]he object once so impeccable in its material order, has acquired new meanings and new moods. Our feelings have become concerned, and we have changed and changed our art. The objects now are images of ourselves, not comfortable, appropriate likenesses, but you and me and that man over there in the corner seen in our private meanings, seen inside out." As e. e. cummings said about his poems, in a passage quoted in the exhibition catalogue, "All they hope to do is to suggest that particular awareness without which no human spirit ever dreams of rising from such unmysteries as thinking and believing and knowing."[28] The premise that artists and poets have a common concern with ideas and images was demonstrated anew by Hamilton in this exhibition, the first major project of its type. Developing the theme, the ideas put forward in *Object and Image* have been reiterated and expanded at the Gallery in *Dante Gabriel Rosetti and the Double Work of Art*, organized by Maryan Ainsworth, now senior research fellow in paintings conservation at the Metropolitan Museum of Art, and *Words for Images: A Gallery of Poems*, organized by John Hollander, Sterling Professor of English, and Joanna Weber, assistant curator of european and contemporary art, in 2001. *Object and Image* embodies the Gallery's continuing commitment to generating exhibitions that advance thought and scholarship about art.

Lamont Moore's most important exhibition from the perspective of building the collection was *Pictures Collected by Yale Alumni* in 1956. Originating with an idea proposed by two Yale classmates, Thomas R. Coward and Shreve Cowles Badger, B.A. 1919, the exhibition was a collaboration between alumni, notably Stephen Carlton Clark, George Dix, James Fosburgh, and E. Coe Kerr, Jr., and Gallery staff, especially two curators, Charles Seymour, Jr., and George Heard Hamilton. Theodore Sizer, former curator and director of the Gallery, who was then at work on a history of the arts at Yale, provided an introduction to the catalogue in which he focused on the Alumni Hall loan exhibition of 1858 as a prototype—nearly a century before—for this alumni exhibition. The 1956 exhibition, which included two hundred fifty works of art, was shown only at Yale. Once again the show drew record attendance: 29,000 visitors in approximately six weeks.

Pictures Collected by Yale Alumni was as close to a comprehensive exhibition of European and American art as the Gallery has ever done. The one hundred eighty-four paintings in the exhibition ranged from the fifteenth through the twentieth centuries, including works by Memling, Bosch, Cranach, El Greco, Hals, Rembrandt, Boucher, Fragonard, Chardin, Hogarth, Gainsborough, Guardi, Stubbs, Goya, Reynolds, Earl, Stuart, Copley, Constable, Turner, Delacroix, Corot, Daumier, Courbet, Eakins, Homer, Whistler, Manet, Degas, Monet, Pissarro, Gauguin, van Gogh, Renoir, Cézanne, Seurat, Vuillard, Sargent, Shinn, Picasso, Matisse, Léger, de Chirico, Hartley, Marsh, Klee, Braque, de Kooning, Pollock, Motherwell, Nicholson, Wyeth, and many more. Watercolors and drawings by many of these artists, along with Ingres, Prendergast, Rosetti, and others not represented among the paintings completed the exhibition.

Loans were drawn from Yale alumni and Yale families across the United States, among them some of the most prominent collectors in the country. Many were or became some of the Gallery's most generous donors, among them Arthur G. Altschul, Richard Brown Baker,

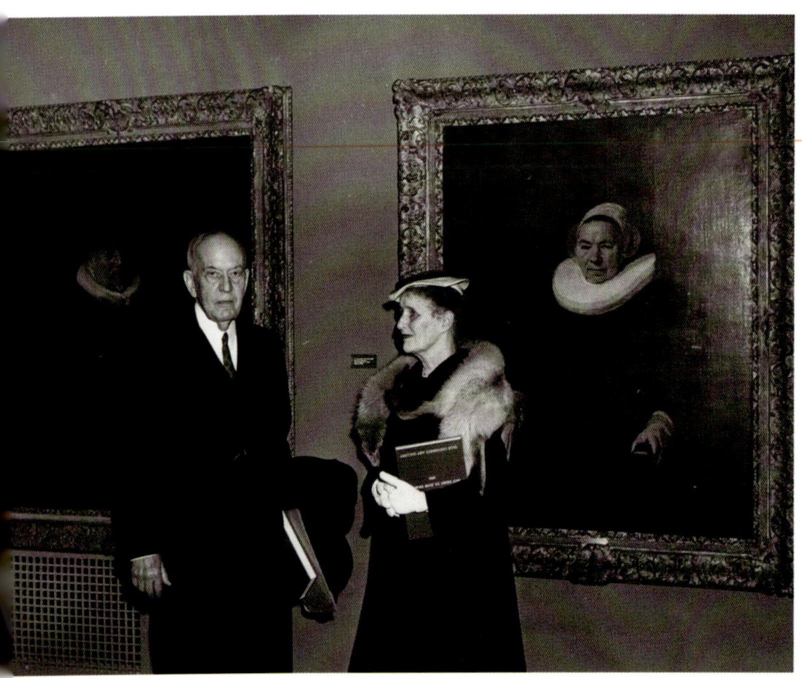

FIG. 150
Mr. and Mrs. Stephen Carlton Clark with the Franz Hals portraits in the 1956 exhibition
Photograph courtesy Yale University Art Gallery Archives

Molly and Walter Bareiss, Stephen Carlton Clark, Ralph Coe, George Hopper Fitch, James W. and Mary Fosburgh, A. Conger Goodyear, Lauder Greenway, Leonard C. Hanna, Frederick W. and Susan Morse Hilles, Mr. and Mrs. Seymour H. Knox, Robert Lehman, Mr. and Mrs. Paul Mellon, Mr. and Mrs. Paul Moore, Mr. and Mrs. Charles S. Payson, Hannah D. and Louis M. Rabinowitz, Mr. and Mrs. Joseph Verner Reed, Edith Malvina K. Wetmore, and Mr. and Mrs. John Hay Whitney.

What made this exhibition especially important was the number of paintings in it that were ultimately given or bequeathed to the Gallery. Among them were Hieronymus Bosch, *Intemperance* (fig. 132), and Lucas Cranach the Elder, *Crucifixion with the Converted Centurion* (fig. 133), gifts of Hannah D. and Louis M. Rabinowitz; Frans Hals, the pair of portraits of *De Heer and Mevrouw Bodolphe* (figs. 150 and 150a), Edouard Manet, *Jeune Femme allongée en costume espagnol* (fig. 151), Winslow Homer, *The Mill* (formerly *Morning Bell* [fig. 152]), Thomas Eakins, *Will Schuster and Dave Wright Going Shooting (Rail Shooting)* (fig. 153, for which a drawing already existed in the Garvan Collection), all part of the Stephen Carlton Clark bequest in 1961; John Singleton Copley, *Mr. and Mrs. Benjamin Pickman*, bequest of Edith Malvina K. Wetmore; Edouard Vuillard, *The Kitchen*, lent by Philip L. Goodwin and given in his honor by members of his family; and Gustave Courbet, *Source of the River Loue*, gift of Molly and Walter Bareiss. British paintings lent by Paul Mellon came to Yale with the founding gift for the Yale Center for British Art, and several French Impressionist paintings were given to the Gallery. Fewer of the drawings and watercolors from the exhibition are now at Yale, but John Marin, *Tree, Cape Split*, came to Yale as part of the Philip L. Goodwin Collection in 1958, and the Edward Hopper watercolor *House of the Fog Horn* (fig. 154) was given by George Hopper Fitch in 1973.

Among the prints, Charles Y. Lazarus (B.A. 1936) donated a group of Géricault etchings, including *Entrance to the Adelphi Wharf* (1821; fig. 155). This donation and subsequent gifts of Géricault prints made by Lazarus were celebrated in the exhibition *The Graphic Art of Géricault* in 1969.[29] In the introduction to the catalogue, Andrew Carnduff Ritchie, the director, and

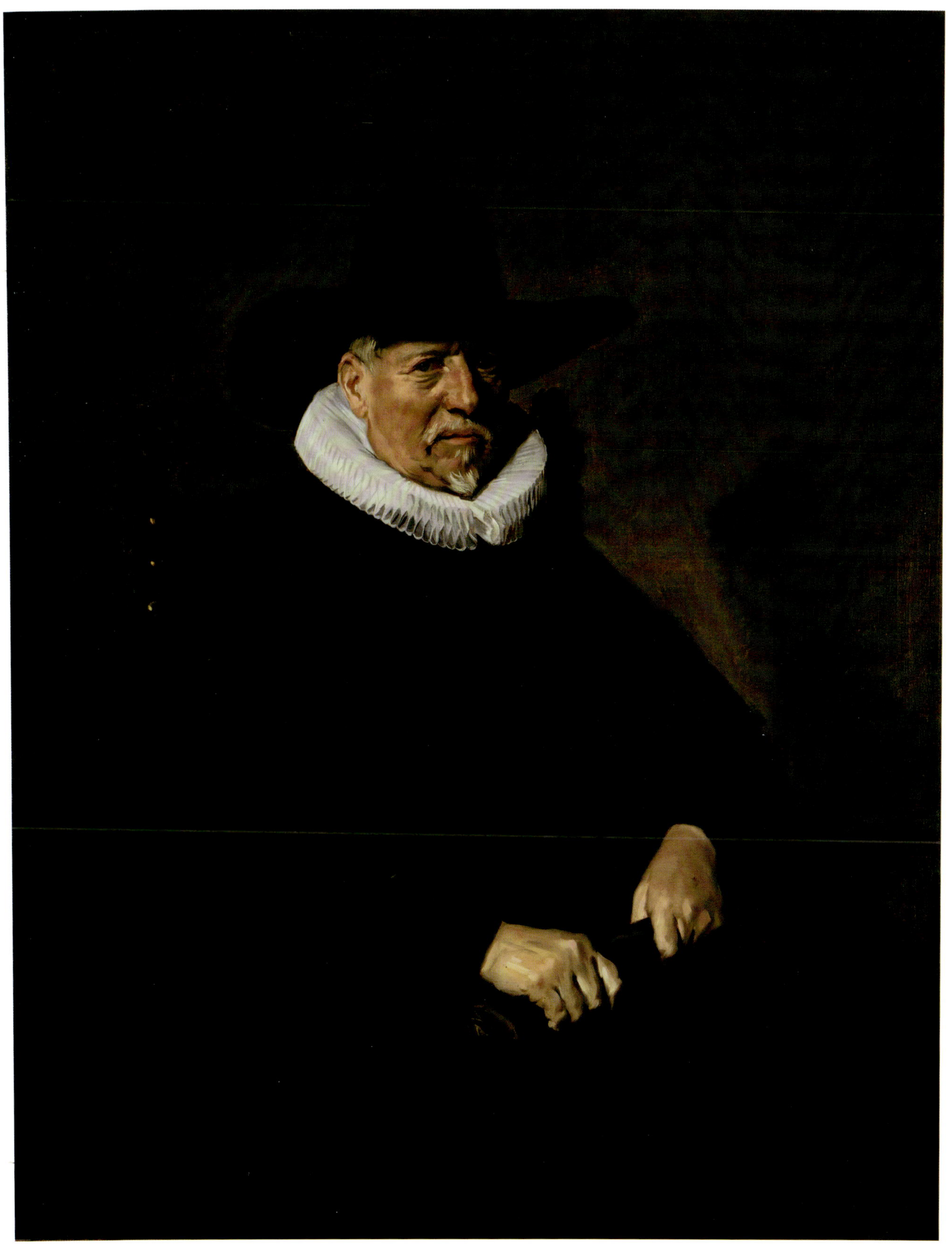

FIG. 150a
Frans Hals
De Heer Bodolphe, 1643
Oil on canvas, 122.4 x 97.5 cm
Bequest of Stephen Carlton
Clark, B.A. 1903
1961.18.23

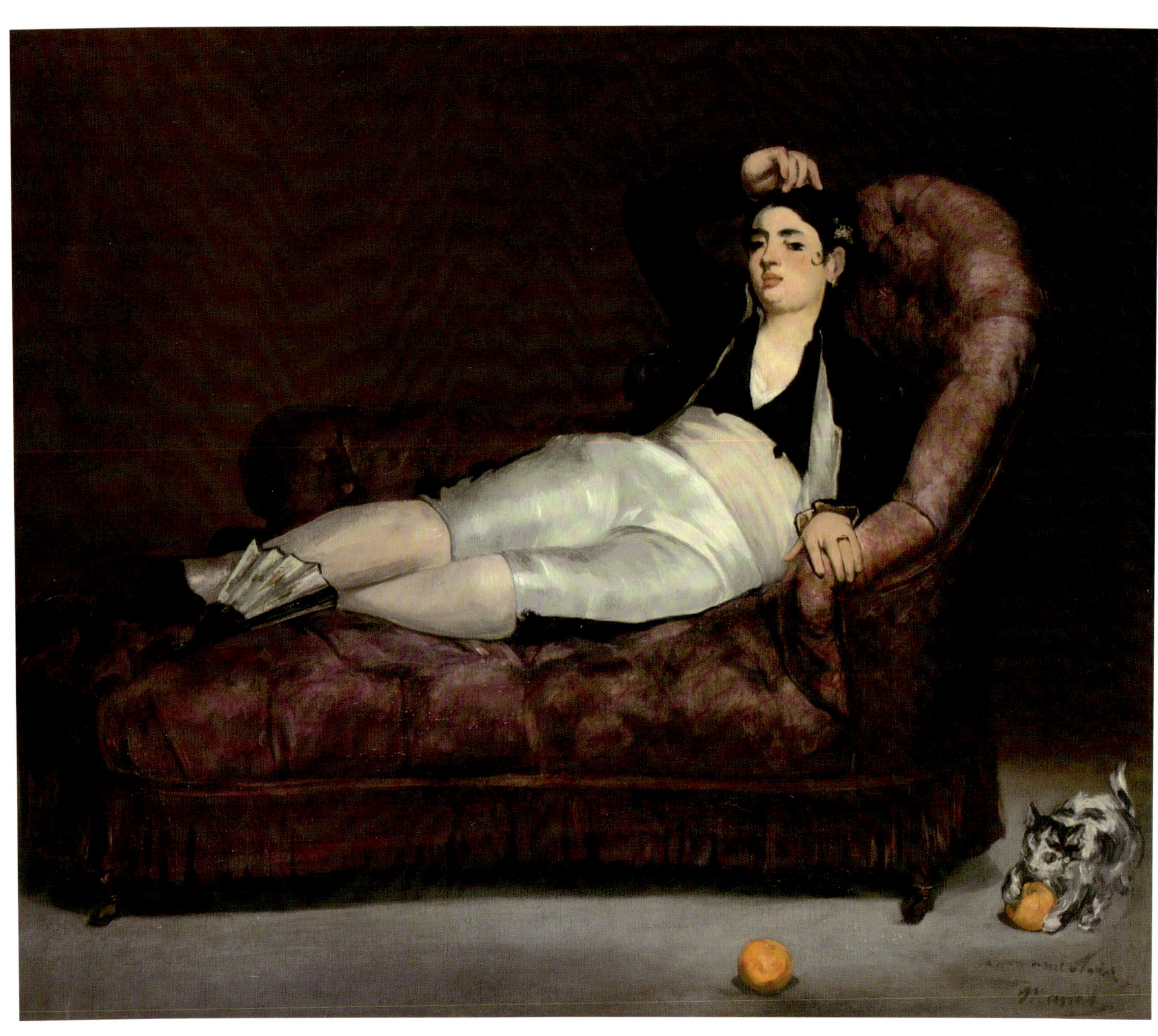

FIG. 151
Edouard Manet
Young Woman Reclining in Spanish Costume (Jeune Femme allongée en costume espagnol), 1862–63
Oil on canvas, 94.7 x 113.7 cm
Bequest of Stephen Carlton Clark, B.A. 1903
1961.18.33

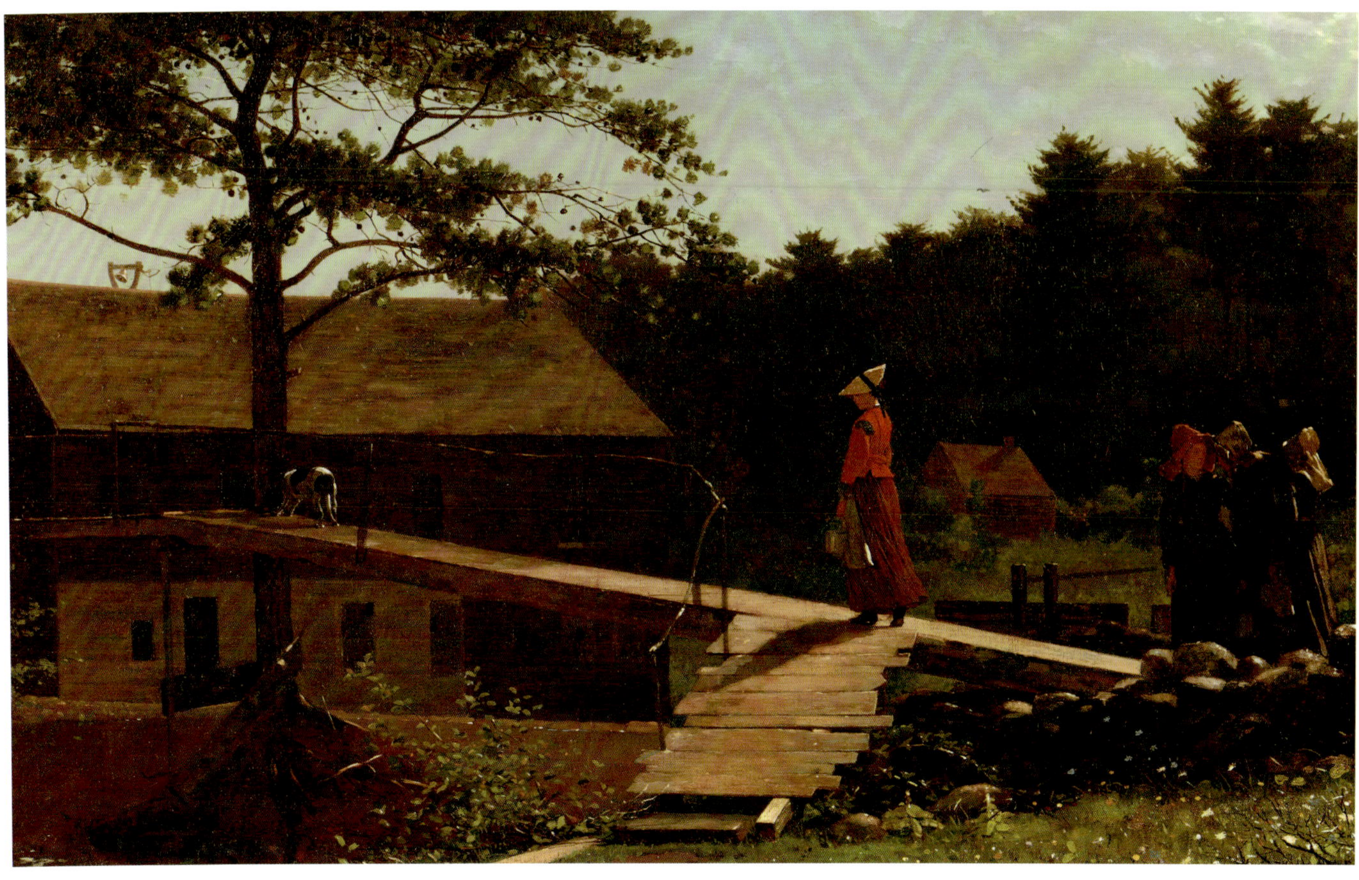

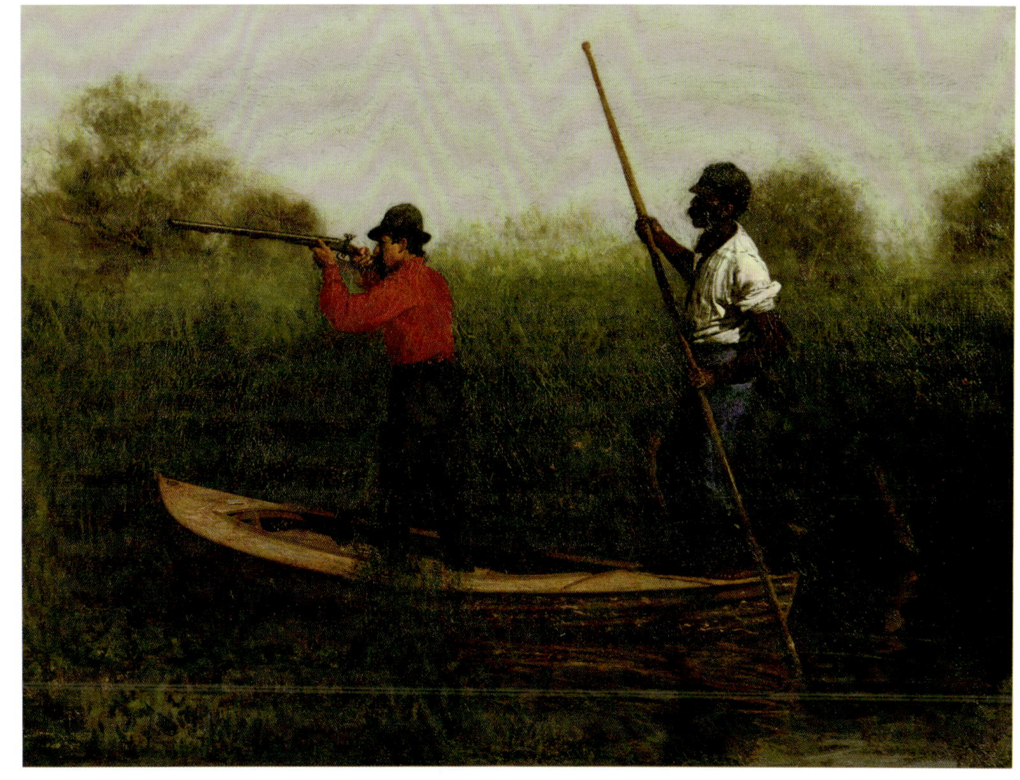

FIG. 152
Winslow Homer
The Mill (formerly *Morning Bell*), 1871
Oil on canvas, 61 x 96.8 cm
Bequest of Stephen Carlton Clark, B.A. 1903
1961.18.26

FIG. 153
Thomas Eakins
Will Schuster and Dave Wright Going Shooting (Rail Shooting), 1876
Oil on canvas, 56.2 x 76.8 cm
Bequest of Stephen Carlton Clark, B.A. 1903
1961.18.21

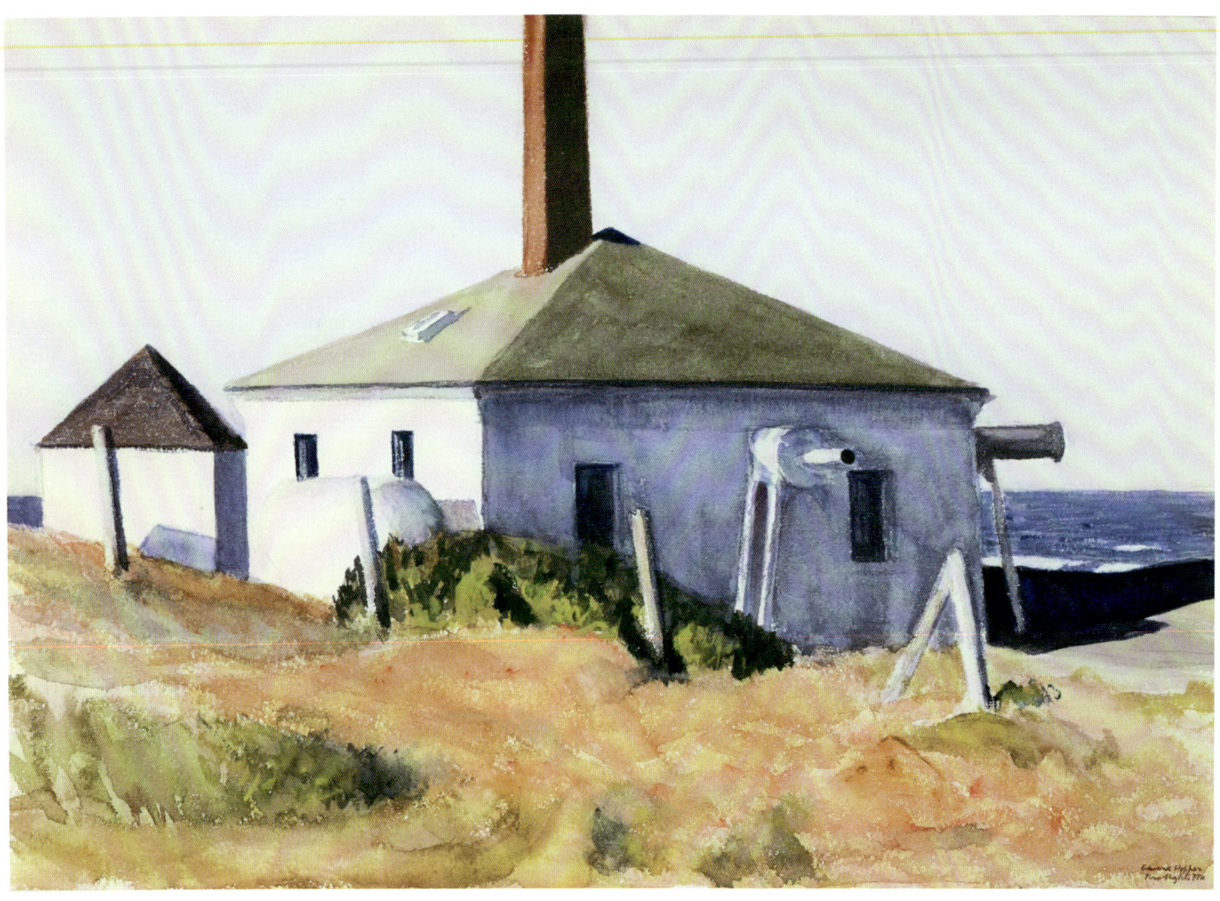

FIG. 154
Edward Hopper
House of the Fog Horn, No. 3, 1929
Watercolor over graphite, 35.4 x 50.6 cm
Gift of George Hopper Fitch, B.A. 1932
1973.149

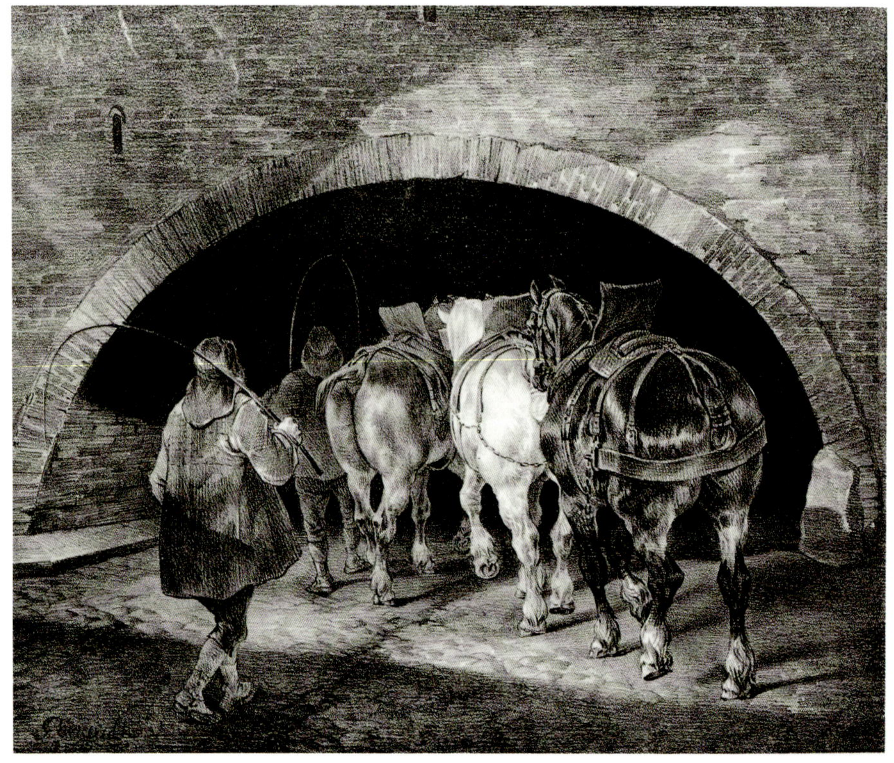

FIG. 155
Théodore Géricault
Entrance to Adelphi Wharf, 1821
Lithograph, 25.6 x 30.8 cm
Gift of Charles Y. Lazarus, B.A. 1936
1956.3.24

Alan Shestack, the curator of drawings and prints, noted, "Mr. Lazarus' interest in Géricault and his knowledgeable collecting of Géricault material was first stimulated during his undergraduate years at Yale, when he studied the history of prints under the inspired teaching of the late Theodore Sizer. We can think of no finer way Mr. Lazarus could have paid tribute to his former teacher than by assembling a print collection of consistently high quality for the enlightenment and education of future generations of students at Yale." The exhibition was organized by Kate H. Spencer as part of her program as a Ford Foundation Fellow studying museum techniques at the Gallery, a grant obtained by Andrew Carnduff Ritchie that in this case funded one of many opportunities students have had for decades to organize exhibitions in the prints and drawings department. The 1956 alumni exhibition also enriched the teaching program, offering originals to study for final exams in place of the usual slides and photographs (fig. 156).

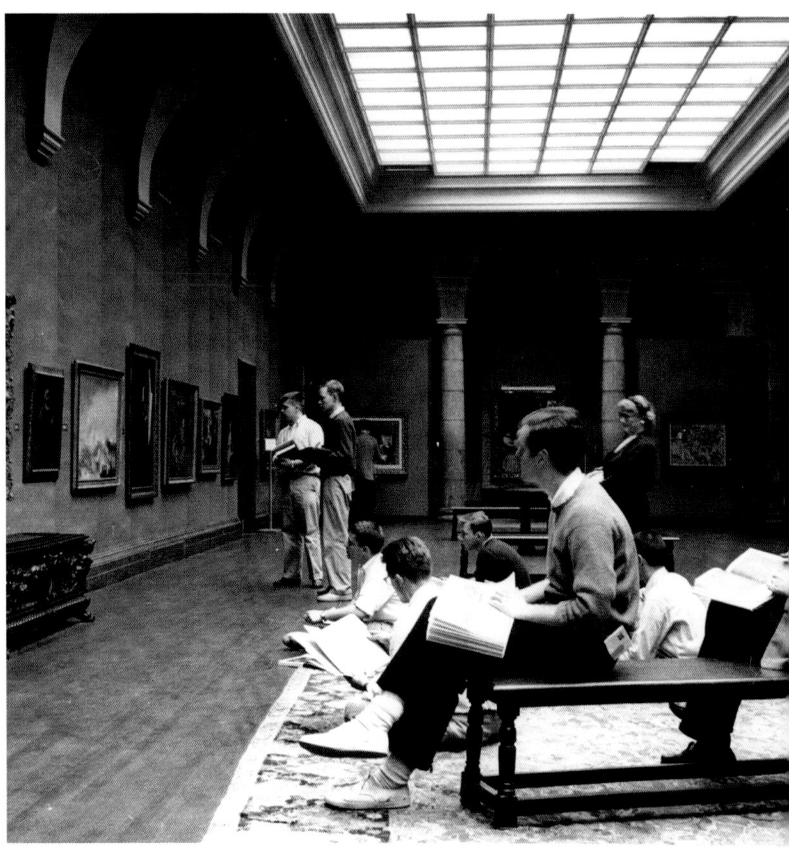

FIG. 156
Students studying for the final exam in History of Art 12 (introductory course) in the 1956 exhibition
Photograph courtesy Yale University Art Gallery Archives

Involved as the Gallery's director with students as well as alumni, in the academic year 1954/55 Lamont Moore founded an undergraduate group called The Georgians, which was devoted to collecting and appreciating the fine arts and to promoting and collecting art at Yale. Many trips to the homes of private collectors were organized for the group. Members were encouraged to emulate the illustrious collectors and donors among their alumni predecessors at Yale, such as Stephen Carlton Clark, Robert Lehman, Paul Mellon, John Hay Whitney, Walter Bareiss, and others. Among other activities, The Georgians sponsored an exhibition in 1956 of *Paintings by Graham Sutherland and Drawings by Henry Moore*. Their second exhibition, in 1957, was a mixed-media loan show of contemporary art borrowed from artists and galleries in New York, followed by an exhibition of sculpture later that year. The organization did no further exhibitions and did not last beyond the end of the decade.

A second major exhibition effort of 1956 was *Masterworks from Yale University*, a loan show organized with other collecting institutions at Yale for the Chicago Festival and shown at the Art Institute of Chicago. The Gallery lent works from the Jarves and Griggs Collections, the Société Anonyme, the Garvan Collection, and

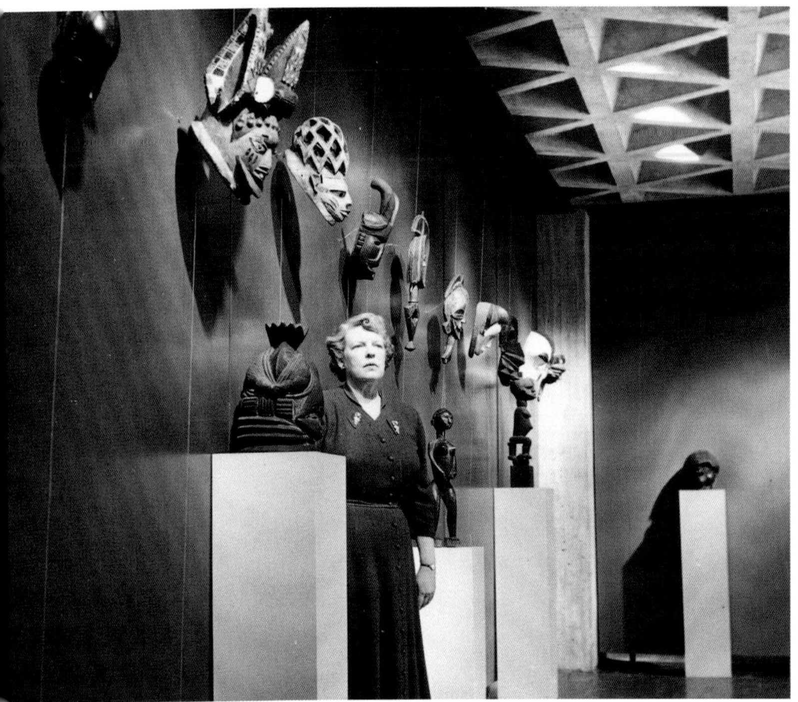

FIG. 157
Mrs. Ralph M. Linton in the exhibition *African Art from the Linton Collection*, 1954
Photograph courtesy Yale University Art Gallery Archives

the collections of African, Chinese, and Japanese art. Other Yale collections represented were Sterling Library, the School of Music Library, and the Western Americana Collection. Chicago was a major focus of fund-raising in the 1940s and '50s, and an exhibition such as this was a vivid reminder to alumni in Chicago of the richness of Yale's collections. The catalogue included excerpts from Wilmarth S. Lewis, *The Yale Collections*, a comprehensive overview of the University's holdings published in 1946.

Another way in which the Yale collections were kept in the public eye and in the minds of potential donors was through the loan of individual works to museums throughout the country. Most commonly these were furniture from the Garvan Collection, and such loans were very much in the spirit of Mr. Garvan's original wishes for the collection. In 1956, Lamont Moore noted in a report to the University Council Committee that one of the projects for the coming year would be to check on the condition of some nine hundred pieces of furniture that were out on loan.[30]

Some of the new acquisitions made after the opening of the Kahn building represented the introduction of new fields in the Gallery's collections. An exhibition in March and April 1954 marked the gift of the Linton Collection of African Art to the Gallery (figs. 144 and 157), the first African art to enter the permanent collection and still the core of the Gallery's African holdings.[31] African objects had entered the Peabody Museum of Natural History's collection at Yale as early as the 1880s, but the choice of the Gallery for the Linton Collection appears to have been a conscious statement that these objects were art, not just anthropological specimens. The exhibition, the first of African art at Yale, included over one hundred and fifty sculptures selected from the collection. Formed by Dr. Ralph M. Linton, Sterling Professor of Anthropology, over a period of twenty years, the collection included works from West and Central Africa (figs. 158 and 159). Professor Linton published widely in the fields of African anthropology and art, and he was among the first to dispel the idea of African art as "primitive." Linton was interested in African carvings as sculpture and in their makers as artists. As Gallery Director Lamont Moore recorded in his preface to the catalogue, Professor Linton was not

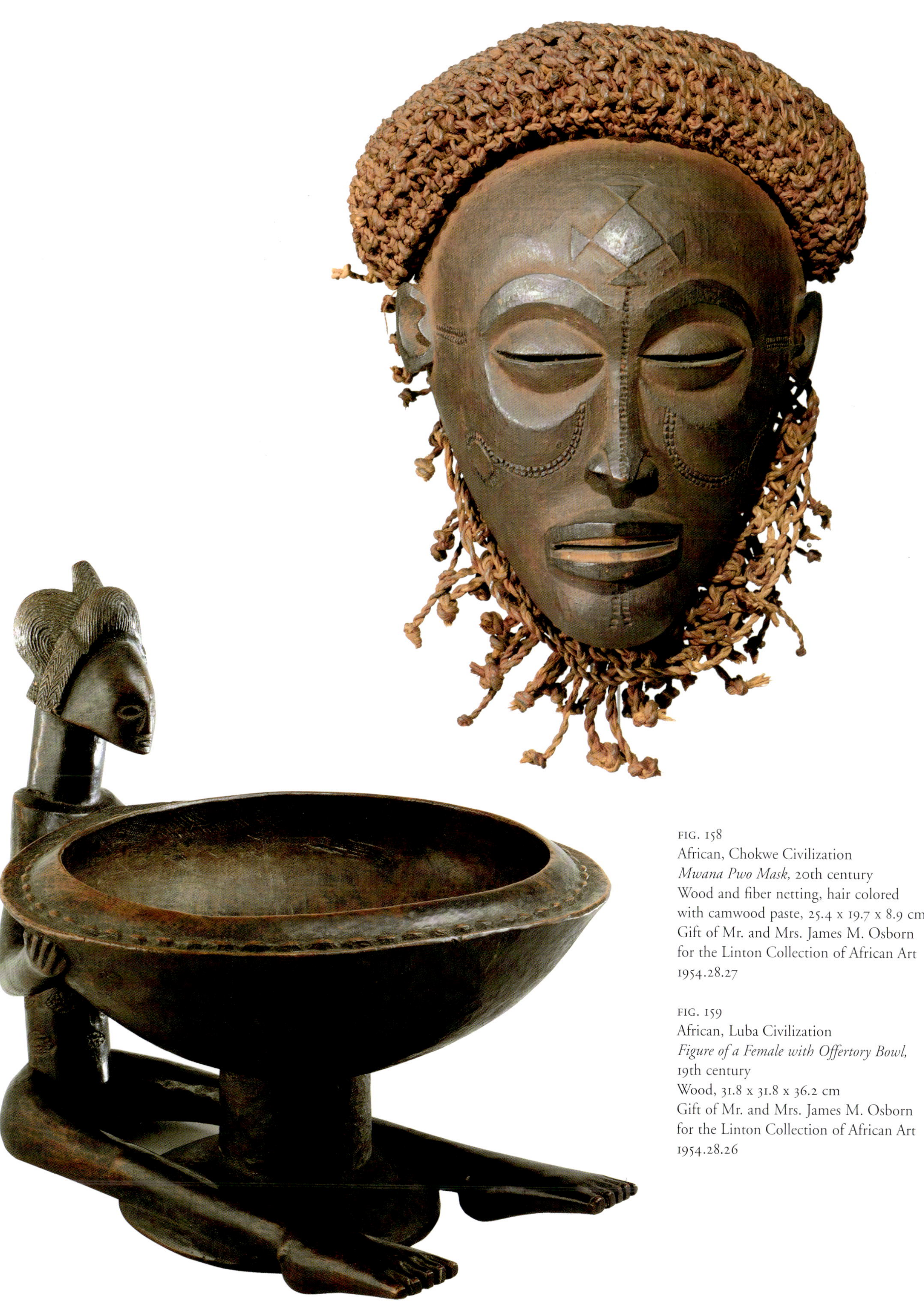

FIG. 158
African, Chokwe Civilization
Mwana Pwo Mask, 20th century
Wood and fiber netting, hair colored with camwood paste, 25.4 x 19.7 x 8.9 cm
Gift of Mr. and Mrs. James M. Osborn for the Linton Collection of African Art
1954.28.27

FIG. 159
African, Luba Civilization
Figure of a Female with Offertory Bowl, 19th century
Wood, 31.8 x 31.8 x 36.2 cm
Gift of Mr. and Mrs. James M. Osborn for the Linton Collection of African Art
1954.28.26

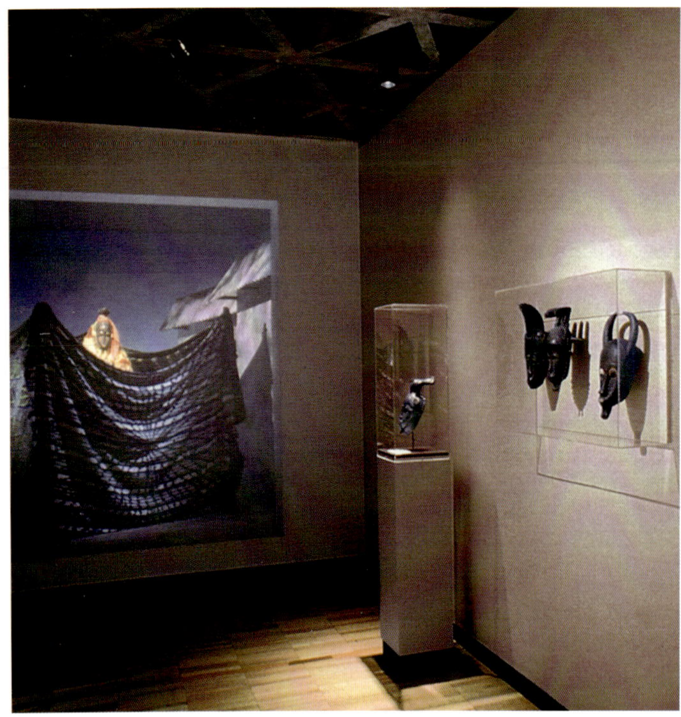

FIG. 160
Baule: African Art/Western Eyes, 1997
Photograph courtesy Yale University Art Gallery Archives

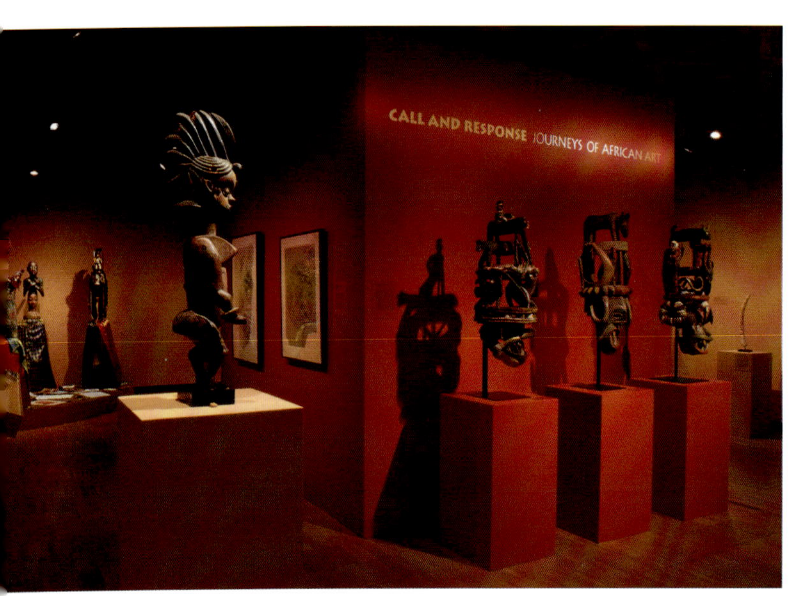

FIG. 161
Call and Response: Journeys of African Art, 2000/2001
Photograph courtesy Yale University Art Gallery Archives

only a scholar and collector, but also a master woodcarver, studying through direct personal experience the medium favored by African artists. Designed as a celebratory loan exhibition, the show became a memorial to Dr. Linton, who died suddenly in December of 1953. It was reviewed by David McCullough (B.A. 1955), today a well-known historian and then a staff writer for the *Yale Daily News*. The collection was subsequently donated by Mr. and Mrs. James M. Osborn in honor of Dr. and Mrs. Linton. Mr. and Mrs. Osborn gave additional objects to enrich the Linton Collection in 1955, 1959, and 1960; Hazel Osborn donated a Zamble mask in 1974; a son, Thomas, gave several pieces in 1980, and another son, J. Marshall, gave a Dan mask in 1984.

Other African art exhibitions have followed. In 1986, Allen Wardwell (B.A. 1957) curated an exhibition of African sculpture at the University of Pennsylvania Museum that he then brought to Yale.[32] Deeply interested in both African and Precolumbian art, the former director of the Asia Society, and a member of the Gallery's Governing Board until his sudden death in 1999, Allen Wardwell was a valued adviser and donor to the Gallery in many fields. In 1997 Susan Vogel, founder and first director of the Museum for African Art in New York and director of the Yale University Art Gallery from 1995 to 1997, organized the landmark exhibition *Baule: African Art/Western Eyes* (fig. 160).[33] This exhibition was the first to bring together a comprehensive collection of Baule sculpture. It was also the first major contextual exhibition of Baule art, using recreations of African environments to reveal the African understanding of their art. Most recently, *Call and Response: Journeys of African Art* (fig. 161), an exhibition organized by Bárbaro Martínez-Ruiz, Lyneise Williams, and Sarah Adams, three graduate students working with Robert Farris Thompson, the Colonel John Trumbull Professor of the History of Art, was shown at the Gallery in 2000/01, with a catalogue featuring an essay by Professor Thompson. Drawing on the Gallery's holdings and private collectors, *Call and Response* considered the ways that migrations and other interchanges in Africa and the world have transformed African art. The year 2000 also marked the establishment of the Yale University Art Gallery–Van Rijn Archive of African Art, sponsored by James Ross (B.A. 1960), representing the start of what will ultimately grow into a major archival resource for the University and the field. Critical to the future of African art at Yale was the endowment in 2000 by Charles B. Benenson (B.A. 1933) of the position of curator of African art, leading to the establishment of an African art department at the Gallery. The future also holds promise of significant African collections destined for the Gallery.

The second new field into which the Gallery's collections entered in the 1950s was Precolumbian art. Like African art, the art of Mesoamerica and South America was increasingly appreciated and studied during this period, as scholars and archaeologists discovered and excavated growing numbers of sites and from them began to understand the cultures that produced Precolumbian art. As these objects escaped the association with primitivism that had characterized the view of them in the 1920s and '30s and became the focus of study for their own cultural and artistic merit, universities like Yale began to increase their Precolumbian holdings in both their art and anthropology collections.

The first Precolumbian objects to be exhibited at the Gallery as art were the collections of Peruvian textiles given by Mrs. William H. Moore for the Hobart Moore Memorial Collection in 1937 (fig. 162) and the George Hewitt Myers Collection of around one hundred fifty pieces of Peruvian pottery that was placed on loan to the Gallery in 1939, where it remains today. A selection from these collections was shown in 1940, with similar objects from Yale's Peabody Museum of Natural History. A loan exhibition of Precolumbian art prepared by the Brooklyn Museum and circulated by the Museum of Modern Art in New York was shown at Yale in 1942. This exhibition included sculpture as well as ceramics and textiles. It is likely that the special interest in this field was generated by George Kubler (B.A. 1934, M.A. 1936, PH.D. 1940), later a renowned scholar of Precolumbian art, who had recently joined the Yale faculty in history of art in 1938.[34] Professor Kubler was also devoted to the art and architecture of colonial Latin America, and it was thus probably at his suggestion that an exhibition on that subject was organized by the Gallery and shown in 1942, a month after the Brooklyn Precolumbian show. There was also significant interest in the region for political and

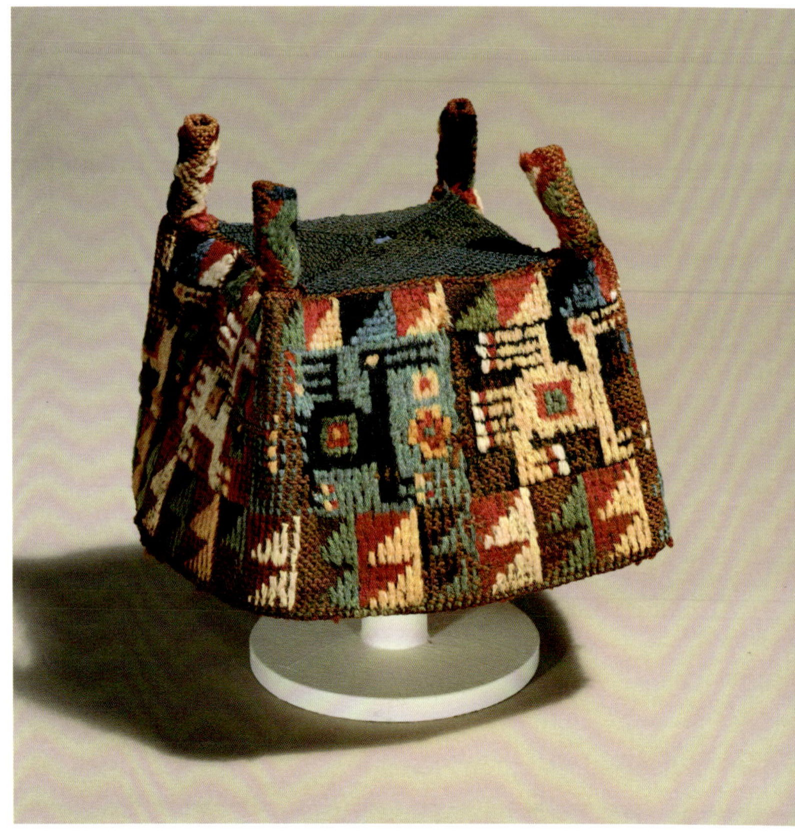

FIG. 162
Peruvian, Nazca Culture (Huari)
Wool Pile Cap, 1100–1550 A.D.
Llama or alpaca wool and cotton, wool pile, 8.3 x 3.2 cm
The Hobart and Edward Small Moore Memorial Collection, Gift of Mrs. William H. Moore
1937.4589

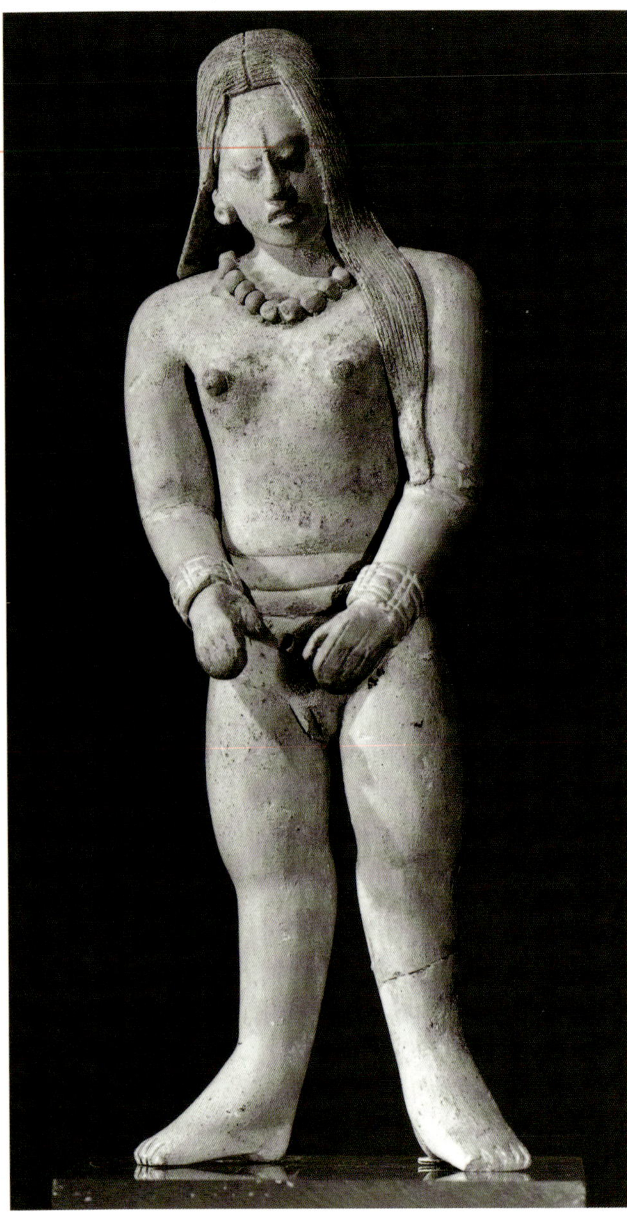

FIG. 163
Maker unknown
Jaina Standing Woman, 600–900 A.D.
Terracotta, 22.8 x 8.3 x 7.1 cm
Gift of the Olsen Foundation
1958.15.9

geopolitical reasons during World War II, adding an incentive for exhibitions in Latin American art of any period. Professor Kubler was named curator of Precolumbian and Primitive art in 1959 and was listed as such until October 1972.

Aside from textiles, early acquisitions of Precolumbian art by the Gallery were modest. A Nazca (Peru) whistle-spouted vessel in the shape of a seated woman was purchased for the collection in 1942 as a gift of the Associates in Fine Arts. In 1956, Professor Kubler donated a fine Nazca bowl with cat-deity figures to the Gallery, continuing the tradition of faculty donations to the collection so frequent in the nineteenth century.

The heart of the Gallery's Precolumbian collection is the collection of Dr. and Mrs. Fred Olsen. Although not a Yale graduate, Olsen was a New Haven area resident and developed a close relationship to Professor Kubler. The first Olsen gifts came to the Gallery in 1958, and they immediately brought some objects of exceptional quality to the collection. Among them, three classic Maya terracotta figurines from Jaina Island, Guatemala, stand out (figs. 163–65), but there were also West Mexican figures and figural groups, a stone hacha from a ballgame court in Veracruz, and stone reliefs from Veracruz and Tlaxcala. Olsen, who collected in a dozen different fields, also donated Egyptian and Coptic art to the Gallery. Trained as a scientist and with a Ph.D. from Washington University in St. Louis, Olsen was a "leading industrial chemist who helped revolutionize the manufacture of gunpowder in World War II."[35] After his retirement as a vice president at Olin Industries in 1956, Olsen devoted himself to collecting, assembling one of the most comprehensive collections of Arawak artifacts as he and his wife, Florence, traveled by dugout in the remote jungles of Venezuela, Surinam, and Guyana.

In 1973, faced with the need for funds to pay medical bills, Mr. Olsen sold the best pieces remaining in his collection, offering them first to Yale. With the encouragement of Professor Kubler, the Stephen Carlton Clark, B.A. 1903, Fund made it possible for Alan Shestack, director of the Gallery since 1971, to acquire more than eighty of these objects, several of which have remained the core of the Gallery's holdings

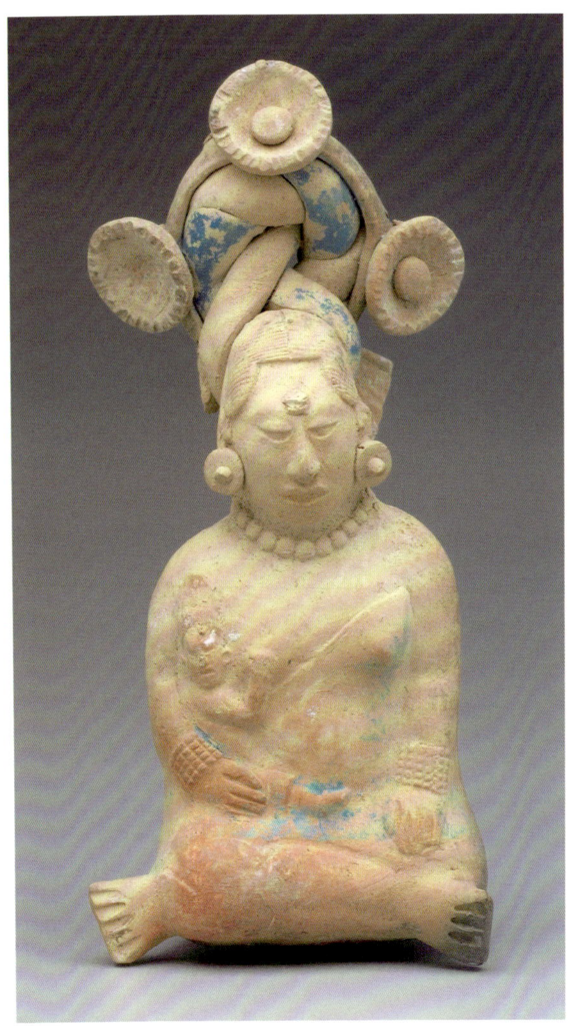

FIG. 164
Maker unknown
Jaina Seated Woman with Child,
600 – 900 A.D.
Terracotta, 17.8 cm
Gift of the Olsen Foundation
1958.15.10

FIG. 165
Maker unknown
Jaina Standing Warrior,
600 – 900 A.D.
Terracotta, 18.1 cm
Gift of the Olsen Foundation
1958.15.11

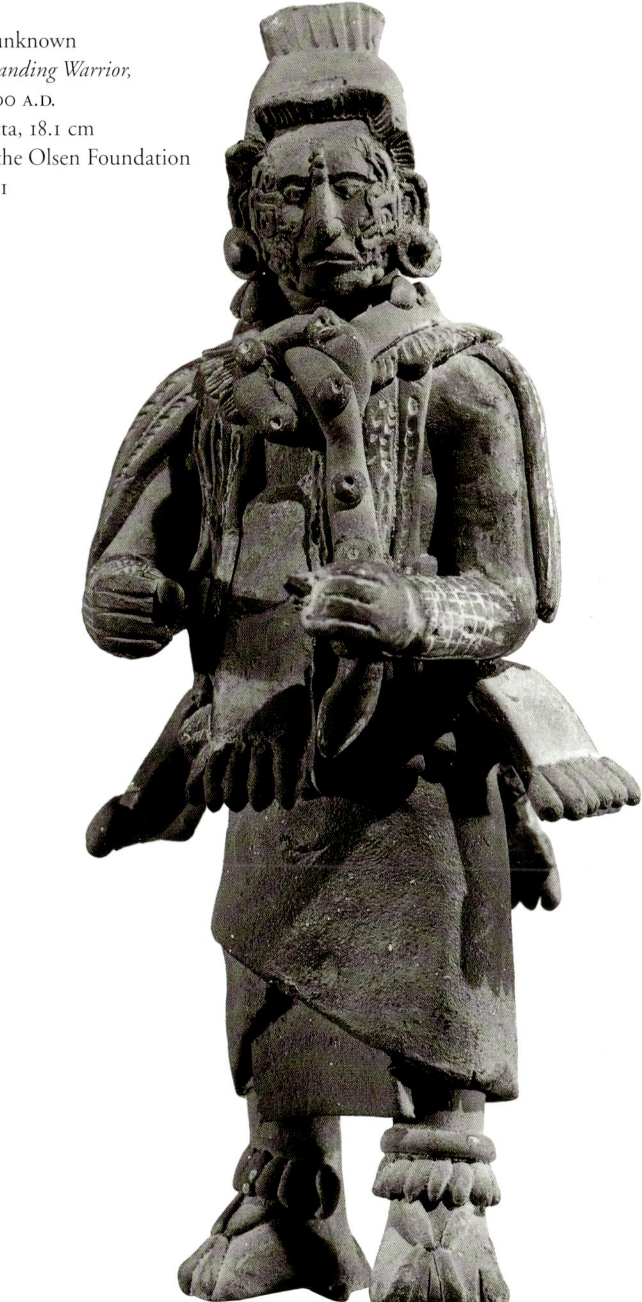

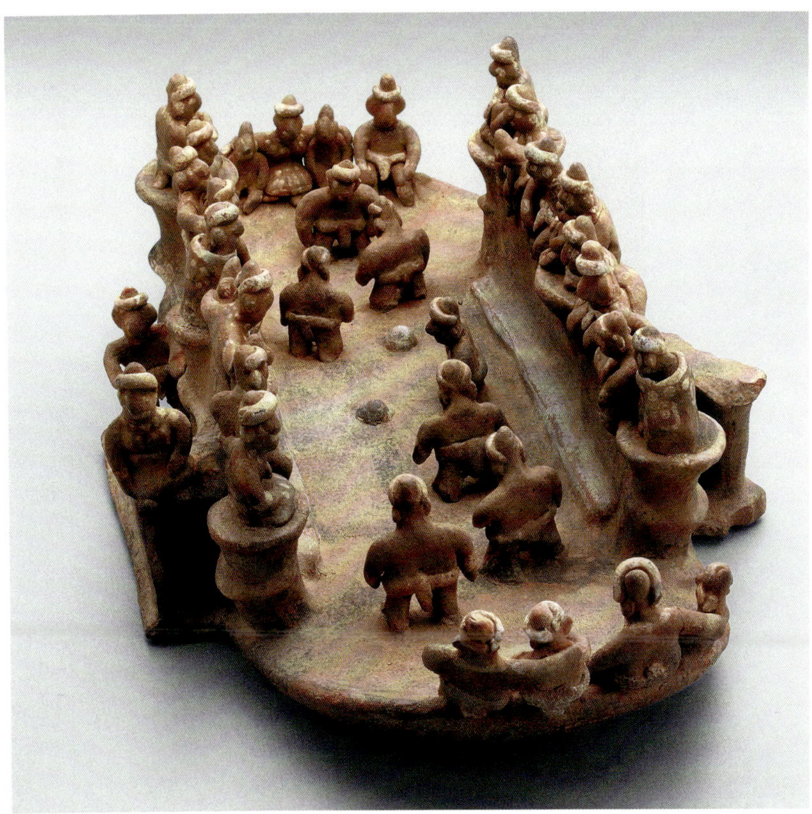

FIG. 166
Unknown maker
Nayarit Ball Game with Spectators,
100 B.C.–A.D. 250
Terracotta, 45.1 x 26.0 cm
Stephen Carlton Clark,
B.A. 1903, Fund
1973.88.26

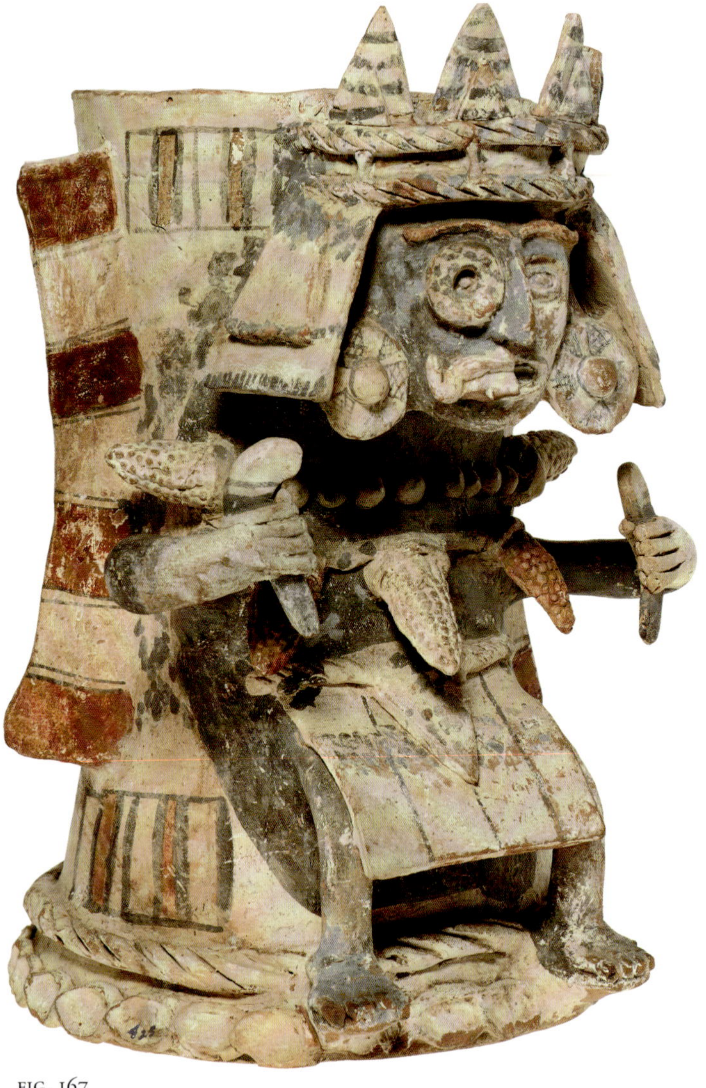

FIG. 167
Maker unknown
Aztec Brazier with Effigy of Corn Deity, A.D. 1400–1500
Terracotta, 40.8 x 31.0 x 31.5 cm
Stephen Carlton Clark, B.A. 1903, Fund
1973.88.14

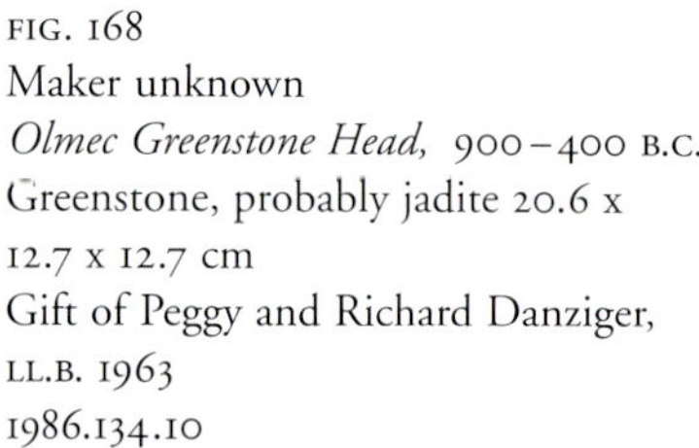

FIG. 168
Maker unknown
Olmec Greenstone Head, 900–400 B.C.
Greenstone, probably jadite 20.6 x 12.7 x 12.7 cm
Gift of Peggy and Richard Danziger, LL.B. 1963
1986.134.10

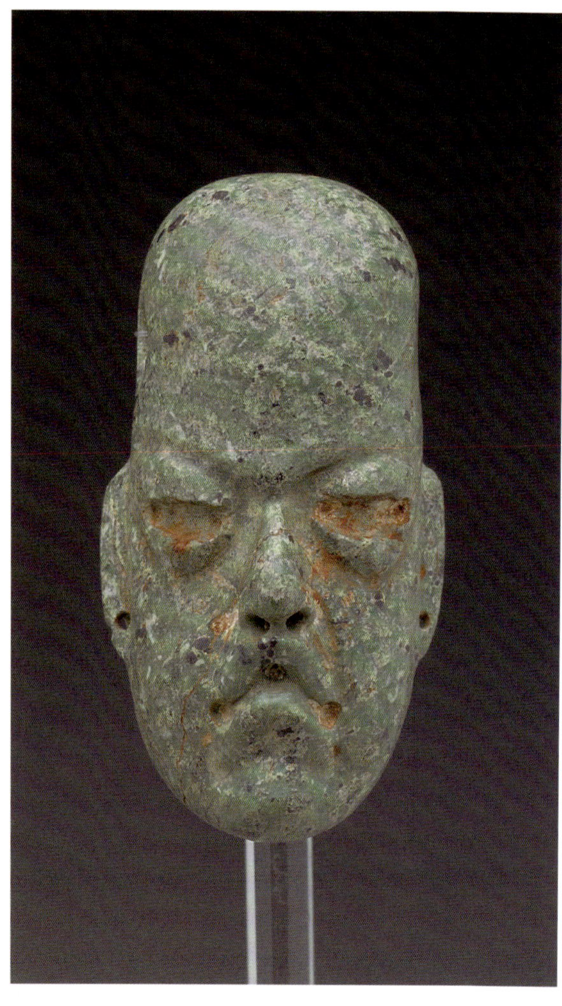

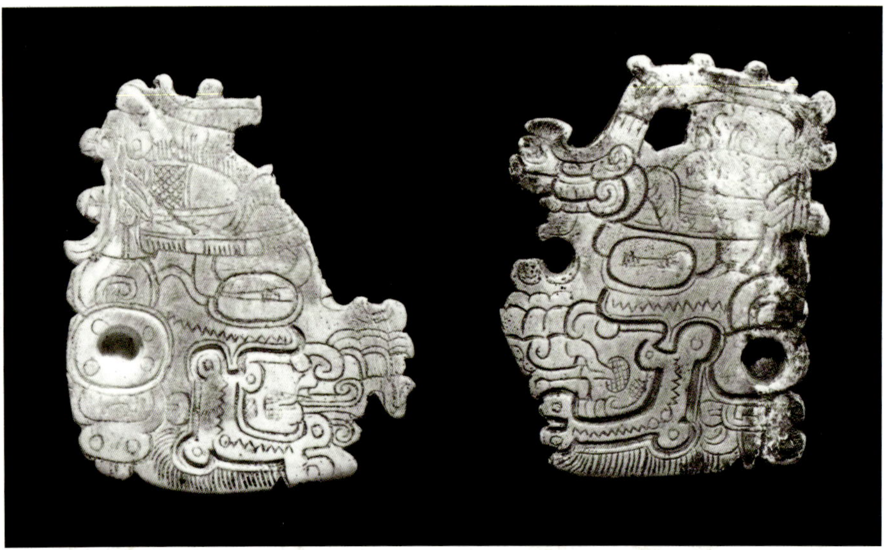

FIG. 169
Maker unknown
Mayan Ear Flares, A.D. 50–450
Conch shell with cinnabar, 4.8, 5 cm
Gift of Mr. and Mrs. Allen Wardwell, B.A. 1957
1988.91.1, 1991.45.1

and permanent display. Foremost among the 1973 purchases is the terracotta *Ballcourt Scene* (fig. 166), a model of the ballgame that provides a thematic link among many of the objects in the Yale collection. A carved stone Maya stele, several additional Jaina figurines, Maya painted vessels, and Aztec sculpture and vessels (fig. 167) are among the other works in this group. Olsen, born in England in 1891, survived to see his major pieces become the treasures of the Gallery's collection, and died in Guilford, Connecticut, in 1986.

The most important among subsequent gifts and purchases of Precolumbian art have come in conjunction with the reinstallation of the collection in 1988. A collaborative effort between Professor Mary Miller (PH.D. 1981) of the history of art department, her students, and the Gallery, this new installation represented the first complete rethinking of the display since 1962. Moving the collection out of the second floor of the Gallery, where it had been shown with African art in spaces adjacent to early twentieth-century painting and sculpture in an anachronistic survival of the view of Precolumbian and African art as "primitive," the 1988 installation placed Precolumbian art next to the art of the ancient Mediterranean, with which it shares a great vase painting tradition and similar methods of interpretation and study. Gifts from Peggy and Richard Danziger (LL.B. 1963), notably a fine Olmec greenstone head (fig. 168) and a *Laughing Boy* from Veracruz, and the Maya carved shell earflare of a human face given by Mr. and Mrs. Allen Wardwell enriched the new display in critical ways. The Wardwell earflare was one of a pair, and when, against all odds, its lost mate came on the market several years later, the Wardwells kindly purchased it for the Gallery to reunite the pair (fig. 169). Subsequent purchases have added, among others, a painted Maya vessel and a rare carved Maya femur.

The separation of the Gallery from the School of Fine Arts took place in 1955, at the direction of Yale President A. Whitney Griswold. For Griswold, who had taken office in 1950, this move was part of a major reorganization of the arts at Yale. The Division of the Arts, created in 1947 to unify the arts at Yale, was dissolved, and replaced by the University Council on the Arts, with rotating chairs, which was to advise the president on matters concerning music and the visual arts. There was also a Committee on the Art Gallery, a subcommittee of the University Council. The Art Gallery, which had been part of the Division of the Arts, became autonomous and a self-governing institution within Yale similar to the library or the Peabody Museum of Natural History. The School of Fine Arts was renamed the School of Architecture and Design, whose program would continue to include painting, sculpture, graphic arts, architecture, and city planning. The School of Drama also became a separate school.

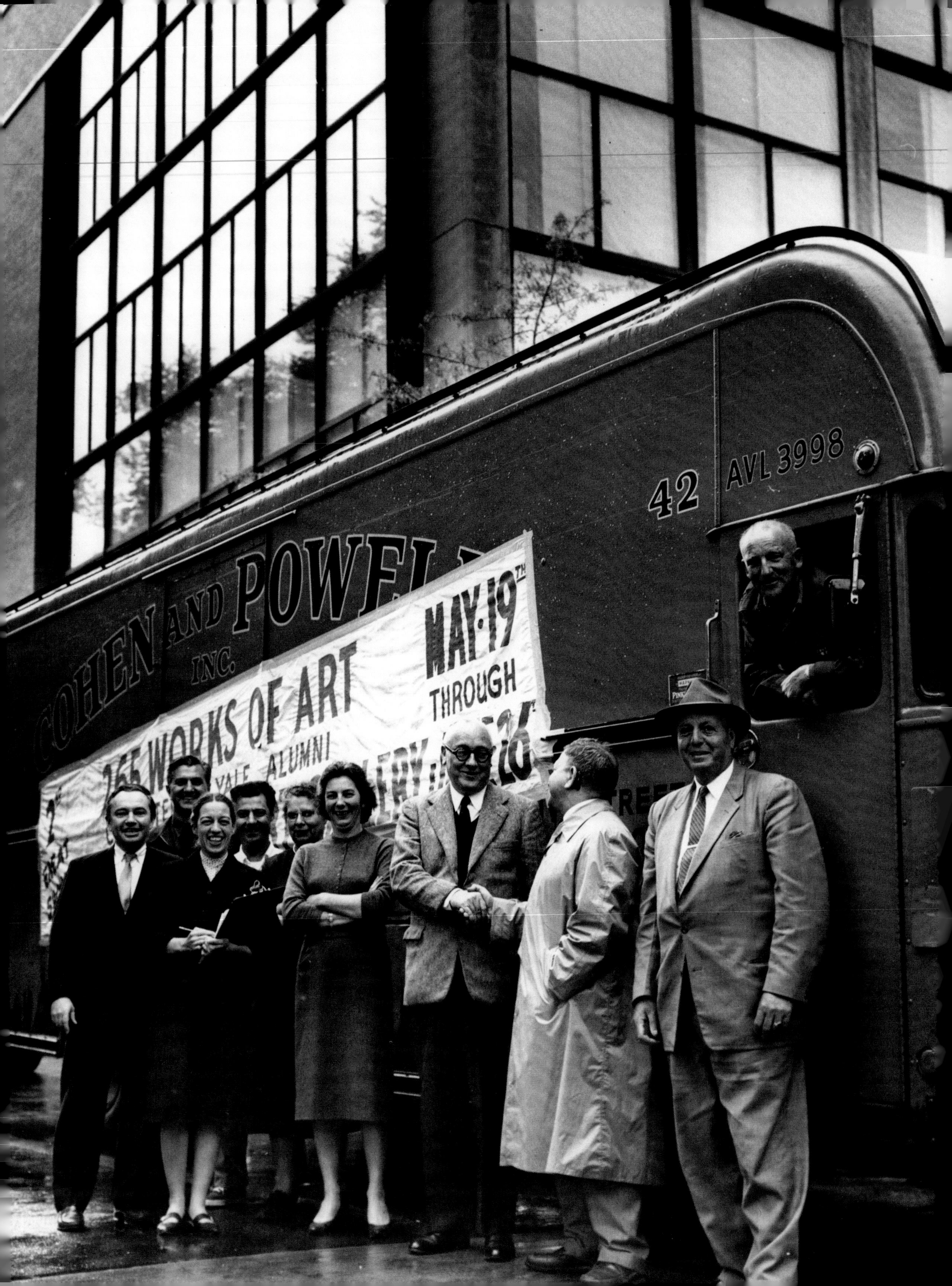

COHEN AND POWEL
INC.
265 WORKS OF ART
YALE ALUMNI
MAY 19TH
THROUGH
42
AVL 3998

CHAPTER 12

A Magnet for Visitors and Art

Andrew Carnduff Ritchie (fig. 170) succeeded Lamont Moore as director in July 1957. Ritchie came to Yale from the Museum of Modern Art, where he had served as director of the Department of Painting and Sculpture. Born in Scotland, he earned a Ph.D. from the Courtauld Institute of Art in London, and held museum and teaching appointments, including as director of the Albright Art Gallery in Buffalo, in several institutions prior to joining the MoMA staff in 1949. Ritchie was a dedicated museum professional, and a director with a vision. He was eager to expand the collections aggressively, and he continuously stressed the need to fill gaps in sixteenth- and seventeenth-century painting and sculpture, Greek, Roman, and Egyptian sculpture, and major twentieth-century European and American art. He raised significant sums for acquisitions. He was also fortunate that his arrival coincided with that of the Leonard C. Hanna, Jr., B.A. 1903, Fund, designated for acquisitions but unrestricted as to field, the largest acquisition fund to have been given to the Gallery up to that point. He personally undertook buying trips to London and elsewhere in which he acquired works in fields ranging from ancient Etruscan to modern American art. Such an omnivore occasionally has to digest mistakes, and there were a few antiquities that turned out to be less old than they should have been, but by and large, Ritchie's purchases were meaningful additions to the collection.

Ritchie encouraged his curators to be active in seeking gifts, and campaigned to attract major gifts and bequests himself. Results such as the Rabinowitz bequest in 1959, the Clark bequest in 1961, Walter Bareiss's major donation of prints in 1957, the *Draped Seated Woman* by Henry Moore (gift of Mr. and Mrs. Alex Hillman), two works by Maillol (*L'Air*, gift of Mr. and Mrs. Henry J. Heinz II, and *Torso of a Young Woman*, gift of A. Conger Goodyear, B.A. 1899), and other gifts are indicative of the positive response. Many of these gifts reflected long-standing relationships between donors and the Gallery; others began new ones. Ritchie recommended to the Yale Corporation that a new Acquisitions Committee be appointed, and in 1958 the Corporation did so, naming Stephen Carlton Clark, James W. Fosburgh, Robert Lehman, Wilmarth Lewis, Mrs. Paul Moore, Irving S. Olds, and G. Lauder Greenway to serve.

FIG. 170
Andrew Carnduff Ritchie and Art Gallery staff meeting the works of art arriving for the 1960 alumni exhibition, April 1960
Photograph courtesy Yale University Art Gallery Archives

John Canaday (M.A. 1932), a Yale graduate whose memories of the Gallery as a student were of excellent early American collections and the Jarves pictures, and of a museum that "combined a kind of Ruskinism shined up with Berensonian polish and the implication that New England was still a sturdy elysium of elm-shaded streets where the solid citizens of a British colony strode in knee-breeches,"[1] wrote in the *New York Times* in 1961 of the profound transformation that had taken place. Noting the commitment to broadening the program of the museum and the scope of its collections that emerged with the shift to modernism in the 1940s, Canaday credits Ritchie with many of the acquisitions that carried the transformation forward with works of art of the highest quality in every field from Asian and Mesoamerican to American and European. In Canaday's view, it was the consistently high standard that Ritchie adhered to in his purchases—"Mr. Ritchie has no patience with the idea that a proper acquisition for a university museum is the 'good study piece,' which means a good typical example of a period or school that offers every demonstrable point for instruction but lacks the undemonstrable quantity that differentiates a meaningful work of art from a satisfactory exercise"[2]—that sets the Yale Art Gallery apart from other university museums. Later, as described below, Canaday wrote about the exhibition installed at the Gallery to celebrate these acquisitions.

Ritchie's vision extended to the Gallery itself, and he was concerned with both practical and aesthetic issues. Air conditioning was installed in the first three floors of the Kahn building, and in the third floor exhibition galleries of the Swartwout building. Basement art storage was fireproofed. A kitchen, restroom, and superintendent's tool room were installed on the first floor. Some functional reorganization of space was undertaken, changing office, study, storage, and classroom space into exhibition galleries. A study room for Precolumbian and African art was carved out of the exhibition space in the west half of the second floor of the Kahn building, and the prints and drawings department was rearranged to provide more study space. The west and a large portion of the south walls of the new gallery spaces on the first, second, and third floors were paneled over, hiding the original Kahn surfaces, and the signature Kahn stair silo was boxed in with walls. There were practical reasons for some of this. Enclosing the stair silo created more storage space. The west walls were completely glass, and the sun streaming through them in the afternoon created serious problems for the air conditioning. In addition, covering the glass with panels vastly increased the amount of space available for hanging pictures and exhibiting other art. Art had previously been hung on and installed in front of the original cinderblock walls (fig. 146). The new panels were generally painted white, transforming the dark gray Kahn surfaces into something more like MoMA. Whatever Ritchie's specific reasons—and many of his donors were active at MoMA and likely attuned to its aesthetic—the changes met with positive responses, although not universally, and the reinvigorated exhibition spaces continued to attract major gifts and bequests.

The permanent collections were exhibited throughout the first three floors of Kahn and the Swartwout building, with the basement and fourth floor of Kahn continuing to be devoted to architecture and graphic design. Modern art was shown on the first floor of Kahn, in expanded gallery space. On the second floor, new galleries were devoted to the early twentieth century, including the Société Anonyme Collection, adjacent to African and Precolumbian art from the Linton, Olsen, and Osborn Collections (fig. 171). These galleries replaced studios, a classroom, and office space for architecture and city planning, which had moved to Weir Hall. The third floor contained Renaissance, later European, and Asian art in Kahn and American and ancient art in the Swartwout building. The Associates Room was created and the registrar's office was relocated on the first floor. By spring of 1960, these gallery renovations were complete. Attendance grew, exceeding 100,000 in the 1959/60 academic year.

Ritchie appointed new senior staff for several departments. Appointing curators with outstanding professional and scholarly qualifications was a priority for Ritchie, and he sought candidates in both Europe and the United States. George J. Lee was named curator of Oriental art in 1959, the first full-time curator in this field. He was joined for his first year by Nelson I. Wu as curator of Chinese painting. Trained at Harvard (B.A. 1940), Lee served on the staff of the Fogg Art

Museum from 1942–49, the last year as assistant curator of Oriental art. For the decade before coming to Yale, he was curator of Oriental art at the Brooklyn Museum. Lee was curator at Yale until his death in 1976, joined in his last years and then succeeded by Mary Gardner Neill (PH.D. 1981). Appointed curator soon after the death of Ada Small Moore, one of the Gallery's greatest benefactors and donors to Asian art, he benefited from Mrs. Moore's dual bequest of works of art and of two endowment funds, one for the acquisition and the other for the care and maintenance of Asian art. Lee's focus was on scholarship and care of the collections, which resulted in publications on the permanent collection and in special exhibitions on both Chinese and Japanese art. Among these was his exhibition *The Edo Culture in Japanese Prints* in 1972, based on the Yale collection, and combining visually appealing works of art with social history. The Gallery's director, Alan Shestack, wrote that "Japanese prints probably represent the most elegant and tasteful examples of inexpensive popular art ever produced." The emphasis of the exhibition, as Shestack noted, was "on the role of these printed images as mirrors of Japanese culture."[3]

Egbert Haverkamp-Begemann became curator of drawings and prints in 1960. Begemann had been curator of drawings of the Boymans van Beuningen Museum in Rotterdam, then a lecturer and researcher at Harvard before coming to Yale. Both curators began work on acquisitions and on catalogues of parts of the permanent collection. Ritchie hired Stanton Loomis Catlin as assistant director, needing a professional to manage the day-to-day operation of the Gallery while he was traveling in search of art and funding.

Building the collection was a primary focus for Ritchie, and he continued to pursue both purchases and gifts with intensity. He staged frequent exhibitions of recent acquisitions as an effective way to draw attention to the new additions to the collection and to inspire even more donations. John Canaday's review in the *New York Times* of the exhibition celebrating the 1959–60 acquisitions is indicative of the interest that the art world took in the Yale Art Gallery's growing collection.[4] Canaday characterized the show as "an exhibition that should add envy-green to the college colors of

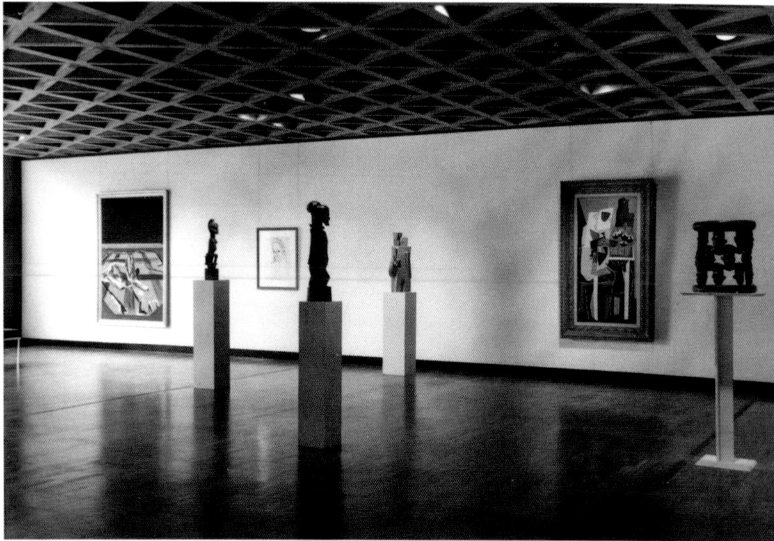

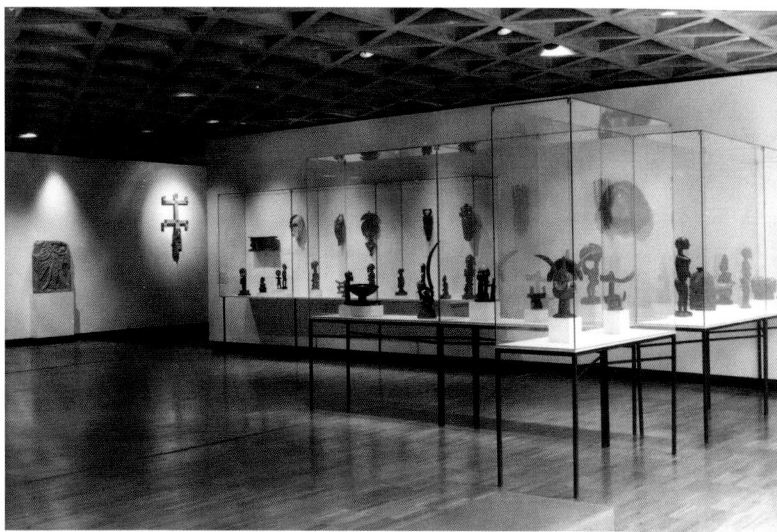

FIG. 171
Permanent collection installation, 2nd floor, ca. 1958/59
Photographs courtesy Yale University Art Gallery Archives

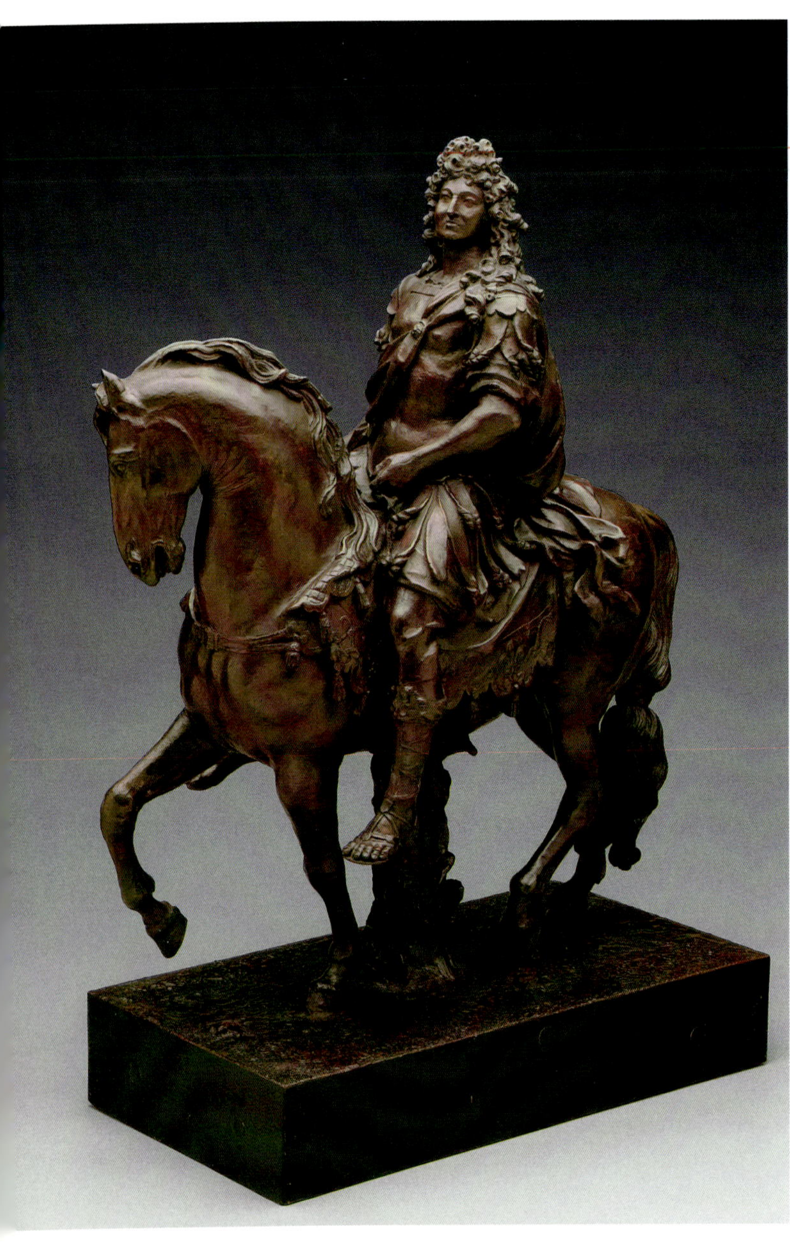

FIG. 172
François Girardon
Maquette for the Equestrian Statue of Louis XIV, ca. 1687
Wax, 81.3 x 29.2, L. 59.7 cm
Gift of Mr. and Mrs. James W. Fosburgh, B.A. 1933, M.A. 1935
1959.56

many a school." Describing the exhibition as a selection from more than 350 works of art acquired by the Gallery in the previous two years, Canaday reported that the ratio of gifts and purchases was around 2 to 1. Noting that the acquisitions ranged from a Japanese vase from the first millenium B.C. to contemporary painting and sculpture, he cited purchases of works by Valdés Leal, Claude Lorrain, Sir Joshua Reynolds, and John Trumbull, and gifts and bequests of works by Braque, Maillol, and Hieronymus Bosch. Particularly noteworthy, and the piece Canaday chose to illustrate, was the maquette for an equestrian statue of Louis XIV by François Girardon, the gift of Mr. and Mrs. James W. Fosburgh (B.A. 1933; fig. 172). Modeled in wax and described as unique by the Gallery, "it justifies the use of that dangerous adjective if anything does," in the reviewer's opinion, especially since the monumental bronze counterpart for the Yale wax version, erected in Paris in 1699, was destroyed by French revolutionaries in 1792.

Canaday noted that the Gallery's purchase policy, as described by Ritchie, "is planned to fill gaps left by donations." In Canaday's own view, the gifts and bequests received in 1959–60 "represent not only a biennial coup but also a happy augury. In the field of institutional collecting, the old saw that them that has, gets, holds true. Donors like to know that the works of art they relinquish will find their permanent home in the best of company, and for Yale the caliber of recent acquisitions has resulted in a snowballing of a once static, if pleasant, museum." Ritchie and the Gallery's supporters could not help but have been pleased and encouraged by this review, and Canaday's reputation as an augur remained untarnished for years afterward.

In 1960, Stephen Carlton Clark died, leaving the Yale Art Gallery a bequest of art that more than fulfilled Canaday's prophecy. Clark, a graduate of the class of 1903 and long a member of the Gallery's circle of major donors and advisers, had already given the Gallery a number of important works, especially works on paper. His first gifts, in 1930, included watercolors by Edward Hopper, Charles Burchfield, and Arthur B. Davies, drawings by Robert Henri and Joseph Stella, and paintings by George Luks. In 1954, Clark donated a painting by Picasso and drawings by Matisse and Orozco, followed in 1958 by Picasso's *First Steps* (fig. 173) and paintings by

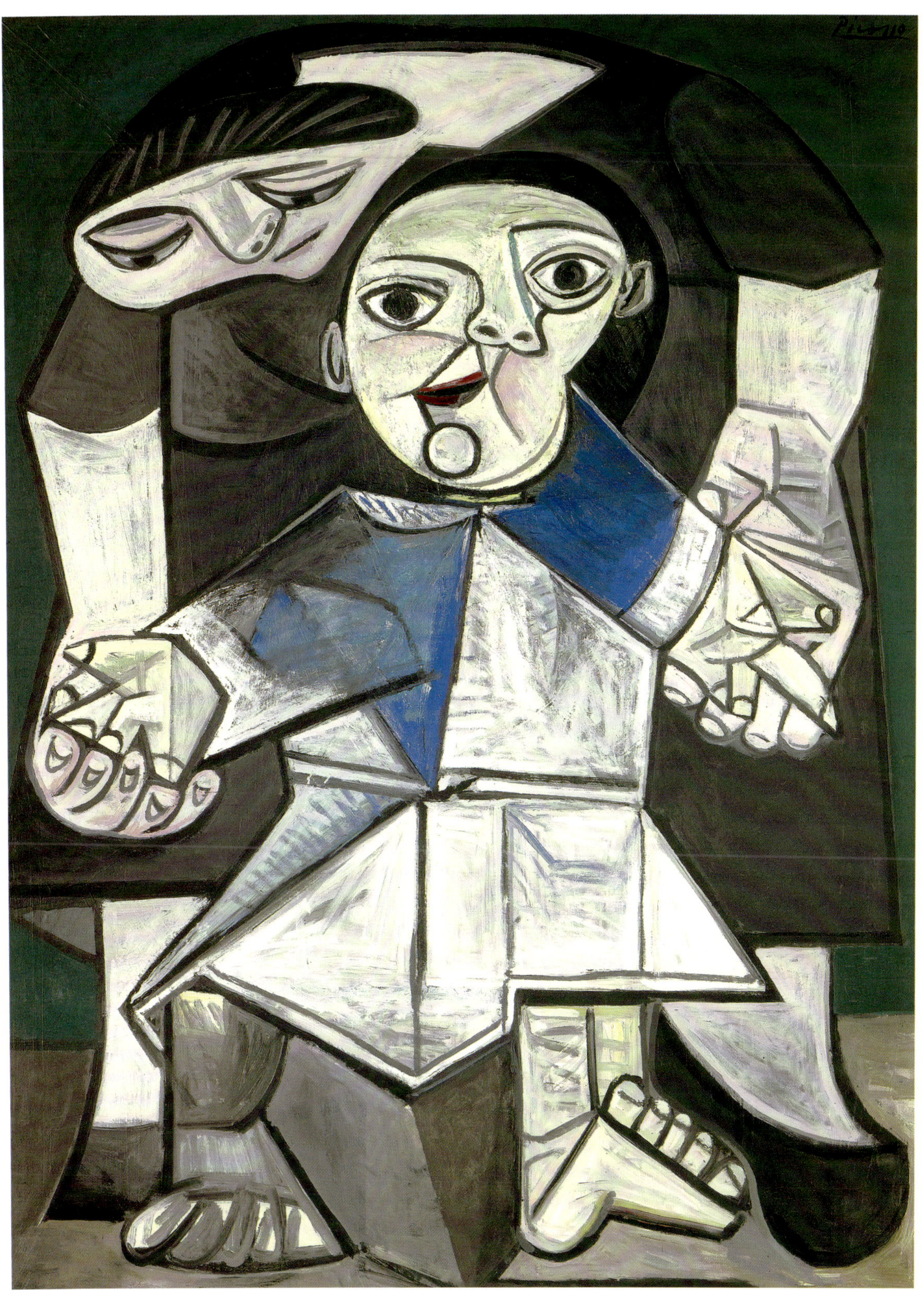

FIG. 173
Pablo Picasso
First Steps, 1943
Oil on canvas, 130.2 x 97.1 cm
Gift of Stephen Carlton Clark,
B.A. 1903
1958.27

two twentieth-century British artists, Francis Bacon and Stanley Spencer.

The bequest that Clark left the Gallery was extraordinary. In numbers, it included thirty-four objects, twenty-three paintings, six drawings, and five prints, but this modest total disguises the incredible quality of the works in the group. Some, including important paintings by Manet (fig. 151) and Hals (figs. 150 and 150a), had been part of the 1956 alumni exhibition, as noted above. There were two additional European paintings—namely, an early Corot, *The Harbor of La Rochelle (Le Port de La Rochelle)* of 1851, and the painting that is probably the most renowned work of art in the Gallery's collection, Vincent van Gogh's *Night Café* (fig. 174). There were five drawings and five prints by George Bellows. But it was the American paintings in the bequest that truly transformed the Gallery's holdings in two areas of this field.

Prior to the Clark bequest, Yale's American paintings consisted of the Trumbull Collection, numerous portraits, the Whitney Collection of Sporting Art, a small number of late nineteenth- and early twentieth-century paintings in the Garvan Collection, the American works in the Société Anonyme Collection and the Dreier bequest, and a few isolated but important gifts such as the Benjamin West *Agrippina Landing at Brundisium with the Ashes of Germanicus* (fig. 131). The collection remained weak in nineteenth-century art, and had no major works of the mid-twentieth century. The Clark bequest added eight paintings by Thomas Eakins (fig. 175, *Kathrin: Girl with a Cat*, and fig. 153), three by Winslow Homer (fig. 176, *A Game of Croquet*, and fig. 152), and four by Edward Hopper. The Hoppers in particular, consisting of *Rooms by the Sea*, *Rooms for Tourists*, *Sunlight in a Cafeteria* (fig. 177), and *Western Motel*, are considered among the artist's most important works, although three of them are very late and the group as a whole is thus not representative of his entire career. Not only were gaps filled, but they were filled with works of the highest quality, setting a standard for subsequent acquisitions. A portrait of *Mrs. John Powell* by Copley and two by Bellows, *Lady Jean* and *Katherine Rosen*, completed the list of paintings in the bequest. As a whole, the Clark bequest established for paintings what the Garvan Collection had already established for decorative arts, the principle that a teaching collection must go beyond acquiring mere examples to providing the very best works of art produced in every field.

The Stephen Carlton Clark, B.A. 1903, Fund, a $1 million endowment for acquisitions, was part of the bequest in response to a plea from Ritchie for an endowment for acquisitions. As a member of the Acquisitions Committee, Clark was well aware of the reality of the need. The Clark Fund has been used since 1964 to acquire works in this spirit for fields ranging from Precolumbian, Chinese, and ancient Greek and Roman art through European and American paintings, drawings, prints, and photographs. Acquisitions made with the fund such as Marcel Duchamp, *The Bride Stripped Bare by Her Bachelors, Even (Large Glass)*, a hand-colored photograph collage purchased in 1981 for its relation to Duchamp's work in the Société Anonyme Collection, and two studies for Hopper's *Sunlight in a Cafeteria*, bought in 1987, demonstrate the Gallery's commitment to buying works that complement existing holdings as important enrichments of a teaching collection.

Throughout the 1960s significant acquisitions continued to arrive, attracted by the unremitting campaigns of a dynamic director and the expanded and renovated Gallery space. Ritchie was a magnet for art. *Recent Gifts and Purchases*, a special exhibition of the acquisitions of the year 1963, took place in early 1964—a recent acquisitions show with the *Bulletin* as the illustrated checklist became an annual event for some time after this. The *Bulletin* for 1964 listed 636 works added to the collection the previous year.

Other special exhibitions honored important private collectors who had connections to Yale. These exhibitions provided the opportunity for faculty to teach from and students to study and do research on important works to which they would otherwise have had little or no access, in the ideal conditions of having them installed in the galleries where they took classes. Thus *Neo-Impressionists and the Nabis in the Collection of Arthur G. Altschul* in 1965 (fig. 178) was recorded in a catalogue by Professor Robert L. Herbert and the students of his graduate seminar. Later in 1965, *British Paintings and Drawings in the Paul Mellon Collection* presented a selection of two hundred works from the

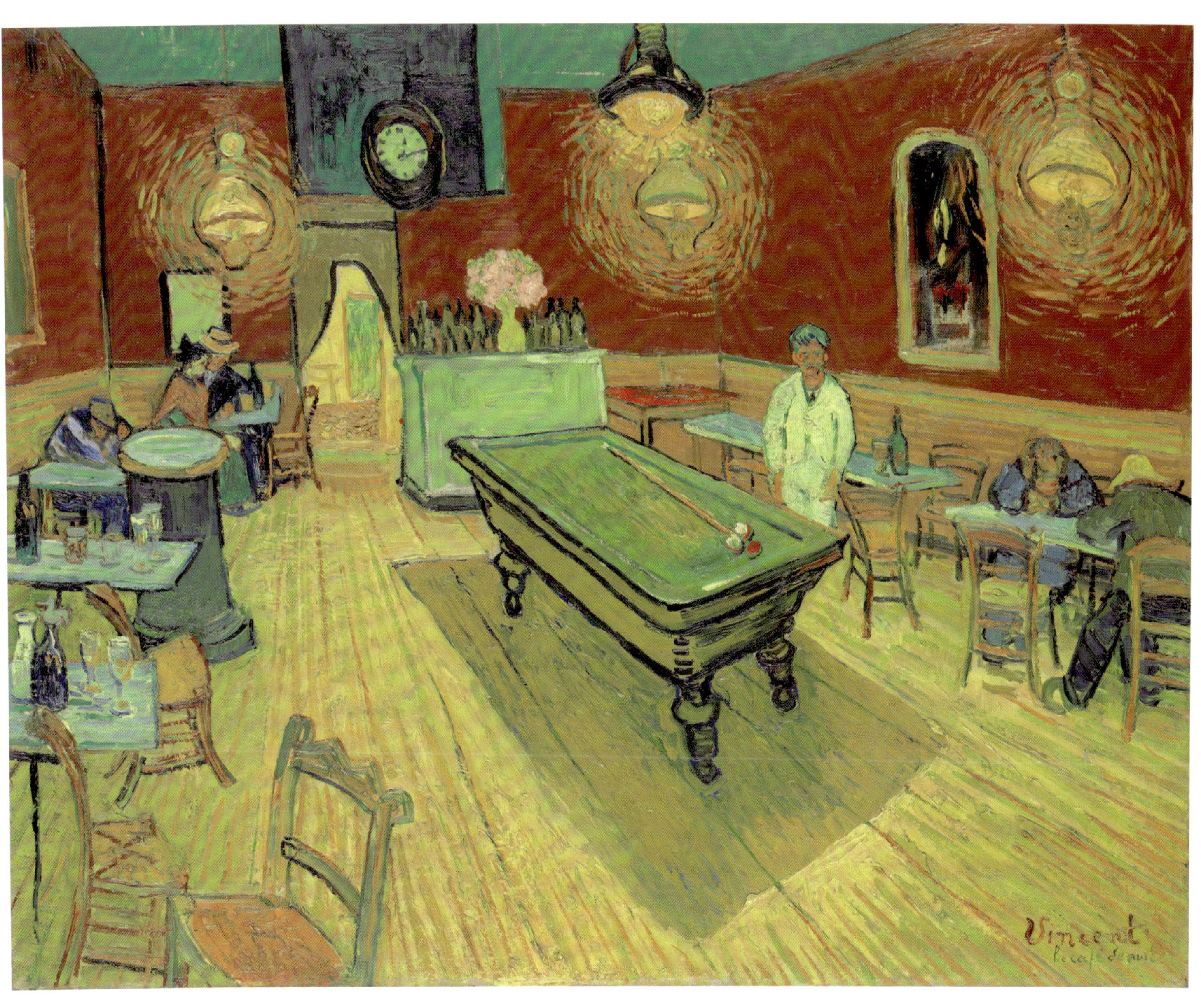

FIG. 174
Vincent van Gogh
Night Café (Le Café de nuit), 1888
Oil on canvas, 72.4 x 92.1 cm
Bequest of Stephen Carlton Clark,
B.A. 1903
1961.18.34

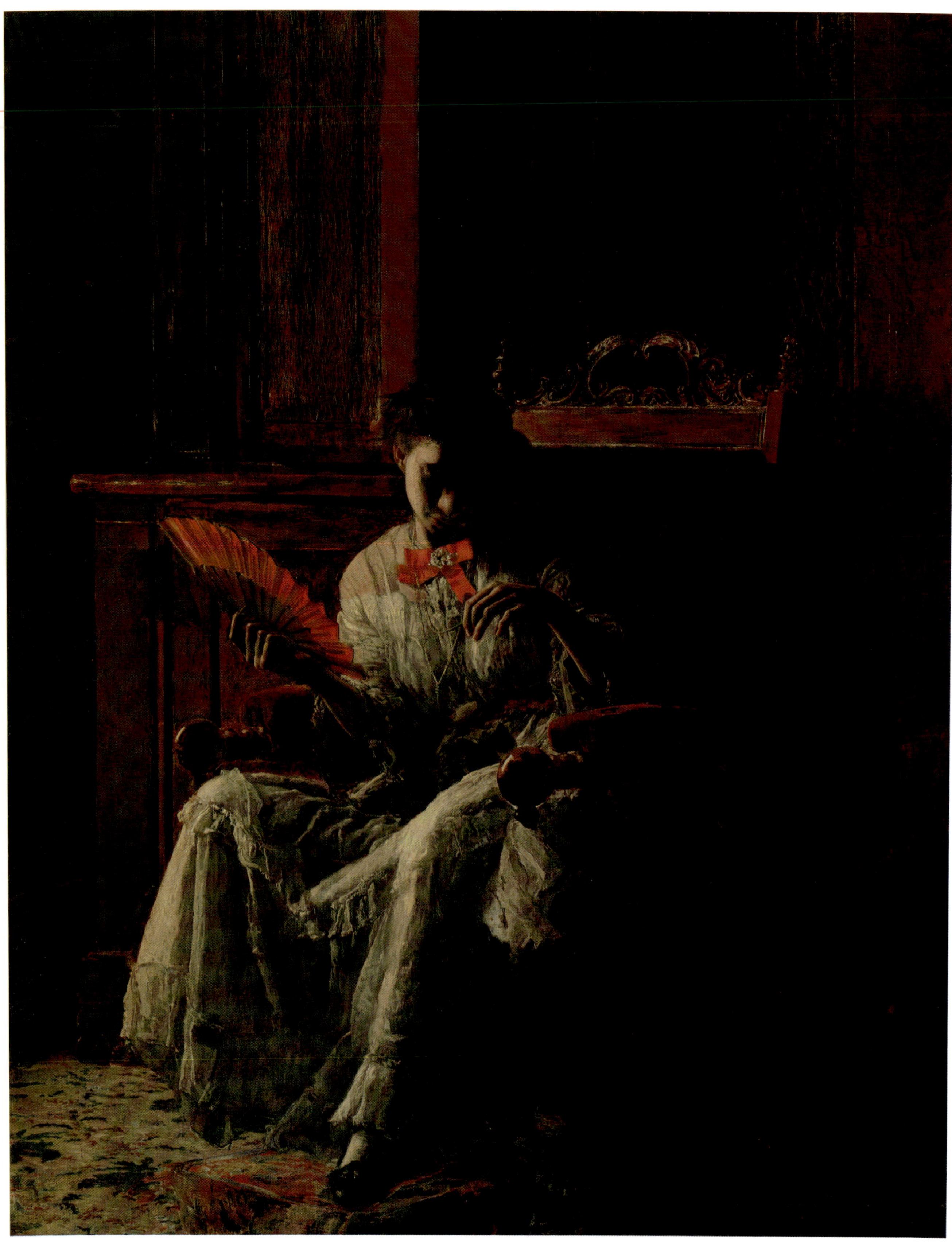

FIG. 175
Thomas Eakins
Kathrin: Girl with a Cat, 1872
Oil on canvas, 165.1 x 133.4 cm
Bequest of Stephen Carlton Clark, B.A. 1903
1961.18.17

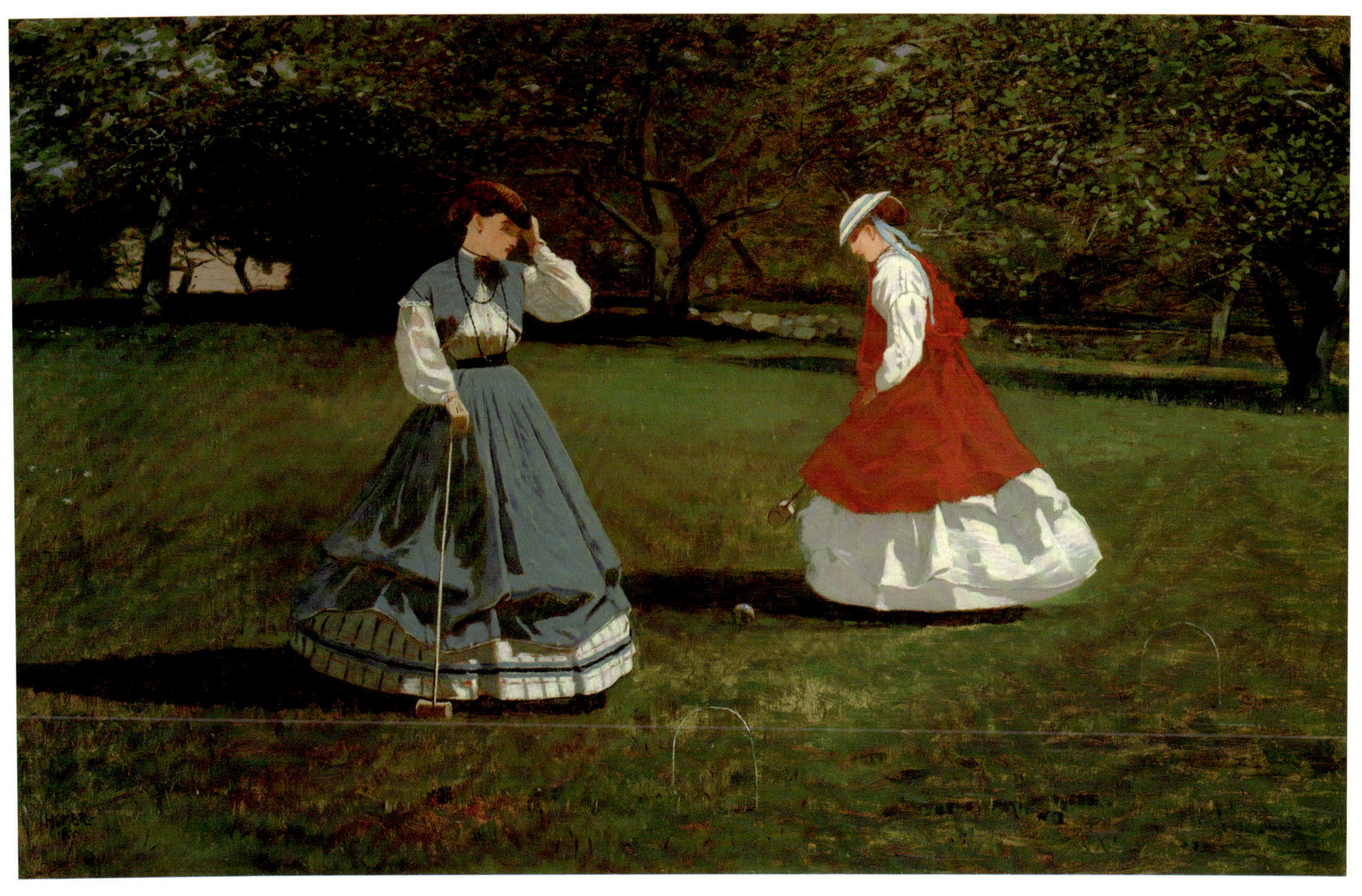

FIG. 176
Winslow Homer
A Game of Croquet, 1866
Oil on canvas, 60.3 x 87.9 cm
Bequest of Stephen Carlton Clark,
B.A. 1903
1961.18.25

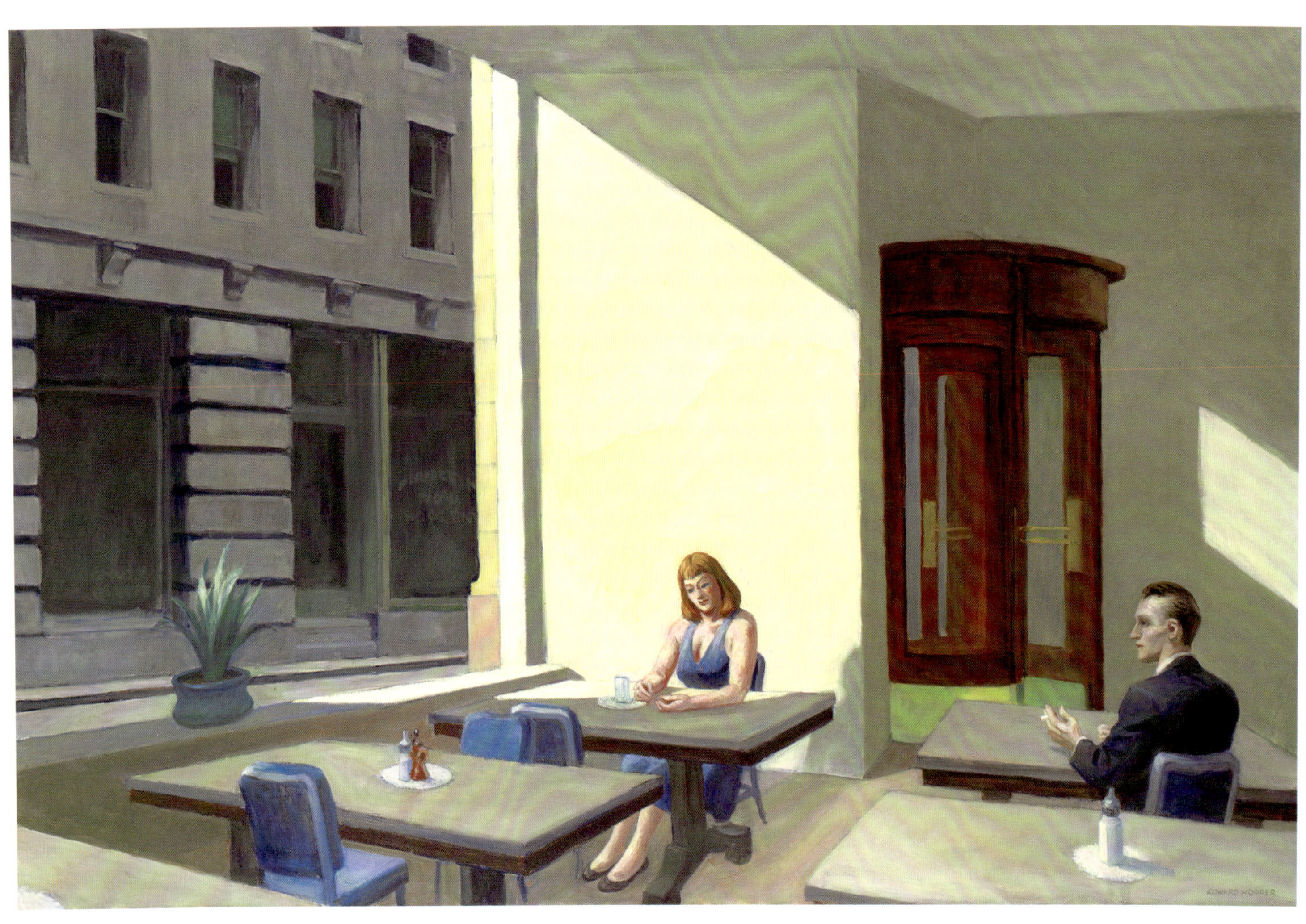

FIG. 177
Edward Hopper
Sunlight in a Cafeteria, 1958
Oil on canvas, 102.1 x 152.7 cm
Bequest of Stephen Carlton Clark, B.A. 1903
1961.18.31

premier private collection of British art in America. For many, this was the first glimpse of the collection that Mr. Mellon would ultimately give to Yale as part of the founding of the Yale Center for British Art.

In 1966, the Gallery received a bequest of paintings and drawings from Edith Malvina K. Wetmore. The majority of the paintings were French, including works by Seurat, Bonnard, Vuillard (*Woman before a Mirror*), Redon, and Henri Fantin-Latour, but an important pair of portraits by Copley, *Benjamin Pickman* and *Mrs. Benjamin Pickman* (Mary Toppin), was part of the bequest. Miss Wetmore, known as a francophile and described by the *New York Times* as one of the last dowagers of Newport, was born in 1870 in Switzerland.[5] The daughter of George Peabody Wetmore, governor of and later United States senator from Rhode Island, Edith Wetmore was a founder of the Newport Casino Theater and a fellow in perpetuity of the Metropolitan Museum of Art in New York. At her death, her Newport estate, Chateau-sur-Mer, was designated for the Society for the Preservation of New England Antiquities, and she bequeathed funds to Yale to increase professors' salaries. Also part of this bequest was an important group of nineteenth-century French drawings. The Wetmore drawings included the charming *Portrait of Mlle. Marcotte* by Jean-Auguste-Dominique Ingres (fig. 179), particularly prized for teaching, as well as works by Seurat (*L'Echo*, fig. 180), Daumier, Caillebotte, Couture, and Guys. Although not well known as an art collector, Miss Wetmore bequeathed paintings and drawings that remain among the Gallery's treasured holdings.

WORKS ON PAPER

An important collection of Old Master works entered the prints and drawings department in 1961, donated anonymously to Yale in 1957 and transferred from the library to the Gallery. This collection consisted of six albums of Old Master drawings collected by John Percival, first Earl of Egmont (1683–1748). Egmont, an Irish peer, was a lifelong friend of Bishop Berkeley, one of the early important donors to Yale through his gift in 1736 of his farm in Rhode Island and a library of nine hundred books, the finest single library to have come to America at the time. Berkeley was certainly

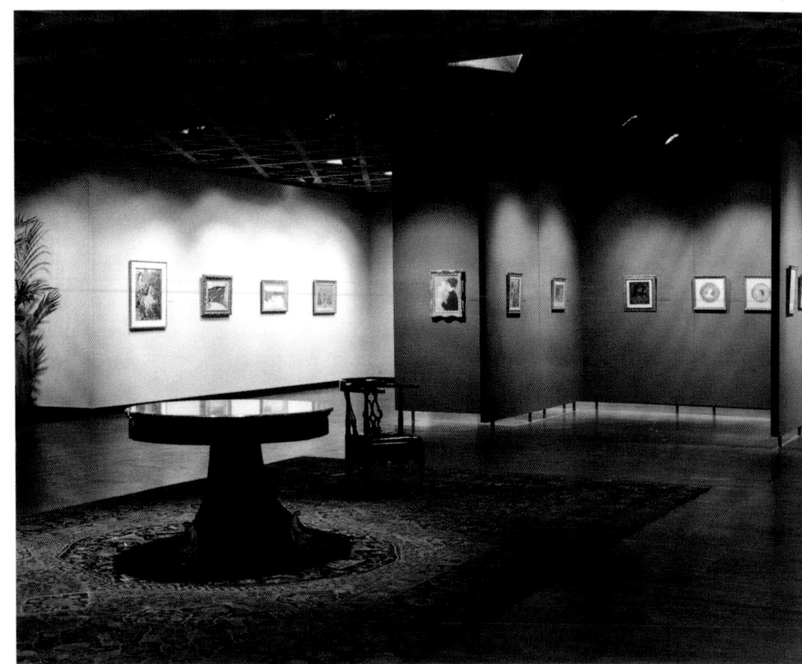

FIG. 178
Neo-Impressionists and the Nabis in the Collection of Arthur G. Altschul, 1965
Photograph courtesy Yale University Art Gallery Archives

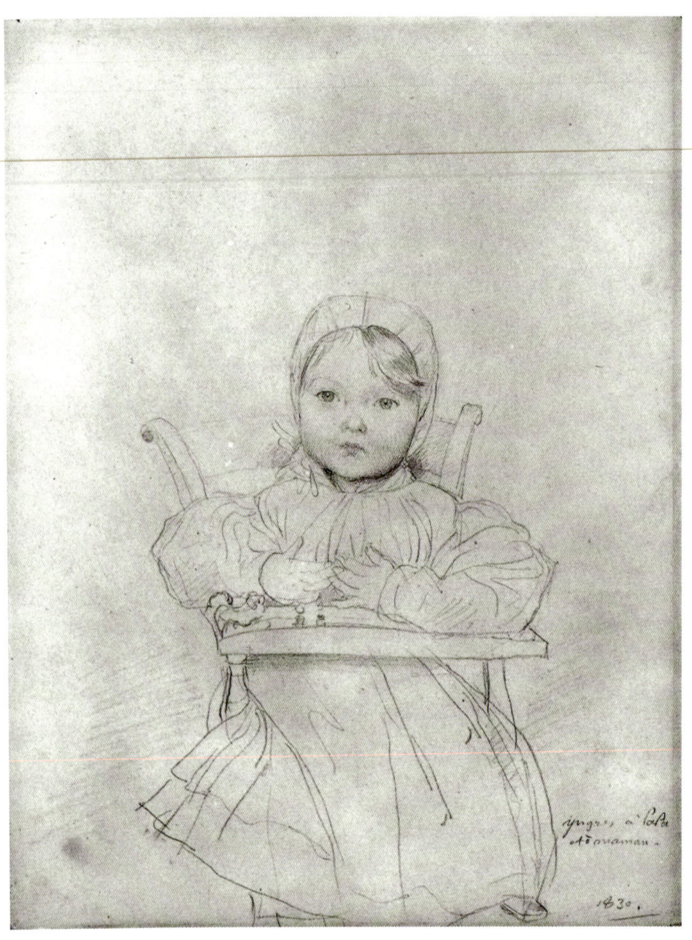

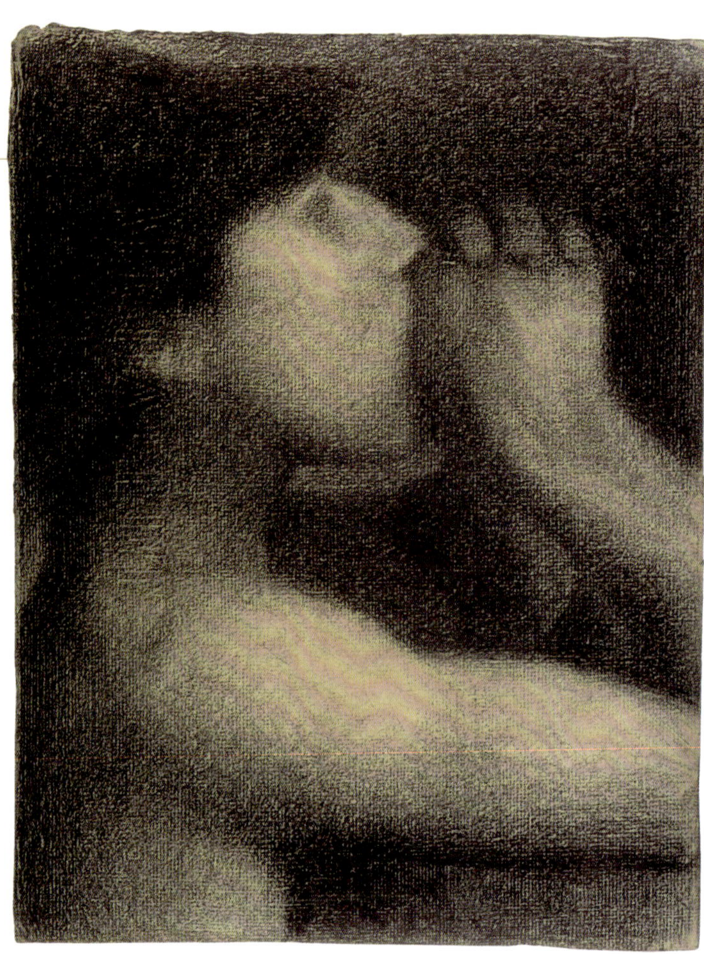

FIG. 179
Jean-Auguste-Dominique Ingres
Portrait of Mlle. Marcotte, 1830
Graphite, 24.5 x 19.1 cm
Bequest of Edith Malvina K. Wetmore
1966.80.7

FIG. 180
Georges Pierre Seurat
L'Echo, study for *Une Baignade, Asnières*, 1882–83
Black conté crayon, 31.2 x 24 cm
Bequest of Edith Malvina K. Wetmore
1966.80.11

FIG. 181
Maarten de Vos
Jonah Thrown Overboard, ca. 1589
Pen and brown ink and brown wash over sketch in black chalk heightened with white, 28. x 22.3 cm
Egmont Collection, Yale Library Transfer
1961.65.51

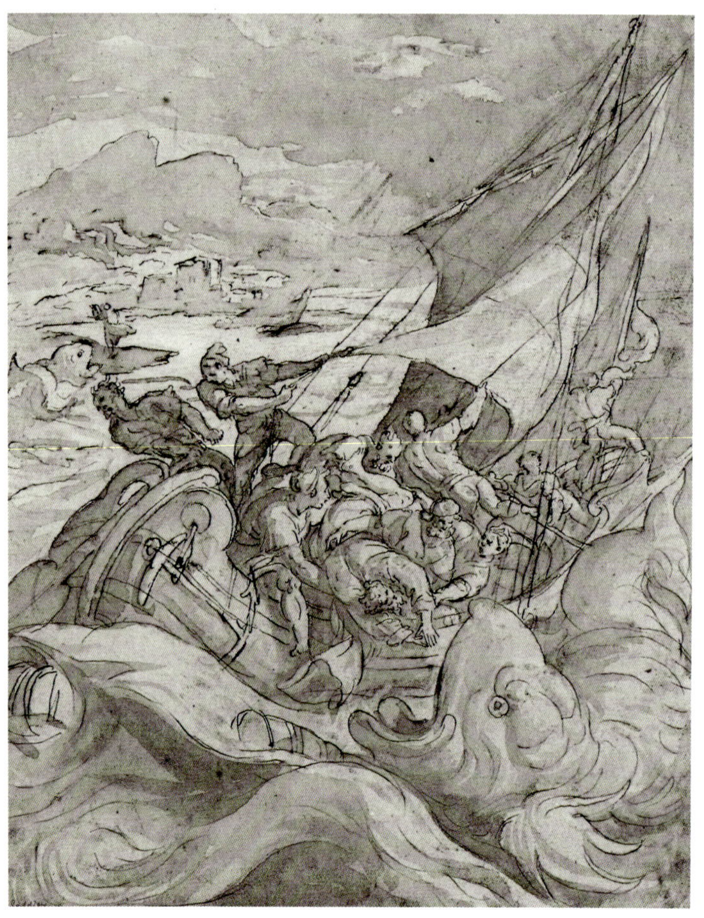

instrumental in forming parts of Egmont's collection, and it is likely that the Bishop acquired many of the Italian drawings in the collection during his residence in Rome. The Egmont albums contain 543 drawings ranging from the sixteenth to the mid-eighteenth centuries and representing the work of artists from virtually every European nation.

The Egmont Collection is particularly strong in Dutch and Flemish drawings and it forms the backbone of the Gallery's collection in this field. Maarten de Vos (fig. 181), Abraham Bloemaert, Jacques de Gheyn II, Jan van Goyen, Cornelis Hendriksz Vroom, Pieter Lastman, Ferdinand Bol, and Gebrand van den Eeckhout are among the artists represented in the collection. Although it does not boast drawings by Rembrandt or Rubens, the Egmont Collection, by its clear effort to be comprehensive, reveals the complexity of the artistic schools surrounding these great masters. In addition, Italian drawings, notably *St. Catherine* by Filippo Bellini, *Apollo Killing the Python* by Luca Cambiaso, and *Portrait of an Old Man* attributed to Bernini, and French drawings, among them the *Virgin and Child* by Jacques Bellange and *Two Women* by Simon Vouet, are included.

The transfer of the Egmont albums occurred barely a year after Egbert Haverkamp-Begemann was appointed curator of drawings and prints. Begemann and Anne-Marie Logan, a noted drawings scholar who served as assistant curator of drawings and prints from 1967–71 and as acting curator for a year after Begemann left in 1971 to teach at New York University, worked through the 1960s on their comprehensive catalogue *European Drawings and Watercolors in the Yale University Art Gallery: 1500–1900*, and it was published in 1970. In the course of their research on the Egmont drawings for this catalogue, Begemann and Logan reattributed 361 of the drawings. Their work inspired gifts to the collection and they encouraged the Gallery to purchase Old Master drawings to complement current holdings in time for inclusion in the catalogue. Supported by the Everett V. Meeks Fund, begun in 1956, drawings by Jacob Jordaens (fig. 182), Jan Breughel the Elder, Jan Muller, Taddeo and Frederico Zuccaro, Pompeo Batoni, Antoine Watteau, Hubert Robert, and François Boucher, among others, were purchased. In 1961 alone, twenty-three drawings, including eight by Gainsborough and

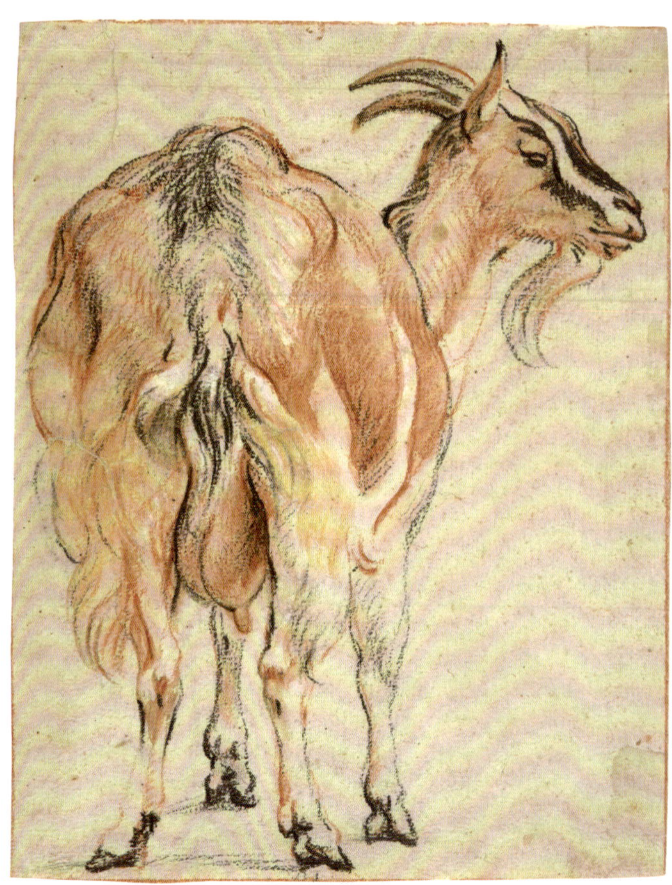

FIG. 182
Jacob Jordaens
Goat, ca. 1628–41
Red, black, and yellow chalk, touches of red and brown wash, heightened with white, 25.4 x 19.9 cm
Everett V. Meeks, B.A. 1901, Fund
1963.9.39

seven by Millet, and ten prints were purchased with the Meeks Fund. This momentum continued after the catalogue appeared, with further acquisitions using the Meeks and Maitland F. Griggs Funds well into the 1970s.

Alan Shestack was named to succeed Begemann as curator of drawings and prints in 1968 and held the position until he became director of the Yale Art Gallery in 1971. Previously on the curatorial staff of the National Gallery of Art and the Philadelphia Museum of Art, Shestack combined scholarship with extensive museum experience and commitment to high professional standards. A specialist in works on paper from the fifteenth and sixteenth centuries in northern Europe but equally interested in photography and contemporary art, Shestack produced exhibitions and added to the collection in all of these areas. Some of the exhibition projects begun during this brief term as curator were completed only after he became director. Notable among these were the exhibition *Prints of Dürer and His Time* (1974), and the major traveling exhibition *Hans Baldung Grien* (1981). The exhibition on Hans Baldung Grien was the first monographic study on this important German mannerist artist, and in its placement of the artist's work in the context of Dürer and other contemporary German artists, it broke new ground in the study of German art of the early Renaissance. A collection of German Expressionist prints donated by Walter and Molly Bareiss in 1969 remains outstanding among the acquisitions for the department.

James D. Burke succeeded Alan Shestack as curator in 1972. The title of the position was changed in 1978 to curator of prints, drawings, and photographs. Harvard-educated with a specialty in seventeenth-century Dutch paintings and drawings, Burke shared Shestack's interest in photography and contemporary art as well as in the art of northern Europe. His purchases for the collection reflected this. Representative were two drawings by Jacques-Louis David, *Drum Set in Battersea Park* by Claes Oldenburg, three lithographs by James Rosenquist, a woodcut by the sixteenth-century German artist Michael Ostendorfer, and a portfolio of ten photographs by Diane Arbus, all purchased, along with other works, during 1973–74. Encouraged by Burke, a gift from Richard L. Menschel of ninety photographs by Aaron Siskind in 1977 marked the beginning of the Gallery's photography collections, followed in the same year by a large transfer of photographs from Yale's Sterling Memorial Library.

Exhibitions organized by graduate students were encouraged by both Burke and Shestack, among them *American Drawing, 1970–1973* (Christina Cahill, now the director of the Norton Gallery, West Palm Beach), *Sixteenth Century Italian Drawings* (John Caldwell, a collaboration with Edmund P. Pillsbury, curator of European painting at Yale and a specialist in Italian drawings), *Darkness into Light: The Early Mezzotint* (Ellen D'Oench, later professor and curator of prints at Wesleyan University), and *Dante Gabriel Rosetti and the Double Work of Art* (Maryan Ainsworth, now senior research fellow, paintings conservation, at the Metropolitan Museum of Art). Burke's photography exhibitions included *William Henry Jackson: Photographer of the American West*, and *Color Photography—Inventors and Innovators, 1850–1975*. His most significant exhibition as curator was *Charles Meryon: Prints & Drawings*, shown at Yale, Toledo, and Saint Louis in 1974–75. Meryon's views of Paris chronicled the city and evoked its atmosphere with unparalleled skill, and some of his images are among the most familiar views of the city. This exhibition was the first monographic presentation of this remarkable French draftsman and printmaker, with a catalogue that remains the standard work on the artist. As a result of his work on the exhibition, Burke found the preparatory drawing (fig. 183) for an etching already in the Yale collection (fig. 184) and acquired it for the permanent collection.

In 1984, a major bequest of more than two hundred Old Master prints and drawings was made by Ralph Kirkpatrick (Hon. M.A. 1965), a renowned harpsichordist and member of the Yale faculty. This generous bequest joined the gifts of nearly a hundred prints and drawings that this dedicated collector of European Old Master and twentieth-century prints and drawings had given to the Gallery between 1954 and 1982. The bequest included prints by Cézanne, *The Bathers*; Delacroix, *The Blacksmith* (fig. 185); Vuillard, *Interior*; Redon, *The Wing*; and Rembrandt, *The Death of the Virgin*. *Ralph Kirkpatrick In Memoriam*, an exhibition of the Kirkpatrick gifts and bequests, took place at the Gallery shortly after the donor's death in 1984. In the

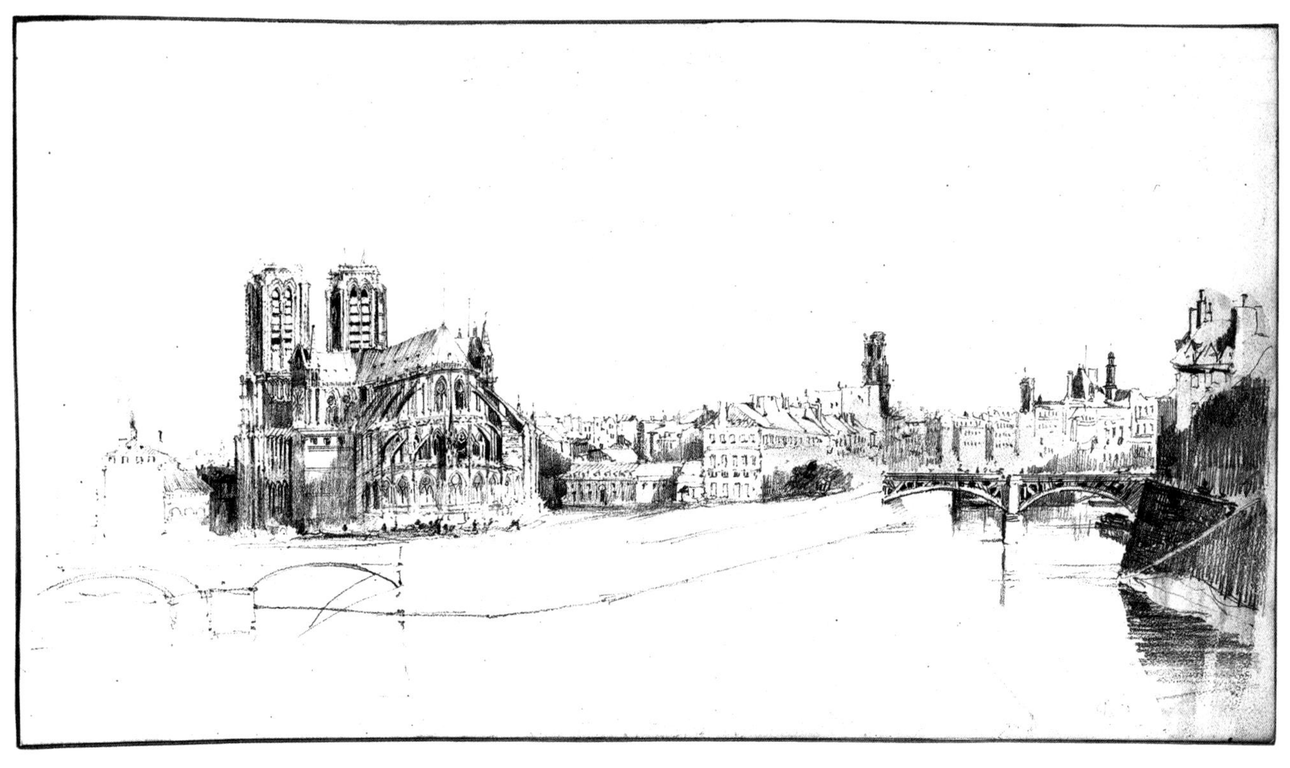

FIG. 183
Charles Meryon
L'Abside de Notre Dame de Paris, 1847
Graphite fixed with gum arabic, 21.2 x 38.8 cm
Everett V. Meeks, B.A. 1901, Fund
1973.59

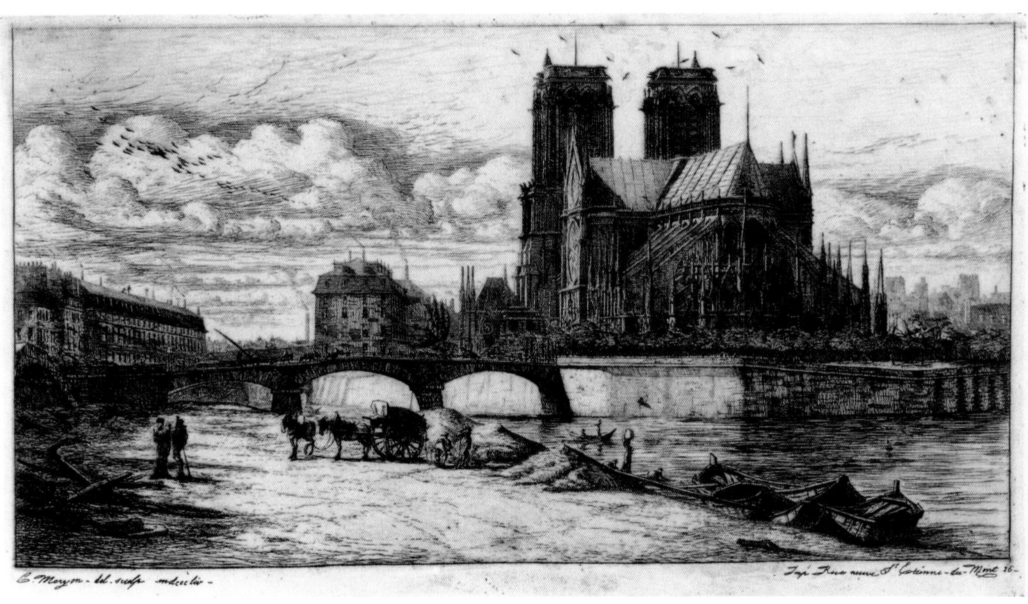

FIG. 184
Charles Meryon
The Apse of Notre Dame, 1854
Etching, 14.9 x 28.9 cm
Gift of "A Lover of Prints"
1928.346

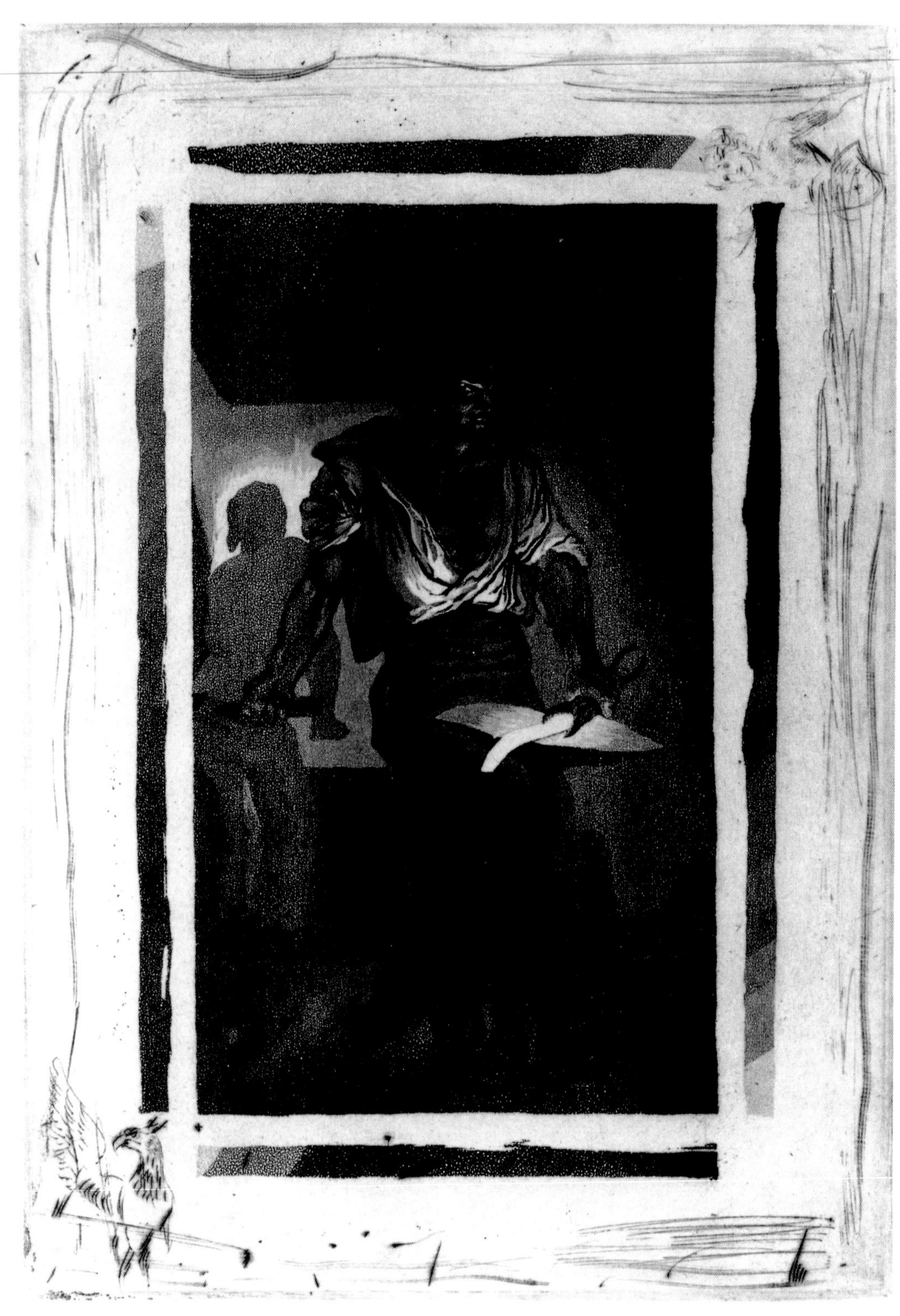

FIG. 185
Eugène Delacroix
The Blacksmith, 1833
Etching and aquatint, 57.2 x 40.6 cm
Bequest of Ralph Kirkpatrick
1984.54.56

"Tribute" that Alan Shestack wrote for the catalogue, he said, "I believe most people thought of Ralph solely as a musician—a virtuoso performer, interpreter, and teacher of keyboard music—but he was also a Renaissance man with keenly developed taste in art and literature. . . . He was always eager to talk about prints, about the literature on the history of graphic art, or about print exhibitions he had seen during his travels as a concert performer. Indeed, it was often on concert tours, especially those which took him abroad, that he bought prints, often spending most of his fee or honorarium on a rare etching or lithograph." Richard S. Field, curator of prints, drawings, and photographs and organizer of the exhibition, wrote, "Ralph collected art as an art historian might have. . . . For this man, collecting was a personal matter, . . . a fulfillment of a career not chosen."

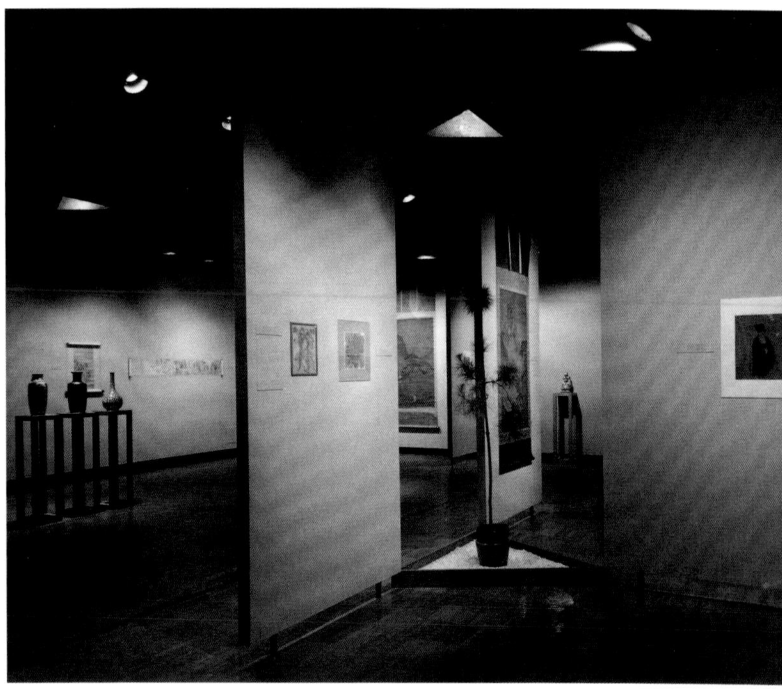

FIG. 186
Chinese Paintings at Yale, 1963
Photograph courtesy Yale University Art Gallery Archives

ASIAN ART

George J. Lee, curator of Oriental art, published the first comprehensive catalogue of the Asian art at the Gallery in 1970. Although entitled *Selected Far Eastern Art in the Yale University Art Gallery*, Lee's catalogue encompassed the full range of Chinese, Japanese, and Korean art at Yale and included nearly five hundred objects including paintings, jades, ceramics, bronzes, sculpture, textiles, ivory, lacquer, and works on paper.

The primary focus for acquisitions of Asian art in the 1960s and '70s was Chinese painting. An exhibition *Chinese Paintings at Yale* (fig. 186) was staged in the spring of 1963 to celebrate the acquisition of nearly forty paintings over the previous dozen years. Building on the foundation laid by Mrs. William H. Moore with her gifts in 1937 and 1952 and her bequest in 1955, curators George Lee and Mary Gardner Neill collaborated with Professor Richard Barnhart, who had joined the faculty in 1967, to build the collection. *Autumn Landscape* by Lan Ying (1653; fig. 187) entered the collection in 1967 as an anonymous gift in honor of Professor Nelson Wu from two professors of Chinese history at Yale, scholars giving a work of art in honor of another distinguished scholar. Examples of all of the major painting types, including hanging scrolls, album leaves, and fan paintings were acquired by purchase during this period.

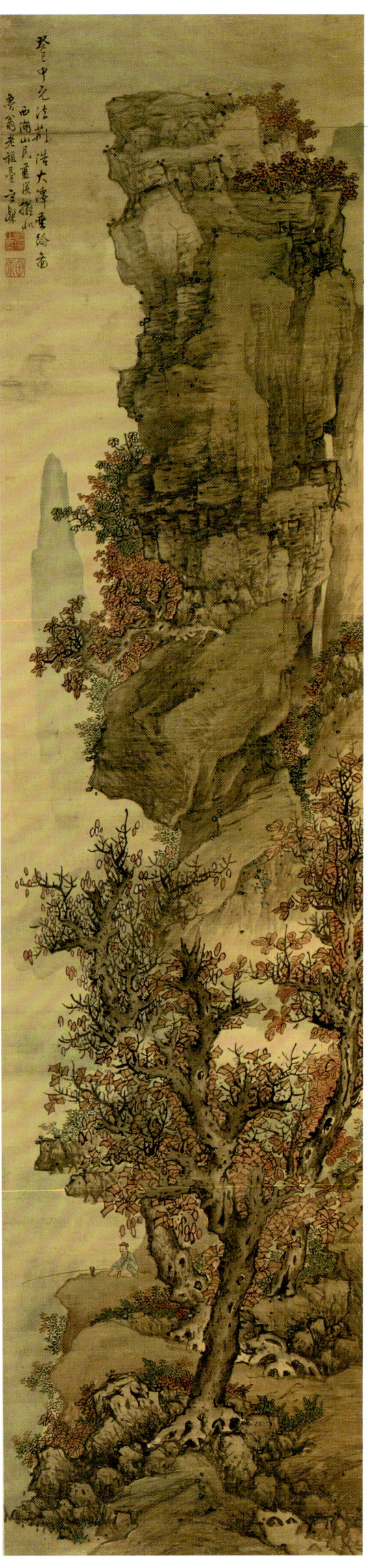

FIG. 187
Lan Ying
Autumn Landscape, 1653
Hanging scroll, ink and color on silk, 195.0 x 48.5 cm
Anonymous Gift in honor of Nelson Wu
1967.75

FIG. 188
Chin Nung
Plum Blossom and Calligraphy, 1761
Hanging scroll, ink on paper
Leonard C. Hanna, Jr., B.A. 1913, Fund
1976.26.2

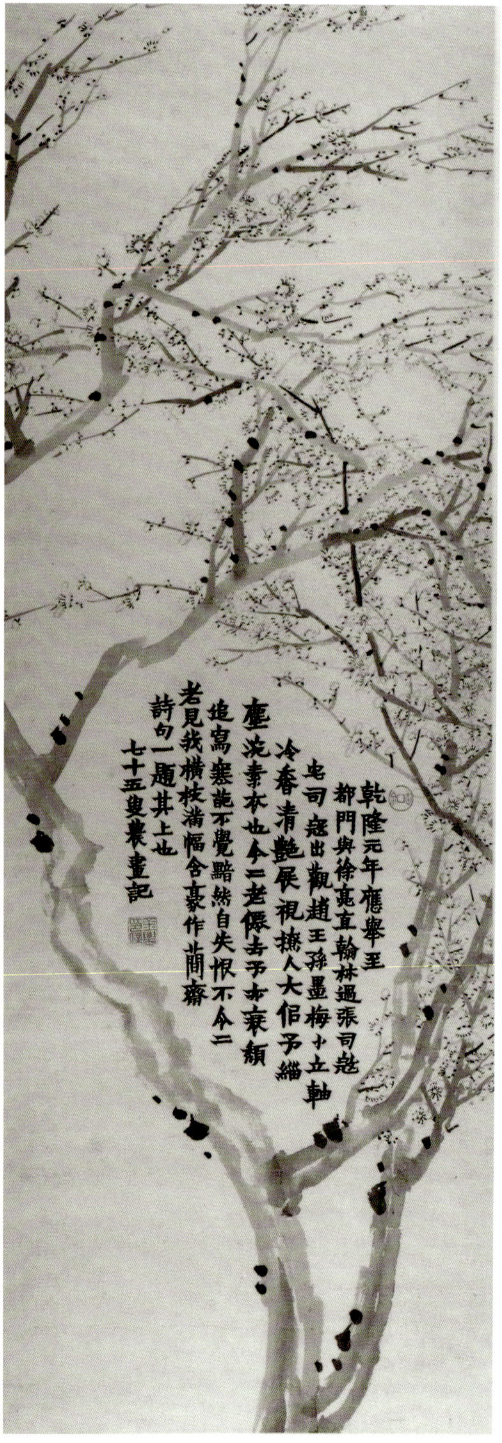

A significant group of paintings was purchased in 1976. Included were the *Landscape in the Style of Huang Kung-wang* by Wang Shih-min (1638), *Eight Landscapes in the Styles of Old Masters* by Wang Chien (1669), and *Plum Blossom and Calligraphy*, an important hanging scroll by Chin Nung (fig. 188). *Plum Blossom and Calligraphy* was exhibited in *Traces of the Brush*, a substantial loan exhibition of calligraphy organized in 1977 for Yale and Berkeley by Shen C. Y. Fu, professor of Chinese art at Yale, in collaboration with his wife, Marilyn Fu, Mary Gardner Neill, associate curator of Oriental art, and a Yale graduate student, Mary Jane Clark. The catalogue offered a preliminary outline of a comprehensive history of Chinese scripts, an important contribution to scholarship in the field. *Plum Blossom and Calligraphy*, along with others depicting related subjects, became the focus of another major loan show, *Bones of Jade, Soul of Ice: The Flowering Plum in Chinese Art*, in 1985. Curated by Maggie Bickford, a doctoral candidate at Princeton, and Mary Gardner Neill, who had become curator of Oriental art in 1978, *Bones of Jade* combined new scholarship with a thematic approach to the material that made the exhibition especially successful for the public as it traveled from Yale to Berkeley and Saint Louis.

Many of the new acquisitions of Chinese paintings were featured in the traveling exhibition *The Communion of Scholars: Chinese Art at Yale*, organized by Mary Gardner Neill in 1982–83 and shown at the China Institute in New York, the Museum of Fine Arts, Houston, and Yale. *The Communion of Scholars* was the first traveling exhibition to bring the Yale collection of Chinese art to large audiences outside of New Haven. In addition to paintings, the exhibition included Changsha and later ceramics, bronzes, jades, and sculpture, and a special section on scholars' objects. In his preface to the catalogue, Alan Shestack, the Gallery's director, honored the collaboration among the three institutions and among the worldwide network of scholars who contributed their expertise to the research on the collection: "*The Communion of Scholars*—what an appropriate title for an exhibition of works of art from a university museum, and what an accurate description of the collaborative effort which has gone into the preparation of this catalogue! Such a 'communion' is, of course, a basic purpose of the university, and we at Yale are pleased to have brought about this exhibition and catalogue, and to have been the catalyst which stimulated the scholarly collaboration and exchange in the field of Chinese art which the catalogue represents."[6] Recently, under David Ake Sensabaugh, curator of Asian art, and Sadako Ohki, assistant curator, the focus for purchases has broadened to include sculpture and ceramics, although major paintings continue to come to the collection as gifts.

DIRECTORS

Alan Shestack (fig. 189) succeeded Andrew Carnduff Ritchie as director in 1971. Coming from the position of curator of drawings and prints at the Gallery, he brought to his fourteen-year tenure a commitment to scholarship and the use of the Gallery's collections in teaching, and with his background at the Philadelphia Museum and the National Gallery, a commitment to continuing the professional standards of the major American museums that Andrew Ritchie had brought to Yale. In his report to the President and Fellows of Yale in 1974, covering the first three years of his term, he wrote with pleasure of the seminars on American painting since World War II (taught by Theodore Stebbins, curator of American painting) and Greek vase painting (taught by J. J. Pollitt, professor of Classics and history of art), which would both result in Gallery exhibitions with scholarly catalogues largely written by the graduate students in the seminars. He also reported that he was teaching a graduate seminar in museum practices, with field trips funded by the National Endowment for the Arts, that by 1974 was in its third year.[7]

Expansive in his own vision of what the Gallery could be, Shestack encouraged his curators to think the same way, and was unfailingly supportive of curators in their efforts to create innovative and important exhibitions and programs and make major acquisitions for the collection. Exhibitions such as the remarkable *Towards Independence*, organized for the bicentennial in 1976 and the first exhibition of American art to travel to London, and the groundbreaking installation of the Garvan collections in 1973 and other activities in American art happened with Shestack's enthusiastic support at every turn (see chapter 14 for both).

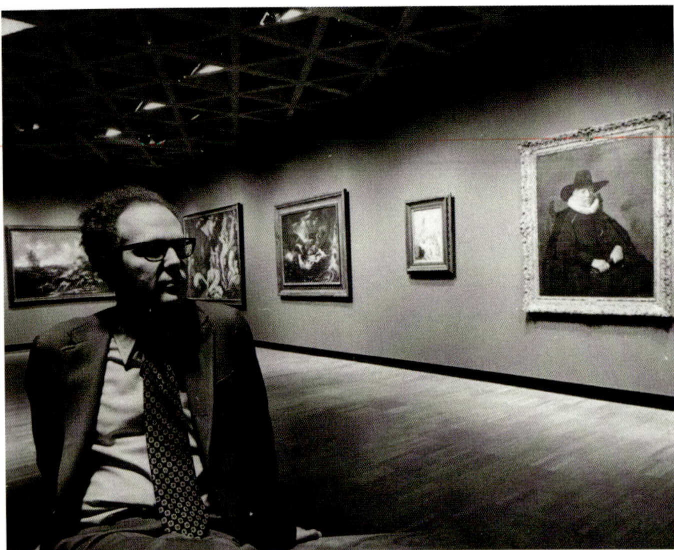

FIG. 189
Alan Shestack, 1971
Photograph courtesy Yale University Art Gallery Archives

Major acquisitions, none surpassing the Katharine Ordway Collection of modern art, bequeathed with an endowment in 1980 (see chapter 13), but including indisputable landmarks such as the gift by Paul Mellon (B.A. 1929) of French paintings by Delacroix, Monet, Degas, Pissarro, Cézanne, Boudin, Vuillard (fig. 190), and others; the important paintings and drawings that came as a bequest from Mary C. and James W. Fosburgh (B.A. 1933, M.A. 1935); the sixty-four paintings by Josef Albers given to the Gallery by Anni Albers and the Josef Albers Foundation (fig. 191); the John P. Axelrod, B.A. 1968, Collection of American Art, comprising more than four hundred prints and drawings by artists working between the wars; and the significant additions to the modern sculpture collection made by Susan Morse Hilles all came to Yale with Shestack's encouragement and active personal involvement. Exploring another of his own interests and focusing on a part of the collection without a curator to urge its development, he purchased important pieces of African sculpture in 1972 and 1982. Encouraging the curators to make major acquisitions, he supported, among others, the purchase of notable nineteenth- and twentieth-century American still-life paintings and, for the ancient art collection, an Athenian *Black-Figure Amphora* attributed to Group E, a *Red-Figure Calyx Krater* by the Aegisthus Painter, and a *Portrait of Demosthenes*, the famous Athenian orator.[8]

Alan Shestack, now deputy director of the National Gallery of Art, is a thoughtful spokesman for professional practices in art museums and a respected analyst of the role of the modern art museum director. During his term as director at Yale, he served as president of the Association of Art Museum Directors. In 1978, he wrote a pivotal article on art museum directors, "The Director: Scholar and Businessman, Educator and Lobbyist," for *Museum News*, published by the American Association of Museums and considered the fundamental periodical in the field.[9] In this article, he addressed the question "Who should run museums?," discussing how museums should be managed and how museum directors should be trained. Under his leadership, the AAMD had undertaken a study of directorial training, its history, present state, and future direction and needs. The results of the study indicated that the majority of directors had come out of curatorial departments, and

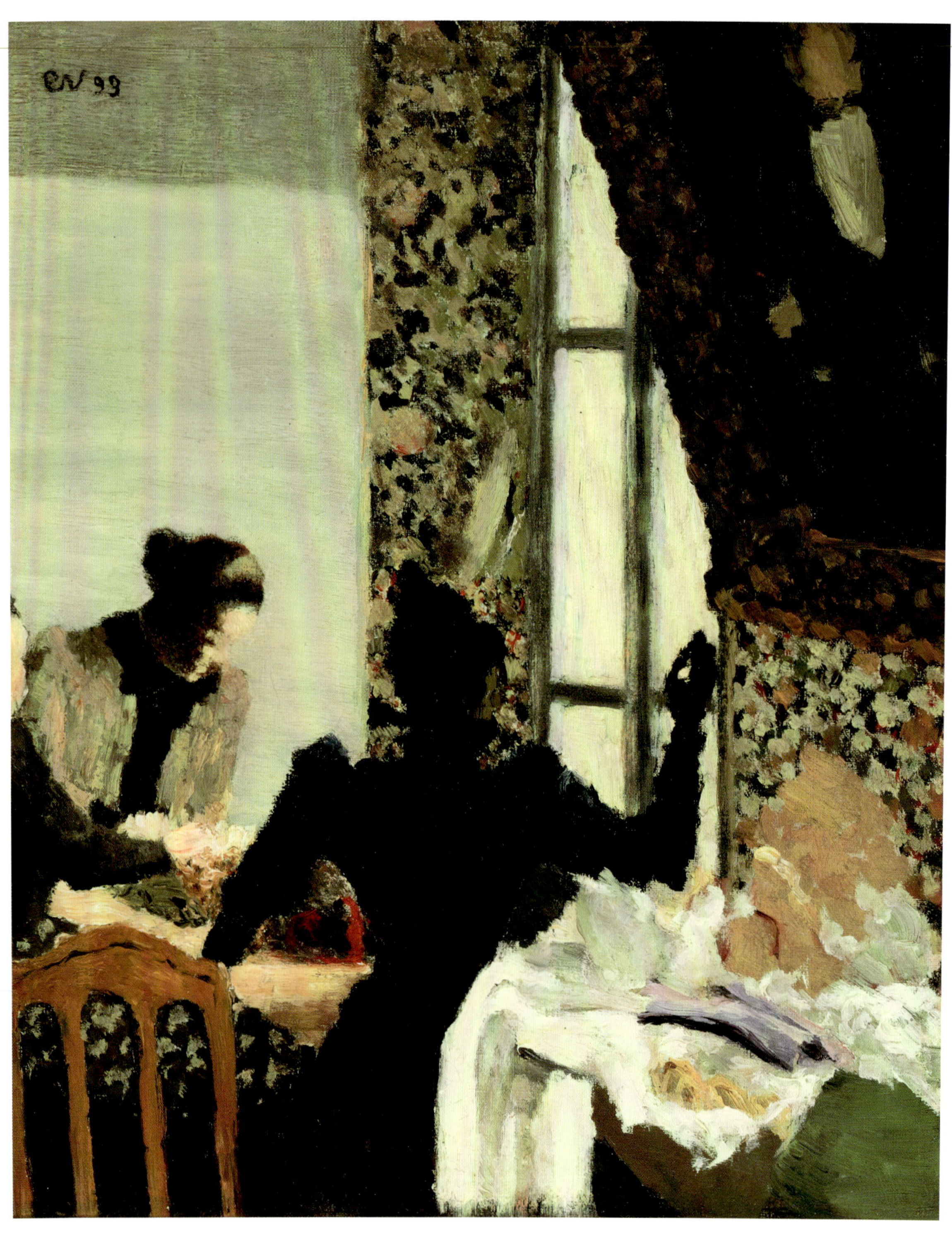

FIG. 190
Edouard Vuillard
The Thread (L'Aiguilée), 1893
Oil on canvas, 41.6 x 33.3 cm
Gift of Mr. and Mrs. Paul
Mellon, B.A. 1929
1983.7.6

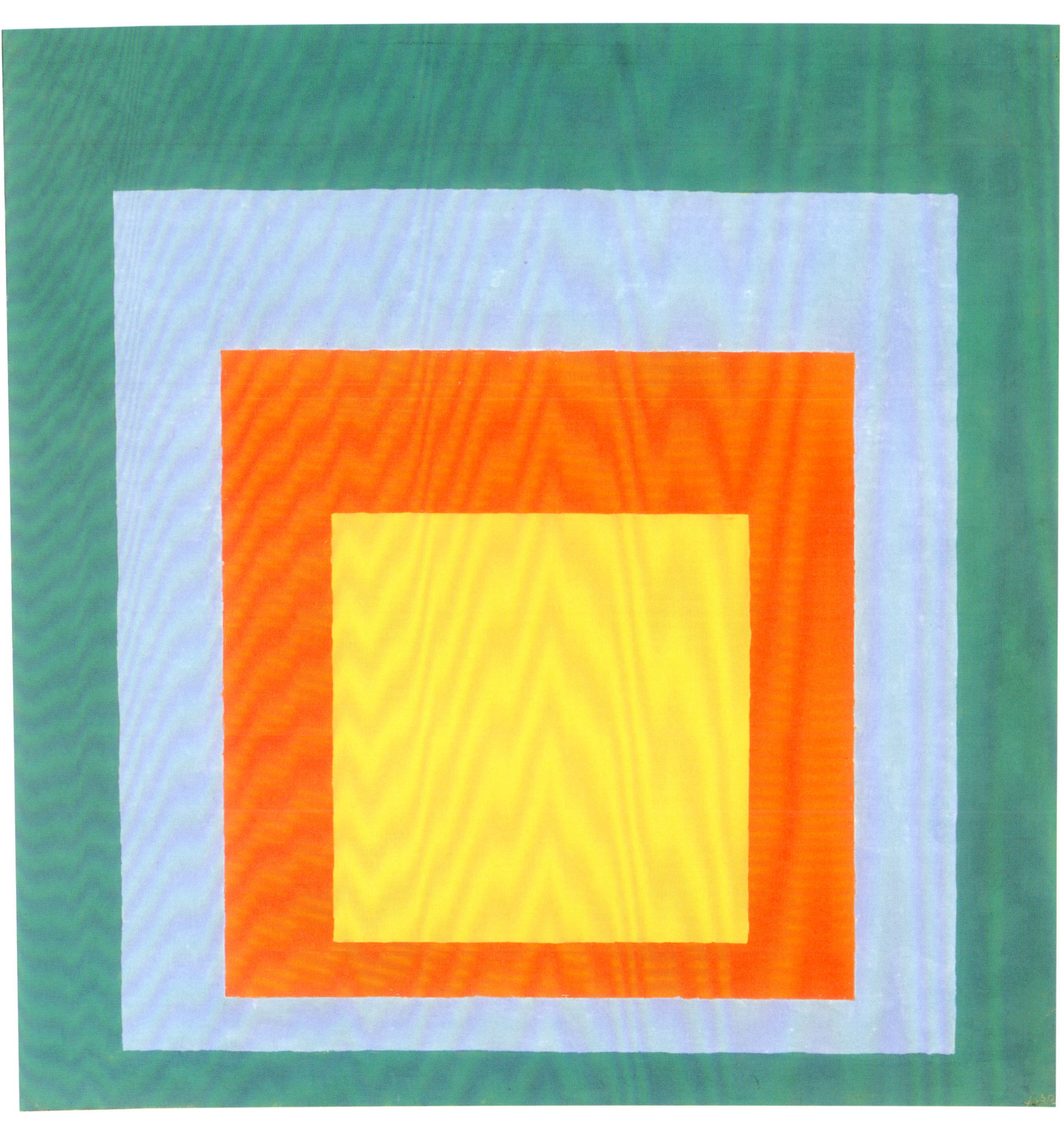

FIG. 191
Josef Albers
Homage to the Square, 1950
Oil on masonite, 52.4 x 52.4 cm
Gift of Anni Albers and the Josef Albers Foundation
1977.160.33

many directors who took part in the study attributed their success to the inspiration of the director under whom they worked. Many also cited the importance of experience in museum work as students—the very sort of experience offered at the Yale Art Gallery.

Shestack's memorable description of the modern art museum director in 1978—"He must function as art historian and connoisseur, businessperson and fund-raiser, diplomat, politician, lobbyist, personnel manager, publisher, architectural consultant, restaurateur, educator, after-dinner speaker and—as one director recently described his role—resident psychoanalyst"[10]—was if anything more appropriate when the article was reprinted in 1984, and is probably even more so today. "The success or failure of the museum often depends on how clearly the director perceives a problem and its ramifications," he wrote, "how well he understands the viewpoints of all parties, and how well he is able to articulate these positions to the board."[11] Despite this recognition of management skills as key to success, in answer to the fundamental question of whether the director should be an administrator or an art historian, Shestack did not hesitate to reinforce the need for a director with a passion for and serious knowledge of art:

> Administrators who have not studied art history and who do not have a deep, abiding love for the art objects in their care are likely to make uninformed decisions that do not further the mission of communicating the art of the past and present. To do this effectively and with integrity, the chief administrator must be sensitive to art historical issues. It is not enough for an administrator to turn to subordinates for advice on acquisitions, conservation, exhibitions or publications. Effective administration is essential, but the role of administration is to enable museums to serve their primary purpose, to educate and to provide enjoyment in the visual arts. It is of little value to have a smooth-running ship if it does nothing but pursue a meaningless course.[12]

After Alan Shestack's departure from Yale in 1985, Anne Coffin Hanson, John Hay Whitney Professor of the History of Art and a noted Manet scholar, served as acting director until the end of 1986. Always one of the most active users of the Gallery's collections in her teaching, Professor Hanson clearly relished the even more direct involvement in Gallery exhibitions and acquisitions that the role of director offered. She was personally engaged in several of the exhibitions that took place during her tenure, designing and overseeing the installation for *The Woven and Graphic Art of Anni Albers* and *Antonio Sant' Elia*, the latter reflecting her long-standing interest in Italian Futurism. A focus on twentieth-century art characterized the majority of exhibitions shown while she was at the helm, among them the important *Art for "The Masses" (1911–1917): A Radical Magazine and Its Graphics* and the accompanying show *Prints by Artists of "The Masses,"* exhibitions of works from Richard Brown Baker's modern art collection, Richard Field's traveling exhibition *Richard Hamilton: Image and Process*, and a number of exhibitions drawn from the permanent collection. The main exception was the blockbuster exhibition *Winslow Homer Watercolors*, organized by Helen A. Cooper, curator of American paintings and sculpture, which opened at the National Gallery of Art before coming to Yale. Anne Hanson, like Alan Shestack, encouraged curators to make major purchases, supporting the acquisition of a Japanese six-paneled screen by Yamamoto Soken entitled *Teika's Poems on Flowers and Birds of the Twelve Months* (ca. 1690–92), and an ancient bronze statuette of the *Tyche of Antioch*, after the famous statue of the goddess by the Greek sculptor Eutychides.

Mary Gardner Neill's distinguished record of acquisitions and exhibitions as the head of the Asian department led to her appointment as director of the Gallery in January 1987 (fig. 192). Among the major exhibitions that were organized or shown during Neill's directorship were *A Taste for Angels: Neapolitan Painting in North America, 1650–1750*; *Word in Flower: The Visualization of Classical Literature in Seventeenth-Century Japan*; *The Art Museums of Louis I. Kahn*; *Childe Hassam: An Island Garden Revisited*; *Master of the Lotus Garden: The Life and Art of Bada Shanren* (fig. 193); *Eva Hesse: A Retrospective*; *Felix Vallotton: A Retrospective*; and *Discovered Lands, Invented Pasts*. The permanent collections of ancient and Precolumbian art were completely reinstalled in 1988 in contiguous galleries on the ground floor, expanding the ancient

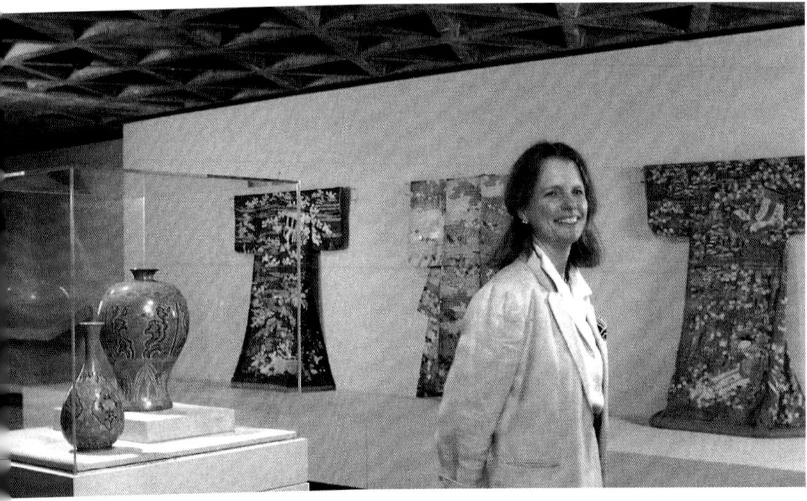

FIG. 192
Mary Gardner Neill, 1995
Photograph courtesy Michael Marsland

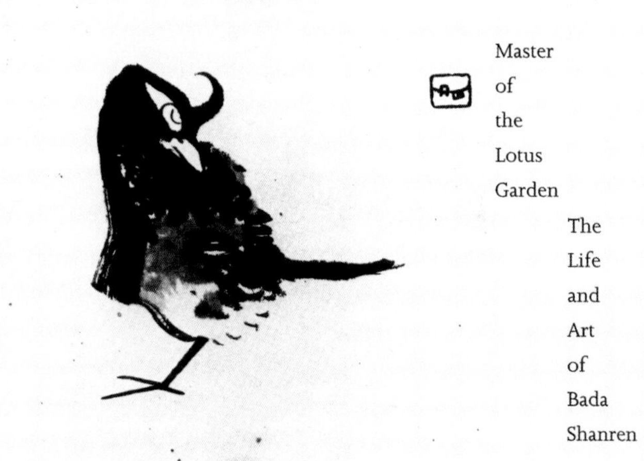

FIG. 193
Invitation to *Master of the Lotus Garden: The Life and Art of Bada Shanren*, 1991
Courtesy Yale University Art Gallery Archives

galleries and reinterpreting the Precolumbian collection, as described above.

Education, outreach, and public programs were priorities during Neill's administration. Janet Saleh Dickson (fig. 194), curator of education, frequently taught classes herself and also oversaw the growth of the docents program, increasing their professional training. She added several new types of programming to the Gallery's regular offerings, notably a weekly Wednesday lunchtime lecture series called Art à la Carte, and the Sunday Series, a richly varied program of lectures and performances. Departing from earlier reliance on lectures for weekend programming, the new Sunday Series focused heavily on the performing arts, a real innovation for the Gallery as New Haven's museum. Other programs brought in artists for workshops and classes. Visiting lecturers included artists, scholars, poets, art critics, and museum professionals, many of them world renowned. Trained in modern art and a painter herself, Janet Dickson brought contemporary art to a broad audience within the New Haven community, sharing her enthusiasm about this and other fields with Gallery visitors of all ages.

Major gifts arrived while Mimi Neill was director, including notable Chinese and Japanese paintings donated by H. Christopher Luce (B.A. 1972), more than five hundred modern American photographs given by George Hopper Fitch (B.A. 1932), and sixty-six significant contemporary paintings and works on paper by contemporary German and Austrian artists given by Walter and Molly Bareiss. Important purchases ranged from ancient Roman portraits of *Caligula*, the Gallery's first portrait of a Roman emperor, and *Avidia Plautia*, mother of the emperor Lucius Verus, to Thomas Hart Benton's *Weighing Cotton* and *Stacks*, a commissioned site-specific work by Richard Serra.

Working closely with Henry J. Heinz II (B.A. 1931) and Walter Bareiss, chairmen in succession of the Governing Board, Mimi Neill made unprecedented progress in endowing key parts of the Gallery's basic mission at a critical point in its financial history. Especially memorable were the endowment of the Henry J. Heinz II Directorship and Conservation Fund in 1987, combining conservation with the endowed directorship given by Mr. Heinz in 1982; the Mary C.

and James W. Fosburgh (B.A. 1933, M.A. 1936) and Paul Mellon (B.A. 1929, LL.D. 1967) Publication Fund; and the National Endowment for the Arts challenge grant for endowment, designated for the creation of a department of conservation. Of equal value to the Gallery's mission were endowments for the general support of specific departments, such as American Arts from Mabel Brady Garvan; Prints, Drawings, and Photographs from John P. Axelrod (B.A. 1968); and a number of unrestricted endowments, including the Leslie Cheek, Jr., General Support Fund and the Thomas T. Solley (B.A. 1950) Director's Discretionary Fund. Through the generosity of Henry J. Heinz II, Robert Lehman, Leslie Cheek, Jr., Kurt and Arlette Seligmann, and others who donated funds for conservation and collection maintenance, the care of every part of the collection is supported by endowed funds. Mimi's focus on collection care included security, improvement of storage conditions, and the beginnings of plans for the expansion of the museum. Mimi served as director until 1994 when she left for the Seattle Art Museum, where, now Mary Gardner Gates, she has brought her dynamic energy and style to the post of director.

The conservation department that was created as a result of the NEA challenge grant has become both a fundamental part of the Gallery's operation and a center for teaching and research. Kristin Hoermann, the first conservator to head the new department, set up the new studio, the first modern facility for painting conservation at Yale. Now two conservators, Mark Aronson and Patricia Sherwin Garland, care for the paintings and oversee outside conservation of sculpture, decorative arts, Asian art, African art, and classical and Precolumbian antiquities, while Theresa Fairbanks-Harris is the conservator for works on paper for both the Gallery and the Yale Center for British Art. Courses in conservation are taught regularly, using both the Gallery and BAC collections and facilities.

Key to the Gallery's ability to treat large and important parts of the collection in spite of the small size of its staff has been the extraordinary collaboration with the conservation departments of the J. Paul Getty Museum and the financial support of the J. Paul Getty Trust. The trust has funded two major projects, the conservation of Yale's ancient Athenian vases in preparation

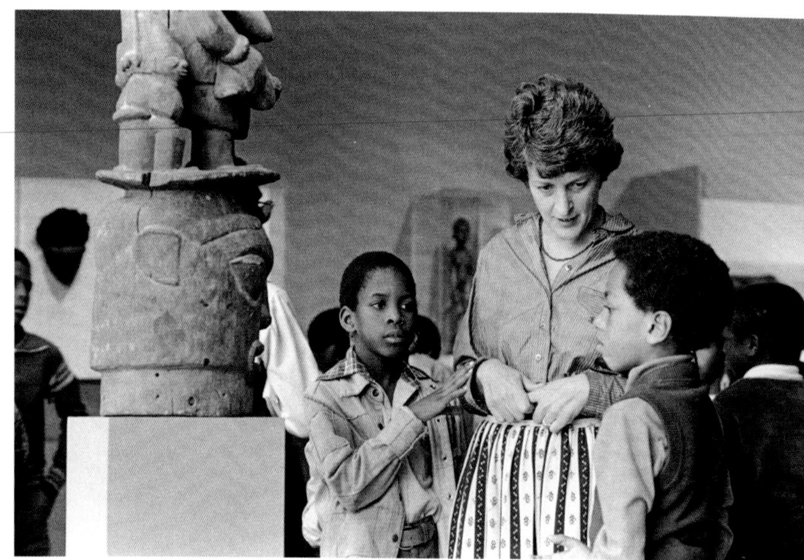

FIG. 194
Janet Saleh Dickson teaching in the African art galleries, 1988
Photograph courtesy Yale University Art Gallery Archives

for their publication in the *Corpus Vasorum Antiquorum*, and the study and treatment of the American miniatures in preparation for the exhibition and book *Love and Loss: American Mourning Miniatures* and the catalogue of Yale's miniature collection to follow. Since 1998, a special collaboration between Yale's paintings conservators, Mark Aronson and Patricia Garland, and their colleagues in painting conservation at the Getty Museum, Mark Leonard, Andrea Rotha, Elisabeth Mention, and Yvonne Szafran, has focused on the early Italian paintings in the landmark Jarves Collection and those given by Maitland Griggs and Robert Lehman. This project has involved the exchange of conservators as well as paintings between Yale and the Getty, and it has brought together an international team of conservators and scholars who have studied and treated the paintings, revealing much that was unknown about the works of art, the techniques by which they were made, and the circumstances in which they were created. Much of this research contributes new information to the field. The paintings themselves are rejuvenated. Several have new attributions as a result of this work, most notably two fragments of an altarpiece that are now recognized as being by Fra Angelico (fig. 134) and joining fragments from the same altarpiece in the Getty Museum's collection. The relationship continues through the involvement of the antiquities conservation department at the Getty, where Jerry Podany and his colleagues will undertake the treatment and remounting of the massive city mosaic from Gerasa, the ancient city in Jordan excavated in part by Yale in the 1920s and '30s (fig. 105), making it possible to display this monument for the first time in more than sixty years.

Jules D. Prown served as interim director during much of 1994, ably overseeing operations, acquisitions, and an exhibition program that included the major Chinese painting exhibition, *The Jade Studio: Masterpieces of Ming and Qing Painting and Calligraphy from the Wong Nan-p'ing Collection*, organized by Richard Barnhart, professor of History of Art, and Colin Mackenzie, curator of Asian art; *An Obsession with Fortune: Tyche in Greek and Roman Art*, organized by Susan Matheson and featuring essays by both graduate students and internationally renowned scholars, and *Charles Demuth: Poster Portraits 1923–1929*, organized by Robin Jaffee Frank, about which more will be said later. Prown addressed the critical need to upgrade the Gallery's computer systems and install a collections management system, an initiative that led to the adoption of *The Museum System* as the Gallery's database software. Efforts to formulate a master plan for renovation and possible expansion of the Gallery moved forward in collaboration with the Polshek and Partners architectural firm. Acquisitions included several purchases, notably a *Portrait of Menander*, the Greek comic poet of the fourth century B.C.; Chris Burden *America's Darker Moments*; a preparatory drawing by Jean-Léon Gérôme for his painting *Ave Caesar, Morituri te Salutant*, already in the Yale collection; and a Yuan Dynasty scroll painting of two doves from ca. 1350. Important gifts included several Tang Dynasty figures from the Lawrence and Regina Dubin Family Collection and sixty-five American, British, and French photographs from George Hopper Fitch.

Susan Mullin Vogel (fig. 195) became director of the Gallery in 1995, coming to Yale from New York, where she was the founder and director of the Museum for African Art. Her expertise brought a renewed focus on the Gallery's African art collections. An important early twentieth-century Baule portrait mask from the Ivory Coast, *Portrait Mask of a Woman*, was purchased for the collection in 1996, as was an appliqué banner, some fifty-four feet long, made in the 1950s by Fante artists from Ghana and showing a priestess with a retinue of musicians, a paymaster balancing scales, fishermen, and harvesters in a palm grove. Her seminal exhibition *Baule: African Art/Western Eyes* (fig. 160) and the extensive educational programs associated with it brought in significant new audiences from both Yale and New Haven.

Frederick R. Mayer (B.A. 1950) became chairman of the Governing Board in 1995, succeeding Walter Bareiss. Under his leadership, the Governing Board, working with Susan Vogel and the Gallery staff, began to address the financial challenges of endowing curatorships and other staff positions and the planning and funding of the renovation and expansion that had been proposed for the Gallery. Based on a University Report prepared in 1995 by a distinguished committee chaired by Jules

Prown, expansion of teaching, gallery, and storage spaces had been adopted as a priority by the University, as part of an overall plan for the entire Arts Area at Yale.

Frederick and his wife, Jan, who had bought a house in New Haven, especially wanted to foster the growth of the public education and outreach programs for the city, and in 1996 they endowed a fund to establish the Jan and Frederick Mayer Curator of Education. Mary Kordak, who now holds this position, and her colleagues have continued to expand the school and docent programs with ever-increasing numbers of school groups and teacher workshops (fig. 196), as well as adult groups and students from schools and colleges throughout the area. The Gallery's exceptional group of docents was honored by the State of Connecticut in 2001. The Student Gallery Guides, a new and instantly successful program organized by Ellen Alvord, associate curator of education, has brought an energetic core of Yale College students to the Gallery to give tours of the collections to other Yale students and the public.

Acquisitions in all fields were made and received, often specifically tied to teaching or exhibitions. A fine collection of drawings and personal documents by Charles Demuth, discovered by Robin Jaffee Frank, associate curator of American paintings and sculpture, as part of her research for the exhibition *Charles Demuth: Poster Portraits 1923–1929*, was donated to the Gallery by Dr. and Mrs. William R. Hill in honor of Richard Weyand, for many years Demuth's closest friend. The photography collection continued to grow through donations by George Hopper Fitch. Fifteen major Abstract Expressionist paintings were donated by Richard Brown Baker, a gift that was celebrated in the exhibition *Collecting with Richard Brown Baker*, organized by Sasha Newman, the Seymour Knox, Jr., Curator of European and Contemporary Art. Interested in contemporary art as well, Susan Vogel encouraged the gifts of Thurston Twigg-Smith, featured in the 1997 exhibition *Hawaiian Eye*, organized by Daphne Deeds, curator of exhibitions and programs. An important ancient Greek vase from South Italy by the Hoppin Painter with a scene related to a tragedy by Aeschylus and a portrait of a young Roman girl were purchased for the ancient art collection, the first because of its connection to the teaching of Greek literature, the latter

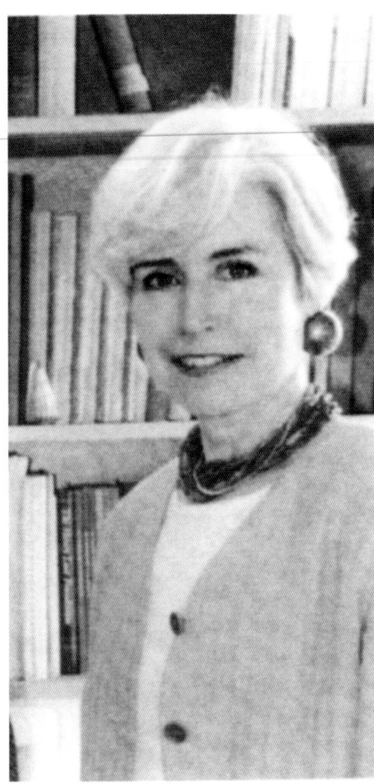

FIG. 195
Susan Mullin Vogel 1995/96
Photograph courtesy Yale University Art Gallery Archives

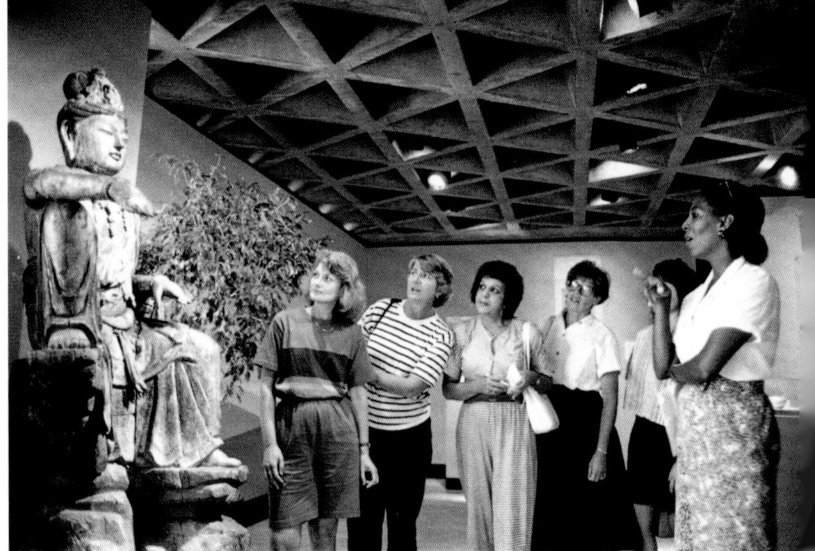

FIG. 196
Mary Kordak conducting a teacher workshop in the Asian Gallery, 1992
Photograph courtesy Yale University Art Gallery Archives

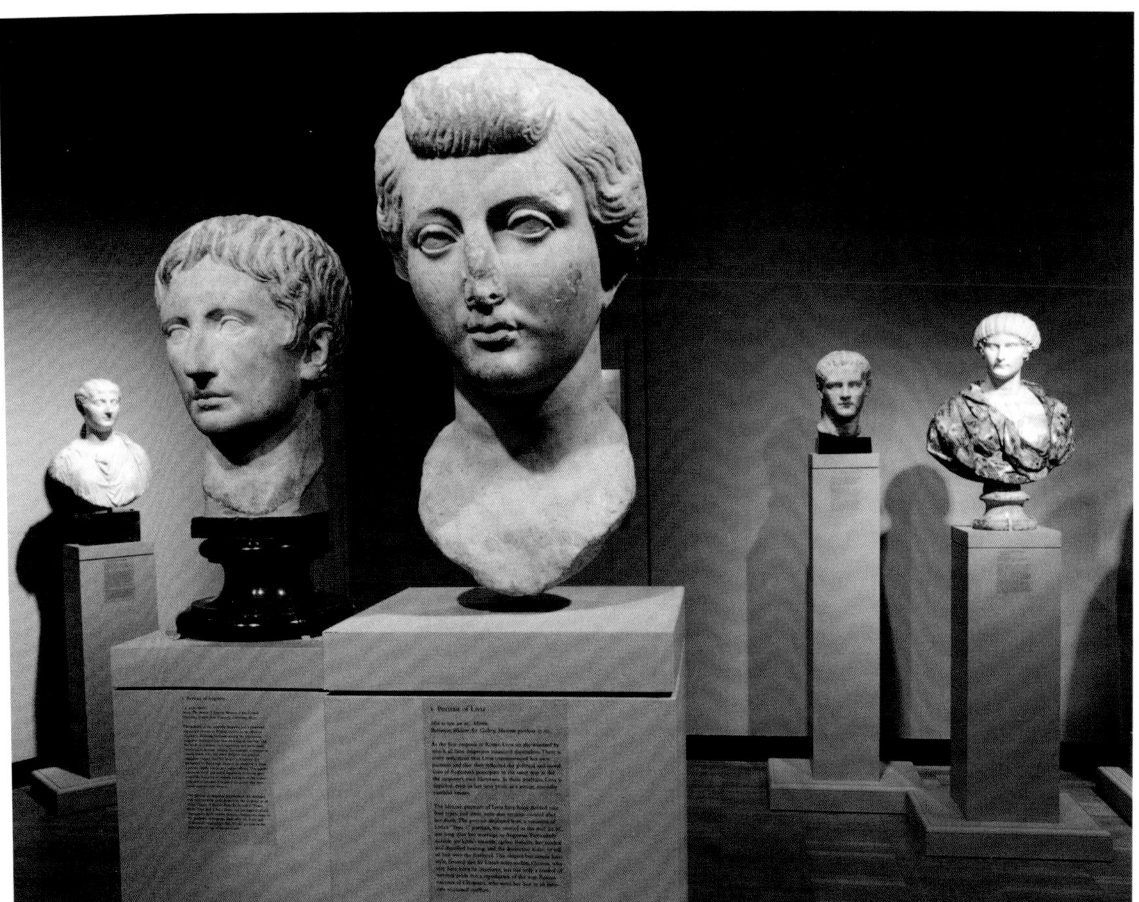

FIG. 197
I, Claudia: Women in Ancient Rome, 1996
Photograph courtesy Yale University Art Gallery Archives

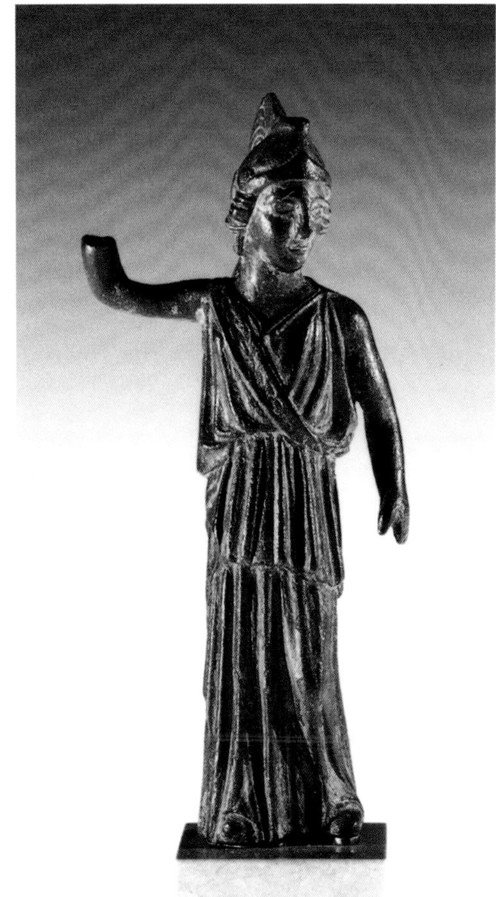

FIG. 198
Athena, 5th century B.C.
Bronze, 10.8 x 5 x 2.6 cm
Gift of Ruth Elizabeth White
1988.80.10

as part of the development of an exhibition on women in ancient Rome.

The endowment fund establishing the Molly and Walter Bareiss Curator of Ancient Art was donated by the Bareisses in 1996, crowning a commitment to the development of ancient art at the Gallery that extended back to the seminar and exhibition *Greek Vases at Yale* more than twenty years before. This was a landmark year for ancient art at Yale, marked also by the opening of *I, Claudia: Women in Ancient Rome* (fig. 197), the most ambitious ancient art exhibition ever undertaken by the Gallery. Curated by Diana E. E. Kleiner, Deputy Provost for the Arts and Dunham Professor of Classics and History of Art, and Susan B. Matheson, curator of ancient art, the exhibition was the first to examine the lives of Roman women as revealed in art. Bringing together 175 imperial and private portraits and other images of women in marble and bronze, coins, glass, paintings, jewelry, textiles, and objects used by women in their daily lives, the exhibition and catalogue explored the lives of women from empresses to slaves, from young girls to old women, considering the roles of women in Roman society and the way these roles were represented in art. Innovative in the contextual and thematic nature of both its content and installation, *I, Claudia* brought a new approach to the exhibition of Roman art as it sought to show what it was like to be a woman in ancient Rome. The exhibition traveled to the North Carolina Museum of Art, Raleigh, and the San Antonio Museum of Art, whose respective curators of ancient art hold Ph.D.s from Yale.

Two years after the opening of *I, Claudia*, the generosity of a modern woman provided the last major landmark for the ancient art collection in the twentieth century, the Ruth Elizabeth White Fund for the purchase and publication of works of Greek, Roman, and Etruscan art for the permanent collection. Miss White had no prior connection to Yale or the Gallery when she visited the museum in 1988 and saw the newly installed galleries of ancient art, a field in which she had long collected, and by her own admission it was the visit itself that inspired her to donate her collection and establish the endowment as a bequest to Yale. Among the works that she gave is her *Athena* (fig. 198), one of the few fifth-century Greek bronzes in Yale's collection, and the endowment has already been used to purchase a major Roman portrait and a Hellenistic Greek bronze, both important enhancements to the teaching program.

After Susan Vogel left Yale to pursue a career in filmmaking, Helen A. Cooper served as acting director for nearly a year with grace, good sense, and a welcome collegiality and good humor. Not wanting to lose momentum in planning for the Gallery renovation and expansion during the transition to a new director, she formed two successive staff committees representing all parts of the Gallery's operations and launched a year-long self study of the Gallery's facilities and operations. Chaired by Richard S. Field, associate director and curator of prints, drawings, and photographs, and Susan Matheson, curator of ancient art, these committees produced reports that became the basis for the subsequent programming of the Gallery expansion. The major exhibition during Helen Cooper's term was the two-part presentation of later twentieth-century art at Yale, *Now and Then: Art at Yale Since 1945*, and *Now and Later*, organized by Joachim Pissarro, the Seymour Knox, Jr., Curator of European and Contemporary Art. *Gifts from Walter and Molly Bareiss in Celebration of His 80th Birthday* marked another landmark in the extraordinary relationship between the Gallery and Walter Bareiss.

Having reached the 1990s in this chapter for many of the Gallery's departments and collections, we must step back in the next two chapters to resume the stories of modern and American art at Yale.

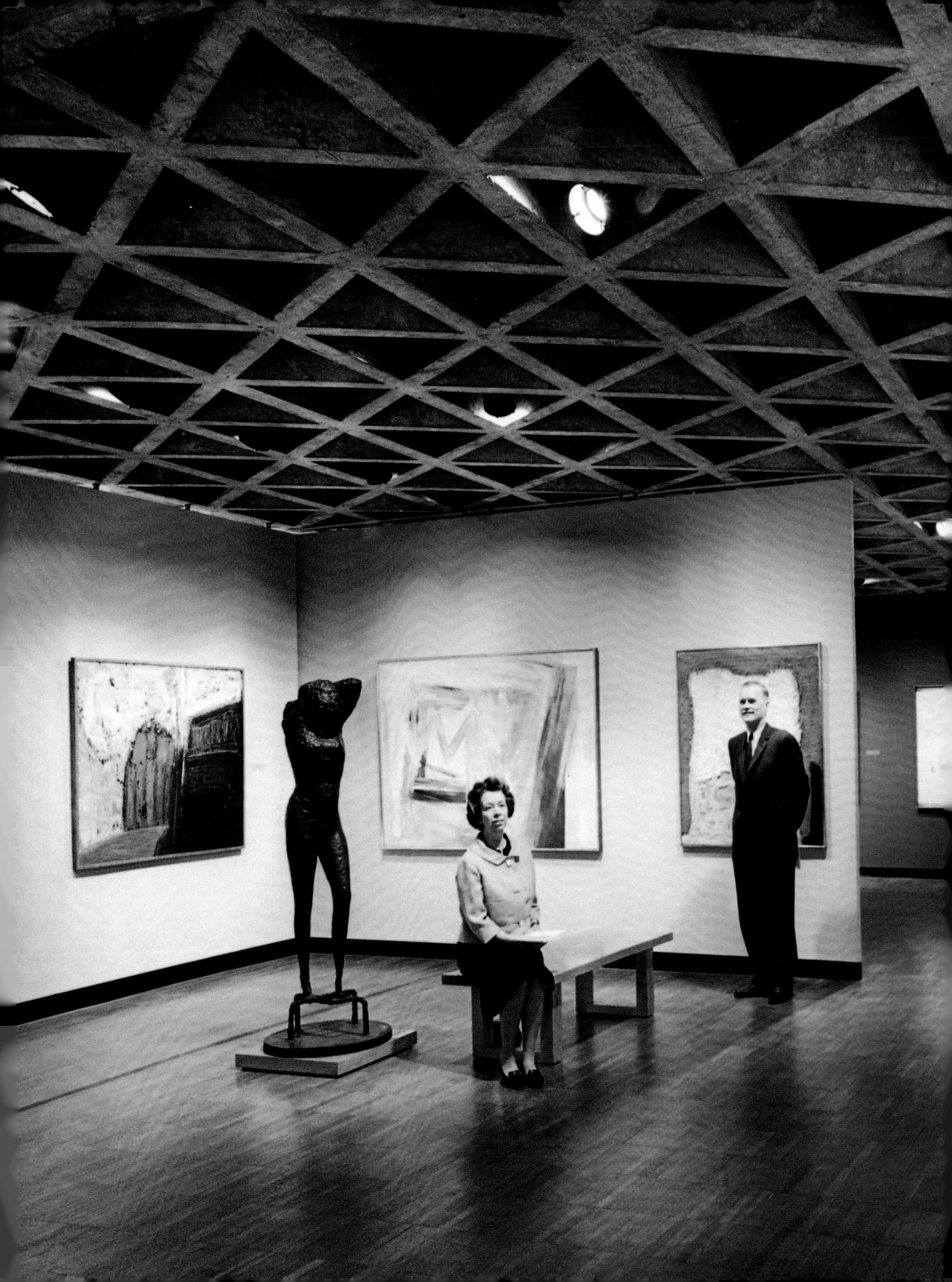

CHAPTER 13

Modern and Contemporary

The opening of the building designed by Paul Rudolph for the School of Art and Architecture in November 1963 freed the Kahn building for the sole use of the Art Gallery. The new A&A building housed the departments of painting, sculpture, graphic design, architecture, and city planning, as well as the Art and Architecture Library. Rudolph's building was praised as a prime example of the "Brutalist" style, and it retains that reputation today. In celebration of the dedication of the new building, the Gallery mounted a special exhibition, *The Work of Paul Rudolph, Architect.* The catalogue, with an introduction by Vincent Scully, listed thirty-nine works by Rudolph, as shown in models, drawings, and photographs.

With the architecture and graphic design departments moving out, the fourth floor and the basement of Kahn became available to the Gallery for exhibition space. So did the main exhibition gallery (the Sculpture Hall) on the first floor of the Swartwout building, which had been used for the art library between 1953 and 1963. The Sculpture Hall reverted to its original function, and additional large sculpture was exhibited in the courtyard behind the Kahn building. In the spring of 1964, the director, assistant director, the prints and drawings department, and the Asian department moved to the fourth floor of the Kahn building. The third floor, including both Kahn and Swartwout, was dedicated to European and American art. The basement galleries were assigned to contemporary art, representing a renewed commitment to the work of living artists.

Yale's commitment to its School of Art was reflected in the expansion of the School's program as it moved into its new building. The Gallery's response was a renewed dedication to modern and contemporary art. Building on the support of the work of living artists that stretched back to the acquisition of the Trumbull paintings, and on the prominence in the field of early twentieth-century art that the Société Anonyme Collection brought to Yale, Andrew Ritchie and his successor, Alan Shestack, both deeply devoted to modern art, assigned permanent galleries and temporary exhibition space, as well as time and money, to the display and acquisition of contemporary art. The endowment of the Seymour H. Knox, Jr., Curator of European and Contemporary Art in 1988 was inspired by Seymour

FIG. 199
Susan Morse Hilles and Richard Brown Baker in the exhibition *Two Modern Collectors*, 1963
Photograph courtesy Yale University Art Gallery Archives

Knox's love of contemporary art. This endowment, which took place while Mary Gardner Neill, who became director in January 1987, was in office, was the culmination of a relationship between Knox and the Gallery, fostered by Andrew Ritchie, that stretched back through his many years of service on the Governing Board. Ritchie had known Knox in Buffalo, when Ritchie had been on the staff of the Albright-Knox Art Gallery and Seymour Knox had held the family seat on the Albright-Knox's Board, and later at MoMA, where Ritchie was curator and Knox was one of a number of Yale graduates on that museum's board. Other Yale alumni on the MoMA board were also significant supporters of modern art at the Gallery. Subsequent support for contemporary art has come in the form of gifts of art and acquisition funds from a growing number of alumni and friends. In spite of the physical and administrative separation of the School from the Gallery, links between the two remain strong, the Gallery collections used for teaching and students from the School involved in the Gallery's exhibitions and programs.

Loan exhibitions of contemporary art from private collectors and New York galleries had been instituted by John Ferguson Weir in the late nineteenth century, and they remained the primary method of bringing contemporary art to Yale and to the city in the mid-twentieth. As was the case with the earlier loan exhibitions, recent ones have sometimes resulted in the addition of exhibited works to the Gallery's permanent collection. Exhibitions that focused on individual collectors fostered relationships that have been extremely beneficial to the Gallery's collections. Prominent among the collectors so featured have been Richard Brown Baker, Susan Morse Hilles, Molly and Walter Bareiss, and Thurston Twigg-Smith. Other exhibitions have shown works owned by larger groups of alumni, and still others have exhibited works created by Yale faculty and Yale-trained artists.

From late May through August 1963, while the Rudolph Art and Architecture building was being completed, a special exhibition celebrating two of Yale's great collectors of modern art, Richard Brown Baker and Susan Morse Hilles, was installed in the first floor east galleries of the Kahn building. *Two Modern Collectors* included fifty-three mid-twentieth-century paintings and sculpture from their collections (fig. 199). Although both Hilles and Baker had exhibited works from their collections at the Gallery before, this was the first time that a special exhibition had been devoted to them. Initially, Baker was reluctant to participate, but Hilles won him over. In a letter to Andrew Ritchie, who had proposed the idea of the exhibition to him, Baker wrote,

> Scarcely two hours after writing you this morning to present my objections to the idea of a joint presentation, I chanced to run into Sue [Hilles], whose immense enthusiasm for the idea melted some of my reservations. I gather that the contemplated show would not be very large, would not pretend to include only "top" things but would aim at informal liveliness. Sue urged me to forget my Pollock, Dubuffet, etc. I inferred that in her conception neither of us would be loaning works Yale has already exhibited, but would be showing newer, less familiar artists to try to wake New Haven up. I rather warmed to the notion of such an unofficial, informal little show . . . that might appear under such a title as "Contemporaries from Two Collectors" and attempt primarily to be an interesting, avant-garde exhibit rather than a resume of each of our collections.[1]

Included at the end of the letter was a list of paintings, drawings, watercolors, and collages for Ritchie and Sue Hilles to consider as they selected what would be shown from both collections. And on this basis the exhibition went forward.

Andrew Ritchie, in his statement announcing the exhibition, spoke of Baker and Hilles as "friends whose taste seems to complement each other" but who pursued individual directions.[2] Particularly important about both, in Ritchie's view, was "their courage in exploring new modes of expression and their desire to encourage younger artists in a most concrete way—by purchase of their work." Both Hilles and Baker, who each began collecting seriously in 1954, continued to support young artists throughout the following decades of their active collecting. Hilles, who had attended art schools from 1925–29, describes her collecting as follows in the introduction to the exhibition catalogue:

Two resolutions made thirty years apart have greatly influenced the contents of my collection. I decided to be selective about museum viewing when I was in Munich in 1924. My aim was to spend more time looking at the works of art which had significance for me. To accomplish this aim, I had to train myself to glance at and quickly pass by paintings or sculpture which I judged to be of lesser importance. "A good eye" will be the end result of spending more time on viewing good or great art. Bad art is like bad literature—it takes up space and clutters the mind.

My recent resolve of 1955 was to buy the work of living artists (fig. 200). By this resolution I limit the field of collecting, keeping myself free from striving for a representative collection. I also help the artist earn his living. I enjoy myself playing my own hunches about buying. While an artist is alive, it is impossible to make a final evaluation of his work. Therefore his prices may or may not be reasonable and his work may or may not have staying power for the future. I always hope and think I've bought a "winner."[3]

Baker's statement about his collecting was more philosophical, but it was similarly focused on the work of living and often unknown artists and the need to support them. His words speak equally to the need for collecting by individuals and museums:

Born a New Englander, I am suspicious of collecting—any kind. It breathes self-indulgence. Self-denial is our Puritan goal. Yet in mid-twentieth-century America, not to be a collector may be as sinful as to be one. After all, a collector is an individual who knows and keeps—who cares. By the millions exist non-collectors who can afford but are indifferent . . . if we had such people only, most of the products society fabricates would be discarded once their novelty passed. . . .

We enjoy at present an economy of surpluses. Consider the fine arts . . . I speculate that not one in a thousand of our living self-styled artists enjoys a following that can be counted on to buy annually as much as one third of his output. . . . I do not contend that these works should be bought. Like

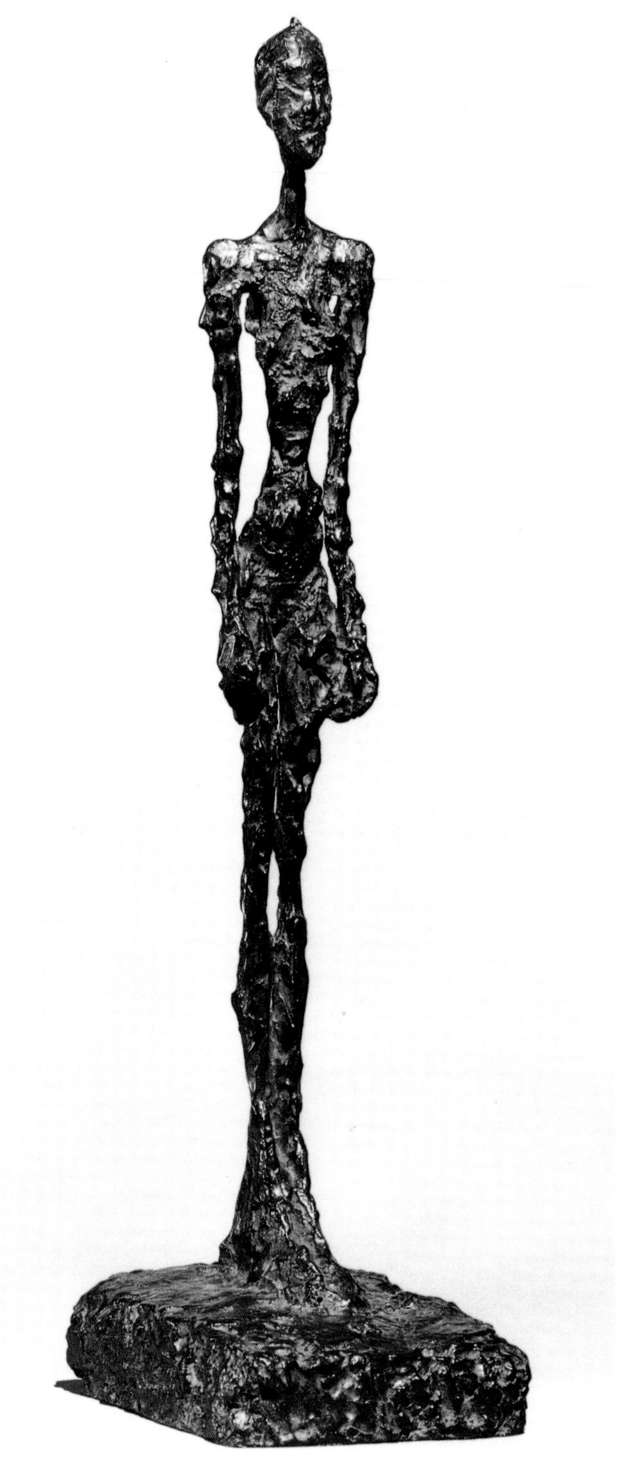

FIG. 200
Alberto Giacometti
Standing Woman, 1956
Bronze, 72 x 18 x 23 cm
Gift of Susan Morse Hilles
1984.50

anyone who specializes, I have diminished my capacity to take pleasure in what my experience suggests is bad or mediocre art. I prefer a bare wall to a bad picture.

> Yet for the health and enrichment of society people should go on trying their utmost to create art. As in 1763 and 1863, 1963 will see most of these efforts fail. Those that succeed count; they count very much. The individuals capable of creative power are important people. They merit an appreciative audience. On various levels they require support if their potential is to incubate.
>
> To feel a stirring enthusiasm, a recognition of the universal in the unknown, a conviction that one is confronting fresh, genuine art, when beholding the creation of a stranger who as yet lacks reputation, is an experience not often available. It is one to seek. When I have it I feel exalted; something has been added to me. The feeling is pure, ennobling. The decision to buy, should my means permit it, is an affirmation that the uniqueness, the quality, expressed by this unfamiliar artist, is recognized by me.[4]

Others noted the importance of the exhibition. *Art in America* published a special article on the exhibition entitled "Two in the Front Row," revising the contents of the September–October issue to permit the addition of the article.[5] Stuart Preston, reviewing the exhibition for the *New York Times*, characterized the exhibition as a survey of the last decade of painting and sculpture, and described the Gallery as having "brought off a resounding coup by securing the loan of two outstanding collections."[6]

According to Preston, the two collections "exert a double appeal, both for the merit and interest of works of art included, and for demonstrating the never-to-be-overlooked fact that no amount of enlightened museum, or other official collecting can possibly replace the value—the more idiosyncratic the better—of individual judgment. How often must museum directors envy the happy irresponsibility of the private collector. And what gnashing of directorial teeth when expert 'consensus' backs the wrong horse while a flight of fancy leads to a pot of gold." Focusing primarily on Abstract Expressionism, the exhibition offered "isolated as in a laboratory demonstration, excellent examples of the kind of abstraction that, almost overnight, made America a pathfinder and world leader in art during the decade 1948–58." But as Preston pointed out, Hilles and Baker were not collecting to create a "museum" or to create art history. These are "two collectors who are not primarily concerned with anticipating the judgement of posterity; with establishing an immutable pantheon, or with striving for 'representative' collections. Their aims are more modest and far more personal, namely to exercise personal taste and judgement and to form the fruitful role of patron of living art and artists."

Both Hilles and Baker continued to collect in this vein for decades after this exhibition. It is a mark of their eye for originality and quality that so many of the artists who were relatively unknown when these two astute buyers purchased their work are now household names. Works from the Baker and Hilles collections have been exhibited at Yale as individual loans and as the basis for subsequent exhibitions, and both of these enlightened patrons of the arts have been remarkably generous donors to Yale.

For Richard Brown Baker, the 1963 exhibition was the first in a series of Yale shows and publications focusing on his collection. *Richard Brown Baker Collects!*, an exhibition of 1975 that grew out of a graduate seminar taught the previous year by Theodore E. Stebbins, Jr., curator of American painting, included works from the 1950s but focused largely on work created from 1960–74. Featured were some of the signature paintings from Baker's collection, notably Pollock's *Arabesque* and four major paintings by Roy Lichtenstein. Also present were works that chronicled his collecting of post–Abstract Expressionist artists, including Beal, Dine, Johns, Rosenquist, Tuttle, and Twombly, almost all of which he bought in the year they were produced.

Another exhibition, *Collecting with Richard Brown Baker: From Pollock to Lichtenstein*, was staged in 1995, curated by Sasha M. Newman, the Seymour H. Knox, Jr., Curator of European and Contemporary Art. Beginning with the purchase of the Pollock *Arabesque* in 1955, this exhibition focused on the months between December 1955 and January 1957 as a critical period in the development of Baker's collection. During this period,

FIG. 201
Franz Kline
Wanamaker Block, 1955
Oil on canvas, 199.4 x 180.3 cm
Gift of Richard Brown Baker
1994.91.1

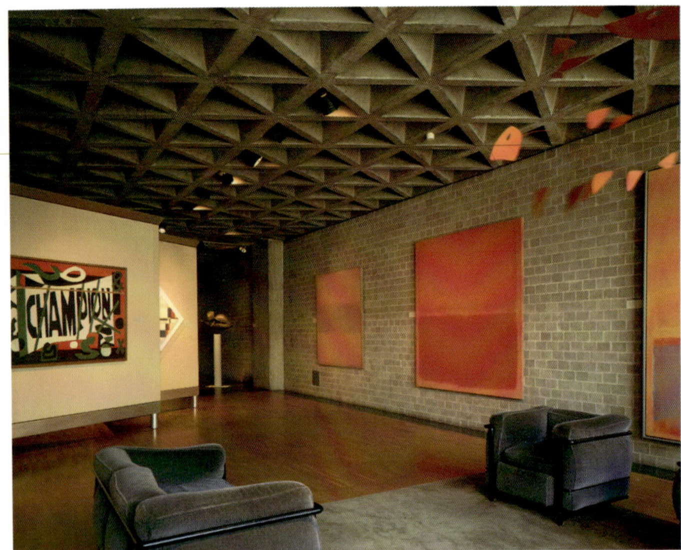

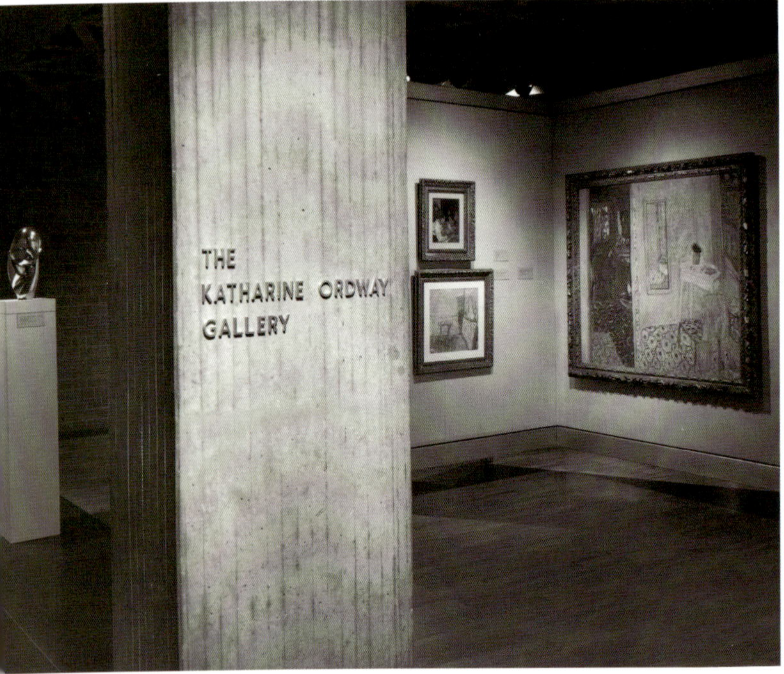

FIG. 202
Katharine Ordway Gallery, ca. 1980
Photographs courtesy Yale University Art Gallery Archives

Baker also purchased Franz Kline's *Wanamaker Block* (1955; fig. 201) and major works by Dubuffet, Tapies, Stankiewicz, and Hofmann, among others. Excerpts from Baker's journal and letters, published as part of the exhibition catalogue, reveal a passionate collector—"An overwhelming urge to see pictures rather than muck about the U.N. led me to traipse around in the damp all today visiting galleries. My acquisitive instinct hasn't weakened."[7] In a letter to his mother, he wrote, "So much about paintings is likely to bore you. But modern art has established itself with me as a consuming interest, and I must apologize if the interest spills over."[8] The modern art that filled his apartment has been his lifelong companion, which he has generously shared with his friends and Yale students alike. It has spilled over into the galleries at Yale where it will continue to inspire students and "wake New Haven up," as Richard Brown Baker would wish.

KATHARINE ORDWAY

The bequest by Miss Katharine Ordway to the Yale University Art Gallery in 1980 was a major milestone for its collection of twentieth-century art (fig. 202). Miss Ordway's decision, encouraged by Alan Shestack, to bequeath her outstanding collection and a supporting endowment to Yale resulted in a quantum leap in the Gallery's holdings of twentieth-century art and its ability to add to this key part of its collection. Miss Ordway's bequest comprised more than 150 twentieth-century paintings, sculptures, prints, and drawings, along with a few earlier paintings and several Asian and Precolumbian works. It complemented the Société Anonyme Collection, carrying on the tradition of modern art that was already strong at Yale while at the same time adding new artists to the Gallery's collection.

Included in the Ordway Collection, for example, were Yale's first major works by Mark Rothko, three important oils: *Untitled*, 1954, *Untitled (Orange)*, 1957, and *No. 3*, 1967 (fig. 203). The last was bought in January 1968, no more than a few months after it was finished. These three paintings, now mainstays of the Yale collection, were joined in 1986 by an earlier oil *Untitled*, 1947, and a drawing in indigo ink and acrylic, *Untitled*, ca. 1968, as gifts of the Rothko Foundation. Together, these holdings comprise a representative and

FIG. 203
Mark Rothko
No. 3, 1967
Mixed media on unprimed canvas,
205.1 x 193 cm
The Katharine Ordway Collection
1980.12.23

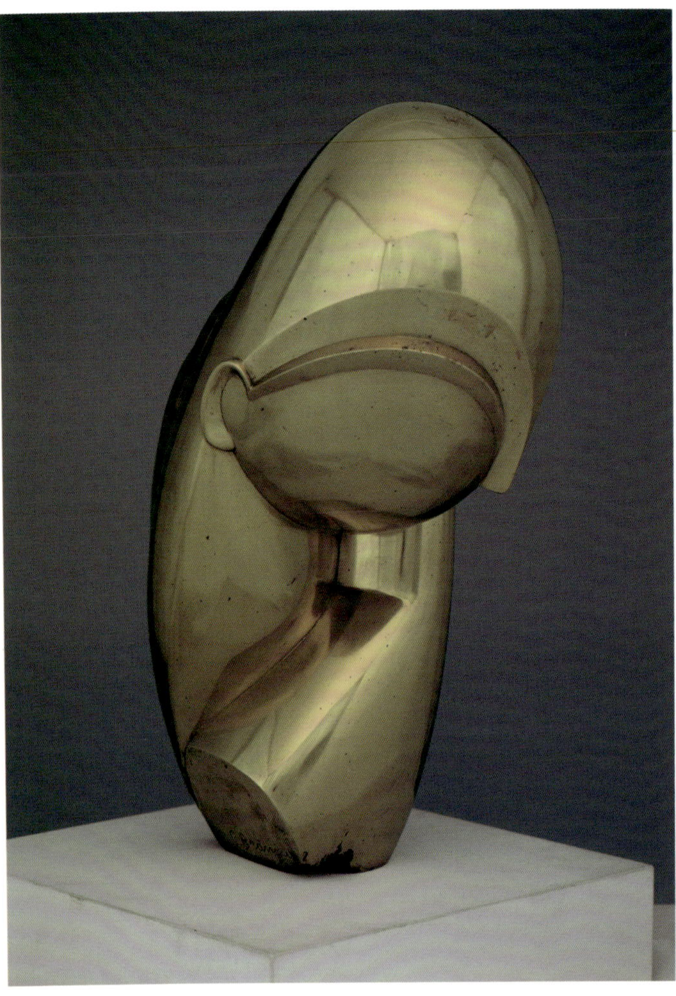

FIG. 204
Constantin Brancusi
Mlle. Pogany II, 1925
Polished bronze, 55.8 x 47.7 cm
The Katharine Ordway Collection
1980.12.16

significant group of the artist's work, reassembled at the college in which Rothko was an undergraduate in the early 1920s.

Miss Ordway bought many of her most important works at or near the time of their creation, often before the artist had achieved fame. In his introduction to the catalogue of the exhibition held at the Gallery to celebrate the Ordway Collection, Alan Shestack wrote, "From the beginning of her collecting in the 1920s, Miss Ordway exercised her own judgment, showing remarkable independence and foresight. For instance, she saw Brancusi's *Mlle. Pogany* [fig. 204] while it was still in the studio and bought it directly from the artist in 1925. . . . Her handsome Gorky [*The Betrothal*, 1947, fig. 205] was purchased at a charity auction in 1949 [two years after it was painted] purely for the love of the picture, and her Pollock painting was bought from Betty Parsons in 1948, the year it was painted, long before Pollock became a household name." This Pollock painting (*Number 4*, 1949) and a drawing by the artist in enamel on gesso (*Number 14: Gray*, 1948; fig. 206) were probably acquired by Miss Ordway at the same time. They were shown together at the Betty Parsons Gallery in early 1949, and both have been exhibited extensively since then in the United States and abroad.

There were other firsts besides the Rothkos in the Ordway bequest. The Gorky *Betrothal* was the first work by that artist to come to Yale, as was Henri Rousseau's *The Canal* (1905). Also a Yale first was a fine Salomon van Ruysdael *View of Alkmaar*, ca. 1650, the sole Old Master painting in the bequest. Other Ordway paintings, such as the Bonnard and Vuillard, for example, provided important complements to the Gallery's existing holdings.

In addition to the bequest of her collection, Miss Ordway left an endowment to the Gallery for a publication of her collection,[9] conservation of it, and its growth that has been used to purchase more than eighty works of twentieth-century art. The first acquisition made with the Ordway Fund was *Schwitzki's Syntax* by Stuart Davis (1961; fig. 207), characteristic of what the artist called his "Color-Space-Compositions." Purchased from the Davis estate, it is again the first work by the artist to come to Yale. Subsequent acquisitions with the Ordway Fund have included Duchamp's

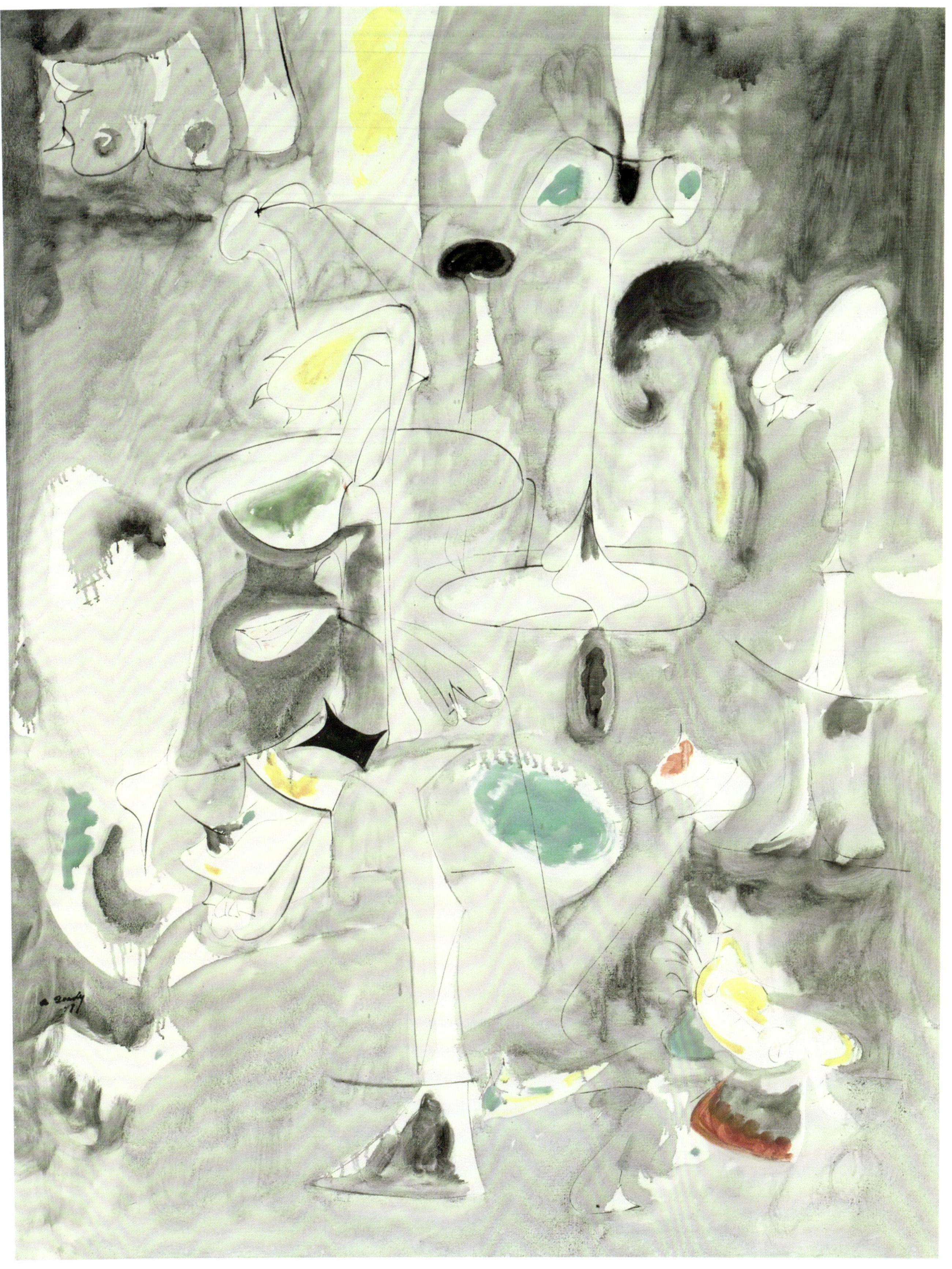

FIG. 205
Arshile Gorky
The Betrothal, 1947
Oil on canvas, 128.9 x 101.6 cm
The Katharine Ordway Collection
1980.12.45

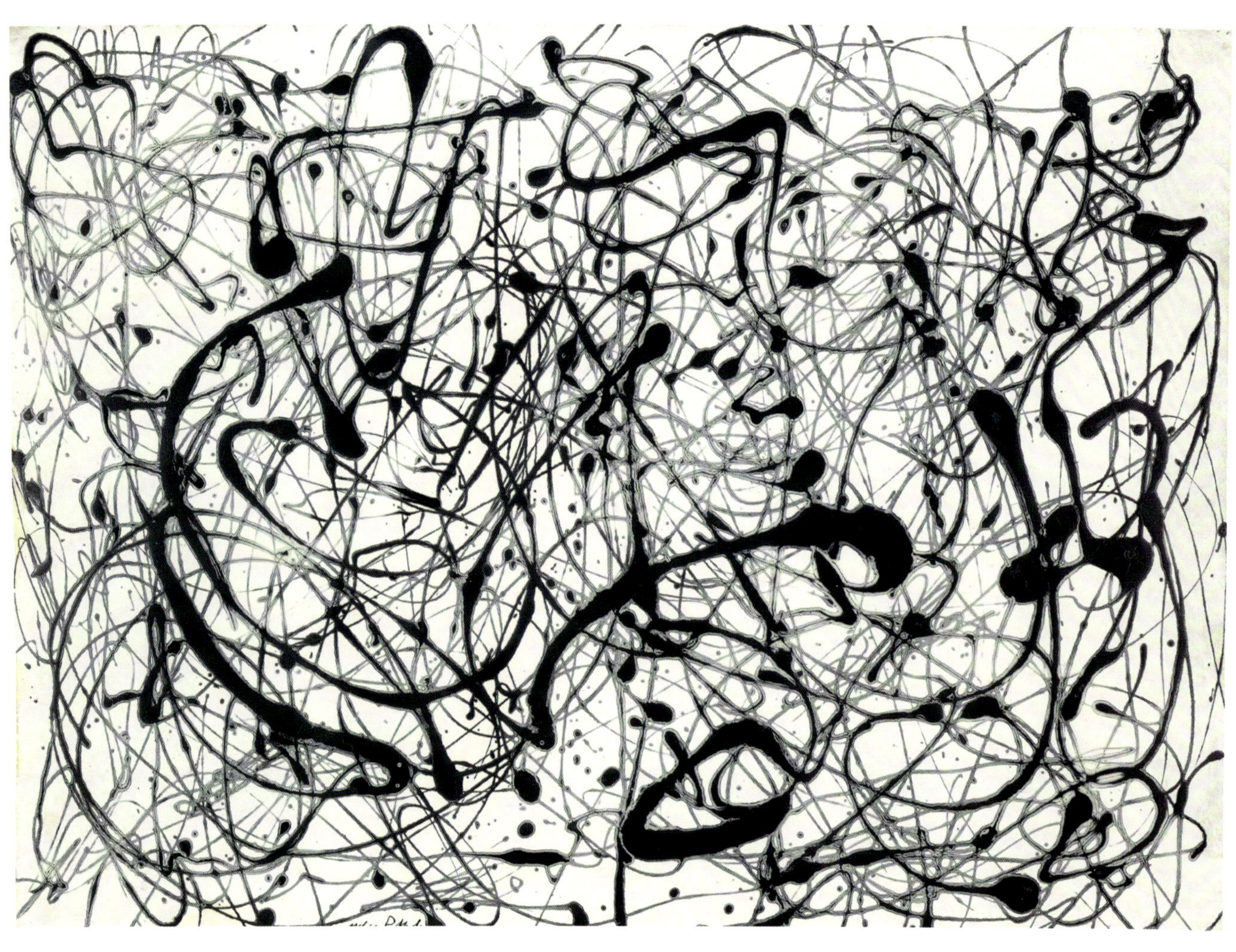

FIG. 206
Jackson Pollock
Number 14: Gray, 1948
Enamel on gesso on wove paper,
57.8 x 78.8 cm
The Katharine Ordway Collection
1980.12.74

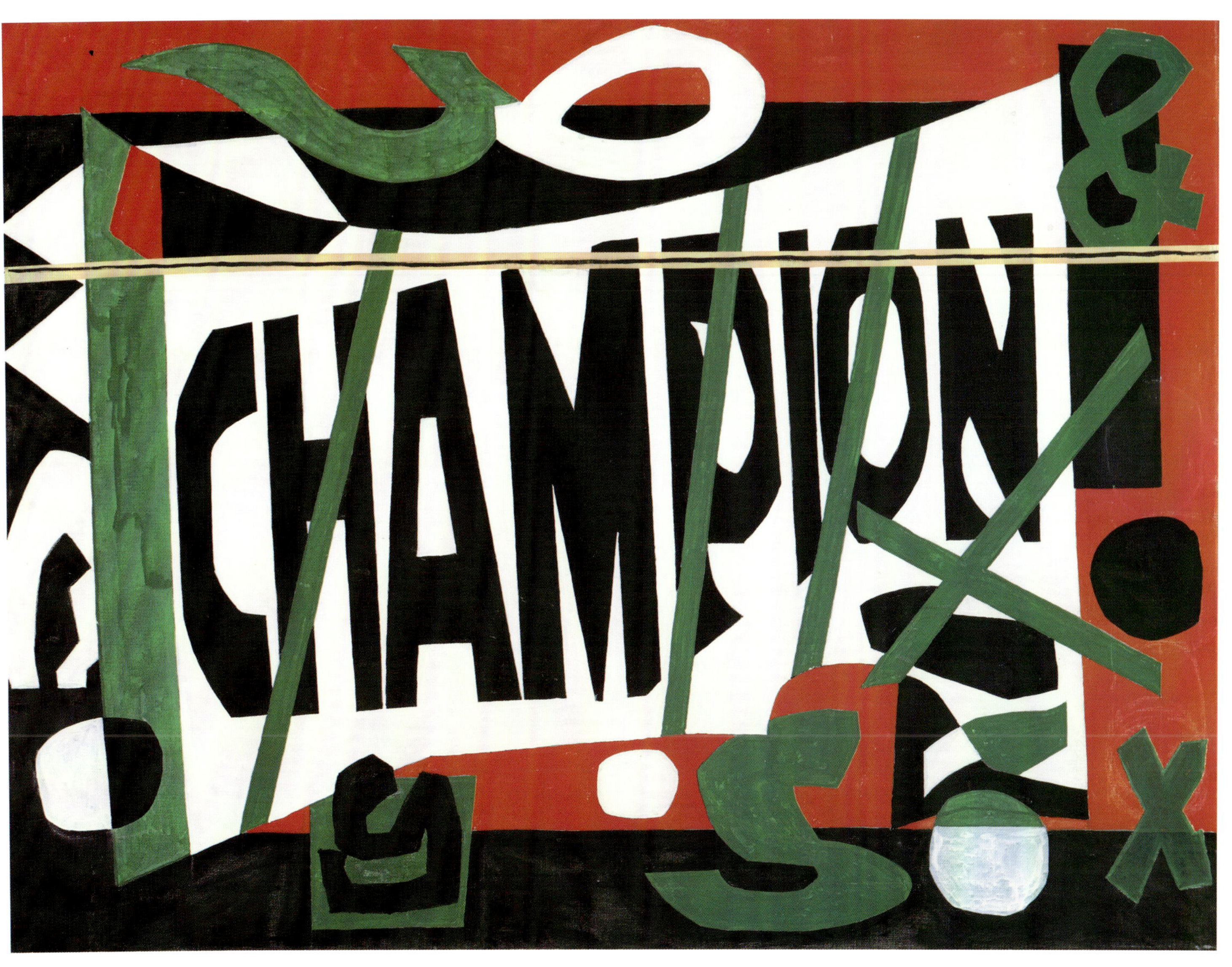

FIG. 207
Stuart Davis
Schwitzki's Syntax, 1961
Oil and wax emulsion on canvas,
106.7 x 142.2 cm
The Katharine Ordway Fund
1980.84

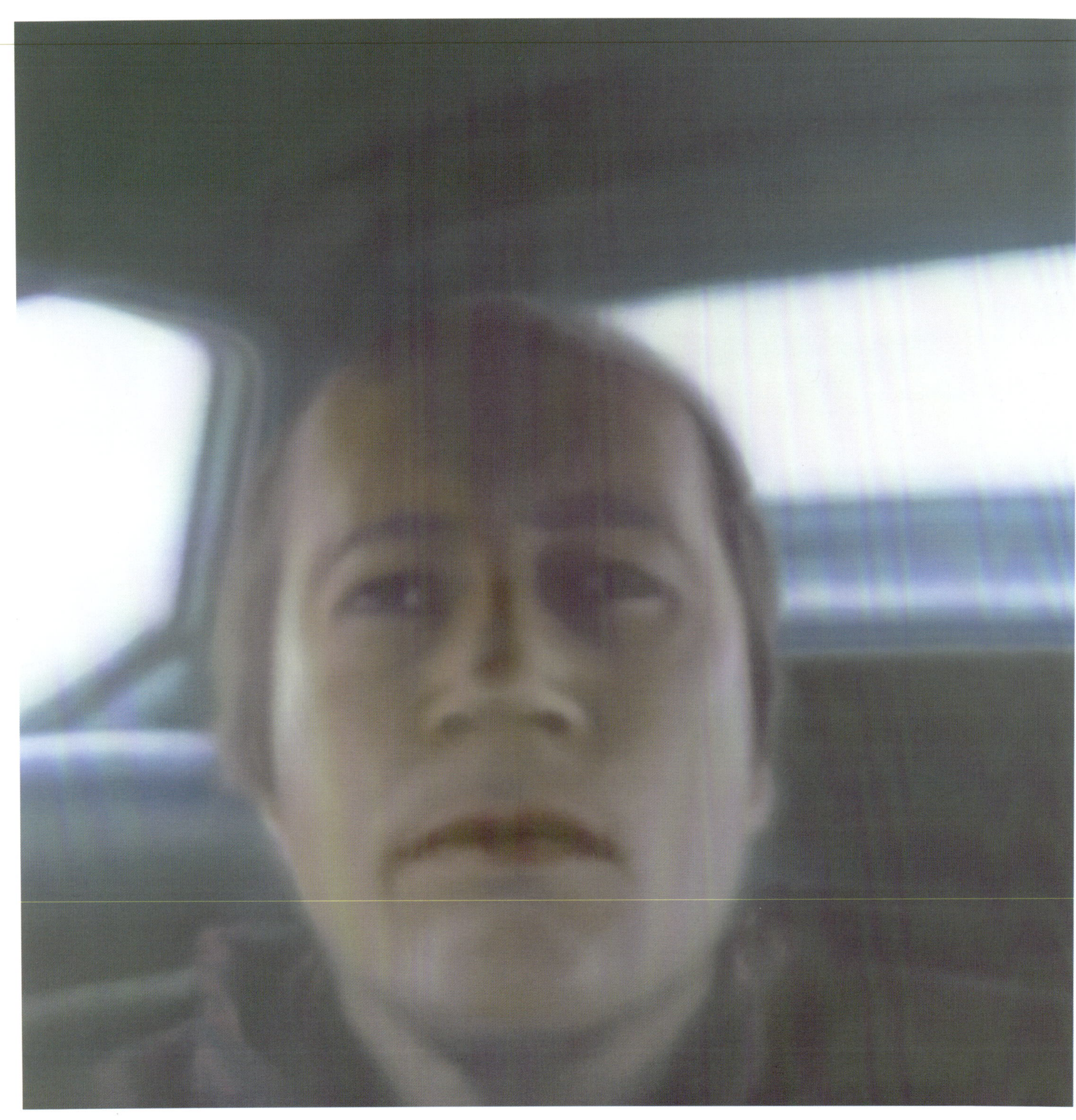

FIG. 208
Gerhard Richter
Bildnis Holger Friedrich, 1972
Oil on canvas, 140 x 140 cm
Gift of Molly and Walter Bareiss,
B.S. 1940S
1991.58.81

Standard Stoppages and *Stacks* by Richard Serra (M.F.A. 1964), as well as works by Degas, Severini, Sol LeWitt, Jacob Lawrence, Lorna Simpson, and Joseph Beuys, among numerous others.

German and Austrian Contemporary Art from the Bareiss Collection, organized by Sasha Newman, the Seymour H. Knox, Jr., Curator of European and Contemporary Art, and shown at the Gallery in 1989, broadened the parameters of Yale's contemporary exhibitions beyond the American focus that had characterized the majority of them since the 1950s. In so doing, this exhibition revived the recognition of Germany as an important producer of contemporary art that had already been acknowledged by Katherine Dreier. The exhibition included only a part of the contemporary German and Austrian art that Molly and Walter Bareiss have collected; nevertheless, it demonstrated the comprehensive and multifaceted nature of the collection and the intensity with which Walter Bareiss commits himself to the artists who interest him, often collecting their works in many media and in substantial depth. Gerhard Richter, Georg Baselitz, Joseph Beuys, Arnulf Rainer, Anselm Kiefer, and Hermann Nitsch were all featured in the exhibition. Richter's *Bildnis Holger Friedrich* (fig. 208) was given by Molly and Walter Bareiss in 1991, while the Katharine Ordway Fund was used to purchase *Green Violin and Telephone S[ender]—R[eceiver]* by Joseph Beuys and *Untitled (Poured Picture)* by Hermann Nitsch.

Although this was the first exhibition devoted exclusively to the Bareiss Collection, loans and gifts from these extraordinary friends of the Gallery have been noted in these pages time and again—there is not a single department at the Gallery that has not been enriched by a gift from Molly and Walter Bareiss. Major gifts have ranged from an Etruscan bronze mirror through a Degas drawing to ancient and contemporary Asian ceramics. Paintings, drawings, and prints from the Bareiss Collection have featured in all of the Yale alumni collectors' exhibitions since 1956, and the Bareisses have lent countless works over the years for exhibitions and courses in a broad range of fields. They have repeatedly hosted seminars of Yale students at their home, providing a remarkable environment for learning. The 1975 exhibition *Greek Vases at Yale*, for

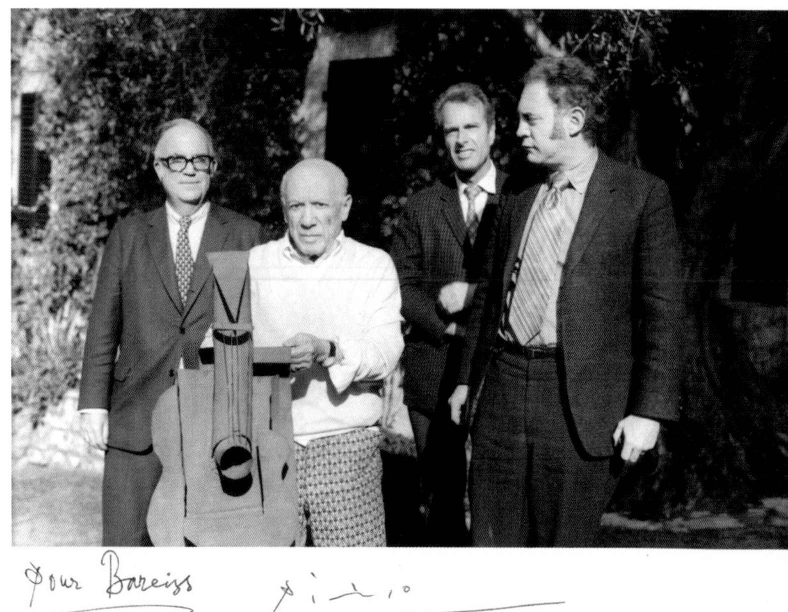

FIG. 209
Jacqueline Roque
Walter Bareiss with Pablo Picasso, Ernst Beyeler, and William Rubin, 1969
Gelatin silver print, 23.8 x 29.8 cm
Gift of Walter and Molly Bareiss, B.S. 1940S
1999.9.31

example, a collaboration between the Gallery and J. J. Pollitt, professor of Classics and history of art, grew out of such a seminar, giving graduate students in both departments a unique opportunity to study and publish outstanding Greek vases in the Bareiss Collection. Continuing this interest in Greek art, the Bareisses have funded the endowment of the Molly and Walter Bareiss Curator of Ancient Art, the post that the author of this volume is honored to hold.

Walter Bareiss's association with the Gallery began even before he enrolled as a student at Yale. "When I applied for Yale, my father and I came from Europe by boat and obviously the first thing we did after we had the interview, we went to the gallery and looked at the pictures . . . and that was very impressive." He returned to the Gallery often as a student, and remembers, "The most impressive thing was the Jarves collection. . . . It was the only place where you could get real Renaissance pictures." Equally memorable was his meeting with Marcel Duchamp, "a great experience by itself" for an undergraduate who was just beginning to collect artist-illustrated books. Since then, he has maintained a lifelong commitment to the Gallery, serving as a member of its Governing Board for half a century, and as chairman from 1987–1995. Perhaps best known as a collector of modern art, something he has been doing since he was a teenager, he has served as a trustee and as acting director of the Museum of Modern Art. In 1969 he presided over the acquisition by MoMA of Picasso's famous cardboard maquette guitar (1912), recorded in a photograph (fig. 209) taken by Jacqueline Roque (Picasso's third and last wife) showing the artist with Bareiss, William Rubin (MoMA's celebrated curator), and Ernst Beyeler (Picasso's dealer at the time). The photograph is inscribed "Pour Bareiss." The Gallery celebrated Bareiss's eightieth birthday in 1999 with an installation of gifts and loans of modern German, British, and American art from his collection. He, characteristically, celebrated by giving drawings by Matisse, Degas, Picasso, Giacometti, Moholy-Nagy, and Caroll Dunham to the Gallery's prints and drawings collection and works of art to three more of the Gallery's departments.

A West Coast focus has dominated the formation of another Yale collection that is coming to the Gallery as a gift, that of Thurston Twigg-Smith (B.E. 1942). A fifth-generation Hawaiian, Twigg-Smith began supporting and collecting local Honolulu artists as part of an effort to revive the family newspaper, the *Honolulu Advertiser*, in the late 1940s. "One of the things I felt strongly about was that we should be part of the community, and although we weren't making any money, I thought it would be good public relations to establish a foundation to support local artists."[10] In thus urging the paper's board to support local artists by acquiring their work, Twigg-Smith initiated one of America's earliest corporate art collections. When the committee failed to agree on which works to buy, Twigg-Smith began to purchase them himself, beginning his lifelong collecting of contemporary art. Later, as publisher of the *Advertiser*, he established regular exhibitions of local artists in the newspaper's building, from which the members of the paper's corporation would purchase one or two works for the corporate collection. Ultimately, the *Advertiser*'s collection became the nucleus of the Honolulu Museum of Contemporary Art, which Twigg-Smith founded in 1961, the year he became editor of the paper.

Celebrated in the 1997 exhibition *Hawaiian Eye: Collecting Contemporary Art with Thurston Twigg-Smith*, the Twigg-Smith Collection explores, as described in the exhibition catalogue, neo-figuration and post-conceptualism in the art of the 1980s, while looking back to their sources in the 1960s and ahead to what followed in the 1990s. The collection includes works by Wayne Thiebaud (fig. 210), Alex Katz, David Hockney, Jim Dine, Vija Celmins, and Robert Arneson, and a large percentage of Bay Area and southern California painters and sculptors. In an interview with Daphne Deeds, curator of the exhibition, Twigg-Smith commented, "Giving art is the best part of all giving because you're giving something that's going to be permanent and remain visible and useful to the community. I think I get more joy out of gifts of works of art than any other philanthropic endeavor."[11] Most recently, contemporary exhibitions have focused on work by New York artists, as in *Objective Color*, organized by Jennifer Gross, Seymour H. Knox, Jr., Curator of European and Contemporary Art, and photography, in shows curated by Director Jock Reynolds.

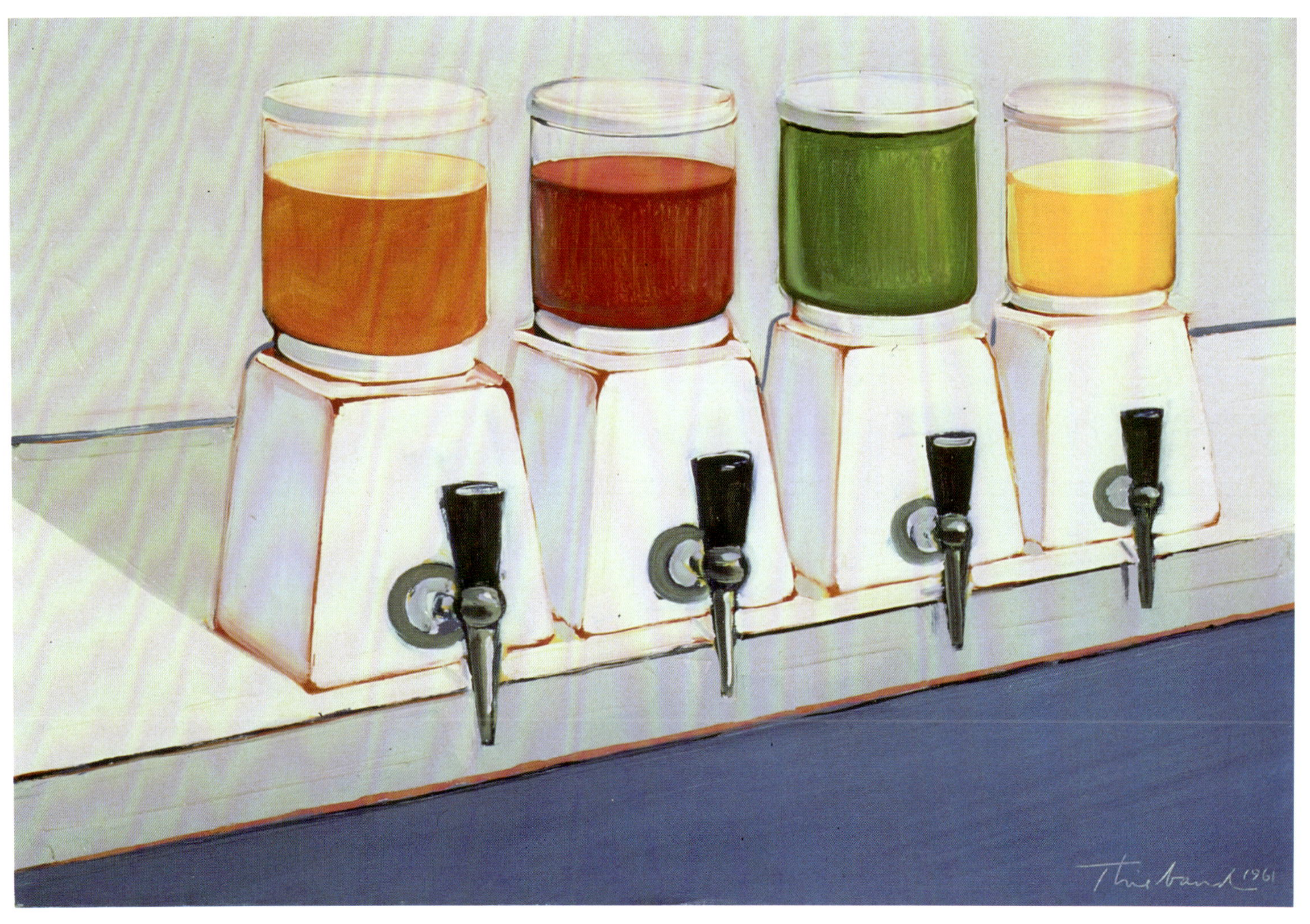

FIG. 210
Wayne Thiebaud
Drink Syrups, 1961
Oil on canvas
Promised gift of Thurston and
Sharon Twigg-Smith

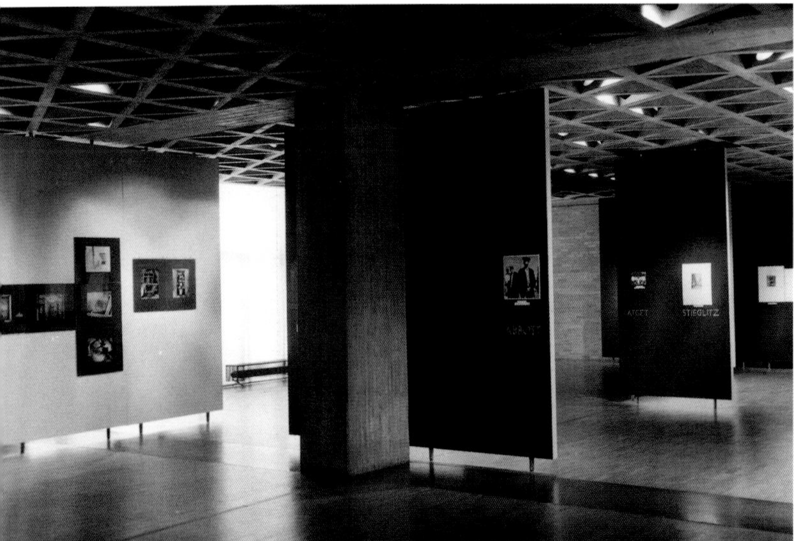

FIG. 211
Four Photographers, 1955
Photograph courtesy Yale University Art Gallery Archives

PHOTOGRAPHY

In the fall of 1955, the Gallery mounted an exhibition, *Four Photographers* (fig. 211), to draw attention to the section of photography recently established in the Department of Graphic Arts and directed by Herbert Matter. Although the manuscripts and archives department and other collections of the Yale Library contained, published, and exhibited photographs, and there had been exhibitions of architectural and documentary photographs at the School of the Fine Arts in the late nineteenth and early twentieth centuries, this was the first major exhibition of photography as an art form at the Gallery. *Four Photographers* marked the beginning of a new level of interest in the medium that would result in subsequent exhibitions and in a growing collection of photographs that are widely used for teaching. Eugène Atget, Berenice Abbott, Clarence John Laughlin, and Alfred Stieglitz were the four photographers in the 1955 exhibition. Included in the exhibition was a letter from Abbott to Lamont Moore suggesting that Yale might want to buy her collection of Atget photographs and perhaps collaborate in publishing a book on Atget. This was not done, but the boat had been launched.

There are other collections of photographs at Yale, but the Gallery's collection is of a different sort and serves a different purpose. The photographic holdings of Yale's Manuscripts and Archives Collection, the Beinecke Rare Book and Manuscript Library, and other branches of the library such as the African, Near Eastern, and Judaica Collections are primarily historical and documentary in nature, although the Beinecke Collection, for example, contains photographs by well-known photographers like Alfred Stieglitz. The Gallery's collecting philosophy has been more closely tied to the teaching of photography in the School of Art and as a field of art history, and acquisitions are frequently made to support these two areas of study. Thus historic photographs by the pioneers in the field are of equal importance to those being made by talented students today, and both are being added to the collection. Outstanding photographs already existed in the Gallery's collection prior to the 1955 exhibition. The Société Anonyme Collection, for example, is rich in photographs, especially those of Man Ray (fig. 212), one of the Société's founders.

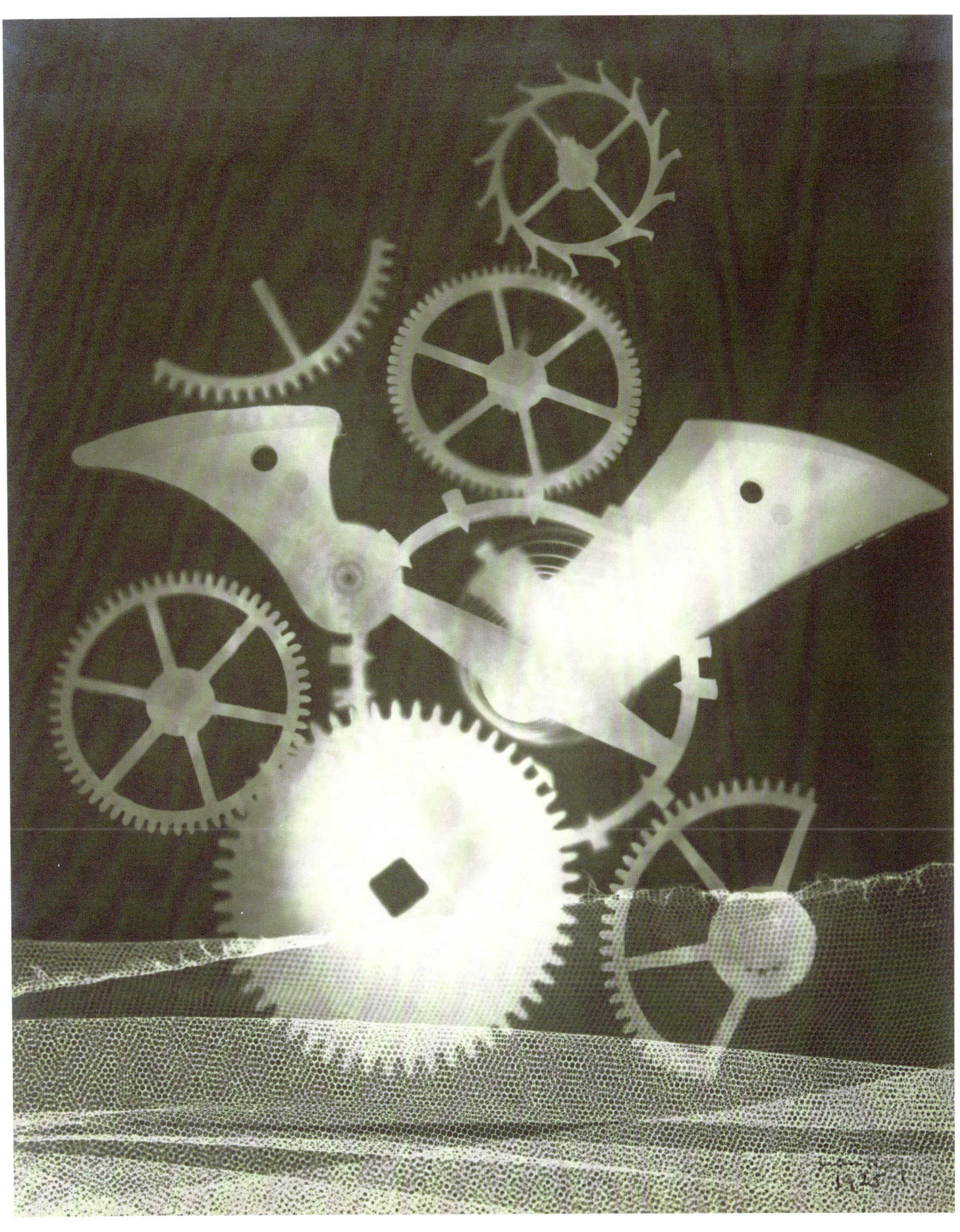

FIG. 212
Man Ray
Clock Wheels, 1925
Rayograph, 28.3 x 22.9 cm
Gift of Collection Société
Anonyme
1941.655

FIG. 213
Eugène Atget
Pendant l'Eclipse – 1912, 1912,
printed later by Berenice Abbott
Gold chloride-toned print,
17.1 x 22.4 cm
Gift of Russell Lynes, B.A. 1932
1977.53.9

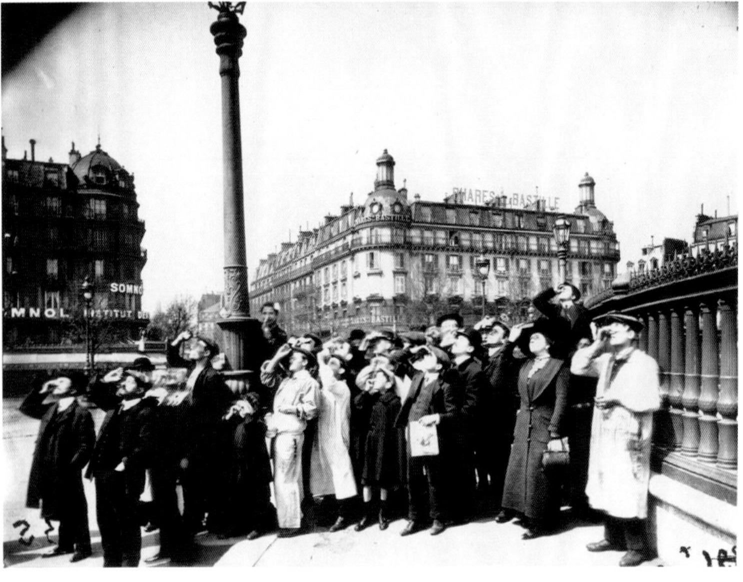

FIG. 214
Berenice Abbott
Exchange Place, ca. 1935
Vintage gelatin silver print,
23.2 x 18.4 cm
S. Sidney Kahn, B.A. 1959, Fund
1975.103

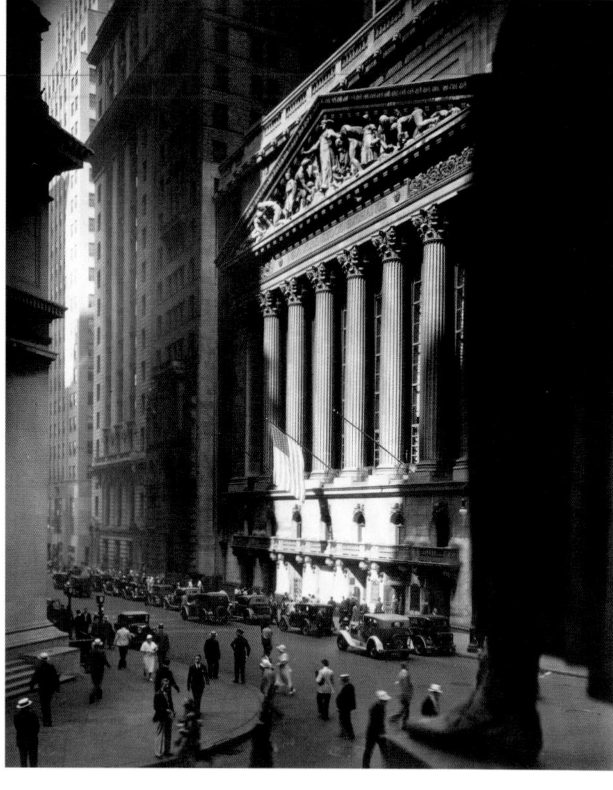

Particularly beginning in the 1970s, however, Alan Shestack as director and James D. Burke as curator of prints and drawings campaigned avidly to add to the collection through purchase and gift, and Richard S. Field carried on the campaign as curator of prints, drawings, and photographs in the 1980s and '90s, buying representatively from the nineteenth century to the present. With Jock Reynolds as director and Richard Benson as dean of the School of Art, the close collaboration between the Gallery and the photography program in the School has intensified, and as a result the collection is growing at an even faster rate, with a particular emphasis on work that can inspire students as the work of one photographer has often inspired another (figs. 213–20). The collection now numbers nearly three thousand images. Throughout this period of intense growth, the collection has been supported by generous gifts of photographs and funding from Yale alumni and other friends, notably George Hopper Fitch, S. Sidney Kahn, and Richard Benson.

A varied exhibition program in photography has characterized the past twenty years and, under Jock Reynolds, photography exhibitions have increased in range and number. Exhibitions featuring the work of Paul Caponigro, John T. Hill, Jerry Uelsmann, Bruce Davidson, Walker Evans, Wynn Bullock, Aaron Siskind, Harriet S. V. Thorne, Robert Frank, Roni Horn, Paul Outerbridge, Lois Conner, James Latimer Allen, and others have drawn the attention of students, scholars, and collectors. Exhibitions of historical photographs such as *Philadelphia Naturalistic Photography, 1885–1906*, *William Henry Jackson: Photographer of the American West*, and *Appropriated Lands: Photography and the Great Surveys of the American West, 1867–1879*; thematic exhibitions such as *Photographers Look at Buildings*, *Imaging African Art*, and *Portraiture and the Harlem Renaissance: The Photographs of James L. Allen*; exhibitions focusing on portraiture and the body; exhibitions on specific processes, such as *Color Photography—Inventors and Innovators, 1850–1975*, and *American Daguerreotypes from the Matthew R. Isenburg Collection*; and several teaching exhibitions on the history of photography have rounded out the program.

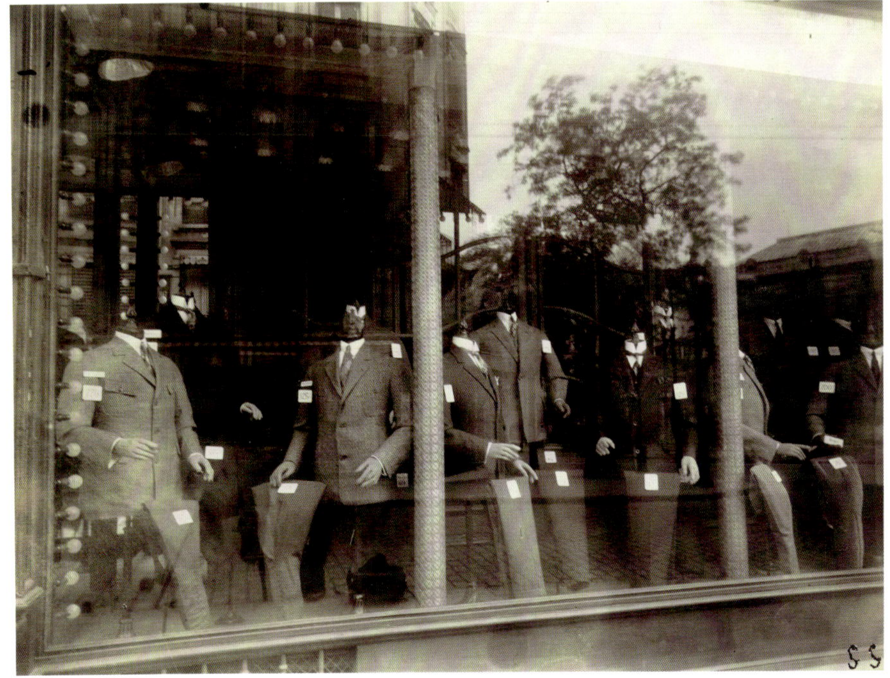

FIG. 215
Eugène Atget
Avenue des Gobelins, ca. 1925–27
Vintage albumen print,
17.8 x 22.4 cm
Gift of Lunn Gallery/Graphics
International Ltd.
1973.13.2

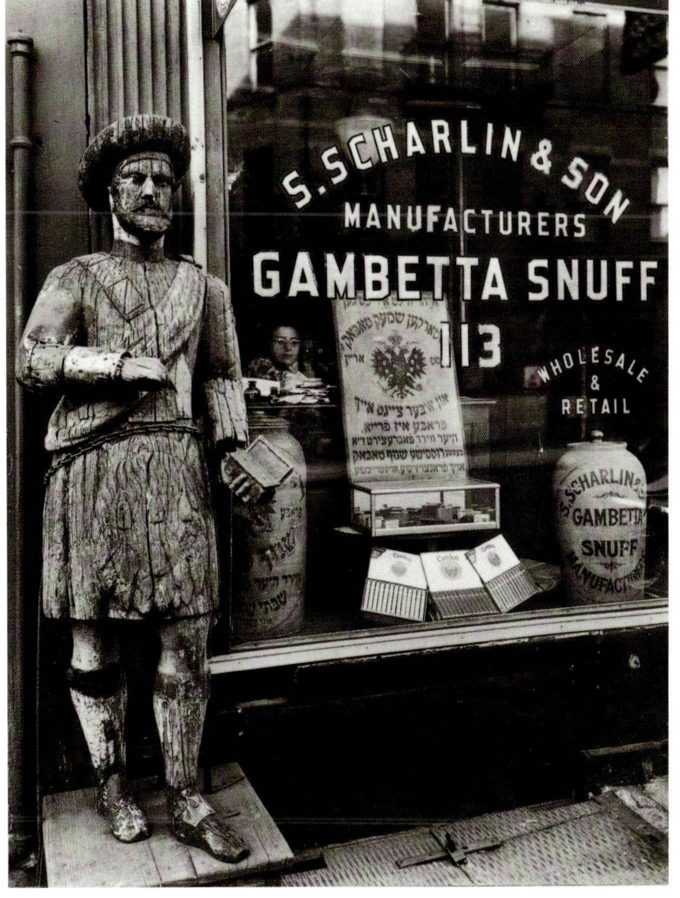

FIG. 216
Berenice Abbott
Snuff Shop, 113 Division Street, Manhattan, January 26, 1938
Vintage gelatin silver print,
23.8 x 18.7 cm
Purchased with Funds from the
National Endowments for the Arts
and the Charina Foundation
1988.78.1

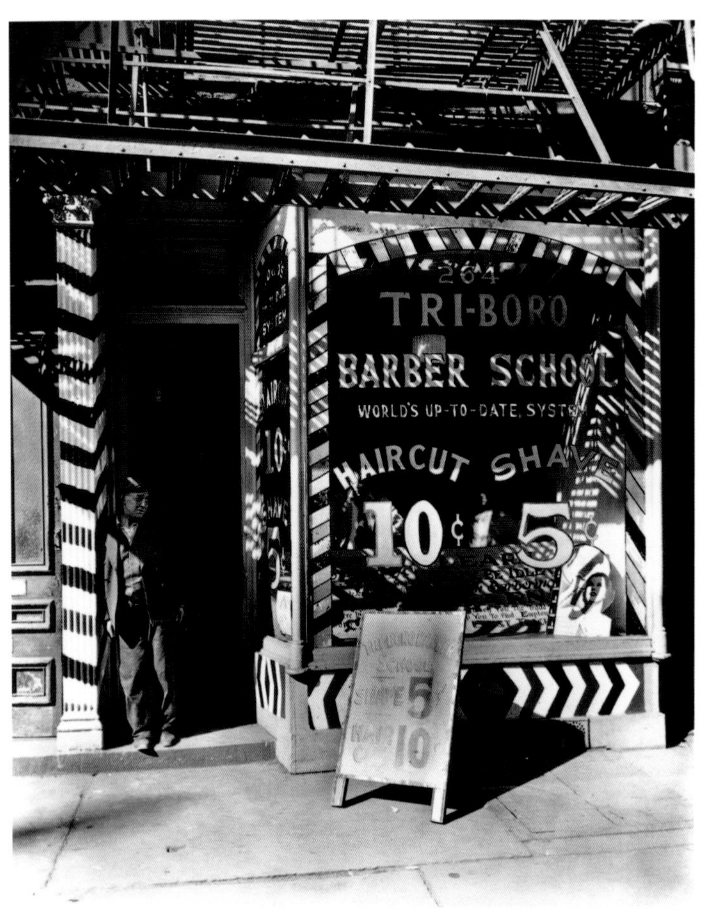

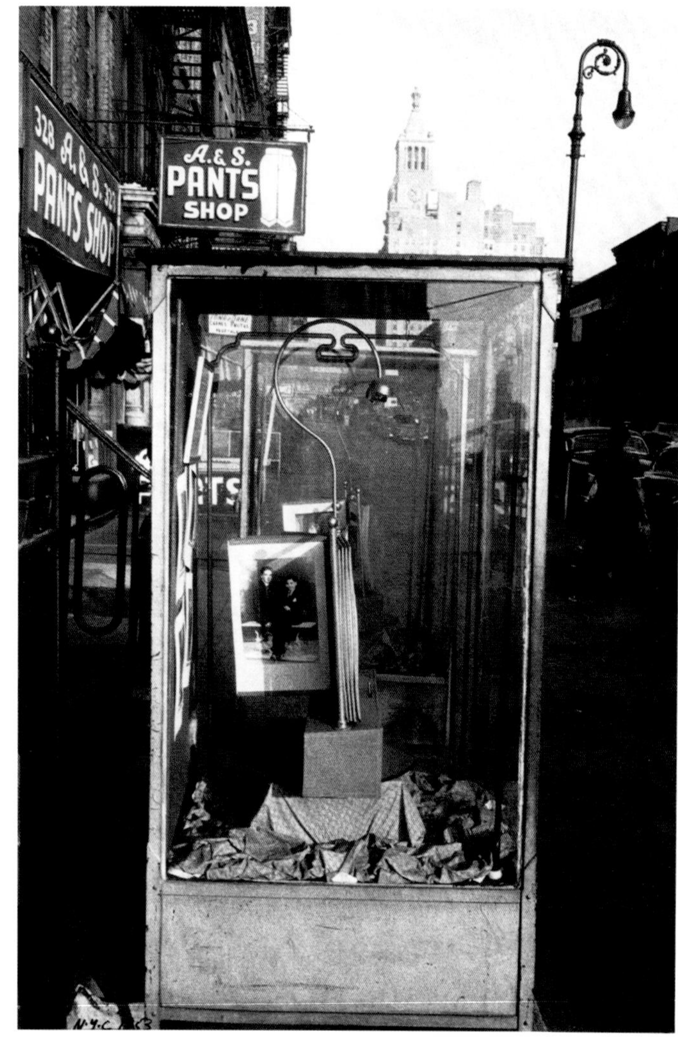

FIG. 217
Berenice Abbott
Triboro Barber School, ca. 1935
Vintage gelatin silver print,
25.2 x 20.2 cm
The Henry S. Cooper, B.A. 1956,
Contemporary Print Purchase Fund
1975.104

FIG. 218
Robert Frank
N.Y.C 1953 [A&S Pants], 1953
Gelatin silver print, 35.6 x 27.9 cm
Gift of the Ethné and Clive Gray
Family Collection
1999.42.3

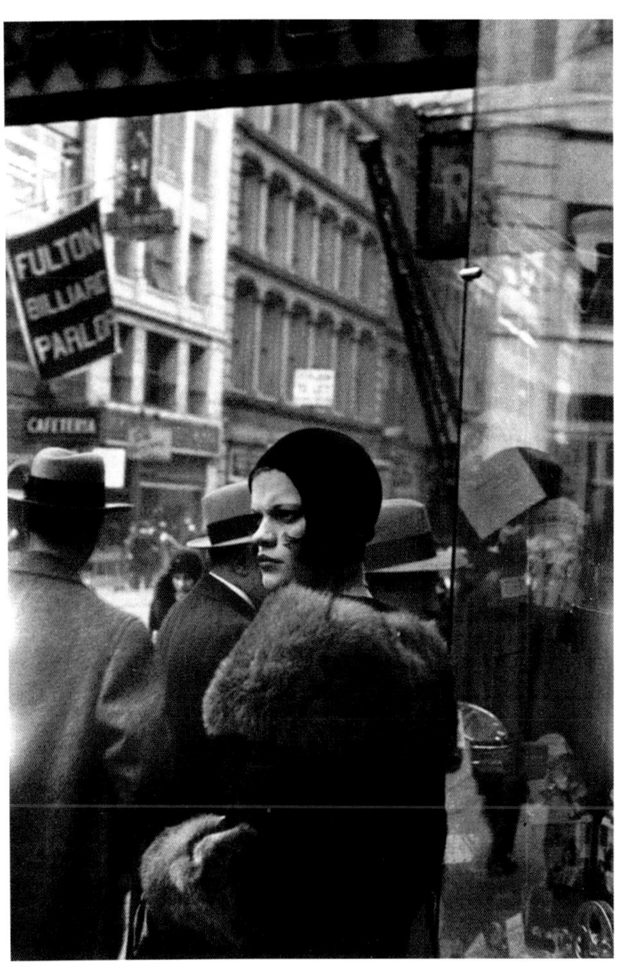

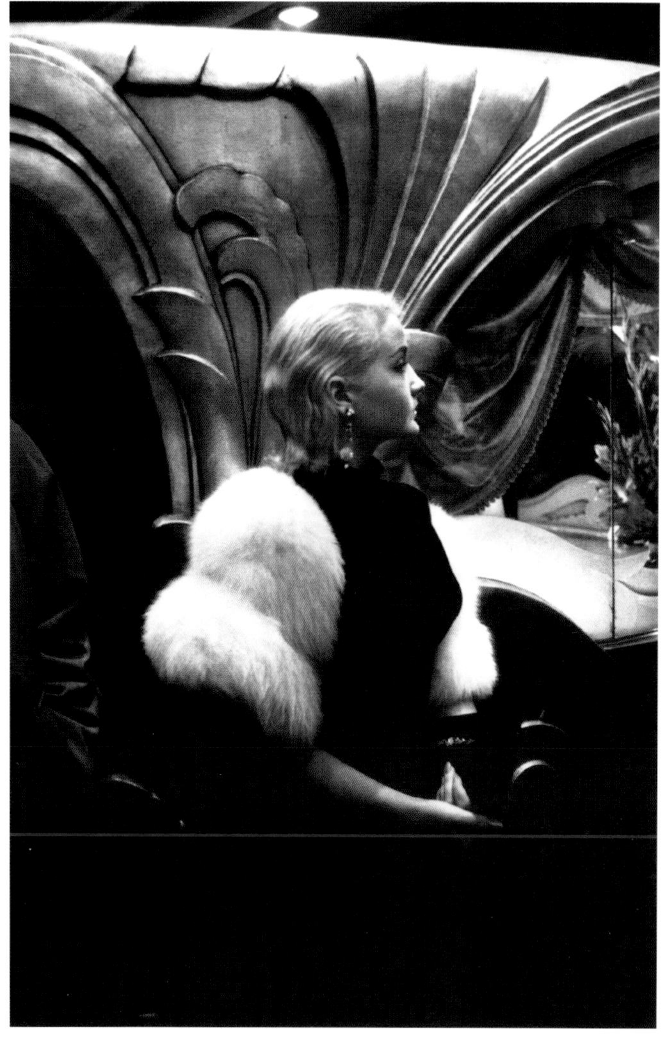

FIG. 219
Walker Evans
Girl in Fulton Street, New York, 1929,
printed later
Gelatin silver print, 24.1 x 16.5 cm
Yale University Art Gallery Purchase
1981.55.1

FIG. 220
Robert Frank
Movie Premiere, Hollywood, 1955
Gelatin silver print, 35.2 x 27.9 cm
Purchased with the aid of funds from
the National Endowment for the Arts
and the Susan Morse Hilles
Matching Fund
1981.4

On rare occasions, works of contemporary art have been commissioned by Yale. In 1968, Stuart Wrede, a graduate student in the Yale School of Architecture, approached several of his fellow students with the idea of commissioning a sculpture from Claes Oldenburg (B.F.A. 1951). Inspired by a statement by Herbert Marcuse to the effect that if any of Oldenburg's apparently unfeasible monuments were ever built—a huge banana in the center of Times Square, for example—it would signal the revolutionary end of society as we know it, and looking for a suitable protest against certain policies at Yale, Wrede and his colleagues decided to proceed. Together with Oldenburg, two faculty members from the architecture school (Vincent Scully and Charles Brewer), two art students, and a lawyer, they formed the Colossal Keepsake Corporation to oversee and implement the commission and make a gift of the work to Yale. The artist donated his time and the corporation paid for materials. The result was the famous *Lipstick* (fig. 221). In its original form, the red top of the lipstick was soft and inflatable. Officially titled *Lipstick (Ascending) on Caterpillar Tracks*, the sculpture has been described as a "barometer for the mood on campus," and a "stolid witness to the volatile nature of American history" in the decade of the 1960s.[12] Oldenburg chose Hewitt Quadrangle (also known as Beinecke Plaza), specifically a quadrant near Woodbridge Hall, which housed the President's office, as the site for his sculpture. Its design and location cloaked in secrecy until the day of its installation, the *Lipstick* immediately became the target of protesters. Nevertheless, it remained on its site until deterioration forced the artist to order it removed in 1970. In 1974, after long negotiations in which Alan Shestack, Vincent Scully, and Theodore Stebbins, curator of American painting, were especially active, it was returned to Yale, given to the Art Gallery, and installed in Morse College. It remains at Morse aside from occasional trips to other institutions as a loan for special exhibitions, including to the Gallery for its tercentennial exhibition.

Other special commissions include *Stacks* (1990; fig. 222), by Richard Serra, a very personal evocation of the use of the Art Gallery's Sculpture Hall as the art library during the artist's time at Yale, and *Wall Drawing* by Sol LeWitt (1993).

Several monographic exhibitions have advanced scholarship on major American artists, making significant contributions to the field. Helen A. Cooper organized *Eva Hesse: A Retrospective*, which was shown at Yale (fig. 223) and at the Hirshhorn Museum in Washington, D.C. Mixing Hesse's sculptures with her drawings and her own writing about her work, this exhibition remains fundamental to the study of the artist. Recently, Robert (B.F.A. 1961, M.F.A. 1963) and Sylvia Mangold (B.F.A. 1961) have donated a sculpture (*Untitled*) by Hesse (B.F.A. 1959) to the Gallery in Helen Cooper's honor, acknowledging the importance of both the artist and the exhibition and accompanying monograph.

Similarly, *Mel Bochner: Thought Made Visible, 1966–1973*, organized in 1995 by Richard S. Field, curator of prints, drawings, and photographs, and shown at Yale, Brussels, and Munich, was a major retrospective exhibition of Bochner's work accompanied by an equally comprehensive catalogue. Several of the works included in the Bochner exhibition have also entered the Gallery's collection. These two major exhibitions, both of which filled the entire first floor of the Kahn and Swartwout buildings, embody the high level of scholarship that has distinguished exhibitions both large and small that have been organized for decades by the Yale Art Gallery.

Occasionally a major addition to another branch of the University's collections has had a direct impact on the Gallery. The acquisition by the Beinecke Library of the archives of Filippo Tommaso Marinetti, the founder of Futurism, made Yale a center for the study of Futurism and stimulated interest in the Futurist Movement among faculty and students. Anne Coffin Hanson, John Hay Whitney Professor of History of Art, taught several graduate seminars on Futurism, and they developed into the Gallery's exhibition *The Futurist Imagination* (1983).[13] Focusing on Futurist graphic design and drawings, and drawing extensively from the Marinetti Archive, the exhibition featured work by many of the movement's other major participants, including Boccioni, Carrà, and Severini. Graduate students were directly involved in the exhibition: six wrote the catalogue essays, while others assisted with research. Work on the exhibition spawned another key relationship for the Gallery, that with Lydia Winston Malbin, who opened her home to the students and

FIG. 221
Claes T. Oldenburg
Lipstick (Ascending) on Caterpillar Tracks, 1969, reworked 1974
Painted steel body, aluminum tube and fiberglass tip, 670.6 x 594.4 x 332.7
Gift of the Colossal Keepsake Corporation
1974.86

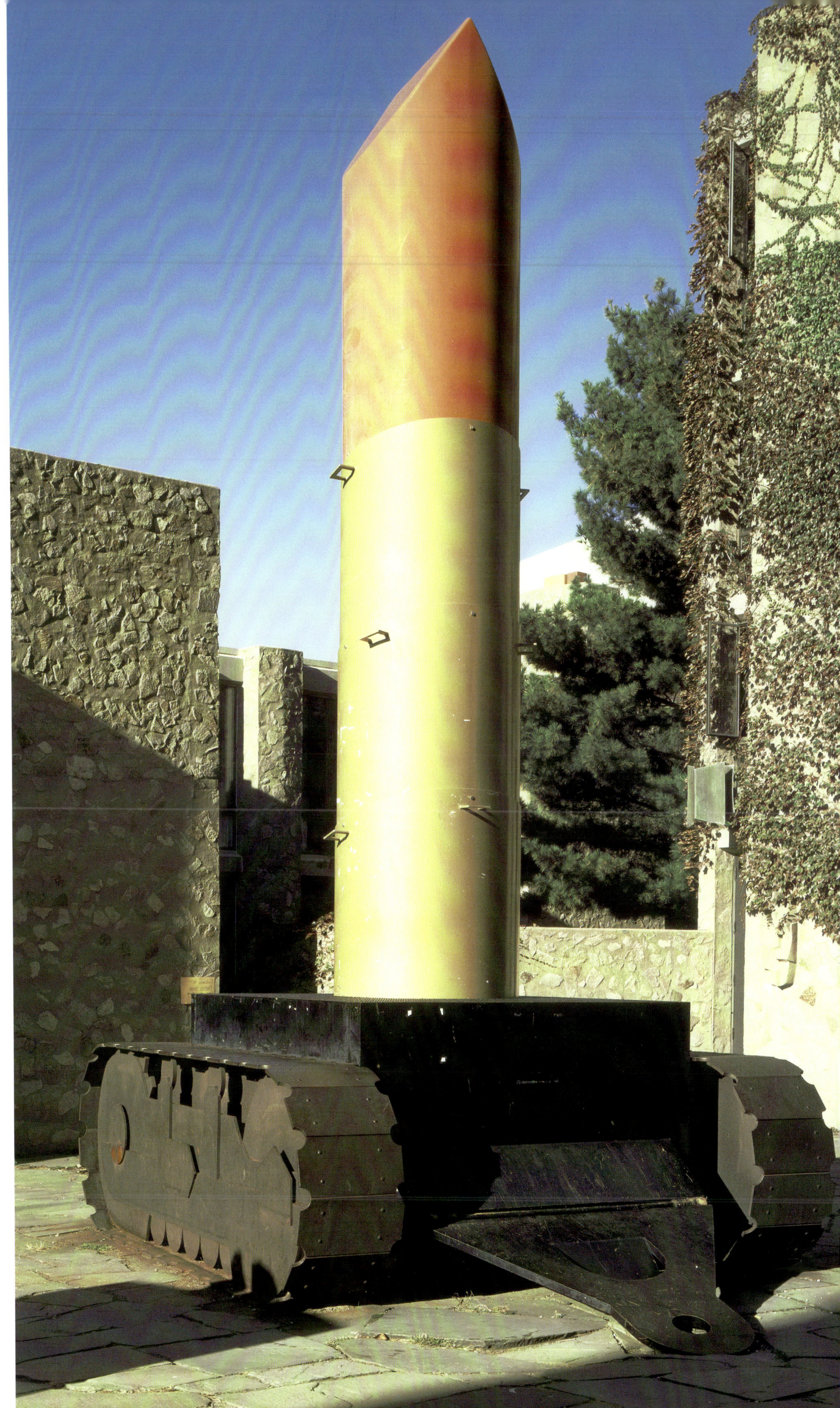

FIG. 222
Richard Serra
Stacks, 1990
Rolled steel, two elements, each
236 x 244 x 25 cm
The Katharine Ordway Fund
1990.2.1

lent generously to the exhibition from her extraordinary collection of Futurist material. Some years later, the Malbin Archive came to Yale, and in 1988 Professor Hanson, again working with a graduate student, William Valerio, organized an exhibition of works on paper from the Malbin collection, *The Graphic Art of Umberto Boccioni.*

Collections held by the other museums and the libraries at Yale have often been integral to and sometimes the focus of Gallery exhibitions. *Gifts to Osiris: Ancient Egyptian Art at Yale* (1987), which celebrated the publication of Gerry Scott's catalogue of Yale's Egyptian art, written while he was a graduate student working in the Gallery's ancient art department, drew heavily, as did the catalogue, on the collections of the Peabody Museum of Natural History. *Charles Demuth: Poster Portraits, 1923–1929* (1994) focused on the portraits and supporting documentation in the Beinecke Rare Book and Manuscript Library. The Beinecke Library, the Yale Center for British Art, the Lewis Walpole Library, and the Manuscripts and Archives Collection at Sterling Memorial Library have been extraordinary resources and generous lenders for many Gallery exhibitions, none more so than *Modern Gothic: The Revival of Medieval Art* (2000), the majority of which was drawn from these four collections in concert with that of the Gallery.

Arguably the exhibition that most closely linked the Gallery and its donors with the School of Art and its alumni was *Yale Collects Yale*, organized by Sasha Newman in 1993.[14] The idea for the exhibition—works of painting and sculpture created by Yale School of Art alumni that were in the collections of Yale alumni—was, in Newman's own words, "a preposterous one," but, as she also notes, "one that would probably not have been possible at any other institution." More than sixty Yale graduates holding degrees ranging from B.A., B.S., PH.D., LL.D., J.D., and M.D. to every variety of degree from the schools of art, architecture, and design lent more than 130 works of art by Yale artists. The exhibition revealed not only the extraordinary number of Yale artists who are at the top of the profession, but the continuation of a pattern of collecting among Yale alumni that is both prescient and brave. Many of the collectors and artists in the exhibition continue to be generous donors to the Gallery.

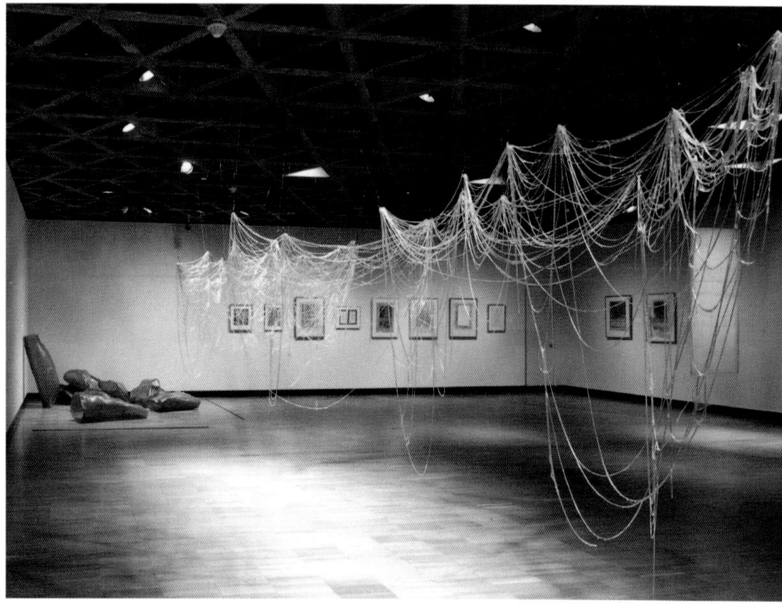

FIG. 223
Eva Hesse: A Retrospective, 1992
Photograph courtesy Yale University Art Gallery Archives

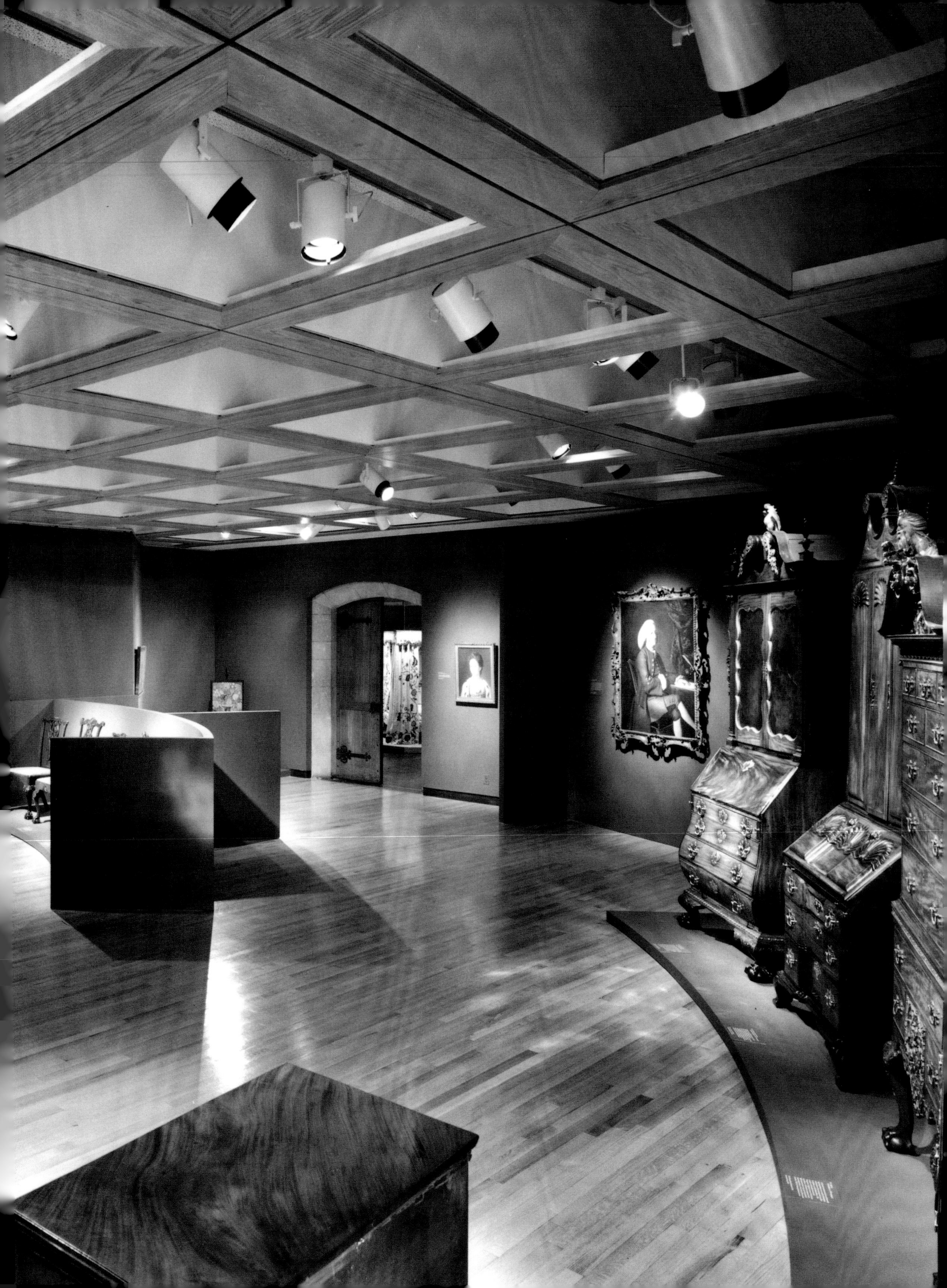

CHAPTER 14

"Towards Independence"

Other portions of the American collections were receiving attention in the late 1950s and 1960s. Mabel Brady Garvan provided significant financial support for the collections and programs, especially in the late 1950s. In 1959, at the urging of Mrs. Garvan, a special advisory committee on the Garvan Collection was formed as a subcommittee of the University Council Committee on the Art Gallery. The chairman of the committee, Irving S. Olds (B.A. 1907), wrote to Charles F. Montgomery, the director of the Henry Francis DuPont Winterthur Museum, in a letter inviting him to join—clear evidence linking Montgomery to the Garvan Collection more than a decade before he became its curator—that the committee was being formed "with a view to having the Garvan Collection serve the most useful purpose at Yale and carry out as far as possible the original objectives of the donors."[1] Serving on the committee in addition to Olds and Montgomery were Mrs. Garvan, her son Anthony N. B. Garvan, who was on the staff of the Smithsonian Institution, other museum professionals, collectors, Yale faculty, the director of the Gallery, and the curator of the Garvan Collection, Meyric Rogers. Mrs. Garvan and the Garvan Committee took an active role in the use and development of the Garvan Collection, urging its publication and ensuring its prominence at Yale and nationwide.

Meyric R. Rogers had been appointed curator of the Garvan and Related Collections only recently, in 1958; he held the post until he retired in 1964. Rogers had had a distinguished career as director of the Baltimore Museum of Art and the City Art Museum of St. Louis, and as curator of American decorative arts at the Art Institute of Chicago prior to coming to Yale. His *American Interior Design*, a survey of the development of decorative arts in the United States, appeared in 1947, and he had been visiting lecturer in the history of art at Yale in the winter of 1956. In 1960, he arranged a special installation of early American silver celebrating the thirtieth anniversary of the Garvan gift to Yale. Focusing on the silver and gold from the Garvan Collections, the installation also included complementary pieces of Garvan furniture and works in other media, as well as loans and gifts from other generous patrons.

At the time Rogers arrived, plans were under way to publish the Garvan Collections, and in order to facilitate

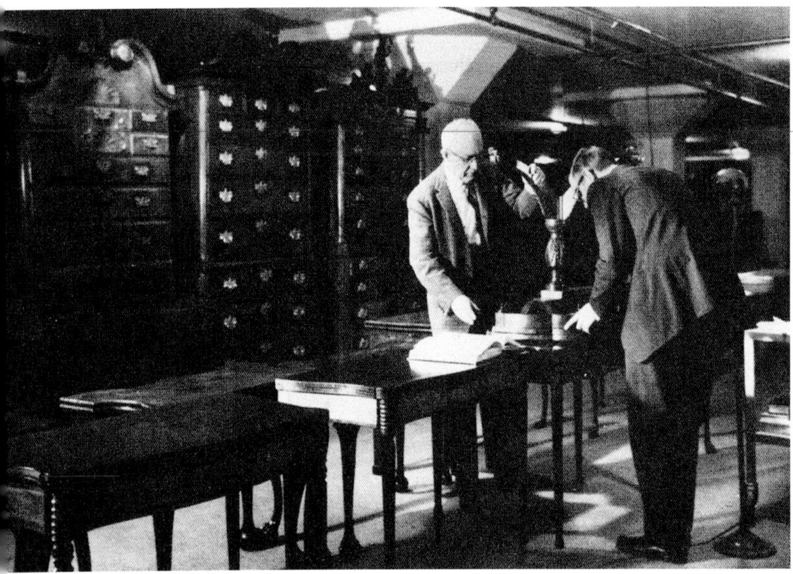

FIG. 224
Meyric Rogers and J. Kirk in the Furniture Study, ca. 1962
Photograph courtesy Yale University Art Gallery Archives

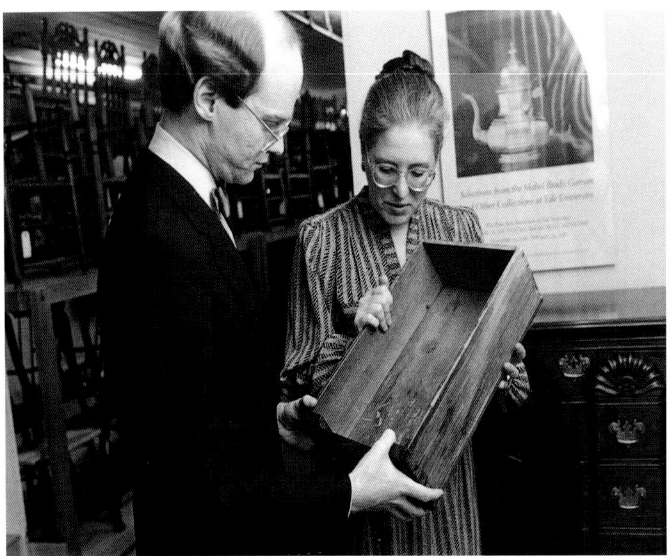

FIG. 224a
Patricia E. Kane and David L. Barquist in the Furniture Study, looking for signs of forgery, 1985
Photograph courtesy Yale University Art Gallery Archives

this project, it was determined to bring all of the Garvan pieces scattered around the country on loan to historic houses and other museums back to New Haven for study, research, and conservation. These several hundred objects could not be housed in existing Gallery storage or exhibition space in a way that would make examination, treatment, and study possible—a new and different kind of space was necessary for the collection. A 10,000-square-foot open space was found in the basement of the Yale University Press building, half a block away from the Gallery on York Street, and here Rogers created the Garvan Furniture Study in 1960/61 (figs. 224 and 224a). Rogers installed some 700–800 pieces of furniture in the new study facility, arranging them in rows by form and period, revealing the chronological development of style and technique and permitting detailed examination of each object.

Initially conceived as a research facility for those preparing the collection catalogues, the Garvan Furniture Study was immediately recognized as a superb teaching tool, and it has been used by Yale classes at all levels ever since. It now displays around 1,000 pieces of predominantly American furniture, including reproductions and fakes, and houses a conservation lab and a photography studio, serving visiting scholars and collectors as well as students. Loft-like in its flexibility as a space, the Furniture Study has been rearranged from time to time to adapt to changing teaching methods. On one occasion, in 1971, the students of the undergraduate course "History of Art 50b: Introduction to American Decorative Arts" organized an installation called *American Arts at Yale: 1971–1651*, arranging a selection of the furniture into groups that moved backward into time and showing related objects with it. This move toward what is now a standard process of "contextualization" was a departure from the traditional formal chronological display that preceded it, and it reflected the directions in which the faculty and curators (Jules Prown, Charles Montgomery, and Theodore Stebbins, Jr.) were going at the time. The Furniture Study has remained a fundamental resource for teaching and research at Yale, simultaneously a laboratory and a library of objects.

The drive to publish the Garvan Collection resulted in an initial catalogue of the pewter collection in 1965, but the intensive research and often time-consuming conservation needed for these objects meant that it was 1970 before the other catalogues began to appear. A two-volume catalogue of the silver was published in that year, followed by a four-volume catalogue of all of the furniture, completed in 1992. Complete checklists of American paintings and sculpture have also been published.[2]

Following the extraordinary additions to the American paintings collection that came with the Stephen Carlton Clark bequest in 1961, George Bellows's *The Rope*, or *Builders of Ships* was a gift to the collection in 1962, *Coney Island Beach* by Reginald Marsh was donated by his widow in 1963, and *Bob's Head Steer* by Georgia O'Keeffe was given in 1965. A Samuel F. B. Morse drawing of *Marpessa*, from a *Judgment of Jupiter*, was purchased with the John Hill Morgan Fund in 1963; a Childe Hassam watercolor, *Back of the Old House*, was given by Mr. and Mrs. George Hopper Fitch in 1969; and *Drawing*, 1946, by Arshile Gorky was given by Julien Levy in 1967.

Hiram Powers's *Greek Slave* was purchased in 1962 (fig. 225). Executed in 1851 for the villa of Russian Prince Demidoff, in San Donato, Italy, the Yale statue was the fifth version of Powers's 1844 image of a Christian Greek woman offered for sale in a Turkish market during the Greek war of independence. Powers said of what most considered his greatest work,

> I remembered reading an account of the atrocities committed by the Turks on the Greeks during the Greek revolution. . . . During the struggle the Turks took many prisoners, male and female, and among the latter were beautiful girls, who were sold in the slave markets of Turkey and Egypt. These were Christian women, and it is not difficult to imagine the distress and even despair of the sufferers while exposed to be sold to the highest bidders. But as there should be a moral in every work of art, I have given to the expression of the Greek Slave that trust there could still be in a Divine Providence for a future state of existence, with utter despair of the present, mingled with somewhat of scorn for all around her. She is too deeply concerned to be aware of her nakedness. It is not her person but her

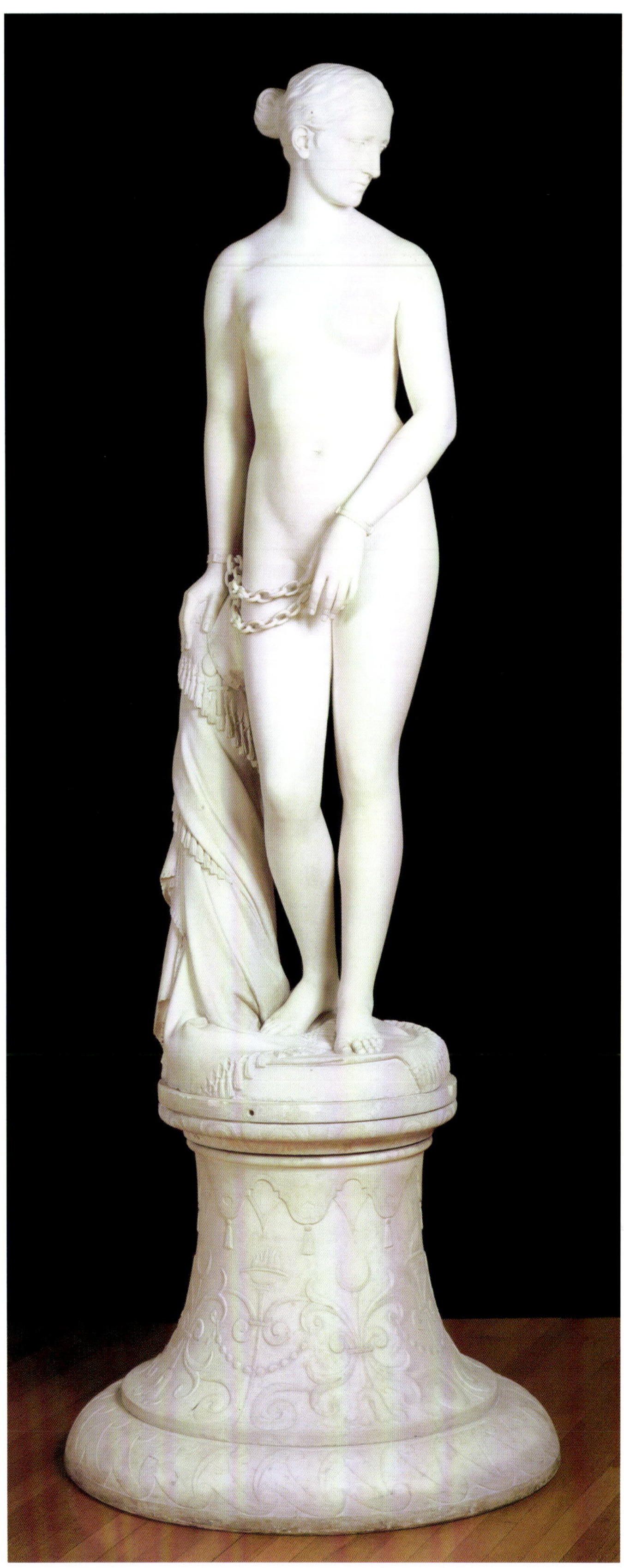

FIG. 225
Hiram Powers
The Greek Slave, 1851, after an original of 1844
Marble, 165.7 x 53.3 x 46.4 cm
Olive Louise Dann Fund
1962.43

spirit that stands exposed, and she bears it all as Christians only can.[3]

One of the most fabled works of American sculpture of the nineteenth century—it was displayed at the Crystal Palace Exhibition in London in 1851, and it was said that 50,000 visitors a day paid 25 cents to see it in one American showing—the *Greek Slave* was copied innumerable times for popular consumption. As one contemporary scholar has said, "By the end of the century, the *Greek Slave* had become synonymous with respectable, even staid, taste."[4] Henry James said of it, "so undressed, yet so refined, even so pensive, in sugar-white alabaster, exposed under little glass covers in such American homes as could bring themselves to think such things right."[5] It has also been called "American art's first anti-slavery document in marble."[6] It remains a key monument in American neoclassical art and one of the Gallery's most popular works.

In 1962/63 Jules David Prown (Hon. M.A. 1971) served as curator designate and in July 1963 became curator of the Garvan and Related Collections of American Art, succeeding Meyric Rogers, who retired in July of 1964 and continued as curator emeritus until 1971. Trained at Harvard, Jules Prown began teaching at Yale in 1961, and enjoyed a distinguished career as professor of history of art in the fields of British and American art and material culture. His particular prominence in the training of several generations of graduate students who have gone on to careers in teaching and museums was closely tied to his emphasis on teaching and learning from original works of art, which made him one of the most dedicated users of the Gallery's collections. As curator, Prown was responsible for American paintings and sculpture as well as decorative arts. In this role, he oversaw the major reinstallation of the American collections on the third floor of the Swartwout building in 1964, made possible by the transfer of the Jarves Collection from these galleries to the newly vacated third floor of the Kahn building. He also made the improvement of the records of the collection a priority, overseeing the completion of a card catalogue of American prints, and encouraged the completion of collection catalogues, started under Meyric Rogers at the instigation of Mabel Brady Garvan, including the catalogue of pewter by the new associate curator, Graham Hood, a catalogue of the silver completed by Graham Hood and Kathryn Buhler, and the start of a catalogue on furniture by the assistant curator, John Kirk. American painting and sculpture was to be incorporated into the general Gallery catalogue, planned to be published with a grant from the Ford Foundation.

Prown never stopped teaching, and this focus directed his thinking about the collections and their role in the academic program. In his report on the American collections to the Art Gallery Associates in May 1964, he outlined his view of the philosophy and policy of the use of the collections, a pioneering view that embraced the broader fields of American history and American material culture, was readily endorsed by the University, and became the basis for Yale's distinction in teaching American art:

> [The Gallery's policy] is based on a belief that collections such as these can be fruitfully used in teaching for the development of aesthetic sensibility among undergraduates—teaching them to use their eyes and to learn to enjoy the pleasures of seeing. It is further based on a conviction that art objects are a heritage of things from the past; that art objects are vehicles of ideas as well as pleasure, reflecting certain values, attitudes, and concepts of the people who made them; and that art objects are, therefore, important historical materials. Finally, it is felt that the history of American art is an important field of study within the broader context of Western art history, and it is believed that because of Yale's extensive and superb collections of American art, we are uniquely equipped to carry forth the study the history of American art here on both the undergraduate and graduate level.[7]

As Prown's philosophy for using the American collections embraced fields of study beyond the history of art, so, as he noted, did Yale's president, Kingman Brewster, recognize the value of the University's collections for its entire teaching program in a statement made in his inaugural address.[8]

In Prown's last year as curator, he organized the Gallery's penultimate major exhibition to date of art owned by Yale alumni, *American Art from Alumni Collections.* Drawn from the collections of sixty-five Yale alumni, among them Paul Mellon, Arthur G. Altschul, Henry J. Heinz II and his son H. John Heinz III, and John Hay Whitney, all major donors to the Gallery, the show included 144 paintings, drawings, watercolors, and sculptures by 96 artists. It covered the span of around 200 years from an anonymous portrait of James Pierpont of 1711 to *Club Night* by the Ashcan school painter George Bellows, and it included major works by well-known artists, among them Whistler, Mary Cassatt, John Singer Sargent, Benjamin West, and Winslow Homer. Prown, writing about the exhibition in *Art News,* stated that it "also includes a number of little known or recently discovered works by major artists and some fascinating paintings of high quality by virtually unknown artists," and "is intended to provide a resource for teaching and research in the field."[9] A graduate seminar of twelve students worked with these new discoveries and hidden treasures, researching attributions, dates, and style, using the exhibition as their laboratory as they prepared essays for publication. A picture book illustrating all of the works shown as well as a limited edition of a hardcover catalogue with full entries by the graduate students accompanied the exhibition.

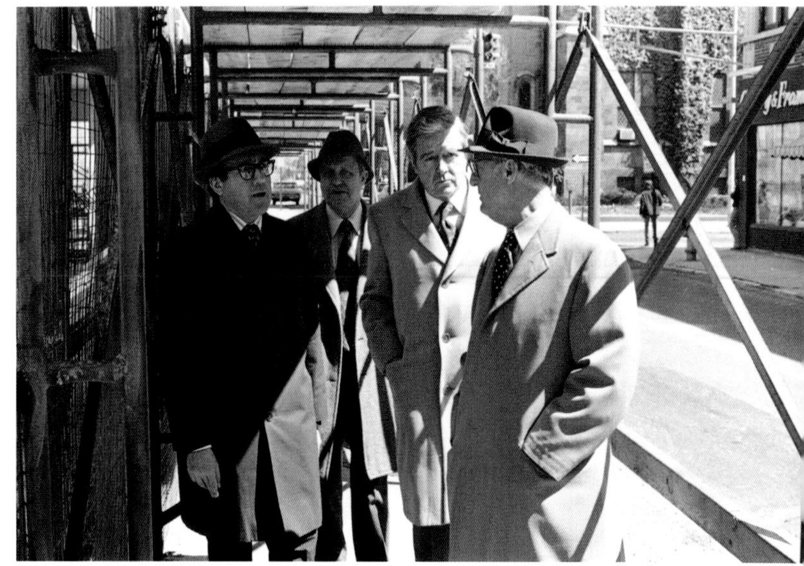

FIG. 226
Jules Prown, Louis Martz, Kingman Brewster, and Paul Mellon (left to right) during construction of the Yale Center for British Art, 1976/77
Photograph courtesy Yale University Art Gallery Archives

Prown has had the unique opportunity to serve as the director of both the Yale Center for British Art, a post he resigned his curatorship to assume in July 1968, and the Yale Art Gallery as interim director from June through December of 1994. The Yale Center for British Art, established as part of the extraordinary gift by Paul Mellon to Yale of his world-renowned collection of British art and designed as both a museum for the collection and a study center for British art, was a landmark in the history of Yale's collections and teaching mission. Architecturally, the center is the perfect complement to the Art Gallery: Louis I. Kahn's last museum stands directly across the street from his first. Given the close link between British and American art, the collections of the two institutions are complementary as well. As director of the BAC, Prown oversaw construction (fig. 226), and the building opened in 1977 with the inaugural exhibitions *The Pursuit of Happiness: A View of Life in Georgian England,* and *English Landscape*

Watercolors 1630–1850. Prown returned to teaching in 1975/76 and was named the Paul Mellon Professor of the History of Art in 1986.

The separate post of curator of American paintings, last held by John Hill Morgan until his death in 1945, was revived in 1971 with the division of the American departments into two parts (paintings and sculpture, and decorative arts) and the appointment of Theodore E. Stebbins, Jr. (B.A. 1960) as curator. In the interim, American paintings had been under the care of the curator of paintings, George Heard Hamilton, and then of Jules Prown, as part of the umbrella portfolio of the Garvan and Related Collections of American Art. Stebbins had been appointed as associate curator of the Garvan and Related Collections in 1968, succeeding Hood, and he continued in this capacity through the start of the term of the new curator of the Garvan Collections, Charles Montgomery.

In Stebbins's own view, the focus of his tenure as curator of American paintings (1971–77) was collection growth: "During this period special emphasis was placed on acquisition, particularly in the nineteenth century; the most serious gaps existed here, and it was apparent that they would have to be filled quickly or not at all. The major purchase was of Frederic E. Church's *Mt. Ktaadn* [fig. 227], and we also acquired fine landscapes by Gifford, Cole, Bierstadt and Durand, genre and figure subjects by Mount, Eastman Johnson, and Hovenden, and still lifes by Harnett, Vedder, and de Scott Evans, among others."[10] Such a campaign continued the Gallery's founding tradition of strength in American paintings, and responded effectively to the need to build a comprehensive American painting collection for teaching. At the same time, Stebbins was actively involved with teaching, research, exhibitions, and installations, and enjoyed a close collaboration with his colleagues in the American decorative arts department.

Charles F. Montgomery (Hon. M.A. 1970), appointed curator of the Garvan and Related Collections of American Art and professor of history of art in 1970, began his career at Yale in 1969 as a visiting lecturer. Montgomery came to Yale with impressive credentials as a scholar, teacher, and museum director, having published catalogues and dozens of articles on American furniture, silver, and other decorative arts, taught at the Universities of Pennsylvania and Delaware, and served as director at Wintherthur from 1954–61. *American Furniture: The Federal Period* remains a benchmark in the field. Committed to scholarship and teaching from original objects, Montgomery taught and mentored scores of students at Yale, training many of today's foremost teachers, curators, and collectors of American decorative arts. Alan Shestack said of him, "no other single individual has done so much to provide both popular and scholarly instruction in the American arts."[11] As impressive as was his knowledge about objects, Montgomery was probably most engaging as a teacher because he loved objects and responded to them first on an emotional level, a contagious passion that inspired students and collectors alike. In "Some Remarks on the Practice and Science of Connoisseurship,"[12] he stated, "When first looking at an object, it is important to let oneself go and try to get a sensual reaction to it. I ask myself: Do I enjoy it? Does it automatically ring true? Does it sing to me?" Going on to study material, form, style, skill and workmanship, attribution, date, condition, context, and history of ownership, he concluded with questions for the connoisseur that could as readily apply to any type of object or work of art: "Is it important as a thing of beauty? Is it rare, typical, or illustrative of the culture that produced it?" Although written for collectors, these questions were at the heart of Montgomery's teaching, and they inspired his exhibitions and scholarship as well.

Not long after beginning his tenure as curator, Montgomery began planning a complete reinstallation of the American collections. Funded by Mabel Brady Garvan, the project was inspired by Mrs. Garvan's wish to have more of the collection on view. No additional space was to be allotted to the collection, however, so Montgomery turned to the design firm of Chermayeff and Geismar and the architectural firm the Cambridge Seven to devise a way to get more material into the existing space. Working with Patricia E. Kane and Margaretta Lovell, specializing in the decorative arts collections, and Theodore Stebbins, curator of American paintings, Montgomery created a pioneering contextual installation of American art entitled *American Arts and the American Experience* (fig. 228). This installation was nothing short of revolutionary in the way in

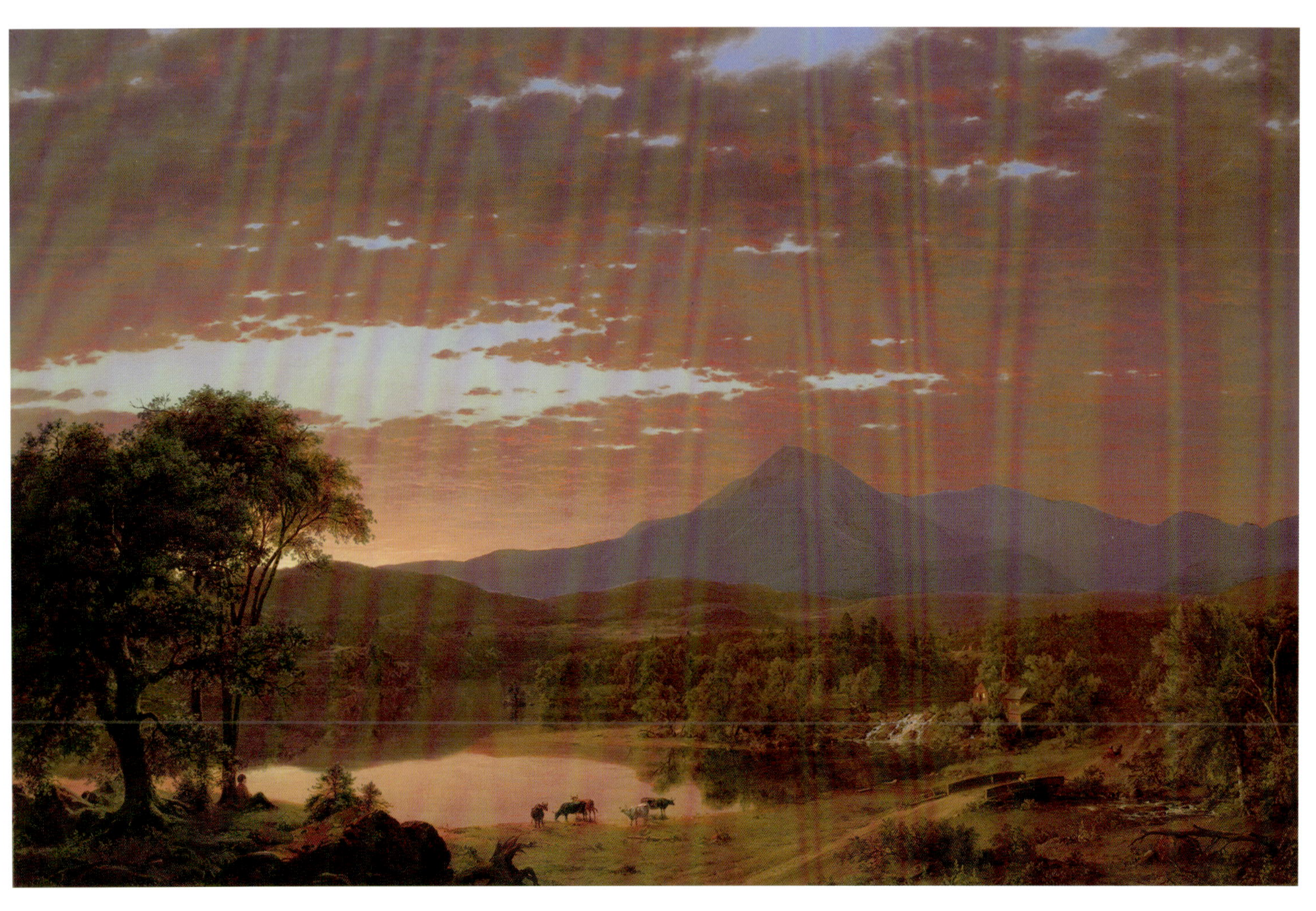

FIG. 227
Frederic Edwin Church
Mt. Ktaadn, 1853
Oil on canvas, 92.1 x 140.3 cm
Stanley B. Resor, B.A. 1901, Fund
1969.71

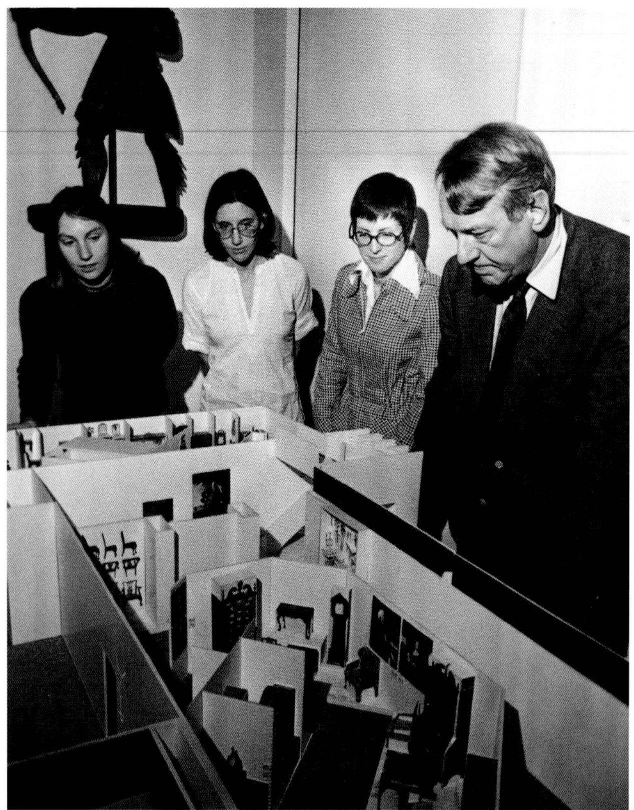

FIG. 228
Charles F. Montgomery, Patricia Kane, Louise Lippincott, and Margaretta Lovell (right to left) with the model for the installation, 1973
Photograph courtesy Yale University Art Gallery Archives

which decorative arts were displayed (figs. 229 and 230). It was called an "extraordinary installation" by Hilton Kramer, in his review for the *New York Times*.[13] Chermayeff was best known as a graphic designer, and the installation had, as was often noted, the feeling of a page layout, with furniture mounted on walls in arrangements that evoked, in Kramer's words, "the pages of a mail-order catalogue. . . . In a single display area devoted to 10 Windsor chairs of the 18th and early 19th century, for example, only two chairs sit on the floor of the display area, while the others are attached to the walls of the enclosure in rising tiers."[14] As striking and even unsettling as this was visually, it had a significant didactic purpose, allowing the viewer to examine not only the way a chair, for example, was used, but, by being able to view its underside, how it was made. Chermayeff's design also permitted the display of a far greater number of objects than had been possible in the same space with traditional exhibition techniques—some 1,500 objects in all, double what had been there before. Among the space-saving techniques used in the installation was another "first," the adaptation of a Remington Rand "Lektriever," a set of shelves designed to revolve like a Ferris wheel that was normally used to store office files, to display dozens of spoons, teapots, tankards, mugs, and other flatware and small objects, in a space no larger than a tall closet. Looking through a window at a shelf of objects, the visitor could view shelf after shelf with the push of a button.

Similarly revolutionary was the rejection of traditional period rooms in favor of a mazelike sequence of intimate whitewashed spaces combining furniture and silver and other small objects with paintings and interpretive material. Instead of a series of individual rooms each requiring the visitor to stop and enter, there was a continuous flow of space and time. Conceived with the goal of making as much of the collection accessible to students as possible and exploiting the sheer number of objects on view to display them in ways that would allow maximum study of each without handling it, the Montgomery/Chermayeff installation was first and foremost a teaching enterprise. Considered by Kramer and others as less sympathetic to the paintings than to the three-dimensional works, the Chermayeff design was particularly influential on installations of decorative arts

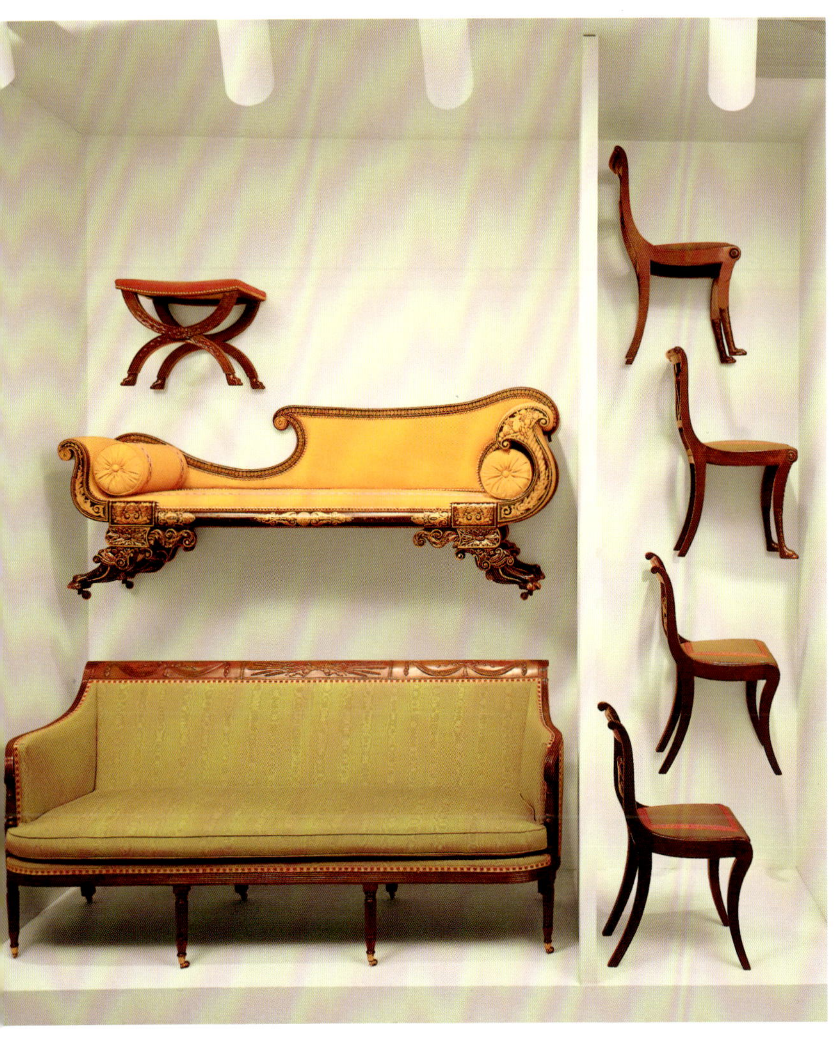

FIG. 229
Chermayeff and Geismar and the Cambridge Seven, designers
American Arts and the American Experience installation, 1973
Photograph courtesy Yale University Art Gallery Archives

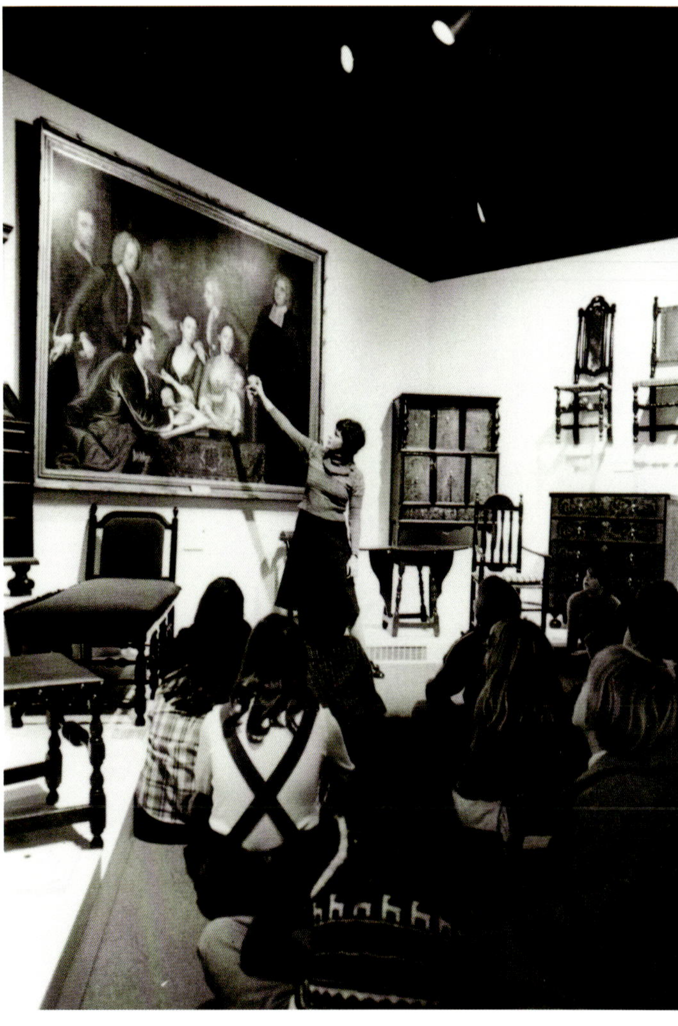

FIG. 230
Janet Saleh Dickson, Curator of Education, teaching in the new installation
Photograph courtesy Yale University Art Gallery Archives

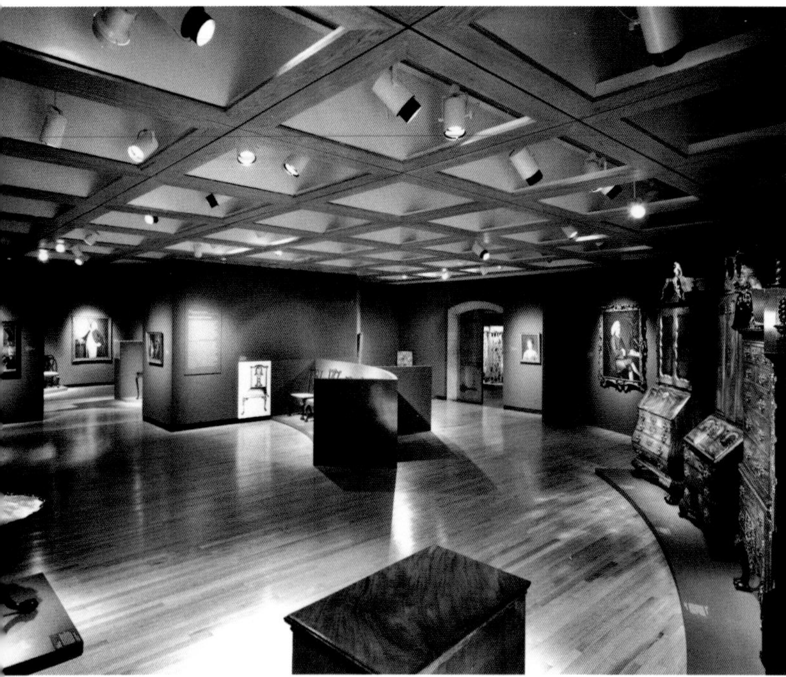

FIG. 231
American Art: 1750–1800, Towards Independence, 1976
Photograph courtesy Yale University Art Gallery Archives

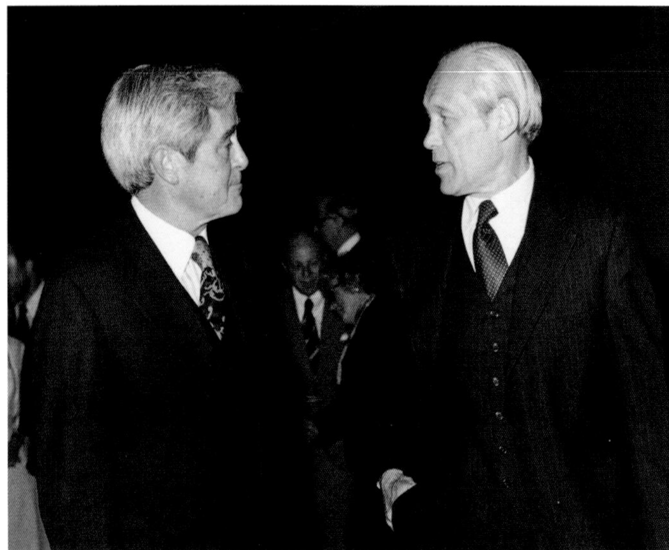

FIG. 231a
Yale President Kingman Brewster (left) and Robert McNeil at the opening of *Towards Independence*
Photograph courtesy Yale University Art Gallery Archives

in other museums. The installation remained on view until 2000.

Montgomery was also intense in his efforts to add to the collections through gift and purchase, to ensure the care of the collection through securing funding from the Dobson Foundation for conservation of the decorative arts, and to continue work on the publication of the collection catalogues begun under Rogers and continued under Prown. Catalogues published during Montgomery's tenure included Edwin A. Battison and Patricia E. Kane, *The American Clock, 1725–1865*, and Patricia E. Kane, *300 Years of American Seating Furniture*.[15] Among the outstanding acquisitions during Montgomery's tenure were important additions to the pewter collection, a special interest of his, notably two early dishes by Edmund and John Dolbeare.

TOWARDS INDEPENDENCE

The bicentennial of the United States was marked at the Gallery by an unprecedented special exhibition of American art. At the invitation of Sir John Pope-Hennessy, the Yale University Art Gallery organized *American Art: 1750–1800, Towards Independence* (fig. 231 and 231a), to be shown during the bicentennial year at Yale and at the Victoria and Albert Museum in London. This was the first major exhibition of eighteenth-century American art to be shown in London. Although nearly one-fifth of the exhibition came from the Yale collection, Her Majesty the Queen, the British Museum, and sixty-seven public and private collections from all over America also lent objects to it.

The choice of Yale to organize such an exhibition was an obvious one. First, Yale had been in the forefront of collecting American art since well before 1776, and it was well known for having one of the best collections of American art in the world. Second, the Gallery had a distinguished tradition of scholarship in the field, ensuring that the exhibition and its catalogue would make a significant contribution to scholarship. Third, through the British Art Center in New Haven and its affiliate, the Paul Mellon Centre for British Art in London, Yale was a major center for British scholarship in America.

A Yale steering committee consisting of Charles Montgomery, Jules Prown, and Theodore Stebbins planned the exhibition and selected the objects. John Walker, former director of the National Gallery in Washington, and Roy Strong, who succeeded Pope-Hennessey as director of the Victoria and Albert Museum, were instrumental in securing loans. The project was carried out by a characteristically broad and creative team of Art Gallery staff, students, and faculty, consisting of the steering committee; Patricia E. Kane, associate curator of American decorative arts, who was co–general editor with Montgomery; Frank Goodyear, Jr., curator, Pennsylvania Academy of the Fine Arts and acting curator of American paintings at Yale during 1974–75; Margaretta Lovell, curatorial assistant in the department of American decorative arts; and several graduate students and interns. Much of the research for the catalogue was done in a graduate seminar taught at the Gallery by Charles Montgomery. It seems to have been a key experience for many of these students, encouraging them to go on to museum careers.

The goal of the exhibition, as Alan Shestack wrote in his introduction to the catalogue, "was to bring together over two hundred works of art to demonstrate the excellence and variety of artistic production in America during the years of transition from the late colonial period to that of independence, and also to suggest how certain characteristics intrinsic to American art reflect some different aspects of the American national character."[16] Including paintings, prints, drawings, furniture, silver, glass, ceramics, metalwork, and textiles, the exhibition showed the range and diversity of American art. In decorative arts it examined such ideas as the difference between "city" and "country" styles and "functional" vs. "ornamental" design, while in paintings and drawings it explored the values and ideals of American society as it marched toward independence. On every level, as Jules Prown pointed out in his catalogue essay, the change of style in American art as a result of independence is dramatic, a complete shift from European rococo to neoclassical, sensuous worldly visual delights transformed into austere abstractions. The catalogue served both as an introduction for the British public to this and other fundamentals of American art and culture between 1750 and 1800 and as a historical narrative of each major category of American art, illustrated by the individual works in the exhibition.

AFTERMATH

Less than two years after the close of *Towards Independence*, Charles Montgomery died. At the time of his death, which was totally unexpected, he was in the midst of his next major exhibition project, *Silver in American Life*. The exhibition was being organized in conjunction with the American Federation of Arts, and it was designed to travel to a dozen museums in the United States and Canada. Like *Towards Independence*, this exhibition had something of a missionary purpose. The Gallery wanted to share some of its magnificent American collection with communities across the country. It also wanted to tell the story of American silver as completely as possible, and the extraordinary scope of the Yale collection placed the Gallery in an ideal position to accomplish this goal. It was a particularly fitting project for the Gallery because of the goals that Francis Garvan had expressed for his collection when he gave it to Yale, namely that it "should be mobilized and circulated throughout the country" so that it could be "rendered more accessible." It was in this spirit that Charles Montgomery conceived the exhibition and in the same spirit that Gerald W. R. Ward and Barbara McLean Ward, who had been working closely with Montgomery on the project, undertook to complete it in memory of their mentor.

The exhibition addressed every aspect of the use, study, and appreciation of American silver, from ores, mining, and refining, through tools and workshop practices, trade, craft, mechanization, function, money, religion, jewelry, and style. It included furniture as a context for the silver, providing an opportunity for a tea service to be displayed on a suitable tea table and for a cupboard to be arranged in a display of the family's treasures. "Smitten with silver fever," as Mark Twain described the frenzied Nevada silver miners, thousands of visitors came to the exhibition in twelve cities between 1979 and 1982 before much of the heart of Yale's collection returned to New Haven, Mr. Garvan's wishes creditably honored.

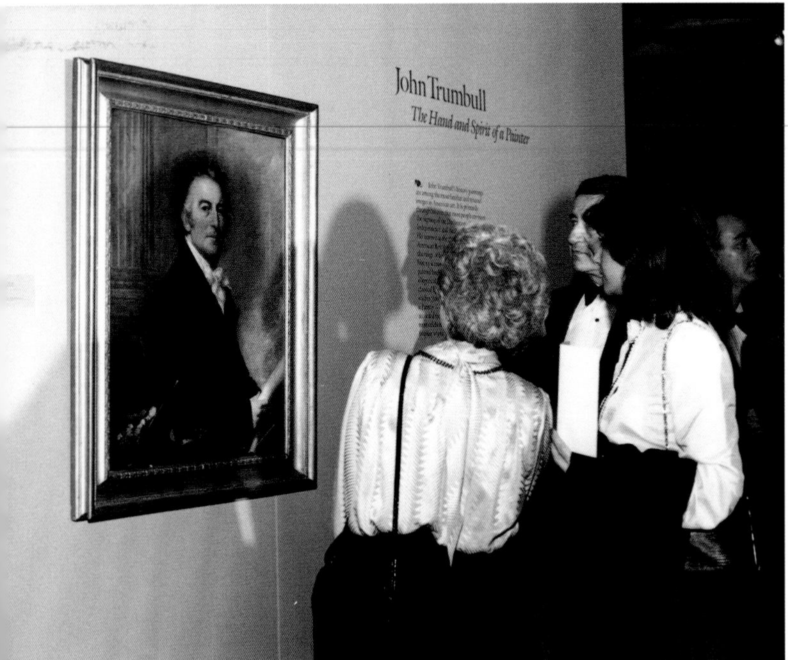

FIG. 232
John Trumbull: The Hand and Spirit of a Painter, 1982
Photograph courtesy Yale University Art Gallery Archives

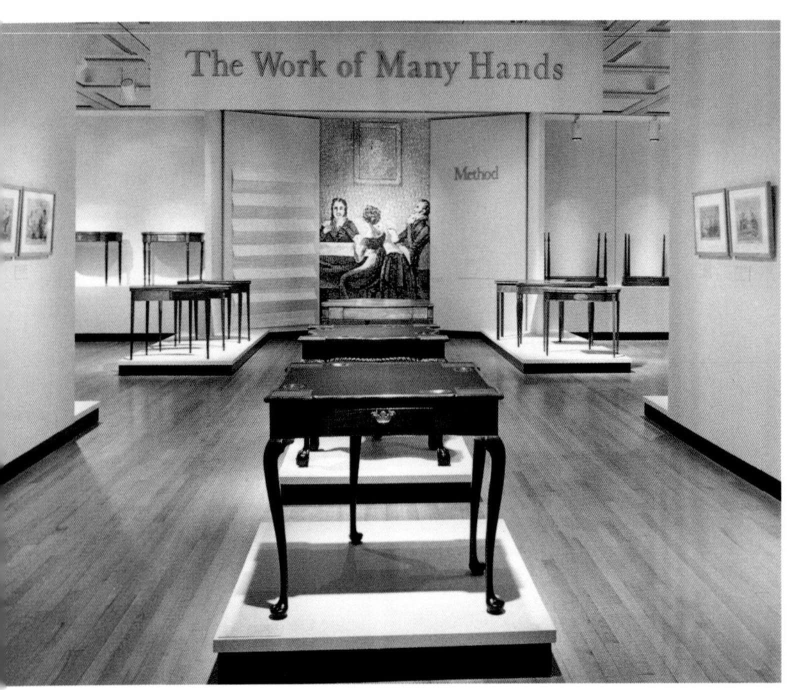

FIG. 233
The Work of Many Hands: Card Tables in Federal America 1790–1820, 1982
Photograph courtesy Yale University Art Gallery Archives

AMERICAN ARTS IN THE 1980S AND 1990S

Charles F. Montgomery was commemorated in 1980 with the establishment in the Department of History of Art of a professorship of American decorative arts named in his honor. The first endowed chair in this field in America, the named professorship recognizes Montgomery's dedication to scholarship and his extraordinary success in teaching from original objects in a museum setting. Like John Marshall Phillips before him, Montgomery trained a generation of scholars and curators in the field, using a collection of the highest quality to teach scholarship of the highest standard. Funded by a gift from Mr. and Mrs. Robert L. McNeil, Jr. (B.S. 1936; fig. 231a), the professorship ensures that decorative arts will be a permanent part of the Yale curriculum. The simultaneous establishment of the Center for the Study of American Art and Material Culture, also funded by the McNeils and headed by the Montgomery professor, responded to Robert McNeil's wish, as described by Alan Shestack in his report to the Garvan Committee, that his gift be "a stimulus to utilizing works of art as cultural documents, . . . to coordinate Art Gallery activities and collections with other related areas, especially American History and Literature, but not excluding subjects such as technology and economics, . . . [and] to integrate the Garvan Collection more thoroughly with humanistic teaching in the American field."[17] It has provided a continuing forum for faculty, museum professionals, and graduate students from fields including history of art, American studies, anthropology, archaeology, architecture, religious studies, geophysics, and applied mechanics to discuss shared interests and develop collegial projects for research, publication, and exhibition.

Throughout the decade of the 1980s, the American arts department carried out an exceptional number of exhibition and publication projects. In 1982, the major monographic exhibition *John Trumbull: The Hand and Spirit of a Painter* (fig. 232), curated by Helen A. Cooper, drew on faculty and students in all branches of American studies at Yale to create a dialogue among disciplines that would result in a complete picture of Trumbull, his career, and his art. Jules Prown taught a graduate seminar on Trumbull while the exhibition was being put up, giving the students the chance to examine the paintings in detail, including their backs, many of which still preserved their numbers from the original hanging in the Trumbull Gallery in 1832. Honoring Trumbull in 1982 could not fail to be a suitable celebration of the sesquecentennial of the Gallery. The exhibition brought a number of significant gifts into the collection, including a self-portrait of the artist from 1802.

The Work of Many Hands: Card Tables in Federal America 1790–1820 (fig. 233), curated by Benjamin Hewitt, Gerald W. R. Ward, and Patricia E. Kane, took place the same year, also honoring the Gallery's 150th anniversary. As Alan Shestack wrote in the director's foreword, "One of the primary functions of a university museum is to present exhibitions which are the result of important new research. [This exhibition] breaks new ground in the field of American decorative arts. Based on Benjamin Hewitt's ten-year computer study of one specific furniture form, it is unprecedented in its statistical method of analyzing American furniture."[18] Inspired by Charles Montgomery's *American Furniture: The Federal Period*, Hewitt, a psychologist as well as a collector, adapted scientific analysis to the study of furniture, using a consistent set of characteristics to analyze each table. Tabulating the results permitted the definition of regional workshops and the attribution of undocumented tables to them. *The Work of Many Hands* became a prototype for subsequent studies of other types of furniture; it was a pioneering step in what is now a standard computer-based method of study.

Exhibitions originating in seminars or organized by graduate students have often shaped their careers. Two exhibitions of American prints organized in 1983 and 1985 directed the path of one doctoral candidate, Rebecca Zurier, for example, and led to scholarly recognition and a teaching career. The first, *American Prints, 1900–1950*, which grew out of a seminar taught by Richard S. Field, curator of prints, drawings, and photographs, featured the gifts of John P. Axelrod (B.A. 1968). In the exhibition, Field aimed to present a unified view of American printmaking of the period, maintaining that "almost all American prints of 1900–1950 presented recognizable images of America to a broad public, and further, that the vast majority of these prints were informed by the subjects, techniques, styles, and even the audiences of the illustrator."[19] This thesis divided American and European print scholars. Axelrod welcomed the dispute: "A little controversy never hurt an exhibition."[20] Zurier, part of the seminar, wrote an essay for the catalogue. The second exhibition, *Art for "The Masses" (1911–1917): A Radical Magazine and Its Graphics*, was curated by Zurier. It featured a Greenwich Village–based magazine whose graphics were a virtual portfolio of works by the Ashcan school. As a result of this exhibition Zurier has specialized in the Ashcan school, later producing an exhibition on Ashcan artists for the Smithsonian Institution. *At Home in Manhattan: Modern Decorative Arts, 1925 to the Depression*, was also organized by a graduate student, Karen Lucic (then Davies). Exploring a neglected period in American decorative arts as revealed in the primary sources of the period, *At Home in Manhattan* was the first major exhibition devoted to American design of the modern era. Lucic has gone on to become one of the foremost experts in this field.

Two exhibitions on the work of Winslow Homer, *The Croquet Game* and *Winslow Homer Watercolors,* were shown in 1984 and 1986. The first initiated a series of "single-subject exhibitions" that have included *Charles Demuth: Poster Portraits 1923–1929*, *Childe Hassam: An Island Garden Revisited*, and *Thomas Eakins: The Rowing Pictures*. Both of the Homer exhibitions were organized by Helen A. Cooper, Holcombe T. Green Curator of American Painting and Sculpture. *Winslow Homer Watercolors* celebrated the 150th anniversary of the artist's birth, and it presented the largest selection of Homer watercolors ever offered for public view. Shown first at the National Gallery and the Amon Carter Museum, *Winslow Homer Watercolors* met with critical praise as well as public acclaim. At Yale, the Homer watercolors exhibition was a true blockbuster, with visitors lined up around the corner onto High Street waiting to get in. *Charles Demuth: Poster Portraits*, organized by Robin Jaffee Frank, associate curator of American Paintings and Sculpture, was described by the *New York Times* as a "blockbuster disguised as a small show."[21] The exhibition offered important new insights into Demuth's work through the examination of the literary context of the portraits, made possible by the rich collections of the Beinecke Rare Book and Manuscript

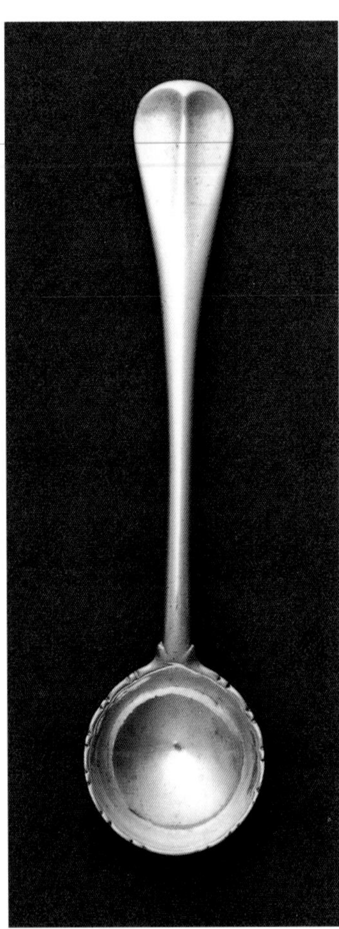

FIG. 234
Samuel Minott
Salt Spoon, ca. 1775
Silver, L. 91 mm
Gift of Philip M. Kossack
1985.87.1371

Library at Yale, generously loaned to the Gallery on this as on many other occasions.

In 1992, the Yale University Art Gallery collaborated with the Thomas Gilcrease Institute of American History and Art in Tulsa, Oklahoma, to create the important and provocative exhibition of American landscape painting *Discovered Lands, Invented Pasts: Transforming Visions of the American West.*[22] Focusing on the "discovery" that Europeans and Americans viewed themselves as making of the American West and the wonder that it inspired, on the erasure of Native American and other non-European peoples and women and the physical manifestations of Euroamerican settlement from paintings to preserve the idea of a pristine wilderness, and on the invention of a past that would define the term "American" for the various peoples who inhabited these western lands, the exhibition raised complex and difficult questions about American identity and the content of American landscape painting. The emphasis on American landscape paintings as constructions expressing specific ideas rather than factual reports and the new readings and revisionist interpretations of many chestnuts of American painting that resulted from this exhibition sparked heated discussion and often dispute in the field, but many of the issues raised remain at the heart of research and thought about American art today. Helen A. Cooper organized the exhibition, which was developed in conjunction with the book written by an interdisciplinary team from Yale (Jules D. Prown, Howard R. Lamar, William Cronon, and Susan Prendergast Schoelwer); the National Gallery of Art (Nancy K. Anderson); Amherst College (Martha A. Sandweiss); and the University of Victoria, British Columbia (Brian W. Dippie), in collaboration with George Miles, curator of the Yale Collection of Western Americana in the Beinecke Rare Book and Manuscript Library, an institution whose partnership was fundamental to the success of the project.

Scholarship and the growth of collections go hand in hand in the Gallery, and this has certainly been the case in American art. The permanent collection has been considerably enriched as a scholarly resource beginning in 1984 by the donations of more than 7,000 pieces of American silver flatware and other objects by Carl R. Kossack (B.S. 1931, M.A. 1933) and his sons

Frederick, Alan, and Philip (fig. 234). In a 1988 exhibition of Kossack silver organized by Patricia E. Kane, curator of American decorative arts, David L. Barquist, associate curator of American decorative arts, and Aline L. Zeno, two hundred of the pieces were shown, including spoons, tongs, platters, pitchers, toast racks, fish slicers, and pocket watches. Rita Reif, reviewing the exhibition for the *New York Times*, called it "a notable collection, amassed on a teacher's salary."[23] Reif quotes Kossack, who was a professor of mathematics at Southern Connecticut State University in New Haven until his retirement in 1976, on the formation of his collection: "I began buying silver right after World War II. . . . I have always had a subscription to the Metropolitan Opera, and we would come in early before the Saturday matinee to browse in the silver shops of 47th Street."[24] His first purchase was a German tankard, but he soon concentrated exclusively on American silver, which was both more plentiful and more reasonably priced. Although Kossack's collecting methods might not seem systematic to a curator—"You never know what you are going to find, so it is not a good idea to look for only the work of a certain silversmith or period. Wherever you go, you look in every shop, and that's how you find things unexpectedly"[25]—the results have been no less productive. According to Kane, more than half of the makers in the Kossack Collection are new to Yale's holdings, and the Kossack Collection contains several previously unknown forms as well as previously unrecognized variant maker's marks used by known silversmiths. The daunting scale of the collection is a significant part of its value for teaching and research, and its encyclopedic nature makes it what Kane has described as "the single most important source of primary evidence relating to nineteenth-century American silver."[26] A resource for scholars of silver and the certain source for new and revised information on individual makers, the collection is of equal value for the teaching of broader issues relating the silversmith's craft to the social history of the nineteenth century.

Continuing the tradition of scholarship in American decorative arts that has seen catalogues and checklists published from 1973 through 1992 on chairs, looking-glasses, case furniture, tables, pewter, clocks, paintings, and sculpture in the Yale collection, in 1998 Patricia E. Kane published the monumental study *Colonial Massachusetts Silversmiths and Jewelers: A Biographical Dictionary Based on the Notes of Francis Hill Bigelow & John Marshall Phillips*, a volume that draws heavily on the Kossack Collection. The American miniatures have been exhaustively studied by Robin Jaffee Frank, resulting in the traveling exhibition *Love and Loss: American Portrait and Mourning Miniatures* in 2000, the promised bequest of an important collection of mourning miniatures by Devida Deutsch, and a forthcoming catalogue of the entire collection. In 2001, David L. Barquist organized the traveling exhibition *Myer Myers: Jewish Silversmith in Colonial New York*. Based on his Yale dissertation, the exhibition and catalogue provide the first comprehensive scholarly study of the artist and his times.

Exhibitions featuring important collections of American art have enriched the Gallery's teaching program. Notable among these was *A Private View: American Paintings from the Manoogian Collection* (fig. 235), organized by Helen A. Cooper and Nancy Rivard Shaw, curator of American art at the Detroit Institute of Arts, and shown at these museums and at the High Museum in Atlanta in 1993. Richard Manoogian (B.A. 1958) and his wife, Jane, have formed an exemplary collection of American paintings. Beginning in the 1970s with contemporary art, the Manoogians ultimately focused on nineteenth-century American painting, assembling what the exhibition curators described as a collection that "follows in the proud tradition of earlier private collections of American art."[27] The collection includes paintings by many of the best-known American artists—Thomas Cole, Albert Bierstadt, Thomas Moran, Raphaelle Peale, Martin Johnson Heade, John Singer Sargent, William Merritt Chase, and Childe Hassam. Joining the curators in writing for the exhibition catalogue was a talented group of graduate students, a number of whom have gone on to museum careers.

George Hopper Fitch (B.A. 1932) has been one of the Gallery's most generous donors and loyal advisers for nearly fifty years, and a member of the Gallery's Governing Board since 1972. Two exhibitions, in 1980 and 1997, have celebrated his extraordinary gifts of American twentieth-century watercolors to Yale.[28] Beginning with his gift of a watercolor by George Grosz

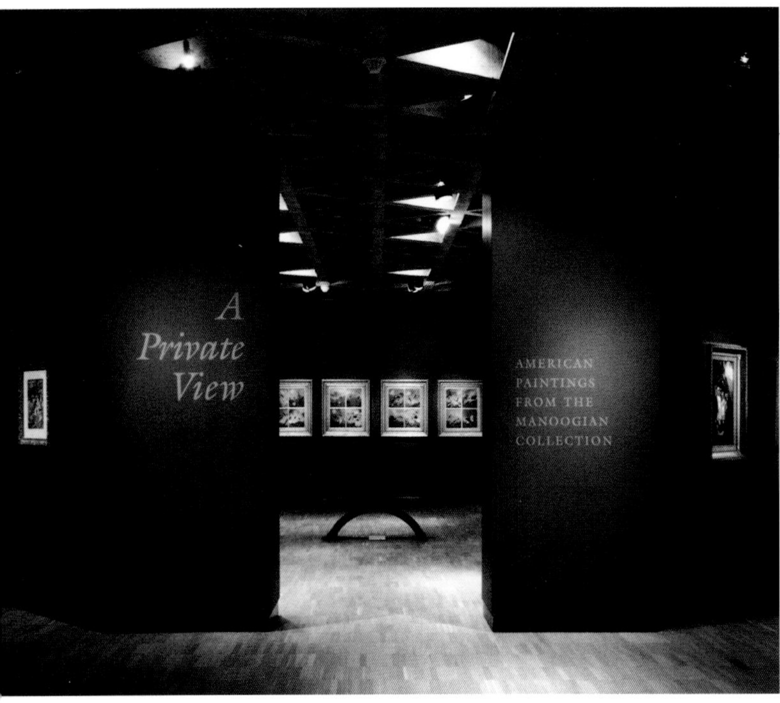

FIG. 235
A Private View: American Paintings from the Manoogian Collection, 1993
Photograph courtesy Yale University Art Gallery Archives

in 1953, George Hopper Fitch has donated dozens of watercolors (fig. 236), drawings, and prints, and hundreds of photographs to the Gallery, enriching both its collections and its teaching program. Splendid watercolors by O'Keeffe, Sheeler, Hopper (fig. 154), Prendergast, Hassam, Hartley, and many others have been presented to the Gallery, transforming the collection. He was encouraged at first to make these gifts by his second wife, Muriel, who told him, "George, get rid of all those things under your bed and let the students learn from them." "Give a thing and it is yours forever," was his statement at the opening of the 1980 exhibition of his gifts, expressing the philosophy that has guided his generosity to Yale. These words became the title of the 1997 exhibition organized by Elisabeth Hodermarsky, assistant curator of prints, drawings, and photographs, honoring George Hopper Fitch on the occasion of his sixty-fifth reunion at Yale.

A remarkable gift of nineteen American landscape and genre paintings was made in the early days of 1992 by Teresa Heinz in memory of her husband, Senator H. John Heinz III (B.A. 1960). As Mary Gardner Neill described in her director's report in the Gallery *Bulletin*, paintings included in the gift, "like Francis Edmonds' *The Organ Grinder* (fig. 237) and Francis Guy's *Utilizing a Spare Moment*, with their depictions of the joys and virtues of simple life, were immensely popular in their own day and will be central to any discussion of the pre–Civil War period in History of Art and American History classes. Landscapes range from the dark, evocative mystery of a George Inness to the pastoral calm of a Jasper Cropsey. And three works by Martin Johnson Heade and two by Sanford R. Gifford enable us for the first time to show the breadth of these artists' respective visions. Offering firsthand exposure to magnificent works by some of America's greatest artists, the Heinz gift has immeasurably expanded the teaching possibilities of the collection; in its range and depth, it serves as a fitting legacy to John Heinz's deep love of American art."[29]

Endowments for acquisitions have been key to the collection's growth, and the substantial bequest by the artist Simeon Braguin in 1999 for the purchase of works of art by living American artists ensures the future growth of American art. The first work bought with the

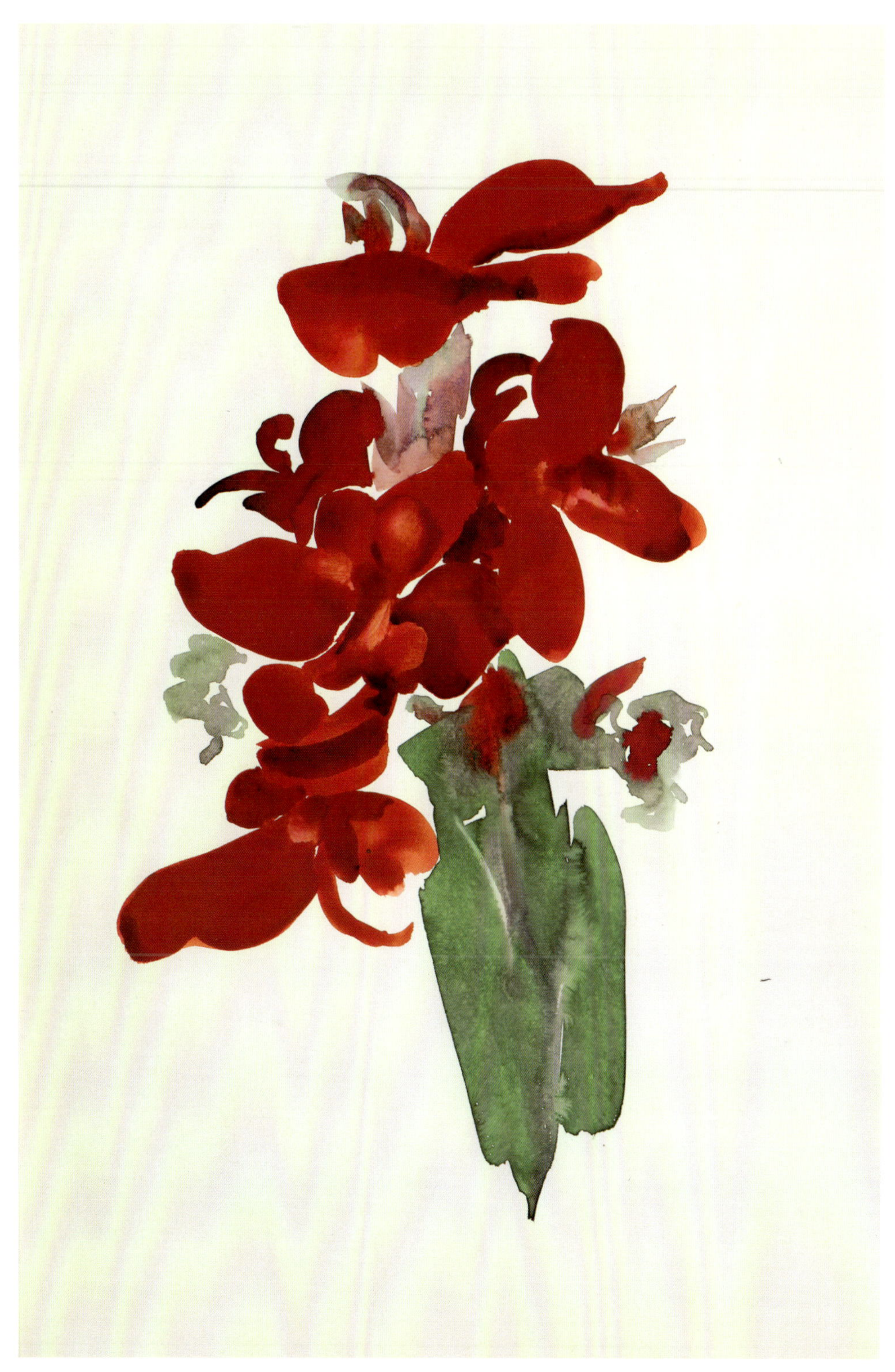

FIG. 236
Georgia O'Keeffe
Red Canna, 1920
Watercolor on wove paper, 49.2 x 33 cm
Gift of George Hopper Fitch, B.A. 1932, and Mrs. Fitch
1979.111

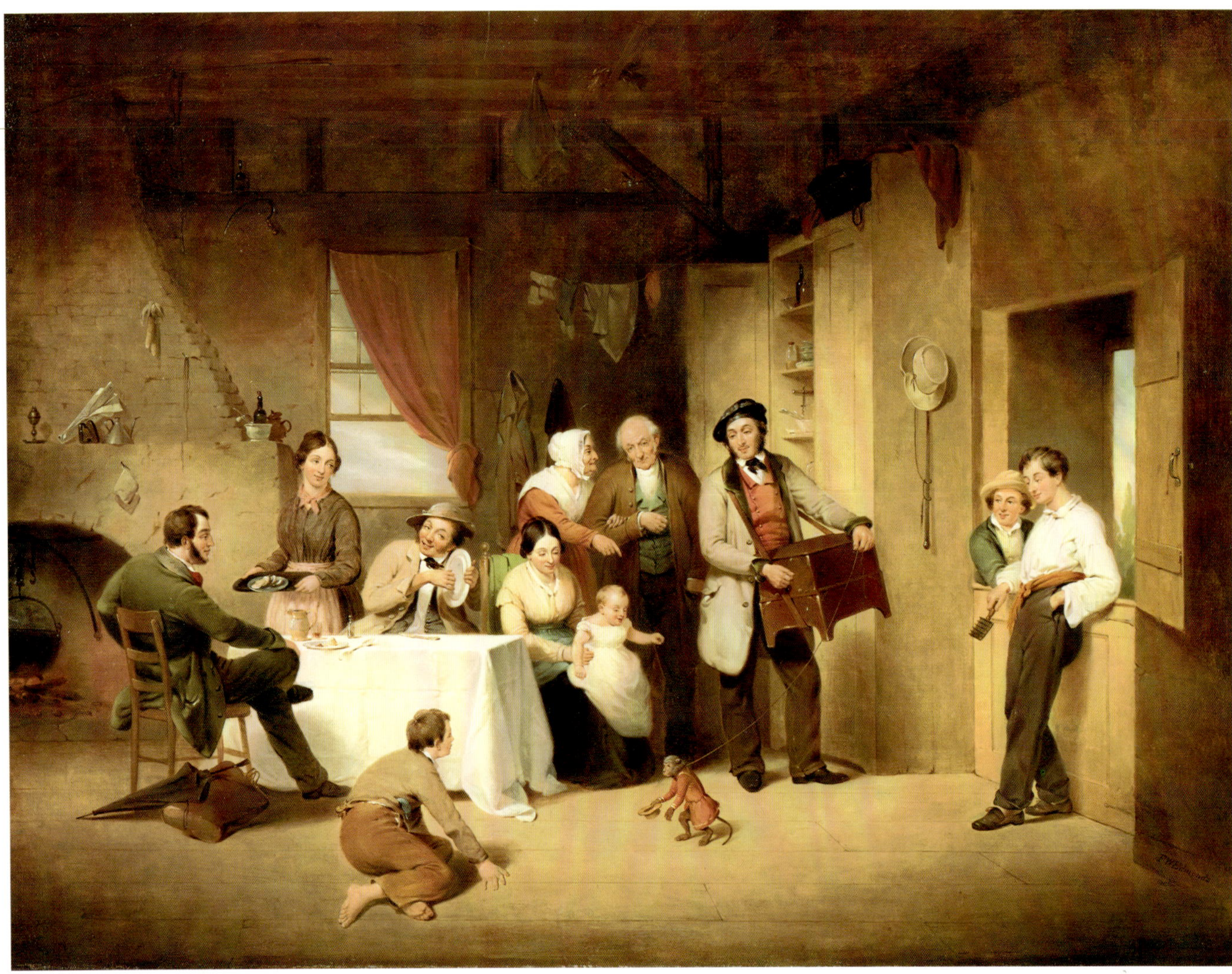

FIG. 237
Francis Edmonds
The Organ Grinder, ca. 1850
Oil on canvas, 80.6 x 106 cm
Gift of Teresa Heinz in memory of her husband H. John Heinz III, B.A. 1960
1992.5.6

Simeon and Janet Braguin Fund was the sculpture *123454321 Cross and Tower* by Sol LeWitt, acquired in 1999 (fig. 238).

Equally important are the recent endowments and pledged endowments of curatorial positions in several fields, creating the Allan (B.A. 1957) and Alice Kaplan Associate/Assistant Curator of American Paintings and Sculpture, the Friends of American Arts Curator of American Decorative Arts (which will become the Patricia E. Kane Curator of American Decorative Arts upon Patricia Kane's retirement from the post), the Benjamin Hewitt Associate Curator of American Decorative Arts, the Lionel Goldfrank, III (B.A. 1965) Curator of Early European Art, the Robert L. Solley (B.A. 1976) Curator of Prints, Drawings & Photographs, and the Frances and Benjamin Benenson Foundation Curator of African Art.

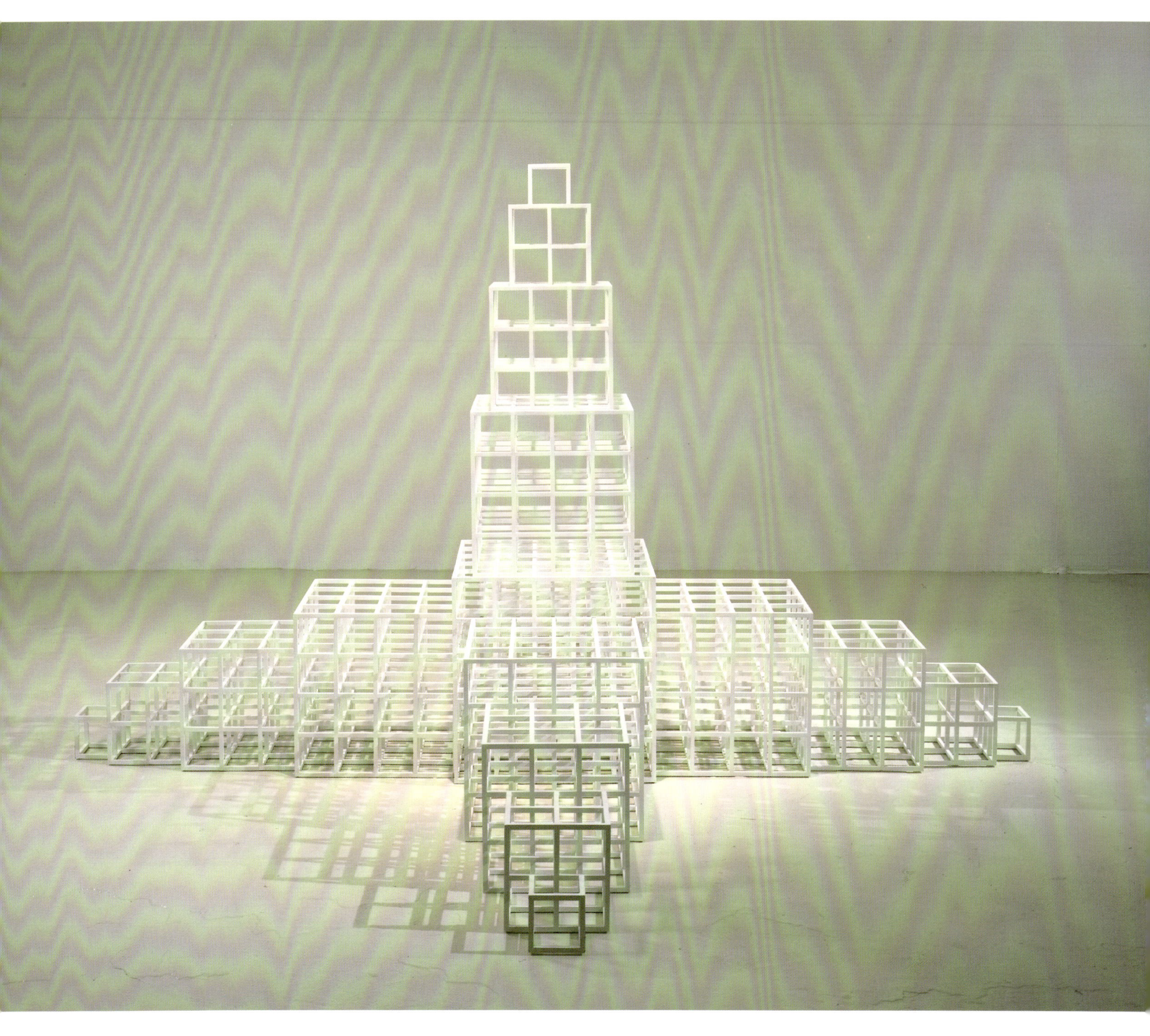

FIG. 238
Sol LeWitt
123454321 Cross and Tower, 1984
Wood painted white
182.9 x 304.8 x 304.8 cm
The Janet and Simeon Braguin Fund
1999.37.1a-e

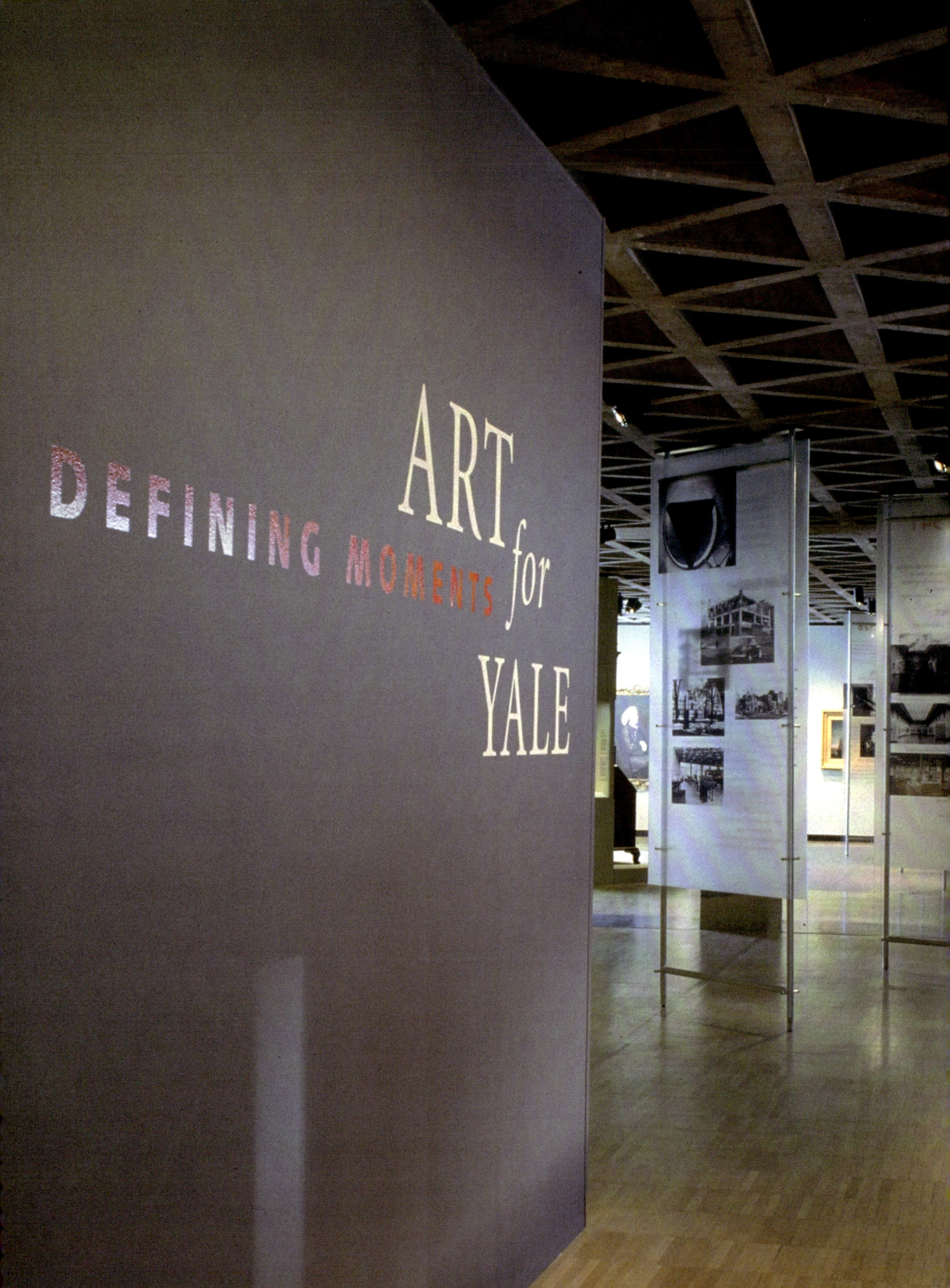
ART
DEFINING MOMENTS
for
YALE

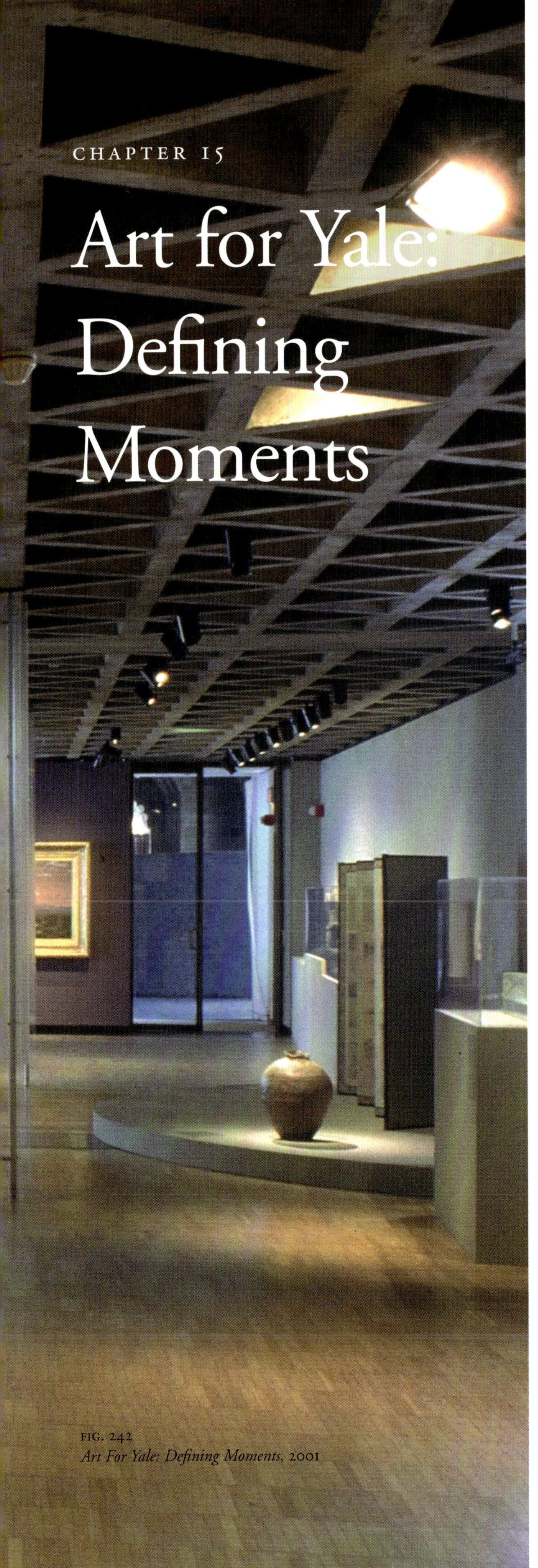

CHAPTER 15

Art for Yale: Defining Moments

FIG. 242
Art For Yale: Defining Moments, 2001

Jock Reynolds has been director of the Yale Art Gallery since 1998 (fig. 239). Director of the Addison Gallery of American Art at Phillips Academy Andover before coming to Yale, he has organized notable exhibitions on American art and photography and published extensively in these fields. His primary calling, however, is not as an art historian but as an artist, particularly as a sculptor and photographer, making his appointment as director the first in more than seventy-five years to name a practicing artist to the post. For an institution whose beginnings with Trumbull and Weir are so closely tied to the creation of art, this was a fitting appointment at this historic moment.

In just a short time Jock Reynolds has accomplished much. He has focused primarily on two things, the planning and funding for the growth of the Gallery and its staff and the celebration in 2001 of the Tercentennial of Yale. Along the way, he has enriched the collections, urged and shepherded the reinstallation of the permanent galleries in every department, enlarged and encouraged the Gallery's collective family and friends, and expanded and intensified its interaction with the School of Art and colleagues throughout the University.

The expansion and renovation of the Gallery that is now under way is the largest ever undertaken by the institution. As part of the University's project for the entire Arts Area, the Gallery will renovate its landmark Louis Kahn building and expand into and renovate all of Egerton Swartwout's 1928 Gallery of Fine Arts and P. B. Wight's 1864 School of the Fine Arts, now known as Street Hall. In addition, a second building, within short walking distance of the present complex, will be built for the Gallery as an art study center, drawing on the model of the American decorative arts department's Furniture Study at 149 York Street. Reynolds summarized the goals of the project in his article "Renewing a Teaching Mission, Restoring an Architectural Legacy, and Building for the 21st Century,"[1] reflecting the Gallery staff's shared commitment to enhancing the accessibility of the collections through increased exhibition space, object classrooms within the Gallery, and readily accessible collection storage for faculty, students, and staff. For the three buildings on Chapel Street, this will be accomplished, in collaboration with the distinguished architectural firm Polshek Partnership L.L.P.,

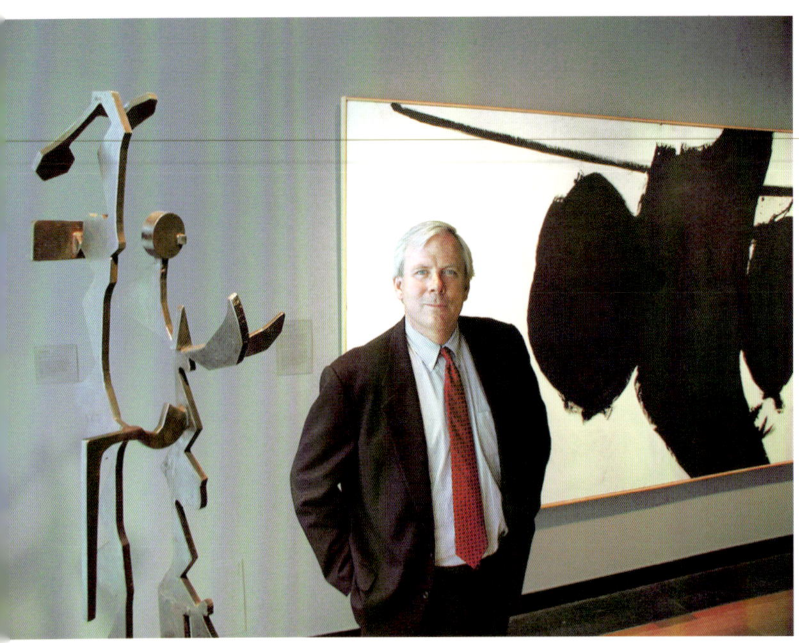

FIG. 239
Jock Reynolds, 2000
Photograph courtesy Yale University Art Gallery Archives

within a historically sensitive renovation that will recover the magnificent exhibition spaces now hidden by adaptation of these buildings over more than a century of varied use. Funding for this project, and for the growth of the staff that operating the expanded facilities and program will require, is well along, thanks to the generosity of the Gallery's many devoted friends. These extraordinary donors have taken to heart the principle stated by President Richard Levin of "the responsibility of one generation to nurture and protect the culture, the ideas and the arts for generations to come."[2]

The reinstallation of the permanent collection by each of the Gallery's curatorial departments has been a key part of the planning process for the renovation. The most ambitious of these has been the complete reinstallation of the American paintings and sculpture and American decorative arts collections, which opened in 2001 (figs. 240 and 241). The first overall reinstallation of the American collections since 1973, this project was developed by Patricia E. Kane, curator of American decorative arts, and Helen A. Cooper, Holcombe T. Green Curator of American Paintings and Sculpture, and their colleagues, in collaboration with faculty and students. The revealing of the original appearance of Egerton Swartwout's main exhibition gallery on the third floor of his 1928 Gallery of Fine Arts transformed the mazelike presentation of American decorative arts of the 1973 Chermayeff installation into a soaring exhibition gallery for paintings and sculpture. The Trumbull Gallery continues to evoke the appearance of Colonel Trumbull's 1832 picture gallery, while American decorative arts are now shown in smaller spaces more suited to their domestic scale. Interpretive installations offer a social and art-historical context for the objects.

The Gallery celebrated Yale's Tercentennial with three special exhibitions in 2001. Two were exhibitions of works on paper organized by Suzanne Boorsch, curator of prints, drawings, and photographs. The first, *Circa 1701: Printed Portraits from the Time of Elihu Yale,* paid homage to Yale's founder. The second, *A Moment Ongoing: The Legacy of Everett V. Meeks*, presented some of the many drawings and prints that have been purchased with the Everett V. Meeks Fund, an endowment for the purchase of Old Master works on paper that was named for the colorful dean of the School of Art and

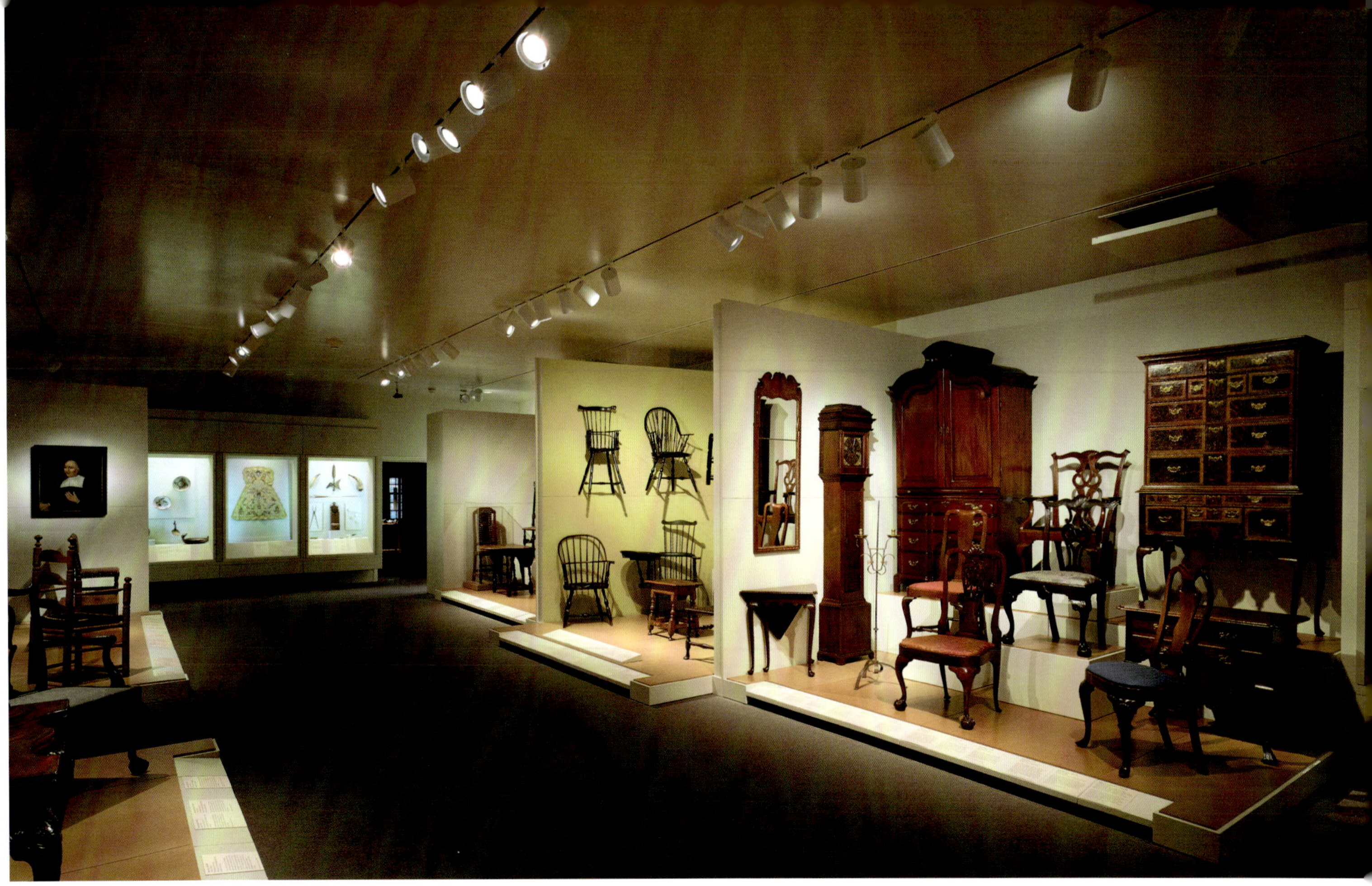

FIG. 240
Reinstallation of the American Galleries, 2001
Photograph courtesy Yale University Art Gallery Archives

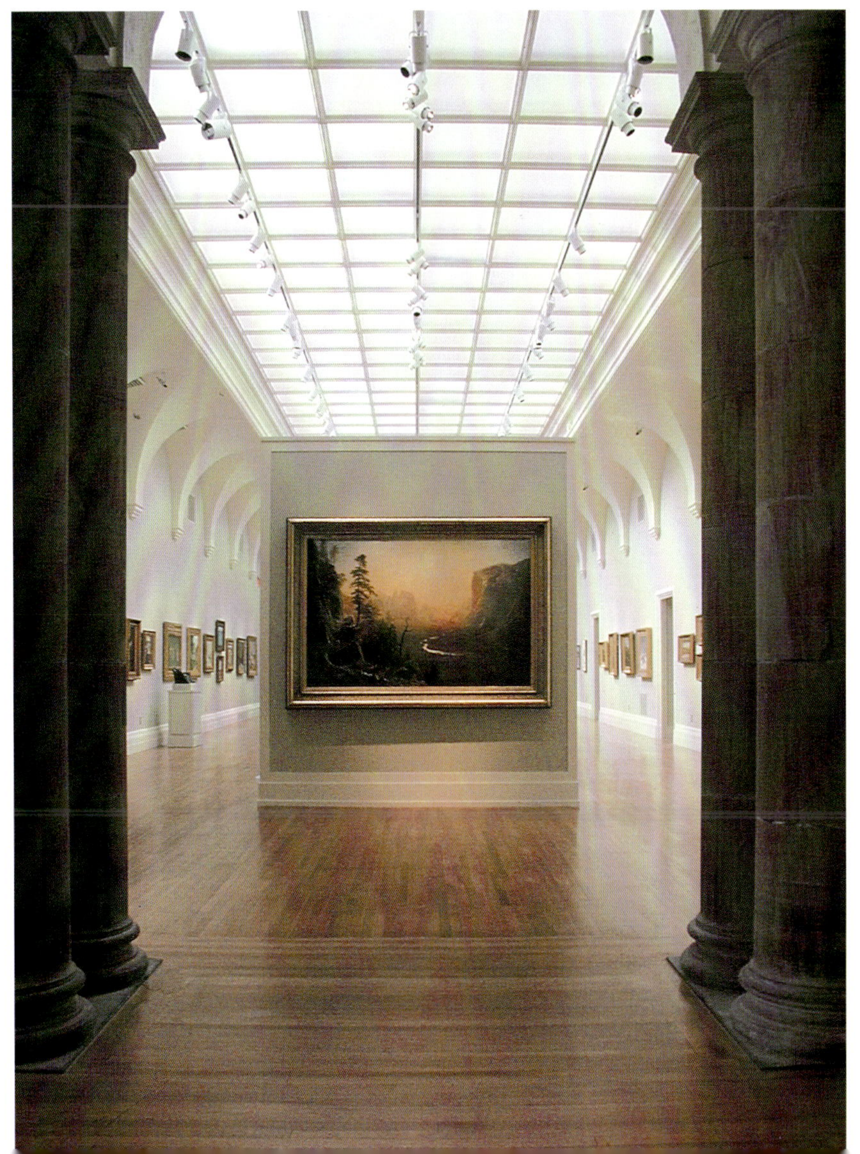

FIG. 241
Reinstallation of the American Galleries, 2001
Photograph courtesy Yale University Art Gallery Archives

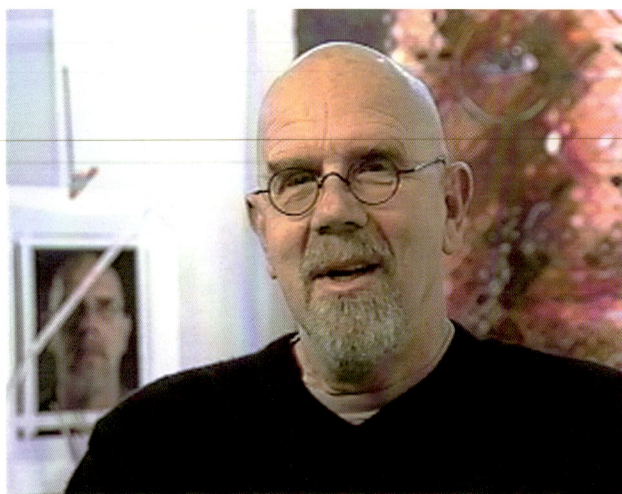

FIG. 243
Chuck Close in his studio, video interview
Photograph courtesy Yale University Digital Media Center for the Arts

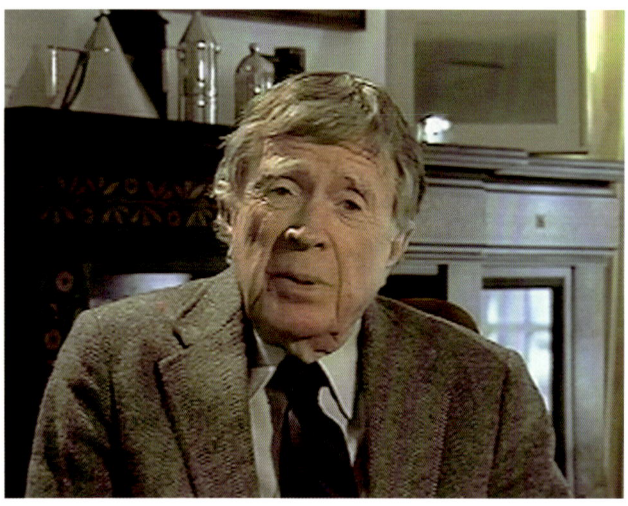

FIG. 244
Vincent Scully, video
Photograph courtesy Yale University Digital Media Center for the Arts

FIGS. 245–253
Art For Yale: Defining Moments, 2001
Photographs courtesy Yale University Art Gallery Archives

Gallery director in the 1920s and '30s. Many of the Gallery's most important purchases in this field have been made with this fund, adding immeasurably to the value of the collection for teaching.

The major effort for the Tercentennial was *Art for Yale: Defining Moments* (fig. 242), an unprecedented exhibition organized by Helen Cooper offering a panorama of the collections, donors, staff, faculty, and students that have together made the Gallery what it is today.[3] Structured as a path through time and elegantly designed by Sarah Buie, the exhibition filled the entire first floor, leading the visitor from the Gallery's beginnings with the collegiate collection and the Trumbull paintings through the defining moments in its history to the present day. Significant works from every part of the collection were chosen by Cooper in collaboration with the curators of the other departments. A narrative timeline snaked through the galleries on translucent panels modeled after the "pogo panels" of the Kahn building. A list of titles of major exhibitions appeared as a spiral on the floor. The names of all donors of works of art to the collection—more than 3,000 of them—were listed on panel after panel covering windows and walls throughout the gallery space. Quotations screened on walls from donors, faculty, students, docents, children, security guards, alumni/ae, artists, and staff brought many voices to the exhibition. A video showed interviews (fig. 243) with a similarly broad group. Another video, featuring Vincent Scully (fig. 244), Sterling Professor Emeritus of the History of Art, opened the exhibition celebrating the founding, collections, history, and architecture of the Gallery.

This richly varied display of exceptional works of art (figs. 245–53) and the unparalleled history of collecting and teaching art narrated in the exhibition were memorable, but it is the voices quoted on the walls that best revealed the way in which the Gallery has enriched people's lives. In those that follow, accompanied by views of the exhibition, the reader will find the pleasure and learning that have been derived from what Jock Reynolds has called "the first place in America where university officials saw the value of exposing students and faculty and members of the New Haven community itself directly to works of art and having that be an integral part of an education. . . . whenever possible the best works of art that can be assembled."[4]

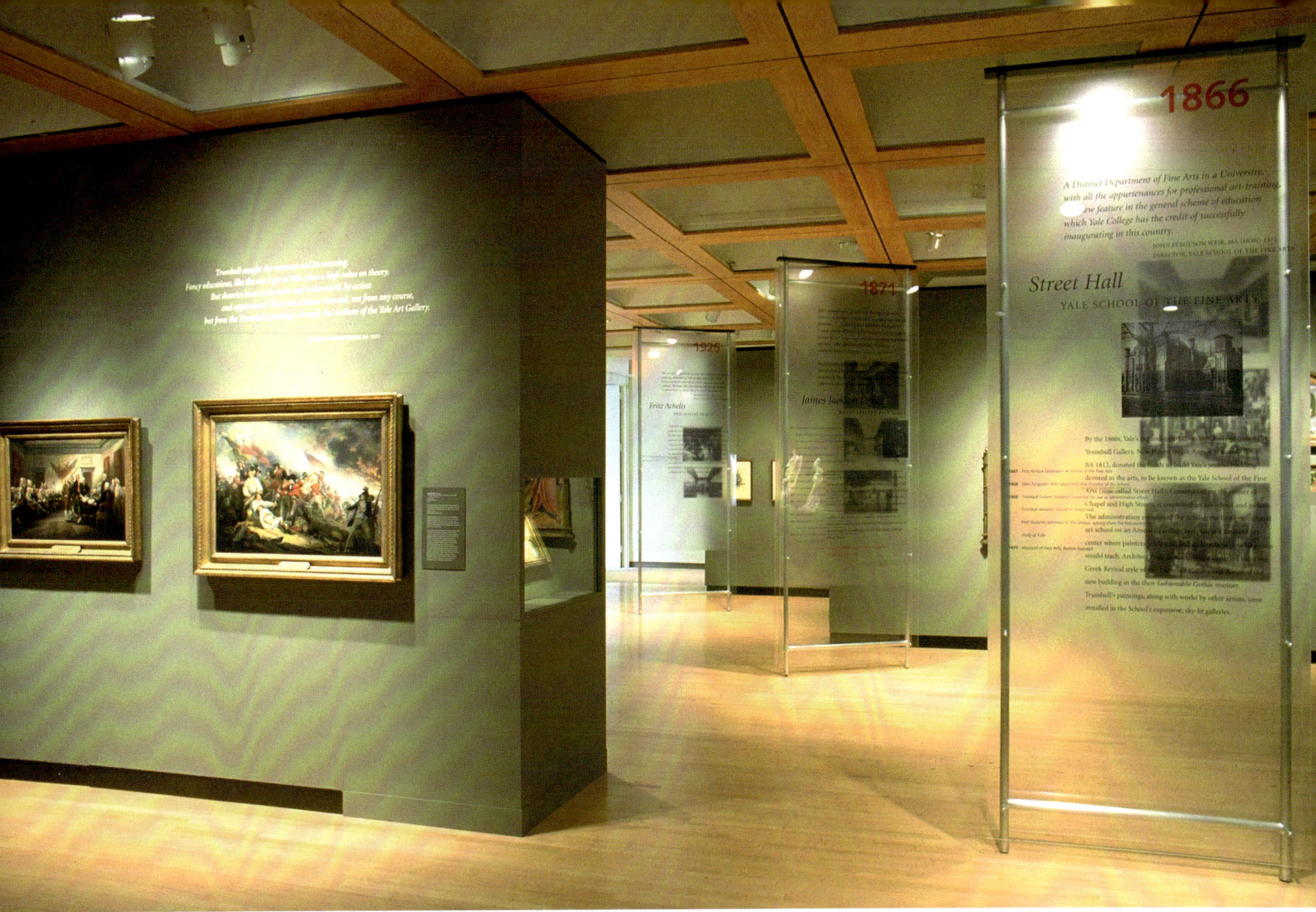

VOICES ON THE WALL

The original work of art—what can it teach? The assignment that ignited my serious interest in the history of art was a paper I had to write for George Heard Hamilton. Write about a painting in the Gallery—that was all we were told. I stood in front of some of the big fish, the *Night Café* by van Gogh and the *Brooklyn Bridge* by Joseph Stella, but I shied away from their intensity and completeness. I was drawn by another picture by van Gogh, painted in 1887 when he was an impressionable Dutch lay missionary newly arrived in Paris . . . struggling to find his own way of painting. . . . I could see that the dots stretched, became impulsive longer strokes that radiated the light and revealed the energy of the artist, who let his hand express his exuberance. This is a moment—this picture—when van Gogh found the means not just to depict a scene, but also to express his own reaction to it. This would quickly become his language, and there it was in front of me, its first expression, I stayed up all night to write about it—not, for once, because the paper was late, but because of sheer excitement.

JOHN WALSH, B.A. 1961, *former director of the J. Paul Getty Museum; member of the Art Gallery Governing Board*

As students, we were incredibly privileged to get behind the scenes and be involved in every aspect of doing an exhibition. The opportunity to be in daily contact with works of art and the people who spend their lives studying them continues to be a model for me in the way I approach my own work.

WILLIAM HOWZE, B.A. 1967, M.A. 1978, *documentary filmmaker*

When I came to Yale I knew so little about contemporary art and certainly even less about American art that the courses I took, the lectures I heard and the trips I took were quite a revelation to me.

WALTER BAREISS, B.S. 1940s, *member of the Art Gallery Governing Board*

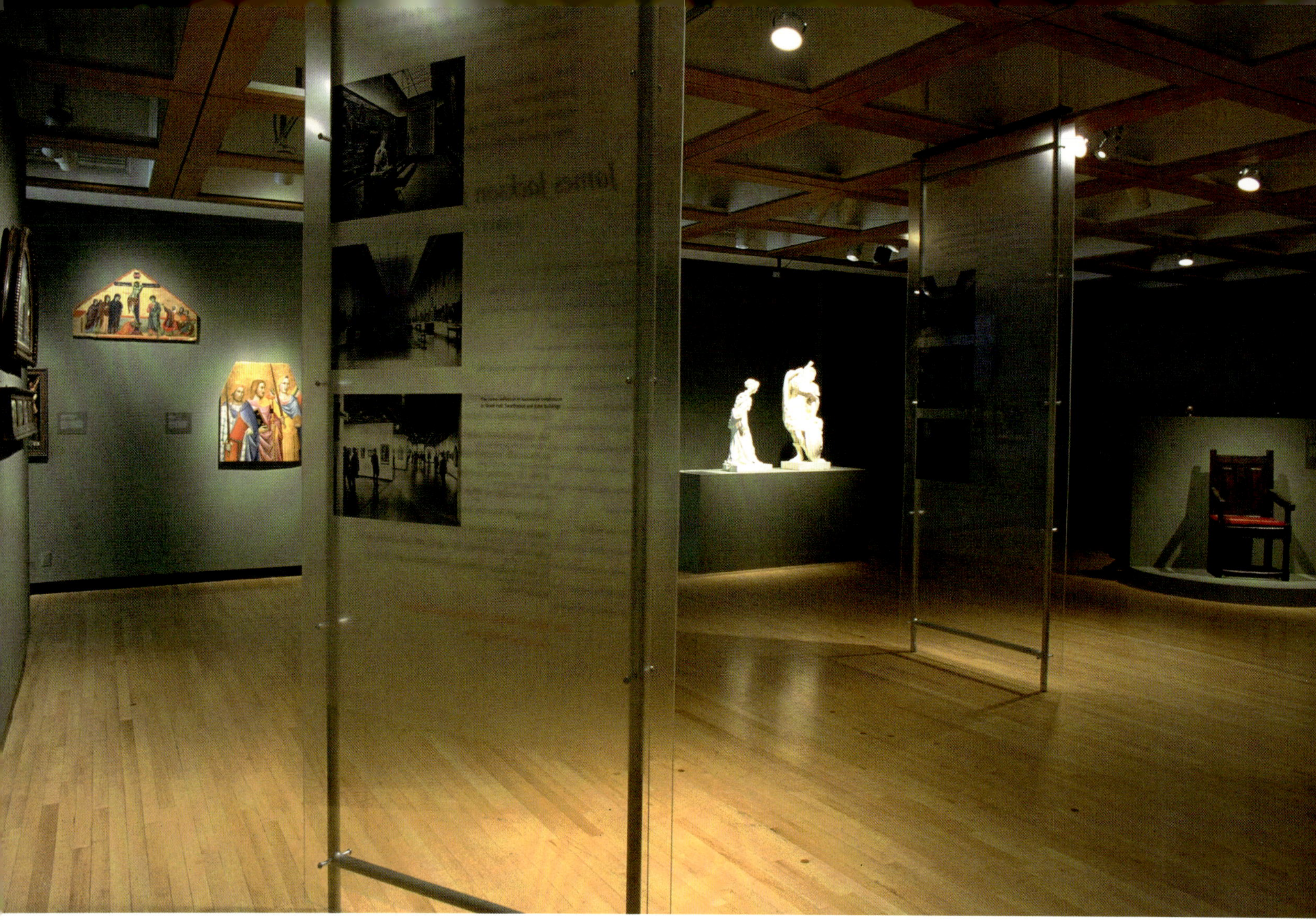

From Louis Kahn's wonderful building to the depth and quality of its collection, the museum provides an intimate setting for visual artists to extend their education. The two paintings by the Master of the Osservanza, the Van Gogh *Night Café*, and Manet's *Young Woman in Spanish Costume* are personal favorites and deep and lasting influences. While I was in the graduate program, Brice Marden came to lecture and visit studios. After a short discussion of the issues of my work Brice asked if I wanted to go over to the museum and look at the Mondrians. We spent a good hour looking at them interspersed by Brice's terse but insightful comments about surface, light, and the obsessive vision of one of the earliest, most influential abstract painters. It was one of the most productive hours in my academic experience.
DAVID ROW, B.A. 1972, M.F.A. 1975

All those images at Yale: *Tu m'*, *Rooms by the Sea*, *First Steps*, *The Knife Grinder* . . . you INCULCATED them into me. . . . You played a big role in sparing me a life as a feeble electrical engineer. Instead, I went into the record business, opening a discotheque, wrote songs, did some painting, and now develop computer software. During all this time, I have been a passionate collector.
NORMAN DOLPH, B.E. 1960, *writing to George Heard Hamilton on his 90th birthday*

An overwhelming number of Yale alumni are more than collectors: they are moving forces in the art life of their communities. . . . One ventures to attribute much to the Yale experience . . . a climate in which appreciation . . . in the arts was considered part of the intelligent, cultivated man's equipment.
ALINE B. SAARINEN, *New York Times, 1956*

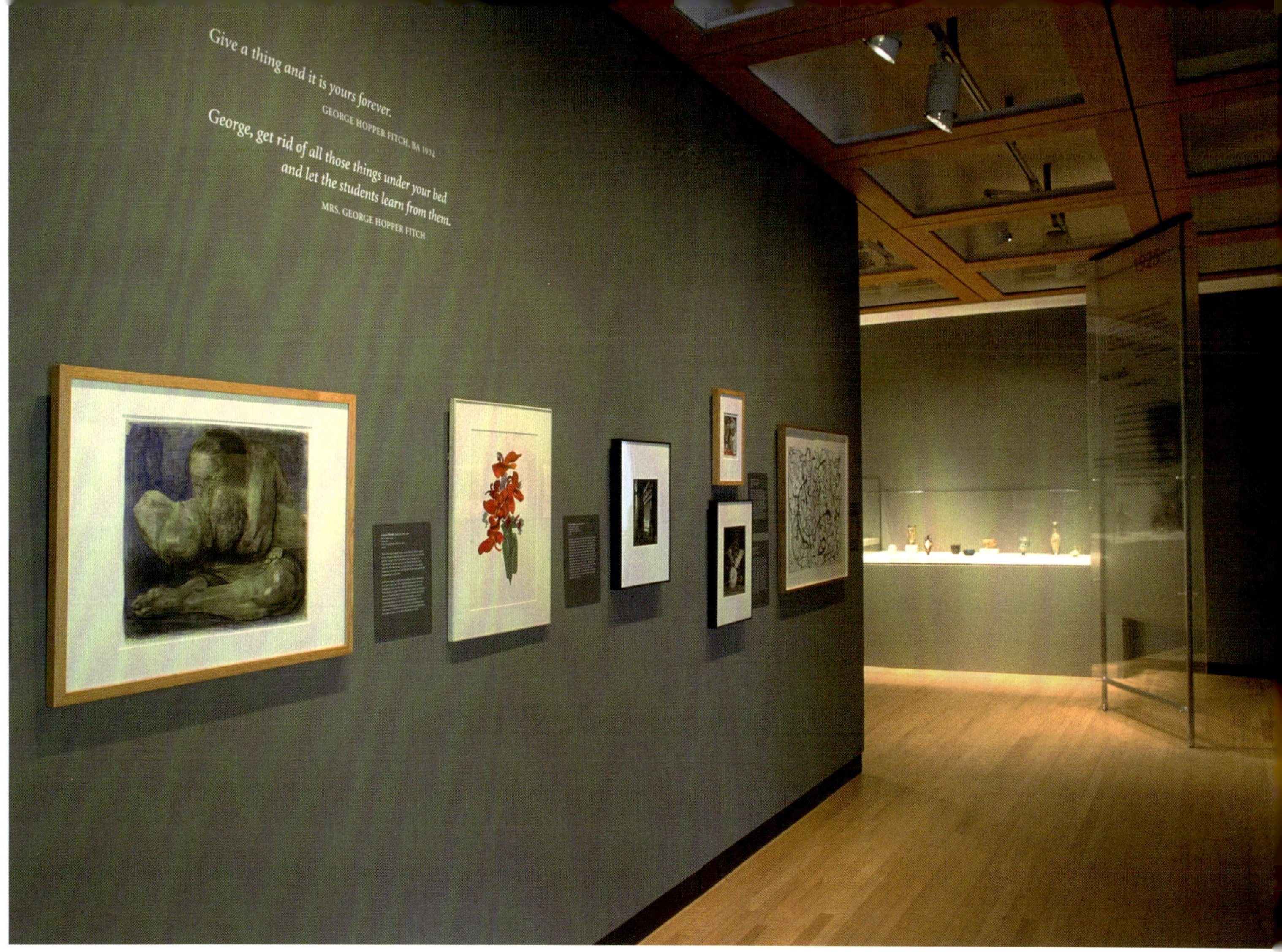

There is no intellectual or emotional substitute for the authentic, the original, the unique masterpiece.
PAUL MELLON, B.A. 1929, L.L.D. 1967

We were really fortunate in that the Gallery often does projects involving graduate students at different levels, you know, research assistants, etc., etc. But in our case, we were given the opportunity to actually mount an exhibition working with someone from the Gallery.
LYNEISE WILLIAMS, *graduate student, history of art*

We have lots of classes from all over the state that come here, and the students can actually visualize something they've learned about in school. That's really fun to see their faces when they see something, understand something.
DEBBIE BERNARD, *security guard*

One of my favorite kinds of assignments . . . is to take an object that arrives here in some state of incompleteness. I've had students working very effectively and most recently digitally in reconstructing objects and scanning in missing parts, say that they would find in the art library, bringing them to inform this ancient object and to bring it back to life. . . . I think that students by having the opportunity to spend repeated time with an object, time first with a professor or a teaching assistant and then to come back and to work with it on their own, begin to see the way that an object out of the past, one for which we have no texts, almost no archaeological knowledge, can come to be like a text from the past, and that as they begin to spend time with it, it begins to open up worlds upon worlds.
MARY ELLEN MILLER, PH.D. 1981, *Vincent Scully Professor of the History of Art*

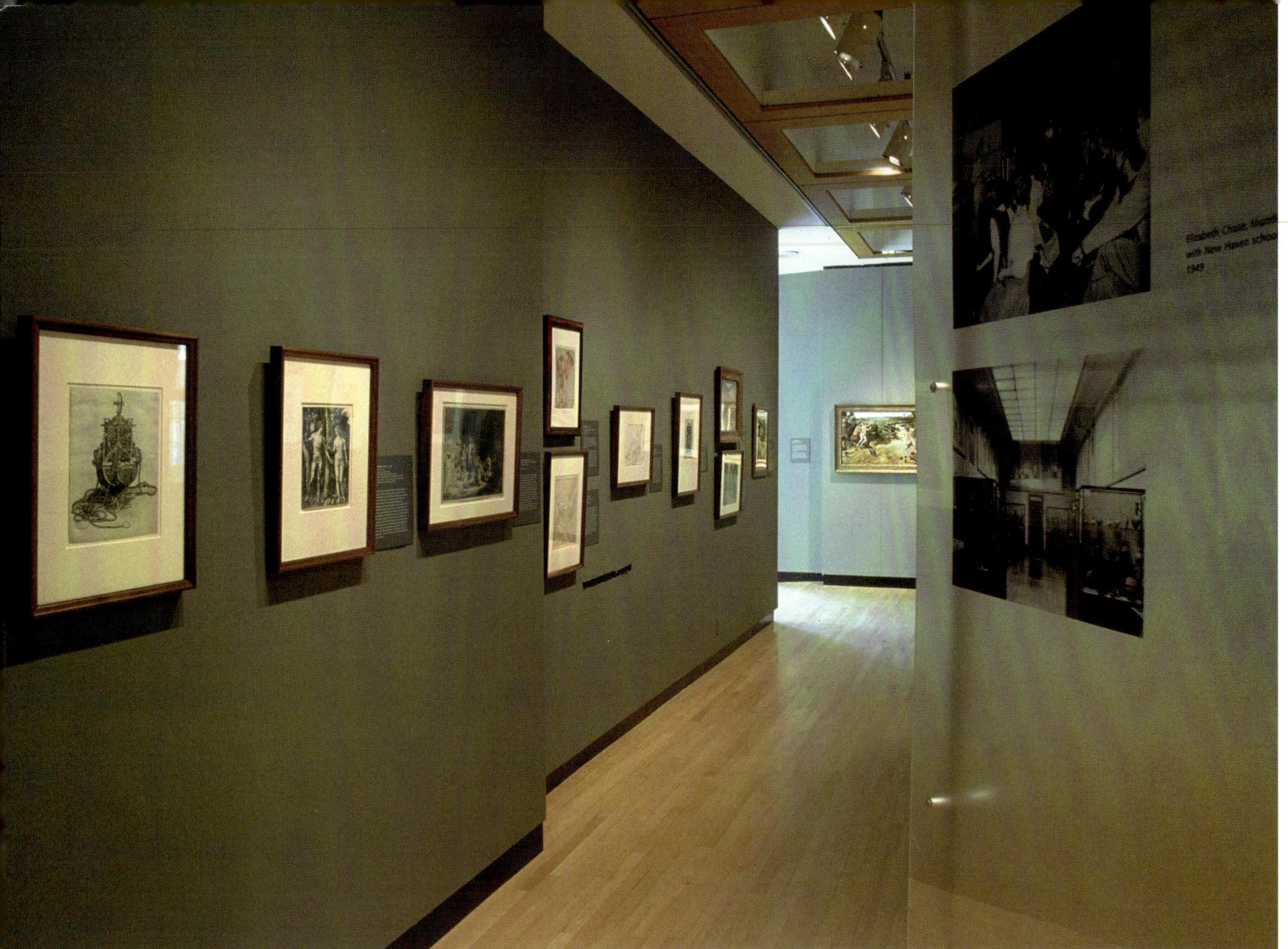

For me, the Art Gallery was an important part of my Yale experience. I think it's such a rare resource to have a museum with works of art of such high quality available and that art itself is a primary source. We don't have to just look at books or the written word—pictures are also primary and sometimes tell us more about a culture, about life, and touch very directly in terms of the way people lived, the way they felt. For me, art is that essential bridge between the past and the present.
STEVEN KOSSACK, B.A. 1972, *member of the Art Gallery Governing Board*

We get such a variety of people, and since I came here, I've seen that now we have more of the community coming in, more of every background—the inner city children, they're bringing their families in, and I like to see the mix of cultures now, more so than ever. . . . You can almost write a book about what people say and do and how everyone sees the art in different ways.
CLAUDIA MATHIEU, *security guard*

I came to the Art Gallery for the first time for a teaching section, for a survey course of world art, from prehistory to the Renaissance, and I haven't really left since. As an undergraduate I've been allowed and encouraged to work on projects that I would never have imagined working on. I wrote an acquisition proposal for a Roman portrait bust which the University did end up acquiring last year. That was an unbelievable experience. I think I've had the best entry-level museum experience that anybody could imagine. I don't think that there's any museum in the world that could have afforded me more opportunities.
RICHARD GROSSMANN, B.A. 2001, *research assistant in ancient art*

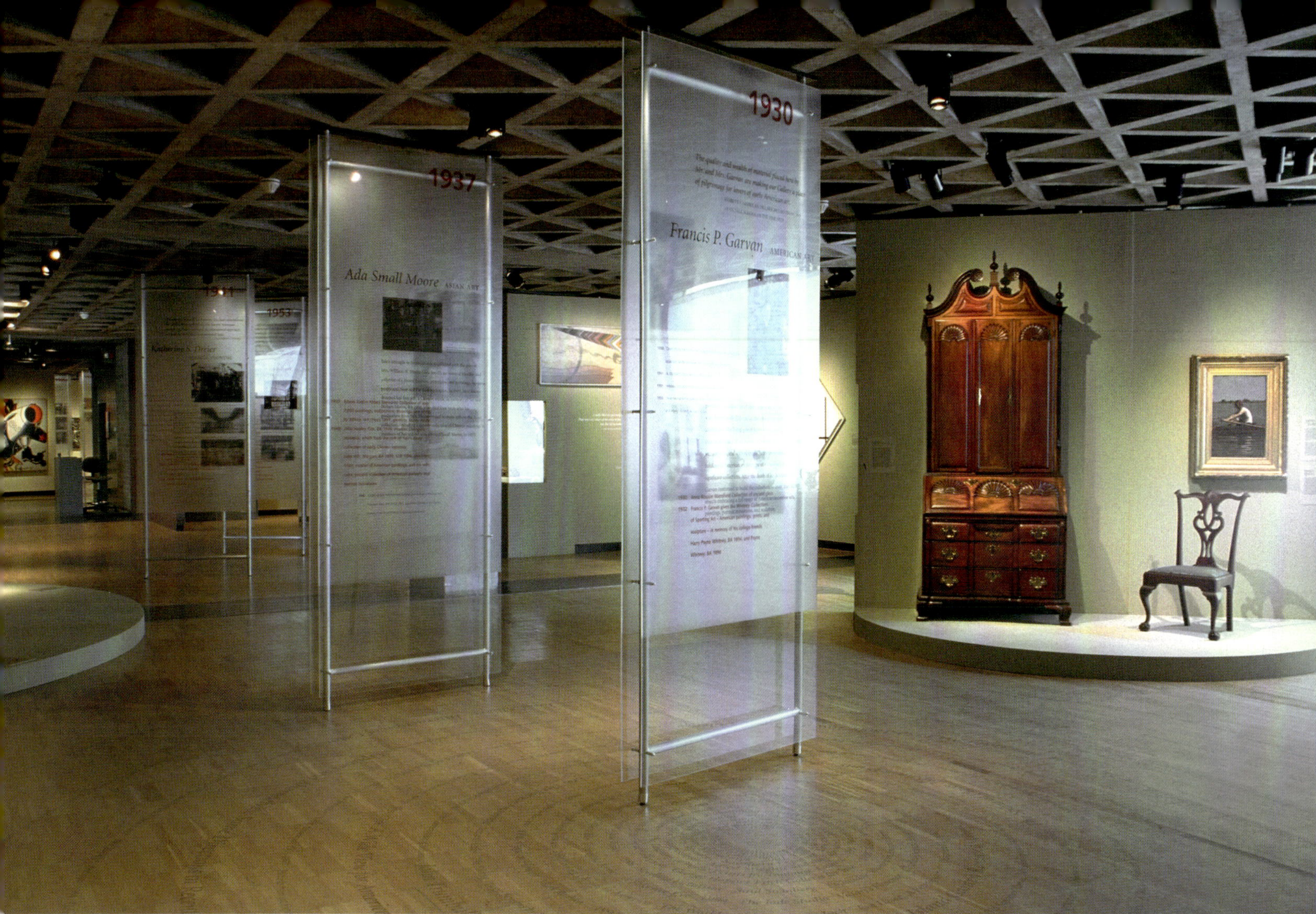

We have programs for all kinds of people that come into the museum. For children, for talented and gifted children, for handicapped children, for children who are mentally challenged. Some of those programs have been the best in terms of orchestrating because the satisfaction and the pleasure that these objects give these kids are so visible, so important.
MARY KORDAK, *curator of education*

The Jarves Collection was so different from what I was studying at law school. It was a refuge.
RICHARD DANZIGER, LL.B. 1963, *member of the Art Gallery Governing Board*

Jarves was not disposed to scatter a collection so valuable in its collective character as an illustration of the development of early Christian art and a school for the American art student.
New York Tribune, November 10, 1871

I was taking courses from Charles Seymour, who was a professor of Italian Renaissance paintings . . . and I really fell in love with a pair of Sienese paintings by the Master of the Osservanza. . . .There was a purity and a kind of hyperrealism about them.
H. CHRISTOPHER LUCE, B.A. 1971, *member of the Art Gallery Governing Board*

. . . all art museums should be allied with a University; . . . our young, studying in the university, with the chance to study and understand, are the hope of art in our country.
FRANCIS P. GARVAN, B.A. 1897, M.A. (HON.) 1922

As collections and lectures become progressively easier to retail by wire, all the more reason for some universities to focus on those elements of study and of learning which require the sharing of live experience. Art, artifact and manuscript can be identified on a television screen at a far distance, but critical perception and evaluation require intimacy with the original. Day after

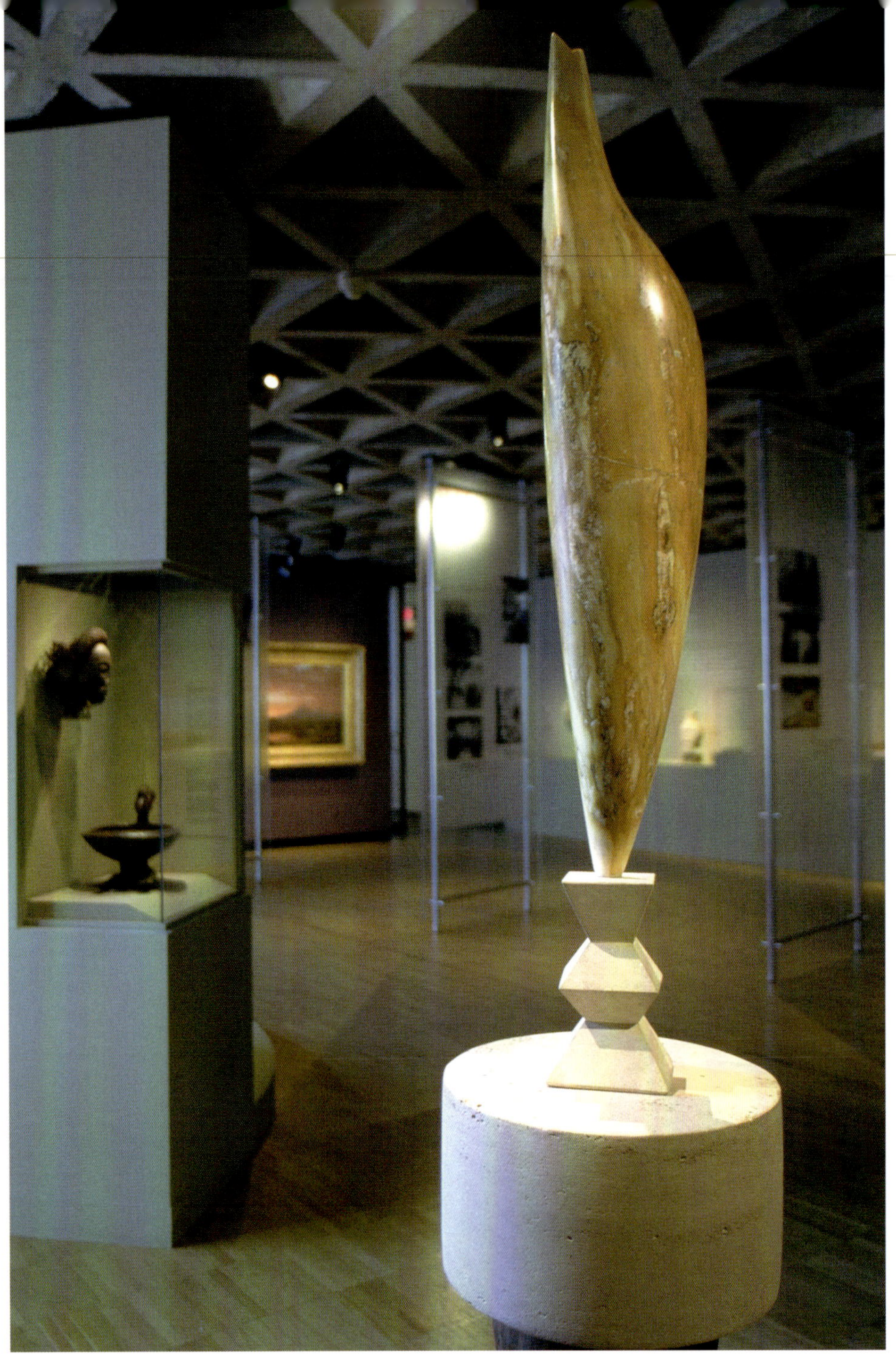

tomorrow it may be the rare collection, not the massive assembly of researchable words and data, which will become the intellectual asset whose location matters.
KINGMAN BREWSTER, *President of Yale,* 1963–77, *inaugural address*

Yale is the best place in the world to teach American art. Nowhere else can you find the comprehensive kind of collection we have. A lot of students get a passion for American art because of the way we teach it and because of the access they have to the Gallery's collection.
JULES D. PROWN, M.A. (HON.) 1971, *Paul Mellon Professor Emeritus of the History of Art*

To be able to meet and talk to Marcel Duchamp was a great experience by itself. It was this very period of my undergraduate studies at Yale when I began collecting on a small scale books, illustrated with original works of art.
WALTER BAREISS, B.S. 1940S, *member of the Art Gallery Governing Board*

. . . to awaken an understanding and comprehension of what a living Force Art is in the world and how essential to the Life of the Nation.
KATHERINE DREIER *to Theodore Sizer*

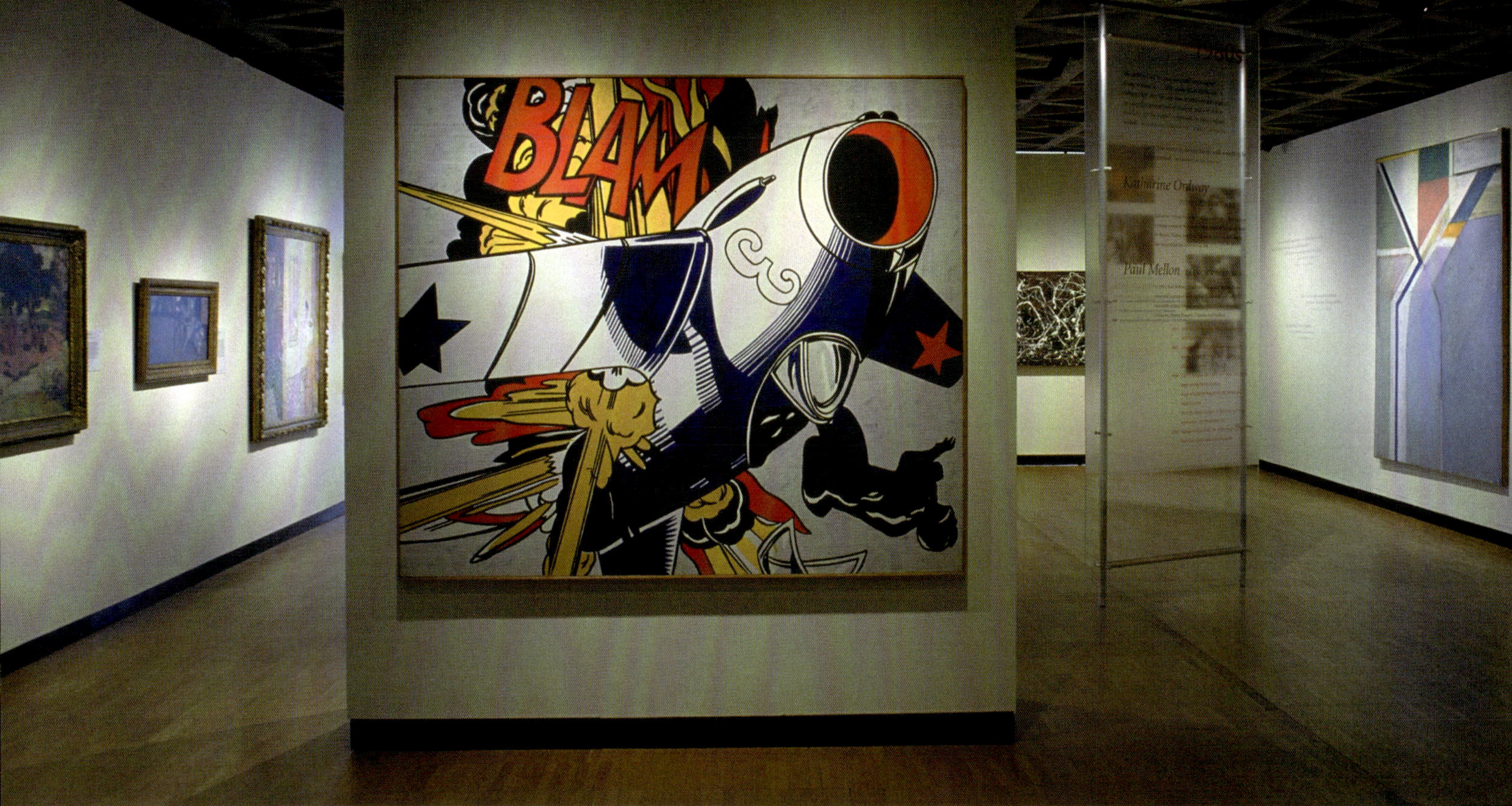

An original has subtleties and qualities that a reproduction will never have.
RICHARD BROWN BAKER, B.A. 1935, *member of the Art Gallery Governing Board*

I enjoyed seeing the old furniture. I never thought there would be furniture. The hawk claws are so neat I can't keep my eyes off of it.
MILFORD STUDENT, *Orange Avenue School*, 1998

Many, many of the greatest curators and artists throughout this country and abroad have trained here. Anyone who is knowledgeable about the arts in America knows that this place is a great source for learning and study and creative ferment.
JOCK REYNOLDS, *Henry J. Heinz II Director*

When I got home it took me 5–10 minutes to tell my mom about each painting. My mom enjoyed hearing about it so much that she has decided to go herself this weekend and discover the magic of the Yale Art Gallery.
MILFORD STUDENT, *Orange Avenue School*, 1998

The Yale Art Gallery is free—it costs nothing. As a result, it is a great resource for people in the New Haven community, and we encourage people to use this resource. It's just invaluable. We have a lot of programs for the students, we have evening gatherings for the community, and we really encourage the participation of the New Haven community. . . . The reason that I became a docent is because of my art historical background. . . . I have a master's in history of art and I am very privileged, I think, to be able to use that information at the Yale Art Gallery. . . . I've learned so much. It's an ongoing process of learning. I don't know half of what I should know, but we're always learning about the collections.
NIKKI TOOLE, *docent*

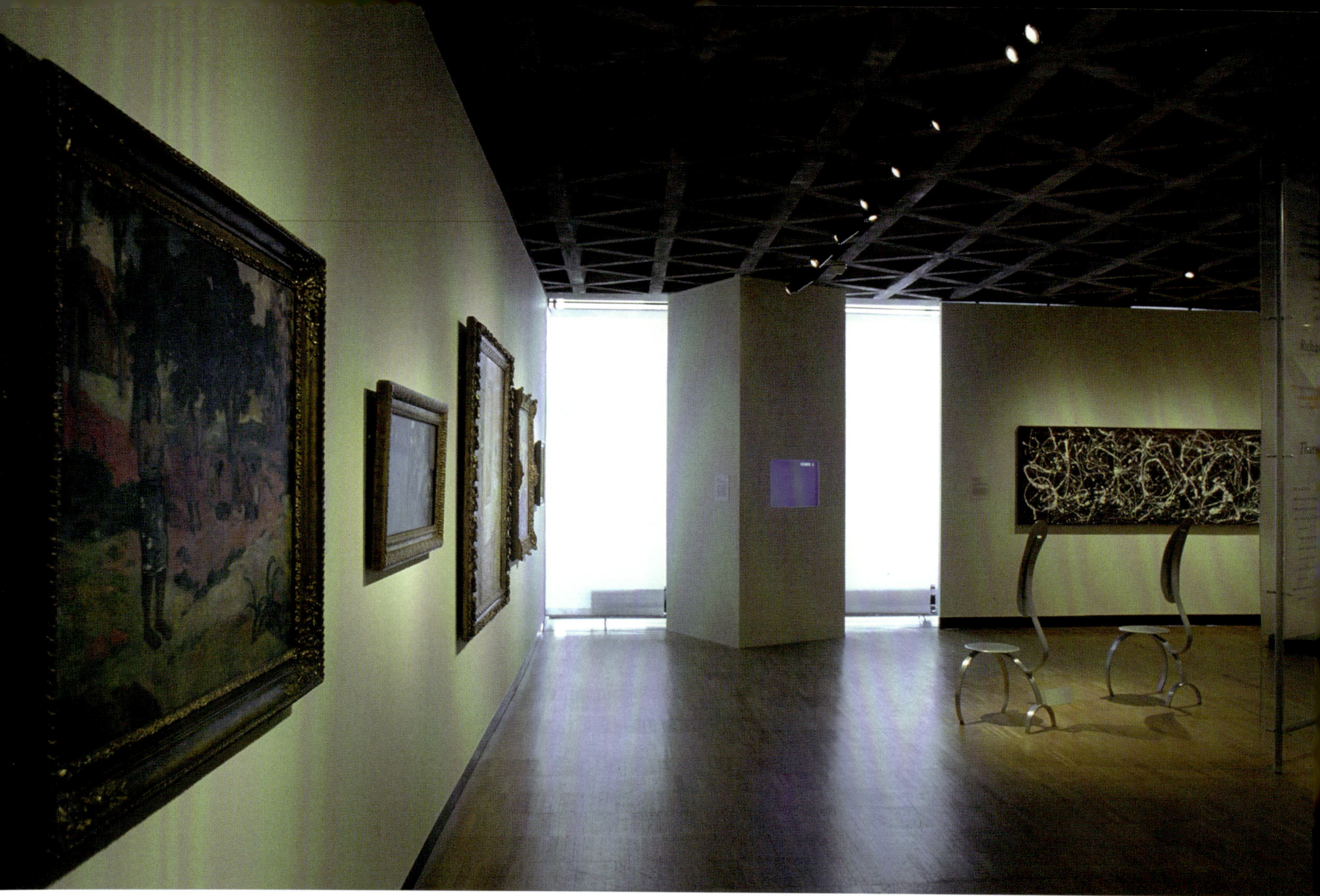

I'm a collector by nature. It's like reaching for a peanut every few minutes.
RICHARD BROWN BAKER, B.A. 1935, *member of the Art Gallery Governing Board*

You really don't fully understand a work of art until you live with it. I hope that these gifts will allow Yale students and faculty and the New Haven community to begin living with art that has meant so much to me.
THURSTON TWIGG-SMITH, B.E. 1942, *member of the Art Gallery Governing Board*

Give a thing and it is yours forever.
GEORGE HOPPER FITCH, B.A. 1932, *member of the Art Gallery Governing Board*

George, get rid of all those things under the bed and let the students learn from them.
The late MRS. GEORGE HOPPER FITCH

I have no talents, I don't know very much. But I think I can recognize quality when I see it.
STEPHEN CARLTON CLARK, B.A. 1903

The group of works I'd say I responded to most as an undergraduate were things given by Stephen Clark, which included a wide variety of European paintings, which were all joined because Clark had a great eye. They were things that I found tremendously exciting as works of art.
STEVEN KOSSACK, B.A. 1972, *member of the Art Gallery Governing Board*

For me, the Art Gallery felt like an extension of the School of Art which was in Street Hall. The art library and the art history department were adjoined to the museum in the space where the LeWitt and Serra are now installed. The printmaking department was situated downstairs in the museum. So there was real a physical link between the school and the museum. I would catch a quick look at works of art on exhibit as I dashed from one class to another. Sometimes I would slow down my looking and one time I was moved to write a poem about the Duchamp painting *Tu m'*.
SYLVIA PLIMACK MANGOLD, B.F.A. 1961

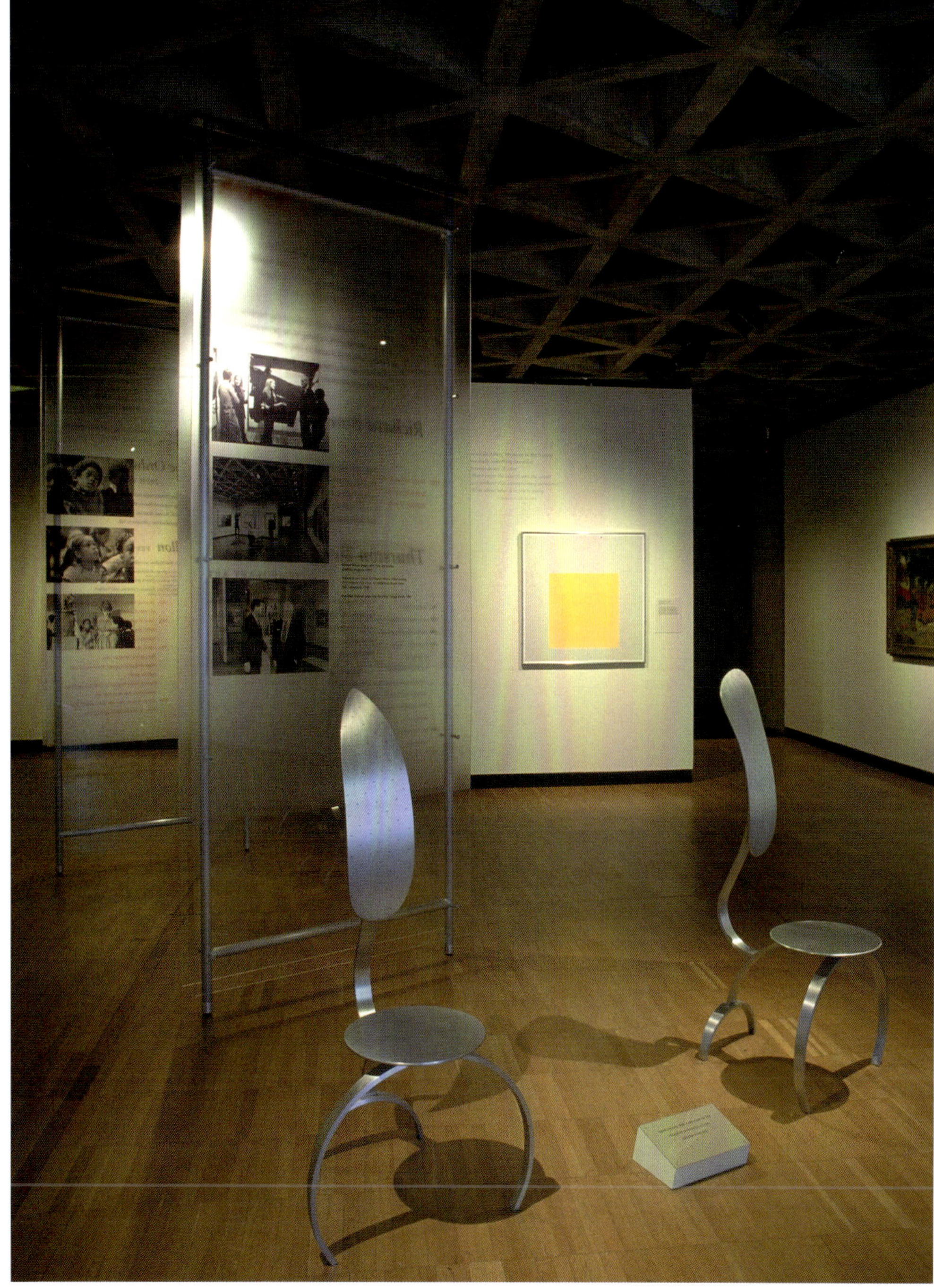

The quality of the students we attract and the accomplishments of our graduates are directly attributable to the fact that they can walk across the street to the Art Gallery and have contact with masterpieces anytime they want. I wouldn't even want to think about teaching painting without this kind of access.
DAVID PEASE, M.A. (HON.) 1983, *Street Professor Emeritus of Painting and former Dean, Yale School of Art*

I would say it's a tremendous set of treasures and you are really missing one of the great assets in the university. Whether or not you take a course just go there and see what's there.
JOSEPH G. FOGG III, B.A. 1968, *member of the Art Gallery Governing Board*

I learned that sometimes it's not how art looks it's what you think about it.
MILFORD STUDENT, *Orange Avenue School*, 1998

I felt pulled toward the Gallery—it was a space I enjoyed being in and I always felt better after I spent some time there.
LIONEL GOLDFRANK III, B.A. 1965, *member of the Art Gallery Governing Board*

ENDNOTES

CHAPTER 1

INTRODUCTION: THE COLLEGIATE COLLECTION

1. On the history of collegiate collections, see Jean C. Harris, *Collegiate Collections, 1776–1876*, exhibition catalogue, Mount Holyoke College Art Museum, June 15–December 15, 1976.

2. The Bowdoin College collection was bequeathed by James Bowdoin III in 1811 as a collection; it precedes the Trumbull collection but not Yale's earlier acquisitions of portraits. The Bowdoin pictures were displayed in the college's Massachusetts Hall until Richard Upjohn's Chapel was built in the 1840s and a room within it dedicated to showing the collection. This room was called the Walker Art Gallery, and the pictures were shown there until the new Walker Art Building was built in 1894; see Harris, *Collegiate Collections*, 26–27. The Dartmouth collection began in 1772. It is not known where it was displayed until 1791, when it was installed with the fossils in part of the library in Dartmouth Hall. Here it stayed until 1811, when it was placed in storage for sixteen years, after which the paintings were shown in Thornton Hall and the fossils in Dartmouth Hall. The paintings were transferred to Reed Hall in 1839, joined there by the Assyrian reliefs when they were acquired in 1856, moved to the new library in 1884, and finally united with the Art School in the newly constructed Carpenter Hall in 1929; see Harris, *Collegiate Collections*, 29–30.

The Yale claim for priority is based on the fact that Yale was the first to build a building specifically for its art collection. As Betsy Fahlman states, "The Trumbull Gallery was not the first art museum in America or even the first collegiate collection, but it was the first campus structure in the United States designed specifically as an art museum." See Betsy Fahlman, "Art Displays in New Haven: Edward Sheffield Bartholomew and Yale's Exhibition of 1858," *Journal of the New Haven Colony Historical Society* 38 (Fall 1991): 29.

3. On early attitudes toward collecting in America, see Neil Harris, *The Artist in American Society: The Formative Years, 1790–1860* (New York: G. Braziller, 1966).

4. The collection bequeathed to Bowdoin College in 1811 was a notable exception, in that it included 133 European paintings and drawings, many of which were not portraits; see Harris, *Collegiate Collections*, 26–28.

5. *Bulletin of the Associates in Fine Arts at Yale University* 3, no. 2 (December 1928): 33, "apparently executed by a Colonial coach painter after engravings." See also the letter from Theodore Sizer to George Croce, October 29, 1954, citing J. Cooper as possibly English and an eighteenth-century painter; Manuscripts and Archives Collection, Sterling Memorial Library, Yale University (hereafter cited as Yale MS&A), Sizer Papers, MS 453.

6. On Nehemiah Strong, see F. B. Dexter, *Biographical Sketches of the Graduates of Yale College* (New York: H. Holt and Company, 1896), 2:383–88, as cited by Harris, *Collegiate Collections*, 43, cat. no. 34.

7. See *Connecticut Portraits by Ralph Earl, 1751–1801*, exhibition catalogue, Gallery of Fine Arts, Yale University, August 1–October 15, 1935, 28, cat. no. 35; also cited by Harris, *Collegiate Collections*, 43, cat. no. 34. On the painter, see also Elizabeth M. Kornhauser et al., *Ralph Earl: The Face of the Young Republic* (New Haven: Yale University Press, 1991).

8. On Augur and Jocelyn in New Haven, see Rollin G. Osterweis, *Three Centuries of New Haven, 1638–1938* (New Haven: Yale University Press, 1953), 234. On Jocelyn, see also Bernard Heinz, "Nathaniel Jocelyn: Puritan, Painter, Inventor," *Journal of the New Haven Colony Historical Society* 39 (Summer 1993): 1–44.

9. For Trumbull as architect, see Irma B. Jaffe, *John Trumbull: Patriot-Artist of the American Revolution* (Boston: New York Graphic Society, 1975), 290–96; Paul Venable Turner, *Campus: An American Planning Tradition* (Cambridge: MIT Press, 1984), 38–43; Erik Vogt, "The Trumbull Gallery," *Yale Bulletin* 2000, 26–45.

10. 1797.1.

11. Osterweis, *New Haven*, 307.

CHAPTER 2

COLONEL TRUMBULL AND HIS COLLECTION

1. On Trumbull, see John Trumbull, *Autobiography, Reminiscences and Letters by John Trumbull from 1756 to 1841* (New Haven, 1841), written at the urging of Benjamin Silliman; Theodore Sizer, ed., *The Autobiography of Colonel John Trumbull: Patriot-Artist, 1756–1843* (New Haven: Yale University Press, 1953); Jaffe, *Trumbull*; and Helen A. Cooper, *John Trumbull: The Hand and Spirit of a Painter*, exhibition catalogue, Yale University Art Gallery, October 28, 1982–January 16, 1983.

2. See Cooper, *Trumbull*, 76–81, cat. nos. 25 and 26, on which this narrative is based.

3. On Trumbull's portraits, see Oswaldo Rodriguez Roque in Cooper, *Trumbull*, 94–105 (essay), 106–72, cat. nos. 33–124 (entries).

4. On Trumbull and the Academy, see Jaffe, *Trumbull*, 207–8, 264–75.

5. Paul Staiti, "Ideology and Politics in Samuel F. B. Morse's Agenda for a National Art," in *Samuel F. B. Morse: Educator and Champion of the Arts in America* (New York: National Academy of Design, 1982), 17, n. 14.

6. Yale MS&A, Silliman Family Papers, MS 450; Silliman's recollections of Trumbull, entitled "Reminiscences" and dated June 18, 1857–April 3, 1858, are written into a small notebook, originally in the Mabel Brady Garvan Collection, Gift of Francis P. Garvan (B.A. 1897) in 1930. On Silliman, see Chandos Michael Brown, *Benjamin Silliman: A Life in the Young Republic* (Princeton: Princeton University Press, 1989). Trumbull, in his autobiography (edited by Theodore Sizer), says that he first suggested the idea of having the pictures go to Yale to Mr. Alfred Smith, a friend of his from Hartford; how the idea got from Smith, who had no Yale connection, to Yale, Trumbull does not reveal (Sizer, ed., *Trumbull Autobiography*, 285). Sizer (n. 6) notes that Smith was a trustee (1842) and president (1856) of the Wadsworth Atheneum, so the link may have been between Smith and Daniel Wadsworth. Smith was Daniel Wadsworth's lawyer and Trumbull's friend. Trumbull also states that

he first thought of giving them to Harvard; a letter to Josiah Quincy about this is preserved at Harvard (284, n. 5). The material quoted in this paragraph is taken from the "Reminiscences," part 2, 9–10.

7. On the bank and its failure, see Osterweis, *New Haven*, 259. The building was designed by Ithiel Town in 1824 in Greek Revival style.

8. Quoted from the indenture between Trumbull and Yale; see below, n. 9.

9. The indenture is preserved in the Treasurer's Records, Yale MS&A, YRG 5-A, RU 151. It is quoted in Trumbull's autobiography (Sizer, ed., *Trumbull Autobiography*, 285–89). The document is written into the Yale Corporation Records of August 18, 1835, but the agreement is recorded as having been accepted by the Corporation on September 13, 1831, which marks the official date of acceptance.

10. Namely, *The Death of General Warren at the Battle of Bunker's Hill, 17 June 1775*; *The Death of General Montgomery in the Attack on Quebec, 31 December 1775*; *The Declaration of Independence, 4 July 1776*; *The Capture of the Hessians at Trenton, 26 December 1776*; *The Death of General Mercer at the Battle of Princeton, 3 January 1777*; *The Surrender of General Burgoyne at Saratoga, 6 October 1777*; *The Surrender of Lord Cornwallis at Yorktown, 19 October 1781*; and *General George Washington Resigning His Commission, Annapolis, 23 December 1783*.

11. Namely, *Our Savior with Little Children*; *The Woman Accused of Adultry*; *Madonna and Child with St. John the Baptist*, copied from Raphael; *St. Jerome*, copied from Correggio; *Infant Savior*; *St. John and the Lamb*; *Holy Family*; and *Maternal Tenderness*.

12. "Reminiscences," as quoted in Sizer, ed., *Trumbull Autobiography*, 375; see also Jaffe, *Trumbull*; Cooper, *Trumbull*; and Vogt, "Trumbull Gallery," 26–45.

13. Beinecke Rare Book and Manuscript Library, Yale University. Sizer, ed., *Trumbull Autobiography*, 376; Roger Hale Newton, *Town & Davis, Architects, Pioneers in American Revivalist Architecture: 1812–70* (New York: Columbia University Press, 1942); Amelia Peck et al., *Alexander Jackson Davis: American Architect 1803–1892* (New York: Rizzoli International Publications and The Metropolitan Museum of Art, 1992); and Vogt, "Trumbull Gallery," 37, fig. 7.

14. "Reminiscences," as quoted in Sizer, ed., *Trumbull Autobiography*, 377. The letter from which Silliman quoted (1831) includes sketches and notes on sizes; Yale MS&A, Trumbull Papers, MS 596.

15. *Connecticut Journal*, Tuesday, October 30, 1832, 3 (clipping in the collection of the New Haven Colony Historical Society).

16. Osterweis, *New Haven*, 238–40.

17. The Dickens visit is recorded in *American Notes* (London: Chapman and Hall, 1842), 183.

18. For the roster of visitors, see Osterweis, *New Haven*, 307–9. Osterweis (308) places the Jackson visit on June 15, 1833, citing the *New Haven Register* of June 15 and 22, and the *Connecticut Journal* of June 18, 1833; Silliman's date of 1837 in the "Reminiscences," 33, ("[The stairs] were not carpeted until the visit of General Andrew Jackson in 1837"), seems less reliable, although Silliman's mention at least confirms the visit.

19. Yale MS&A, Silliman Papers, MS 450. The letter is to Maria Trumbull Silliman Barker Church from her mother, Harriet Trumbull Silliman (wife of Benjamin Silliman), October 16, 1839. Henrietta's message is a postscript, signed "Hattie." Sizer correctly says that she is Henrietta Frances Silliman, later Mrs. James Dwight Dana.

20. Silliman, "Reminiscences," part 1, 40.

CHAPTER 3
THE MISSIONARY, THE *WOLF*, AND THE 1858 EXHIBITION

1. *Catalogue of Paintings, Belonging to Yale College, Deposited in the South Room of the Trumbull Gallery* (New Haven: printed by B. L. Hamlen, printer to the College, 1852).

2. Ibid., cat. no. 59, gives this credit line.

3. For the history of the acquisition of these reliefs by Yale and other institutions, the present location of the reliefs, and their original location in the palace, see John B. Stearns, *Reliefs from the Palace of Ashurnasirpal II* (Graz: Ferdinand Berger & Söhne, 1961).

4. On Williams, his family, his missionary activities at Mosul, and the acquisition of the reliefs for Yale, see Elizabeth Dunbar, *Talcott Williams: Gentleman of the Fourth Estate* (Brooklyn: Robert E. Simpson & Son, 1936), 43–82, especially 53–54.

5. For Samuel and Frederick Williams, see Dunbar, *Williams*, and for their gifts of Chinese art, see below, chapter 4.

6. Letter from W. F. Williams to Leonard Bacon, June 15, 1853, Yale University Art Gallery Archives (hereafter YUAG Archives).

7. Ibid.

8. Letter from W. F. Williams, still in Mosul, to Leonard Bacon, February 1, 1854, YUAG Archives.

9. Ibid., n. 6.

10. On the biblical connection, see "Rocks of Unevangelized Lands," in Stearns, *Reliefs*, 1–3. On the modern history of the reliefs, see also John Malcolm Russell, *From Nineveh to New York* (New Haven: Yale University Press, 1997).

11. *Catalogue of the Works of Art Exhibited in the Alumni Building, Yale College, 1858* (New Haven: Thomas J. Stafford, Printer, 1858), second edition, note on page 15 at the end of the catalogue. D. W. (Daniel Wadsworth) Coit was the uncle of Daniel Coit Gilman, the College Librarian.

12. Fahlman, "Art Displays," 29.

13. *Catalogue, 1858*, "Note."

14. *Resignation* is reproduced in Fahlman, "Art Displays," 30; the image is from the New Haven Colony Historical Society's archives. Thanks are due to Robin Jaffee Frank for confirming the fraternal relationship. The primary contemporary source on the exhibition is Daniel Coit Gilman, "Art Exhibition at Yale College; review of the *Catalogue of the Works of Art Exhibited in the Alumni Building, Yale College* (New Haven, 1858)," *The New Englander and Yale Review* 16 (November 1858): 807–16.

15. On the acquisition of there statues, see Fahlman, "Art Displays."

16. All previous quotes from Gilman, "Exhibition at Yale College."

17. All cited by Fahlman, "Art Displays," nn. 33–41.

18. As quoted in Gilman, "Exhibition at Yale College," 807.

19. Ibid., 814.

20. Ibid., 814.

21. Ibid., 816.

CHAPTER 4
THE YALE SCHOOL OF THE FINE ARTS

1. Augustus R. Street's letter of March 24, 1864, transcribed into the Records of the Corporation, Yale College Register, March 29, 1864, Yale MS&A, YRG I-A, RU 307, HM 49.

2. John F. Weir, "Yale School of the Fine Arts," in William L. Kingsley, *Yale College*, 2 vols. (New York: Henry Holt, 1879), 2:141.

3. A further encouragement may have come from Nathaniel Jocelyn, the well-known New Haven portrait painter, from whom Street took painting lessons. A statement to this effect attributed to Street was published in 1877, when Jocelyn was still alive, although it is not clear to whom Street made the statement. See Heinz, "Jocelyn," 41, n. 2; and Fahlman, "Art Displays," 39. Jocelyn was given a studio in the School of Art in 1866 and he taught and painted there until his death in 1881. Jocelyn's own New Haven studio burned in 1849.

4. Weir, "Yale School of the Fine Arts," 2:140.

5. See n. 1.

6. Quoted from a copy of Augustus Street's will dated September 25, 1863. Treasurer's Records, Yale MS&A, YRG 5-B, RU 151.

7. See n. 1.

8. Daniel Coit Gilman, "The Jarves Collection in the Yale School of the Fine Arts," *The New Englander and Yale Review* 27 (1868): 179, no source given.

9. Quoted from the "Minutes of the Art Council," March 1866, Yale MS&A, YRG 18A, RU 189; transcription by Josephine Setze from the original minutes into the bound "Minutes of the Governing Board," Book 4, meeting of September 20, 1945, YUAG Archives.

10. Ibid.

11. Ibid., January 1867, as above, n. 9.

12. John Ferguson Weir, "The Fiftieth Anniversary of the School of the Fine Arts, Yale University" (New Haven: Yale University Press, 1916), 10. Yale MS&A, John Ferguson Weir Papers, MS 550.

CHAPTER 5
THE JAMES JACKSON JARVES COLLECTION

1. Quoted in Francis Steegmuller, *The Two Lives of James Jackson Jarves* (New Haven: Yale University Press, 1951), 231.

2. Quoted by Steegmuller, *Jarves,* 229–30.

3. The first Italian art to enter the Metropolitan consisted of a collection of drawings assembled, coincidentally, by James Jackson Jarves; it came to the museum in 1881. Most of the Metropolitan's Italian paintings came later from the Lehman Collection.

4. On Norton, Jerome, and Corcoran, and other failed efforts to place the pictures, see Steegmuller, *Jarves,* 169–95.

5. Letter from Norton to Jarves, December 8, 1867, quoted by Steegmuller, *Jarves*, 233.

6. Quoted by Gilman, "Jarves Collection," 179, no source given.

7. Ibid., 178.

8. Russell Sturgis, Jr., *Manual of the Jarves Collection of Early Italian Pictures Deposited in the Galleries of the Yale School of the Fine Arts. Being a Catalogue, with Descriptions of the Pictures Contained in That Collection, with Biographical Notices of Artists and an Introductory Essay, The Whole Forming a Brief Guide to the Study of Early Christian Art* (New Haven: Yale College, 1868).

9. *Descriptive Catalogue of the Paintings Now on Exhibition at the Institute of Fine Arts, 625 Broadway, comprising the celebrated pictures of the well-known Dusseldorf Gallery, with several interesting additions, and the Unique Jarves Collection of Old Masters* (New York: Joseph Russell, Printer, 1860; also 1861).

10. *The College Courant* 1 (February 26, 1868), 197.

11. *The College Courant* 4 (March 6, 1869), 145.

12. *Catalogue of the Jarves Collection of Early Italian Pictures, Deposited in the Galleries of the Yale School of the Fine Arts. To be Sold at Auction in the Galleries at Yale College, New Haven, Conn., on Thursday, November 9th, 1871. Sale to commence at 10 o'clock. Joseph Leonard, Auctioneer, Boston* (Boston: W. F. Brown & Co., Printers, 1871).

CHAPTER 6
NEW TEACHERS, OLD MASTERS, AND OLD POTS

1. Kingsley, *Yale College*, 2:44.

2. Weir, "Fiftieth Anniversary," 14; President's Report, "Yale College in 1871," June 1871, 19.

3. President's Report, "Yale College in 1870," June 1870, 23.

4. Excerpts, Minutes of the Faculty, Yale School of the Fine Arts, June 30, 1874. YUAG Archives.

5. Ibid., October 9, 1888 through June 6, 1892. YUAG Archives.

6. Minutes of the Art Council, October 24, 1878. YUAG Archives.

7. Excerpts, Minutes of the Faculty, March 26, 1891, YUAG Archives.

8. Ibid., June 3, 1891, YUAG Archives.

9. Extracts from the minutes of the Corporation Relating to the School of the Fine Arts. Yale MS&A, John Ferguson Weir Papers, MS 550.

10. "New Galleries at Yale, Art School Open," *New Haven Register*, February 17, 1911, Yale MS&A, Weir Papers, MS 550.

11. 1911.1, 2, 8, 10; 1913.676, 677.

12. *Reports of the Course of Instruction in Yale College . . .* (New Haven: Printed by Hezekiah Howe, 1828), Yale MS&A.

13. The house is now the property of Albertus Magnus College.

14. Weir, "Fiftieth Anniversary," 21.

15. Ibid.

16. Excerpts, Minutes of the Faculty, Yale School of the Fine Arts, December 8, 1916, YUAG Archives.

17. All this on Porter in the Records of President Arthur Twining Hadley, Yale MS&A, YRG 2-A RU 25, as quoted in Linda Seidel, "Kingsley Porter: Legend and Legacy," in Craig Hugh Smyth and Peter M. Lukehart, eds., *The Early Years of Art History in the United States* (Princeton: Princeton University Press, 1993), 101.

17. Fahlman, "Art Displays," 41.

CHAPTER 7
THE GALLERY OF FINE ARTS

1. On the architectural history of the Gallery of Fine Arts by Egerton Swartwout, see Patricia E. Kane, "Egerton Swartwout's Gallery of Fine Arts at Yale University," *Yale Bulletin* 2000, 68–87, on which the following is based.

2. The title was changed from director to dean during the academic year 1918/19.

3. See Kenneth Edmunds, "The Simplification of Architectural Practice as Illustrated in the Methods Employed by Egerton Swartwout in Designing the Gallery of Fine Arts," *Architecture* 55, no. 3 (November 1927): 127–36.

4. As quoted in Kane, from Edmunds, "Simplification of Architectural Practice," 132.

5. "Program, Gallery of Fine Arts, Draft Copy," May 1925, 1. YUAG Archives.

6. *Yale Bulletin* 2, 2 (June 1927): 27.

7. Letter from Maitland F. Griggs to George Parmly Day (University Treasurer), 8 June 1929, YUAG Archives. Confirmed in the Treasurer's Report 1928–29, 29.

CHAPTER 8
FRANCIS P. GARVAN AND MABEL BRADY GARVAN COLLECTIONS OF AMERICAN ART

1. "Dean Meeks Praises Gift," *New York Times,* June 22, 1930, 3.

2. On Garvan see G. W. R. Ward, P. E. Kane, H. A. Cooper, *Francis P. Garvan, Collector* (New Haven, 1980), published as a tribute to him on the fiftieth anniversary of the gift of the Mabel Brady Garvan Collection to the Yale Art Gallery.

3. *Made in America Monthly* 5 (November 1941); YUAG Archives.

4. Charles Messer Stowe, "This Country Needs Collectors, Is Opinion of Francis P. Garvan," *New York Sun,* July 26, 1930, 6.

5. Ibid.

6. Ibid.

7. Ibid.

8. Patricia E. Kane, "Francis P. Garvan: Collector of American Decorative Arts," in Ward et al., *Garvan,* 28.

9. Letter from Francis P. Garvan to Francis H. Bigelow, December 24, 1916; YUAG Archives.

10. Letter from Francis P. Garvan to Edward B. Reed, December 24, 1929; copy in YUAG Archives.

11. Stowe, "This Country Needs Collectors," 6.

12. Letter from Francis P. Garvan to George Parmly Day, Treasurer of Yale, June 6, 1930; copy in YUAG Archives.

13. See note 10.

14. Letter from President James Roland Angell to Francis P. Garvan, June 30, 1928, Yale MS&A, Angell Papers, YRG 2A, RU 24.

15. Theodore Sizer, "John Marshall Phillips, 1905–1953," reprinted from *The Walpole Society Note Book* (1953), 5.

16. *Parade Magazine,* July 19, 1948.

17. Described by Sizer, "Phillips," and in "John Marshall Phillips," *National Cyclopaedia of American Biography*, vol. 50 (New York, 1968): 303–4.

18. Letter from Frank B. Stone to Patricia E. Kane, March 11, 1999, YUAG Archives, Garvan Collection.

19. On Myer Myers, see David L. Barquist, *Myer Myers: Jewish Silversmith in Colonial New York*, exhibition catalogue, Yale University Art Gallery, September 14–December 30, 2001, and other venues.

20. David L. Barquist, *American and English Pewter at the Yale University Art Gallery* (New Haven: Yale University Art Gallery, 1985), 13.

21. Letter accompanying the gift, quoted by Helen A. Cooper, "Francis P. Garvan, Collector of Paintings, Prints & Sculpture," in Ward et al., *Garvan,* 45.

22. On Abbey, see *Edwin Austin Abbey, 1851–1911,* exhibition catalogue, Yale University Art Gallery, December 6, 1973–February 17, 1974, and other venues; Lucy Oakley, *Unfaded Pageant: Edwin Austin Abbey's Shakespearean Subjects*, exhibition catalogue, Miriam and Ira D. Wallach Art Gallery, Columbia University, 1994; dissertation by Baird Jarman, Yale University, forthcoming, whom I thank for his assistance.

CHAPTER 9
DIGGING AND TEACHING

1. *Yale Bulletin* 3, 2 (December 1928): 26.

2. Ibid.

3. On Yale's Egyptian collections, see Gerry D. Scott, *Ancient Egyptian Art at Yale* (New Haven: Yale University Art Gallery, 1986).

4. On the Dura-Europos excavations, see Clark Hopkins, *The Discovery of Dura-Europos* (New Haven: Yale University Press, 1979), with references to the excavation reports and additional bibliography.

5. On the glass collection, see Susan B. Matheson, *Ancient Glass in the Yale University Art Gallery* (New Haven: Yale University Art Gallery, 1980).

6. President's Report, 1927–28, 121.

7. Yale MS&A, Theodore Sizer Papers, MS 453.

8. *Yale Alumni Weekly* 43 (December 8, 1933): 1.

9. *Yale Alumni Weekly* 45 (January 11, 1935): 373.

10. *New Haven Register*, June 23, 1935.

11. *Yale Bulletin* 9, 1 (June 1939): 28.

CHAPTER 10

KATHERINE DREIER AND THE SOCIÉTÉ ANONYME

1. On the succession of Goodwin designs for this building, see Susan B. Matheson and Elise K. Kenney, "Prologue to Kahn: The Philip Goodwin Design," *Yale Bulletin* 2000, 88–103.

2. On the Société Anonyme Collection, see Robert L. Herbert, Eleanor S. Apter, and Elise K. Kenney, eds., *The Société Anonyme and the Dreier Bequest at Yale University: A Catalogue Raisonné* (New Haven: Yale University Press, 1984). The narrative that follows is drawn from the introduction to this volume.

3. Frederick Hartt, *Yale Daily News*, January 15, 1942; unidentified review, January 13, 1942; both Yale MS&A, Art School Scrapbooks.

4. Herbert et al., *Société Anonyme*, 28.

5. Ibid., 31.

6. Ibid.

7. Obituary, *New York Times*, July 18, 1945. See also A. Elizabeth Chase, "The John Hill Morgan Memorial Exhibition of American Art, February 22–March 25 [1946]," *Yale Bulletin* 14, 1 (March 1946): 2–3, and John Marshall Phillips, "The Morgan Miniatures," 9, 3 (June 1941): 2.

8. Obituary, *New York Times*, April 28, 1957; see also Charles Seymour, Jr., "Louis Mayer Rabinowitz," *Yale Bulletin* 23, 3 (September 1957): 10–14.

9. Minutes of the Governing Board of the Art Gallery, June 5, 1947, YUAG Archives.

10. *National Cyclopaedia of American Biography*, vol. 50 (New York, 1968): 303–4; on John Marshall Phillips and the Art Gallery, see also the special issue, *Yale Bulletin* 21, 1 (October 1953).

CHAPTER 11

"A NEW BUILDING FOR THE ARTS AT YALE"

1. On the Kahn building, see Patricia Cummings Loud, *The Art Museums of Louis I. Kahn* (Durham, N.C.: Duke University Press, 1989); and Alexander Purves, "The Yale University Art Gallery by Louis I. Kahn," *Yale Bulletin* 2000, 104–13.

2. "Order and Form," *Perspecta* 3 (1955): 47.

3. As quoted in Henry S. F. Cooper, "The Architect Speaks," *Yale Daily News, Special Supplement: The New Art Gallery and Design Center* (November 6, 1953), 2.

4. *Perspecta* 3 (1955): 47.

5. Ibid.

6. Vincent J. Scully, Jr., "Somber and Archaic; Expressive Tension," *Yale Daily News, Special Supplement*, 10.

7. As quoted in the *New Haven Register*, November 1, 1953, YUAG Archives.

8. As quoted in Cooper, "The Architect Speaks," 2. The Kahn quotes in the next paragraph are from the same source.

9. Frederick Gutheim, "Modern Architecture at Yale," *New York Herald Tribune*, November 28, 1953, 10.

10. Maude Kemper Riley, "Yale: A Tent in Concrete," *Art Digest* 28 (1954): 13, 25.

11. Gutheim, "Yale."

12. "A Wall of Glass . . . A Wall of Brick," *Yale Daily News, Special Supplement*, 7–8.

13. Avery Faulkner, "The Student Speaks," *Yale Daily News, Special Supplement*, 4.

14. Riley, "Tent in Concrete," 25.

15. Lamont Moore, *"Pictures for a Picture" of Gertrude Stein as a Collector and Writer on Art and Artists*, exhibition catalogue, Yale University Art Gallery, February 11–March 11, 1951; Baltimore Museum of Art, March 21–April 21, 1951.

16. Part of the Collection of American Literature at Yale University.

17. Gertrude Stein, *What Are Masterpieces* (Los Angeles, CA: The Conference Press, 1940), 27, 28, 29, as excerpted in Moore, *Stein*, 13–14.

18. Moore, *Stein*, 14.

19. Exhibition catalogue subtitle; April 10–May 17, 1953, published as an issue of the *Yale Bulletin* 20, 3 (1953).

20. "Tradition in Art: Civic Retrospective," *Interiors* (June 1953), 10.

21. Aline B. Louchheim, "City Planning through the Ages: Yale Exhibition Traces Man's Effort to Find Livable Solution," *New York Times*, April 19, 1953, section 10, 9.

22. Quoted in Louchheim, "City Planning."

23. Ibid. [anonymous reviewer, not Tunnard].

24. Personal communication, August 20, 2001.

25. Jacques Maritain, *Creative Intuition in Art and Poetry* (New York: Pantheon Books, 1953), 3.

26. "Art and Artists: Yale Links Pen, Brush and Chisel," *New York Herald Tribune Book Review*, June 6, 1954, 18.

27. George Heard Hamilton, *Object and Image in Modern Art and Poetry*, exhibition catalogue, Yale University Art Gallery, April 30–June 14, 1954, n.p.

28. From e. e. cummings, *i, six nonlectures* (1953), quoted in Hamilton, *Object and Image*, by permission of Harvard University Press.

29. Kate H. Spencer, *The Graphic Art of Géricault*, exhibition catalogue, Yale University Art Gallery, February 5–March 30, 1969.

30. Lamont Moore, Report to University Council, May 1956, Yale MS&A, Griswold Papers, YRG 2A, RU 22.

31. Adelin Linton and Claire Vernick, *The Linton Collection of African Sculpture: An Exhibition*, Yale University Art Gallery, March 13–April 18, 1954.

32. Allen Wardwell, *African Sculpture from the University Museum, University of Pennsylvania*, exhibition catalogue, Philadelphia Museum of Art, November 23, 1986–February 8, 1987.

33. Susan Vogel, *Baule: African Art/Western Eyes*, exhibition catalogue, Yale University Art Gallery, August 30, 1997–January 4, 1998.

34. George A. Kubler, ed., *Pre-Columbian Art of Mexico and Central America* (New Haven: Yale University Art Gallery, 1986) remains the only comprehensive catalogue of the collection.

35. Obituary, *New York Times*, November 11, 1986, B6; see also the *New Haven Register*, November 11, 1986, 28.

CHAPTER 12
A MAGNET FOR VISITORS AND ART

1. John Canaday, "Adieu, Academe: Or, Changing Ideas on the Function of University Art Museums," *New York Times,* January 15, 1961, section 10, 11.

2. Ibid.

3. George J. Lee, *The Edo Culture in Japanese Prints*, exhibition catalogue, Yale University Art Gallery, October 19–November 26, 1972.

4. John Canaday, "Art: Acquisitions of Yale Gallery," *New York Times,* January 10, 1961, Scrapbook, YUAG Archives.

5. Obituary, *New York Times,* March 11, 1966, 34.

6. Mary Gardner Neill, *The Communion of Scholars: Chinese Art at Yale*, exhibition catalogue, China House Gallery, China Institute in America; Houston, Museum of Fine Arts; and Yale University Art Gallery, October 5, 1982–April 17, 1983, 9.

7. Alan Shestack, Annual Report, Yale University Art Gallery, 1973–74, YUAG Archives.

8. A special issue of the *Yale University Art Gallery Bulletin* published in 1987 honored Alan Shestack with a series of articles celebrating major acquisitions made while he was director.

9. *Museum News* 12 (1978): 27–31, 89–91, reprinted with an afterword in *Museum News* 62 (1984): 66–70.

10. Ibid., 27.

11. Ibid., 29.

12. Ibid., 31.

CHAPTER 13
MODERN AND CONTEMPORARY

1. Letter from Richard Brown Baker to Andrew Carnduff Ritchie, November 10, 1962, YUAG Archives.

2. Press release, Yale University News Bureau, May 22, 1963.

3. *Two Modern Collectors: Susan Morse Hilles and Richard Brown Baker*, exhibition catalogue, Yale University Art Gallery, May 22–September 1, 1963, 5.

4. Ibid., 38.

5. Memorandum from Caroline Rollins to Stanton Catlin, assistant director under Andrew Ritchie, May 27, 1963, YUAG Archives.

6. Stuart Preston, "Two Private Collectors in a Public Place," *New York Times,* August 18, 1963, section 10, 16.

7. Richard Brown Baker journal, April 1955, as quoted in the 1995 exhibition catalogue, 13.

8. Letter from Richard Brown Baker to his mother, April 17, 1955, as quoted in the 1995 exhibition catalogue, 14.

9. Alan Shestack and Lesley K. Baier, *The Katharine Ordway Collection* (New Haven: Yale University Art Gallery, 1983).

10. As quoted in Daphne Deeds, *Hawaiian Eye: Collecting Contemporary Art with Thurston Twigg-Smith*, exhibition catalogue, Yale University Art Gallery, February 2–June 15, 1997, 5.

11. Ibid., 2.

12. Susan P. Casteras, *The "Lipstick" Comes Back*, exhibition catalogue, Yale University Art Gallery, October 17–November 30, 1974, 24.

13. Anne Coffin Hanson, ed., *The Futurist Imagination: Word + Image in Italian Painting, Drawing, Collage and Free-Word Poetry*, exhibition catalogue, Yale University Art Gallery, New Haven, April 13–June 26, 1983.

14. Sasha M. Newman, *Yale Collects Yale: 1950–1993*, exhibition catalogue, Yale University Art Gallery, April 30–July 31, 1993.

CHAPTER 14
"TOWARDS INDEPENDENCE"

1. Letter from Irving S. Olds to Charles F. Montgomery, October 23, 1959; YUAG Archives, Garvan Collection.

2. The authors and titles of these catalogues are listed in the bibliography, p. 268.

3. Letter from Hiram Powers to E. W. Stoughton, 1869; photostat in New York Public Library scrapbook on Hiram Powers, as quoted in Samuel A. Roberson and William H. Gerdts, "'. . . so undressed, yet so refined . . .' The Greek Slave," *The Museum* 17 (1965) 4. I thank Robin Jaffee Frank for this and the following two references.

4. Joy S. Kasson, *Marble Queens and Captives: Women in Nineteenth-Century Sculpture* (New Haven: Yale University Press, 1990), 48.

5. Henry James, *William Wetmore Story and His Friends*, 2 vols. (Boston: Houghton Mifflin, 1903): 114 15.

6. Freeman Murray, as quoted in the tabloid published in conjunction with the Garvan installation of 1973; the probable source, although I have been unable to consult it, is: Freeman Henry Morris Murray, *Emancipation and the Freed in American Sculpture*, Washington, D.C., 1916. Reprinted Freeport, N. Y.: Books for Libraries Press, 1972, as cited by Vivien M. Green, "Hiram Powers's Greek Slave: Emblem of Freedom," *American Art Journal* 14 (Autumn 1982), pp. 31–39. My thanks to Robin Jaffee Frank and Amy Kurtz Lansing for this reference.

7. "Report on the American Collections," May 5, 1964, 1; YUAG Archives.

8. Prown quotes this statement in his report of 1964 (see n. 7); it is quoted below in chapter 15, p. 255–56.

9. Jules Prown, "The Rediscovery of America, 1," *Art News* 67 (May 1968): 30–33.

10. Introduction, Theodore E. Stebbins, Jr., and Galina Gorokhoff, comp., *A Checklist of American Paintings at Yale University* (New Haven: Yale University Art Gallery, 1982), xviii–xix. See also Theodore E. Stebbins, Jr., "Collecting American Art for Yale, 1968–1976: A Curatorial Report," *Yale Bulletin* 36 (1977), 1–17.

11. Alan Shestack, "Foreword," in B. M. Ward and G. W. R. Ward, *Charles F. Montgomery and Florence M. Montgomery: A Tribute* (New Haven: Yale University Art Gallery, 1978), 9.

12. Published in *The Walpole Society Note Book* in 1961, reprinted in Ward and Ward, *Montgomery*, 17–29.

13. Hilton Kramer, "Art: An Extraordinary Installation," *New York Times*, June 2, 1973, section L, 27.

14. Ibid. Actually, the installation contained other types of Windsor furniture besides chairs, and a chair and a bench, rather than two chairs, stood on the floor.

15. Full titles are given in the bibliography, 268.

16. Charles F. Montgomery and Patricia E. Kane, eds., *American Art: 1750–1800, Towards Independence*, exhibition catalogue, Yale University Art Gallery, April 3–May 23, 1976; Victoria and Albert Museum, July 15–September 26, 1976, 9.

17. Alan Shestack, Report to the Garvan Committee, March 14, 1973, YUAG Archives.

18. Benjamin A. Hewitt, Gerald W. R. Ward, Patricia E. Kane, *The Work of Many Hands: Card Tables in Federal America, 1790–1820*, exhibition catalogue, Yale University Art Gallery, March 25–May 30, 1982.

19. Richard S. Field, in Richard S. Field, Rebecca Zurier, et al., *American Prints, 1900–1950: An Exhibition in Honor of the Donation of John P. Axelrod,* B.A. *1968*, exhibition catalogue, Yale University Art Gallery, May 10–September 31, 1983, 7.

20. As quoted in *A Great Panorama: Celebrating Twenty-Five Years of American Arts at Yale* (New Haven: Yale University Art Gallery, 1998), 26.

21. William Zimmer, "Shedding Light on the Cryptic Portraits of Charles Demuth," *New York Times*, October 30, 1994, Connecticut section, 22.

22. *Discovered Lands, Invented Pasts: Transforming Visions of the American West*, exhibition: Helen A. Cooper, Yale University Art Gallery, Gilcrease Museum, and Buffalo Bill Historical Center, June 15, 1992–April 11, 1993; book: Jules David Prown, Nancy K. Anderson, William Cronon, Brian W. Dippie, Martha A. Sandweiss, Susan Prendergast Schoelwer, and Howard R. Lamar (New Haven: Yale University Press and the Yale University Art Gallery, 1992).

23. "Yale Enriches Its Silver Trove," *New York Times,* March 27, 1988, 42.

24. Ibid.

25. Ibid.

26. Press release, typescript [1988] YUAG Archives.

27. Helen A. Cooper and Nancy Rivard Shaw, *A Private View: American Paintings from the Manoogian Collection*, exhibition catalogue, Yale University Art Gallery and the Detroit Institute of Arts, April 3–July 31, 1993, 9.

28. *American Watercolors from the Collection of George Hopper Fitch*, exhibition catalogue, spring 1980 issue of the *Yale Bulletin*, April 13–August 31, 1980, and *Give a Thing and It Is Yours Forever: George Hopper Fitch Collects for Yale*, May 6–June 8, 1997.

29. *Yale Bulletin* 1992, 7.

CHAPTER 15
ART FOR YALE: DEFINING MOMENTS

1. On this project, see Jock Reynolds, "Renewing a Teaching Mission, Restoring an Architectural Legacy, and Building for the 21st Century," *Yale Bulletin* 2000, 114–24.

2. See note 4, below.

3. The exhibition was shown only at Yale, from April 19–August 19, 2001. This book complements the exhibition.

4. This and all subsequent quotes in this chapter were collected for the Gallery's exhibition *Art for Yale: Defining Moments* by the exhibition's curator, Helen Cooper, from letters, other written sources, and personal interviews and are used by permission.

Selected Bibliography

This list includes catalogues and major checklists of the permanent collection, as well as exhibition catalogues and selected articles that serve as reference publications of the collection. In addition, exhibition catalogues mentioned in the text are cited in full here. Unless stated otherwise, catalogues were published by the Yale University Art Gallery.

GENERAL

Biographical Sketches of the Graduates of Yale College. F. B. Dexter. 6 vols. New York: H. Holt and Company, 1885–1912.

Bulletin of the Associates in Fine Arts; Yale University Art Gallery Bulletin. Vol. 1– . New Haven, 1926– .

The Yale Collections. Wilmarth Lewis. New Haven: Yale University Press, 1946.

Yale University Portrait Index: 1701–1951. New Haven, 1952.

On the history of the architecture of the Yale University Art Gallery, see the articles by Vincent Scully, Erik Vogt, Alexander Purves, Patricia E. Kane, Elise K. Kenney, Victoria J. Solan, Jock Reynolds, and Susan B. Matheson in the *Yale University Art Gallery Bulletin,* 2000.

PERMANENT COLLECTION CATALOGUES, HANDBOOKS/GUIDES TO THE PERMANENT COLLECTIONS

Catalogue of Paintings by Colonel Trumbull . . . Now Exhibiting in the Gallery of Yale College . . . . John Trumbull, ed. New Haven, 1832, 1835, 1852, 1860, 1864; also published with an introduction in the *American Journal of Science,* 1840, 213–50.

Catalogue of Paintings, Belonging to Yale College, Deposited in the South Room of the Trumbull Gallery. New Haven: printed by J. Peck, 1835.

Catalogue of Paintings, Belonging to Yale College, Deposited in the South Room of the Trumbull Gallery. New Haven: printed by B. L. Hamlen, printer to the College, 1852.

Catalogue of Works of Art in the Permanent and Loaned Collections of the Yale School of the Fine Arts. New Haven, 1871.

A Catalogue, with Descriptive Notices, of the Portraits, Busts, etc. Belonging to Yale University. New Haven, 1892.

Selected Paintings and Sculpture from the Yale University Art Gallery. Andrew Carnduff Ritchie and Katharine B. Neilson. New Haven, 1972.

Yale University Art Gallery: Selections. Alan Shestack, ed. New Haven, 1983.

Handbook of the Collections, Yale University Art Gallery. New Haven, 1992. Works acquired before 1990.

AMERICAN

Paintings by John Trumbull at Yale University. John Hill Morgan. New Haven, 1926.

American Gold 1700–1860. Exhibition catalogue. Yale University Art Gallery, 1963.

"American Pewter: Garvan and Other Collections at Yale." Graham Hood. *Yale University Art Gallery Bulletin.* 1965.

American Silver: Garvan and Other Collections in the Yale University Art Gallery. 2 vols. Kathryn Buhler and Graham Hood. New Haven, 1970.

The American Clock 1725–1865: The Mabel Brady Garvan and Other Collections at Yale University. Edwin A. Battison and Patricia E. Kane. Greenwich: New York Graphic Society Limited, 1973.

Edwin Austin Abbey, 1851–1911. Kathleen Foster, ed. Exhibition catalogue. Yale University Art Gallery, 1973.

300 Years of American Seating Furniture: Chairs and Beds from the Mabel Brady Garvan and Other Collections. Patricia E. Kane. Boston: New York Graphic Society, 1976.

A Checklist of American Paintings at Yale University. Theodore E. Stebbins, Jr., and Galina Gorokhoff. New Haven, 1982.

American and English Pewter at the Yale University Art Gallery. David L. Barquist. New Haven, 1985.

American Case Furniture in the Mabel Brady Garvan and Other Collections at Yale University. Gerald W. R. Ward. New Haven, 1988.

American Sculpture at Yale University. Paula B. Freedman with Robin Jaffee Frank. New Haven, 1992.

American Tables and Looking Glasses in the Mabel Brady Garvan Collections at Yale University. David L. Barquist. New Haven, 1992.

"A Great Panorama": Celebrating Twenty-Five Years of American Arts at Yale. New Haven, 1998.

ANCIENT

The Rebecca Darlington Stoddard Collection of Greek and Italian Vases. Paul V. C. Baur, ed. New Haven: Yale University Press, 1922.

The Excavations at Dura-Europos, Preliminary and Final Reports. Various authors. New Haven: Yale University Press; Los Angeles: University of California Press; Ann Arbor: University of Michigan Press, 1929 – 2001.

Gerasa: City of the Decapolis. Paul V. C. Baur, ed. New Haven: Yale University Press, 1938.

Ancient Glass in the Yale University Art Gallery. Susan B. Matheson. New Haven, 1980.

Dura-Europos: The Ancient City and the Yale Collection. Susan B. Matheson. New Haven, 1982; revised, 2001.

Ancient Egyptian Art at Yale. Gerry D. Scott, III. New Haven, 1986.

Pre-Columbian Art of Mexico and Central America. George A. Kubler, ed. New Haven, 1986.

Greek Vases: A Guide to the Yale Collection. Susan B. Matheson. New Haven, 1988.

ASIAN

Selected Far Eastern Art in the Yale University Art Gallery. George J. Lee. New Haven: Yale University Press, 1970.

The Communion of Scholars: Chinese Art at Yale. Mary Gardner Neill. New York: China Institute in America, Inc., 1982.

EUROPEAN AND CONTEMPORARY

Manual of the Jarves Collection of Early Italian Pictures Deposited in the Gallery of the Yale School of the Fine Arts. Being a Catalogue, with Descriptions of the Pictures Contained in That Collection, with Biographical Notes of Artists and an Introductory Essay, The Whole Forming a Brief Guide to the Study of Early Christian Art. Russell Sturgis, Jr. New Haven, 1868.

A Descriptive Catalogue of the Pictures in the Jarves Collection Belonging to Yale University. Osvald Sirén. New Haven, 1916.

Katherine S. Dreier and Marcel Duchamp. *Collection of the Société Anonyme: Museum of Modern Art 1920.* George Heard Hamilton, ed. New Haven, 1950.

The Rabinowitz Collection of European Paintings. Charles Seymour, Jr. New Haven, 1961.

Early Italian Paintings in the Yale University Art Gallery. Charles Seymour, Jr. New Haven, 1970.

The Katharine Ordway Collection. Alan Shestack and Lesley K. Baier. New Haven, 1983.

The Société Anonyme and the Dreier Bequest at Yale University: A Catalogue Raisonné. Robert L. Herbert, Eleanor S. Apter, and Elise K. Kenney, eds. New Haven: Yale University Press, 1984.

PRINTS, DRAWINGS, AND PHOTOGRAPHS

European Drawings and Watercolors in the Yale University Art Gallery: 1500–1900. Egbert Haverkamp-Begemann and Anne-Marie Logan. New Haven, 1970.

EXHIBITION CATALOGUES CITED IN THE TEXT

Catalogue of the Works of Art Exhibited in the Alumni Building, Yale College, 1858. New Haven: Thomas J. Stafford, Printer, 1858.

First Annual Exhibition of the Yale School of the Fine Arts, Founded as a Department of Yale College, by the Late Augustus Russell Street of New Haven, Conn. New Haven: J. H. Benham & Son, Printers, 1867.

Paintings, Landscapes, and Marines by American Artists from the Collection of Robbins Battell, Norfolk. New Haven, 1882.

Federal Art in New England. 1937.

Portraits of Distinguished New Haveners. Yale University Art Gallery Bulletin. 1938.

Masterpieces of New England Silver: 1650–1800. John Marshall Phillips. 1939.

Art of Australia, 1788–1941. Sidney Ure Smith O.B.E., ed. New York, 1941.

The John Hill Morgan Memorial Exhibition of American Art. Yale University Art Gallery Bulletin. 1946.

Exhibition of Painting and Sculpture by the Directors of the Société Anonyme Since Its Founding, 1920–1948. Yale University Art Gallery Bulletin. 1948.

The Smibert Tradition. John Marshall Phillips. 1949.

"Pictures for a Picture" of Gertrude Stein as a Collector and Writer on Art and Artists. Lamont Moore. 1951.

Ars in Urbe. Lamont Moore and Christopher Tunnard. 1953.

Object and Image in Modern Art and Poetry. George Heard Hamilton. 1954.

African Art from the Ralph M. Linton Collection. Adelin Linton and Claire Vernick. 1954.

Pictures Collected by Yale Alumni. Lamont Moore and Theodore Sizer. 1956.

Masterworks from Yale University. Lamont Moore, and excerpts from Wilmarth Lewis, *The Yale Collections* [1946]. 1956.

Chinese Paintings at Yale. George C. Lee. 1963.

The Work of Paul Rudolph, Architect. Vincent Scully. 1963.

Two Modern Collectors: Susan Morse Hilles and Richard Brown Baker. Andrew Carnduff Ritchie, Susan Morse Hilles, and Richard Brown Baker. 1963.

Neo-Impressionists and the Nabis in the Collection of Arthur G. Altschul. Robert L. Herbert and graduate students in History of Art. 1965.

Painting in England 1700–1859 from the Collection of Mr. and Mrs. Paul Mellon. Basil Taylor. 1965. With separate plate volume.

English Drawings and Watercolors from the Collection of Mr. and Mrs. Paul Mellon. Andrew Carnduff Ritchie. 1965.

American Art from Alumni Collections. Jules D. Prown and graduate students in History of Art. 1968.

The Graphic Art of Géricault. Kate H. Spencer. 1969.

The Edo Culture in Japanese Prints. George C. Lee. 1972.

Sixteenth Century Italian Drawings: Form and Function. John Caldwell and Edmund P. Pillsbury. 1974.

Charles Meryon: Prints & Drawings. James D. Burke. 1974.

The "Lipstick" Comes Back. Susan P. Casteras. 1974.

Inventors and Innovators in Color Photography 1850–1975. James D. Burke. 1975.

Greek Vases at Yale. J. J. Pollitt, Susan B. Matheson, and graduate students in History of Art and Classics. 1975.

Richard Brown Baker Collects! Theodore E. Stebbins, Jr., and graduate students in History of Art. 1975.

Darkness into Light: The Early Mezzotint. Ellen D'Oench. 1976.

Dante Gabriel Rossetti and the Double Work of Art. Maryan Ainsworth. 1976.

American Art 1750–1800: Towards Independence. Charles F. Montgomery and Patricia E. Kane, eds. 1976.

Traces of the Brush: Studies in Chinese Calligraphy. Shen C. Y. Fu, Marilyn Fu, Mary Gardner Neill, and Richard M. Barnhart. 1977.

Silver in American Life. Gerald W. R. Ward and Barbara McLean Ward. 1978.

American Watercolors from the Collection of George Hopper Fitch. Yale University Art Gallery Bulletin. 1980.

Hans Baldung Grien: Prints and Drawings. James H. Marrow and Alan Shestack. 1981.

John Trumbull: The Hand and Spirit of a Painter. Helen A. Cooper. 1982.

The Work of Many Hands: Card Tables in Federal America 1790–1820. Benjamin Hewitt, Gerald W. R. Ward, and Patricia E. Kane. 1982.

Philadelphia Naturalistic Photography, 1865–1906. Mary Panzer. 1982.

The Communion of Scholars: Chinese Art at Yale. Mary Gardner Neill. New York: China Institute in America, Inc., 1982.

American Prints, 1900–1950: An Exhibition in Honor of the Donation of John P. Axelrod, B.A. *1968.* Richard S. Field and graduate students in History of Art. 1983.

At Home in Manhattan: Modern Decorative Arts, 1925 to the Depression. Karen Davies. 1983.

The Futurist Imagination: Word + Image in Italian Painting, Drawing, Collage, and Free-Word Poetry. Anne Coffin Hanson, ed., and graduate students in History of Art. 1983.

Richard Hamilton: Image and Process. Richard S. Field. London: The Tate Gallery, 1983.

The Croquet Game. David Park Curry. 1984.

Ralph Kirkpatrick In Memoriam. Richard S. Field. 1984.

Bones of Jade, Soul of Ice: The Flowering Plum in Chinese Art. Mary Gardner Neill and Maggie Bickford. 1985.

Art for "The Masses" (1911–1917): A Radical Magazine and Its Graphics. Rebecca Zurier. 1986.

Winslow Homer Watercolors. Helen A. Cooper. 1986.

A Taste for Angels: Neapolitan Painting in North America, 1650–1750. Judith Colton and George Hersey. 1987.

The Graphic Art of Umberto Boccioni. Anne Coffin Hanson and William Valerio. 1988.

Word in Flower: The Visualization of Classical Literature in Seventeenth-Century Japan. Carolyn Wheelwright. 1989.

American Daguerreotypes from the Matthew R. Isenburg Collection. Richard S. Field and Matthew R. Isenburg. 1989.

German and Austrian Contemporary Art from the Bareiss Collection. Sasha M. Newman. 1989.

The Art Museums of Louis I. Kahn. Book: Patricia Loud. Durham, North Carolina: Duke University Press, 1989.

Childe Hassam: An Island Garden Revisited. Helen A. Cooper. 1990.

Felix Vallotton: A Retrospective. Sasha M. Newman. New York: Abbeville Press, 1991.

Master of the Lotus Garden: The Life of Bada Shanren. Mary Gardner Neill and Richard M. Barnhart. 1991.

Eva Hesse: A Retrospective. Helen A. Cooper. New Haven: Yale University Press, 1992.

Discovered Lands, Invented Pasts: Transforming Visions of the American West. Book: Jules Prown, Nancy K. Anderson, William Cronon, Brian W. Dippie, Martha A. Sandweiss, Susan Prendergast Schoelwer, and Howard R. Lamar. New Haven: Yale University Press, 1992.

Yale Collects Yale: 1950–1993. Sasha M. Newman. 1993.

A Private View: American Paintings from the Manoogian Collection. Helen A. Cooper, Nancy Rivard Shaw, and graduate students in History of Art. 1993.

The Jade Studio: Masterpieces of Ming and Qing Painting and Calligraphy from the Wong Nan-p'ing Collection. Richard M. Barnhart and Colin Mackenzie. 1994.

An Obsession with Fortune: Tyche in Greek and Roman Art. Susan B. Matheson, ed. *Yale University Art Gallery Bulletin.* 1994.

Charles Demuth: Poster Portraits 1923–1929. Robin Jaffee Frank. 1994.

Collecting with Richard Brown Baker: From Pollock to Lichtenstein. Sasha M. Newman. 1995.

Mel Bochner: Thought Made Visible, 1966–1973. Richard S. Field. 1995.

Thomas Eakins: The Rowing Pictures. Helen A. Cooper. 1996.

I, Claudia: Women in Ancient Rome. Diana E. E. Kleiner and Susan B. Matheson, eds. 1996.

Hawaiian Eye: Collecting Contemporary Art with Thurston Twigg-Smith. Daphne Deeds. 1997.

Baule: African Art/Western Eyes. Susan Mullin Vogel. New Haven: Yale University Press, 1997.

Now and Then: Art at Yale Since 1945; Now and Later. Joachim Pissarro and Thomas Crow. 1998.

Portraiture and the Harlem Renaissance: The Photographs of James L. Allen. Camara Dia Holloway. 1999.

Call and Response: Journeys of African Art. Sarah Adams, Barbaro Martinez-Ruiz, and Lyneise Williams. 2000.

Imaging African Art: Documentation and Transformation. Daniell Cornell. 2000.

Modern Gothic: The Revival of Mediaeval Art. Susan B. Matheson and Derek D. Churchill. 2000.

Love and Loss: American Mourning Miniatures. Robin Jaffee Frank. 2001.

Myer Myers: Jewish Silversmith in Colonial America. David L. Barquist. 2001.

Exhibitions 1858–2001

ELISE K. KENNEY

This list records exhibitions shown at the Yale University Art Gallery and its antecedents. For the early exhibitions, especially those before 1930, dates, title or subject, and organizer are given when known. Italics indicate titles of exhibitions, as recorded in archival and published sources. Roman type describes exhibition content when precise titles are not known. Catalogues, books, checklists, and brochures published in conjunction with an exhibition are noted. Catalogues of exhibitions mentioned in the text of this book are cited in full in the *Selected Bibliography*, pp. 267–70. The list of exhibitions gives what is known at this time; it will be amended as new information becomes available.

(*) An asterisk
marks a traveling exhibition organized by the YUAG or one for which the Art Gallery had a principal collaborative role.

(†) A dagger
denotes circulating exhibitions whose content, organization, interpretative material, and itinerary were overseen by a non-YUAG arts organization or museum.

Information about the exhibitions has been drawn from Registrar's records; published catalogues; Arts Council and Faculty Minutes, 1866–1928; Governing Board minutes, 1940-; Annual Reports to the President, 1868–1986; Director's Annual Reports, 1940–; the YUAG *Bulletin,* 1926—; the YUAG Archives; and the Yale University Library, MS&A.

1858–75

June 18–August 14, 1858
Works of Art Exhibited in the Alumni Building, Yale College 1858. Catalogue

Summer 1867
First Annual Exhibition of the Yale School of the Fine Arts, Founded as a Department of Yale College, by the Late Augustus Russell Street of New Haven, Conn. Loan show and works owned by the College. Catalogue

January 1869
Annual Exhibition of the Yale School of the Fine Arts

January 1870
Annual Winter Exhibition

June 9–September 20, 1870
Second Annual Exhibition of the Oil Paintings and Other Works of Art Temporarily Loaned to the Yale School of the Fine Arts

Winter–January 1871
Works of Art in the Permanent and Loaned Collections of the Yale School of the Fine Arts

July 8–October 17, 1871
Third Annual Exhibition

Winter 1872
Annual Exhibition of Student Work

June 23–Summer 1873
Fourth Annual Exhibition

January 1874
Winter Exhibition

June 17, 1874
Fifth Annual Exhibition of the Yale School of the Fine Arts

May 1–June 1875
Annual Summer Exhibition. Catalogue

1876–1900

January 1876
Winter Exhibition

July–September 1876
Annual Summer Exhibition

April–June 1877
Exhibition of 28 oil paintings loaned by Henry E. Russell

June 5, 1879
Annual Summer Exhibition

June 1–July 1, 1882
Paintings, Landscapes, and Marines by American Artists from the Collection of Robbins Battell, Norfolk. Catalogue

June 1886
Loan Exhibition and Student Work

Summer 1886
Exhibition of Paintings from New York City

June 1887
Annual Exhibition of Student Work

June 4, 1888
Pictures and Sketches of F. T. Langzettel

June 1889
Exhibition of Student Work

1890
Summer Exhibition

June 1891–Summer 1891
Exhibition of Student Work

January–February 1892
Winter Exhibition, J. Twachtman paintings and studies

May–July 1892
Summer Exhibition, John La Farge

Spring 1894
† *"The Century Magazine" and "Scribner's." Designs by Leading Illustrators*

June 1894
Edwin Howland Blashfield, N.A.

June 1894
F. Hopkinson Smith, Watercolors and Charcoals

Summer 1894
Exhibition of Student Work

November 1–December 1, 1894
† *Exhibition of Illustrative Art: "The Century" and "Scribner's" Magazines*

May–June 1895
Exhibition of 150 Japanese Prints

Fall 1896
† *300 Examples of Illustrative Art, Lent by "The Century" and "Scribner's" Magazines*

Summer 1898
Exhibition of 300 Designs Lent by John La Farge

November 1, 1898– December 1?, 1899
† *Drawings Lent by the "New York Herald," "Scribner's," "Century," "McClure's," and "Colyer's Weekly"*

April 7–26, 1899
Exhibition of 300 Designs Lent by John LaFarge

Fall 1899
Exhibition of Works of Mr. Will H. Low

1901–25

May 1901–After Commencement
Retrospective exhibition of artists formerly pupils of the School

September 1901
Bicentennial Exhibition of American paintings which covered the time of the College's existence, from Smibert to Innes

Summer 1903
Exhibition of Student Work

Summer 1904
Annual Exhibition of Student Work

June 1–15, 1905
Japanese Print Exhibition. Selections from Private Collections in New Haven, New York, and Boston

Late 1905–Early 1906?
Paintings from the Collection of Mr. George S. Palmer of New London, Conn.

May 31–June 26, 1907
Etchings and Engravings from New York Collections and Dealers

May–June 1908
Exhibition of the Paintings of Professor John Niemeyer, A.N.A. in recognition of his 37 years of teaching at the Art School

May 1909
Biennial Loan Exhibition. La Farge, Joaquin Sorolla, y Bastida, Cabanel, Emil Carlsen, Howard Pyle, Hassam, Robert Reid, Cecilia Beaux, English and American illustrators

Spring 1909 or 1910?
Annual Exhibition of Student Work

June 1912
Annual Exhibition of Student Work

December 1912–June 1913
Winter Exhibition, 350 Etchings and Engravings by Jacques Callot

December 7–13, 1913
Paintings, Drawings, Sculpture, William Sergeant Kendall, M.A., A.N.A.

February 25–March 11, 1914
Collection of Lithographs of Greek Temples by Joseph Pennell

April 8–26, 1914
Paintings of the New Haven Paint and Clay Club

March–April 19, 1915
Annual Exhibition of the New Haven Paint and Clay Club

June 1915
Exhibition of Photographs of Greek and Mediaeval Architecture

April 3–23, 1916
Fifteenth Annual Exhibition of the New Haven Paint and Clay Club

April 1–22, 1917
Sixteenth Annual Paint and Clay Club Exhibition

April 1–21, 1918
Seventeenth Annual Paint and Clay Club Exhibition

March 11?–21, 1919
Paintings and Drawings by Jean Julien Lemordant

March 31–April 20, 1919
Eighteenth Annual Paint and Clay Club Exhibition

April 10–May 7, 1920
New Haven Paint and Clay Club Exhibition

March 28–April 17, 1921
New Haven Paint and Clay Club Exhibition

April 4–23, 1922
New Haven Paint and Clay Club Exhibition

November 11–December 20, 1922
Oils and Pastels Henry Davenport

January 5–20, 1923
34 Watercolor Sketches of Travels in Naples, Amalfi, Capri by Irene Weir, B.F.A. 1906

January 25, 1923
14 Still Life Compositions by Russell Cheney, B.A. 1904

February 3–17, 1923
32 Miniature Portraits on Ivory by Charles Turrell of London

February 21–28, 1923
Exhibition of Student Work

March 18–April 8, 1923
Twenty-Third New Haven Paint and Clay Club Exhibition

April 10–11, 1923
Competition Drawings for the Chicago Tribune Tower

May 6–16, 1923
Drawings by John H. Niemeyer, A.N.A. (Street Professor of Drawings, Emeritus)

May 23–June 23, 1923
†Designs, Sketches, and Working Drawings of Professor Ezra Winter's Recent Decorative Work. Cunard Building, New York City, and the Eastman Theatre, Rochester, New York

May 25–July 1, 1923
Exhibition of Student Work

Spring 1924
Exhibition of the New Haven Paint and Clay Club

June 1924
**Exhibition: Mural Paintings, Screens and Landscapes by Bancel La Farge*

October 27–November 9, 1924
**Small Paintings of Morgat, Brittany, by Henry Davenport*

February 14–March 1, 1925
Sixth Annual Exhibition of the Architectural Club of New Haven

1926–30

June and July 1926
26th Annual Exhibition of New Haven Paint and Clay Club

December 12–16, 1926
Art School Exhibition of Watercolors by Perry M. Duncan

January 1–March 1927
Fifty Prints: Dürer and Rembrandt
Watercolor Sketches by Edwin A. Park
Paintings and Drawings by J. J. Lemordant

Spring 1927
Fifty-nine Drawings by Ingres, Courtesy of de Hauke and Company

Spring 1929
Collection of the Late John Davenport Wheeler, Yale 1858S, of New Haven

Spring 1929
George Hewitt Myers, Yale 1898, Loan of Near and Far Eastern Rugs
35 Japanese Prints, Ukiyo'é School, Lent by Howard Mansfield, Yale 1871
New Gifts, Duncan Phillips, Yale 1908
Bellotto Painting, Edward B. Greene, Yale 1900
Canaletto Etchings and Tiepolo Drawings

1929–30
Exhibition of 50 Prints from the American Institute of Graphic Arts

Late 1920s
†Circulating shows by MoMA, AFA (American Federation of Arts), and Smithsonian Museum frequently exhibited

January 10, 1930[?]
Garvan Collection Gift

May 14–21, 1930
John Henry Niemeyer Retrospective

September 19–October 10, 1930
Exhibition of Student Work

November 11–20, 1930
Modern Japanese Wood Block Prints

November 21–December 15, 1930
†17th and 18th Century British Watercolors, Lent by the Pennsylvania Museum of Art

1930
Pueblo Indian Drawings by Oqiva Pi from the Collection of Dr. Pierce Baker

1931–35

January 3–17, 1931
†British Woodcuts and Wood Engravings. National Gallery of Canada. Catalogue

January 19–31, 1931
Violet Oakley N.A. Catalogue

February 4–18, 1931
Modern Austrian Woodcuts and Color Prints. National Gallery of Canada

March 21–28, 1931
Charles J. Connick of Boston, Watercolor Sketches and Cartoons for Stained Glass Windows

April 27–May 3, 1931
† Viennese Architects. Brooklyn Museum of Art

End of Summer–Late September 1931
American Decorative Arts of the Nineteenth Century. Garvan Collection and Recent Acquisitions

October 5–17, 1931
Deane Keller

November 2–9, 1931
Watercolors and Paintings by Eugene Kingman

November 9–22, 1931
†Second International Exhibition of Lithographs and Wood Engraving. Art Institute of Chicago

December 14, 1931
Paintings by Paul Dougherty

February 22–May 15, 1932
George Washington Bicentennial Exhibition. Catalogue

February 22–May 15, 1932
Twelve Pieces of Silver: Cornelius Kierstede 1675–1753

March 7–26, 1932
Type Designs and Book Illustration. Lent by Philip Hofer, New York Public Library

April 16–May 1, 1932
Works by H. Emerson Tuttle. Catalogue?

October 29–November 17, 1932
Hundredth Anniversary Exhibition. Checklist

November 18–December 2, 1932
Exhibition of Chinese Rubbings

December 28, 1932–January 15, 1933
Book Illustrations and Photographs of Romantic Revival Architecture

1933–34
Exhibitions of Public Works of Art Project under Bancel LaFarge

January 7–31, 1933
Modern French and American Paintings

January 21–April 16, 1933
Examples of the Work of Johannis Nys of Philadelphia (active 1700–1723). From the Mabel Brady Garvan Collection and other loans

February 4–March 12, 1933
†*German Facsimile: Color Prints of Old Master French Paintings, 1375–1905*

February 18–March 14, 1933
Loan Exhibition of Chinese Paintings

March 7–19, 1933
†*Photographs of Greece By Charles Harris Whitaker*

March 11–June 10, 1933
Franklin Roosevelt Silver. From the Mabel Brady Garvan Collection

March 20–April 2, 1933
Contemporary South African Painting Lent by Charles T. Loram

April 5–30, 1933
†*Art in Relation to Sports.* American Federation of Arts

May 1–14, 1933
Drawings by Madame René Cheruy

October 18–31, 1933
Contemporary Woodcuts. Catalogue

November 6–19, 1933
Paintings by Ellen Starbuck of New Haven

November 11–December 2, 1933
Photographs of Greece. Lent by Arnold Genthe

January 2, 1934
Portraits of Early New Haven Physicians. Pamphlet

January 6–21, 1934
Paintings and Watercolors by Salvatore De Maio, F.A.A.R., B.F.A. 1930, Lent by the Artist

January 22–February 10, 1934
Photographs of Early American Historical Houses

January 22–February 25, 1934
Reproductions of Mediaeval Goldsmiths' Work

January 27–February 10, 1934
Exhibition of Contemporary Silver by Georg Jensen

February 1934
Photographs of Persian Architecture. Lent by American Institute for Persian Art and Archaeology

February 14–28, 1934
Paintings by Deane Keller, F.A.A.R.

February and March 1934
Early American Historical Prints Lent by Francis P. Garvan, Class of 1897

March 1–14, 1934
Prints by H. Emerson Tuttle

March 3–17, 1934
Early Museum Architecture

March 24–April 1, 1934
Exhibition of Drawings and Models for Buildings Designed by Graduates of the Yale School of Architecture

April 17–30, 1934
Paintings and Drawings, especially pastels by Mrs. Charles Warren

April 17–30, 1934
Views of Old Russia by Leonid and Rima Brailowsky

May 5–26, 1934
Replicas in Tempera of Egyptian Wall Paintings of the New Kingdom (XVII–XIX Dynasties)

May 20–June 30, 1934
Exhibition in Honor of the Centenary of the Death of Lafayette

October 6–21, 1934
Rubbings from Chinese Tombstones

October 1934
Architecture: Photographs of French Cathedrals by Clarence Ward of Oberlin College

November–December 2, 1934
Historic American Buildings Survey of Massachusetts

November 3–17, 1934
†*American Cities of the '30s, '40s, '50s, before the Civil War, Photos by Berenice Abbott.*

University Architectural Exhibitions

November 15–30, 1934
Photographs by Ansel Adams

December 1934–January 1935
†*Armor and Arms from the Metropolitan Museum of Art*

December 3–16, 1934
Watercolors by Wayland W. Williams, Yale 1910

December 1934
Christmas Story in Art

January–February 10, 1935
Russian Ballet Designs; Lifar and Diaghileff [sic]

January 24–February 9, 1935
Oil Paintings by Richard A. Rathbone, B.F.A. 1928

February 16–March 3, 1935
Watercolors by Eliot O'Hara's Class

February 22–April 5, 1935
85 Garvan Prints

March 1935
Romanesque Churches of Apulia, Photographs, Wesleyan Architectural Exhibition. Catalogue

April 14–28, 1935
Photographs of Early Washington Architecture

April 14–28, 1935
Bird Portraiture. Watercolors by Henry H. Townsend, 1897

June 1–September 30, 1935
Paintings by John Trumbull and Samuel Finley Breese Morse Connecticut Tercentenary, 1635–1935. Catalogue

June 1–July 22, 1935
Connecticut Portraits by S. F. B. Morse Connecticut Tercentenary, 1635–1935. Same catalogue as above exhibition

August 1–October 15, 1935
Connecticut Portraits by Ralph Earl, 1751–1801 Connecticut Tercentenary, 1635–1935. Catalogue

August 1–October 1, 1935
Early Connecticut Silver 1700–1830 Connecticut Tercentenary, 1635–1935. Catalogue

August 1–October 1, 1935
Silver and Prints from the Mabel Brady Garvan Collection. Connecticut Tercentenary, 1635–1935

October 6–20, 1935
Drawings and Photographs of Work of Miss Marion Coffin, Landscape Architect

October 20–November 17, 1935
Exhibition of Chinese Paintings

October 22–31, 1935
Exhibition of Work of Members of Pi Alpha Society of the Yale School of the Fine Arts

November 1–15, 1935
†*Bookbindings by Ignatz Wiemeler.* MoMA

November 5–12, 1935
†*Le Corbusier—Architecture.* MoMA

December 9, 1935–January 6, 1936
†*Photos of 19th Century Houses, by Walker Evans.* MoMA

December 7, 1935–January 15, 1936
"Measured Drawings" Photographs

1936–40

February 2–16, 1936
Edwin Cassius Taylor Memorial Exhibition

February 4–18, 1936
Modern Painting in Color Reproduction

March 2–15, 1936
Exhibition of Modern Paintings, Drawings & Sculpture Owned in New Haven

April 12–26, 1936
†*Modern Architecture, Photographs.* MoMA

May 16–June 16, 1936
Gaylord D. Richmond, Deane Keller, George Davidson, George Savage

October 6–16, 1936
Exhibition of Prints by the "American Artists Group"

October 16–November 30, 1936
Exhibition of Living American Art

November 1–13, 1936
Reproductions of Paintings and Drawings by Leonardo da Vinci

November 15–30, 1936
Work of the Federal Art Project of Connecticut

November 20–30, 1936
Landscapes by Students of Mr. George Davidson of Waterbury

December 1–15, 1936
Photographs of Sculpture by Carl Millès

December 17–22, 1936
Work by Members of the Pi Alpha Society

December 22–31, 1936
Reproduction of Famous Paintings on Christmas Subjects, "The Christmas Story"

January 1–15, 1937
Living American Art

January 15–31, 1937
Exhibition of Work of Gilbert Banever

February 1–13, 1937
**Collegiate Schools of Architecture*

February 7–March 7, 1937
Exhibition of Paintings, Watercolors, and Etchings by Reginald Marsh

February 18–March 4, 1937
19th Century French Paintings. Catalogue: YUAG *Bulletin*

February 23–March 6, 1937
†*Lithographs and Etchings by William Woollett*

March 15–April 6, 1937
Flower Paintings by Mabel H. La Farge and Isabelle H. Tuttle

March 15–April 18, 1937
American Genre Painting and Victoriana from the Garvan Collection

March 15–31, 1937
Drawings and Photographs Prepared by the Historic American Building Survey

April 1–15, 1937
International Travel Posters

April 24–May 15, 1937
Drawings made for the American Index of Design (Decorative Arts), WPA Federal Art

May 2–June 7, 1937
**Early English Watercolors (1770–1850)*

May 1937
Student Exhibition of Drawings for Rome Academy Collaborative Problem

May 15–22, 1937
Exhibition of New York World's Fair Architectural Competition Drawings Sponsored by World's Fair, New York 1939, Inc.

June 15–September 15, 1937
Summer Exhibition of Work by Students in the Yale School of Fine Arts

September 16–30, 1937
†*Annual Exhibition of California Society of Etchers.* California Society of Etchers

October 6–16, 1937
Prints by "American Artists Group" of New York City

October 10–31, 1937
Paintings by Living American Artists

October 26–31, 1937
†*British Architecture of Today (Photographs).* Association of Collegiate Schools of Architecture by Royal Institute of British Architects

November 21–December 11, 1937
Federal Art in New England. Catalogue

December 12, 1937–January 3, 1938
Reproductions of Dutch Painters

December 16, 1937–January 9, 1938
American Artists Group (Prints)

January 3–24, 1938
Reproductions of Italian Sculpture

January 9–31, 1938
**Exhibition of Paintings of Elsie Rowland Chase*

January 10–22, 1938
Faculty Watercolor Show

January 25–February 3, 1938
†*Pittsburgh Plate Glass Competition. Photographs.* American Federation of Arts

February 4–18, 1938
†*Posters by E. McKnight Kauffer.* MoMA

February 6–12, 1938
Yale Photographic Club

February 22–March 5, 1938
Student Work

February 22, 1938
Textiles from the Hobart Moore Memorial Collection

February 22, 1938
Alumni University Day Special Exhibition

February 22–June 15, 1938
The Greene Collection of Portrait Engravings

March 5–20, 1938
Photographs of Work by Women Architects: Carina Eaglesfield Mortimer, Bertha Mather McPherson, Theodate Pope-Riddle

April 1–30, 1938
Sculpture by Anna Hyatt Huntington. Catalogue

April 11–24, 1938
Exhibition of British Calligraphy and Illumination. Catalogue

April 27–May 6, 1938
Photographs by Watson Webb, Jr. Yale 1938

May 7–20, 1938
Photographs of Mexico by Donald R. Laidig

May 7–19, 1938
Work of the Pi Alpha Society

May 10–June 22, 1938
Pardee-Morris Paintings. Lent by New Haven Colony Historical Society, exhibited at New Haven Public Library for the New Haven Tercentenary

May 23–28, 1938
George E. Kidder-Smith—Architectural Photographs

May 24–June 4, 1938
Photographs and Drawings of the Work of New Haven Architects

June 1–11, 1938
New Haven Progress. Decorative arts and photographs lent by the Yale Art Gallery and exhibited at Coxe Memorial Gymnasium for the New Haven Tercentenary

June 6–11, 1938
Rome Academy Collaborative Drawings

June 16–September 1938
Summer Exhibition of Work by Students of the Yale School of Fine Arts

July 5–September 18, 1938
Portraits of Distinguished New Haveners. Catalogue: YUAG *Bulletin*

September 6, 1938
Miniature Fire Engines

October 3–21, 1938
†*Exhibition of Alvar Aalto—Architecture and Furniture.* MoMA

October 16–30, 1938
Bert Bruestle, Saxton Burr, Armin Hemburger, and Herbert Thoms

October 23–November 1, 1938
Maynard Workshop Photos of Modern and Historic Houses

November 1–6, 1938
Annual Photography Exhibition

November 2–30, 1938
Walters Art Gallery—Photographs of Their Objects

November 6–15, 1938
†*National Exhibition of Representative Buildings.* American Federation of Arts

December 1–15, 1938
Modern German Church Architecture

December 1–29, 1938
**Herman Armour Webster, Yale 1900s.*

January 2–14, 1939
American Artists—Great Prints

January 4–17, 1939
Faculty Watercolors

January 8–22, 1939
William Sergeant Kendall Exhibition

January 22–February 5, 1939
La Farge Memorial Exhibition

February 13–21, 1939
National Intercollegiate Photographic Exhibition. Yale Photography Club. Checklist

March 9–22, 1939
Paintings, Drawings, and Pastels by Edwin Austin Abbey. The Edwin Austin Abbey Collection. Catalogue

March 15–31, 1939
Watercolors by Aldis B. Browne

March 15–30, 1939
American Crewel Embroidery

March 26–May 7, 1939
**Chinese Antiquities from Ch'ang-sha China Lent by John Hadley Cox, B.A. 1935.* Catalogue

April 2–16, 1939
WPA Artists—Pictures, Pottery, and Sculpture of Connecticut Artists

April 19–25, 1939
Commercial Printing

April 25–May 2, 1939
Annual New Haven Camera Club. Yale Photography Club

May 1939
Prints and Woodcuts by Charles Wilson Smith, Yale 1917

May 1–15, 1939
†*Daumier and Gavarni.* Western Association of Art Museum Directors. Checklist

May 17–30, 1939
†*Seventh Watercolor Exhibition.* American Federation of Arts

Through June 11, 1939
Exhibition of 25 Pastel Portraits by E. A. Abbey

Through June 11, 1939
Watercolors by Members of Eliot O'Hara's Class

June 18–September 10, 1939
Masterpieces of New England Silver: 1650–1800. Catalogue

Summer 1939
Washingtoniana. Lent by de L. Kountze, Yale 1899

October 1–15, 1939
Block Prints in Color

October 18–November 8, 1939
Facsimiles of 16th, 17th, and 18th-Century French Drawings

October 27–December 3, 1939
Ship Prints of the 18th and 19th Centuries from the Garvan Collection

November 12–26, 1939
Work by Members of the Yale Undergraduate Art Club

November 26–December 8, 1939
Paintings, Watercolors, and Drawings by Herbert J. Gute, Yale 1933

December 8, 1939–January 12, 1940
Print Masterpieces

December 11–21, 1939
Contemporary Finnish and Swedish Architecture

December 13, 1939–January 10, 1940
The Making of a Mural: Studies for the Harrisburg Lunettes by Edwin Austin Abbey

December 15, 1939–January 13, 1940
Christmas Story in Art

December 20, 1939–January 3, 1940
Mediterranean and Near Eastern Embroideries from the Hobart Moore Memorial Collection

December 21, 1939–January 14, 1940
Pieter Breugel, the Elder

January 1–15, 1940
Connecticut Domestic Wall Decoration and Inn and Tavern Signs. WPA, Connecticut Art Project, Index of American Design

January 1–17, 1940
Exhibition of Faculty Watercolors by Theodore Sizer, Everett Meeks, Deane Keller, Emerson Tuttle

January 17–February 25, 1940
Eighteenth Century Italian and English Landscape Painting. Catalogue, YUAG *Bulletin*

January 23–February 8, 1940
Prints from the University Collections

February 11–18, 1940
Photographs of Houses and Gardens from the Maynard Workshop

February 22–28, 1940
Alumni Day Exhibition. Work by Students and Recent Accessions

February 26–March 12, 1940
Portraits of Chinese Types by Graham Peck

March 1–14, 1940
Modern Architecture in Switzerland Presented by the Graduate Group in Architecture to Show the Voices-Methods-Aims of the Movement in Switzerland

March 1–30, 1940
Modern British Silver Plate from the London Guilds. Lent from the World's Fair

March 15–31, 1940
Paintings by George J. Marinko, Jr., Yale 1933, and Aldos B. Browne, Yale 1934

March 31–April 7, 1940
National Collegiate Exhibition of Pictorial Photography

April 1–30, 1940
Paintings by Childe Hassam

April 1–May 12, 1940
Exhibition of Peruvian Pottery and Textiles from the Collection of George Hewitt Myers

April 8–15, 1940
Watercolors by Edwin Avery Park, B.F.A. 1928
Abstractions by Charles W. Smith, 1917

April 8–May 15, 1940
**Historic and Modern English Silver Plate.* British silver plate kept for safekeeping during the war

April 15–30, 1940
Paintings by Oscar Weisbuch B.F.A. 1932

April–May 28, 1940
†*14 Subjects by van Gogh.* Holland House

May 6–12, 1940
Combined Exhibition Yale Photography Club and New Haven Camera Club

May 11–31, 1940
Three Centuries of "Memento Mori"

May 15–30, 1940
Photographs of Contemporary French Architecture

May 17–June 9, 1940
Theatre Arts Exhibition

July 1940
Recent Accessions

Summer Exhibition
Work by the Students in the Departments of Architecture, Drama, Painting, and Sculpture

October 20–November 3, 1940
Contemporary Japanese Prints of Far Eastern Art, Lent by John D. McLaughlin, Boston

November 6–December 8, 1940
Contemporary British Painting

December 2, 1940–Spring 1941
The Lelia A. and John Hill Morgan Collection of American Miniatures

December 8, 1940–January 12, 1941
Print Masterpieces 1450–1800 from the University Collections

December 15, 1940–January 13, 1941
Christmas Story in Art

1941

January 4–20, 1941
†*Modern Sculptors and Painters.* The Federation of American Painters and Sculptors, Inc.

January 10–February 25, 1941
Chinese Paintings from the Collection of Ada Small Moore (Mrs. William H. Moore). Brochure

February 1–17, 1941
Chinese Flower Exhibition by the New Haven Garden Club

March 1941
Faculty Exhibition, School of the Fine Arts

March 4–31, 1941
Printed Textiles in the Mabel Brady Garvan Collection

April 28–May 19, 1941
Picasso's "Seated Man." Loan from MoMA

April 28–May 10, 1941
The Architectural Works of George Howe of Philadelphia

May 1–31, 1941
Turkish and Greek Island Embroideries

May 1–31, 1941
Reproductions and Self-Portraits

May 16–June 8, 1941
Bookplates, Prints

May 20–June 4, 1941
Watercolors by Herbert Gute's Class

June 14–September 1941
Recent Additions to the Moore Collection of Textiles

July 3–September 1941
Recent Accessions

Summer 1941
Paintings of Asiatic Costumes by Countesse d'Aumale

July 13–September 1941
Annual Exhibition of the Works of the Students in the Departments of Architecture, Drama, Painting, and Sculpture

October 11–November 23, 1941
Early American Pottery, Glass, and China

November 5–December 7, 1941
Harmony, Balance, and Rhythm in Textile Design

1942

January 13–February 22, 1942
Modern Art—Société Anonyme Painting

January 16–February 13, 1942
Pagan Imagery in Renaissance Art

January–March–May 1942
Chinese Textiles
Writing as a Motive in Textile Design
Textiles from North Africa and the Greek Islands

January–February 1942 Architecture exhibitions, each approximately two weeks long
Modern Architecture for the Modern School
Ancient Architecture in Colombia
Models in Color Camouflage Treatments for Industrial Plants
Camouflage Materials
Blitzed Architecture in London Lent by the British Information Service

Winter and Spring 1942
Birth of a Bomber. Lent by the British Information Service
Photographs of Contemporary Brazilian Architecture
Paintings by Edwin Austin Abbey Illustrating Shakespeare's Plays

March 2–22, 1942
**Art of Australia 1788-1941.* Catalogue

March 11–April 16, 1942
†*Pre-Columbian Art—Ceramics, Textiles, Sculpture.* MoMA

April 15–June 14, 1942
Our Navy in Action

May 1–17, 1942
Photos of Murals and Sculpture

May 10, 1942
East Indian Textiles of the 19th Century

May 23–June 14, 1942
Latin American Colonial Textiles, Paintings, Ceramics

Summer 1942
5000 Years of Picture Making

December 1942
Christmas Story in Art

1943

January 9–February 7, 1943
†*Emblems of Unity and Freedom.* American Index of Design Exhibition, Metropolitan Museum of Art

May 15–July 7, 1943
†*National War Poster Exhibition.* Lent by Artists for Victory, Inc.

June 1943
Work of Students in the School of the Fine Arts

? Summer 1943
†*Plastics Today and Tomorrow.* Organized by magazine, *Plastics*

July 1943–July 1944 Architecture exhibitions, each approximately two weeks
The Wooden House in America
†*Stockholm Builds, Brazil Builds.* MoMA
The Architecture of William Wilson Wurster
Contemporary Architectural Renderings
Nineteenth Century Railroad Stations
Integration of Modern Art and Science

Fall 1943–Spring 1944 Photography exhibitions, each approximately two weeks
Photography Exhibitions from the British Information Services, the Netherlands Information Services, and the Belgian Information Center
Photographs by Phillip Hanson Hiss
Bali, Contemporary Photographs
Photographs of China by Fritz Henle, lent by the American Federation of Arts

October 16–November 8, 1943
Arts and Sciences

October 16–November 8, 1943
Modern Exhibition—Painting and Architecture

November 2–8, 1943
National Art Week

1944

Winter–Spring 1944 Textile exhibitions, each approximately two weeks
Turkish Velvets and Embroideries
Embroideries of India, Persian Safavid Silks
Peruvian Textiles
Textiles of Bali and Its Neighbors
The Diagonal Lattice as a Textile Motive
Tie and Dye Techniques of India, Japan and Peru
Metal Cloths of India; and Chinese Textiles

Spring 1944
Annual Exhibition of the Work of Members of the Brush and Palette Club

March 1–15, 1944
†*Holland under the Nazis.* Holland House Corporation, New York

March 11–April 16, 1944
**Canadian Art 1760–1943.* Catalogue: YUAG *Bulletin.* Art Gallery of Ontario

April 19–30, 1944
Animal Sculpture by Herbert Hazeltine

May–August 13, 1944
Eighteen Paintings by Robert Doherty

Spring 1944
Italian Paintings from the Collection of Maitland F. Griggs, B.A. 1896

Spring 1944
Modern Art of Mexico and Cuba
Oriental Rugs, from the Collection of George Hewitt Myers, B.A. 1898
Russian War Posters lent by Holland House Corporation

November 1–7, 1944
American Art Week

December 4–17, 1944
Aspects of Greek Civilization

1945

January 8–29, 1945
Aspects of Italian Civilization

January 29–February 18, 1945
Aspects of French Civilization

February 15–March 31, 1945
The British-American Goodwill Exhibition. Presented by Artists for Victory, Inc. Catalogue

March–April 1945
Duchamp—Duchamp-Villon—Villon Exhibition. Catalogue: YUAG *Bulletin*

March–April 1945
Power in the Pacific

June 19, 1945
Italian Exhibition. Catalogue: YUAG *Bulletin*

November 2–December 20, 1945
†*Building in the USSR*

1946

January 10–February 11, 1946
The Art of Medicine

February 22–March 25, 1946
The John Hill Morgan Memorial Exhibition of American Art. Catalogue: YUAG *Bulletin*

March 4–16, 1946
†*California Photographs by Roger Sturtevant.* Architectural League of New York

March 21–May 5, 1946
Exhibition of Japanese Obi Silks. Collection of the late Helen Wells Seymour

Spring 1946
Exhibiton of Far Eastern Textiles. Bequest of Louise Wallace Hackney

April 5–May 5, 1946
Exhibition of Contemporary Sculpture: Objects and Constructions. Catalogue: YUAG *Bulletin*

May 18–June 3, 1946
Graphic Tectonic Prints: Josef Albers

November 1–15, 1946
Unit Furniture. MoMA

November 15–December 31, 1946
H. Emerson Tuttle Prints and Drawings

November 16, 1946
The American Scene in Pottery and Prints from the Garvan Collection

1947

January 6–February 3, 1947
Modern Art in Advertising. Catalogue

February 13–26, 1947
†*Paintings Looted from Holland by the Nazis.* Netherlands Embassy. Catalogue

March 7–30, 1947
American Painting and Sculpture. Whitney Museum of American Art

April 2–20, 1947
The Fine Arts under Fire—Photography

April 8–27, 1947
**Medicine in Art—Prints from the Collection of Dr. Clements C. Fry*

May 6–25, 1947
Connecticut Watercolor Society

June 7–22, 1947
Prints from the Mabel Brady Garvan Collection

June 7–September 1947
Masterpieces of Painting and Decorative Arts from the Mabel Brady Garvan Collection

June 7–September 1947
Recent Accessions of the Gallery

June 28–September 1947
Paintings from the Collection Société Anonyme

September 14–20, 1947
Exhibition of Textiles from Some U.N. Nations

October 11–November 16, 1947
Eighteenth Century French Arts and Eighteenth Century French Silks

November 3–9, 1947
St. Denis

November 10–16, 1947
†*Venice. Life* magazine

November 17–23, 1947
Landscapes. Student exhibition

November 18–30?, 1947
American Genre Prints

November 25–30, 1947
Houses by Carl Koch. School of Architecture exhibition

December 1–15, 1947
Work of Louis Sullivan

December 16, 1947–January 18, 1948
Yale Archaeology 1947. Dura-Europos, St. Denis, Tepeaca, and the Viru Vallery of Peru

December 17, 1947–January 4, 1948
The Christmas Story in Art

December 1947
Bible Exhibition

1948

January–March 21, 1948
Textile Room exhibitions, Chinese textiles from the Hobart Moore Memorial Collection

January–February 1948
Fakes and Forgeries

January 4–February 23, 1948
An Exhibition Illustrating the Development of Modern Painting

January 5–12, 1948
†*Architectural Education 1947.* Architectural League of New York

January 13–18, 1948
†*The Age of Enlightenment. Life* magazine

January 19–25, 1948
†*Photographs of California Architecture.* American Institute of Architects

March 1–15, 1948
Graziani's "A Mural in the Making." Springfield Art Museum

March 5–April 11, 1948
Exhibition of Painting and Sculpture by the Directors of the Société Anonyme Since Its Founding, 1920–1948. Catalogue: YUAG *Bulletin*

April 19–May 2, 1948
†*Egypt. Life* magazine

April 20–May 15, 1948
Modern Mexican Painting from Colorado Springs Fine Arts Center

May 1948
†*Embroideries Made in Greece during the War.* American Friends of Greece

May 15–29, 1948
The Artist and Social Communication

May 21–June 6, 1948
Select Americana. Exhibition for Walpole Society meeting

June 9, 1948
Summer Exhibition of Recent Accessions, especially gifts of silver

Summer 1948
Italian Church Vestments

October 5–November 7, 1948
Three Centuries of American Textiles

October 16–22, 1948
Americana: Exhibition of Early American Arts and Crafts

October 22–November 4, 1948
Visual Approach to History: Chartres and Carcassonne. Teaching exhibition

October 30–November 29, 1948
Annual Exhibition of Connecticut Arts Association

November 1–December 5, 1948
Masterpieces from the Permanent Collections

November 12–December 12, 1948
Masterpieces of Nineteenth Century French Painting Belonging to Yale Alumni

November 15–28, 1948
**Modern House Comes Alive: Architecture and Decorative Arts.* Bertha Schaefer Gallery

December 4, 1948–January 15, 1949
Winter Scenes in Paintings and Prints

December 6, 1948–January 16, 1949
The Dress of Kings. Christmas exhibition

1949

January 13–February 13, 1949
Sculpture Since Rodin. Catalogue: YUAG *Bulletin*

January 19–February 13, 1949
**Painting Towards Architecture: The Story of Space.* Miller Company of Meriden

February 21–March 13, 1949
A Center for UNESCO. First postwar Collaborative Problem of Departments of Architecture, Painting, and Sculpture

February 21–April 17, 1949
Recent Accessions

February 21–27, 1949
Painting and Sculpture: Works from the Collections of Undergraduate Associates in Fine Arts

March 1, 1949
Société Anonyme

March 15–28, 1949
Faust on the Stage: An Historical Survey. Drama school

March 15, 1949
Architecture: Saarinen

March 17–April 18, 1949
Sports and Games

March 18–April 10, 1949
Drawings of Modern Masters

April 11–June 5, 1949
Industrial Arts

April 15–May 8, 1949
Yale Moderns. Student exhibition

April 19–May 22, 1949
Modern Design: A Search for Appropriate Form

April 26–May 1949
Sven Markelius—Architectural Designs

May 10–22, 1949
Paintings, Sculpture and Drawings by Undergraduates of Yale University

May 17–June 5, 1949
Japanese Prints: 1650–Present

June 14–October 1949
Recent Accessions

June 17–21, 1949
Annual Exhibition of the Division of the Arts at Yale: Painting, Sculpture, Architecture, History of Art, Drama

June 19–Summer 1949
Elihu Yale and the Collegiate School

Fall 1949
Goethe's Faust I on the Stage. School of Drama

October 8–November 20, 1949
The Smibert Tradition. Catalogue: YUAG *Bulletin*

October 8–November 20, 1949
Smibert's Influence—Early Works of Trumbull

October 8–November 20, 1949
Eighteenth-Century Textiles

October 22–29, 1949
The American Stove Company Building

October 26–November 4, 1949
Carcassonne and Chartres. Teaching exhibition

November 11–20, 1949
†Architecture: The Terrace Plaza Hotel. Skidmore Owings & Merrill exhibition

November 14–January 9, 1950
European and American Watercolors of the 18th, 19th and 20th Centuries from Yale's Permanent Collections

November 22, 1948–January 1, 1950
Flowers in Persian Textiles

November 23–December 4, 1949
Friday Afternoon Sketches by Students in the School of the Fine Arts

November 28, 1949–January 1, 1950
Josef Albers, Paintings

November 30, 1949–January 30, 1950
Plastics

December 1949
Prints by Jacques Callot Lent by the Pierre Berres Gallery, New York, Supplemented by Yale's Collections

December 12, 1949–January 1, 1950
Stage Design by Donald Oenslager

1950

January 4–February 5, 1950
Embroidered and Woven Trimmings

January 7–30, 1950
Angers Sculpture

January 10–18, 1950
Prophet of the Modern: Drawings, Watercolors, Books, Manuscripts by John Ruskin, 1819–1900. Ruskin Society exhibition

January 12–February 23, 1950
Museum Class Exhibition

January 17–February 23, 1950
Recent Accessions

January 20–February 12, 1950
An Idea Center for Plastics: Selected Models from the Collaborative Problem

January 30–February 13, 1950
Architecture by George Howe

February 7–March 5, 1950
Printed Japanese Fabrics

February 7–23, 1950
Design for Television

February 22–March 19, 1950
35 American Painters of Today. Catalogue: YUAG *Bulletin*

February 26–April 3, 1950
Prints from Yale Collections

March 1–15, 1950
Architecture of H. Hamilton Harris

March 1–April 2, 1950
Aspects of Wall Decoration

March 9–April 2, 1950
Satin Weaves

April 4–30, 1950
Non-Objective Design in 18th Century Textiles

April 4–May 7, 1950
Exhibition on the Occasion of the 30th Anniversary of the Société Anonyme

April 17–May 21, 1950
**French Paintings of the Latter Half of the Nineteenth Century from the Collections of Alumni and Friends of Yale.* Catalogue: YUAG *Bulletin*

May 1–June 5, 1950
Japanese Priests' Robes from the Collection of Mrs. William H. Moore

June 1–30, 1950
Six Centuries of Prints

June–August 1950
Changing exhibitions of student work

Fall 1950–Spring 1951 Special exhibitions, each about 2 weeks
Prints After Paintings of John Trumbull
Laces of the 18th and 19th Centuries
Architecture of Elting and Schweikher
European Prints
Japanese Prints
Flower Designs in Textiles
Three and a Half Centuries of Printmaking
†*1950 AIA National Honor Awards.* American Federation of Arts
Recent Textile Accessions

September 25–October 29, 1950
Contemporary Church Architecture

October 19–November 18, 1950
Prospects: An Exhibition of English Landscape Watercolors from English and American Private Collections. Catalogue

November 5–December 3, 1950
Models from a Collaborative Problem: Exhibition of Architecture of Former Yale Students

November 20–December 7, 1950
Architecture and the City Plan

December 9, 1950–January 9, 1951
†*Visual Education for Architects.* American Federation of Arts

December 9, 1950–January 7, 1951
Printed Cottons, Past and Present

1951

January 1–31, 1951
Lithographs from the Collection

January 16–February 4, 1951
17th-Century Textiles in India and Persia

February 11–March 11, 1951
**"Pictures for a Picture" of Gertrude Stein as a Collector and Writer on Art and Artists.* Catalogue

February 22–March 18, 1951
Japanese Prints, Gift of Mrs. William H. Moore

February 22–March 18, 1951
French 17th and 18th Century Engravings and Color Prints from the George Binet Gallery, New York

March 7–April 8, 1951
Japanese Priests' Robes, Gift of Mrs. William H. Moore

March 13–April 13, 1951
†*Paintings from the Caves of the Thousand Buddhas.* American Federation of Arts

March 14–26, 1951
Architects Collaborative Problem

March 1951
Works of John F. Ward

April 12–May 6, 1951
†*Art Sacré.* Catalogue. American Federation of Arts

April 12–May 6, 1951
18th-Century Church Vestments Collected by James Jackson Jarves

April 18–May 16, 1951
Puppets in American Theatre

April 23–May 7, 1951
The Painter's Departure: Current Trends as Reflected in the Paintings of Maud Morgan, Jackson Pollock and Others. Brochure

May 1–31, 1951
Prints from the J. Paul Oppenheim Memorial Collection of Contemporary American Prints

May 7–28, 1951
19th and 20th Century Prints. Teaching exhibition

May 8–June 4, 1951
Flower Designs in Textiles from Europe and the Middle and Far East

May 10–31, 1951
1951 AIA National Honor Awards

May 15–27, 1951
Gallery Highlights and Flower Compositions

June 9, 1951–October 21, 1951
Yale Worthies. Publication of the *Yale University Portrait Index, 1701–1951*

June 1951
Survey of History of Printing from Relief Blocks

September 1–October 31, 1951
Oriental and Occidental Woodcuts

October 2–November 4, 1951
Masterpieces from the Moore Collection of Textiles

October 27–November 4, 1951
S. F. B. Morse: Scientist and Artist

October 27–November 23, 1951
†*Pottery of Bernard Leach and Associates.* Institute of Contemporary Arts

November 7–December 2, 1951
Weaving and Embroidery in Turkey

November 9–25, 1951
Connecticut Contemporary Painting. Connecticut Arts Eastern States Exposition

December 15, 1951–January 20, 1952
Master Prints in the Yale Collections

1952

February 5–March 2, 1952
Textiles of the Italian Renaissance

February 8–March 2, 1952
Craftsmanship in American Silver from the Yale Collections

February 15–March 2, 1952
Mannerism and Baroque: Italy, Spain, Holland

March 2–17, 1952
Design and Structural Aspects of the Crystal Palace

March 5–16, 1952
†*Industrial Design.* Olivetti Typewriter Company

March 5–21, 1952
Chinese Painting

March 17–April 13, 1952
Textiles of Ancient Peru

March 25–June 1, 1952
Rediscovered Italian Paintings at Yale. Catalogue

April 10–25, 1952
Nineteenth-Century Art. Teaching exhibition

April 14–June 1, 1952
Rhythm in Textile Design

April 22–May 10, 1952
Yale Silver at Knoedler's

April 30–May 14, 1952
Paintings Prints, Drawings, and Sculpture by Pablo Picasso from Private Collections

May 1–21, 1952
Twentieth-Century Art. Teaching exhibition

Summer 1952
Recent Accessions
Student work

September 30–October 25, 1952
Bible Stories in Art

October 1–31, 1952
Japanese Priests' Robes

October 10–31, 1952
Print Class Exhibition

October 10–November 5, 1952
Athletes in Bronze and Plaster at the Payne Whitney Gymnasium

October 17–November 5, 1952
Form, Image, Design. Teaching exhibition

October 31–November 6, 1952
Carcassonne. Teaching exhibition

October 31–November 30, 1952
People and Politics

November 1–30, 1952
Grandmother's Shawls and the Oriental Types that Inspired Them

November 1, 1952–January 4, 1953
Modern Mexican and Guatemalan Weaving

December 1, 1952–January 1, 1953
Four Centuries of Lace

December 15, 1952–February 1, 1953
In Memory of Katherine S. Dreier, 1877–1952: Her Own Collection of Modern Art

December 15–January 7, 1953
Medieval Art. Teaching exhibition

1953

January 3–February 1, 1953
Tapestry as Technique

February 16–March 15, 1953
Design in Industry. Institute of Contemporary Art. Catalogue

February 22, 1953
Portraits of George Washington for Alumni Day

March 1953
Indian and European Embroidered Muslin

March 1953
One Hundred Years of Theatrical Posters

April 1–16, 1953
Form in Art. Teaching exhibition

April 10–May 17, 1953
Ars in Urbe

April 17–May 3, 1953
French Textiles: Original Reproductions

May 1–31, 1953
Persian Trimming Bands and Striped Designs

June 4–28, 1953
Collections (Books and Pictures) of the Class of 1933

June 6–July 1, 1953
Recent work by students in the Division of the Arts

June 6–July 31, 1953
Recent Accessions

June 6–Summer 1953
The Coronation of Edward VII: Pastel Portraits by Edwin Austin Abbey

November 6–29, 1953
A New Building for the Arts at Yale. Special exhibition. Plans and construction photographs of Yale University Art Gallery and Design Center by Louis I. Kahn

November 20–December 31, 1953
Collaborative Graphic Arts Project

November 26, 1953–January 3, 1954
Lamplight-Portable Lamp Design

1954

January 4–25, 1954
Modern Prints

January 15–February 22, 1954
Watercolors by John Marin 1870–1953

February 3–March 7, 1954
Scenes from Shakespeare in Paintings and Prints

February 26–March 15, 1954
19th and 20th Century Japanese Silks

March 12–April 18, 1954
The Linton Collection of African Sculpture. Catalogue

April 30–June 14, 1954
Object and Image in Modern Art and Poetry. Catalogue

October 14–November 28, 1954
Palmyrene and Gandharan Sculpture. Catalogue

November 10, 1954
Student Exhibition by Charles Rosen. Drama School

December 1, 1954–January 1, 1955
Presented for Christmas

December 1954–January 1955
Matisse

December 1954 Special exhibitions, 2 weeks each
Architecture Drawings by P. Jobison
Drawings of Mies van der Rohe

1955

January 19–February 13, 1955
Recent Accessions

February 8–April 7, 1955
Objects from the Cooper Union Museum

February 16–March 20, 1955
20th Century Drawings: An Exhibition. Brochure

April 4–25, 1955
†*Pictures of the Floating World: Three Centuries of Japanese Prints.* Smithsonian Institution

May 7–June 5, 1955
Americana: Furniture, Silver, Pottery

June 13–September 1955
Student work

September 14–October 9, 1955
Four Photographers: Abbott, Atget, Clarence John Laughlin, Stieglitz

October 20–November 20, 1955
Portraits of Interiors. Brochure

November 1–25, 1955
Fabrics by Frank Lloyd Wright

November 30, 1955–January 1, 1956
Contemporary Finnish Design

November 30, 1955–January 1, 1956
Presented for Christmas

December 1955
Christmas 1955

1956

January 19–February 23, 1956
Dada: Forty Years After

February 15–March 18, 1956
Designs of the Mimbreños. Catalogue

February 22, 1956
Dedication of The Hobart and Edward Small Moore Memorial Collection of Near and Far-Eastern Art Objects

April 12–May 20, 1956 (extended to June 18)
Josef Albers: Painter and Teacher. A Retrospective Exhibition

April 20–June 18, 1956
Masterworks from Yale University. Special exhibition for the Art Institute of Chicago. Catalogue included excerpts from Wilmarth S. Lewis, *The Yale Collections,* 1946

May 3–June 18, 1956
An Exhibition: Paintings by Graham Sutherland, Sculpture and Drawings by Henry Moore. Brochure

May 8–June 18, 1956
Pictures Collected by Yale Alumni. Catalogue

June 1956
Roman and Early Christian Glass

September 27–October 22, 1956
Vocabulary in Form. Teaching exhibition

September 27–October 22, 1956
Medical Prints and Drawings from Collection of Dr. Clements C. Fry

October 2–14, 1956
†*French Children's Paintings.* French Cultural Services, New York

Fall 1956
Department of the History of Art. Teaching exhibitions

November 8, 1956–December 9, 1956
†*Donald Oenslager: Stage Designer and Teacher.* Catalogue. American Federation of Arts

December 13, 1956–January 3, 1957
†*Eskimo Art III.* Smithsonian Institution exhibition

1957

January 10–February 24, 1957
Exhibition of 1956 Accessions by Gift and Purchase

February 27–March 13, 1957
Second Exhibition by The Georgians: Contemporary Artists. Brochure

February 28–March 17, 1957
Two Sculptors: Bertoia and Noguchi

March 14–April 14, 1957
†*Contemporary Finnish Architecture.* Smithsonian Institution

April 12–May 27, 1957
Twenty Watercolors

May 7, 1957
60 Prints and Drawings from Yale Art Gallery Collections, Renaissance to Present

Summer 1957
Sculpture. Georgians exhibition

September–October 1957
Form in Art. Teaching exhibition

November 1957
†*Exhibition of Venetian Villas.* Soprintendenza ai Monumenti Medievali e Moderni, Venice

December 1957
Watercolors and Drawings from the Permanent Collection

December 1, 1957–April 5, 1958
Student Work. School of Drama

December 2–16, 1957
†*Skyscrapers, Photographic Plans, Diagrams, and Texts.* MoMA

1958

January 1–February 7, 1958
Société Anonyme Exhibition

January 31–February 19, 1958
†*Leonardo da Vinci.* International Business Machines

February 22–May 1, 1958
Yale University Art Gallery: Recent Acquisitions

February 1958
Sculpture and Paintings from the Gallery Collection of Modern Art

March 8–August 31, 1958
Olsen Collection of Ancient Central American Art

May 1–11, 1958
Calotypes of David Octavius Hill and Robert Adamson

June 9–July 7, 1958
Design, Painting, and Sculpture, Architecture. Student exhibition

August 8–31, 1958
Paintings and Sculpture from the Gallery's Modern Collections

September 12–November 9, 1958
Principles of Form in the Visual Arts. Department of the History of Art. Teaching exhibition

October 10–November 9, 1958
Photographs of Peru by John Cohen and Mexican Textiles from the Harriet Engelhardt Memorial Collection

November 1, 1958–January 1959
The Philip L. Goodwin Collection Exhibition

November 19, 1958–January 18, 1959
Drawings by Rico Lebrun

1959

January 30–Summer 1959
Selections from the Permanent Collection

February 4–April 12, 1959
Recent Gifts and Accessions of 1958

March 12–May 17, 1959
The Ernest Steefel Collection of 20th Century Graphic Art. Catalogue

April 17–25, 1959
†*Robert Edmond Jones: Designs for the Theatre.* American Federation of Arts

May 7–21, 1959
Exhibition of Paintings by Students and Faculty of the Department of Fine Arts, New Asia College, Hong Kong

June 5–September 20, 1959
Student work

September 2–November 1, 1959
Selections from the Permanent Collection: Paintings and Sculpture

September 22–October 25, 1959
Principles of Form in the Visual Arts. Department of the History of Art. Teaching exhibition

November 18, 1959–March 13, 1960
The Louis and Hannah Rabinowitz Bequest

December 10, 1959–January 10, 1960
Pictorial Weavings by Anni Albers. Catalogue

1960

February 19–March 27, 1960
Musical Instruments at Yale. Catalogue

March 24–May 24, 1960
American Prints, 1950–1960

April 6–May 22, 1960
Selections from the Gallery Collections of Oriental and Western Art

May 18–June 1960
Early American Silver: The Mabel Brady Garvan Collection 30th Anniversary Exhibition

May 19–June 26, 1960
Paintings, Drawings and Sculptures Collected by Yale Alumni. Catalogue

June 13–July 10, 1960
1950–60 Annual Exhibition of Students' Work. School of Art and Architecture

August 1–October 16, 1960
Works from the Gallery Collections of 20th-Century Art

September 20–December 1960
Principles of Form. Teaching exhibition

October 25–December 31, 1960
Fry Collection of Medical School Prints

1961

January 12–March 26, 1961
Recent Acquisitions and Purchases

Spring 1961
The Olsen Collection of Pre-Columbian Art

April 27–September 3, 1961
Paintings and Sculpture from the Albright Art Gallery

June–August 1961
School of Architecture. Student exhibition

September 1961–February 1962
Language of Form. Teaching exhibition

October 12–November 26, 1961
The Stephen C. Clark, B.A. *1903, Bequest*

December 6, 1961–February 4, 1962
Contemporary Paintings from New York Galleries

1962

February–May 20, 1962
100 Gifts and Purchases

March 17–April 15, 1962
Theodore Sizer: 50 Years of Creative Work

May 1–27, 1962
†*Tiepolo Drawings from the Victoria and Albert Museum, London.* Catalogue. Smithsonian Institution

Summer 1962
School of Art and Architecture. Student exhibition

September 4–November 4, 1962
Language of Form. Teaching exhibition

October 11, 1962–January 6, 1963
Color in Prints. Catalogue: YUAG *Bulletin*

December 7, 1962–March 3, 1963
Recent Gifts and Acquisitions

December 1962–January 1963
Variations on a Persian Bowl

December 1962–January 1963
Alumni Works

1963

February 14–May 8, 1963
Chinese Paintings at Yale. Brochure

March–May 26, 1963
Selections from the Collection of Drawings

March 23–April 14, 1963
Joseph Albers: Interaction of Color. Book

April 1–July 5, 1963
American Gold from 1700–1860. Catalogue

May 22–September 1, 1963
Two Modern Collectors: Susan Morse Hilles and Richard Brown Baker. Catalogue

June 7–July 7, 1963
Student Exhibition. Architecture

September 19–October 20, 1963
Department of the History of Art. Teaching exhibition

November 9, 1963–January 6, 1964
The Work of Paul Rudolph, Architect. Catalogue

November 9, 1963–January 6, 1964
Recent Paintings by Jack Tworkov. Catalogue

1964

January 30–April 12, 1964
Recent Gifts and Purchases, 1963

March 3–23, 1964
Scientific Instruments from the David Wheatland Collection

March 22–May 3, 1964
Loan Exhibition of Collection of Julian Levy: Ernst and Gorky

April 22–June 7, 1964
Drawings from the Janos Scholz Collection. Catalogue

September 17–November 2, 1964
The Language of Form in the Visual Arts. Teaching exhibition

October 14–November 8, 1964
Four Centuries of Theater Design, Drawings from the Donald Oenslager Collection. Catalogue

November–December 27, 1964
Gabor Peterdi, Paintings, Drawings and Prints

November 1964
55 Dürer Prints

November 1964
Ukiyo-e Prints

1965

January 13–February 15, 1965
Contemporary Art at Yale: 1. Art and Architecture Faculty

January 21–March 14, 1965
Neo-Impressionists and the Nabis in the Collection of Arthur G. Altschul. Catalogue

March 1965
Acquisitions, 1964

March 3–April 4, 1965
Contemporary Art at Yale: 2. Art and Architecture Faculty

April 15–June 20, 1965
English Drawings and Watercolors from the Collection of Mr. and Mrs. Mellon; Painting in England, 1700–1850. Catalogues

September 16–October 24, 1965
Language of Form in the Visual Arts. Teaching exhibition

September 24–November 30, 1965
Dutch and Flemish Drawings of the Sixteenth and Seventeenth Centuries

October 13–November 28, 1965
Photography in America: 1850–1965. Catalogue

November 17, 1965–January 2, 1966
Contemporary Art at Yale: 3. Art and Architecture Faculty

December 22, 1965–January 13, 1966
Travel in Nineteenth-Century America: Prints from the Mabel Brady Garvan Collection

1966

January 25–March 20, 1966
**The Art of Latin America Since Independence.* Catalogue. University of Texas Art Museum

February 16–April 1, 1966
Recent Gifts and Purchases, 1965

February 16–September 15, 1966
Prints and Drawings from the Collection of Allen Evarts Foster, B.A. *1906*

April 13–May 22, 1966
Contemporary Art at Yale: 4. Art and Architecture Faculty

May 21–June 19, 1966
Designs for the Stage by Yale Drama School Alumni

September 14–October 31, 1966
Language of Form in the Visual Arts. Teaching exhibition

October 25, 1966–January 8, 1967
German Expressionist Prints from the Collection of Walter Bareiss. Catalogue

October 25, 1966–January 8, 1967
Animals and Plants in the Graphic Arts

1967

January 1967
Garvan Silver Collection

January 19–February 25, 1967
Recent Acquisitions and the Wetmore Bequest

January 19–February 19, 1967
Contemporary Art at Yale: 5. Art and Architecture Faculty

January 25–March 25, 1967
Prints and Drawings from the Collection of Frank Altschul

February 19, 1967
Gavarni Prints

March 5–April 9, 1967
Italian Drawings from the Princeton Art Museum. Catalogue

March 30–May 8, 1967
Contemporary Art at Yale: 6. Art and Architecture Faculty

May 4–June 18, 1967
The Helen W. and Robert M. Benjamin Collection. Catalogue

June 7–October 29, 1967
Whistler and the English Tradition in Etching

September 19–December 3, 1967
Language of Form in the Visual Arts. Teaching exhibition

October 12–December 3, 1967
Exchange Exhibition from the Fogg Art Museum

December 1967
Watercolors on View

December 1967
Yale University Art Gallery Acquisitions

1968

January 11–February 11, 1968
Recent Gifts and Purchases, 1967

January 19–May 1, 1968
Eighteenth Century Venetian Etchings

February 26–May 5, 1968
Islamic Art at Yale

April 25–June 16, 1968
American Art from Alumni Collections. Catalogue

May 6–September 15, 1968
Exhibition of Twentieth Century Prints and Drawings

May 9–June 23, 1968
Contemporary Art at Yale: 7. Art and Architecture Faculty

September 12–December 8, 1968
French Drawing: Watteau to Matisse

September 26–December 21, 1968
The Language of Form. Teaching exhibition

November 1–December 5, 1968
†Festival Designs by Inigo Jones. Catalogue. International Exhibitions Foundation

December 16, 1968–January 19, 1969
Portrait Prints and Drawings: Dürer to Picasso

December 20, 1968–February 9, 1969
Recent Gifts and Purchases, 1968

1969

February 5–March 30, 1969
The Graphic Art of Géricault. Catalogue

February 27–April 13, 1969
**African and Afro-American Art: The Transatlantic Tradition.* Museum of Primitive Art

April 8–June 15, 1969
Etchings of Rembrandt

June 3–September 7, 1969
Graphic Art of Picasso

June 3–August 17, 1969
Selections from the Collection of the Société Anonyme

June 24–September 7, 1969
French Prints of the Nineteenth Century

September 7–December 20, 1970
The Art of Jacques Villon

September 24, 1969–January 25, 1970
Language of Form in the Visual Arts. Teaching exhibition

October 9–November 16, 1969
**Prints and Drawings of the Danube School.* Catalogue

October 16, 1969–January 4, 1970
Contemporary Prints

October 25–December 14, 1969
Selections from the Collection Société Anonyme

December 4, 1969–March 1, 1970
Recent Gifts and Acquisitions

1970

January 27–March 30, 1970
Master Prints of the 15th and 16th Centuries

March 12–May 10, 1970
19th and 20th Century Prints—The Recent Gifts of Mr. and Mrs. Walter Bareiss B.A. *1940.*

April 30–June 14, 1970
**Recent Sculpture by James Rosati: 1963–1969.* Catalogue.

May 15–31 1970
Yale Art School Faculty Exhibition for the University Fund for Justice

May 27–June 21, 1970
Paintings Sculpture and Photographs by the Graduating Class of the Art School

August 11–30, 1970
Math Model Buildings Competition

September 14–December 1970
The Art of Jacques Villon

September 23–January 1971
Language of Form in the Visual Arts. Teaching exhibition

October 14–November 22, 1970
**German Painting of the 19th Century.* Catalogue

November 18, 1970–January 1, 1971
A New Look at Old Silver

1971

January 12–March 14, 1971
Contemporary American Prints

February 5–28, 1971
Recent Gifts and Purchases

March 4–April 25, 1971
Younger Painters and Sculptors from New York Galleries

March 11–April 25, 1971
Master Drawings and Watercolors from the Permanent Collection. Book, *European Drawings and Watercolors, 1500–1900,* 2 vols.

March 11–May 17, 1971
Print. Teaching exhibition

March 16–May 9, 1971
Print Connoisseurship

March 23–May 9, 1971
**Prints: The Problem of the Multiple Image*

May 6–June 20, 1971
**Salute to Mark Rothko.* Checklist

May 18–September 5, 1971
Baroque Prints and Drawings

May 25–June 20, 1971
Work by the Graduating Class of the Yale Art School

Spring 1971
Art of the 20s, Teaching exhibition

June 1971–June 1974
**The American Arts at Yale 1971–1651.* Catalogue

Summer 1971
Société Anonyme Collection. Teaching exhibition

September 13–October 31, 1971
Prints by Josef Albers

September 26, 1971–January 30, 1972
Language of Form in the Visual Arts. Part 1, *Change in Western Arts: From Paleolithic to Baroque*; Part 2, *Plastic Arts of Yoruba.* Teaching exhibitions

October 13–November 28, 1971
The Graphic Art of Albrecht Dürer

October 28–December 12, 1971
Manet and His Contemporaries

November 4, 1971–January 8, 1972
Picasso Drawings from the Collection of Mr. and Mrs. Walter Bareiss

December 8, 1971–January 16, 1972
Walker Evans: Forty Years, An Anthology of Taste. Checklist

1972

January 18–March 19, 1972
Evolution of Landscape in the Netherlands

January 26–March 5, 1972
The World between the Ox and the Swine

February 15–May 14, 1972
Surrealist Paintings. Teaching exhibition

March 15–April 23, 1972
William Blake Watercolor Designs for the Poems of Thomas Gray. Catalogue. First exhibition shared with Yale Center for British Art

March 28–May 21, 1972
Drawings from the Permanent Collection

April 19–August 31, 1972
Italian Primitives: The Case History of a Collection and Its Conservation. Catalogue

May 18–Summer 1972
Recent Gifts and Purchases

May 26–June 20, 1972
Work of Graduating M.F.A. *Students*

May 30–September 24, 1972
European Posters 1880–1920

September 14, 1972–February 1973
Cubism. Teaching exhibition

October 10–November 20, 1972
Exhibition of Watercolors by John M. Stanley from the Paul Mellon Collection

October 19–November 26, 1972
The Edo Culture in Japanese Prints. Catalogue

December 5, 1972–February 3, 1973
American Drawings from the Collection

December 14, 1972–March 5, 1973
Four Directions in Modern Photography: Bruce Davidson, John T. Hill, Paul Caponigro, Jerry N. Uelsmann. Catalogue

1973

January–May 1973
Department of the History of Art. Teaching exhibition

February 13–April 8, 1973
16th-Century European Prints

April 4–May 16, 1973
Contemporary New York Artists: Jasper Johns, "White Flag"

April 4–May 16, 1973
Options and Alternatives: Some Directions in Recent Art. Checklist and catalogue

April 24–September 16, 1973
Currier and Ives: Scenes from the American Imagination.

May 30–June 10, 1973
Art School Graduating M.F.A. Student Exhibition

June 1973
American Arts and The American Experience. Opening, redesigned Garvan and American art galleries. Tabloid

Summer 1973
Contemporary Prints and Drawings

September 1973–Spring 1974
Prints, Drawings, Collages, Collection Société Anonyme. Teaching exhibition

September 27–November 18, 1973
Wynn Bullock/Aaron Siskind: Photographs

October 9–November 25, 1973
American Drawing 1970–1973. Tabloid

December 6, 1973–February 17, 1974
Edwin Austin Abbey (1852–1911). Catalogue

December 11, 1973–February 3, 1974
The Cubist Image in the Graphic Arts
American Drawings from the Yale Collections

1974

January 15–May 5, 1974
Art of the Twentieth Century

February 12–April 22, 1974
Prints of Dürer and His Time

March 4–April 28, 1974
Contemporary American Paintings

March 28–June 2, 1974
7 Realists: Bailey, Fish, Hanson, Mangold, Pearlstein, Posen, Weisenfeld. Catalogue

May 7–September 8, 1974
Sixteenth-Century Italian Drawings: Form and Function. Catalogue

May 16–26, 1974
Art School M.F.A. Graduate Student Exhibition

June 3–28, 1974
Forgeries and Restorations in American Furniture. Checklist, *The American Clock 1725–1865.* Catalogue and checklist

September 17–October 26, 1974
Contemporary Realist Prints

October 17–November 30, 1974
The "Lipstick" Comes Back. Catalogue

October 24–November 24, 1974
Prints and Drawings. Teaching exhibition

November 12, 1974–January 19, 1975
Nineteenth-Century French Etchings

November 20, 1974–January 19, 1975
**Charles Meryon: Prints & Drawings. Catalogue*

1975

January 21–March 16, 1975
Dutch Religious Art of the Seventeenth Century. Catalogue

February 12–April 6, 1975
The Kashmir Shawl. Catalogue

April 1–May 27, 1975
Collage. Catalogue

April 15–June 16, 1975
Walker Evans: Photographs

April 23–July 13, 1975
Richard Brown Baker Collects! Catalogue

June 10–Fall 1975
Early 20th Century American Realist Prints, Drawings and Watercolors. Catalogue

July 12, 1975–February 7, 1976
Contemporary Paintings

September 17–November 2, 1975
The Ideal of Feminine Beauty in Japanese Prints

September 24–October 29, 1975
William Henry Jackson: Photographer of the American West. Book

September 30, 1975–April 15, 1976
Seventeenth Century Chinese Painting. Teaching exhibition

November 11, 1975–January 11, 1976
Color Photography—Inventors and Innovators, 1850–1975. Catalogue

November 19, 1975–January 18, 1976
Greek Vases at Yale. Catalogue

1976

January–May 12, 1976
Oriental Art. Teaching exhibition

February 1–27, 1976
17th-Century Chinese Painting Exhibition

February 3–April 11, 1976
Darkness into Light: The Early Mezzotint. Catalogue.

April 3–May 23, 1976
**American Art 1750–1800: Towards Independence.* Catalogue

April 23–June 13, 1976
Recently Acquired Drawings and Watercolors: 1973–1976

July 1, 1976–March 1977
Contemporary Works from the Yale University Art Gallery Collection

July 6–August 22, 1976
Architectural Drawings for Modern Public Buildings in New Haven. Catalogue

July 24–September 5, 1976
†*Presidential China.* Smithsonian Institution

September 2–October 17, 1976
German Expressionist Prints

September 22–November 14, 1976
Dante Gabriel Rossetti and the Double Work of Art. Catalogue

October 26, 1976–January 2, 1977
Scenes of Nature: Prints and Drawings of Dutch Landscape

November 3, 1976–January 3, 1977
Japanese Literati Painting. Teaching exhibition

December 1, 1976–January 23, 1977
Fifty Years of Stage Design: Drawings by Donald Oenslager and His Students

1977

January 11–February 27, 1977
French Drawings

January 25–September 11, 1977
Sculpture, Painting, Works on Paper. Teaching exhibition

February 9–March 13, 1977
Five Years of Collecting Photographs

February 23–April 17, 1977
300 Years of American Seating Furniture: Chairs and Beds from the Mabel Brady Garvan and Other Collections at Yale University. Book

March 8–May 23, 1977
Prints of Eugène Delacroix. Catalogue

April 6–June 27, 1977
**Traces of the Brush: Studies in Chinese Calligraphy.* Catalogue

May 13–July 10, 1977
The Eye of the Beholder: Fakes, Replicas, and Alterations in American Art Silver. Catalogue

June 8–August 20, 1977
Paris Theater Life 1880–1900

September 7, 1977–January 22, 1978
Etchings: From Dürer to Dine

September 9–October 9, 1977
†*Folk Art and Crafts of the Deep South.* Smithsonian Institution

September 9, 1977–January 29, 1978
Painting, Sculpture. Teaching exhibition

October 13, 1977–January 28, 1978
Recent American Art from the Woodward Foundation

1978

January 1978
Painting, Sculpture. Teaching exhibition

January 18–March 5, 1978
Home Away from Home, Student Period Rooms ca. 1877. Brochure

January 19–27, 1978
Wildlife: Prints, Drawings, Paintings: An Art Gallery Bestiary

January 31–March 30, 1978
Material Culture: Oil, Stitchery, Quilts. Yale Center for American Art and Material Culture

February–March 5, 1978
Home Away from Home: Student Rooms at Yale: 1870–1910. Yale Center for American Art and Material Culture

February 15–March 26, 1978
Numerals: 1924–1977

February 23–April 1, 1978
The Art of Josef Albers. Catalogue.

March 7–April 23, 1978
'Til Death Do Us Part: Design Sources of Eighteenth-Century New England Tombstones. Yale Center for American Art and Material Culture

March 28–June 6, 1978
A Survey of American Photographs 1840–1940. Yale Center for American Art and Material Culture

March 31–April 23, 1978
The Artist as Inventor

April 4–June 11, 1978
From Theater to Landscape: French Prints and Drawings of the Eighteenth Century

April 4–June 15, 1978
Excavations of St. Denis

April 4–May 28, 1978
Samuel F. B. Morse: The Artist As Inventor. Yale Center for American Art and Material Culture

April 7–June 6, 1978
Design to Persuade: Poster Art. Yale Center for American Art and Material Culture

April 13–June 4, 1978
**Federico Barocci: Selected Drawings and Prints.* Catalogue

May 2–June 7, 1978
Toys, Tools and Carvings: Eskimo Artifacts. Yale Center for American Art and Material Culture

June 15–August 31, 1978
Contemporary Paintings

June 20–September 3, 1978
Femmes: French Prints and Drawings 1880–1900. Catalogue

August 14, 1978–February 25, 1979
Rhode Island Furniture: 1740–1820. Yale Center for American Art and Material Culture

September 6–December 25, 1978
Prints and Drawings. Teaching exhibition

September 12–October 29, 1978
**Faces of the Japanese Theatre*

September 19, 1978–January 15, 1979
Pictures from an Expedition: Early Views of the American West. Yale Art Gallery and Yale Center for American Art and Material Culture. Catalogue

October 5–November 26, 1978
**Jackson Pollock—New Found Works.* Catalogue

October 17–November 21, 1978
Maat: The Order of the Universe. Catalogue

October 24, 1978–April 16, 1979
Chinese Paintings from the Collection of Wang Nan-Ping

November 14, 1978–January 14, 1979
The Prints of Albrecht Dürer

November 15, 1978–February 18, 1979
Southern Furniture: Baltimore to Charleston. Yale Center for American Art and Material Culture

December 13, 1978–January 21, 1979
Prints and Drawings of the Seventies

1979

January–June 1979
Four Twentieth Century Artists: Jacques Villon, Kurt Schwitters, Man Ray, and El Lissitsky

January 30–April 16, 1979
Photographers Look at Buildings

February 7–March 18, 1979
†*Imperial China: Photography 1846–1912.* Catalogue. American Federation of Arts

March 30–June 18, 1979
All That Glisters: Brass in Early America. Yale Center for American Art and Material Culture. Catalogue

April 5–September 23, 1979
Paintings and Sculpture from the Mary C. and James W. Fosburgh Bequest

April 25–May 15, 1979
American Art and Artifacts: The Interpretation of Objects. Yale Center for American Art and Material Culture

April 25–June 24, 1979
Cloth and Class: The Prestige of Fabric. Catalogue

Spring 1979–January 16, 1980
Modernism. Teaching exhibition

May 2–June 24, 1979
The Photographs of Harriet V. S. Thorne. Catalogue

Summer 1979
Italian Drawings 1550–1750. Teaching exhibition

July 10–August 26, 1979
Contemporary American Drawings Since 1945

September 8, 1979–January 20, 1980
A Century of Tradition and Innovation in American Decorative Arts: 1830–1930. Brochure

September 11, 1979–January 6, 1980
Questioning Things: The Problems of Meaning in American Art and Artifacts. Teaching exhibition

September 19–November 18, 1979
Gavarni: The Carnival Lithographs. Catalogue

September 20–December 31, 1979
John Trumbull. Teaching exhibition

October–November 1979
Impressionism, Neo-Impressionism, and Post-Impressionism. Teaching exhibition

October 17–December 2, 1979
Mondrian and Neo-Plasticism in America. Catalogue

November 28, 1979–January 27, 1980
Anne Ryan: Collages

December 19, 1979–February 10, 1980
Recent Acquisitions: Decorative Arts, 1976–1979

December 20, 1979–May 18, 1980
Patterns: Dress and Japanese Life

1980

February 13–April 6, 1980
**Rembrandt and His Followers: Prints from the Yale and Wesleyan University Collections.* Catalogue

February 28–April 13, 1980
†Real and Imaginary Beings: The Netsuke Collection of Joseph and Edith Kurstin. Catalogue

Spring 1980
History of Photography. Teaching exhibition

Spring 1980
African Sculpture. Teaching exhibition

April 4–June 29, 1980
Tons of Type: Two Hundred Years of American Letterpress Broadsides. Yale Center for American Art and Material Culture. Checklist

April 23–August 31, 1980
American Watercolors from the Collection of George Hopper Fitch. Catalogue: YUAG *Bulletin*

May 8–September 28, 1980
A Wide View for American Art: Francis P. Garvan Collector. 50th Anniversary Exhibition. Catalogue

May 12–July 13, 1980
Seeing Rather than Dreaming: Coronation Sketches by Edwing Austin Abbey. Yale Center for American Art and Material Culture. Brochure

June 25–October 26, 1980
Technique and Tradition of Indonesian Textiles. Extensive wall labels

Fall 1980
Opening of Katharine Ordway galleries and collection. Catalogue

September 1–December 22, 1980
Dada, Surrealists—Precursors and Followers. Teaching exhibition

September 10–October 26, 1980
The Intimate Vision of Edouard Vuillard. Brochure

October 23–January 4, 1981
† "The Most Remarkable Scenery": Thomas Moran's Western Watercolors. Catalogue

November 18, 1980–January 11, 1981
† To See Big Within Small: Chinese Album Leaves and Fans from the Collection from Boston Museum of Fine Arts. Catalogue

November 18, 1980–January 11, 1981
Selected Japanese Prints

1981

January 21–March 15, 1981
Walker Evans and Robert Frank: An Essay on Influence. Catalogue

January 29–March 29, 1981
20 Artists: Yale School of Art 1950–1970. Catalogue

March 31–June 7, 1981
The Spread of Dürer's Woodcut Style. Catalogue

Spring 1981
German Expressionism, Andean Objects. Teaching exhibitions

April 23–June 16, 1981
** Hans Baldung Grien: Prints and Drawings.* Catalogue

May 14–September 13, 1981
A Sense of Pattern: Textile Masterworks from the Yale University Art Gallery Collection. Catalogue

July–August 23, 1981
† Charles Marville: Photographs of Paris at the Time of the Second Empire. Alliance Française and Musée Carnavalet. Catalogue

September 2–November 9, 1981
Department of the History of Art. Teaching exhibition

September 8–November 8, 1981
† Late Entries to the Chicago Tribune Tower Exhibition. Catalogue

September 27–November 15, 1981
Goya's "Los Caprichos." Catalogue

November 4–December 12, 1981
† A Masterpiece Closeup: Raphael's 1520 Transfiguration. Polaroid exhibition

November 9, 1981–April 27, 1982
Italian Panel Paintings. Teaching exhibition

November 25, 1981–January 24, 1982
A Generous Benefactor: Prints from the Lydia Evans Tunnard Collection

1982

January 27–March 28, 1982
** German Drawings of the 60s.* Catalogue

January 28–September 12, 1982
Indian Sculpture from the Collection of Alice and Nasli Heeramaneck. Catalogue

February 10–April 4, 1982
Philadelphia Naturalistic Photography, 1885–1906. Catalogue

February 23–April 28, 1982
Sparing No Detail: James Gamble Rogers' Drawings for Yale University 1913–1935. Catalogue

March 24, 1982–January 2, 1983
Life in an Eastern Province. The Roman Fortress at Dura-Europos

March 25–May 30, 1982
The Work of Many Hands: Card Tables in Federal America. Catalogue and brochure

April 15–June 15, 1982
Emblem for an Era: Selected Images of American Victorian Women from the Yale University Community, 1837–1911. Illustrated pamphlet

April 21–September 13, 1982
Recent Acquisitions: Contemporary Prints

May 6, 1982–January 2, 1983
The Sacred Heritage of Tibet. Illustrated booklet

May 18–August 31, 1982
Prints by Contemporary Sculptors. Catalogue

September 20–November 30, 1982
German Woodcut Book Illustration 1460–1540: Selections from the Paul Mellon Collection at the Yale Center for British Art

October 5, 1982–April 17, 1983
**The Communion of Scholars: Chinese Art at Yale*. Catalogue

October 7, 1982–January 16, 1983
John Trumbull: The Hand and Spirit of a Painter. Catalogue and brochure

October 28, 1982–January 16, 1983
**Silver in American Life: Selections from the Mabel Brady Garvan and Other Collections at Yale University*. American Federation of Arts

December 15, 1982–February 20, 1983
On Reading Prints: Complex Narratives and Meanings in Five Centuries of Printmaking, A Study in Print Iconology. Catalogue

1983

March 7–May 1, 1983
Turn-of-the-Century Photographs by Robert Demachy 1894–1914. Catalogue

April 13–June 26, 1983
The Futurist Imagination: Word + Image in Italian Painting, Drawing, Collage, and Free-Word Poetry. Catalogue

May 10–August 31, 1983
American Prints 1900–1950: An Exhibition in Honor of the Donation of John P. Axelrod, B.A. 1968. Catalogue

Spring 1983
Art in the Machine Age. Teaching exhibition

May 19–September 18, 1983
Nineteenth-Century French Prints from the Permanent Collection

September 23–November 20, 1983
Selections from the History of Photography

November 10, 1983–February 5, 1984
At Home in Manhattan: Modern Decorative Arts, 1925 to the Depression. Catalogue

November 23, 1983–January 3, 1984
Modern Photographers After 1960

1984

January 12–March 4, 1984
†Seventeenth Century Dutch Prints from Daily Life. Catalogue

February 1–March 25, 1984
**The Artistic Revival of the Woodcut in France 1850–1900*. Catalogue. Brochure

March 1–May 6, 1984
The Spirit of Place: Japanese Paintings and Prints 16th–19th Centuries. Catalogue

April 5–June 10, 1984
French Drawings: Acquisitions 1970–1984. Catalogue

Spring 1984
Expressionism, Dada. Teaching exhibition

April 18–June 24, 1984
**Winslow Homer: The Croquet Game*. Catalogue

April 25–August 31, 1984
Art for a New Era: The Société Anonyme Collection: 1920–1950. Book: Catalogue raisonné; tabloid

June 15–August 9, 1984
Sets and Series: Prints from the Low Countries. Catalogue

August 15–October 15, 1984
† The Prints of Barnett Newman. Catalogue

September–December 1984
Pop Art Painting. Teaching exhibition

September–December 1984
Art in the Machine. Teaching exhibition

September–December 1984
History of Photography. Teaching exhibition

October 11, 1984–January 6, 1985
** The Folding Image: Screens by Western Artists of the Nineteenth and Twentieth Centuries*. Catalogue

October 25, 1984–March 3, 1985
Ralph Kirkpatrick In Memoriam. Catalogue

1985

March 27–June 9, 1985
**Natural and Pastoral Themes by Barbizon Printmakers*. Catalogue

April 18–June 16, 1985
**Bones of Jade, Soul of Ice: The Flowering Plum in Chinese Art*. Catalogue

May 22–September 15, 1985
**Artists in Tune with Their World: Popular Artists of the Americas from the Selden Rodman Collection*. Catalogue

June 19–September 1, 1985
Nineteenth-Century French Lithography

September 17–November 3, 1985
Prints and Drawings by Contemporary Artists: Recent Acquisitions

October 10–December 8, 1985
†Richard Hamilton: Image and Process. Catalogue

November 7, 1985–January 2, 1986
† Celestial Images: Astronomical Charts from 1500–1900. Catalogue

December 18, 1985–January 12, 1986
Welcome Back: Works from the Collection of Richard Brown Baker

1986

January 8–March 9, 1986
**Art for "The Masses" (1911–1917): A Radical Magazine and Its Graphics*. Catalogue

January 9–March 9, 1986
Prints by Artists of "The Masses"

January 30–March 23, 1986
† The Woven and Graphic Art of Anni Albers. Catalogue

March 18–May 4, 1986
The Shape of Chic: Fashion and Hairstyles in the Floating World. Catalogue

April 8–June 15, 1986
Interiors and Exteriors: Contemporary Realist Prints. Catalogue

April 8–June 15, 1986
Salute to Spring: 20th Century Art from the Collection

April 17–June 7, 1986
† Old Master Drawings from the John and Alice Steiner Collection

May 6–June 15, 1986
Working in the Floating World. Catalogue

June 20–August 24, 1986
The Good Old Summertime: American Prints and Drawings: 1850–1910. Catalogue

June 20–August 10, 1986
Selections from the Collection: 1982–1987

August 25, 1986–January 1987
Russian Art, the Duchamps. Teaching exhibition

August 29–October 19, 1986
Photography. Teaching exhibition

September 10–November 4, 1986
**Winslow Homer Watercolors*. Catalogue

September 16–November 6, 1986
†Antonio Sant'Elia: Architectural Drawings. Brochure

October 28, 1986–January 1, 1987
**The Art of Teaching: Sixteenth-Century Allegorical Prints and Drawings*. Catalogue

November 21, 1986–March 8, 1987
Selections from the Collection: 20th Century Sculpture

December 11, 1986–March 9, 1987
Chinese Folk Art: The Small Skills of Carving Insects. Catalogue

1987

January 13–March 18, 1987
The Afterlife of a Rivalry: Raphael vs. Michaelangelo. Brochure

January 27–May 11, 1987
Collage, Montage, and Assemblage in 20th Century Art. Teaching exhibition

February 18–April 19, 1987
Gifts to Osiris: Ancient Egyptian Art at Yale. Book, *Ancient Egyptian Art at Yale*

March 4–May 31, 1987
Contemporary Chinese Paintings

March 25–May 31, 1987
Contemporary American Artists in Print. Catalogue

April 1–May 31, 1987
Charles Sheeler—American Interiors. Catalogue

June 10–September 5, 1987
Acquisitions 1982–1987: European and American Drawings

June 17–August 9, 1987
Contemporary American Art 1960–1980

June 24, 1987–January 8, 1988
Recent Acquisitions 1976–1986

August–November 1987
Russian Constructivism in the 20th Century. Teaching exhibition

September 9–November 29, 1987
**A Taste for Angels: Neapolitan Painting in North America, 1650–1750.* Catalogue

September 15–November 1, 1987
Master Drawings from the Permanent Collection

September–December 1987
Modern Art: Art in the Machine Age. Teaching exhibition

October–November 1987
Edouard Manet. Teaching exhibition

November 6, 1987–January 9, 1988
From Mannerism to Classicism: Printmaking in France 1600–1660. Catalogue

December 9, 1987–January 20, 1988
†*A Graphic Muse: Prints by Contemporary American Women.* Catalogue

December 1987
American Art, 1960 to the Present

December 1987
Chinese Art: New Additions to the Yale Collection

1988

January 19–March 20, 1988
French Drawings from the Permanent Collection 1600–1800. Catalogue

February 9–March 28, 1988
Selections from the Collections

February 11–June 12, 1988
American Silver from the Kossack Collection. Brochure

February 23–April 4, 1988
Bright Color, Bold Ink: Stylistic Diversity in Momoyama Art. Brochure

March 29–June 5, 1988
†*Gian Domenico Tiepolo and the "Flight into Egypt."* Catalogue

April 12–June 5, 1988
†*Foirades/Fizzles: Echo and Allusion in the Art of Jasper Johns.* Catalogue

April 19–June 12, 1988
Continuity and Change: Five Contemporary Chinese Artists

Spring 1988
Art of the American West. Teaching exhibition

June 14–August 7, 1988
20th Century Painting and Sculpture from the Collection

June 21–September 4, 1988
Images of New Haven

Summer 1988
Summertime USA: Post 1950 Art

September 9–November 6, 1988
†*Evocative Images: African Sculpture from the University of Pennsylvania Museum and the Yale Art Gallery.* Catalogue

September 13–October 30, 1988
The Graphic Art of Umberto Boccioni: Selections from the Lydia Winston Malbin Collection. Brochure

November 17–January 8, 1988
†*The World in Miniature: Engravings by the German Little Masters: 1500–1550.* Catalogue

Fall 1988
History of Photography. Teaching exhibition

Fall 1988
Late Nineteenth-Century French Art. Teaching exhibition

December 2, 1988–January 15, 1989
†*In Pursuit of the Dragon: Traditions and Transitions in Ming Ceramics*

1989

January 18–March 18, 1989
Expressionist Prints: Nolde to Kokoschka

February 2–March 19, 1989
German and Austrian Contemporary Art from the Bareiss Collection. Catalogue

February 10–March 10, 1989
Sixteenth Century Italian Prints. Teaching exhibition

February 28–June 1, 1989
Gesture and Expression: The Language of Art in the Age of Revolution. Teaching exhibition

February 28–June 12, 1989
David to Delacroix. Teaching exhibition

March 9–June 11, 1989
Toward an Urban View: The Nineteenth-Century American City in Prints. Catalogue

April 16–June 4, 1989
†*The Sforza Court: Milan in the Renaissance 1450–1535.* Catalogue

Spring 1989
Age of Michelangelo. Teaching exhibition

June 16–August 31, 1989
Fred Sandback Sculpture. Catalogue

June 20–August 27, 1989
New Acquisitions and Promised Gifts in Photography: Fabrications and Mediations

September 2–October 22, 1989
Confronting the Uncomfortable: Questioning Truth and Power. Catalogue

September 22–November 12, 1989
Word in Flower: The Visualization of Classical Literature in Seventeenth-Century Japan. Catalogue

November 10, 1989–January 2, 1990
American Daguerreotypes from the Matthew R. Isenburg Collection. Catalogue

Fall 1989
Topics in Modern Art: Russian Art. Teaching exhibition

Fall 1989
Sixteenth-Century Italian Drawings. Teaching exhibition

Fall 1989
Dada and Surrealism. Teaching exhibition

December 2–31, 1989
Mark Rothko: The Multiforms. Brochure

1990

January 15–March 3, 1990
Paul Outerbridge, A Singular Aesthetic: Photographs and Drawings 1921–1941. Catalogue

January 27–March 11, 1990
† *The Art Museums of Louis I. Kahn.* Book

March 30–July 29, 1990
The Plow and the Harrow: Van Gogh and Millet. Brochure

April 4–June 10, 1990
**Childe Hassam: An Island Garden Revisited.* Catalogue

April 19–June 3, 1990
† *Kobayashi Kiyochika: Artist of Meiji.* Catalogue

Spring 1990
Art after 1968. Teaching exhibition

Spring 1990
Berlin in the 1920s. Teaching exhibition

June 12–September 9, 1990
The Preparatory Process: Drawings for Paintings and Prints in the Yale Art Gallery Collection. Catalogue

July 1–September 16, 1990
† *Abstraction/Geometry/Painting: Selected Painting in America Since 1945*

September 15–November 4, 1990
Watercolor in America: Part I, The 18th and 19th Centuries. Catalogue

September 26–October 21, 1990
American Abstraction in the 60's & 70's: From the Permanent Collection

September 29–December 9, 1990
† *Eastman Johnson: The Cranberry Harvest: Island of Nantucket.* Catalogue

November 6, 1990–January 2, 1991
† *Scenes and Sequences: Recent Monotypes by Eric Fischl.* Catalogue

November 15, 1990–January 13, 1991
The Watercolor in America: Part II, The Early 20th Century. Catalogue

1991

January 25–March 24, 1991
**Master of the Lotus Garden: The Life and Art of Bada Shanren, 1626–1705.* Catalogue

January 31–March 12, 1991
Private Delights: The Drawings of Mary Bell

March 14–April 21, 1991
Simeon Braguin Paints

April 4–June 2, 1991
Vision and Continuity: Italian Drawings from the Permanent Collection, 1550–1800. Catalogue

April 19–September 22, 1991
The Preparatory Process: Art in the Making. Catalogue

April 26–September 29, 1991
"Noble Simplicity and Silent Greatness": Neoclassical Art from 1700 to 1900. Catalogue. Brochure, *New Haven " Classical Tour"*

Spring 1991
The High Renaissance: Art, Letters and Faith. Teaching exhibition

Spring 1991
Early 20th-century Russian Art. Teaching exhibition

June 14–September 8, 1991
Chiseled, Gouged, and Cut: Woodcuts from the Permanent Collection

September 7–November 10, 1991
Art or Theory? Minimal and Conceptual Prints

October 23, 1991–January 5, 1992
**Felix Vallotton: A Retrospective.* Catalogue

November 19, 1991–January 12, 1992
† *The Pear: French Graphic Arts in the Golden Age of Caricature.* Catalogue

Fall 1991
Art, Community and Culture. Teaching exhibition

Fall 1991
Age of Michelangelo. Teaching exhibition

Fall 1991
David to Delacroix. Teaching exhibition

Fall 1991
Abstract Expressionism. Teaching exhibition

1992

January 17–April 19, 1992
Pattern and Invention: Ornament Prints: 1500–1800. Catalogue

February 1–March 22, 1992
Looking Glasses in America, 1725–1850. Book, *American Tables and Looking Glasses in the Mabel Brady Garvan and Other Collections at Yale University*

February 8–March 11, 1992
Recent Accessions

March 3–July 31, 1992
**The World Within a Square Inch: The Art of Chinese Seal Carving.* Brochure

April 15–July 31, 1992
**Eva Hesse: A Retrospective.* Catalogue

May 1–July 31, 1992
Beyond Rembrandt: Dutch Drawings at Yale 1500–1700. Catalogue

Spring 1992
Selections from An Uncertain Grace: Photographs by Sebastião Salgado

Spring 1992
Italian Art of the XVIth century. Teaching exhibition

September 1–December 6, 1992
Appropriated Lands: Photography and the Great Surveys of the American West, 1867–1879

September 19, 1992–January 3, 1993
**Discovered Lands, Invented Pasts: Transforming Visions of the American West.* Book

Fall 1992
History of Photography. Teaching exhibition

Fall 1992
Italian Art in the XVIth century. Teaching exhibition

1993

January 5–March 7, 1993
Prints, Drawings, Photographs, and Watercolors: Three Years of Acquisitions

January 15–March 15, 1993
Contemporary Art After 1965

January 15–March 15, 1993
David von Schlegell: "Immanences." Brochure

February 6–April 11, 1993
† *The Cosmic Dancer: Shiva Nataraja.* Catalogue

March 25–July 31, 1993
At the Dragon Court: Chinese Embroidered Mandarin Squares from the Schuyler V. R. Cammann Collection. Brochure

April 3–July 31, 1993
**A Private View: American Paintings from the Manoogian Collection.* Catalogue

April 30–July 31, 1993
Yale Collects Yale: 1950–1993. Catalogue

September 1–November 28, 1993
A Primer of Printmaking Processes

September 10–November 21, 1993
**South of the Border: Mexico in the American Imagination, 1914–1947.* Catalogue

Fall 1993–February 27, 1994
The Dancing Brush: Chinese and Japanese Calligraphy from the H. Christopher Luce Collection

December 10, 1993–March 6, 1994
A Selective Eye: Paintings and Sculpture from the Collection of Susan Morse Hilles. Catalogue

December 10, 1993–March 6, 1994
Post-Painterly Abstraction: Years of Transition

1994

January 11–March 20, 1994
Testing the Limits: New Print Portfolios. Brochure

February 1–April 10, 1994
**Collection in Context: Gorky's "Betrothals."* Catalogue

April 7–June 12, 1994
**Wright Morris: Origin of a Species.* Catalogue

April 7–June 12, 1994
†Alone in a Crowd: Prints of the 1930s and 1940s by African-American Artists from the Collection of Dave and Reba Williams. American Federation of Arts. Catalogue

Spring 1994
Architecture of the French. Teaching exhibition

Spring 1994
Introduction to the History of Western Art. Teaching exhibition

April 9–July 31, 1994
**The Jade Studio: Masterpieces of Ming and Qing Painting and Calligraphy from the Wong Nan-p'ing Collection.* Catalogue

April 14–May 15, 1994
Vasari's Florence: Artists and Literati at the Medicean Court. Catalogue

May 1994
American Figure Paintings. Teaching exhibition

September 1–December 31, 1994
An Obsession with Fortune: Tyche in Greek and Roman Art. Catalogue: YUAG *Bulletin*

September 16, 1994–January 8, 1995
Charles Demuth: Poster Portraits 1923–1929. Catalogue

September 17, 1994–January 8, 1995
Art and Design of the Twenties: Selections from the Permanent Collection

Fall 1994
The Age of Rubens and Rembrandt. Teaching exhibition. Brochure

1995

January 20–March 26, 1995
Reinventing the Emblem: Contemporary Artists Recreate a Renaissance Idea. Catalogue

February 10–April 16, 1995
†Painting the Maya Universe: Royal Ceramics of the Classic Period. Catalogue

April 4–July 16, 1995
**Prodigal Son Narratives 1480–1980.* Catalogue

April 26–July 9, 1995
†Roni Horn: Inner Geography. Catalogue

Spring 1995
Venice and Rome: From Tintoretto to Caravaggio. Teaching exhibition

Spring 1995
A la Mode: Women and Fashion in Late 19th Century French Prints and Drawings. Teaching exhibition

Spring 1995
Western Art from the Renaissance to the Present. Teaching exhibition

May 19–September 13, 1995
Collecting with Richard Brown Baker: From Pollock to Lichtenstein. Catalogue

June 7–July 11, 1995
Drawings by Children from the Celentano School in Honor of the Special Olympics

Summer–Fall 1995
Across Cultures: Interactions in Asian Art

September 1–23, 1995
America's Darker Moments

September 30–October 23, 1995
Impressionism in America. Teaching exhibition

September 30–December 3, 1995
Homer and Eakins: Twenty-Six Works from the Permanent Collection. Teaching exhibition

October 12–December 31, 1995
**Mel Bochner: Thought Made Visible 1966–1973.* Catalogue, 2 brochures

October 20, 1995–January 7, 1996
**Severini Futurista 1912–1917.* Catalogue and brochure

December 15, 1995–April 28, 1996
Compassion and Transcendence in Buddhist Art

1996

February 3–March 3, 1996
American Allegorical Prints: Constructing an Identity. Catalogue

February 3–July 21, 1996
Art and Society in Massachusetts, 1620–1776

February 3–July 31, 1996
First Masters of American Silver: The Craft of the Silversmith in Colonial Massachusetts Catalogue. Book: *Colonial Massachusetts Silversmiths and Jewelers: A Biographical Dictionary Based on the Notes of Francis Hill Bigelow & John Marshall Phillips*

February 17–May 5, 1996
Bodies: Figure and Ground in American Photography. Teaching exhibition

February 17–May 5, 1996
Art in the Western Tradition: The Renaissance to the Present. Teaching exhibition

March 26–June 9, 1996
†Saul Steinberg: About America. Fifty Drawings from the Collection of Sivia and Jeffrey Loria. Catalogue

May 4–June 9, 1996
Bradbury Thompson Exhibition

May 11–September 15, 1996
Tastes and Traditions: Japanese Arts of the Edo Period, 1615–1868. Brochure

September 6–December 1, 1996
**I, Claudia: Women in Ancient Rome.* Catalogue Fall 1996
The Age of Michelangelo. Teaching exhibition

Fall 1996
Marinetti and Futurism. Teaching exhibition

Fall 1996
Foundations of Chinese Art. Teaching exhibition

October 11, 1996–January 14, 1997
**Thomas Eakins—The Rowing Pictures.* Catalogue

October 29, 1996–July 1997
Treasures of Chinese and Japanese Art from the Permanent Collections

November 23, 1996–March 16, 1997
Paper Support: Recent Acquisitions of Prints, Drawings, and Photographs and Artists' Books

1997

January 21–May 21, 1997
Natural/Unnatural: Renaissance to the Present. Teaching exhibition

January 21–May 21, 1997
American Photography and the Other Arts: Modernism and the Camera. Teaching exhibition

January 27–May 17, 1997
From Tropical Africa to Black America

February 2–June 15, 1997
Hawaiian Eye: Collecting Contemporary Art with Thurston Twigg-Smith. Catalogue

February 10–March 17, 1997
Josef Albers: From the Collection

April 11–June 8, 1997
†*Crossing the Frontier: Photographs of the Developing West, 1849 to the Present.* Catalogue

May 6–June 8, 1997
"Give a Thing and It Is Yours Forever": George Hopper Fitch Collects for Yale

August 30, 1997–January 4, 1998
**Baule: African Art/ Western Eyes.* Catalogue

September 12–December 14, 1997
Paul Cadmus, Visionary Realist. Brochure

September 19–December 14, 1997
Sketches by Italian Masters 1550–1600. Teaching exhibition

September 19–December 14, 1997
The Spirit of the Chinese Brush

September 20–November 30, 1997
†*Munch and Women: Image and Myth.* Art Services International. Catalogue

December 16, 1997–February 1, 1998
Animating the Static—Experiments in Video 1965–1980

December 16, 1997–May 31, 1998
From Tomb to Teahouse: Selections from the Asian Collection

1998

January 27–May 17, 1998
From Tropical Africa to Black America. Teaching exhibition

January 27–May 17, 1998
The Borders of the Renaissance. Teaching exhibition

January 27–May 17, 1998
The Art of the Modern Era. Teaching exhibition

February 10–August 1, 1998
Now and Then: Art at Yale Since 1945. Catalogue

February 14–April 12, 1998
The Age of Rubens and Rembrandt. Teaching exhibition

March 27–July 31, 1998
Now and Later. Second part of ongoing exhibition, *Now and Then*

May 15–July 3, 1998
†*Masami Teraoka: The Floating World Comes of Age.* Arts Management

Spring 1998
25 Years of Collecting American Drawings. Publication, "A Great Panorama": Celebrating Twenty-Five Years of American Arts at Yale

June 9–August 30, 1998
Saints, Sinners, and Scenery: European Genre and Landscape Paintings from the Collection of Dr. Herbert and Monika Schaefer

September 1–December 13, 1998
The Pleasures of Paris: Prints by Toulouse-Lautrec. Brochure

September 22–December 18, 1998
Fin-de-Siècle Symbolist Prints from Manet to Munch

September 22, 1998–February 15, 1999
Spirit and Ritual in Asian Art

October 13, 1998–January 3, 1999
The Unmapped Body: Three Black British Artists. Catalogue

Fall 1998
The Arts of Medieval Islam. Teaching exhibition

Fall 1998
Twentieth-Century Photography. Teaching exhibition

Fall 1998
The Black Atlantic Visual Tradition. Teaching exhibition

1999

January 19–April 11, 1999
Portraiture and the Harlem Renaissance: The Photographs of James Latimer Allen. Catalogue

February 2–May 30, 1999
†*World Within Worlds: The Richard Rosenblum Collection of Chinese Scholars' Rocks* Catalogue

February 9–June 13, 1999
†*Closing: The Life and Death of an American Factory, Photographs by Bill Bamberger.* Book and brochure

Spring 1999
Art in the Golden Age of Television. Teaching exhibition

Spring 1999
Western Art from the Renaissance to the Present. Teaching exhibition

March 23–June 13, 1999
Flora and Fauna in Asian Art

April 6–June 13, 1999
After Looking at Chinese Rocks: Brice Marden's Work in Progress; and *After Looking at Chinese Landscape: Lois Conner's Work in Progress*

May 1–August 8, 1999
Please Be Seated: Contemporary Seating Furniture

May 15–July 5, 1999
Gifts from Walter and Molly Bareiss in Celebration of His 80th Birthday

May 15–June 6, 1999
Dawoud Bey: Photographs

Spring 1999
Stars and Stripes Forever: Popism and American Art 1955–1975. Catalogue

July 20–October 17, 1999
Postmodern Transgressions: Artists Working Beyond the Frame

September 1–December 12, 1999
Figures and Landscapes in Asian Art

September 3–November 28, 1999
Alfred Stieglitz and the Equivalent: Reinventing the Nature of Photography. Catalogue

September 17–December 12, 1999
Figures and Landscapes in Asian Art

November 9, 1999–February 27, 2000
Four Centuries of American Art and Design

December 14, 1999–February 13, 2000
Changing Impressions: Marcantonio Raimondi and Sixteenth-Century Print Connoisseurship. Catalogue

2000

January 10–31, 2000
African American Art. Teaching exhibition

January 11–April 16, 2000
Female Images, Female Lives in Asian Art

January 25–April 9, 2000
†*Jasper Johns: New Paintings and Works on Paper.* Catalogue

January 28–February 27, 2000
Sidney Kahn Memorial Exhibition: Skulls

February 24–April 16, 2000
Contemporary American Prints and Drawings Acquired in Honor of Richard S. Field

Spring 2000
Illusions, Allusions, and Delusions in the Art of Marcel Duchamp

Spring 2000
German Secular Prints. Teaching exhibition

April 4–July 30, 2000
Modern Gothic: The Revival of Medieval Art. Catalogue

April 25–July 31, 2000
**Philip Guston: A New Alphabet.* Catalogue

May 9–July 30, 2000
Imaging African Art: Documentation and Transformation

May 9–August 6, 2000
Dance of the Dragon: Fabulous Beasts in Asian Art

August 15–December 17, 2000
Southern Exposure: Works by Winfred Rembert and Hale Woodruff

August 22–November 26, 2000
The Persistence of Photography in American Portraiture

September 1–November 26, 2000
The Body Politic: The Evolution of Political Satire in Print

September 5–December 10, 2000
The Miniature in the Arts of Asia

October 3–December 31, 2000
**Love and Loss: American Portrait and Mourning Miniatures.* Book

December 15, 2000–March 25, 2001
Call and Response: Journeys of African Art. Catalogue

December 19, 2000–April 1, 2001
Circa 1701: Printed Portraits from the Time of Elihu Yale

2001

January 16–April 1, 2001
Ancients and Moderns in Asian Art I

January 30–March 25, 2001
†*From Caligula to Constantine: Tyranny and Transformation in Roman Portraiture.* Catalogue

February 2–March 25, 2001
Objective Color

Spring 2000
Renaissance to 20th Century. Teaching exhibition

March 24–October 7, 2001
Contemporary Design by Yale Alumni

April 17–September 2, 2001
Ancients and Moderns in Asian Art II

April 19–August 19, 2001
Art for Yale: Defining Moments. Tercentenary Exhibition. Book

April 20–July 15, 2001
A Moment Ongoing: The Legacy of Everett V. Meeks

August 21–November 4, 2001
A Gallery of Poems. Book, *Words for Images: A Gallery of Poems*

Fall 2001
Latin American Art. Teaching exhibition

September 14–December 30, 2001
**Myer Myers: Jewish Silversmith in Colonial New York.* Catalogue

September 28–December 30, 2001
Rediscovering Fra Angelico: A Fragmentary History. Book and brochure

October 2–December 9, 2001
**The Art of Mu Xin: Landscape Paintings and Prison Notes.* Catalogue

October 26, 2001–April 21, 2002
John Singer Sargent: The Painter as Sculptor

November 20, 2001–February 3, 2002
Holland of the Imagination: Dutch Drawings and Prints of the 16th and 17th Centuries. Brochure

Index

Titles of works of art and names of exhibitions are indicated in *italics*. Figure numbers are indicated in *italics* and preceded by the page number on which they appear. The word "donor" in an index entry refers to the occurrence of a name in a credit line for an illustrated work of art. For additional Yale University Art Gallery exhibitions, see *Exhibitions 1858–2001*, pp. 271–94.

Abbey, Edwin Austin, 109, 142; *Coronation of Edward VII*, 109; *Henry VIII*, 109; *King Lear*, 109; Memorial Collection, 109, *104*, 145, 153; *Rebecca and Rowena*, from *Ivanhoe*, 109; Richard, *Duke of Gloucester, and the Lady Anne*, 109, *104*; *The Play Scene in "Hamlet"*, 109; *Twelfth Night*, 109; *Two Gentlemen of Verona*, 109

Abbott, Berenice, 119, 216; *Exchange Place*, 218, *214*; *Snuff Shop*, 219, *216*; *Triboro Barber School*, 220, *217*

Academy, American, of Arts, 14; Trumbull president of, 14

Academy, National, of Design, New York, 9, 14, 38, 41, 43, 55, 64

Achelis, Frederick (Fritz), 64;Collection, 64, 66, 53, 67, 54, 73, 143

Achelis, Frederick George, 64

Adams, Abigail, 132

Adams, Ansel, 119

Adams, John, 12

Adams, Sarah, 164

Addison Gallery of American Art, Phillips Academy, Andover, 118, 124, 247

Aegisthus Painter, 63, 190

Aeschines, portrait of, 33

Ainsworth, Maryan, 155, 184

Albers, Josef, 190; *Homage to the Square*, 192, *191*; Foundation, 190

Albright (Knox) Art Gallery, 171, 202

Alden Wood carvings, 73

Alden, Colonel Bradford, confessionals, 58

Alexandria, Virginia, Episcopal Theological Seminary in, 27

Allen, James Latimer, 218

Allston, Washington, 33; *Jeremiah Dictating His Prophecy*, 40, *35*, 41

Altschul, Arthur G., 155, 201

Altschul, Mrs. Frank, 143

Alumni Hall (Alumni Building), 31, *29*, 34

Alvord, Ellen, 197

American Association of Museums, 190

American Bank Note Company, 9

American Federation of the Arts, 118, 237

American School for Classical Studies at Athens, 78

Amherst College, 27–28, 240

Amistad, 9

Amon Carter Museum, 239

Anderson, Nancy K., 240

André, Major John, 11; self-portrait, 20

Angelico, Fra, 45, 196; *Annunciation*, 134, 137, *134*

Angell, James Roland, 69, 92

Angers, Church of St. Martin, sculptures, 84, *76*, 149

Anne, Queen of England, 6, 85

Arbus, Diane, 184

Arkell, Bartlett, donor, 15, *12*

Arndt, Dr. Paul, 63

Arneson, Robert, 214

Aronson, Mark, 195–96

Art Digest, 149

Art in America, 204

Art Institute of Chicago, 161

Art News, 231

Ashton, Will, 141, *140*

Asia Society, 164

Associates in Fine Arts/Art Gallery Associates, 70, 76, 118, 134, 147; donor, 78, 79, *66*

Association of Art Museum Directors, 190

Assurnasirpal II, reliefs from palace of, 27–29, *24–27*, 74, 84

Atget, Eugène, 216; *Avenue des Gobelins*, 219, *215*; *Pendant L'Eclipse*, 218, *213*

Athena, 198, *198*, 199

Auburn Theological Seminary, 27

Auden, W. H., 154

Augur, Hezekiah, 9, 23–25, 118; *Head of Apollo*, 33; *Resignation*, 33; *Jephthah and His Daughter*, 24, 33, 43

Augur, James, 33

Austin, Henry, College Library, 30, *28*, 34, 73

Avidia Plautia, portrait of, 194

Axelrod, John P., 195, 239; Collection of American Art, 190

Bacon, Francis, 154, 176

Bacon, Rev. Leonard, 28–29; portrait of, 43

Badger, Shreve Cowles, 155

Bail, Louis, 35

Baker, Richard Brown, 155, 193, 197, 200, *199*, 202–206, 257, 258; donor, 205, *201*

Baltimore Museum of Art, 150, 151, 227

Barber, Edwin Atlee, 102

Bareiss, Molly and Walter, 84, 156, 184, 194, 202, 213, 214; Curator of Ancient Art, 199; donors, 212, *208*; Walter, 143, 161, 171, 194, 196, 199, 213, *209*, 251, 256

Barnard, S., views of Charleston, 105

Barney, James Whitney, 115

Barnhart, Richard M., 187, 196

Barquist, David L., 228, *224a*, 241

Barringer Collection, 111

Bartholomew, Edward Sheffield, statues of Demosthenes and Sophocles, 34

Bartolo, Taddeo di, *St. Jerome*, 134, 138, *135*

Bartolo, Taddeo di, *St. John the Baptist*, 134, 138, *136*

Baselitz, Georg, 213

Bassert, Francis, 102

Batoni, Pompeo, 183

Battell, Robbins, 57

Battison, Edwin A., 236

Baule, *Portrait Mask of a Woman*, 19

Baur, Professor Paul V. C., 63, 116

Beal, Jack, 204

Begemann, Egbert Haverkamp-, 173, 183

Bellange, Jacques, *Virgin and Child*, 183

Bellinger, Alfred R., 145

Bellini, Filippo, *St. Catherine*, 183

Bellows, George, 97, 102, 176; *Lady Jean*; 176; *Katherine Rosen*, 176; *The Rope (Builders of Ships)*, 229; *Club Night*, 231

Benenson, Charles B., 164

Benenson, Frances and Benjamin, Foundation, Curator of African Art, 244

Bennett, John II, *Sword*, 99

Benson, Richard, 218

Benton, Thomas Hart, *Weighing Cotton*, 194

Berkeley, Bishop, 181, 183

Berkeley, University Museum, 189

Berlin Painter, 62, *49*, 63,

Bernard, Debbie, 253

Bernini, Gian Lorenzo *Portrait of an Old Man*, 183

Betts, F. J., 31, 42

Beuys, Joseph, 213; *Green Violin and Telephone S[lender]—R[eceiver]*, 213

Beyeler, Ernst, 213, *209*; 214

Bible: *Isaiah*, Book of, 29

Bible: *Judges*, Book of, 25

Bickford, Maggie, 189

Bierstadt, Albert, 43, 232, 241; *Yosemite Valley*, 47

Bigelow, Francis Hill, 91, 241

Blakelock, Ralph Albert, *Moonlit Landscape with Indians*, 105

Blin, Peter, possibly by, 6, *4*

Bloemaert, Abraham, 183

Boardman and Company, 102

Boccioni, Umberto, 222

Bochner, Mel, 222

Bol, Ferdinand, 183

Bonnard, Pierre, 181, 208

Boorsch, Suzanne, 248

Bosch, Hieronymus, 155, 174; *Intemperance*, 134, 135, *132*, 156

Boston, *Chest of Drawers*, 92, *81*

Boston Athenaeum, 33, 46

Boucher, Francois, 155, 183

Boudin, Eugène Louis, 190

Bowdoin College, 3, 27, 28

Boymans van Beuningen Museum, 173

Braguin, Simeon, bequest, 242; and Janet, Fund, 244, 245, *238*

Brancusi, Constantin, *Mlle. Pogany II*, 126, 208, 204; *Yellow Bird*, 126, *122*

Braque, Georges, 150, 155, 174

Bray, John E., donor, 25, *23*

Breughel, Jan, the Elder, 183

Brewer, Charles, 222

Brewster, Kingman, 230, 231, *226*, 236, *231a*, 255–56

Bril, Paulus, 31

British Museum, 236

Brix, Maurice, 96

Brooklyn Museum of Art, 91, 117, 132, 165

Brothers in Unity, 30, 34

Brown, John, 92

Brown, John George, *Illustrations for "Tom Sawyer,"* 105

Bruce, Patrick Henry, 124, 126

Bucci, Signore, 46

Buckland, William, portrait of, 105, *99*

Buell, Abell, 118

Buhler, Kathryn, 230

Buie, Sarah, 250

Bull, C. Sanford, 132

Bull, Ludlow S., 112, 116, 145; donor, 113, *106*

Bulletin of the Associates in Fine Arts (see also *Yale University Art Gallery Bulletin*), 71, 73, 74, 75, 84

Bullock, Wynn, 218

Burch, Cornelius van der, *Beaker*, 99, *89*

Burchfield, Charles, 174

Burden, Chris, *America's Darker Moments*, 196

Burke, James D., 184, 218

Cahill, Christina, 184

Caillebotte, Gustave, 181

Calder, Alexander, 126

Caldwell, John, 184

Calhoun, John C., 132

Caligula, portrait of, 194

Cambiaso, Luca, *Apollo Killing the Python*, 183

Cambridge Seven, 232, 234–35, *228–30*

Campendonk, Heinrich, 126
Canaday, John, 172, 173–74
Caponigro, Paul, 218
Carrà, Carlo, 222
Carrère and Hastings, 69
Cassatt, Mary, 31
Catlin, Stanton Loomis, 173
Celmins, Vija, 214
Cézanne, Paul, 150, 155; *The Bathers*, 184
Champney, Benjamin, 32, *30*, 33
Chardin, Jean-Baptiste-Simeón, 155
Charina Foundation, donor, 219, *216*
Chase, A. Elizabeth, 116, *114*, 116–17, 118, 119, 145,
Chase, William Merritt, 241
Cheek, Leslie, Jr., General Support Fund, 195
Chermayeff & Geismar, 232–33, 248, 234–35, *228–30*
Chicago, Art Institute of, 227
Chien, Wang, *Eight Landscapes in the Styles of the Old Masters*, 189
China Institute in New York, 189
Christiansen, Hans, 100
Church, Frederic Edwin, 33; *Mt. Ktaadn*, 232, 233, *227*; *Ruins at Baalbek*, 57, 58, *45*
Cimabue, 45
Cincinnati, Society of, donor, 9
Cinqué, 9
Civil War, American, 35
Clark, Mary Jane, 189
Clark, Stephen Carlton, 143, 155, 156, *150 & 150a*, 161, 171, 174, 258; bequest, 156, 158–59, *151–53*, 171, 176, 229; Fund, 166, 168, *166*, *167*, 176; Mr. & Mrs., donors, 175, *173*
Cleveland Museum of Art, 73
Clinton, De Witt, portrait of, by John Trumbull, 14
Clinton, Governor George, portraits of, by John Trumbull, 14
Close, Chuck, 250, *243*
Coe, Ralph, 156
Coit, D. W., drawings by, 30
Cole, Thomas, 33, 34, 153, 241; *View of the White Mountains, New Hampshire*, 57
College Courant, 47
Colossal Keepsake Corporation, 222; donor, 223, *221*
Cone, Etta and Dr. Claribel, 151
Coney, John, 91; *Monteith Bowl*, 100, *95*
Congregational Church, 6–7, 27
Connecticut College, 124
Connecticut State Legislature, 15, 18
Connor, Lois, 218
Constable, John, 155
Cook, Clarence, 46
Cooper, Helen A., 193, 199, 222, 238, 239, 240, 241, 248, 250
Cooper, Henry S., Contemporary Print Purchase Fund, 220, *217*
Cooper, J., 6
Copeland, Elizabeth, 100
Copley, John Singleton, 11, 85, 155; *Benjamin Pickman, Mrs. Benjamin Pickman*, 156, 181; Mr. and Mrs. Isaac Smith, portraits of, 84, 86–87, *77a & b*, 132; *Mrs. John Powell*, 176
Corcoran, William Wilson, 46
Corot, Jean Baptiste Camille, 155; *The Harbor of La Rochelle* (*Le Port de La Rochelle*), 176
Courbet, Gustave, 155; *Source of the River Loue*, 156
Courtauld Institute of Art, 171
Couture, Thomas, 181
Covert, John, 126
Coward, Thomas R., 155
Cox, John Hadley, 83–84; donor, 84, *75*
Cranach, Lucas, the Elder, 155; *Crucifixion with the Converted Centurion*, 134, 156, 136, *133*
Crawford, Thomas, *Demosthenes, Homer, and Cicero*, 23, 43, 321; *Demosthenes*, 24, *20*
Crivelli, Carlo, 134
Crivelli, Vittore, 134, 140, *138*
Cronon, William, 240
Cropsey, Jasper F., 43, 242
Crosby, Sumner McKnight, 142, 145
cummings, e. e. , 154
Currier & Ives, 97, 102, 143
Curtis, Daniel, 102
Curtis-Rose House, Branford, Connecticut, 85

Daggett, Naphtali, 41
D'Amico, Frederick, 170, *170*
Dana, Richard Henry, 59
Dann, Olive Louise, Fund, 229, *225*
Danziger, Richard, 55; and Peggy, 168, 169, *168*, 255
Dartmouth College, 3, 27
Daumier, Honoré, 155, 181
Davenport Limner, 6, *5*, 7, 85,
Davenport, John, 7, 85; portrait of, 6, *5*
David, Jacques-Louis, 184
Davidson, Bruce, 218
Davies, Arthur B., 174
Davies, Karen (see Lucic, Karen)
Davis, Alexander Jackson, 18, 23, 31; and Ithiel Town, *Design for "Pinacotheca for Col. Trumbull,"* 19, *18*
Davis, Stuart, *Schwitzki's Syntax*, 208, 211, *207*
Day, Jeremiah, 15, 38; portrait of, 20, 30
de Chirico, Giorgio, 155
de Gheyn, Jacques, II, 183
de Kooning, 155
de Vos, Maarten, 182, *181*, 183
Deeds, Daphne, 197, 214
Degas, Edgar Hilaire Germain, 155, 213, 214
Delacroix, Eugène, 155, 190; *The Blacksmith*, 184, 186, *185*
Deming, Mr., of Hartford, 34
Demosthenes, portrait of, 34, 190
Demuth, Charles, 197
Deskey, Donald, 100
Detroit Institute of Arts, 241
Deutsch, Devida, 241
Dickens, Charles, visit to New Haven, 21
Dickson, Janet Saleh, 194, 195, *194*, 235, *230*
Dine, Jim, 204, 214
Dippie, Brian W. , 240
Dix, George, 155
Dobson Foundation, 236
D'Oench, Ellen, 184
Dolbeare, Edmund and John, 236
Dolph, Norman, 252
Domenichino (Domenico Zampieri), 31
Dougherty, Raymond P., 116
Douglas, Frederick, visit to New Haven, 21
Dreier, Katherine S., 120–26, *118*, *120*, 142, 151, 213, 256; bequest, 150, 176; memorial exhibition, 143, 153
Dubin, Lawrence and Regina, Family Foundation, 196
Dubuffet, Jean, 202
Duccio, 45
Duchamp, Marcel, 121–26, *118*, 143, 214, 256; *Rotary Glass Plates*, 125, *121*; *Standard Stoppages*, 208–209; *The Bride Stripped Bare by Her Bachelors, Even (Large Glass)*, 176; *Tu m'*, 126, 127, *123*, 252, 258
Duchamp-Villon, 125, 126, 143
Dummer, Jeremiah, 91; candlesticks, pair of, 100, *94*
Dunham, Carol, 214
Dura-Europos, 112–17, *109–11*
Durand, Asher B., 33, 232
Durer, Albrecht, 64, 184; *Adam and Eve*, 64, 67, *54*
Durrie, George H., 118
Dwight, Timothy, portrait of, 9
Dzubas, Friedel, 126

Eagle Bank of New Haven, 15
Eakins, Thomas, 102, 155; *John Biglin in a Single Scull*, 102, 104, *98*; *Kathrin: Girl with a Cat*, 176, 178, *175*; *Taking the Count*, 103, *97*; *Will Schuster and Dave Wright Going Shooting*, 156, 159, *153*
Earl, Ralph, 7, *6*, 118, 155; donor, 7, *6*; portrait of Baron von Steuben, 99, *92*; portraits by, 20, 85
Eastlake, Sir Charles, 46
Eaton, Daniel Cady, 53
École des Beaux-Arts, Paris, 37, 57
Edgell, Simon, 102
Edmonds, Francis, *The Organ Grinder*, 242, 244, *237*
Egmont Collection, 182, *181*, 183
Egmont, John Percival, Earl of, 181, 183
El Greco, 155
Eliot, T. S., 154
Elizabeth II, Queen of England, 236
Elliott, C. L. , 33
Ennion, 115
Ernst, Max, 126
Eutychides, *Tyche of Antioch*, 193
Evans, de Scott, 232
Evans, Walker, 218; *Girl in Fulton Street, New York*, 221, *219*

Fabriano, Gentile da, *Madonna and Child*, 46, *38*
Fairbanks-Harris, Theresa, 195
Fantin-Latour, Henri, 181
Faulkner, Avery C., 149
Feldman, Hyman I., 69
Fellowes, Richard S., 42, 59
Field, Richard S., 187, 193, 199, 218, 222, 239
First Church (Congregational), New Haven, 28
Fisher, Alexander Metcalf, 7–8, 7, *7*
Fitch, George Hopper, 84, 156, 160, *154*, 194, 196, 197, 214–42, 258; Mrs., 84, 242, 258
Flagg, J. B., 43
Fogg Art Museum, Harvard University, 172
Fogg, Joseph G., III, 259
Foote, John, 38
Ford Foundation, 161, 230
Fosburgh, James, 155, 171; and Mary Cushing, 156, 190; and Mary Cushing, donors, 174, *172*; and Mary Cushing, and Paul Mellon Publication Fund, 195
Fragonard, Jean-Honoré, 155
Frank, Robert, *Movie Premiere, Hollywood*, 221, *220*
Frank, Robert, 218; *N.Y.C. 1953 (A&S Pants)*, 220, *218*
Frank, Robin Jaffee, 196, 197, 239, 241
Franklin, Benjamin, 6, *3*
Friends of American Arts, Curator of American Decorative Arts, 244
Fu, Marilyn, 189
Fu, Shen C. Y., 189
Fueter, Daniel Christian, *Rattle*, 100, *93*

Gabo, Naum, 124, 126; *Construction in Space with Balance on Two Points*, 126; *Linear Construction*, 154, *149*
Gainsborough, Thomas, 155, 183
Galaxy, 46
Garland, Patricia Sherwin, 195–96
Garstin, Mrs. Dalton V. , donor, 76, *61*
Garvan Collection, 89–108, 102–103, 117, 116, 132, 143, 141, 145, 156, 161, 162, 176, 227–28, 230, 238; Garvan and Related Collections of American Art, 232
Garvan Committee, 227, 238
Garvan Furniture Study, 228, 247
Garvan, Anthony B., 227
Garvan, Francis P., 115, 118, 119, 237, 255; portrait of, 90, *78*; and Mabel Brady, 74, 85, 89–108
Garvan, Mabel Brady, 89, 195, 227, 230, 232
Gates, Mary Gardner (see also Neill, Mary Gardner), 195
Gaugin, Paul, 55
Gehry, Frank, 100
Genauer, Emily, 154–55
George I, King of England, 4, *1*
George, Prince of Denmark, 6
Georgians, The, 161
Gerasa, 74, 111, 113, 115, 116, 196; mosaic from, 112, *105*
Géricault, Theodore, *Entrance to the Adelphi Wharf*, 156, 160–61, *155*
Gérôme, Jean-Léon, *Ave Caesar, Morituri te Salutant*, 196
Ghiberti, Lorenzo, bronze doors, plaster cast of, 41, 48
Ghirlandaio, Ridolfo, 45; *Lady with a Rabbit*, 48, 52, *42*
Giacometti, Alberto, 214; *Standing Woman*, 203, *200*
Gibbs Collection of Minerals, 15, 29
Gifford, Sanford R., 43, 232, 242; *On the Winooski River*, 57
Gilcrease, Thomas, Institute of American History and Art, 240
Gilman, Daniel Coit, 31, 34–35, 38, 42, 47
Giotto, 45
Girardon, Francois, *Maquette for the Equestrian Statue of Louis XIV*, 174, *172*
Goldfrank, Lionel, III, 259; Curator of Early European Art, 244
Goodrich, Chauncey A., 15
Goodwin, Philip L., 121–22, 126, 141, 147, 153, 156
Goodyear, A. Conger, 156, 171
Goodyear, Charles, 118
Goodyear, Frank, 237
Gorham Manufacturing Co., 100
Gorky, Arshile, *Drawing*, 229; *The Betrothal*, 208, 209, *205*
Graff, Washbourne, and Dunn, 100
Graves, Michael, 100, 101, *96*

Gray, Ethné and Clive, Family Collection, 220, *218*
Green, Holcombe T., Curator of American Paintings and Sculpture, 239
Greene, Carl G., 170, *170*
Greene, George W. , 34
Greene, Henry and Charles Sumner, 100
Greenough, Horatio, *Aeschines*, 58; *The Angel Abdiel*, 33, *31*, 58; *Angel Warning St. John*, 58; Aristides, 33
Greenway, G. Lauder, 156, 171
Grien, Hans Baldung, 184
Griggs, Maitland Fuller, 70, 76, 84, 196, bequest, 134, 138, *135*, *136*; Collection, 121, 161; donor, 76, 78, *65*; Fund, 84, 86–87, *77a&b*, 132, 134, 139, *137*, 184
Gris, Juan, 151
Griswold, A. Whitney, 169
Gropius, Walter, 152
Gross, Jennifer, 214
Grossmann, Richard, 254
Grosz, George, 241
Group E, 63, *51*, 190
Guardi, Francesco, 155
Guggenheim, Solomon R., 126
Gutheim, Frederick, 148
Guy, Francis, *Utilizing a Spare Moment*, 242
Guys, Constantin, 181

Hadley, Arthur Twining, 64
Halicka, Alice, 126
Hals, Frans, 155, 176; *De Heer and Mevrouw Bodolphe*, 156, 157, *150 & 150a*
Halsey, R. T. H., 91
Hamilton, Alexander, portrait of, by John Trumbull, 14
Hamilton, George Heard, 124–25, 132, *130*, 141, 143, 145, 153–55, 232, 251, 252
Hamilton, James, *Capture of the "Serapis" by John Paul Jones*, 105
Hamilton, Richard Heard, 154, *149*
Hanna, Leonard C., Jr, , 143, 156; Fund, donor, 63, *51*, 171
Hanson, Anne Coffin, 193, 222, 225
Harkness, Edward S., 66, 70, 71
Harnett, William, 232
Harrisburg, Pennsylvania, Capitol rotunda, 109
Hart, William, 43
Hartley, Marsden, 155, 242
Hartt, Frederick, 124–25
Harvard University, 11, 64, 172, 173, 184, 230 (see also Fogg Art Museum)
Haskell, Dr. Henri Byron, 28
Hassam, Childe, 64, 241, 242; *Back of the Old House*, 229
Hatch, Mary Mills, 145
Havemeyer, Electra (Webb), and James Watson Webb, 143
Heade, Martin Johnson, 241, 242
Heinz, H. John, III, 231, 242, 244, *237*
Heinz, Henry J., II, 231; Director, 194; Mr. and Mrs., 171
Heinz, Teresa, 242; donor, 244, *237*
Hekking, William, 123
Henri, Robert, 105, 174; *Street Scene with Snow (57th Street, New York)*, 107, *101*
Herbert, Robert L., 176
Hering, Henry, 74
Hesse, Eva, *Untitled*, 222
Hewitt, Benjamin, 239; Associate Curator of American Decorative Arts, 244
Heyne, John Christoph, 102
High Museum of Art, Atlanta, 241
Hill, Dr. and Mrs. William R., 197
Hill, John T., 218
Hilles, Susan Morse, 190, 200, *199*, 202–206; donor, 203, *200*, 221, *220* ; and Frederick W., 156
Hillhouse, family, 9
Hillhouse Professor of Greek, 45
Hillhouse, James, portrait of, 20
Hillman, Mr. and Mrs. Alex, 171
Hirshhorn Museum, 222
Hoadley, George, 7
Hockney, David, 214
Hodermarsky, Elisabeth, 242
Hoermann, Kristin, 195
Hogarth, William, 155
Hollander, John, 155
Homer, Winslow, 155, 231, 239; *A Game of Croquet*, 176, 179, *176*; *The Mill* (formerly *Morning Bell*), 156, 159, *152*
Honolulu Advertiser, 214
Hood, Graham, 230
Hopkins, Clark, 116
Hopper, Edward, 174, 142, 242; *House of the Fog Horn*, 156, 160, *154*; *Rooms by the Sea*, 176, 252; *Rooms for Tourists*, 176; *Sunlight in a Cafeteria*, 176, 180, *177*; *Western Motel*, 176
Hoppin Painter, 197
Hoppin, James Mason, 57, 58, 59
Horn, Roni, 218
Houston Museum of Fine Arts, 189
Houston, Senator Sam, visit to New Haven, 21
Hovenden, Thomas, 232
Howe, George, 147–48
Howze, William, 251
Hubert, George, 74
Hughes, Robert Ball, portrait of John Trumbull, 25, *22*, 43
Hunt, Richard Morris, 43
Huntington, Daniel, 41, 43
Hurd, Jacob, 99; *Two-Handled Cup (Tyng Cup)*, 97

Ingres, Jean-Auguste-Dominique, 155; *Portrait of Mlle. Marcotte*, 181, 182, *179*
Inness, George, 33, 57, 242
Ives, Chauncey Bradley, 118; portrait by, 23; portrait of Ithiel Town, 19, *17*; portrait of Jeremiah Day, 30

J. Paul Getty Museum, 195–96
J. Paul Getty Trust, 195
Jackson, President Andrew, visit to New Haven and Trumbull Gallery, 21
James, Henry, 230
Jarves Collection, 35, 45–53, 55, 59–60, 72–73, 56, 121, 134, 143, 149, 161, 196, 214, 230, 255
Jarves Gallery, 56
Jarves, James Jackson, 45–53, 255
Jarvis, John Wesley, portrait by, 85
Jefferson, Thomas, 12; and John Trumbull, *Declaration of Independence*, 13, *11*
Jerome, Chauncey, 118
Jerome, Leonard W., 45
Jewett, William, and Samuel Lovett Waldo, portrait of Trumbull, 12, *9*
Jocelyn, Nathaniel, 9, 25, 42, 43, 118; portrait by, 20, 38, *32*; portrait of Benjamin Silliman, 25
Johns, Jasper, 204
Johnson, Eastman, 232
Johnson, Philip, 153
Johnson, Samuel, *Freedom Box*, 99, *91*
Jones, E. Alfred, 116
Jones, Luther Maynard, 47
Jordaens, Jacob, 183, *182*

Kahn, Louis I., 122, 141, 144, 146, *143a & b*, 147–49, 148, *145*, 153, 231, 247
Kahn, S. Sidney, 218; Fund, donor, 218, *214*
Kakabadzé, David, 126
Kalo Shops, 100
Kan, Jin, 80, *67*
Kandinsky, Wassily, 124, 126, *Small Yellow*, 128, *125*
Kane, Patricia E., Curator of American Decorative Arts, 244
Kane, Patricia E., 100, 228, *224a*, 232, 236, 237, 239, 241, 248
Kaplan, Allan and Alice, Associate/Assistant Curator of American Paintings and Sculpture, 244
Karasz, Ilonka, 100
Katz, Alex, 214
Keller, Deane, 118
Kelly, J. Frederick, 85
Kendall, William Sergeant, 64, 69
Kensett, J. F., 33, 43
Kerr, E. Coe, Jr., 155
Kimball, G. D., 149
Kimbell Art Museum, 147
Kingsley, William L., 30, *28*, 31, 53
Kiphuth, Robery J. H., 145
Kirchner, Ludwig, 126
Kirk, John, 228, *224*, 230
Kirkpatrick, Ralph, 184, 186–87; bequest, 186, *185*
Klee, Paul, 126, 155
Kleiner, Diana E. E., 199
Kleophrades Painter, 61
Kline, Franz, *Wanamaker Block*, 205, *201*, 206
Kneeland, Dr. Yale, Jr., 84
Kneller, Sir Godfrey, portrait of George I, 3, 4, *1*, 20, 85
Knittle, Rhea Mansfield, 102
Knox, Mr. & Mrs. Seymour H., Jr., 156
Knox, Seymour H., Jr., curator of European and Contemporary Art, 197, 201–202,
Kordak, Mary L., 197, *196*, 197, 255
Kossack, Carl R., 240
Kossack, Frederick, Alan, and Philip, 241
Kossack, Philip M., donor, 241, *234*
Kossack, Steven, 254, 258
Kramer, Hilton, 234
Kubler, George, 165–66

Lafayette, General the Marquis de, 9, 119, 115
Lamar, Howard R., 240
Lancaster Highchest, 92, 94, *83*
Landi, Neroccio di Bartolommeo de', *Annunciation*, 48, 53, *43*
Lang, Louis, 43
Lastman, Pieter, 183
Laughlin, Clarence John, 216
Lawrence, Jacob, 213
Layard, Austen Henry, 27
Lazarus, Charles Y., 156, 160, *155*, 161
Leal, Valdés, 174
Lee, George J., 172–73, 187
Leffingwell Professorship of Painting and Design, 55, 64
Legare, John Berwick, Esq., 25
Léger, Ferdinand, 124, 155; *Composition No. VII*, 129, *126*; *The Viaduct*, 126
Lehman, Robert, 115, 134, 143, 156, 161, 171, 195, 196; donor, 140, *138–39*
Lehmbruck, Wilhelm, 126
Lemuel Hopkins, Dr., portrait of by John Trumbull, 64, 65, *52*
Leonard, Mark, 196
Levin, Richard, 248
Levy, Julien, 229
Lewis, Josephine Miles, 58
Lewis, Wilmarth S., 123, 147, 162, 171
LeWitt, Sol, 213, 258; *123454321 Cross and Tower*, 244, 245, *238*; *Wall Drawing*, 222
Lichtenstein, Roy, 204
Lincoln, President Abraham, visit to New Haven, 21
Lindsley, Harrison Wheeler, 57
Linonian Society, 30, 34
Linton, Ralph, 162–164, *144*, *157–59*; Mrs. Ralph, 148, *144*, 162, *157*; Linton Collection, 172
Lippincott, Louise, 234, *228*
Lipschitz, Jacques, *Guitar Player in Chair*, 126
Lipschitz, Jacques, 124, 150
Lissitsky, El, 126
Livingston, Edward, portrait of by John Trumbull, 14
Livingston, Robert, 14
Lobdell, Dr., 28
Lockwood, Greene & Company, 118
Lockwood, Luke Vincent, 91
Logan, Anne-Marie, 183–84
Lohmann, Carl A., 64, 66, 145
Lorrain, Claude, 31, 174
Lothrop, Isaac, donor, 5, *2*
Loucheim, Aline B. (see also Saarinen, Aline B.), 153
Lovell, Margaretta, 232, 234, *228*, 237
Luce, H. Christopher, 194, 255
Lucic, Karen, 239
Luks, George, 174
Lunn Gallery/Graphics International Ltd., donor, 219, *215*
Lynes, Russell, donor, 218, *213*

Mackenzie, Colin, 196
Magdalen, Master of the, *Madonna and Child*, 48
Maillol, Aristide, 174; *L'Air*, 171; *Torso of a Young Woman*, 171
Malbin, Lydia Winston, 222; Archives, 225
Malevich, Kasimir, *The Knife Grinder*, 252
Manet, Edouard, 155, 176, 193; *Jeune Femme allongée en costume espagnol* (*Young Woman Reclining in Spanish Costume*), 156, 158, *151*, 252
Mangold, Robert, 222
Mangold, Sylvia Plimack, 222, 258
Manoogian, Richard, 241; Jane, 241
Mansfield, Burton, 114; Anna Rosalie Mansfield Collection, 114
Manship, Paul, 102
Marc, Franz, 126
Marcuse, Herbert, 222
Marden, Brice, 252

Marin, John, *Tree, Cape Split*, 156
Marinetti, Filippo Tommaso, Archives, 222
Maritain, Jacques, 154
Marsh, Dwight W., 28
Marsh, Othniel C., 111
Marsh, Reginald, 155; *Coney Island*, 229
Martinez-Ruiz, Barbaro, 164
Martz, Louis, 231, *226*
Marvell, I. K., 34
Massaccio, 45
Massys, Quentin, 134
Mather, Cotton, mezzotint portrait of, 108
Matheson, Susan B., 196, 199
Mathieu, Claudia, 254
Matisse, Henri, 155, 174, 214
Matter, Herbert, 216
Maverick, Peter, *Freedom Box*, 99, *91*
Mayer, Frederick R., 196–97; Jan, 197; Jan and Frederick, Curator of Education, 197
McAdam, John, donor, 20, *19*
McCance, T., Jr., 149
McCarthy, Frank, 102
McCracken, William, donor, 20, *19*
McCullogh, David, 164
McKenzie, Robert Tait, 102
McKie, Judy, 100
McNeil, Robert, Jr., 236, *231a*; Mr. & Mrs. Robert, Jr., 238
Meeks, Everett V., 69–70, *55*, 74, 75, 89, 115, 118, 123, 134; 141, *140*; Fund, 183–84, 248; Fund, donor, 185, *183*
Mellon, Paul, 143, 161, 181, 190, 231, *226*, 253; Centre for British Art, London, 236; Mr. & Mrs. Paul, 156; Professor of History of Art, 232; Yale Center for British Art, 231–32
Members of the Yale Art Museums, 71
Memling, Hans, 155
Menander, portrait of, 196
Menschel, Richard L., 184
Mention, Elisabeth, 196
Meryon, Charles, 185, *183–84*
Metropolitan Museum of Art, 46, 53, 91, 109, 112, 116, 118, 119, 132, 181
Miles, George, 240
Miller, Mary Ellen, 169, 253
Millet, Jean Francois, 183
Minott, Samuel, 241, *234*
Missionaries, American Christian, 27–29
Mitchell, Donald Grant, 34, 41
Moholy-Nagy, Laszlo, 124, 214
Mondrian, Piet, 126, 130, *127*, 252; *Composition*, 130, *127*; *Fox Trot* paintings, 124
Monet, Claude, 155, 190
Montgomery, Charles F., 100, 227, 228, 232–34, 234, *228*, 236, 237, 239; Professor of History of Art, 238
Moore, Ada Small (Mrs. William H.), 78–82, 81, *69*, 115, 173, 187, 165; donor, 81–82, *68*, *70–74*
Moore, Bishop Paul, Jr., 78
Moore, Edward Small, 80
Moore, Fanny Hanna, 83
Moore, Henry, *Draped Seated Woman*, 171
Moore, Hobart, 80
Moore, Hobart and Edward Small, Collection, 115, *112, 113*
Moore, Hobart, Memorial Collection, 145, 165, *162*
Moore, Lamont, 143, 145, 147, 148, *144*, 150, 151–53, 155, 162, 216
Moore, Paul, 83; Mr. & Mrs. Paul, 156; Mrs. Paul (Fanny Hanna), 147, 171; portrait of Baron von Steuben, donor of, 99
Moran, Thomas, 241
Morgan, John and Lelia Hill, 126, 132; donors, 132, *129*
Morgan, John Hill, 141, 232; Fund, 229
Morse, Samuel F. B., 14, 58, 117; donor, 40, *35*, 41, *36*; *Dying Hercules*, 41, *36*; *Marpessa*; *Judgment of Jupiter*, 229; portrait by, 15, *12*; portrait of, 43; portraits by, 7, 20, 85
Mosul, Iraq, 27–28
Motherwell, Robert, 154, 155
Moulthrop, Reuben, 7
Mount Holyoke College, 124
Mount, William Sidney, 232
Muller, Jan, 183
Munhall, Edgar, 170, *170*
Museum for African Art, New York, 164, 196
Museum News, 190
Museum of Fine Arts, Boston, 53, 112, 189
Museum of Modern Art, 118, 121–22, 126, 142, 152, 165, 171, 172, 202, 214
Museums, university art, 35; oldest, 3
Myers, George Hewitt, 84, 116, 145, 165
Myers, Louis Guerineau, 102
Myers, Myer, 99, 241

Nadelman, Elie, *Classical Head*, 108, *102*; *Patricia Garvan*, 108
Nagel, Charles, Jr., 116, 118
National Endowment for the Arts, 189, 195; donor, 219, *216*, 221, *220*
National Gallery of Art, Washington, D. C., 143, 150, 184, 189, 190, 237, 239, 240
Neill, Mary Gardner (see also Gates, Mary Gardner), 173, 187, 189, 193, 194, *192*, 195, 202, 242
New Englander and Yale Review, 47
New Haven, 37, 63
New Haven Colony Historical Society, 9, 118
New Haven Paint and Clay Club, 64
New Haven Register, 59–60, 117
New Haven Sketch Club, 35
New Haven, Board of Aldermen, 71
New Haven, Chapel Street, 37, 39
New Haven, Citizens of, donor, 24, *21*
New Haven, Cutler's Art Shop, 35
New York Daily Tribune, 46,47
New York Herald Tribune, 148, 154
New York Times, 118, 153, 172, 173, 181, 204, 234, 241, 252
New York Tribune, 255
Newman, Sasha M., 197, 204, 213, 225
Newport, Rhode Island, Townsend-Goddard *Desk and Bookcase*, 92, *82*
Nicholson, Ben, 155
Niemeyer, John H., 55
Nitsch, Hermann, 213; *Untitled (Poured Picture)*, 213
Nolde, Emil, 124
North Carolina Museum of Art, 199
North, William L., 99
Norton, Charles Eliot, 46–47
Nung, Chin, *Plum Blossom and Calligraphy*, 188, *188*, 189

Obrisset, John, 25
Officina Alessi, 100, 101, *96*
Ohki, Sadako, 189
O'Keeffe, Georgia, 242; *Bob's Head Steer*, 229; *Red Canna*, 243, *236*
Oldenburg, Claes, *Drum Set in Battersea Park*, 184; *Lipstick (Ascending) on Caterpillar Tracks*, 222, 223, *221*
Olds, Irving S., 171, 227
Olsen, Fred, 112, 167–69; donor, 113, *107*; Olsen, Mr. and Mrs. Fred, 166; Olsen Collection, 172; Olsen Foundation, 166–67, *163–65*
Ordway, Katharine, 126, 190, 206–13; Collection, donor, 207–210, *203–206*; Fund, 208–209, 213, 224, *222*; Fund, donor, 211, *207*
Orozco, José Clemente, 174
Osborn, Mr. & Mrs. James W., 164; Collection, 172; Hazel, 164; J. Marshall, 164; Thomas, 164
Osservanza Triptych, Master of the, 252, 255; *Temptation of St. Anthony*, 48, 50–51, *41a & b*
Ostendorfer, Michael, 184
Outerbridge, Paul, 218

Packard, Lewis R., 45
Paestum, temple, cork models of, 20, *19*
Painter of Munich 2335, 63
Paolo, Giovanni di, *Madonna and Child with Saints Jerome and Bartholomew*, 134
Parsons, Betty, 208
Parthenon, plaster casts of sculpture from, 41, 43, 73,
Payson, Mr. & Mrs. Charles, 156
Peabody and Stearns, Boston, 63
Peale, Charles Willson, 14; *Mrs. George Washington* (Martha Dandridge Custis), 105; *William Buckland*, 105, *99*
Peale, Raphaelle, 241
Pease, David, 259
Pelham, Peter, *Cotton Mather*, 108
Pelham-Keller, Frances H., 170, *170*
Pelletreau, Elias, *Tankard*, 41, *37*
Pennsylvania Academy of the Fine Arts, 237
Percival, John, Earl of Egmont, 181, 183
Perkins, Charles C., 43
Perspecta: The Yale Architectural Journal, 147
Peters, Dr. William Thompson, donor, 19, *17*, 23
Petryn, Andrew, 145
Philadelphia Museum of Art, 184, 189
Phillips Collection, 143
Phillips, John Marshall, 96–97, *86*, 100, 116, 119, 141, 143, 145, 147, 150, 238, 241
Picasso, Pablo, 150, 155, 213, *209*, 214; *First Steps*, 174, 175, *173*, 252
Pier, Garrett Chatfield, 112, 115
Pierpont, James, portrait of, 231
Pierson, Rev. Abraham, 25
Pillsbury, Edmund P., 184
Pissarro, Camille, 155, 190
Pissarro, Joachim, 199
Plaster casts, 33, 39–40, *34*, 43, 56
Podany, Jerry, 196
Polk, James, visit to New Haven, 21
Pollaiuolo, Antonio, *Battle of the Nudes*, 134, 139, *137*; *Hercules and Deianira*, 48, 49, *40*, 134
Pollitt, J. J., 189, 214
Pollock, Jackson,155, 202, *Arabesque*, 204; *No. 4*; *Number 14: Gray*, 208, 210, *206*
Polshek Partnership L.L.P., 196, 247
Pope-Hennesey, John, 236, 237
Popova, Liubov, 126
Porter, Arthur Kingsley, 64
Porter, John Addison, 31
Porter, Noah, 41, 53, 55
Potwine, John, *Flagon*, 92, *80*
Pound, Ezra, 154
Poussin, Nicholas, 31
Powers, Hiram, *Greek Slave*, 229–30, 229, *225*
Prendergast, Maurice, 155, 242
Preston, Stuart, 204
Prown, Jules David, 100, 196, 228, 230–32, 231, *226*, 236, 237, 238, 240, 256

Quidor, John, *Ichabod Crane Flying from the Headless Horseman*, 105, 106, *100*

Rabinowitz, Hannah D., 134
Rabinowitz, Louis M., 132–34, *131*; donor, 132–33, 135, *130–34*; bequest, 171; Collection, 134; and Hannah D., 156
Rainer, Arnulf, 213
Raphael, 31, 34, 45
Ray, Man, 122, 124, 216; *Clock Wheels*, 217, *212*; *Lamp Shade*, 126, 127, *124*
Redon, Odillon, 181; *The Wing*, 184
Reed, Mr. & Mrs. Joseph Verner Reed, 156
Rehoboth Church, silver from, 99
Reif, Rita, 241
Rembrandt, 155; *Christ Preaching (La Petite Tombe)*, 64, 66, *53*; *Christ with the Sick around Him* (*The Hundred Guilder Print*), 64, 143; *The Death of the Virgin*, 184; *The Windmill*, 64
Remington, Frederic, 102; *Spurring his Horse in Pursuit*, 58; *The Scream of the Shrapnel at San Juan Hill*, 58, 59, *46*
Renoir, Pierre Auguste, 155
Resor, Stanley B., Fund, 233, *227*
Revere, Paul II, *Bloody Massacre, Boston, 1770*, 108, *103*; *Waiter*, *Tankard*, *Teapot*, *Pitcher*, 92, *79*
Reynolds, Jock, 214, 218, 247–48, 248, *239*, 250, 257
Reynolds, Sir Joshua, 155, 174
Richards, William Troost, 43
Richardson, George, 102
Richardson, Joseph, Sr., *Tea Kettle on Stand*, 98, *88*, 99
Richardson, Leslie, 116
Richter, Gerhard, 213; *Bildnis Holger Friedrich*, 212, *208*, 213
Riggs, T. Lawrason, 78; donor, 80, *67*
Riley, Maude Kemper, 149
Ritchie, Andrew Carnduff, 156, 161, 170–71, *170*, 172, 174, 176, 189, 201, 202
Rivard, Nancy, 241
Robert, Hubert, 183
Rogers, James Gamble, 70
Rogers, John, groups, 43, 108
Rogers, Meyric R., 100, 227–28, 228, *224*, 230, 236
Rollins, Caroline, 142, 145, 170, *170*
Roque, Jacqueline, 213, *209*, 214
Rosenquist, James, 184, 204
Rosetti, Dante Gabriel, 155
Ross, James, 164
Rostovtzeff, Michael Ivanovitch, 112, *109*, 145
Rotha, Andrea, 196
Rothko Foundation, 206
Rothko, Mark, 154, 208; *No. 3*, 207, *203*; *Untitled, 1947*, 206; *Untitled, 1954*; *Untitled (Orange), 1957*; *No. 3, 1967*, 206; *Untitled, ca. 1968*, 206

Rousseau, Henri, *The Canal*, 208
Row, David, 252
Rowe, Margaret T. J., 145
Rubin, William, 213, 214, *209*
Rudolph, Paul, 75, 147, 153, 201
Rush, Benjamin, 6, *3*
Ryerson Fund for Lectures, 117, 143

Saarinen, Aline B. (see also Loucheim, Aline B.), 252
Saarinen, Eero, 147, 153
Saint Louis, City Art Museum, 189, 227
Salisbury, Edward Elbridge, 31, 33, 34, 38, 41, 43, 45, 55, 58, 64; donor, 33, *31*
San Antonio Museum of Art, 199
Sanderson, Robert, 91; and John Hull, Wine Cup, 99, *90*
Sandweiss, Martha A., 240
Sargent, John Singer, 155, 231, 241
Sawyer, Charles H., 143, 145, 147, 150
Schanker, Louis, 126
Schoelwer, Susan, 240
Schwitters, Kurt, 124, 126
Scott, Gerry D., III, 225
Scott, Sir Walter, *Ivanhoe*, 109
Scully, Vincent, 147, 149, 152–53, 201, 222, 250, *244*
Seattle Art Museum, 195
Seligmann, Kurt and Arlette, 195
Sensabaugh, David Ake, 189
Serra, Richard, 258; *Stacks*, 194, 213, 222, 224, *222*
Setze, Josephine, 170, *170*; *Yale University Portrait Index*, 143
Seurat, Georges, 155, 181; *L'Echo*, 181, 182, *180*
Severini, Gino, 124, 213, 222
Seymour, Charles, Yale President, 123, 125, 145
Seymour, Charles, Jr., professor and curator, 142, 145, 155, 255
Seymour, George Dudley, 85
Shan, Li, 80
Sheeler, Charles, 242
Sheffield Scientific School, 57
Sherman, Roger, portrait of, 20, 85
Shestack, Alan, 161, 166, 173, 184, 187, 189, 190, *189*, 193, 201, 206, 207, 218, 222, 232, 237, 238, 239
Shih-min, Wang, *Landscape in the Style of Huang Kung-wang*, 189
Shinn, Everitt, 155
Sill, Miss Elizabeth, donor, 64, 65, *52*
Silliman, Alfred Wild, and Benjamin IV, donors, 12, *9*
Silliman, Benjamin, 14–15, 18, 29, 35; portrait of, 15, *12*, 20, 43
Silliman, Benjamin, Jr., 31
Silliman, Benjamin IV, and Alfred Wild, donors, 12, *9*
Silliman, Harriet, 14
Silliman, Mrs. Hepsa Ely, 35
Simpson, Lorna, 213
Simpson, William Kelly, 112; donor, 113, *108*
Siskind, Aaron, 184, 218
Sizer, Theodore, 74, *59*, 115, 117, 123, 132, *130*, 134, 141, *140*, 155, 161, 64, 73, 74, 75, 96
Skinner, Aaron Nicholas, 31
Smibert, John, 97, 142; *Bishop Berkeley and His Entourage (The Bermuda Group)*, 5, *2*, 6, 20, 85, 235, *230*; *Edward Winslow*, 105
Smith, Helen Wade, 145
Smith, Mr. & Mrs. Isaac, portraits of, 132
Smithsonian Institution, 227, 239
Société Anonyme Collection / Collection Société Anonyme, 122–31, 141, 142, 145, 149, 151, 153, 161, 172, 176, 216; donor, 217, *212*
Société Anonyme: Museum of Modern Art 1920, 123–31, 201, 206
Society for the Preservation of New England Antiquities, 181
Soken, Yamamoto, 84; *Teika's Poems on Flowers and Birds of the Twelve Months*, 193
Solley, Robert L., Curator of Prints, Drawings, and Photographs, 244
Solley, Thomas T., Director's Discretionary Fund, 195
Southern Connecticut State University, New Haven, 241
Spencer, Kate H., 161
Spencer, Stanley, 176
Stebbins, Theodore E., Jr., 189, 204, 222, 228, 236
Steichen, Edward, 64
Stein, Gertrude, 150–52; Collection, 151
Stein, Leo, 150
Stella, Joseph, 124, 126, 174; *Brooklyn Bridge*, 251; *Spring (The Procession)*, 131, *128*
Stephens, Ferris J., 145
Stephens, Frederic W., 61
Sterling and Francine Clark Art Institute, 153
Steuben, Major General Frederic Wilhelm Augustus, Baron von, *Freedom Box* and *Sword*, 99
Stevens, Wallace, 154
Stickley, Gustav, 100
Stieglitz, Alfred, 216
Stiles, Ezra, 25
Still, Clyfford, 154
Stoddard, Louis E., 63
Stoddard, Rebecca Darlington, 61, 63; donor, 62, *49–50*; Collection, 66, 73, 116
Stoeckel, Carl, 57; Ellen Battell, and Trust, Estate, 57
Stone, Edward Durrell, 121
Stone, Frank B., 97, 102
Storrs, John Henry Bradley, 126
Stowe, Charles Messer, 89
Stowe, Harriet Beecher, 46
Street Hall, 247
Street, Augustus Russell, 31, 33, 37–42, 55, 70; family, 9, 57; portrait of, 38, *32*, 43
Street, Caroline Mary Leffingwell (Mrs. Augustus Russell), 37–42, 55, 56; donor, 38, *32*
Strong, Rev. Nehemiah, portrait of, 7, *6*, 20
Strong, Roy, 237
Stuart, Gilbert, 7, 11, 14, 155; portrait by, 85; portrait of Benjamin Silliman by, 25; portrait of John Trumbull by, 11
Stubbs, George, 155
Student exhibitions, 41
Sturgis, Russell, Jr., 47, 53
Sueharu, Fukami, *View of Distant Sea II*, 84
Swartwout, Egerton, 60, 70–71, 74, 247; Gallery of Fine Arts, 72, *58*, 74, *60*
Szafran, Yvonne, 196

Taft, William Howard, 64
Tait, Arthur F., 102
Teniers, David, *Jephthah and His Daughter*, 31
Textile Museum, Washington, D. C., 84
The Nation, 47
Thiebaud, Wayne, 214; *Drink Syrups*, 215, *210*
Thomas, Dylan, 154
Thompson, Robert Farris, 164
Thorne, Harriet S. V., 218
Tiepolo, Giandomenico, 134
Tiepolo, Giovanni Battista, *Merit and Fame*, 134, 140, *139*; *Polymnia, The Muse of Religious Poetry*, 134; *Thalia and Melpomene, The Muses of Comedy and Tragedy*, 134
Tiffany & Co., 100
Toole, Nikki, 257
Town, Ithiel, 18, 23, 31, 118; portrait of, 19, *17*, 23
Townsend-Goddard, *Desk and Bookcase*, 92
Trinity Church on the Green, New Haven, 23
Trinity Church, New York, 43
Troye, Edward, 102
Trumbull Collection, 14–15, 18, 39, 42, 56, 100, 117, 176, 201, 238–39
Trumbull Gallery, 3, 9, 14, 18, 19, *16*, 20, 23, 29–30, 30, *28*, 38, 39, 58, 248
Trumbull, Faith, mother of John, 11
Trumbull, Governor Jonathan, father of John, 11; portrait of, 9
Trumbull, John, 3, 11–21, 31, 58, 74, 117, 118, 119, 174, 238, 247; campus plan, 1872, 9; death and burial, 21; *Death of General Montgomery in the Attack on Quebec*, 17, *14*; *Death of General Warren at Bunker Hill*, 16, *13*; *Declaration of Independence*, 12, 13, *10*, 14, 117; designs Trumbull Gallery, 18; lectures in front of his pictures, 57; lectures in Trumbull Gallery, 21; *Lieutenant Thomas Grosvenor and his Negro Servant*, 105; miniature portraits by, 18, *15*; moves to New Haven, 21; *Norwich Falls (or The Falls of the Yantic at Norwich)*, 105; paintings, 74; portrait of, 12, *9*; portrait of Dr. Lemuel Hopkins by, 64, 65, *5*; portraits by, 9; Revolutionary War pictures, 9, 12, 73; teacher of Benjamin West, 132; and Sarah, bodies moved to School of the Fine Arts, 39
Trumbull, Lt. Governor Jonathan, donor, 9
Tunnard, Christopher, 152–53
Turner, Joseph Mallord William, 155
Tuttle, H. Emerson, 115, 118
Tuttle, Richard, 204
Twain, Mark, 237
Twigg-Smith, Thurston, 197, 202, 214, 258; and Sharon, donors, 215, *210*
Twining, Stephen, 15
Twombly, Cy, 204
Tyche, 115
Tyng, Commodore, 97; portrait of, by an unknown artist, 105; Mrs. Commodore, portrait of, by John Smibert, 105

Uelsmann, Jerry, 218
Union Theological Seminary, Utica, N.Y., 27–28
University of Delaware, 232
University of Pennsylvania, 112, 164, 232
University of Victoria, British Columbia, 240
Upjohn, Richard, 43

Valerio, William, 225
van den Eeckhout, Gebrand, 183
van Dyck, Anthony, 31, 134
van Gogh, Vincent, 155; *Night Café*, 176–77, *174*, 251, 252
van Goyen, Jan, 183
Van Name, Addison, 45
van Ruysdael, Salomon, *View of Alkmaar*, 208
Vanderlyn, John, portrait by, 20
Vedder, Elihu, 232
Victoria and Albert Museum, 236, 237
Villon, Jacques, 125, 126, 143
Vogel, Susan Mullin, 164, 196, 197, *195*
Vouet, Simon, *Two Women*, 183
Vroom, Cornelis Hendriskz, 183 197, *195*
Vuillard, Edouard, 155, 190, 208; *Interior*, 184; *The Kitchen*, 156; *The Thread (L'Aiguilée)*, 191, *190*; *Woman Before a Mirror*, 181

Wadsworth, Daniel, 15
Waldo, Samuel Lovett, and William Jewett, portrait of John Trumbull by, 12, *9*
Walker, John, 237
Walker, Ralph T., 100
Walsh, John, 251
Walworth, Sarah, 75
Wang Mian, 80, 83, *74*
Ward, Barbara McLean, 237
Ward, Gerald W. R., 237, 239
Wardwell, Allen, 164; Mr. and Mrs. Allen, donors, 168, 169, *169*
Warren, Mrs. Charles, 118
Warren, Robert Penn, 154
Washington, George, portrait(s) of, by John Trumbull, 8, *8*; 9, 14
Washington, George, 11, 102, 119
Watteau, Antoine, 183
Weber, Joanna, 155
Webster, Daniel, visit to New Haven, 21
Weir, Irene, 58
Weir, John Ferguson, 37, 41, 42, 43, 53, 55, 56–60, 63, 64, 69, 75, 202, 247; in studio, 56, *44*; portrait of, 60, *47*; portrait of Samuel Wells Williams, 76, *61*; *The Gun Foundry*, 55
Weir, Julian Alden, 55, 64
Weir, Robert Walter, 55, 58, 60
Wesleyan University, 124
West, Benjamin, 11, 12, 31, 231; *Agrippina Landing at Brundisium with the Ashes of Germanicus*, 132–134, *130*, *131*, 176; *Cicero Discovering the Tomb of Archimedes*, 132; *Death of General Wolfe at the Heights of Abraham*, 132; *Self Portrait*, 132, *129*; student of John Trumbull, 132
Wetmore, Edith Malvina K., 143, 156, 181
Wetmore, George Peabody, 181
Weyand, Richard, 197
Wheeler, Davenport, Collection, 60
Wheeler, J. Davenport, 59
Whiffenpoofs, 66
Whistler, James Abbott McNeill, 155, 231
White, Andrew Dickson, 34
White, H. Wade, 126
White, Ruth Elizabeth, 199; Acquisition and Publication Fund, 199; donor, 198, *198*
Whiting Palestinian Collection, 61, *48*, 73, 114
Whiting, John David, 61
Whitney Collection of Sporting Art, 102, 176
Whitney, Eli, 7, 118; portrait of, 20
Whitney, Henry Payne, 102

Whitney, John Hay, 161, 231; Mr. & Mrs. John Hay, 156

Whitney, Payne, 102

Wight, Peter Bonnett, 38, 47, 56, 72, 247; School of the Fine Arts, 38, *33*, 39, *34*, 48, *39*

Will, Henry, 102

Williams College, 27, 28, 153

Williams family, donors, 83

Williams, Frances Wayland (Mrs. Frederick Wells), 76, 119; donor, 77, *64*

Williams, Frederick Wells, 27, 57, 75, 76, 119; collection, 77, *65*; donor, 77, *62*

Williams, Lyneise, 164, 253

Williams, Rev. Elisha, 7

Williams, Samuel Wells, 27, 57, 60, 74; collection, 73, 77, *62*; portrait of, 76, *61*

Williams, Wayland Wells, 76, 119; collection, 77, *64*

Williams, William Carlos, 154

Williams, William Frederic, 27–29, *26*, 76

Winslow, Edward, portrait of, by John Smibert, 105; *Sugar Box*, 92, 95, *84*, 96, 97, 105; *Two-Handled Covered Cup*, 92, 95, *85*

Winterthur, Henry Francis DuPont, Museum, 227

Wolf, The, 29

Women, art education for, 37–38; at Yale School of the Fine Arts, 57

Woolsey, family, 9

Woolsey, Theodore, 38, 41, 42, 55

Wrede, Stuart, 222

Wu, Nelson I., 172, 187

Wyeth, Andrew, 155

Yale Alumni Weekly, 117

Yale Babylonian Collection, 61

Yale Center for British Art, 181, 195, 225, 231–32, 236; exhibitions: *English Landscape Watercolors 1630–1850*, 231–32; *The Pursuit of Happiness: A View of Life in Georgian England*, 231

Yale College, 57

Yale College: Collegiate Collection, 3–9

Yale College: Connecticut Hall, 15

Yale College: Old Brick Row, mid-19th century, 29

Yale College: Old Campus, mid-19th century, 29–30, *28*

Yale College: School of the Fine Arts, 37–43, 123, 169

Yale Corporation, 123, 145, 147, 171; Prudential Committee, 45

Yale Daily News, 47, 147–149, 164

Yale Glee Club, 147

Yale Lekythos Painter, 63

Yale Oinochoe Painter, 62, *50*; 63

Yale School of Divinity, 57

Yale School of Law, 57

Yale School of Medicine, 57

Yale School of the Fine Arts, 57, 145; courses for undergraduate credit, first in 1891, 57

Yale University, Tercentennial, 3

Yale University: Architecture, department of, 69; professorship endowed, 58

Yale University: Art Council, 41, 42, 47, 55, 56

Yale University: Beinecke Plaza, 222

Yale University: Beinecke Rare Book and Manuscript Library, 114, 216, 222, 225, 239, 240

Yale University: Calhoun College, 132

Yale University: Center for the Study of American Art and Material Culture, 238

Yale University: Classics, Department of, 63, 73, 112, 116

Yale University: Coxe Cage, 118

Yale University: Day Mission Library, 73

Yale University: Department of Design, 149

Yale University: Divinity School, 61

Yale University: Division of the Arts, 143, 145, 169

Yale University: Lewis Walpole Library, 225

Yale University: Linsly-Chittenden Hall, 30

Yale University: Manuscripts and Archives Collection, Sterling Memorial Library, 216, 225

Yale University: Memorial (Woolsey) Hall, 63, 66, 73

Yale University: Morse College, 222

Yale University: Norfolk School of Music, 117

Yale University: Osborn Botanical Laboratory, 73

Yale University: Osborn Hall, 61

Yale University: Osborn Zoological Laboratory, 73

Yale University: Peabody Museum of Natural History, 61, 111–12, 165, 169, 225

Yale University: Phelps Hall, 73

Yale University: Saybrook College, 124

Yale University: School of Architecture, 118

Yale University: School of Architecture and Design, 169

Yale University: School of Art, 225

Yale University: School of Art and Architecture, 201

Yale University: School of Drama, 169

Yale University: School of Music Library, 162

Yale University: Sterling Memorial Library, 30, 114, 118, 162, 184

Yale University: University Council Committee on the Art Gallery, 227

Yale University: University Council on the Arts, 169

Yale University: Weir Hall, 70, 73

Yale University: Yale Babylonian Collection, 116, 145

Yale University: Yale Collection of Western Americana (Beinecke), 162, 240

Yale University Art Gallery: Acquisitions Committee, 171, 176

Yale University Art Gallery Bulletin (see also *Bulletin of the Associates in Fine Arts*), 142, 145, 153, 176, 242

Yale University Art Gallery: Governing Board, 66, 83, 196, 202, 214

Yale University Art Gallery: Print Department, 64

Yale University Art Gallery: Endowed Positions: Bareiss, Molly and Walter, Curator of Ancient Art, 156 ; Benenson, Frances and Benjamin Foundation, Curator of African Art, 244; Friends of American Arts, Curator of American Decorative Arts, 244; Goldfrank, Lionel, III, Curator of Early European Art, 244; Green, Holcombe T. Green , Curator of American Paintings and Sculpture, 239; Heinz, Henry J., II, Director, 194; Hewitt, Benjamin, Associate Curator of American Decorative Arts, 244; Kane, Patricia E., Curator of American Decorative Arts, 244; Kaplan, Allan and Alice, Associate/Assistant Curator of American Paintings and Sculpture, 244; Knox, Seymour H., Jr., Curator of European and Contemporary Art, 201; Mayer, Jan and Frederick , Curator of Education, 197; Solley, Robert L., Curator of Prints, Drawings, and Photographs, 244

Yale University Art Gallery: Exhibitions: 1858 Exhibition, 31–35, 37, 38, 42, 155; 1867 Exhibition, 42–43, 55; 1870 Exhibition, 55; *A Moment Ongoing: The Legacy of Everett V. Meeks*, 248; *A New Building for the Arts at Yale: The Yale University Art Gallery and Design Center*, 149; *A Private View: American Paintings from the Manoogian Collection*, 241, 242, *235*; *A Taste for Angels: Neapolitan Painting in North America*, 193; *African Art from the Linton Collection*, 162, *144*, *157*; *American Art and the American Experience*, 232, 234, *228*; *American Art from Alumni Collections*, 231; *American Art: 1750–1800, Towards Independence*, 189, 226, 236, *231*, 236–37; *American Arts at Yale: 1971–1651*, 228; *American Cities of the '30s, '40s, '50s*, 119; *American Daguerreotypes from the Matthew R. Isenburg Collection*, 218; *American Drawing, 1970–1973*, 184; *American Prints, 1900–1950*, 239; *An Obsession with Fortune: Tyche in Greek and Roman Art*, 196; *Antonio Sant'Elia*, 193; *Appropriated Lands: Photography and the Great Surveys of the American West*, 218; *Architecture and the City Plan*, 152; *Architecture: Photographs of French Cathedrals*, 119; *Ars in Urbe*, 152–53, *148*; *Art for "The Masses"(1911–1917): A Radical Magazine and Its Graphics*, 193, 239; *Art for Yale: Defining Moments*, 246–47, *242*, 250–59, *245–53*; *Art of Australia, 1788–1941*, 134; *At Home in Manhattan: Modern Decorative Arts, 1925 to the Depression*, 239; *Baule: African Art/ Western Eyes*, 164, *160*, 196; *Bones of Jade, Soul of Ice: The Flowering Plum in Chinese Art*, 189; *British Paintings and Drawings in the Paul Mellon Collection*, 176; *Call and Response: Journeys of African Art*, 164, *161*; *Charles Demuth: Poster Portraits 1923–1929*, 196, 197, 225, 239; *Charles Meryon: Prints & Drawings*, 184; *Childe Hassam: An Island Garden Revisited*, 193, 239; *Chinese Paintings at Yale*, 187, *186*; *Circa 1701: Printed Portraits from the Time of Elihu Yale*, 248; *Collecting with Richard Brown Baker: From Pollock to Lichtenstein*, 197, 204; *Color Photography—Inventors and Innovators, 1850–1975*, 184, 218; *Contemporary Silver by Georg Jensen*, 118; *Craftsmanship in American Silver from the Yale Collections*, 143; *Dante Gabriel Rosetti and the Double Work of Art*, 155, 184; *Darkness Into Light: The Early Mezzotint*, 184; *Discovered Lands, Invented Pasts: Transforming Visions of the American West*, 193, 240; *Duchamp — Duchamp-Villon — Villon*, 142, 143, *142*; *Early American Historical Prints*, 118; *Eva Hesse: A Retrospective*, 193, 222, 225, *223*; *Exhibition in Honor of the Centenary of the Death of Lafayette*, 119, *115*; *Exhibition of Chinese Paintings*, 118; *Exhibition of the Collection of the Société Anonyme Museum of Modern Art: 1920*, 124, *119–20*; *Federal Art in New England*, 118; *Felix Vallotton: A Retrospective*, 193; *Four Photographers*, 216, *211*; *German and Austrian Contemporary Art from the Bareiss Collection*, 213; *Gifts from Walter and Molly Bareiss in Celebration of His 80th Birthday*, 199; *Gifts to Osiris: Ancient Egyptian Art at Yale*, 225; *Greek Vases at Yale*, 199, 213–14; *Hans Baldung Grien: Prints and Drawings*, 184; *Hawaiian Eye: Collecting Contemporary Art with Thurston Twigg-Smith*, 197, 214; *Holland Under the Nazis*, 121; *Hundredth Anniversary Exhibition*, 117; *I, Claudia: Women in Ancient Rome*, 198, *198*, 199; *Imaging African Art*, 218; *John Hill Morgan Memorial Exhibition of American Art*, 142, *141*; *John Trumbull: The Hand and Spirit of a Painter*, 238, *232*; *Love and Loss: American Mourning Miniatures*, 196, 241; *Master of the Lotus Garden: The Life of Bada Shanren*, 193, 194, *193*; *Masterpieces of New England Silver*, 119, *116*; *Masterworks from Yale University*, 161–62; *Mel Bochner: Thought Made Visible*, 222; *Modern Gothic: The Revival of Medieval Art*, 225; *Myer Myers: Jewish Silversmith in Colonial New York*, 241; *National War Poster Exhibition*, 121; *Neo-Impressionists and the Nabis in the Collection of Arthur G. Altschul*, 176, 181, *178*; *New Haven Progress*, 118; *Now and Then: Art at Yale Since 1945; Now and Later*, 199; *Object and Image in Modern Art and Poetry*, 153–55; *Objective Color*, 214; *Our Navy in Action*, 121; *Painting and Sculpture by the Directors of the Société Anonyme*, 125; *Paintings by Graham Sutherland and Drawings by Henry Moore*, 161; *Philadelphia Naturalistic Photography, 1885–1906*, 218; *Photographers Look at Buildings*, 218; *Photographs of Persian Architecture*, 118; *Pictures Collected by Yale Alumni*, 155–61; *"Pictures for a Picture" of Gertrude Stein as a Collector and Writer on Art and Artists*, 150–52, *147*; *Portraits of Distinguished New Haveners*, 118; *Portraiture and the Harlem Renaissance: The Photographs of James L. Allen*, 218; *Prints by Artists of "The Masses"*, 193; *Prints of Dürer and His Time*, 184; *Ralph Kirkpatrick In Memoriam*, 184, 187; *Recent Gifts and Purchases* (1964), 176; *Richard Brown Baker Collects!*, 204; *Richard Hamilton: Image and Process*, 193; *Rubbings from Chinese Tombstones*, 119; *Silver in American Life*, 237; *Sixteenth Century Italian Drawings*, 184; *The Art Museums of Louis I. Kahn*, 193; *The Christmas Story in Art*, 119; *The Communion of Scholars: Chinese Art at Yale*, 189; *The Croquet Game*, 239; *The Edo Culture in Japanese Prints*, 173; *The Futurist Imagination*, 222; *The Graphic Art of Géricault*, 156; *The Graphic Art of Umberto Boccioni*, 225; *The Jade Studio: Masterpieces of Ming and Qing Painting and Calligraphy from the Wong Nan-p'ing Collection*, 196; *The Smibert Tradition*, 142; *The Work of Many Hands: Card Tables in Federal America 1790–1820*, 238, *233*, 239; *The Work of Paul Rudolph, Architect*, 201; *The Woven and Graphic Art of Anni Albers*, 193; *Thomas Eakins: The Rowing Pictures*, 239; *Traces of the Brush: Studies in Chinese Calligraphy*, 189; *Twelve Pieces of Silver: Cornelius Kierstede 1647–1753*, 118; *Two Modern Collectors*, 202; *William Henry Jackson: Photographer of the American West*, 184, 218; *Winslow Homer Watercolors*, 193, 239; *Word in Flower: The Visualization of Classical Literature in Seventeenth Century Japan*, 193; *Words for Images: A Gallery of Poems*, 155; *Yale Bicentennial*, 58; *Yale Collects Yale*, 225

Yale, Elihu, 3, 4, 2, 25, 85; donor, 4, *1*

Yellin, Samuel, 74

Ying, Lan, *Autumn Landscape*, 187, 188, *187*

Young, Henry, 55

Zeeman, Enoch, portrait by, 85

Zeno, Aline L., 241

Zuccaro, Taddeo and Frederico, 183

Zurier, Rebecca, 239